WAR AND ECONOMY IN
THE THIRD REICH

WAR AND ECONOMY IN THE THIRD REICH

R. J. OVERY

CLARENDON PRESS · OXFORD

Oxford University Press, Great Clarendon Street, Oxford OX2 6DP

Oxford New York

Athens Auckland Bangkok Bogota Bombay
Buenos Aires Calcutta Cape Town Dar es Salaam
Delhi Florence Hong Kong Istanbul Karachi
Kuala Lumpur Madras Madrid Melbourne
Mexico City Nairobi Paris Singapore
Taipei Tokyo Toronto
and associated companies in
Berlin Ibadan

Oxford is a trade mark of Oxford University Press

Published in the United States by
Oxford University Press Inc., New York

First published in Clarendon Paperback 1995

British Library Cataloguing in Publication Data
Data available

Library of Congress Cataloging in Publication Data
Overy, R. J.
War and economy in the Third Reich / R. J. Overy.
p. cm.
Includes bibliographical references and index.
1. Germany—Economic conditions—1918-1945. 2. Germany—Economic
policy—1918-1933. 3. Germany—Economic policy—1933-1945. I. Title.
HC286.3.0943 1994
338.943'009'043—dc20 93-5380
ISBN 0-19-820599-6

3 5 7 9 10 8 6 4 2

Printed in Great Britain
on acid-free paper by
Bookcraft (Bath) Ltd.,
Midsomer Norton, Avon

For Emma, Becky, and Jonathan,
who have grown up with it all

PREFACE

THE present work is the fruit of twenty years of research and writing on the German economy under Hitler. It covers the period as a whole, from the early recovery in 1932/3 to the final stages of the German war economy. Some of the chapters grew out of conference papers; two of them, on Krupp and on rationalization in the German war economy (Chapters 4 and 11), have not been published before. The rest of the chapters reproduce journal articles. They all reflect a chronological progression in my interests, from asking questions about the role of rearmament and of non-military sectors in the German recovery, to emphasizing the very great efforts made to convert the German economy to war purposes after 1939. Naturally enough over the course of twenty years I have changed my mind about a lot of things, and learned a great deal. I blush at the infelicities of expression and uncritical assumptions of the early pieces. I hope there remains sufficient consistency here to avoid the danger that the conclusions of one chapter cancel out the evidence supplied in another. I have tried in the Introduction to link the different pieces together, and to suggest ways in which the subject has developed during the time the essays were written.

The only changes I have made involve textual inconsistencies or particularly jarring expressions. Otherwise they remain as they were published, and I am very grateful to the publishers and editors involved for permission to reproduce them. I would also like to express my thanks to numerous colleagues and friends who have argued these issues through, or have suggested fresh avenues, or have just plain disagreed. My work is all the richer for that. I would also like to thank the staff of the archives and libraries that I have worked in for their courtesy and helpfulness. I would particularly like to thank the staff, past and present, of the Imperial War Museum, where I first worked on my doctoral thesis in 1970, on records which have long since been restituted to Germany, and where I have continued to work on and off ever since. Finally I would like to thank my daughter, Becky, who typed a large part of the manuscript, and who no doubt wishes, like a great many others, that I would finally rationalize my own work practices and buy a computer.

R.O.

King's College, London
October 1992

ACKNOWLEDGEMENTS

I AM grateful to the following for permission to reproduce previously published material: Oldenbourg Verlag for 'Blitzkriegswirtschaft? Finanzpolitik, Lebensstandard und Arbeitseinsatz in Deutschland 1939–1942'; from *Vierteljahrshefte für Zeitgeschichte*, 3 (1988); the Economic History Society and Basil Blackwell Publishers for 'Cars, Roads and Economic Recovery in Germany 1932–38', *Economic History Review*, 2nd ser. 28 (1975), and 'Hitler's War and the German Economy: A Reinterpretation', *Economic History Review*, 2nd ser. 35 (1982); Oxford University Press for 'Germany, "Domestic Crisis" and War in 1939', *Past and Present*, 116 (1987); Macmillan Educational for 'Hitler's War Plans and the German Economy', published in R. Boyce and E. Robertson (eds.), *Paths to War* (London, 1990); Leicester University Press for 'Goering's "Multi-National" Empire', published in A. Teichova and P. Cottrell (eds.), *International Business and Central Europe 1919–1939* (1984); Cambridge University Press for 'Transportation and Rearmament in the Third Reich', in *Historical Journal*, 16 (1973), and 'German Multi-Nationals and the Nazi State in Occupied Europe', published in A. Teichova and M. Levy-Leboyer (eds.), *Multi-Nationals in Historical Perspective* (1986); Frank Cass Ltd. for 'Unemployment in the Third Reich', *Business History*, 29 (1987); Sage Publications for 'Heavy Industry in the Third Reich: The Reichswerke Crisis', in *European History Quarterly*, 15 (1985).

CONTENTS

FIGURES

TABLES

To avoid ambiguity *Milliarden* (US billions) are expressed throughout this book as '000m.

ABBREVIATIONS

BA	Bundesarchiv, Koblenz
BA-MA	Bundesarchiv-Militärarchiv, Freiburg-im-Breisgau
BHO	Berg- und Hüttenwerkgesellschaft OstmbH
BIOS	British Intelligence Objectives Sub-Committee
CIOS	Combined Objectives Sub-Committee
DBFP	*Documents on British Foreign Policy*
DDV	*Der deutsche Volkswirt*
DNVP	Deutschnationale Volkspartei (German Nationalist Party)
DVP	Deutsche Volkspartei (German People's Party)
FO	Foreign and Commonwealth Office Library, London; also Foreign Office files at IWM
IMT	International Military Tribunal, *Trial of the Major War Criminals*, 42 vols. (London, 1949–51)
IWM	Imperial War Museum, London
K-A(L)	Krupp-Archiv (London); copies at Foreign and Commonwealth Office Library, London
KPD	Kommunistische Partei Deutschlands (German Communist Party)
MD	Milch Documents, IWM
Mefo	Metallurgische-Forschungsgesellschaft (a secret state holding company)
MHI	Military History Institute, Carlisle, Pa., USA
NA	National Archives, Washington, DC
NCA	*Nazi Conspiracy and Aggression*, 8 vols. (Washington, DC, 1946)
OKW	Oberkommando der Wehrmacht (German High Command)
RDI	Reichsverband der Deutschen Industrie (German Employers Association)
RIIA	Royal Institute of International Affairs
SA	Sturmabteilung (Storm-troops)
SAK	Salzgitter Konzernarchiv
SD	Sicherheitsdienst (Security Service)
SPD	Sozialdemokratische Partei Deutschlands (German Social Democratic Party)
SS	Schutzstaffel (Black Shirts, led by Himmler)
TWC	*Trials of the War Criminals before the Nuremberg Military Tribunal*, 12 vols. (Washington, DC, 1949)
USSBS	United States Strategic Bombing Survey

VIAG   Vereinigte Industrie-Unternehmungen Aktiengesellschaft (Reich holding company)

VS   Vereinigte Stahlwerke (United Steel)

Introduction: The Nazi Economy in Peace and War

THE place of the German economy in the preparation and prosecution of war is of central importance in any interpretation of the Third Reich. The relationship between war and economy not only involved economic issues but profoundly affected German politics and German military strategy. This reflected Hitler's own view of the economy as primarily an instrument of power. For him the economy was not simply an arena for generating wealth and technical progress; its *raison d'être* lay in its ability to provide the material springboard for military conquest. Hitler held to a widely shared view that in the dog-eat-dog post-war world, prosperity had to be fought for, securing 'the bread of freedom from the hardship of war'.[1]

This instrumental view of the economy allowed Hitler to simplify what were otherwise complicated economic issues. His equation of a strong economy with national revival and military success had obvious implications. It placed a priority on economic revival during the early years of the regime as a precondition for the revival of Germany's international position. It promoted the view, popular among Germany's military élite, that the economy should be treated as a central element in the war capability of the modern state. Future wars, Hitler believed, had to mobilize 'the whole strength of the people'.[2] Economic policy, in this sense, had to be judged by the criterion of strategic necessity as well as social utility. This made Hitler an enemy of free-market economics, and inclined him to the currently fashionable ideas of closed economic blocs and autarky, and ultimately to the idea of seizing 'living-space' and resources by force.

This rejection of economic liberalism had a number of sources. To any German nationalist in the early 1930s it seemed obvious that Germany's current economic ills owed a great deal to the self-interest of the liberal states that dictated peace terms in 1919, and continued to stack the odds against Germany thereafter. Hitler did not think that Germany would find a purely economic solution to her weak position in the world economy: 'the ultimate decision as to the outcome of the world market will lie in power'.[3] Second, there could be no guarantee in a free-market economy that the interests of race or state as Hitler defined them would take priority over the interests of businessmen or consumers. After 1933 the role of the

[1] *Hitler's Secret Book*, intro. T. Taylor (New York, 1961), 15.
[2] Ibid. 46.
[3] Ibid. 99.

state in regulating and directing economic life increased sharply, first in order to encourage economic revival, then to divert economic resources to the growth of German military power. Hitler was a reluctant *dirigiste*, but the logic of his view that the economy, like everything else in German life, had to serve Germany's struggle for existence led, in an unplanned, incremental way, to the establishment of a kind of command economy.

The use of state power to procure the sort of military economy Hitler wanted had important consequences for German politics. The business community, while willing enough to accept state assistance in reviving exports and supplying credit, was in general wary of the trend to economic 'statism' which the speed and scale of rearmament necessitated. Even military leaders were cautious about re-militarization for fear that it would weaken German capitalism or penalize consumers so much that social agitation would result. Faced with the choice between calming these fears or pushing on with rearmament, Hitler chose the latter. As a result the power balance between the party, industry, and armed forces shifted, and Hitler's aim to turn Germany in a short space of time into a military superpower prevailed. It did so at the cost of consumers, as the state forced the diversion of resources to strategic purposes, and, increasingly, at the cost of producers, whose freedom of manœuvre was effectively removed.

In practice, of course, the issues facing the German economy in the 1930s and 1940s were far from simple. Hitler's capacity to reduce economic problems to a series of loosely defined goals provided a political framework of imperative character, but it could not of itself provide the solution. Nor, until Hitler's dictatorship was more secure, did arguments about economic means and ends subside. There was certainly a consensus in the early 1930s about the necessity for economic recovery, but there was no general agreement about how it might be brought about. There was broad social acceptance of the nationalist agenda—rearmament and an end to reparations—but there were clear differences of opinion concerning the pace and nature of rearmament, and the issue of who should control it. During the war Germany's economic performance was inhibited by prolonged arguments about jurisdiction and responsibility. And throughout the period of the Third Reich conflicts about the character and extent of state control over the economy, even within the Nazi Party itself, influenced the evolution of economic policy, and affected economic performance.

It is this relationship between Hitler's vision of an armed economy and the reality of domestic and international circumstances which forms the substance of what follows. The book is based around four major themes, each one of which has been, and remains, an area of historical controversy. The first is the nature of economic recovery in Germany after

1933, and in particular the issue of how much the revival owed to the early onset of rearmament. The second theme, the relationship between German business and the Nazi regime, is linked to the question of recovery if for no other reason than the commonly held assumption that business confidence revived once capitalists had a government they could work with. The following chapters show that the relationship between German capitalism and the Nazi state cannot be reduced to a simple formula, but was a complex one which changed over time. The relationship was also profoundly affected by the third theme, the nature and consequences of German rearmament in the late 1930s. The history of rearmament involves the question of how far German businessmen were responsible for, or profited from, the economic imperialism and military conquests of the regime; but it has also given rise to more serious arguments about whether Hitler intended to arm for limited or total war, and the extent to which the economic burden of rearming provoked domestic social crisis and an opportunistic and aggressive foreign policy.

The last theme, German economic mobilization in the war, is closely linked to interpretations of rearmament in the 1930s. Any discussion of how extensively Germany mobilized for war after 1939 depends to some extent on prior assumptions about the nature of war preparations, and the ability of the Nazi regime to sustain them at particular levels. The widely held view that the Nazi regime rejected mobilization for 'total war' until compelled by military reverses to accept it in 1942, rests on the implicit assumption that Nazi rule was too fragile to sustain higher levels of sacrifice from the German people. Yet the increase in state control, evident throughout the period, does raise the question whether the Nazi leadership was as sensitive to public pressure as the thesis of 'limited war' suggests, and whether the German economy was as prone to crisis under Hitler as is generally accepted. In this sense, arguments about the character of the military economy broaden out into more general arguments about the nature of the Nazi system of control, and the reception of the regime among the wider German population.

GERMAN ECONOMIC RECOVERY

The problems facing the German economy when Hitler came to power in January 1933 were formidable. Over 8 million people employed in 1929 were jobless three years later. Germany avoided international bankruptcy only by defaulting on debts due and the indulgence of her creditors. Industrial production fell to the levels of the 1890s. German trade, on which almost a quarter of the population relied, was halved between 1929 and 1932. The collapse of incomes contributed a great deal to the radicalization of the German electorate after 1929 and the rise of the National Socialist movement to a point where it could vie for power with the established parties.

The Nazi leaders had no magic formula to cure the economy. They were economic nationalists. They favoured protective tariffs, foreign debt reduction, and import substitution to remove what they regarded as debilitating dependence on the world economy. They supported calls for work-creation and labour service with no very clear idea about how to fund them. In general Nazi politicians blamed economic decline on political causes—the influence of Marxism on the labour force, the machinations of international Jewry, the vindictiveness of western politicians; and they offered political solutions—the destruction of organized labour, rearmament, 'biological' politics. The more radical wing of the movement wanted to transcend capitalism and build a new corporate economic order, but there was no clear agreement about what it should look like.

It is not surprising that under the circumstances the Nazi politicians who came to power in 1933 came to rely on existing economic plans and economic institutions to carry them through the first months in office. The regime was committed to providing 'Bread and Work'; Hitler knew well enough that the failure to do so would make other goals difficult to achieve, and would sustain the very social and political instability that had brought him to power in the first place. Yet Hitler never lost sight of the general goal. Meeting with his cabinet colleagues on 9 February to discuss work-creation he emphasized that in the long run 'The future of Germany depends exclusively and alone on rebuilding the armed forces'.[4] It is certainly possible to conclude from this that economic revival mattered to Hitler only to the extent that it provided the means for military revival, but it is not very plausible. There were compelling political arguments for overcoming unemployment and avoiding social unrest; the propaganda promise to rebuild German society and heal the rifts of class war relied on some evidence of state sponsored re-employment. And if Hitler was not a conventional socialist, it is hard to dismiss all his talk of 'community' as mere claptrap.

The difficult thing was to find a mix of policies that would generate re-employment, sustain trade, revive the capital market, and restart investment in industry and agriculture, and would do so without producing fresh pressures on the value of the mark, or the balance of payments. No single economic policy could achieve all this. The rebuilding of the German economy came about, as a Labour Ministry memorandum

---

[4] Sitzung des Ausschusses der Reichsregierung für Arbeitsbeschaffung, 9 Feb. 1933, in K.-H. Minuth (ed.), *Akten der Reichskanzlei: Regierung Hitler 1933–1938*, i. *1933* (Boppard am Rhein, 1983), 62.

put it in December 1934, 'through a multitude of interrelated measures'.[5] How these affected the revival of employment levels is related in Chapter 1 and need not be rehearsed again here. Re-employment on a wide scale stimulated demand and the normal revival of the business cycle. It helped to reduce the hostility of labour following the Nazi destruction of the trade unions and the left-wing political parties. It contributed to a shift in expectations and outlook, as ordinary Germans came to accept that perhaps, after all, Hitler could relaunch the nation as he promised.[6]

At the core of the re-employment strategy lay programmes of state-funded investment for 'work-creation' (*Arbeitsbeschaffung*). Some of this investment was in the form of specific work-creation projects which were labour-intensive. The largest single item in the programme was road and bridge repair and rebuilding. Other funds were used to subsidize house-building and conversion or to stimulate public engineering schemes. It has always been tempting to see these schemes as some form of veiled or 'indirect' rearmament. Hitler's comment at the meeting on 9 February that re-militarization took 'absolute priority' or his comment later in the year that the new motor-roads, the *Reichsautobahnen*, should be developed on 'strategic principles' have been used by historians as prima-facie evidence that work-creation was camouflaged rearmament.[7]

This interpretation is not borne out by the documentary evidence, which demonstrates that the bulk of work-creation funds in the period 1932–4, when the programmes started to be wound up, was spent on civilian projects.[8] Out of RM 1,500m. made available in the first major work-creation schemes, 18 per cent went to projects (building military installations, airfields, etc.) of a military nature. The bulk of funds went on land-reclamation, and road and bridge repair (following four years of declining municipal spending on maintenance). The Post Office and the railways ran their own work-creation schemes, almost all of which involved maintenance and renewal of their infrastructure, and which offered employment to more than 250,000 workers.[9] Government subsidies for house-building and house-repair under the work-creation programmes were even more significant, totalling more than RM 2,000m. in 1933/4

---

[5] Bundesarchiv, Koblenz (BA), R2/18701, Labour Ministry to Finance Ministry, 5 Dec. 1934, 1.

[6] I. Kershaw, *The 'Hitler Myth': Image and Reality in the Third Reich* (Oxford, 1987), esp. ch. 2.

[7] See e.g. H.-E. Volkmann, 'The National Socialist Economy in Preparation for War', in W. Deist *et al.*, *Germany and the Second World War* i. (Oxford, 1990), 222–5.

[8] M. Wolffsohn, 'Arbeitsbeschaffung und Rüstung in nationalsozialistischen Deutschland: 1933', *Militärgeschichtliche Mitteilungen* 27 (1977), 9–19.

[9] BA R2/18701, Reichspostminister to Finance Ministry, 4 Aug. 1934, 'betr. Arbeitsbeschaffungsmassnahmen'; Deutsche Reichsbahn Hauptverwaltung to Finance Ministry, 18 Oct. 1934, 'betr. Sonderarbeitsbeschaffungsprogramme der Deutschen Reichsbahn'.

and doing a great deal to eliminate unemployment among building workers.[10] More important all these schemes were run by officials whose primary interest was in re-employment and the refurbishment of public services. When the War Ministry argued for higher allocations in 1933 it found an unsympathetic ear in the Finance Ministry. While it is no doubt true that limited funds were made available, the bulk of spending in 1933 and 1934 on public, employment-creating projects was non-military in character. Work-creation seems to have been just what it said; short-term programmes to create new jobs and kick-start the economy.

Whether work-creation was ever capable on its own of reviving the German economy, is highly questionable. The revival owed something to a wide range of initiatives, particularly in creating a more favourable set of external economic relations through bilateral trade agreements, debt reduction or default, and, under the terms of the 1934 New Plan, controls over imports. Just as important were the efforts made to stabilize and control the domestic capital market and public finances. In the absence of foreign lending, and with the investment-shyness of private creditors, the government assumed a much greater role in initiating new investment or in giving tax concessions and subsidies to encourage others to invest. Both public-works schemes played a part in the revival of investment, but there were plenty of other projects on which the government was prepared to spend money.

An area of special interest was 'motorization'. The efforts of the government to promote the motor industry and encourage road-building and repair are set out in Chapter 2. The sector revived rapidly, stimulating a whole range of ancillary activities. Road-building, both ordinary roads and the new *Autobahnen*, contributed to the recovery of the construction industry, and absorbed a good deal of casual, unskilled labour which was the hardest unemployment to relieve. The accelerated motorization of Germany reflected the relatively slow growth of motor-vehicle traffic in the 1920s. The 1930s saw a period of 'catching-up', encouraged by cheaper cars, tax concessions, and the revival of middle-class incomes.[11] But it also reflected the general trend to technical modernization in all industrial economies, something which Hitler himself was keen to promote as a tribute to German technical proficiency and a propaganda triumph for the regime. German industry, and the German engineering community,

[10] BA R2/18701, Labour Ministry to Finance Ministry, 22 Dec. 1934, 'Beitrag der Abteilung Siedlungswerk', 6; Deutsche Bau- und Bodenbank, Berlin, 'Die Entwicklung der deutschen Bauwirtschaft und die Arbeitsbeschaffung im Jahre 1933'.

[11] F. Blaich, 'Why Did the Pioneer Fall Behind? Motorisation in German between the Wars' in T. Barker (ed.), *The Economic and Social Effects of the Spread of Motor Vehicles* (London, 1987), 148–64.

welcomed motorization because it promised rapid growth in a vanguard sector with good export prospects.[12]

Of course the 'motorization' of Germany, like work-creation, was not enough on its own to drag the German economy out of recession, though it was clearly a major stimulus to industrial revival and re-employment in the critical early years of the regime. To characterize the expansion of the motor-industry as 'trivial' (as a recent survey of the recovery describes it) seems singularly misplaced for an industry that had become Germany's largest manufacturing employer by 1935, and was by 1938 generating the largest contribution to Germany's manufacturing exports. The road-building programme between 1933 and 1935 consumed almost RM 2,000m., at which point it exceeded expenditure on the German rail network. In the first two years of recovery investment in motor transport and the motor industry matched the early spending on the military.[13]

It is, of course, possible to argue that the road-building and the stimulus to motorization were in fact contributions to the economic rearmament of Germany. No doubt in a very general sense it was recognized that better roads, more experienced drivers, and a larger stock of lorries would be beneficial to an army bent on motorizing itself. It is clear that Hitler was aware from the outset that the new road network was important 'not only on account of motorization, but on grounds of defence', a view that is not acknowledged fully enough in Chapter 2. But it is unrealistic to try to explain a process as complex as motorization through a single cause. Technical modernization of this sort had a momentum of its own; plans to improve Germany's road network predated the Nazi regime by some years. Nor does it seem that the armed forces were all that keen on the new motorways, or very successful in applying the motor vehicle to military needs. The army commander von Fritsch was reported in 1936 to have said that the RM 5,000m. allocated to the *Autobahnen* would have been better spent on refurbishing the railways.[14] Despite the motorization efforts before 1939, the German armed forces remained reliant on rail and horse for the bulk of their transport in the Second World War, particularly on the Eastern Front. The importance of horse transport has long been overlooked. At the beginning of the war German forces had 590,000 horses, by the war's end 1,200,000. During the course of the conflict over 1,200,000 horses were requisitioned in Germany and the occupied

---

[12] For a recent exploration of these issues see J. Herf, *Reactionary Modernism: Technology, Culture and Politics in Weimar Germany and the Third Reich* (Cambridge, 1984); S. Reich, *The Fruits of Fascism: Postwar Prosperity in Historical Perspective* (London, 1990).

[13] H. James, *The German Slump: Politics and Economics 1924–1936* (Oxford, 1986), 384; Blaich, 'Motorisation', 154.

[14] *Akten der Reichskanzlei*, i. 307, 332.

territories. For the invasion of the Soviet Union Germany had 3,350 tanks and 650,000 horses.[15]

These arguments hinge on defining what exactly is meant by rearmament. It has long been accepted that the production and supply of weapons and military equipment, though formally constituting armament, is less than adequate in describing the processes at work in the rearming of any state in the 1930s. It was generally acknowledged that major war required the extensive mobilization of economic resources through the supply of materials, machinery, and labour from the civilian sectors. In this sense, rearmament went well beyond military production. Historians make a distinction here between *direct* rearmament (military output) and *indirect* rearmament (the supply of raw materials, machinery, factory equipment, infrastructure investment, etc. necessary to sustain military output and military capability). The difficult thing is to decide where to draw the line. In the German case any definition is complicated by the fact that Hitler was committed from the outset to remilitarizing the German state and strengthening the economy in ways which would be strategically useful. On this basis, almost anything done by the government in economic affairs was a net contribution to the broader purpose. Yet this renders a definition of indirect rearmament almost meaningless. Clearly much of what went on in the German economy between 1933 and 1935 had a primarily civilian purpose, and was regarded as such by the officials, producers, and consumers involved. To be conceptually useful, indirect rearmament should describe economic activity which has a clear strategic purpose, and which is consciously perceived by the government and the military to be linked to the capacity to make war.

On these criteria a distinction can be drawn between the work-creation programmes of road and bridge repair, which were intended to offer short-term re-employment and restore crumbling public services, and, say, the plans to refurbish the German railways in 1939 in anticipation of heavy military demands in the 1940s.[16] In the first case the link with future plans to prepare the economy for warmaking was almost non-existent; in the second it was the primary purpose. Even a definition like this leaves a grey area where public spending programmes were deliberately camouflaged to hide some military purpose; or where it proves impossible to distinguish in a set of industrial orders between civilian and military clients. But the nature of the evidence will not support a tidy definition, and it would be surprising if it did.

[15] R. L. DiNardo and A. Bay, 'Horse-Drawn Transport in the German Army', *Journal of Contemporary History*, 23 (1988), 130–9.

[16] Second Meeting of the Reich Defence Council, 23 June 1939, in *Nazi Conspiracy and Aggression*, 10 vols. (Washington, DC, 1946), vi. 718–31, for plans to refurbish the railway system.

Both direct and indirect rearmament played some part in the investment-led recovery in Germany, but it was one element in a cocktail of causes, and was by no means the main ingredient. Many of the policies pursued were intended to provide civilian solutions to civilian problems. Rearmament became economically significant when the recovery was well under way, in 1934/5. In this sense recovery was a cause as much as a consequence of further rearmament.

This conclusion begs a very large question. If Hitler saw the German economy as an instrument in the re-militarization of the state, why was rearmament so slow to get going? Why was money and effort expended on reviving the civilian economy in ways which did not obviously have a long-term strategic significance? There are a number of explanations. In the first place Hitler had interests and motives in economic affairs which ran alongside his general desire for a strong, rearmed Germany. His recognition that re-employment was politically expedient has already been noted. He saw work-creation and public investment serving the propaganda boast of social and material rebuilding of the Reich, and compulsory labour service for young people as an avenue to the development of 'community-mindedness'.[17] A recent study by Avraim Barkai on the early years of recovery emphasizes how important ideological concerns were to the party, as efforts were made to construct a more corporatist, state-led economy.[18] Finally, Hitler liked technical modernization for its own sake; he was keen to build the motorways as a hallmark of the new Nazi age, in which he was to play the role of *Bauherr*, of master-builder.[19]

Hitler was also motivated by political prudence. The early programmes of rearmament were disguised in order to avoid complications with powers committed to upholding the Versailles Treaty. Although there was no real secret about the regime's intention to start rearming, it was begun cautiously, to avoid running international risks. There were also domestic dangers. Hitler had a very limited grasp of economic theory, but he knew that inflation was a bad thing. It was not clear at first how military funding could be paid for without running inflationary risks with deficit financing. Until the Reichsbank President, Hjalmar Schacht, came up with the idea of short-term bonds to be redeemed out of future tax revenues as the economy recovered (the so-called Mefo Bills), military spending was not much higher than it had been in the last years of the Weimar Republic. Even then the level of military spending was kept within firm limits partly

[17] Chefbesprechung, 4 Apr. 1933, *Akten der Reichskanzlei*, i. 288–9.
[18] A. Barkai, *Nazi Economics: Ideology, Theory and Policy* (Oxford, 1990), esp. chs. 1, 2.
[19] See esp. J. Thies, 'Hitler's European Building Programme', *Journal of Contemporary History*, 13 (1978); J. D. Shand, 'The Reichsautobahnen: Symbol for the Third Reich', ibid. 19 (1984), 189–98.

to avoid any kind of run on the mark, partly because the Finance Ministry found itself having to pay out a great deal on other areas of public subsidy and investment.

In the second place, there was the problem of mediation. The regime relied on the co-operation of the military leaders, state officials, and non-Nazi ministers, and the willingness of the business community to endorse recovery policies. Much of the detailed work of initiating and implementing economic and financial policy was done by the established economic bureaucracy, in many cases simply continuing policies begun under Weimar governments in the recession. At this level Hitler's general exhortations to think of re-militarization as a first priority were heeded very little. The reports on work-creation prepared by the Labour Ministry and the Finance Ministry show that their priorities were re-employment within a stable financial environment.[20] The issues confronted by the ministerial apparatus—credit collapse, agricultural depression, trade decline, payments difficulties, high unemployment—were not to be solved by the panacea of rearmament, but on their own terms, through a variety of stimuli both conventional and unconventional. The fact that the general result—a drift towards economic nationalist solutions of controlled trade, import substitution, and debt default—ultimately served the interests of large-scale rearmament in the late 1930s seems on the face of it to have been in some measure fortuitous.

The scope for rearmament was also limited by dependence on the military and the business community. The armed forces were happy enough to have a rearming government at last, but they were anxious to control its pace and nature themselves, and in general they favoured a step-by-step approach rather than a rush for military goods. They certainly wanted the civilian sector to be aware of strategic priorities, but the generals did not want to overload the economy so soon after a period of severe crisis, a view which fitted ill with Hitler's ambitions to head a military superpower. Nor were industrialists as enthusiastic about arms orders and thoughts of war; they had had their fingers burned badly in the Great War and the post-war crisis. A sudden switch to arms was fraught with risks, both international, if other states discriminated against Germany for breaking the Treaty, and domestic, if industry found itself over-committed to heavy investment programmes which would peter out once military revival was over.

For all these reasons it proved difficult to transform the economy to war preparation very quickly or extensively. Circumstances imposed economic and political reality on Hitler. Only when the recovery was an

[20] BA R2/18701, Labour Ministry to Finance Ministry, 5 Dec. 1934, 'Arbeitsbeschaffungsmassnahmen', 1–14; Finance Ministry, 'Die Arbeitsbeschaffungs-Massnahmen der Reichsregierung 1932 bis 1935', 2–55.

accomplished fact by 1936, and when the Nazi movement was more politically secure and less dependent on the traditional élites, did it prove possible to accelerate rearmament and restructure the industrial economy and work-force in favour of military priorities.

INDUSTRY IN THE THIRD REICH

The role that German businessmen, either collectively or individually, played in the processes of recovery and re-militarization remains the subject of much debate. The traditional view, established in the 1930s, was that Nazism was the tool of monopoly capitalism, which used the movement at a period of acute crisis in the capitalist system to discipline the work-force, boost profits, and conquer markets. Since the state managed to provide all of these things to some degree, the causal connection was not entirely implausible. Yet the fact that it was the state that came to the rescue also prompted the contrary view, that German business was taken captive by the Nazi state. In this interpretation industry was used simply as an instrument to achieve the state's plans for war and conquest regardless of its actual economic interests. The ability of industry to do anything about this was progressively reduced with the rise of the terror state and the planned economy.

Neither interpretation, thanks to a growing interest in the history of individual firms and businessmen, stands up to critical scrutiny.[21] It has always seemed inherently unlikely that something as incoherent and differentiated as an industrial system could react collectively at a time of acute crisis to push a populist, even anti-capitalist mass movement into power. That is not to say that there were not prominent big businessmen, and a much larger number of smaller businessmen, who supported the Nazi Party and rallied to its call for social and national regeneration (and its promise of tax and interest-rate reduction, and tariff protection). But the problem remains that industry was not a single bloc, with a common political voice or common economic interests. If anything united big business leaders in the recession it was a growing hostility to what was perceived as the self-interest of the political parties and the pro-labour stance of the state, and a desire for a more traditional conservative solution which would restore social order, encourage business initiative, and rebuild Germany's international position. This was the stance taken by Gustav Krupp, whose ambiguous relationship with Nazism is explored in Chapter 4. Krupp's preferred solution was Papen's 'cabinet of barons',

---

[21] See the essay by V. Berghahn, 'Big Business in the Third Reich', *European History Quarterly*, 21 (1991), 97–106.

and a 'national-bourgeois' bloc that would avoid extremism of left or right.[22]

If business leaders had any general responsibility for the rise of Nazism to power, it was primarily in a negative sense, in their widespread disillusionment with the parliamentary system and their failure to give democracy any effective moral support.[23] When German business leaders largely abandoned the attempt to hold the shaky political centre together in 1932, it opened the door to populism sufficiently wide to give Hitler a share of power. But this was not the same as deliberately hoisting Hitler into office as a tool to repair the damage caused to the capitalist economy by the recession. Indeed, many businessmen seem on the evidence to have been wary of the closet anti-capitalism of the rank-and-file Nazis. When Hitler came to power, prominent businessmen reserved judgement on him, sceptical of his chances of achieving economic revival and worried about the prospects for further social and political instability.[24]

During the years that followed, Hitler and the Nazi movement were anything but the tools of German big business. But neither was German business rendered entirely powerless through the crude assertion of the 'primacy of politics' over economic interest. To make sense of the ambiguous and complex relationship between the new regime and German industry the historian must differentiate between industries, and even between firms in the same industry. They did not all react in the same way to the regime, nor were they all treated on the same basis. A recent study of the German motor industry has shown how the economic nationalism of the regime brought special treatment and opportunities for German producers at the expense of the American multi-nationals, Opel and Ford.[25] German businesses responded to the difficulties and opportunities opened up by the Nazi regime primarily as businesses, building up assets, rewarding shareholders, safeguarding markets; but in doing so they were also forced to compete for political favours, or to adopt defensive tactics of their own. German industry before 1933 was among the most highly organized and cartelized industry in Europe; this organization provided some opportunity to influence economic policy, to contest state initiatives,

---

[22] See esp. H. A. Turner, *German Big Business and the Rise of Hitler* (Oxford, 1985); D. Abraham, *The Collapse of the Weimar Republic* (Princeton, NJ, 1981); J. Gillingham, *Industry and Politics in the Third Reich* (London, 1985); R. Neebe, 'Unternehmerverbände und Gewerkschaften in den Jahren der grossen Krise 1929–1933', *Geschichte und Gesellschaft*, 9 (1983), 316–29.

[23] B. Weisbrod, 'Economic Power and Political Stability Reconsidered: Heavy Industry in Weimar Germany', *Social History*, 4 (1979), 241–63.

[24] Turner, *Big Business*, 313–39; P. Hayes, 'Fritz Roessler and Nazism: Observations of a German Industrialist 1930–37', *Central European History*, 20 (1987), 58–79.

[25] Reich, *Fruits of Fascism*, 107–30.

or to operate conservative strategies in the face of an unfavourable world market and uncertainties at home, and it made the crude, instrumental view of industry held by Hitler more bearable.[26]

Nor did the relationship between regime and industry remain constant; the link between the two changed character as the Nazi movement consolidated its position and as Hitler's foreign policy and military ambitions began to dictate the general shape of German public affairs. During the war that relationship changed again as Hitler came to realize that industry had something he wanted, the ability to run the war economy more effectively than the party–military alliance that tried to do so for the first two years of the conflict.

In the early years of the regime economic recovery was a priority. Hitler took the view that industry should be encouraged to help in this process by avoiding anything too revolutionary in economic policy. In an address to party leaders in July 1933, at a time when there was still pressure from within the party to intervene radically in industry, Hitler told them 'the economy must be handled with extraordinary caution'. 'We have the power', he continued, 'to throw out every general director. There are no doubt many who deserve to be chucked out, but we must ask ourselves: can bread be provided for workers like this?'[27] In the end Hitler's view prevailed. The regime set out to win co-operation from industry where it needed it. In return it offered cautious re-employment policies and a restored capital market, an end to trade unions, and political stabilization of a kind. The more socialistic elements in the party were quietened, and economic policy was orchestrated by conservatives, and particularly the head of the Reichsbank, Hjalmar Schacht, who believed that prudent collaboration with the Nazis would bring economic and political benefits for German capitalism.

It is easy to see why businessmen found compelling arguments for accepting the regime on these terms. Having experienced the worst recession in Germany's history, they did not want a return to the social instability of the early 1930s. Government grants and public investment helped to revive flagging trade, and there was little to gain from opposing state policies which were directly linked to rising output and profits. Firms were even prepared to accept much higher levels of state economic intervention than hitherto, on the grounds argued by Schacht in defence of the 'New Plan', that world economic circumstances had brought an end

---

[26] See the recent studies by G. Mollin, *Montankonzerne und 'Dritten Reich': Der Gegensatz zwischen Monopolindustrie und Befehlswirtschaft in der deutschen Rüstung und Expansion 1939–1944* (Göttingen, 1988); P. Hayes, *Industry and Ideology: IG Farben in the Nazi Era* (Cambridge, 1987).

[27] Reichsstatthalterkonferenz, 6 July 1933, in *Akten der Reichskanzlei*, i. 632.

to economic libralism and 'a transition from one economic structure to another', in which planning and state regulation had a much larger part to play.[28]

Yet there were signs of friction during the recovery period as well. Consumer industries recovered much more slowly than heavy industry. Small retail and artisan businesses, which had given a great deal of support to the Nazi Party before 1933, found that the revival of domestic demand was slower than they had hoped, and slower than the overall increase in economic activity. There also existed tension over the other element of the economic nationalist platform, autarky, or self-sufficiency. Krupps's view that autarky did not make economic sense reflected the outlook of a firm that thrived on opening up the world market. Even at IG Farben, the giant chemical firm that eventually benefited considerably from the autarky programme, there were divisions between those directors who favoured export-led revival and a world-market strategy, and those, like Carl Krauch, who wanted a programme of import-substitution and the building of economic 'blocs' to match the protectionism of other large markets.[29] In the party and outside there existed influential circles arguing that the old liberal concept of the open world market had disappeared, and should be replaced by exclusive trading zones, even by the conquest of new resources and markets.

The arguments about autarky owed something to the increased expenditure on armaments in 1935/6, which created strong competition between civilian and military priorities for imports of scarce raw materials, and threatened to slow down both the export revival and the upswing in domestic consumer demand. The business community was divided over this issue too. There were firms, in the new aviation industry in particular, whose economic well-being depended on sustained rearmament. But there were other businesses which adopted what one official later called 'a very reserved attitude' to the opportunities opened up by militarization, partly from fear that rearmament would produce international complications, partly from the belief that military spending was not a sufficient basis on which to build a sustainable economic revival.[30] During 1936 a number of prominent businessmen urged a shift of priority. Albert Vögler, head of the Vereinigte Stahlwerke, Germany's largest steel combine, argued that 'exports should be ranked above the requirements of the armed forces'. His colleague Ernst Poensgen told Hitler's personal economic adviser, Wilhelm Keppler, that he saw 'the necessity for a reduction in armaments',

---

[28] BA R2/540, speech by Schacht, 'Ziele deutscher Handelspolitik', 11 Dec. 1934, 2.

[29] P. Hayes, 'Carl Bosch and Carl Krauch: Chemistry and the Political Economy of Germany 1925–1945', *Journal of Economic History*, 47 (1987), 353–63.

[30] National Archives, Washington, DC (NA), RG 243/entry 32, interrogation of Karl Hettlage, 16 June 1945, 2.

and even Schacht, in a speech some months later, expressed the view that civilian consumption 'must in the future stand in the foreground'.[31]

In 1936 the German economy stood at a crossroads. One direction led to a reintegration into the world economy, higher levels of exports, a revival of domestic consumerism, a reduction in state investment. The other led towards self-sufficiency and controlled trade, military production and more state control. The ultimate destination, according to the economic nationalists and imperialists who favoured it, was the building of a 'large economic region' dominated by Germany, and seized by military force if necessary. No doubt there was some middle way between the two, but Hitler by 1936 was no longer in a mood to compromise. During the summer he turned his back on any moderate option and went all out for autarky and rearmament.

The change in direction in 1936 was a critical one, and not just for the economy. It can be compared with Stalin's decision in 1928 to press on with industrial planning and collectivization, or the sharp break in American economic life produced by the New Deal. Like Stalin, Hitler was pressed into the new course by a combination of economic circumstances, international threats, and pressure from within the party. But like Stalin too, Hitler was ideologically predisposed to choose this course when a choice became necessary. The change was signalled by the Second Four Year Plan publicly announced in October, but it was already under way, with close controls over trade and international payments introduced the previous April, and large new military programmes announced in August. The change in personnel was also significant. The new Plan was placed not under Schacht, but under Hermann Göring, a strong man of the party. Göring welcomed autarky because it gave the regime 'greater manœuvrability and independence' when it came to completing the re-militarization of Germany. He was a champion of rearmament at all costs, and he was sufficiently ambitious and unscrupulous not to let unenthusiastic businessmen stand in the way of achieving the Führer's will.[32]

The new course from 1936 had important consequences for German industry. In the short term it produced a political conflict with the most influential leaders of German heavy industry who were opposed to state pressure to expand domestic production of iron ore as part of the self-sufficiency drive. It was recognized by both sides that much more was involved in the conflict. The background and ramifications of the issue are explored in Chapter 3. What was at stake was the continuing ability of

[31] BA R26I/36, Niederschrift des Gutachten-Ausschusses über Exportfragen, 15 May 1936, 12; R26I/30, Keppler Tageszettel 5 Oct. 1936; R11/318, Ansprache des Dr Schacht auf dem 7 Allgemeinen Sparkassen- und Kommunalbankentag, 29 Sept. 1937, 17.

[32] BA R26I/36, Gutachten-Ausschuss, 30 June 1936, 26.

industry to influence state economic policy, and in particular to prevent anything like the 'nationalization' or 'socialization' of industry. Most businessmen remained committed to the principle of *Gewerbefreiheit*, business freedom. The ideal remained a strong, responsible German state giving autonomy to industry while keeping social conflict within acceptable bounds. This did not exclude state assistance, on which many firms, relied between 1931 and 1936, but it did exclude state interference with corporate decision-making, or direct state control of industrial production.

In practice the decision to promote self-sufficiency and high arms spending made it necessary to extend state control over the economy and eliminate any real room for independent manœuvre that German business still enjoyed. It also brought the state into the direct sphere of production. The failure of the Ruhr industrialists to halt the autarky programme was largely due to the willingness of Göring's new economic apparatus to take the task on themselves. In 1937 the creation of the Reichswerke 'Hermann Göring', established by the state to exploit domestic iron ore, set the pattern for the rest of the Third Reich period. When the regime wanted additional industrial capacity or resources for the military economy which the private sector could not provide, it was created (or conquered) by the state. State ownership of public utilities was already an established fact in Germany, but during the Third Reich state ownership expanded into the productive sector, based around the strategic industries, aviation, aluminium, synthetic oil and rubber, chemicals, iron and steel, and army equipment. Government finances for state-owned enterprises rose from RM 4,000m. in 1933 to RM 16,000m. ten years later; the capital assets of state-owned industry doubled during the same period, and the number of state-owned firms topped 500.[33] The Reichswerke alone engrossed assets worth over RM 5,000m., a process that is described in detail in Chapter 5. During the war the regime toyed with nationalizing the coal industry, insurance companies, and the energy-supply industry. Hitler vetoed these attempts on the ground that the private business form should be retained to avoid excessive bureaucratization, and to encourage 'entrepreneurial' leadership qualities, but when it came to a choice between state policy or private interest, the state usually prevailed.[34]

This process should not be seen in isolation. State intervention and 'planisme' was on the increase in all European economies. Arguments over the nationalization of industry emerged in Italy, France, and Britain in the

[33] BA R7/992, Berichte über den Konzern Reichswerke 'H.G.': 'Schulden der staatlichen Unternehmungen 1933–1943'; NA Microcopy T83, Roll 75, frames 3446065–72, Economics Ministry, 'Der Zuwachs an staatlichen Unternehmungen in Privatrechtsform', n.d. [?mid-1944].
[34] BA R2/31681, Bormann to Speer on socializing energy supply, 27 July 1942.

1930s. Historians now debate whether Britain had a 'managed economy' by 1939, the very term—*die gelenkte Wirtschaft*—adopted by German economists in the 1930s to describe the Nazi economy. Nor should this development be seen as a crude 'dualism', state on one side, industry on the other. The Nazi regime after 1936 was determined to transform the economy in ways which would serve the drive for empire and conquest. Nazi officials found and promoted businessmen who were willing to co-operate with their programmes. Some industrialists accepted that the new direction, viewed with expediency, might bring substantial benefits. Structural shifts in German industry, away from the traditional heavy industries of the Ruhr to the new automotive, chemical, and aviation sectors (much of it in central and southern Germany), reduced the regime's dependence on the old industrial élite. A changing pattern of management accompanied this structural change. The large new firms were run by industrial bureaucrats and technicians with a more narrowly functional perception of their responsibilities. Peter Hayes has recently argued that the 'Nazification' of IG Farben was made easier by the bureaucratic mentality of many of those who ran it, and the easy transfer of personnel between the state economic apparatus and that of industry.[35] Both the Four Year Plan organization and, later, the wartime economic apparatus recruited from the private managerial sector as well as the party and the career civil service. The outcome was a command economy, governed by military priorities, but run by a coalition of state officials, soldiers, party hacks, and industrial technocrats.

For businessmen who did not share the warlike ambitions of the regime, or who disliked the loss of entrepreneurial freedom and the aggressive extension of state responsibility there were still opportunities to defend the interests of the firm, to expand assets at the expense of Jewish owners or the German taxpayer, or, after 1938, to take a share of those industrial spoils not seized by the Reichswerke as the new European order unfolded. The effect of the change in course in 1936/7 was the fragmentation of any common front industry might have had, and the adoption of an attitude of *sauve qui peut*. Industry was regarded entirely instrumentally by party, state, and military, in terms of its ability to provide the sinews of war. Under the 'primacy of politics' industry reacted opportunistically, searching for secure patron–client relationships with the military–state apparatus, building up assets at the state's expense, taking labour from whatever source the state made available, in the end turning a blind eye to atrocity and exploitation. The business community was characterized by a defensive opportunism in the face of state power. This kept the substance

[35] Hayes, *Industry and Ideology*, 379–83.

of German capitalism intact, but at the cost of entrepreneurial independence and unavoidable complicity in the racial and imperialist strategies of the regime's leaders.

REARMAMENT AND FOUR YEAR PLAN

The historical debate about rearmament in the later 1930s, after the new course adopted in 1936 with the Four Year Plan, contains an interesting paradox. Where the arguments about the recovery period insist on giving military spending an exaggerated place, there has been a prevailing tendency to play down the significance of rearmament for the period 1936–9, at just the point when Hitler deliberately embarked on a large-scale programme of direct and indirect rearmament. This view owes a great deal to A. J. P. Taylor's book on the origins of the Second World War which gave wide currency to the work of Burton Klein, an American economist who had worked on the post-war United States Strategic Bombing Survey, and who concluded on the basis of Germany's wartime economic performance that she had been much less thoroughly prepared for war before 1939 than everyone had thought.[36] This fitted neatly with Taylor's own conviction that Hitler had limited ambitions in central Europe, and only needed limited forces to achieve them.

Few historians have accepted Taylor's view that Hitler had limited territorial ambitions, and there is a great deal of convincing evidence that points in the opposite direction. But the argument that rearmament was limited in scope fitted with interpretations of the Third Reich that emphasized its weaknesses, the tendency to confused administration, the proliferation of competing power-centres, fear of alienating the working classes and producing insupportable social crisis. The notions of 'polycracy' and 'weak dictatorship' replaced the totalitarian image. It was argued that limited armaments allowed Hitler to offer guns and butter at the same time. The armed forces reacted by producing the novel conception of *Blitzkrieg*, or 'lightning war'—deploying the limited weapons base in short, sharp campaigns which would optimize Germany's military capability while making few demands on the civilian population. In this way Germany would avoid the mistakes of the First World War and the risks of revolution.[37]

All of these views rested on the assumption that Hitler did deliberately

[36] B. H. Klein, *Germany's Economic Preparations for War* (Cambridge, Mass., 1959); id., 'Germany's Preparation for War: A Reexamination', *American Economic Review*, 38 (1948).
[37] According to J. K. Galbraith, *A Life in Our Times: Memoirs* (London, 1981), 223, the inspiration for the Blitzkrieg economy argument was the economist Nicholas Kaldor, who outlined the hypothesis at a meeting of Bombing Survey staff in Bavaria. For Kaldor's developed view see 'The German War Economy', *Review of Economic Statistics*, 13 (1946).

restrict Germany's military economy during this period in the face of economic and social pressures, and that Klein's economic analysis was therefore valid. The evidential problems with this assumption are explored in detail in Chapter 8. Neither the military nor the economic version of *Blitzkrieg* have stood the test of time. What has emerged is a picture of the economy much more consistent with the large military plans and the visions of conquest at the core of Hitler's thinking. We have already seen that Hitler saw the economy in military terms, and would have liked the direct and indirect rearmament of Germany to move faster after 1933 than it did. Rather than accept reality and limit his ambitions, the change in 1936 signalled Hitler's determination to press on rapidly with high levels of militarization and indirect, economic rearmament. Hitler's view that war must involve 'the whole strength of the people' matched the armed forces' own arguments for broad-based preparation for war, and was echoed in the views of his subordinates who were charged with carrying the programmes out.

Of course it could be argued that here again Hitler was whistling in the wind, promoting a vision of an armed economy that no one took seriously and which begged economic credibility. In other words that it is not enough to locate the *intention* if the circumstances dictated a different course. But there is a very real difference between the early recovery years and the period of the Four Year Plan. From 1936 onwards Hitler began to concentrate political power more firmly in his own hands and those of trusted colleagues. By 1938 the old élites had lost control of the Foreign Office, the armed forces and the economy, and military strategy and economic policy were dictated by Hitler rather than mediated by the old civil service and ministerial apparatus. And this shift was to a considerable degree dictated by Hitler's very desire to press on with large-scale militarization and active territorial expansion, which he felt was being held up by his more timid conservative allies. After 1936 it became much easier for Hitler to turn intention into political fact. By 1939 Hitler's central role in the determination of German state policy was unchallengeable, and it undermines any image of the 'weak dictator' unable to hold his rambling state together.

In the second place there is the overwhelming evidence that Hitler's intentions had very real practical effects, both in the expansion of the armed forces and weapons production, and in the 'indirect' development of the economy for war. What is significant about the new course after 1936 was the regime's recognition that military capability and economic restructuring went hand in hand. The Four Year Plan and rearmament were regarded as ranked the same (*gleichrängig*).[38] Hitler recognized that

---

[38] BA R26IV/5, Vierjahresplan Sitzung 31, 14 Oct. 1938, 2: 'The Four Year Plan belongs with rearmament; it is of equivalent rank with it.'

to be able to make Germany a serious military power, capable of sustaining war with the great powers and conquering 'living-space', it was necessary to make her free from the threat of blockade by building up the domestic production of strategic materials and foodstuffs, and by seizing or integrating the economic resources of central and eastern Europe into a 'greater economic region', very like Japan's 'Co-Prosperity Sphere', which would provide the economic springboard for German imperialism. Rather than indulge the German consumer, the regime controlled imports in favour of strategically necessary goods, kept taxes high, and discriminated against the revival of consumer industries.

The scale and nature of these practical efforts are set out in Chapter 6 and do not need to be reproduced here. But two observations are worth making. First, there still exists considerable uncertainty about what constitutes a high level of direct military spending. By 1938/9 Germany devoted 15 per cent of her GNP to military expenditure, in 1939 23 per cent. There should be no doubt that these are historically high levels of peacetime spending. The European NATO powers at the height of the Cold War devoted between 3 and 7 per cent of GNP to direct military budgets.[39] In 1939 only Stalin's planned economy devoted a higher proportion. Before the First World War, at the time of the first great arms race, German military spending was only 3 per cent of GNP, and 24 per cent of government expenditure. In 1938/9 52 pfennigs of every mark the government spent went on the military budget.[40] To be sure, not all of this was spent on weapons. The military budget was greatly inflated by the urgent building of the Westwall fortifications in 1938–9, and by the mobilization expenses for the Anschluss, the crisis over the Sudetenland, and the occupation of Prague in March 1939. But whether the money was spend on weapons or cement, the military budget diverted resources from the civilian economy.

Second, the argument that rearmament was limited in scale ignores the growing significance of 'indirect rearmament' after 1936. The formal military budget greatly understates the degree to which the German economy was committed to re-militarization in the late 1930s. By looking at the production of finished weapons alone, the impression can be given that Germany had only achieved by 1939 'armament in breadth' (Breitrüstung), that is a limited quantity of battlefield equipment designed for a short campaign. The alternative, what German strategists called 'armament in depth' (Tiefrüstung), relies on evidence that the economic underpinning for sustained warmaking—the machinery, basic raw materials, trained labour, armaments capacity, etc.—is also in

[39] G. Kennedy, The Economics of Defence (London, 1975), 79.
[40] NA Microcopy T178, Roll 15, Finance Ministry, 'Statistische Übersichten zu den Reichshaushaltsrechnungen 1938 bis 1943', Nov. 1944, frame 3671912.

preparation. This was exactly what the programme of autarky and state investment under the Four Year Plan was supposed to achieve, providing the 'productive foundation' on which 'the additional demands of new armaments programmes could be borne'. According to a wartime report on the work of the Four Year Plan since 1936, its inception was based on Hitler's realization that 'to achieve the goal of total mobilization of all economic resources' it was necessary to begin 'a thoroughgoing rebuilding of the present economic structure'.[41]

Indirect rearmament between 1936 and 1939 was in many ways more important than the direct production of military equipment because it was designed to expand the productive economy and trained labour force for the very much larger military programmes ordered by Hitler for the 1940s. It also involved the provision domestically of scarce raw materials essential to future warmaking—synthetic fuel production, synthetic rubber and textiles, aluminium production, domestic sources of iron ore, expanded chemical output to meet the demands for explosives production. The claims that all this made on the German economy were enormous. Between 1936 and 1939 two-thirds of all industrial investment went into war and war-related sectors. The whole industrial economy was distorted in favour of engineering, industrial raw materials, and heavy industrial equipment. The labour market, too, suffered a similar distortion, with shortages in consumer industries and agriculture. By 1939 a quarter of the industrial work-force laboured on orders for the armed forces, but a great many more worked on constructing the new industrial capacity, or on the raw-material programmes of the Four Year Plan, or the building of the Westwall fortifications, or the strategic refurbishment of the railways. The great increase in activity brought more women into the heavy industrial and armaments work-force. Between 1938 and 1941 the number of women employed in chemicals increased by 67 per cent, in the metals industries by 59 per cent, and so on. At Siemens, a major supplier of electrical equipment, the female labour force grew from 10,000 in 1937 to 17,000 in 1939.[42]

This broader conception of war preparation was everywhere in evidence after 1936. The regime was aware of the need to safeguard food supplies, in order to avoid another blockade like the one which had such severe consequences between 1914 and 1918. The Four Year Plan actively promoted the technical improvement of agriculture and the expansion of domestic output, and it promoted the use of immigrant labour to replace German workers who moved to the more lucrative jobs in industry. The

---

[41] BA R261/18, Ergebnisse der Vierjahresplan-Arbeit, Stand Frühjahr 1942, 2, 49.

[42] Military History Institute, Carlisle, Pa. (MHI), Military Intelligence Reports, Reel IX, 'Annual Economic Review, Germany', 22 Mar. 1941, 12–14; D. Winkler, *Frauenarbeit im Dritten Reich* (Hamburg, 1977), 197.

Plan also encouraged large-scale retraining of labour, in skills more necessary for the war effort. A total of 1.2 million workers passed through these programmes before 1939. A systematic industrial index was undertaken by the Economics Ministry, detailing civilian industries suitable for conversion to military production in case of war. Though there existed no central planning agency co-ordinating the indirect preparations for war, the relationship between the different elements seems to have been well understood. The late 1930s saw an increasingly coherent effort to create in a short space of time the economic conditions necessary to sustain large-scale military forces and a strategy of full-scale economic mobilization.

It was also recognized that Germany could not rely on her own resources alone. After 1936 the idea of a larger, German-dominated economic region, fashionable with economic nationalists during the slump, became more widely accepted in party and government circles. Germany's economic diplomacy became geared to increasing Germany's financial and trading presence in eastern and central Europe.[43] By 1939 Germany had secure agreements with Romania, Yugoslavia, Hungary, Slovakia, and, in August, with the USSR to supply food and raw materials on favourable terms. But Hitler wanted physically to control the richer industrial areas of the former German and Austrian empires; and first Austria itself, then the Sudetenland, then Bohemia and, in September 1939, Silesia were brought under direct German rule, and their labour force, raw materials, heavy industry (and gold and foreign currency reserves) added to the economic resource base. Of course there were other elements at work in explaining German territorial expansion—Hitler's obsessive Pan-Germanism, the opportunities opening up in the international arena with the decline of British and French influence, pressure from within the party for a more radical course in foreign policy—but all the captured areas were rich in resources and relatively easy to integrate into the German industrial economy (see Chapters 6 and 11). All of these things, the great increase in direct military spending, the indirect preparation of the economic substructure, the engrossing of the resources of central and eastern Europe, indicate something quite distinct from the idea of limited, 'shop-window' rearmament, for short smash-and-grab wars.

It is sometimes argued that the costs of military build-up on this scale proved insupportable, that Hitler once again found himself the victim of

[43] B.-J. Wendt, *Grossdeutschland: Autarkiepolitik und Kriegsvorbereitung des Hitler-Regimes* (Munich, 1987), esp. ch. 4; E. Teichert, *Autarkie und Grossraumwirtschaft in Deutschland 1930–1939* (Munich, 1984); D. Kaiser, *Economic Diplomacy and the Origins of the Second World War: Germany, Britain, France and Eastern Europe 1930–1939* (Princeton, NJ, 1980), esp. chs. 6, 9; Volkmann, 'National Socialist Economy', 309–15, 323–60.

economic reality. There is no doubt that the adjustment to a state-dominated, rapidly militarizing economy did produce problems in resource allocation and the provisioning of the civilian population. The short world recession of 1938 also hit the German economy in its efforts to boost exports to earn essential imports for the rearmament effort. A recent study has suggested that the critical point in the German trade and payments situation came early in 1938, before Germany seized the gold and foreign exchange resources of Austria.[44] The domestic economy also saw a very slow rate of productivity growth, partly a result of government efforts to get people re-employed as quickly as possible, partly a product of the growing dependence of many firms on state orders, which removed any real incentive to reduce costs or chase foreign competitors. But these were the kind of difficulties faced by all the rearming states in the 1930s—balance-of-payments problems, domestic arguments about budget priorities, a wary industrial response, considerable waste and muddle in the early stages of rearmament. The issue they all faced was how to respond to these difficulties.

In the German case there exists considerable disagreement about the response. It has been argued that the regime deliberately restricted rearmament in order to avoid the domestic consequences of demanding too much of the German civilian population and over-straining an economy in the throes of a delicate recovery. This view, as we have seen, does not take sufficient account of the very large scale of direct and indirect rearmament achieved by 1939, nor of the intentions of the regime's leaders. There is a second, and related, argument which accepts that Germany was arming heavily for war, but suggests that the effort to supply both arms and consumer goods created critical strains which forced Hitler to launch a European war in 1939 to stave off impending social and economic disaster. There are echoes here of the thesis that Germany provoked war in 1914 to preserve the Bismarckian system in the face of popular politics. But this view carries the danger of overstating the nature of the crisis—the strains of rearmament bear no comparison with the very real crisis of 1929–32—and exaggerating the degree of dissent evident in 1939. Some detailed criticisms of both arguments are set out in Chapter 7.[45] Recent research has come to place much more emphasis on the success of the Nazi state in controlling dissent, and winning acquiescence, even among working-class populations hostile to Nazism in 1932. A combination of effective propaganda, full employment, and terror created

---

[44] A. Ritschl, 'Die deutsche Zahlungsbilanz 1936–41 und das Problem des Devisenmangels vor Kriegsbeginn', *Vierteljahrshefte für Zeitgeschichte*, 39 (1991), 103–22.
[45] See too the debate in *Past and Present*, 122 (1989), 200–40.

for the regime a firmer foundation than it had enjoyed at any time since 1933.[46]

This was not a simple or frictionless process. The demands of rearmament led to ever greater claims of the state over the economy, and to much higher levels of state planning than had been thought necessary. Evidence of inefficiency produced state-sponsored rationalization drives, with mixed results.[47] Labour shortages were tackled by encouraging female employment and recruiting foreign workers in Italy, Poland, Yugoslavia, etc.[48] The financial pressures were met by rigid price and wage controls, more careful assessment of public expenditure, and virtual compulsion to get savings banks and other deposit-holders to buy government bonds to fund further spending. The shortages of domestic material resources prompted the trade and military offensive into central Europe. Yet despite all these pressures, the pace of rearmament and economic reconstruction went on in 1939. There is little evidence to suggest that Hitler deliberately limited his military plans, or that the problems they generated pushed him to gamble on war at all costs.

Both these views rest on the central assumption that Hitler wanted a general European war in 1939 and that war preparations, limited or otherwise, were geared to this intention. Yet the outbreak of a general European war in 1939 seems to have been a result of miscalculation on Hitler's part. He wanted to wage his major war three or four years later, when the economy and armed forces were ready. There is no doubt, of course, about his intention to have a local war in 1939 to destroy Poland, once it became clear that the Polish government would not agree to become a virtual satellite of the Reich. Hitler's planning involved a great risk, but a combination of what looked like favourable international circumstances, British and French hesitancy over Danzig, and intelligence sources which indicated western military unpreparedness, persuaded him that the risk was worth taking. His conviction that the western states would not seriously intervene to save Poland was based not on mere wishful thinking, but on what Hitler thought was a reasonable calculation

---

[46] See the discussion in I. Kershaw, *Popular Opinion and Political Dissent in the Third Reich* (Oxford, 1983); D. Peukert, *Inside Nazi Germany: Conformity, Opposition and Racism in Everyday Life* (London, 1987); on the working class see U. Herbert, 'Arbeiterschaft im "Dritten Reich": Zwischenbilanz und offene Fragen', *Geschichte und Gesellschaft*, 15 (1989), 320–60.

[47] R. Hachtmann, *Industriearbeit im 'Dritten Reich': Untersuchungen zu den Lohn- und Arbeitsbedingungen in Deutschland 1933–1945* (Göttingen, 1989), 71–7; P. Kirchberg, 'Typisierung in der deutschen Kraftfahrzeugindustrie', *Jahrbuch für Wirtschaftsgeschichte*, 8 (1969), 117–42.

[48] U. Herbert, *Fremdarbeiter: Politik und Praxis des 'Ausländer-Einsatzes' in der Kriegswirtschaft des Dritten Reiches* (Bonn, 1985), 53–9. In 1937 there were 229,000 foreign workers in Germany, by 1939 398,000.

of western strengths and weaknesses. Nor, it should be said, is there any evidence to suggest that the local war with Poland was part of a strategy of jingoistic diversion, to keep the German working classes from revolt. The Polish campaign was the product of a concerted German drive into eastern Europe. The timing was determined by international and military factors rather than domestic structural pressures.

The thesis of miscalculation is evident from the diaries and memoirs of the time. The recent discovery in Moscow of the missing entries of the Goebbels diary have confirmed the picture. On 21 August the news of the imminent Nazi–Soviet Pact was greeted by Goebbels as 'perfect', since it made the prospect of general war much less likely: 'now we can sleep more easily'. For the next few days Hitler sought to detach Britain from Poland to make doubly sure that the war could be localized. The British leadership gave Hitler enough evidence that they were trying to find a negotiated settlement that he ordered the invasion of Poland on 31 August. 'The Führer', Goebbels wrote, 'does not believe England will intervene.' Even when Britain and France declared war three days later, Hitler told Goebbels that 'there will be only a phoney war in the west'.[49] Goebbels himself, like Göring and the army leaders, thought that there was a greater risk than Hitler said, but the belief that the war could be localized became a conviction. The coming of general European war left Hitler, according to his press chief, Otto Dietrich, 'stunned'.[50]

When war came in September the German economy was not yet ready. The 'armament in depth' was a number of years from completion (see Chapter 6). The large capital projects, oil production, chemicals, the refurbishment of the railways network, were far from complete; the plans for weapons, particularly in the air and the naval rearmament programme, were far from realization. More significant for the argument that Hitler wanted a European war in 1939, there was no preparation for a Western campaign, no 'Schlieffen Plan'. Elaborate plans were made for the conquest of Poland but the unexpected conflict in the west left Hitler and the military chiefs at a loss until von Manstein produced his suggestion for a campaign through the Ardennes forest at the weak hinge of the Anglo-French defensive front. For the next year the economy was weakened by arguments over whether to complete the industrial restructuring or to concentrate on more weapons, while German forces remained short of the tanks, vehicles, bombs, and shells that were to have been provided several years later. Many of the problems and pressures faced by the German war effort were the result, rather than the cause, of the premature outbreak of a large-scale European war.

[49] *Sunday Times*, 12 July 1992, 2: 3.
[50] O. Dietrich, *The Hitler I Knew* (London, 1955), 44.

THE GERMAN WAR ECONOMY

It has long been the convention to divide the history of the German war economy into two distinct phases. During the first, from September 1939 to January 1942, it is argued that the German war effort was deliberately restricted to keep up high levels of civilian consumption; the German armed forces had to make do with current stocks of equipment designed to support short wars of conquest which had to be won in a single military blow. The second phase, from 1942 to 1945, was one of gradual transition to total war, in which the economy was finally converted to war as fully as possible and the civilian consumer forced to accept real economic sacrifices. This shift gave Germany the economic strength to keep going for three years against the combined weight of the three Allied powers.[51]

Like the arguments surrounding the pre-war rearmament effort, this picture of the German war economy rests a great deal on the findings of the US Strategic Bombing Survey. The evidence discovered by the survey showed a low level of armaments production between 1939 and 1942, with high surviving levels of consumer goods production, followed by a sharp increase in output of military equipment from 1942 onwards even in the face of heavy bombing. The survey quickly drew an obvious conclusion, that the German economy must have been mobilized to only a limited degree until the failure in the Soviet Union forced a switch away from consumer goods to military output. This explanatory framework, and the limited statistical evidence that supported it, formed the basis of the *Blitzkrieg* version of the German war effort.[52]

As a source the Bombing Survey must be treated with great caution. In the first place American officials approached the issue in the knowledge that bombing had not been as effective as expected. The German economy had expanded output considerably even when the bombing reached a peak in 1944–5. The discovery that weapons output was relatively low in 1939–41 provided the explanation they were looking for: Hitler had not, after all, armed Germany to the teeth before launching war, and there was plenty of spare industrial capacity to use when bombing started. This explained the apparent paradox of increased bombing and increased German output.[53] Secondly, the survey was carried out under difficult circumstances in a short space of time. Its brief was to report on the effects of bombing, material and moral. Its views on the overall performance of

---

[51] Most recently F. Blaich, *Wirtschaft und Rüstung im 'Dritten Reich'* (Düsseldorf, 1987), 33–55; for a contrary view see R. J. Overy, 'Mobilization for Total War in Germany 1939–1941', *English Historical Review*, 103 (1988), 613–39.

[52] United States Strategic Bombing Survey (USSBS), *Overall Report (European War)*, Sept. 1945, 1–2.

[53] Galbraith, *Memoirs*, 222–7.

the German economy and on German economic policy were the product of interviews with any economic officials or experts the Allies could round up, and as a result were impressionistic and partial. A great deal of the interpretation rested on the evidence of an official from the German Statistical Office, Rolf Wagenführ, who was highly critical of the war effort and who was the source of the claim that Germany enjoyed a 'peacelike war economy' before 1942.[54]

Wagenführ, like the Bombing Survey, based his conclusions on raw data on weapons output and consumer production. He was not in a position to see much of what was going on in the wider economy, and was certainly not privy to the formation of economic and military policy during the war period. More significant, his testimony was contradicted by most of the other major witnesses whom the British and Americans interviewed at the end of the war. The most important was Albert Speer, the Nazi Party architect who was chosen by Hitler to be Armaments Minister in February 1942, and whose period in office coincided with the great increase in German military output. Though Speer later gave the impression that there had been a sharp increase in the German war effort when he took office in 1942, his interviews in 1945 give a rather different version. Speer took the view that the German economy had been mobilized to a relatively high level by 1941 in terms of the degree of industrial capacity and the labour force converted to war work, but that the inefficient and confused management of resources had resulted in levels of arms output much lower than expected. His success in expanding arms output came as a result of using these resources more efficiently and centralizing the war economic apparatus, but not as a result of converting the civilian economy to military production.[55]

This view was echoed in the interviews with officials, businessmen, and engineers who worked in the German economy during the war. Professor Karl Hettlage told his interrogators that there were 'no decisive' reserves of civilian industrial capacity left in 1941 and that the increase in output was due to 'technical rationalization measures, which were more important than any other single measure'.[56] The staff of the Reich Economic Chamber, who worked during the war on establishing national accounts for the war period, provided detailed statistical evidence to show a sharp decline in German *per capita* consumption of goods between 1939 and 1942 and a large increase in the proportion of the economy devoted to

[54] Imperial War Museum (IWM) FD 3057/49, FIAT Report 1312, 'Economic History of the Second World War', by Dr R. Wagenführ.
[55] IWM Box S368, Interrogation reports: Report 86, Speer interrogation, 31 Oct. 1945; Report 54, Speer interrogation, 13 July 1945.
[56] NA RG243 entry 32, Interrogation of Karl Hettlage, 15.

war.[57] Even the Bombing Survey itself reproduced in its numerous statistical appendices evidence that contradicted the central thesis of a two-stage war effort. For reasons that are not entirely clear, the authors of the *Overall Report* on the German war economy chose to ignore this very different interpretation and to accept Wagenführ's figures at face value.

Yet these figures obscure more than they reveal. Wagenführ failed to take into account the fact that the Statistical Office continued to classify industries according to their pre-war category even though many of the 'consumer' industries were converted to war production in 1939. An intelligence report forwarded to Washington in March 1941 from Berlin, based on an article by Hettlage, made the point clearly:

the employment of an unusually large percentage of industrial capacity for wartime purposes is another characteristic of the Reich's wartime economy. The usual demarkation [*sic*] line between arms and munition industries, on the one hand, and peacetime or 'civilian' industries, on the other, is being effaced in a national economy which is so highly mobilized for the purposes of war. Therefore, when the annual reports of companies usually classified as belonging to the group of 'consumer goods industries', indicate a 'satisfactory' or 'record' turnover during the last business year, it does not necessarily mean that they are still engaged in the manufacture of the products ordinarily turned out in peacetime.[58]

By 1941 the armed forces took between 40 and 50 per cent of the output of non-food consumer industries.[59] By June 1940 it was calculated that 43 per cent of the work-force in the civilian industries had been transferred to war contracts.[60] At the same time the quality of consumer goods for the civilian market declined as skilled men were transferred to arms production and civilian producers were forced to improvise. Substitute or *ersatz* materials replaced textiles, leather, or metals needed for military production. Small consumer-goods firms became sub-contractors for the major military suppliers. The German forces' insatiable appetite for uniforms, mess tins, cups, boots, etc. also had to be satisfied by the civilian industries. Even the production of saddles, stirrups, and reins (which has been used as evidence of the survival of inessential consumer production) was absorbed by a military machine which used 1.2 million horses.

The picture from the German side was quite different from the one presented in the Bombing Survey. Civilian consumption fell further and faster than it did in Britain or the United States, and most of the fall came

---

[57] IWM Box S366, FD 3058/49, introduction to R. Grünig, 'Volkswirtschaftliche Bilanz für Deutschland'.

[58] MHI, Military Intelligence Reports, Reel IX, 'Annual Economic Review, Germany: 1941', 31.

[59] IWM FD 5444/45, Protokoll über die Inspekteurbesprechung 22 Feb. 1941 bei OKW, 42.

[60] IWM EDS AL/1571, 'Arbeitseinsatz und Einziehungen in der nicht zum engeren Rüstungsbereich gehörenden Wirtschaft', 9 Jan. 1941, 3.

in the period between 1939 and 1941, despite the acquisition of additional European resources. High taxes, high savings, and a doubling of military spending (with very little growth of GNP), all contributed to limiting the proportion of the economy available for civilian consumption. The effects of economic mobilization during this period are examined more fully in Chapter 9. Whether measured in financial, macroeconomic terms, or in terms of the redistribution of the work-force, or in terms of the conversion of civilian industrial capacity, more of the German economy was converted to war before 1942 than after. Of course as the war went on and Germany faced military defeat the degree of sacrifice became greater, and the regime adopted a combination of do-or-die propaganda and increased terror to keep the population fighting total war. But the basic structure of the wartime economy was set in the first months of war.

How, then, is the low level of weapons production between 1939 and 1941 to be explained? Wagenführ was right to argue that armaments output expanded much more rapidly after 1942 than before. Even here the figures can be misleading. The production of aircraft and artillery did expand slowly; the output of a range of other weapons and equipment, particularly naval production and tanks, grew much more quickly.[61] There appear to be two main explanations. In the first place the German war economy in the early years of war was still committed to high levels of 'indirect' military spending in completing the expensive capital-intensive projects both inside Germany and in the captured areas—synthetic fuel production in Czechoslovakia, aluminium production in Norway, etc. This explains the contrast with Britain, whose smaller industrial base produced more arms from 1939 to 1942. Britain was able to import the fuel oil and raw materials she needed from the outside world, freeing domestic industrial capacity for the manufacture of weapons. The great increase in the output of finished weapons in Germany after 1942 reflected the completion of many of these capital projects, or the decision to curtail them in favour of manufacturing weapons.

The second explanation is political as much as economic. During the first two years of war the economy was managed with an extraordinary degree of muddle and inefficiency. Competition for control of production between the Four Year Plan, the Economics Ministry, the Armaments Ministry (set up under Fritz Todt on 17 March 1940), and the armed forces had a debilitating effect on actual output. The failure to produce any central direction over the flow of labour, machinery, and raw materials led to widespread duplication of effort, wastage, and poor distribution. The real change of direction for the German economy came

---

[61] C. Webster and N. Frankland, *The Strategic Air Offensive against Germany* (London, 1961), iv. 469–70.

in 1941, when Hitler ordered the streamlining and rationalization of production, and in 1942, when he gave his political backing to Speer to centralize production and end the factionalism and bureaucratic egoism which had stifled previous efforts at administrative reform.

The remarkable effects of this rationalization drive cannot be underestimated; they are set out in Chapter 11. Because the economy was so mismanaged, even the most rudimentary improvements in administrative practice and factory methods produced remarkable dividends. According to Karl-Otto Saur, Speer's deputy and an expert in factory rationalization, the reforms made it possible to produce 40,000 tons of army weapons from every 100,000 tons of steel, where previously only 10,000 tons were achieved. By the end of the war German firms 'managed to produce four times the amount of weapons with fewer machines, fewer men and less factory space than before'.[62] The industrial momentum produced by the reforms was finally halted by high levels of bombing and the Allied reconquest of occupied Europe.

The German war economy can be divided into three different stages, though strong continuities are visible throughout the whole war period. The first stage lasted from September 1939 to the summer of 1941. During this period the greater part of the cut-back in civilian consumption during the war was achieved, and the bulk of the conversion of industrial capacity and labour to war and war-related orders carried out. A number of important structural and institutional factors acted to inhibit the effective exploitation of the converted resources: the economic effort of completing the basic industries needed to sustain further warmaking; the economic cost and administrative effort required to incorporate the conquered regions into the German economic system; the uncertainty for industrial and military leaders alike of Hitler's foreign-policy intentions and the outcome of the military campaigns; and finally the high degree of political conflict, jurisdictional confusion, and decentralization in the German war apparatus.

The second stage lasted from the summer of 1941 down to the summer of 1944. During this period efforts were made to rationalize and simplify the war economy and the industries manufacturing weapons. The administrative apparatus was reformed, and a more centralized system for allocating and distributing resources was established. The Four Year Plan and the armed forces were replaced by the Speer ministry and industrial leaders as part of Hitler's effort to reduce the effects of bureaucratization and political infighting on war production. As a result of the reforms, long production runs became possible, weapons were standardized and

[62] IWM Box S368, FIAT Report 90, 1 June 1946, 'The Rationalization of the German Armaments Industry', 6. In German statistics throughout the book 'tons' are to be understood as metric tonnes.

simplified, and output trebled. European labour and resources were exploited more fully, and any uncertainty about the character of the war or the direction of German strategy disappeared.

The third phase ran from the summer of 1944 down to the end of the war. By this stage German production reached its peak. Weapons were produced thereafter from repairing damaged equipment, using up stocks of spares and components, and concentrating production on only the most essential and easily produced equipment. The economy slowly disintegrated during this final stage under the weight of bombing directed against transport, key industries, and oil, and with the gradual loss of European resources. Bombing produced the decentralization of the war economy again and, eventually, the 'regionalization' of the economy as parts of the Reich became virtually cut off from others. Control over the war economy passed increasingly to the SS and the apparatus of terror as the regime resorted to desperate and improvised measures to keep the war effort going.[63] By the end of the war the economy was caught between bombing and invasion on the one hand, and the frantic and brutal efforts of the Party extremists to create a siege economy based on forced labour and underground factories, on the other. In the end only the reluctance of officials and soldiers on the spot prevented Hitler's final call for 'scorched earth' from becoming reality.

CONCLUSION

Hitler's curious blend of Social Darwinism and Wagnerian romanticism explains his willingness to accept, in the end, even the economic suicide of his people. It was a measure of his instrumental view of the economy that he should expect complete sacrifice at the moment of complete defeat. But it would be wrong to see the whole history of war and economy during the Third Reich as a function of Hitler's will. As the system came to centre more and more on the desires of the dictator, and the prospects for alternative strategies became more remote, his influence in economic affairs became more deterministic. But in the early 1930s this outcome was far from clear. The problems facing Germany during the slump and its aftermath were shared by other major industrial economies, and the German response to those circumstances was not unique, let alone a product only of Hitler's thinking or of Nazi ideology.

The slump encouraged a universal drift towards protectionism and self-sufficiency. The pressure of popular domestic politics made it sensible

---

[63] See A. C. Mierzejewski, *The Collapse of the German War Economy 1944–1945* (Chapel Hill, NC, 1988); A. Speer, *The Slave State: Heinrich Himmler's Master Plan for SS Supremacy* (London, 1981).

for all governments to think of saving their own economies at the expense of any concerted, world effort at recovery. In general this meant some kind of tariff structure to keep out imports and protect domestic employment, and greater state management of trade either by securing special bilateral agreements or by establishing a broader, protected economic bloc to replace the free world market. At its most extreme economic nationalism gave rise to demands for the conquest of markets and sources of raw materials, or living-space for populations that could no longer provision themselves effectively because of the fractured world market. Japan's expansion into Manchuria, and the subsequent development of the Co-Prosperity Sphere in east Asia, was the prime example of economically inspired military expansion and 'bloc'-building in the 1930s.[64] But much the same could be seen at work in the efforts of Mussolini's Italy to carve out an African empire and an Italian-dominated economic region in the Middle and Near East, or the calls in Germany to establish a greater economic region in eastern and central Europe to restore an alleged imbalance between population and resources.

Much of this reaction was fuelled by resentment at what Mussolini called the 'plutocratic powers', Britain, France, and the United States, who were perceived to possess easy access to large markets and ample resources in the empire, or, in America's case, the New World. The establishment of protection by Britain in 1932 and the United States in 1930 was taken as evidence that these resources and markets were not going to be shared as they had been in the open world economy before 1914. The policies pursued by German statesmen both before and after 1933 have to be seen in the light of the popular belief that some kind of economic 'new order' was in the making. Even the conservative Schacht admitted that 'the time of economic liberalism in itself is finally gone'.[65] Between 1933 and 1936 the German government dithered about what direction economic nationalism was pushing the economy. Limited rearmament, controlled trade, and greater self-sufficiency were generally accepted as desirable or unavoidable given the nature of European circumstances. What altered the character of the German response was Hitler's insistence that the most radical version of the New Order was what he wanted—military superpowerdom, economic imperialism, a new economic order in Europe brought about by force if necessary, with Germany at its core.

Hilter's decision fitted with what is known of his views on the international system and the relationship between military and economic strength, but it was also occasioned by circumstances. By the mid-1930s

[64] M. Barnhart, 'Japan's Economic Security and the Origins of the Pacific War', *Journal of Strategic Studies*, 4 (1981); J. C. Lebra, *Japan's Greater East Asia Co-Prosperity Sphere in World War II* (Oxford, 1975).

[65] BA R2/540, Schacht speech on the New Plan, 11 Dec. 1934.

the British and French empires were declining as world powers, unable to halt either Italian or Japanese expansion. In the wings were other powers, the United States and the Soviet Union, with great economic and military potential. Hitler's anxious acceleration of rearmament and bloc-formation reflected his desire to fill the vacuum left by Britain and France with a new, German-centred empire before any other state could thwart him. This was an attractive option to the party faithful, and it won recruits among Germany's conservative élites, in the business community, and among German officialdom. During the late 1930s a new coalition of political forces emerged in Germany based on party patronage and allegiance to the Führer's German aims, one which was rooted in a popular nationalism sufficiently strong to stifle resistance to the new course. The Second World War both in Europe and in Asia was a direct consequence of the efforts of radical nationalists in Germany and Japan to construct a new economic and political order.

One result of the option chosen in Germany was the rapid extension of state responsibility for the economy, including state-owned industry. This was true in Italy and Japan also, and was partly a reflection of the difficulty of getting a private, capitalist economy to respond quickly and without complaint to the demands for armaments and heavy industry, partly a product of military intervention in the development of the economy to secure technically advanced weapons to fit military requirements. But it was not all due to rearmament. It is necessary to distinguish the 'militarization' of the economy from other factors affecting the role of the state in economic life. In Germany the state had always played a greater role in economic affairs than was the case in the liberal western economies, and the slump brought the state, willy-nilly, into more active regulation of the private economy. During the 1930s the long-term trend towards greater state economic activity, evident in all advanced economies, operated side by side with the growth of the military command economy, and, indeed, emerged after 1945 little affected by the extreme *dirigisme* of the Nazi regime.

This raises the whole question of continuities, of the extent to which the Third Reich contributed to the economic development and 'modernization' of the German economy. There are obvious ways in which the high level of militarization in the economy contributed to industrial and technological progress, whether in the 'sunrise' sectors of aviation, radio and radar, chemicals, and electronics, or through the training of skilled workers, or through the experience of managers who had run the large, new,

---

[66] W. Carlin, 'Economic Reconstruction in Western Germany 1945–55', in I. Turner (ed.), *Reconstruction in Post-War Germany: British Occupation Policy and the Western Zones 1945–55* (Oxford, 1989), 39–41.

rationalised war factories. The capital stock of Germany in 1945 was larger than it had been in 1933 despite the bombing, and much of it was modernized for military purposes with state money.[66] Of course some progress would have been achieved without high levels of rearmament and without war, and indeed if the export-consumer goods lobby had had its way in 1936, the pace of modernization might have been faster.

But against these contributions must be set the simple fact that Hitler's economic option, like that of the 'new-order' Japanese leaders, was an economic dead-end. It operated on a high level of coercion and enforced social discipline; it worked on false assumptions about the nature of economic well-being—in modern times neither the German nor the Japanese economy has needed 'living-space' to prosper to an unprecedented degree; and by trading on naked conquest both states invited the armed hostility of the rest of the industrial world. Hitler's vision of an armed economy resulted in the dismemberment of Germany, the destruction of most of her major cities, and the death of over 5 million Germans.

I

GERMAN ECONOMIC RECOVERY

1
Unemployment in the Third Reich

WHATEVER its social and economic implications, the problem of unemployment in Germany in the recession and recovery years from 1929 to 1936 was closely bound up with German politics. It was against a background of rapidly rising unemployment that the Nazi Party became a major electoral force. Though it was by no means clear quite how a National Socialist government would tackle unemployment when it came to power in January 1933, there was no doubt in the minds of Germany's new leaders that their own political survival was bound up with the success or otherwise of the 'Battle for Work'. Economic recovery would only occur, Hitler argued, 'if measures are taken again and again with energetic attacks and fanatical tenacity against unemployment'.[1] From 1930 Nazi leaders saw unemployment as a key political issue, to be solved by 'general labour service' and 'general conscription' or by public works; and they feared the effects on Nazi electoral prospects if unemployment were solved by the other parties.[2] The crisis of unemployment was a key plank in the Nazis' growing attacks on the Weimar governments in 1931 and 1932. But having made much of the failure of the 'Party state' to solve the question, the Nazis put themselves in the position in January 1933 of having to make good their promise to provide bread and work.

By early 1933 this task was less daunting than it might have been, for the economy was showing the first slender signs of recovery from the autumn of 1932 onwards. The new government was able to make much propaganda on its own behalf riding on the back of an autonomous upswing in the business cycle, and on the legacy of policies already begun in 1932. Indeed a strategy for work-creation was only introduced in the middle of 1933, so that the initial claims by National Socialist leaders that they were solving unemployment were largely spurious. Nevertheless the desire to do something positive about unemployment was real enough. Hitler wanted economic recovery to be identified in the eyes of the population with his call for national renewal and a new beginning in January 1933.[3] He recognized that it was a precondition for achieving

[1] *Dokumente der deutschen Politik* (Berlin, 1935), i. 209, Führerrede vor dem Generalrat der Wirtschaft, 20 Sept. 1933.
[2] Christie Papers, Churchill College, Cambridge, 180/1/1, Christie to Yencken, 21 Sept. 1930 on interviews with leading Nazis; 180/1/4, Notes of a talk with Göring, '1932'.
[3] Graf Schwerin von Krosigk, 'Aufgaben der Finanzpolitik', *Der deutsche Volkswirt* (*DDV*), 8 (1933/4), 586–7; F. Reinhardt, *Die Arbeitsschlacht der Regierung* (Berlin, 1933), 7–11.

other goals as well: 'If there is success in solving this question, we have created for the new system such a situation that the government can realise step by step its other tasks. Work! Work!'[4]

I

The employment situation inherited by the Nazi government was an extraordinary one. The number of Germans in full-time employment fell from 20 million in the middle of 1929 to 11.4 million in January 1933, a fall of almost 9 million. The total number of registered unemployed rose over the same period from 1.25 million to 6 million (see Table 1.1). The fall in employment was greater than the rise in unemployment because large numbers of workers, particularly women and the long-term unemployed, were removed from the register by 1933. The dimensions of the economic and political crisis in 1932 are easier to understand once it is recognized that the problem was not 6 but 9 million unemployed. Two out of every five Germans employed in 1929 were without work in the winter of 1932–3.

There are a number of special factors in the German case which help to explain the exceptionally high levels of registered unemployment when compared with other European economies. Seasonal unemployment was high in Germany because of the large agricultural sector and the harsher winters, which affected the construction industry in particular. Throughout the 1920s there were always 1.5 to 2 million unemployed in the winter months.[5] The age-structure of the population was also unfavourable. The high pre-war birth-rate meant that higher numbers of young Germans were seeking work in the late 1920s and early 1930s. In the summer of 1932 over a quarter of those unemployed were aged 14–25.[6] Women, too, formed a larger proportion of the work-force in Germany than in other industrial countries, and could legally register as unemployed. Women comprised about 20 per cent of German unemployment in 1932, where in other countries female unemployment tended to be under-recorded or unacknowledged.[7]

But the real cause of Germany's high level of unemployment lay in the weaknesses of the German economy in the 1920s. Shortages of capital

---

[4] K. H. Minuth (ed.), *Akten der Reichskanzlei: Regierung Hitler 1933–1938*, i. *1933* (Boppard am Rhein, 1983), 632, Doc. 180, Reichsstatthalterkonferenz, 6 July 1933.

[5] K. I. Wiggs, *Unemployment in Germany since the War* (London, 1935), 183–4.

[6] F. Baerwald, 'How Germany Reduced Unemployment', *American Economic Review*, 24 (1934), 618–19. In 1910 48% of the population was aged 20–60. In 1925 the figure was 54.6%.

[7] M. Thibert, 'The Economic Depression and the Employment of Women' pt. I, *International Labour Review*, 27 (1933), 449–54.

TABLE 1.1. *Registered unemployed, 1929–1940 ('000)*[a]

	1929	1930	1931	1932	1933	1934
Jan.	2,850.2	3,217.6	4,886.9	6,041.9	6,013.6	3,772.7
Feb.	3,069.7	3,365.8	4,971.8	6,128.4	6,000.9	3,372.6
Mar.	2,483.9	3,040.7	4,743.9	6,034.1	5,598.8	2,798.3
Apr.	1,711.6	2,786.9	4,358.1	5,739.0	5,331.2	2,608.6
May	1,349.8	2,634.7	4,052.9	5,582.6	5,038.6	2,528.9
June	1,260.0	2,640.6	3,953.9	5,475.7	4,856.9	2,480.8
July	1,251.4	2,765.2	3,989.6	5,392.2	4,463.8	2,426.0
Aug.	1,271.9	2,882.5	4,214.7	5,223.8	4,124.2	2,397.5
Sept.	1,323.6	3,004.2	4,354.9	5,102.7	3,849.2	2,281.8
Oct.	1,557.1	3,252.0	4,623.4	5,109.1	3,744.8	2,226.6
Nov.	2,035.6	3,698.9	5,059.7	5,355.4	3,714.6	2,352.6
Dec.	2,850.8	4,383.8	5,668.1	5,772.9	4,059.0	2,604.7
AVERAGE	1,898.6	3,075.5	4,519.7	5,575.4	4,804.4	2,718.3

	1935	1936	1937	1938	1939	1940
Jan.	2,973.5	2,520.4	1,853.7	1,051.7	301.8	159.7
Feb.	2,764.1	2,514.8	1,610.9	946.3	196.3	123.8
Mar.	2,401.8	1,937.1	1,245.3	507.6	134.0	66.2
Apr.	2,233.2	1,762.7	960.7	422.5	93.9	39.9
May	2,019.2	1,491.2	776.3	338.3	69.5	31.7
June	1,876.5	1,314.7	648.4	292.2	48.8	26.3
July	1,754.1	1,169.8	562.8	218.3	38.3	25.0
Aug.	1,706.2	1,098.4	509.2	178.7	33.9	23.1
Sept.	1,713.9	1,035.2	469.0	155.9	77.5	21.9
Oct.	1,828.7	1,177.4	501.8	163.9	79.4	—
Nov.	1,984.4	1,197.1	572.6	152.4	72.5	—
Dec.	2,507.9	1,478.8	994.7	455.6	104.4	—
AVERAGE	2,151.0	1,592.6	912.3	429.4	104.2	43.1

[a] from March 1935 including Saarland; from March 1939 including Sudetenland; from June 1939 including Memel.

Source: Statistisches Jahrbuch für das Deutsche Reich 1940 (Berlin, 1940), 389.

after the inflation of 1923 meant high interest rates and a heavy dependence on foreign funds. The sluggish revival of world trade hit the German economy more than others because of its high export dependence. Agriculture and small businesses were hit by falling prices and high interest charges and taxes. The overall performance of the German economy stagnated between 1913 and 1929, in marked contrast to other industrial economies.[8] The effect of these problems on employment was very different from the British experience. There was far less of the structural and regional unemployment brought about by the collapse of Britain's geographically concentrated export industries. Unemployment in Germany both during the 1920s and during the recession was spread much more evenly across the German provinces and between different economic sectors. Though industrial regions had higher unemployment rates than rural areas, and producer goods suffered a higher loss of manpower than the consumer sectors, these were the conventional features of the industrial business cycle. There is some evidence to suggest that there was growing technological unemployment in the 1920s as firms modernized factory methods and shed labour, though it would be wrong to exaggerate the effects or scope of rationalization. Small and medium-sized firms were discouraged from rationalizing because of the high cost of capital, while some of the rationalized sectors (cars and chemicals, for example) actually expanded their work-force in the 1920s as demand for their products rose.

It has also been argued that German unemployment was made worse by high wages and the political strength of the German trade unions. Again this argument should be treated cautiously. Wages in Germany had barely reached the real levels of 1913 by the late 1920s, and were considerably lower than wage costs in other industrialized countries. What hampered Germany's competitive position was not high wage costs but the failure to invest sufficiently in modernized equipment, the high cost of capital, and the sluggishness of home and foreign demand. It is certainly true that once the recession began to bite in 1930 prices fell faster than wages, so that the peak of real wage rates in the inter-war years for those in employment was reached in 1932. But real wage rates fell faster in Germany during the recession than among any of her major competitors. It seems unlikely that sharper wage cuts would have persuaded businessmen to keep going, since the major part of the crisis was a fall in demand and a slump in prices caused by credit restrictions and the collapse of world trade.[9]

[8] D. Petzina and W. Abelshauser, 'Zum Problem der relativen Stagnation der deutschen Wirtschaft in den zwanziger Jahren', in H. Mommsen, D. Petzina and B. Weisbrod (eds.), *Industrielles System und politische Entwicklung in der Weimarer Republik* (Düsseldorf, 1974), 60–74. See too, D. Petzina, 'The Extent and Causes of Unemployment in the Weimar Republic', in P. Stachura (ed.), *Unemployment and the Great Depression in Weimar Germany* (London, 1986), esp. 33–4, 40–2. In this article Petzina modifies his earlier arguments on stagnation by looking at the structural problems and market rigidities which gave rise to it. He places particular emphasis on the low investment ratio.

[9] Royal Institute of International Affairs (RIIA), *Unemployment: An International Problem* (Oxford, 1935), 126, 259–64; Wiggs, *Unemployment in Germany*, 186–7; G. Bry, *Wages in Germany 1871–1945* (Princeton, NJ, 1960), 22, 362. For a different view on wage rates see J. von Kruedener, 'Die Überforderung der Weimarer Republik als Sozialstaat', *Geschichte und Gesellschaft*, 11 (1985), 358–76, who argues that wages and welfare contributions taken together were too high for the economy in the late 1920s and early 1930s in an environment of sluggish growth and a declining world economy.

Once the German economy turned down in 1928–9 (and it began to do so well before the Wall Street crash in October 1929), employment fell continuously until 1932. Unemployment was higher in the winter months than the summer because of seasonal unemployment, though in 1930–2 the gap between winter and summer employment was only 600,000–700,000 where it had averaged approximately 2 million in the period 1925–9.[10] Nor do the global employment figures show the full picture. Hours of work declined during the recession from an average of 7.67 hours per day in 1929 to 6.91 in 1932. Many workers found themselves on short time during the depression (an estimated 60 per cent of trade-union members in 1931–2), so that real earnings fell much faster than real wage rates. To cope with the recession businessmen preferred to employ women because they were cheaper, so that male employment declined faster than female. In 1928 women made up 33 per cent of the work-force, but 36 per cent in 1932. Female wages in the metal industry in 1931 were 59 per cent of the wages of skilled male workers.[11]

The exceptionally high levels of unemployment in 1930–3 were produced by the near collapse of the German credit system in 1931 and the decline in foreign trade. The withdrawal of loans created a major liquidity crisis, while the value of German exports fell by almost two-thirds between 1929 and 1932. There was little the government could do under the circumstances, though what it did do made the employment situation worse rather than better. Taxes were raised and incomes reduced by decree, and the additional taxation used for unemployment relief. Government spending was cut back and every effort made to avoid fiscal policies that might be construed as inflationary, because of fears of the political repercussions. Local government was forced to lay off workers because of the worsening credit position, and in the end depended on central government for additional funds to meet emergency relief for the long-term unemployed. Government policies in general had the effect of further depressing demand, reducing prices, and squeezing profits. Business confidence ebbed away.[12]

Although there is strong disagreement on exactly when the economy began to turn up again, there is general acceptance that the trough of the

---

[10] Wiggs, *Unemployment in Germany*, 35.

[11] Thibert, 'Economic Depression', 454, 458: J. Grünfeld, 'Rationalisation and the Employment and Wages of Women in Germany', *International Labour Review*, 29 (1934), 605–32.

[12] 'Die Öffentliche Fürsorge im Deutschen Reich', *Wirtschaft und Statistik*, 16 (1936), 82–6 (hereafter *WS*). On the government in the crisis see K. Borchardt, 'Zwanslagen und Handlungsspielräume in der grossen Wirtschaftskrise der frühen dreissiger Jahre', *Jahrbuch der Bayerischen Akademie der Wissenschaften*, Sonderdruck, 1979, 1–24: W. Jochmann, 'Brünings Deflationspolitik und der Untergang der Weimarer Republik', in D. Stegmann, B.-J. Wendt and P.-C. Witt (eds.), *Industrielle Gesellschaft und politisches System* (Bonn, 1978), 97–112.

recession was reached during the course of 1932. Industrial production reached its lowest level in July 1932 and then moved continuously upwards, spurred on by the demand for restocking and helped by lower costs. But the aggregate figure of hours worked in industry was lower in each month between March 1932 and February 1933 than in the preceding year, reaching its lowest point of the depression in January 1933. The number of registered unemployed was higher in December 1932 than in December 1931, but lower from January 1933 onwards.[13] Some level of recovery was assured from the late months of 1932, though the economy was still deep in recession. Some part of the credit for this lies at the door of the government and the Reichsbank for initiating from mid-1932 onwards relief schemes of paid work, and for easing credit conditions while maintaining confidence in the currency, although the effects of both on employment were slight in the short term.[14] And it was only on employment that the Nazi Party had anything very positive to say; their economic plans had a 'work' priority, and Nazi publicists were less inhibited than either Brüning or von Papen by the hostility of orthodox financial and business circles to economic experiments. Unemployment was the most conspicuous and socially damaging consequence of the depression, and was the slowest of the economic indicators to respond to government initiatives.

II

The course of unemployment under the Nazi government reflected the priority Hitler gave to policies that directly promoted work at all costs. Unemployment declined steadily until by 1938 Germany enjoyed a position of full employment. But it is important not to exaggerate the speed and scope of the decline. It is tempting with hindsight to see the elimination of unemployment as an irreversible process set in train with the coming of Hitler's government, but it was by no means a foregone conclusion and was certainly not regarded as such either by politicians or businessmen at the time. Unemployment on a large scale did not disappear in 1933 but averaged 4.5 million over the year, and was 3.7 million at its lowest point in November, helped by the mild winter which permitted building work to continue for longer than usual.[15] Throughout 1934

[13] F.-W. Henning, 'Die zeitliche Einordnung der Überwindung der Weltwirtschaftskrise in Deutschland', in H. Winkel (ed.), *Finanz-und wirtschaftspolitische Fragen der Zwischenkriegszeit* (Berlin, 1973), 135–73.

[14] H. James, *The Reichsbank and Public Finance in Germany 1924–1933* (Frankfurt am Main, 1985), 326–31.

[15] RIIA, *Unemployment*, 69.

unemployment remained close to three million, and was over 2 million for six of the twelve months of 1935. Only in June 1936 did unemployment fall below the level of 1928–9, and in 1937 unemployment was lower in every month than in 1927, the year of lowest unemployment before the slump. The decisive change came in the course of the winter of 1933–4, when unemployment fell by 1.25 million between September and April, against the seasonal trend. During the period from summer 1934 to May 1935 unemployment remained stable and without the introduction of general military conscription and increases in arms expenditure in 1935 might well have remained high throughout the year. Unemployment then declined steadily during 1936, reaching full employment during 1938–9.[16]

Unemployment was thus a major economic and social problem for at least the first three years of the regime, and was historically very high until at least the spring of 1936, although it never returned to the exceptional levels of 1932. Unemployment relief was a large item of expenditure for the local communities and the goverment until the same year (see Table 1.2). Local authorities paid out RM 3,000m. in relief in the financial year 1932/3 and were still paying RM 2,250m. in 1934/5, although the proportion of payments going to the relief of unemployment declined more rapidly. The unemployed as a proportion of those in receipt of relief declined from 66 per cent in March 1933 to 38 per cent in June 1935.[17] This left a substantial financial burden to be borne each year by the Reich government after deduction of local welfare contributions: RM 1,700m. in 1932/3 and RM 1,600m. in 1933/4. Total central funds expended on unemployment relief reached RM 3,100m. and RM 2,800m. in the same years.

The aggregate figures on unemployment tell only part of the story. The increase in employment during the period was higher than the decrease in unemployment, a result of labour not on the register returning to full-time work, and the higher take-up of school leavers each year after 1933. The number of young unemployed declined faster than unemployment among older workers, or unemployment in general.[18] Total employment increased from an average of 12.5 million in 1932 to an average of 18.3 million in 1937, although unemployment fell by only 4.6 million over the same period. Nevertheless unemployment was lower than the 1929 figures by 1936, whereas the employment peak in 1929 was not exceeded until 1939. The figures for total hours worked and the average length of the working

[16] *Statistisches Jahrbuch für das Deutsche Reich, 1939/40* (Berlin, 1940), 189.

[17] WS 16 (1936), 82–7; E. B. Mittelman, 'The German Use of Unemployment Insurance Funds for Works Purposes', *Journal of Political Economy*, 46 (1938), 529–30.

[18] F. Petrick, 'Eine Untersuchung zur Beseitigung der Arbeitslosigkeit unter der deutschen Jugend in den Jahren 1933 bis 1935', *Jahrbuch fur Wirtschaftsgeschichte*, (1967) I. 290. Unemployment among under 25s fell by 61.5% between June 1933 and June 1934 against 46.7% for the population as a whole.

TABLE 1.2. *Unemployment relief expenditure and income, central and local government, 1932/3–1937/8 (RM '000m.)*[a]

	A Reich expenditure	B Local expenditure	C Income, Reich insurance fund	D Local relief income[b]	E Excess of expenditure over income (A + B – C + D)
1932/3	3.15	1.39	1.32	1.02	2.20
1933/4	2.76	1.23	1.54	0.94	1.51
1934/5	2.06	0.79	1.48	0.46	0.91
1935/6	1.63	0.51	1.37	0.31	0.46
1936/7	1.30	0.30	1.54	0.36	–0.20
1937/8	0.72	0.16	1.71	0.24	–1.07

[a] '000m. = US billion.

[b] includes funds for other forms of public relief. Figures for 1932/3 and 1933/4 include special payments from central government.

Sources: WS 16 (1936), 86–7, 852; *Statistisches Jahrbuch für das Deutsche Reich* (Berlin, 1937–1940).

TABLE 1.3. *Employment and hours worked in industry, 1929–1938*

	Total employment[a]	Total hours (1936 = 100)	Average hours per day		
			All ind.	PG[b]	CG[c]
1929	20,750,000	103.6	7.67	7.72	7.61
1930	16,843,000	—	—	—	—
1931	15,020,000	—	—	—	—
1932	12,756,000	54.8	6.91	6.86	6.97
1933	13,436,000	63.0	7.16	7.16	7.15
1934	15,533,000	82.5	7.43	7.53	7.30
1935	16,640,000	90.1	7.41	7.64	7.10
1936	17,839,000	100.0	7.59	7.77	7.37
1937	19,095,000	110.2	7.68	7.87	7.42
1938	20,170,000	119.2	—	—	—

[a] Figure for July. [b] PG = producer goods. [c] CG = consumer goods.
Source: *Statistisches Jahrbuch für das Deutsche Reich* (Berlin, 1930–40).

day reveal the same lag. Total hours worked in industry did not reach the level of 1929 until 1937, a reflection of the slow revival of consumer-goods production after 1933.[19] Average hours worked per day also expanded slowly, and actually fell in 1935 against the figure for 1934 because of the slowdown in consumer output. Again the 1929 figure was not exceeded until 1937 (see Table 1.3), and then only for producer goods rather than consumer production. Although employment expanded rapidly during the 1930s this was helped to some extent by a shorter working day and working week. It took longer for the economy to return to the employment position in 1929 than it did to reduce unemployment.

This pattern was partly a result of the government's determination to reduce the statistics of unemployment as quickly as possible for political reasons, either by encouraging people to leave the unemployment register or by offering 'substitute employment'. The government also sponsored a campaign to reduce the length of the working week in order to spread the available work more widely. These policies were related to but distinct from the general recovery policies and the direct work-creation projects. They were aimed at removing substantial numbers from the unemployment figures as an end in itself or, in the case of military conscription, as a fortuitous by-product of other policies.

[19] By 1938 consumer production was only 7% above the level of 1928 but capital goods were 135% above. See the discussion in C. Nathan and M. Fried, *The Nazi Economic System* (London, 1944), 351–2.

Changes in registration procedures had the effect of removing some of the long-term and female unemployed from the registers, although this practice had served to disguise the true level of unemployment throughout the recession (at its trough employment was 9 million below the level of 1929) and was not a specifically Nazi device. Much more important for removing workers from the register were the schemes of substitute employment for young people, and in particular labour service. Labour service was again not a novelty in Germany, and had been practised elsewhere in Europe before 1933. Its roots went back to the First World War and proposals for community service to sustain a spirit of solidarity and comradeship among young Germans once military service was over. It was taken up in the recession by the Brüning government as part of the battle against unemployment, the *Freiwillige Arbeitsdienst* (Voluntary Labour Service) providing youths with some limited work-experience in land reclamation, road-building and general construction.[20] The Nazi Party was also keen on such schemes and the introduction of some form of labour service became a stock electoral pledge before 1933.[21] In 1931 Konstantin Hierl was appointed Hitler's special commissioner for labour service. He advocated service not simply as an economic necessity, but because it was seen to have educational and propaganda possibilities as well. Labour service was regarded as a means of cementing bonds of loyalty to the racial community by bringing together young men and women from very different walks of life and forcing them to share a common work environment. Once in power the Nazis maintained the existing labour service, linking it with Hitler Youth activity, and finally in June 1935 introduced a law compelling 'all young Germans of both sexes to serve their *Volk* in the Labour Service'.[22]

Before 1935 voluntary labour service became for all intents and purposes compulsory, with the introduction of a number of additional schemes. The first was a special project to provide cheap labour for agriculture, the *Landhilfe*, which was established in the middle of 1933. Under its provisions 16 to 21-year-olds had to spend six months in agricultural work and were given board, lodging, and pocket money in return. The scheme was 'voluntary' though those who turned it down without good cause lost their entitlement to unemployment pay. Between July 1933 and March 1934 the numbers engaged in *Landhilfe* averaged 159,000 (36,000 of whom were girls) and a fixed quota of 160,000 was

[20] H. Köhler, *Arbeitsdienst in Deutschland* (Berlin, 1967), 243–67.

[21] Christie Papers, 180/1/1, interviews with leading Nazis, 21 Sept. 1930.

[22] Dokumente der deutschen Politik (Berlin, 1936), ii. Doc. 77, Rede des Staatssekretär Hierl, 20 June 1934 and iii. 249. Reichsarbeitsdienstgesetz, 26 June 1935; W. Benz. 'Vom freiwilligen Arbeitsdienst zur Arbeitsdienstpflicht' *Vierteljahrshefte für Zeitgeschichte*, 16 (1968), 317–46.

TABLE 1.4. *Substitute employment, 1932–1936*[a]

	Labour	Service	Landhilfe	Landjahr	Landdienst	House-service[b]	Total
	Men	Women					
1932	285,494	—	—	—	—	—	285,494
1933	252,780	10,212	155,939	—	—	—	418,931
1934	237,451	11,556	123,551	22,000	500	5,000	398,058
1935	230,195	12,659	139,232	31,000	3,500	5,000	421,586
1936	265,214		49,441	35,000	14,888	25,000	389,543

[a] Yearly peak.
[b] Additional female labour service.

Source: F. Petrick, 'Eine Untersuchung zur Beseitigung der Arbeitslosigkeit unter der deutschen Jugend in den Jahren 1933 bis 1935', *Jahrbuch für Wirtschaftsgeschichte*, pt. I (1967), 299; F Wunderlich, *Farm Labor in Germany 1810–1945* (Princeton, NJ, 1961), 321–2; WS 16 (1936), 134–7.

established for the scheme. It was an unpopular system, both with the farmers who had to take the new work-force on and with the mainly urban youth who took part. When the job market improved in 1936 the scheme declined rapidly and by 1938 involved only 40,000 workers, who were employed on a more regular wage-labour basis.[23] The Hitler Youth ran a similar scheme for 14 to 25-year-olds, the *Landdienst* (land service). Most of those involved were under 16 and were sent in large groups to help with agricultural work in the summer months, with the day divided between work, political education, and military-style training. In Prussia a rather different plan was introduced through which 14-year-olds had to spend nine months on the land, organized into camps of 60 to 150 children. This 'year on the land' (*Landjahr*) was confined to selected candidates from the cities who were also given political education. *Landjahr* service entitled them to special access to jobs when they left school.[24] Between them these schemes involved around 400,000 young people (see Table 1.4). The main occupation was land reclamation. By 1936 work was under way or completed on 530,000 hectares of land, with projects in all the major Reich provinces.[25]

It is usually argued that these various forms of labour service were primarily designed to reduce overall unemployment figures quickly. While

[23] F. Wunderlich, *Farm Labor in Germany 1810–1945* (Princeton, NJ, 1961), 310–12.
[24] Ibid. 313–14.
[25] Calculated from 'Die deutsche Arbeitsdienst', WS 16 (1936), 136. Land reclamation claimed 53% of all hours worked on labour service in 1935.

there is no doubt that they did contribute to keeping down unemployment among school-leavers it is important not to forget that some form of Reich or community labour service was already in existence before 1933. Indeed the numbers in voluntary labour service before January 1933 were higher than at any point thereafter. In November 1932 some 285,000 Germans were on the scheme, while the highest number in the Third Reich was 252,000 in the middle of 1933 (both figures excluding women). The labour service was used to depress unemployment figures both before and after the seizure of power and did not amount in 1933 to an additional net reduction in numbers. Nor were the other schemes as important as the peak annual figures suggest. Many of those involved were still at school and would not have been counted as unemployed anyway, while outside harvest time the numbers involved were very much smaller. In December 1934 there were 69,000 on *Landhilfe*, in December 1935 82,000,[26] just over half the level in the harvest period. Moreover *Landhilfe* gave harvest and casual work to young workers which would have been done by teams of urban or rural workers (mainly women and children) as a way of supplementing income during the summer and autumn, and was thus not new but transferred employment. Until the late 1930s female labour service remained largely optional. Only a few thousand girls took up voluntary labour service, or the 'year of household service' during 1933–5, leaving a large pool of cheap female labour seeking work at just the time that the government was looking for ways of reducing the number of women in the work-force.[27] Thus the impact on the economy of all these schemes should not be exaggerated; they removed a certain number of young workers and school-leavers for a few months at a time from the job market over and above the level of substitute employment already reached in late 1932, and did little to boost demand since payments were small and partly in kind.

The efforts to remove women from the unemployment registers were equally mixed in their success. The Nazi government from the outset worked to remove women from the labour force and give their jobs to unemployed men, and married men first of all. The criterion used to judge the success of the employment drive was the increase in full-time male employment, and had been so even before 1933. In order to ensure that displaced women workers did not swell the ranks of the unemployed after 1933 efforts were also made to keep women off the unemployment registers or to keep them out of the job market altogether. Fritz Reinhardt, state secretary in the Finance Ministry, announced in February 1934 that it

---

[26] Wunderlich, *Farm Labor*, 321–2.
[27] *WS* 16 (1936), 137; T. W. Mason, 'Women in Germany, 1925–1940: Family, Welfare and Work', *History Workshop*, 1 and 2 (1976), 86–95, for a general view of female labour policy.

was the government's intention to cut the number of women in full-time employment in industry and services from 6 to 3 million.[28] The first major piece of legislation on work-creation in June 1933 was directed at female labour; and the Göring-Plan for employment among married males continued the policy in 1934.[29]

The major device for reducing female employment was the marriage loan. The state offered loans of RM 1,000 free of interest to racially and politically acceptable newly-weds on the condition that the woman gave up her job and undertook not to seek employment again unless her husband's pay dropped below RM 125 a month, or until the loan was paid off (at the rate of RM 10 a month, or eight years). The loan was in the form of certificates to be redeemed at shops selling furniture and household goods so that the scheme would also directly stimulate particular sectors of industry as well. The scheme proved very popular, so much so that the average value of each loan had to be reduced. By the end of 1934 some 365,000 loans were paid out, 183,000 in the first five months of the scheme.[30] Special forms of labour service were also devised that did not pose a threat to male employment. Young girls could volunteer for work as low-paid domestic servants, with a special subsidy paid to employers who took on the additional help. The campaign against two-income families was directed mainly at women, and the propaganda in the Battle for Work played up the place of women in the home and denigrated the growth of female industrial employment.[31]

The overall effect on female employment was mixed. The employment of women was exceptionally high during the depression because female labour was cheap and could protect businesses against the profit squeeze. Contemporary surveys discovered that a high percentage of women in work in industry were there because their husbands were unemployed.[32] As the economy revived it was likely that some of these women would leave employment as their husbands found work. But although the proportion of women at work in industry declined from 30 per cent at the beginning of 1933 to 24 per cent by mid-1936, as more men returned to the work-force, the absolute numbers of women in commercial and industrial employment increased steadily to the outbreak of war, from 5.1

---

[28] *Dokumente der deutschen Politik*, ii. 172, Rede des Staatssekretär im RPM Reinhardt, 20 Jan. 1934.

[29] Ibid. 1. 198–200, Gesetz zur Verminderung der Arbeitslosigkeit vom 1 Juni 1933.

[30] Ibid. 199; ibid. ii. 172, Reinhardt speech; Petrick, 'Untersuchung', 291; *Akten der Reichskanzlei*, ii. 1188–9, Doc. 318. Begründung zum Entwurf eines Gesetzes zur Änderung des Gesetzes über Förderung der Eheschliessungen, 20 Mar. 1934. The average value of the loans declined from RM 730 in Aug. 1933 to RM 560 in Feb. 1934.

[31] J. Stephenson, *Women in Nazi Society* (London, 1975), 79–87; Mason, 'Women in Germany', 96–9.

[32] Thibert, 'Economic Depression', 451.

million in 1933 to 6.5 million in 1938.[33] Most women who were
registered as unemployed in 1932 found their way back into the work-
force after 1933, not into the kitchen. Indeed the numbers of women in
employment was high by comparison with other industrial economies. The
total number of women in the active work-force, including services,
agriculture, and small businesses increased throughout the period from
11.4 million in 1933 to 14.8 million by 1939.[34] Though Nazi promises
may well have appealed to the clerks and skilled workers who were
displaced by women in the recession, the effect of the government's efforts
to reduce female employment was slight. By 1938 the policy was fully
reversed as the government tried to encourage women to take up work to
cope with the labour shortages created by rearmament.[35]

Although the attempt to reduce the unemployment statistics by
substitute employment and campaigns to remove workers from the register
had a limited success between 1933 and 1935, it explains only a small part
of the decline. Many of the schemes proved unpopular after a while. Those
on labour service or *Landhilfe* worked sometimes for only a few months
and then returned to look for regular paid work, so that there was always
a gap between official establishment figures and the actual number on the
projects.[36] Since unemployment declined much faster for younger workers
(aged 16–25) than for other groups, it was tempting to try to get back
into full-time employment.[37] In 1935 this situation was changed with the
introduction of military conscription. This was a form of national service
which it was impossible to avoid, and it took over a million out of the
regular job market over the next two years, accelerating the trend towards
full employment and selective labour shortages which set in during 1937
and 1938.

III

By 1938 Germany was faced with labour shortages rather than
unemployment. During 1938 the number of foreign workers in Germany
increased to 381,000, and by March 1939 to 435,000. In June 1938 there
were only 292,000 registered German unemployed, of which 43 per cent
were classified as unemployable through disability, illness, or psychological

[33] 'Die Frauenarbeit in der Industrie 1933 bis 1936', *WS* 16 (1936), 779–80; *Statistisches Jahrbuch*, 1938, 379.
[34] Ibid. 1937, 23; D. Petzina, 'Die Mobilisierung deutscher Arbeitskräfte vor und während des Zweiten Weltkrieges', *Vierteljahreshefte für Zeitgeschichte*, 18 (1970), 455–6.
[35] Wunderlich, *Farm Labor*, 329–31.
[36] Ibid. 312.
[37] Petrick, 'Untersuchung', 290.

disorder. By the eve of war in August 1939 there were only 33,000 unemployed, so that even those classed as unemployable had been found jobs of some description during 1939.[38] The creation of substitute employment and the attack on female labour was no longer necessary, and was now an impediment to higher levels of productive employment as the demand for higher-paid factory labour increased.

There are a number of ways to explain the fall in unemployment. As we have seen the opportunities to reduce statistical unemployment were limited, and were only introduced from mid-1933 when the downward movement of unemployment was already well under way. The early reduction in unemployment was brought about by a conventional upswing in the business cycle, helped by the changed economic climate in the second half of 1932, and the stimulus of low prices and wages. Though the recovery may well have stabilized at a point short of full employment if left to take its own course as it did in Britain, Germany did not have Britain's structural problems so that any recovery would be spread fairly evenly across the country and between different sectors. Since the main reason for Germany's exceptional unemployment was the credit crisis, the most severe in Germany's history, it was certain that re-employment would occur extensively once the crisis was past.

There is no effective way of measuring how much of the increase in employment was a result of the autonomous working of the business cycle, but most government schemes only began to take effect during late 1933 and 1934, while the more general controls over trade and the capital market were also introduced too slowly to explain the sharp fall in unemployment during the first half of 1933. Nevertheless the direct and indirect policies of the government were important in maintaining the momentum of employment expansion when at certain times during 1933 and 1934 it looked as though recovery might come to a halt. Government intervention was the major reason why the economy moved so rapidly and thoroughly to a position of full employment in contrast to all the other major industrial powers.

The government response to unemployment can be divided between direct and indirect measures. The most important direct measures were the various work-creation schemes introduced during 1932 and 1933. Since the schemes provoked much academic discussion at the time and made much useful propaganda for the Battle for Work, they are worth looking at in some detail. The main object of the work-creation programmes was to provide temporary employment for the long-term unemployed who were no longer covered by insurance and to promote schemes that would

[38] H. Vollweiler, 'The Mobilisation of Labour Reserves in Germany', pt. I. *International Labour Review*, 38 (1938), 448–9.

act as a stimulus to private economic activity. The idea of an 'initial spark' (*Initialzündung*), first popularized by the Brauns Commission investigating the depression in Germany in 1931, was taken up during 1932 and 1933 as the justification for embarking on state-financed programmes which might otherwise have alarmed orthodox financial circles.[39]

Work-creation, like the labour service, was not a Nazi invention. The idea of using relief funds to fund public works went back to the brief recession of 1926, and was maintained every year thereafter, although the sums involved never exceeded RM 40m. per year before 1933.[40] But during 1932 the government supplemented direct relief work with federal work programmes funded directly by the state, primarily through short-term bills which were to be repaid out of future tax revenues when the economy recovered. The first scheme was initiated by Chancellor Brüning shortly before his fall from office in June 1932 at a total cost of RM 165m. On 4 September von Papen, his successor, introduced a second programme worth RM 182m. and in December and January 1932/3 an emergency programme (Sofort-Programm) was brought in by the Reich Commissar for Labour, Günther Gereke, worth RM 500m., increased to RM 600m. in July. The most important of all was the Reinhardt-Programm authorized by the Law for Reducing Unemployment on 1 June 1933, which made RM 1,000m. immediately available for public works.[41] The schemes were aimed at public services and construction, waterways, road-building, bridge repair, etc., much of which had been left undone during the depression because of declining local government income. The funds were distributed by four main Reich agencies, the most important of which was the Deutsche Gesellschaft für öffentliche Arbeiten (Öffa), which administered 60 per cent of the funds released by the government.[42] Details of the finance made available under the work-creation programmes are set out in Table 1.5.

The employment effects of these direct schemes are difficult to ascertain precisely because there was considerable overlap between work-creation, labour service, and additional work-creation schemes funded by the

[39] W. Röpke, 'Trends in German Business Cycle Policy', *Economic Journal*, 43 (1933), 430–41; O. Donner, 'Voraussetzungen und Konsequenzen öffentlicher Arbeitsbeschaffung', *DDR* 7 (1932/3), 1221–2.

[40] Mittelman, 'Unemployment', 530; O. Weigert, 'The Development of Unemployment Relief in Germany' pt. I, *International Labour Review*, 28 (1933), 169–72.

[41] BA R2/18701, Labour Ministry, 'Beitrag zur Denkschrift über die Arbeitsbeschaffungsmassnahman', 1–14; L. Grebler, 'Work-Creation Policy in Germany 1932–1935', pt. I, *International Labour Review*, 35 (1937), 331–8; *DDV* 8 (1933/4), 529–31; K. E. Poole, *German Financial Policies, 1932–1939* (Cambridge, Mass., 1939), 94–100; M. Schneider, 'The Development of State Work Creation Policy in Germany 1930–1933', in Stachura, *Unemployment*, 173–80.

[42] *DDV* 8 (1933/4), 529–31. The other financial institutions involved were the Deutsche Siedlungsbank, Rentenbankkreditanstalt, and the Bau- und Bodenbank.

TABLE 1.5. *Work-creation funds and employment,*
1932–1935

	Expenditure (RMm.)		New jobs
1932–3	1,455	Jan. 1933	23,665
1934	1,985	July 1933	140,126
1935	593	Nov. 1933	400,847
		Jan. 1934	385,275
		Mar. 1934	630,163
		June 1934	392,433

Sources: L. Grebler, 'Work Creation Policy in Germany 1932–1935', pt. II, *International Labour Review*, 35 (1937), 513; F. Baerwald, 'How Germany Reduced Unemployment', *American Economic Review*, 24 (1934), 623.

German railways (RM 991m.) and the Post Office (RM 111m.), all of which used the same sort of suppliers and drew on a common pool of unskilled and semi-skilled labour. The figures of those working directly on the project sites are set out in Table 1.5. The peak was reached in March 1934 with 630,000 workers, but as the funds were gradually used up during 1934 the numbers employed on the projects dropped away to reach less than 200,000 by 1935.[43] To encourage higher levels of employment all work-creation contractors were compelled to operate a forty-hour week, as were other public services, and overtime was banned.[44]

The work-creation employment contributed an estimated 20 per cent to the increase of 2.8 million in employment in 1933–4, though most of it was concentrated in the winter and spring of 1933–4. Like the labour service programme, work-creation took time to get going. Initially there was some distrust of the schemes in business circles, based on a fear of their long-term fiscal effects and on the evidence that the von Papen programmes in particular had no real impact on the rising unemployment levels, though they may well have prevented even higher levels during the winter of 1932–3.[45] There was also a considerable gap between the sums authorized for expenditure and the actual sums taken up. Even by

[43] Grebler, 'Work-Creation', pt. II 513–14; 'Die Entwicklung des Arbeitsmarktes', *DDV* 8 (1933/4), 1280.
[44] 'The Reduction of the Working Week in Germany', *International Labour Review*, 29 (1933), 774–9.
[45] *DDV* 7 (1932/3), 1019–21. In his speech at the Reichsbank on 17 Apr. Schacht warned against over-optimistic expectations from work-creation.

December 1933 only 77 per cent of the von Papen programme had been taken up, and 55 per cent of the Sofort-Programm. The Reinhardt-Programm launched in mid-1933 had allocated only 47 per cent of its funds by December but had only paid out RM 38m., or 4 per cent. Almost 50 per cent of the payments for work-creation were made during 1934 so that there was something like a nine-month to a year lag between establishing a programme and turning it into actual projects employing labour.[46] Some of the major cities where unemployment was highest did not even apply for funds under the Sofort-Programm because of the state of municipal finances.[47] In addition, most of the projects were fairly short term, which may well explain the slowing down in the decline in unemployment during the summer of 1934 and early 1935 as the projects petered out and men looked for long-term employment again. And although they were intened to be labour-intensive, the balance swung towards material costs away from wages in 1933. The von Papen programmes' funds went 44 per cent to wages, 56 per cent to materials, but the Sofort-Programm was divided 38 per cent and 62 per cent respectively.[48]

There is some case for saying that work-creation was a cheap substitute for straight employment relief and did not constitute 'real' jobs. Pay was in the form of certificates which could be exchanged at certain shops for goods and services. Contractors were obliged to provide one warm meal a day.[49] The value of the work certificates was less than the level of minimum relief, which saved the government money, and the certificates did not have to be redeemed immediately, which again helped to cut the government's short-term obligations. But the certificate system also reduced the secondary employment effects which higher wages paid in cash might have produced. It was these secondary effects of work-creation which had provided one of the main arguments for launching them in the first place. Though there is no doubt that the construction industry was stimulated by the schemes, the secondary employment effects elsewhere in the economy were much more muted and encouraged the government to rely more on indirect ways of stimulating employment, which not only proved more effective but were less alarming in appearance to those who disliked economic experiments.

[46] Ibid. 8 (1933/4), 536; Grebler, 'Work-Creation', pt. II, 505–13. For a general discussion of the effects of work-creation see C. Bresciani-Turroni, 'The "Multiplier" in Practice: Some Results of Recent German Experience', *Review of Economic Statistics*, 20 (1938), 76–87.

[47] M. Wolffsohn, *Industrie und Handwerk im Konflikt mit staatlicher Wirtschaftspolitik* (Berlin, 1977), 113. On the state of communal finances see Poole, *Financial Policies*, 13–16.

[48] Wolffsohn, *Industrie*, 113.

[49] *DDV* 7 (1932/3), 1020.

IV

Work-creation was only one weapon in the attack on unemployment after 1933 and was effective only to the extent that there was substantial improvement in the general conditions governing business activity in Germany. Without general signs of business revival and a slow restoration of business confidence it is unlikely that contractors would have been as willing to take up government funds for work projects on the same scale. Part of this revival in business confidence can be attributed to the 'stabilization' of politics promised by the Nazis after January 1933, though it would be wrong to ignore the deep distrust with which many businessmen approached the new government and its economic policies. Part can be attributed to the government propaganda on employment. After January 1933 the government openly promoted work at every opportunity, exhorting businesses to take on extra workers and subsidizing their wage bills, bringing political pressure to bear to get firms to restrict hours of work and overtime; and making noisy propaganda on the importance of re-employment for Germany's political and economic future.[50] During 1933 public opinion was quite prepared to support these initiatives so that there was little political resistance to the employment campaign, in contrast to the difficulties met by both Brüning and von Papen in 1932. In 1933 political conditions were quite different. The trade unions were disbanded in May, and labour's bargaining position emasculated. The other political parties were wound up and all political resistance to government policies on the economy overturned by an assertive and increasingly *dirigiste* administration.

It was in the area of general interventionist economic policies that the government proved most successful, building on the initial efforts made under the last Weimar governments to tackle the major problems of the economy. General policies on trade, finance, and investment helped to sustain and promote the upswing from early 1933 onwards more than the specific policies on work-creation. The credit structure which had ground almost to a standstill in 1931 was stabilized during 1932 and over the following two years credit was generally eased through careful initiatives taken by the government and the Reichsbank in lowering interest rates, consolidating and securing local government debts, and exercising greater control over the banking system. The balance of payments and external debt were also stabilized to avoid any repetition of the crisis of 1930–2. The government not only tackled the problem of public finance, but also eased the capital position of private business. Agriculture was given tax

---

[50] Wolffsohn, *Industrie*, 108–9; L. Zumpe, *Wirtschaft und Staat in Deutschland 1933 bis 1945* (Berlin, 1980), 64–5.

relief and a reduction in the burden of debt, while industry gained subsidies and tax relief for new investment and employment. In September 1932 a system of tax remission was introduced designed to stimulate the productive sectors of the economy by giving government rebates for taxes paid in 1932/3. The rebates came in the form of tax certificates which could be used to pay off taxes in future years or could be used to acquire liquid funds directly from the banking system. In practice many firms used their new liquidity to pay off existing bank loans, but this in itself helped to unblock the arteries of the credit structure. The quantity of tax certificates in circulation reached a peak of RM 1,135m. in March 1934 and declined thereafter as they were paid off by the government (at the rate of one-fifth per year over five years) out of the revenues acquired from the expansion of business and employment.[51]

The government combined a policy of cautious credit creation with the promise that all 'wild experiments' would be avoided. 'The economy', Hitler told a party gathering in July 1933, 'must be treated with extraordinary cautiousness.'[52] In June 1933 the Reichsbank president, Hjalmar Schacht, was put at the head of a special commission charged with supervising and regulating everything to do with the capital markets to ensure that work-creation and other short-term credit schemes did not undermine public credit or confidence in the currency.[53] The effect of the appointment was as much psychological as anything, for the commission never met, and Schacht continued to regulate the capital market in his position as head of the Reichsbank. Although confidence could hardly be described as buoyant during 1933–5, his presence was sufficient evidence of a public determination to promote sensible credit policies and allay fears of inflation. Direct and indirect taxation were kept at the high depression levels and it proved necessary to introduce price and wage controls in order to avoid any risk of the recovery petering out on rising costs and inflationary crisis. Profits were also controlled by limiting their distribution and encouraging reinvestment to expand employment. The government also extended controls over foreign trade. The object was to avoid too rapid an expansion of imports in response to state-created credit and the overvalued mark, which might well have depressed domestic employment or brought on balance-of-payments problems. Work-creation and government investment were concentrated in sectors with a low import content for the same reason. When consumer demand began to expand in 1934, sucking in further imports, even more stringent controls had to be introduced, and the government began to think seriously about

[51] *DDV* 7 (1932/3), 1019.
[52] *Akten der Reichskanzlei*, i. 632, Doc. 180, Reichsstatthalterkonferenz, 6 July 1933.
[53] H. Schacht, *76 Jahre meines Lebens* (Bad Wörishofen, 1953), 399–400.

TABLE 1.6. *Wages: selected statistics, 1929–1938*

	Money hourly wage rates (1913/14 = 100)	Real hourly wage rates (1913/14 = 100)	Real weekly earnings (1925/9 = 100)[a]	Wages as % of National Income
1929	177	115	118	62 (1928)
1930	180	122	—	n.a.
1931	171	125	—	n.a.
1932	144	120	100	64
1933	140	119	104	63
1934	140	116	109	62
1935	140	114	110	61
1936	140	112	112	59
1937	140	112	115	58
1938	141	112	119	57

[a] Adjusted for party levies and other deductions.

Source: G. Bry, *Wages in Germany 1871–1945* (Princeton, NJ, 1960), 331, 362.

programmes of import-substitution. The government's increasingly autarkic views reflected a desire to promote the rapid expansion of domestic output and employment, and to avoid too great a reliance on the world economy after the bruising experiences of the previous decade.[54] Without this wider range of controls and regulations, higher levels of employment would have been postponed, work-creation or not.

The introduction of wage controls helped to reduce wage costs in both public and private employment, continuing the wage reduction policies of the Brüning and von Papen administrations. Wage rates were fixed at the lowest level reached during the recession, and were held steady at depression rates until the late 1930s, declining in real terms between 1932 and 1938 by 6 per cent. Figures for the changes in real rates and earnings are set out in Table 1.6. During the recovery period marginal wage costs were reduced to encourage re-employment. Subsidies were made available to employers in selected sectors, particularly agriculture, reducing wage costs still further.[55] The expansion of national income and output was faster than the expansion of earnings during the 1930s; and profits took a larger share of industrial income after 1933 than before.[56]

[54] K. Mandelbaum, 'An Experiment in Full Employment: Controls in the German Economy 1933–38', in Oxford University Institute of Statistics, *The Economics of Full Employment* (Oxford, 1944), 183–93.
[55] Bry, *Wages*, 235, 262–4; C. W. Guillebaud, *The Economic Recovery of Germany 1933–1938* (London, 1939), 187–92.
[56] G. Stolper, *The German Economy 1870 to the Present* (London, 1967), 150–1; Guillebaud, *Recovery*, 183–5.

To ensure that the work-force did not exert its own pressure on wages the trade unions and traditional wage-bargaining procedures were removed and were replaced with a state-directed system of Labour Trustees who negotiated pay and conditions, setting minimum rates and suppressing any increase in wage levels. Strikes and industrial action were outlawed, and improvements made in the placement procedures of Labour Exchanges to avoid local labour shortages exerting pressure on wage levels. It is difficult to say with certainty how much effect wage costs had on industry's willingness to re-employ, but it was clearly of some significance since industry blamed its poor performance during the recession on excessive wage costs. But German industry did not get all the benefits that low wages might have brought. In the long term low wages should have generated higher export growth but failed to do so because of the overvalued mark and controlled trade. Lower costs and prices should have boosted home demand as well, but high taxes and forced contributions, and increased savings channelled towards government funds, kept retail turnover well below the level of the late 1920s.[57]

Increased government intervention went hand in hand with a large increase in the amount of government demand and investment, some of it directly to stimulate employment, some of it indirectly so. The increased expenditure brought with it a significant increase in public-sector employment in government services and departments. The administration employed 648,000 in 1925 but 1,039,000 in 1939, and total government employment increased from 10.6 per cent to 12.9 per cent of the labour force. The number of local-government employees rose from 544,000 in 1934 to 741,000 in 1938, an increase of 36 per cent in four years.[58] The Nazi Party also increased its employment during the 1930s, setting up its own bureaucratic apparatus. By February 1934 the party had 373,000 functionaries and another 644,000 part-timers excluding the SA and SS, which had officials of their own.[59] Government and party administration between them contributed substantially to new employment after 1933.

The increases in government expenditure, investment, and debt are set out in Table 1.7. In real terms expenditure rose 50 per cent between 1929 and 1934, rising from 15.7 per cent of GNP to 22.9 per cent over the same period,[60] funded by regular budget deficits covered by short-term loans.

[57] *Statistisches Jahrbuch*, 1938, 632.

[58] J. P. Cullity, 'The Growth of Governmental Employment in Germany 1882–1950', *Zeitschrift für die gesamte Staatswissenschaft*, 123 (1967), 202–4; figures on local government employment are calculated from *Statistisches Jahrbuch*, 1935, 453, and 1940, 528–9.

[59] D. Orlow, *The History of the Nazi Party 1933–1945* (Newton Abbot, 1973), 72–3; according to Bresciani-Turroni, "Multiplier", 81, new administrative organizations set up after 1933 created 400,000 new jobs by 1937.

[60] S. Andic and J. Veverka, 'The Growth of Government Expenditure in Germany', *Finanzarchiv*, 25 (1964), 245.

TABLE 1.7. *Government expenditure, revenue, investment, and debt, 1932/3–1938/9 (RM '000m.)*[a]

	Government revenue	Total public revenue	Reich expend.	Total public expenditure	Rearmament	Communications	Total Reich debt	Public investment[b]
1928/9	9.0	14.0	13.0	23.2	0.7	2.6	—	6.6
1932/3	6.6	11.5	9.2	17.1	0.7	0.8	12.3	2.2
1933/4	6.8	12.1	8.9	18.4	1.6	1.3	13.9	2.5
1934/5	8.2	13.3	12.6	21.6	3.2	1.8	15.9	4.6
1935/6	9.6	14.7	14.1	21.9	5.5	2.1	20.1	6.4
1936/7	11.4	16.9	17.3	23.6	10.3	2.4	25.8	8.1
1937/8	13.9	19.6	21.4	26.9	10.9	2.7	31.2	8.4
1938/9	17.7	—	32.9	37.1	17.2	3.8	41.7	10.3

[a] '000m. = US billion.
[b] Calendar years 1928–38.

Sources: C. W. Guillebaud, *The Economic Recovery of Germany 1933–1938* (London, 1939), 218; S. Andic and J. Veverka, 'The Growth of Government Expenditure in Germany since the Unification', *Finanzarchiv*, 23 (1964), 245; R. Erbe, *Die nationalsozialistische Wirtschaftspolitik 1933–1939 im Lichte der modernen Theorie* (Zürich, 1958), 22–3, 54–8; S. Lurie, *Private Investment in a Controlled Economy: Germany 1933–1939* (New York, 1947), 36.

Public investment was greater in total than private investment between 1932 and 1936. Private firms either lacked the capital resources to embark on new investment programmes, or utilized the existing capacity built before 1929 but which had not been fully used during the recession. Private industrial share issues on the German Stock Exchange amounted to a mere RM 19m. between 1932 and 1935; but public loans totalled RM 2,030m.[61] The state deliberately controlled the issue of new private funds, in order to channel investment into labour-intensive sectors like road-building, or to encourage private investment in civil engineering and house-building.

Two areas of public investment were of particular importance in relation to employment. The first was civil engineering, and particularly road-building; the second was rearmament. Investment in roads, both local and national, totalled more than RM 3,500m. from 1933 to 1936, RM 800m. in 1933 and RM 1,200m. in 1934.[62] Most of this expenditure was on the ordinary roads, and not on the *Autobahnen*, the new motorways authorized in 1933, which did not become a significant element until 1935. By the end of 1934 210,000 were employed directly on road-building, with a further 180,000 engaged in secondary activities (planning, haulage, supply, etc.).[63] Work was also carried out on the railway and canal networks, bridges, and public buildings. The effect of all these projects on the wider economy was immediate. Cement production doubled between 1932 and 1934. The index of sales of the major supply industries stood at 18.0 (1928 = 100) in January 1933 but reached 59 by September and 85.7 the following June.[64]

Military expenditure was on the whole less significant than civil engineering in the early stages of the recovery. Only part of the military budget went on facilities and the arms industry, the rest on wages and running costs. Total military expenditure, including the secret rearmament bills, was RM 4,800m. from 1933 to 1935, the bulk of it falling in 1934–5. Of this total only about RM 600m. was spent in 1933 and 1934 on military investment, and RM 1,900m. in 1935.[65] Rearmament began to have a serious effect on employment levels at the point when the civil

[61] Poole, *Financial Policies*, 166; see too R. Erbe, *Die nationalsozialistische Wirtschaftspolitik im Lichte der modernen Theorie* (Zürich, 1958), 67, 108; S. Lurie, *Private Investment in a Controlled Economy: Germany 1933–1939* (London, 1947), 21–4.

[62] R. J. Overy, 'Cars, Roads and Economic Recovery in Germany 1932–38', *Economic History Review*, 2nd ser. 28 (1975), 483.

[63] R. J. Overy, 'Transportation and Rearmament in the Third Reich', *Historical Journal*, 16 (1973), 399.

[64] Overy, 'Cars', 474.

[65] B. H. Klein, *Germany's Economic Preparations for War* (Cambridge, Mass., 1959), 14; Overy 'Cars', 476–7; L. Graf Schwerin von Krosigk, *Staatsbankrott: Finanzpolitik des Deutschen Reiches 1920–1945* (Göttingen, 1974), 230–1.

engineering and work-creation programmes began to peter out in 1935. This can be illustrated by looking at the aircraft industry during the period. Employment in the air industry as a whole was 5,000 in April 1933, 12,000 by October, and then rose sharply to 45,000 by October 1934, reaching 135,000 by April 1936, when it was larger than the German car industry.[66] As orders for aircraft expanded, firms began to pump their own funds into the industry, or to plough back profits, so that by 1936 public investment in the aircraft industry was matched by high levels of private investment too. In 1936 the assets of the industry totalled more than RM 1,000m., with almost half from private sources.[67] It was the same story at Krupp, the major supplier of guns, army equipment, and armour plate. Employment in October 1932 in the Essen works was 26,000; by October 1933 this had risen only to 34,000; but by October 1934 the figure was 51,000, and a year later 76,000.[68]

Of course it is not possible to tell how much of this expanded employment was re-employment. Because the bulk of the work-force was skilled it may well be that workers were attracted from jobs in other sectors of the economy, helping to create the bottlenecks in certain kinds of skilled labour already evident by 1936. There was no shortage of unskilled or semi-skilled labour, but this was less attractive to the arms manufacturers. The most labour-intensive part of rearmament consisted of the rebuilding of military facilities, barracks, airfields, and fortifications, and these became a major employer of labour from 1935 onwards when the work-creation programmes were over. Rearmament attracted significant quantities of labour only after the upswing was under way, and then contributed substantially to sustaining it. Even then not all the expenditure on remilitarization went directly into industry or on generating productive employment. Military expenditure was not the same thing as expenditure on armaments. In 1936 army expenditure on weapons accounted for only 7.6 per cent of the total army budget. In terms of employment it was the large increase in the physical size of the armed forces in 1935 that made the greatest difference. The large capital projects—the Four Year Plan industries, the synthetics programme, the Westwall fortifications—all came later in the 1930s.[69]

Although government expenditure and investment assumed great importance for the economy from 1933 onwards, it was the government's

---

[66] E. Homze, *Arming the Luftwaffe, The Reich Air Ministry and the German Aircraft Industry* (Lincoln, Nebr, 1976), 184.

[67] NA T177, Roll 32, frames 3720914–23, Statistisches Reichsamt, *Die Flugzeugindustrie 1933–1936*; Feb. 1938.

[68] Foreign Office Library, London, Krupp archives, Betriebsberichte 1933/4, 1934/5; Jahresberichte und Bilanzen, 1934/5–1940/1.

[69] On the army budget see BA R2/5156-C, Haushalt des Reichskriegsministerium für das Rechnungsjahr 1937 (Heer).

intention to stimulate private activity as well through selective policies directed at particular industries. According to Reinhardt Hitler wanted to 'overcome the acknowledged lack of purchasing power and incentive and in this way to increase the demand for labour and reduce unemployment'.[70] Kurt Schmitt, Minister of Economics from July 1933 to September 1934, and Schacht, who succeeded him, both hoped that the public efforts to stimulate the recovery would encourage what Schmitt called the 'natural upswing and natural upwards development' in the economy. Schmitt told an audience of economic experts in September 1933: 'The government however is clear about this, that artificial job creation cannot be kept going in the long run, but that it must be solved through a genuine private economic revival of the whole economy, and that only then is a permanent elimination or reduction of the economic crisis produced.'[71] To stimulate these effects the government chose to target particular sectors: house construction, agriculture, and the motor industry. These areas were chosen because of their strategic significance for the economy, and their considerable re-employment potential. The government had no intention of stimulating all industries equally and indiscriminately, and while its policies helped certain key industries they also had the effect of restricting others, notably the major consumer industries.

House construction was helped by a system of subsidies to houseowners initiated by von Papen in September 1932 and expanded during 1933. The scheme paid out some RM 667m. in loans and RM 332m. in direct subsidies on the basis that the owners provide 50 per cent of the cost of house conversion and 80 per cent of the cost of house repair out of their own pockets. It was estimated that an additional RM 2,900m. was spent by the owners themselves. House-building and repair doubled between 1932 and 1934, increasing twice as quickly as other forms of construction.[72] Details on the building industry are set out in Table 1.8. Employment in construction rose from an exceptional trough in 1932, rising faster than all other sectors except agriculture. There were 914,425 building workers registered as unemployed in January 1933, but only 430,787 by October. By June 1934 almost 75 per cent of building workers unemployed in March 1933 were back at work.[73]

[70] *Dokumente der deutschen Politik*, i. 201.

[71] Ibid. 205, Rede des Reichswirtschaftsminister Schmitt, 13 July 1933; *Akten der Reichskanzlei*, ii. 754, Doc. 213, Erste Sitzung des Generalrats der Wirtschaft, 2 Sept. 1933. On the 'boom' in consumer spending see H. James, *The German Slump: Politics and Economics 1924–1936* (Oxford, 1986), 414–15.

[72] WS 16 (1936), 788–9: Grebler, 'Work-Creation', pt. I, 336: Poole, *Financial Policies*, 188–97.

[73] BA R2/18701, Deutsche Bau- und Bodenbank AG, 'Die Entwicklung der deutschen Bauwirtschaft und die Arbeitsbeschaffung im Jahre 1933'.

TABLE 1.8. *House construction and the motor industry: statistics, 1928–1938*

	Number of Dwellings		Housing Invest.	Motor Industry	
	New	Converted	(RM '000m.)[a]	Output	Employment
1928	306,825	23,617	2.82	295,929	83,751
1929	315,703	23,099	2.87	335,553	76,441
1930	307,933	22,327	2.44	189,509	54,153
1931	231,342	20,359	1.19	129,424	46,134
1932	131,160	27,961	0.76	100,639	34,392
1933	132,870	69,243	0.87	158,894	51,036
1934	190,257	129,182	1.35	274,684	80,858
1935	213,227	50,583	1.56	366,072	100,937
1936	332,370	49,904	2.20	449,224	110,148
1937	340,392	31,447	2.00	491,224	123,092
1938	305,526	29,250	2.50	530,737[b]	140,746

[a] '000m. = US billion.   [b] Includes Austria.

Sources: Overy, 'Cars', 483; WS 17 (1937), 494–8; *Statistisches Jahrbuch*, 1940, 643; Klein, *Economic Preparations*, Cambridge Mass., 14.

The motor industry was helped by a series of tax concessions on private and business purchases which dragged the industry out of the recession faster than any other. Production of all vehicles was cut by two-thirds between 1929 and 1932, but by 1935 exceeded the previous output peak achieved in 1929. Moreover there was a switch from motor-cycle sales to car sales as cars became cheaper during the recession, so that the previous peak of car production achieved in 1928 was exceeded by 47 per cent in 1934 and more than 100 per cent in 1935 (see Table 1.8). The boost in vehicle sales, many of which went to business purchasers and farmers, helped to expand motor-industry employment rapidly, reaching the 1928 peak in 1934 and substantially exceeding it in 1935. The spin-off effects of a rapid increase in motorisation were also substantial, since approximately the same numbers were employed in the components industries as in the final assembly plants.[74] If there is a single industrial sector that helped to drag the German industrial economy out of recession during 1933 and 1934, the motor industry has a good claim. Its rapid growth owed something to government policies for agriculture too, for these stimulated rural demand by cutting interest rates and debt charges, lowering taxes and raising prices, and granting tax concessions for new investment.

[74] Overy, 'Cars', 478.

TABLE 1.9. Employment and unemployment, by region, 1933–1937 ('000)

Region	Unemployment (end June)					Employment (end June)				
	1933	1934	1935	1936	1937	1933	1934	1935	1936	1937
East Prussia	76	14	7	4	4	453	535	543	562	576
Silesia	366	195	171	138	58	962	1,122	1,134	1,156	1,233
Brandenburg	752	406	249	175	96	1,805	2,104	2,265	2,371	2,557
Pomerania	86	24	23	12	7	418	509	484	510	529
Nordmark	338	192	127	85	53	867	1,008	1,102	1,174	1,242
Lower Saxony	272	112	67	29	8	891	1,086	1,134	1,238	1,316
Westphalia	390	196	157	114	46	1,093	1,298	1,365	1,462	1,584
Rhineland	667	393	373	276	151	1,499	1,754	1,837	2,152	2,335
Hessen	280	143	125	87	45	693	849	865	932	1,006
C. Germany	387	170	95	54	21	1,179	1,412	1,534	1,633	1,759
Saxony	595	321	265	199	97	1,314	1,551	1,592	1,676	1,811
Bavaria	394	199	140	94	37	1,395	1,640	1,724	1,832	1,950
SW Germany	254	116	78	48	26	1,104	1,300	1,349	1,425	1,520

Source: WS 18 (1938), 47.

Motorization increased more rapidly in rural areas than in cities, reflecting the general improvement in rural demand for industrial goods.

There was also selective help for particular regions as well as for individual industries. This help took the form of locating work-creation projects and other major public works in the more economically backward, primarily agrarian regions. From 1936 onwards a central board was set up to authorize the placing of government contracts in depressed areas. The government also encouraged the relocation of industry, partly to move it away from the danger of bombing, into central and southern Germany. The increase in the labour force in these areas was almost double the national average between 1933 and 1938.[75] The result of these initiatives was that unemployment declined in all major regions at a more or less equal pace between 1933 and 1937, falling furthest in central Germany and East Prussia and the least in Saxony and Silesia.[76] The pattern of regional employment and unemployment is set out in Table 1.9.

It is clear from this discussion that no one policy or single sector can explain the recovery of employment during the period on its own. Government policies have to be considered as a whole, as a 'package' of employment-creating devices designed to sustain the autonomous upswing of the business cycle. It is possible, however, to demonstrate that the

[75] Mandelbaum, 'Full Employment', 197.
[76] 'Die deutschen Wirtschaftsgebieten im Wiederaufbau der Volkswirtschaft', WS 17 (1937), 46–51.

TABLE 1.10. *Unemployment, by economic sector, 1933–1934*

Sector	Unemployed on			% fall
	31 Mar. 1933	31 Mar. 1934	30 June 1934	
Agriculture	238,305	66,144	53,333	22.4
Mining	168,224	106,168	100,246	59.6
Stone	177,556	67,111	57,081	32.1
Metallurgy	886,086	417,287	342,548	38.6
Chemicals	23,106	14,268	12,460	54.0
Textiles	190,167	85,184	70,814	37.2
Clothing	206,915	100,661	97,018	46.8
Paper	48,867	27,446	24,260	50.0
Leather	50,394	24,382	21,497	42.6
Woodworking	276,962	121,151	102,590	37.0
Building	493,260	107,172	139,421	28.2
Transport	339,554	210,670	184,855	54.4
Commerce	427,455	293,178	254,316	59.5
Unskilled labourers	1,220,138	669,735	624,651	51.2

Source: Baerwald, 'How Germany Reduced Unemployment' (n. 6 above), 621.

exceptional speed with which employment expanded owed something not just to the general help given to the business revival through cuts in the marginal cost of capital and labour, but to the selective policies aimed at specific sectors, civil engineering, motorization, agriculture, and house construction. Table 1.10 shows the decline of unemployment in individual industries between 1933 and 1934. The figures reflect government priorities, for heavy industry, agriculture, and building. Help for the motor industry, and for furnishings, through the marriage loan, are reflected in the figures for metallurgy, textiles, and woodworking. Re-employment was slower among the unskilled (despite the work-creation projects) and among white-collar and transport workers. But there were no sectors where there was not significant re-employment during the first eighteen months of the recovery.

V

The rapid reduction of unemployment and the even more rapid expansion of employment had important consequence after 1933. Because of the wage controls and substitute employment there remained large areas of proverty in Germany during the 1930s. Living-standards in general were deliberately suppressed through wage controls and high taxes to prevent the threat of inflation or high demand for imports, but also to encourage re-employment with cheap labour, particularly female and youth labour. For those employed on the work-creation schemes, road-building, labour service, Landhilfe, etc., there was either no cash pay at all, or nominal payment set in some cases below the level of unemployment relief. This left 1.5 to 2 million workers, mainly men, on incomes no better than they were getting when unemployed, and a great many more on the low wage rates of the recession period. The effect of this long-term experience of low income produced growing dissatisfaction and evidence of labour unrest during 1934 and 1935 and was only prevented from developing into a major political threat by increases in hours and earnings from 1935 onwards, and more ruthless policing of the work-force.[77] Low living-standards were the consequence of rapid re-employment in what was still a relatively weak economy, in which consumption was deliberately controlled to release resources for war preparation and large capital projects.

The 'employment' priority of the government after 1933 also had a damaging effect on the productive performance of the economy. Much of the employment in labour-intensive sectors was diverted from manufacturing industry, where it might have been used more productively, into administration, services, or the military. Productivity growth was therefore poor during the 1930s and the multiplier effect of the new employment more muted than it might have been.[78] Firms were not encouraged to rationalize more because capital was scarce and labour cheap; and they operated for much of the time in what was effectively a closed economy or with guaranteed government contracts so that they were not faced with the usual market pressures. This in turn had an unintended long-term effect on Germany's rearmament programme. Under the employment schemes too many workers were pushed into unskilled and semi-skilled sectors and labour mobility, particularly from countryside to town, restricted. The pool of new apprentices fell during the 1930s, creating greater pressure on skilled labour reserves when rearmament was stepped up from 1935, and necessitating extensive retraining schemes later in the decade. The work-force became locked into employment patterns which then had to be broken down again with the switch to large-scale war preparations, and with considerable difficulty. In the face of low wages and high taxes many German workers preferred not to acquire new

[77] T. W. Mason, Sozialpolitik im Dritten Reich (Opladen, 1977), 147–61; I. Kershaw, Popular Opinion and Political Dissent in the Third Reich (Oxford, 1983), 82–95, 120–32.
[78] Bresciani-Turroni, "Multiplier", 83–8; Erbe, Wirtschaftspolitik, 162–3.

skills but to increase household income by expanding the number of wage-earners per household. Where upward labour mobility did occur it was into the state and party bureaucracies where it was lost to rearmament until Speer's efforts to redeploy white-collar workers back into industry later in the war. Industry remained slow to rationalize or shed labour right up to 1939–40, so that the problem of skilled-labour shortages carried over into the war when the government tried to transfer labour rapidly into war industries.[79]

What the government did demonstrate was the political will to reduce unemployment rapidly through state interventionist policies, and its ability to profit from the changed political circumstances that it introduced after 1933. These policies were not the 'Keynesian' recipe for stimulating private consumption and trade, but amounted to setting up a closed economy with strict controls over the capital market, prices, wages, imports, and exports. High levels of government expenditure and investment and selective industrial policies soaked up much of the unemployed, though at the price of low productivity growth, declining competitiveness, and pressures on the balance of payments; at the price, too, of low living-standards, a poor bargaining position for labour as a whole, and the militarization of young workers through compulsory labour service. The government's immediate priority was not, however, balanced economic growth for high living-standards, but economic growth to serve military ends. Overcoming unemployment was seen as an essential political precondition for embarking on large-scale remilitarization, rather than as an economic necessity in its own right. The irony was that less rigorous controls over consumption and less frantic efforts to achieve re-employment quickly after 1933 might well have produced a larger manufacturing base and a work-force more able to cope with the demands of industrialized warfare after 1939.

---

[79] Guillebaud, *Recovery*, 190 on the number of earners per household, which increased from an average of 1.6 in 1933 to 1.8 in 1936. On labour problems see Mason, *Sozialpolitik*, 216–28, 271–82; Petzina, 'Mobilisierung', 443–55. On the effects on rearmament see BA R7/2229, Economics Ministry memorandum by General von Hanneken. 'Richtlinien für die Gestaltung der Fertigung in der Eisen- und Metallverarbeitenden Industrie'. 'The conquest of unemployment', von Hanneken wrote, 'was directly opposed to rationalization.'

2
Cars, Roads, and Economic Recovery in Germany, 1932–1938

IT is an exaggeration', wrote the economist Paul Einzig, 'to attribute the trade revival in Germany exclusively to rearmament... War is not the ultimate weapon in the struggle against the depression.'[1] This was written in 1934. Since then the remarkable scope and strength of the revival in Germany has, despite Einzig, been uncritically attributed to the effects of rearmament at the expense of any real debate on the nature of the recovery. Yet there were a great many other factors at work in the early 1930s which help to explain the character of the revival, not least the accelerated 'motorization' of Germany after several decades of comparatively slow growth.[2] It is the purpose of this chapter to examine the economic effects of motorization in order to demonstrate that the motor-road and the motor vehicle played a significant part alongside rearmament in initiating and sustaining the upswing between 1932 and 1938.

I

Unlike the victors of the First World War, Germany experienced a slow and uneven development in the spread of motor transport in the decade after 1919. Even before 1914 the German motor industry was one of the smallest in Europe, and the lead in motorization was taken by the United States and France. Since Germany was the chief pioneer in the

---

[1] P. Einzig, *The Economics of Rearmament* (London, 1934), 108.
[2] There is not one mention of the developments in the standard works such as A. Bullock, *Hitler: A Study in Tyranny* (London, 1954), and W. L. Shirer, *The Rise and Fall of the Third Reich* (London, 1960), or the economic histories such as A. Schweitzer, *Big Business and the Third Reich* (Bloomington, Ind., 1964), or B. H. Klein, *Germany's Economic Preparations for War* (Cambridge, Mass., 1959). The only general discussion appears in D. Landes, *The Unbound Prometheus* (Cambridge, 1969), 440–51. There are a number of articles which deal largely with the question of motor transport and war preparations. The most important are: P. Kirchberg, 'Typisierung in der deutschen Kraftfahrzeugindustrie und der Generalbevollmächtigte für das Kraftfahrwesen', *Jahrbuch für Wirtschaftsgeschichte*, 8 (1969); H. Handke, 'Zur Rolle der Volkswagenpläne bei der faschistischen Kriegsvorbereitung', ibid. 1 (1962); K. Lärmer, 'Einige Dokumente zur Geschichte des faschistischen Reichsautobahnbaues', ibid. 1 (1962); R. J. Overy, 'Transportation and Rearmament in the Third Reich', *Historical Journal*, 16 (1973).

development and application of the new form of transport, the lag needs to be explained. It was partly a consequence of the density and quality of the German railway network, and the very poor state of many of Germany's roads.[3] It was partly a consequence of fashionable attachment to the horse, and conservative hostility to the mechanical age.[4] Most of all it was the result of the later industrialization of the German states, which produced a society that was less wealthy than Britain, France, or the United States.

This situation persisted in the 1920s.[5] Though the vehicle stock continued to grow across the decade, it was an uneven development, and relied more on the growth of the motor-cycle sector than cars or commercial vehicles.[6] Demand was hit badly by the post-war crisis, the destruction of upper- and middle-class incomes in the inflation of 1923, and the high price of credit thereafter. German agriculture was in a weak state for most of the decade, and failed to provide the stimulus for the motor industry provided by French peasants and American farmers.[7] Nor did the Weimar governments do much to help the infant sector, or to improve the poor road network. The heavy taxes imposed on motor vehicles before the war, when they were regarded as luxuries, remained in force.[8] The scarcity of capital made it difficult for motor firms to find sufficient funds for modernization and expansion, which might have pushed down vehicle prices sufficiently to boost a further area of demand. Only Adam Opel AG, with the help of funds from the parent company, General Motors, was able to convert to new production methods before 1928.[9] There remained a large number of small firms, producing limited numbers of custom-built vehicles. In 1929 there were over 100 different firms producing motor cycles, cars, and lorries.[10] Not surprisingly the

[3] See K. W. Förster, *Verkehrswirtschaft und Krieg* (Hamburg, 1937), 42. For every 100 sq. km. area there were 14.6 km. of railway track in Germany, 11.7 in France, 10.6 in Holland, and 7.4 in Italy.

[4] R. Garrett, *Motoring and the Mighty* (London, 1971), 2–8, 37–49.

[5] For details see 'Automobilbau 1913–33', *DDV* 8: 19 suppl. (1933); 'Die Kraftverkehrswirtschaft', *Wochenbericht des Instituts für Konjunkturforschung* (hereafter *Wochenbericht*), 5: 45 (1933); H.-H. von Fersen, *Autos in Deutschland* (Stuttgart, 1965).

[6] In 1923 there were only 59,409 motor cycles in Germany. In 1929 production alone amounted to 195,686.

[7] By 1929 there were still only approximately 25,000 vehicles in agriculture, though there were over 3m. agricultural holdings.

[8] Cars carried a *Luxussteuer* (Luxury Tax) from 3 Feb. 1910. This was changed to a *Zwecksteuer* (Utility Tax) in 1922, but the high cylinder-tax remained. For further details of the government role see 'Die Investitionen für den Verkehr 1924 bis 1935', *WS* 17 (1937), 331; P. Wohl and A. Albitreccia, *Road and Rail in 40 Countries* (London, 1935), 119–35.

[9] According to a General Motors survey, Opel bought some 80% of its machines and tools between 1924 and 1928, which made it the most advanced motor firm in Germany. See A. P. Sloan, *My Life with General Motors* (New York, 1965), 324–7.

[10] Consolidation took on several shapes. Some firms merged by mutual agreement, such as Daimler and Benz in 1926. Other firms collapsed and were bought up by larger groups or

TABLE 2.1. *Motor-vehicle production in selected countries, 1925–1931* ('000)

Country	1925	1926	1927	1928	1929	1930	1931
Canada	161	205	179	242	263	154	83
France	177	192	191	224	248	222	197
Germany	56	42	106	133	140	85	70
Italy	40	55	65	55	60	48	30
UK	153	180	212	212	239	237	225
USA	4,266	4,301	3,401	4,359	5,358	3,356	2,390

Source: League of Nations, *Review of World Production, 1925–31* (Geneva, 1932).

price of German-made motor vehicles remained considerably higher than those of competitors abroad, and Germany suffered heavy import penetration before the slump. In 1928 40 per cent of all cars sold in Germany were foreign.[11] Most of these came from the United States, and German producers were haunted in the 1920s by the 'amerikanische Gefahr', the American danger, a threat only finally reduced by the imposition of tariffs on foreign imports in 1928.[12]

The motor industry and motor transport in general were hit badly by the depression. Employment was halved and output dropped by over two-thirds, though there was some light in the gloom. American car exports were emasculated; German prices continued to fall; and the demand situation remained much healthier than in the period of currency collapse, for private savings increased and by 1932 car output was rising faster than that of commercial vehicles or motor cycles.[13] The depression also hastened the process of consolidation; more small firms disappeared, while those still in business were left with a quantity of new tools and larger factories acquired at the end of the decade in response to pressure to lower

disappeared altogether. For details of the industry in the 1920s see D. Scott-Moncrieff, *Three-Pointed Star: The Story of Mercedes Benz Cars* (London, 1955); R. Leifmann, *Cartels, Concerns and Trusts* (London, 1932), 267, 312, 321; R. A. Brady, *The Rationalization Movement in German Industry* (Berkeley, Calif., 1933), 142–56; *DDV* 7: 29 (1932/3), 961; *Wochenbericht*, 5 (1933), no. 45, 3.

[11] 'The Automobile Industry in Germany', *Weekly Reports of the German Institute of Business Research* (hereafter *Weekly Reports*; an English-language digest of the *Wochenberichte*), 7 (1934), suppl. to no. 24, 4.

[12] Up until 1928 a loophole in the tariff regulations allowed foreign cars to enter the Reich at only 10% of the duty on whole vehicles through classification of the engine and body as separate 'parts'. Even the finished American product could arrive on the German market some 10% cheaper than its German rival, and was on the whole a more reliable product. See *DDV* 8: 19 (1933/4), 14.

[13] *Vierteljahrshefte für Konjunkturforschung* (1933), pt. B, 20.

TABLE 2.2. *Motor-vehicle production in selected countries, 1933–1938* ('000)

Country	1933	1934	1935	1936	1937	1938
Canada	65	117	173	162	207	166
France	189	181	165	204	201	227
Germany	118	186	248	303	331	340
Italy	40	45	48	45	71	67
UK	286	342	404	461	507	447
USA	1,920	2,753	3,946	4,454	4,808	2,489

Source: Society of Motor Manufacturers and Traders, *The Motor Industry of Great Britain: 1938* (London, 1939).

costs and chase a wider area of demand.[14] The prospects in fact were extremely good. Germany had fallen far behind her European neighbours in the acquisition and use of motor vehicles. Now for the first time there was a chance that German cars would be cheap enough (technical breakthroughs in the 1920s made a car a much more reliable and on the whole cheaper product to maintain) to encourage the spread of the motor vehicle more generally throughout the German economy.

II

The figures for the spread of motor vehicles and the growth of motor transport in Germany after 1933 are not well known. The growth was, however, quite remarkable, compared both with what had been happening before in Germany, and with what was happening in the other major European countries as they struggled out of the depression into some sort of recovery (see Table 2.2 and Table 2.11 at the end of this chapter). The production of vehicles per year trebled between 1933 and 1938 while the production of cars and commercial vehicles actually increased considerably faster, the former at 40 per cent per annum, the latter at 49 per cent. By

[14] Old workshop methods were coming to be replaced by ones which approached the flow-production methods of American factories. By 1924 in the German industry the lag between the supply of the materials and production of the finished vehicle ranged on average from six to nine months. At Ford's in America the figures were minimum 48 hours, maximum fourteen days. By 1929 the average German figures were minimum thirty days, maximum six months. Opel with the most modern plant took the largest slice of the market, producing more than three times the output of the nearest rival. See Institut für Konjunkturforschung, *Kapitalbildung und Investitionen in der deutschen Volkswirtschaft, 1924–1928* (Berlin, 1931), 57; Brady, *Rationalization*, 147.

far the most significant change was the increasing proportion of cars in the total. In 1929, 195,000 motor cycles had been produced but only 95,000 cars. In 1937 the situation was reversed: there were 159,000 motor cycles but 270,000 cars.[15]

The reasons for such a revolution in the fortunes of motor transport were many. Some were rooted in those changes that had already taken place in the late 1920s; moreover, the fact that growth had been so slow before 1929 tended to distort developments after the depression. One of the most important factors was the influence of government on the development of the industry, both through the promotion of good roads and a general enthusiasm for motorization. The methods used were various, from encouraging enrolment in the National Socialist Car Corps to reorganizing and rationalizing the system of road classification and the administration that went with it.[16] Government encouragement was based very largely on the need to produce an economic recovery as the basis for future support for the regime, but it stemmed too from Hitler's own very great interest in motor-vehicle technology and in the role of the motor vehicle in German society.[17] But apart from official support and promotion, major changes in the supply and demand situation prompted a rapid and sudden growth after 1932. It would be a mistake to attribute everything, as the propagandists did, to the efforts of the Nazi regime. The rapid recovery of the sector depended to a certain extent on the general recovery in the business cycle, and also on the growing 'transportation

[15] For details see H. Schleusner, Erzeugungs- und Absatzfragen der deutsche Automobilindustrie (Brandenburg, 1940); 'Die deutsche Kraftfahrzeugindustrie', WS 16: 2 (1936), 2; 'Die Kraftverkehrswirtschaft', WS 19: 3 suppl. (1939); DDV, Special Issue 5 (1934/5), 3–37; Institut für Konjunkturforschung, Die Motor Front Berichtet (Berlin, 1938), and Drei Jahre Motorisierung (Berlin, 1936); O. Blum, Die Entwicklung des Verkehrs (Berlin, 1941).

[16] A. F. Napp-Zinn, 'Die Neugestaltung der Verkehrspolitik im nationalsozialistischen Deutschland', Jahrbuch für Nationalökonomie und Statistik, 141 (1935), and 'Die Entwicklung der Verkehrspolitik im nationalsozialistischen Deutschland 1933–39', ibid. 150 (1939). For a discussion of the Car Corps see P. Meier-Benneckenstein, Partei und Staat, 4 vols. (Berlin, 1941), iv. 389–440.

[17] This interest was largely thanks to the friendship of Jakob Werlin, a Mercedes car salesman, who had first met Hitler in the early 1920s. He was one of the very few of Hitler's intimates who was allowed unrestricted access to the Führer. Like the architecture of Berlin, the spread of motor-car ownership was always to have Hitler's personal attention, and he had long harboured the desire of being the instigator of mass motoring in Germany, as Ford (whom he very much admired) had been in the United States. See J. Werlin, 'Vier Jahre Aufbau in der Motorisierung', Der Vierjahrsplan, 1 (1937), 87, and 'Acht Jahre Motorisierung—Acht Jahre Vorsprung', ibid. 5 (1941), 316. For Hitler's speeches on Motorisierung see Das Archiv (1935), 1737–8; (1936), 1474–9; (1938), 1506–12; and in C. Santoro, Hitler Germany as Seen by a Foreigner (Berlin, 1938), 281. For a general discussion of Hitler and motoring for the masses see W. H. Nelson, Small Wonder: The Amazing Story of the Volkswagen (London, 1967), ch. 2 passim; and K. B. Hopfinger, Beyond Expectation: The Volkswagen Story (London, 1954), chs. 14–15 passim.

TABLE 2.3. *Vehicle ownership in Europe and USA,*
1935 (per 1,000 pop.)

Country	Vehicles[a]	Country	Vehicles[a]
USA	204.5	Switzerland	21.7
France	49.0	Irish Free State	17.8
UK	45.2	Netherlands	17.6
Denmark	41.6	Germany	16.1
Sweden	24.4	Italy	9.5
Norway	22.3	USSR	1.5

[a] Excluding motor cycles.

Source: League of Nations, *World Production and Prices,*
1925–35 (Geneva, 1936), 90.

gap' which encouraged the extension of motor transport at the railhead,
and for delivery and distribution. As one area or sector became
'motorized', so it became more imperative for other sectors to follow suit.
Since the density of motor-vehicle ownership was low in Germany in comparison with other industrial economies (see Table 2.3), there was plenty
of ground to be made up in motorizing the transport system. Though there
remained much horse-drawn traffic in Germany in the 1930s, the horse
could not compete with the motor vehicle, even for short-haul traffic.[18]
For this reason the road-haulage industry developed rapidly during the
1930s. In 1935 the Reichskraftwagenbetriebsverband (Reich Road
Haulage Association) was formed and by 1937 could count almost 35,000
firms.[19] The *Motorisierung* of the 1930s represented a process through
which the communications and distribution sector caught up with the pace
of technological and organizational changes in the actual processes of
production.

These changes were reflected in the pattern of demand and the
distribution of vehicles. The strength of the revival after 1933 expanded
the demand from both large-scale industry and the public sector, including

[18] Wohl and Albitreccia, *Road and Rail*, gives the results of two traffic censuses taken in
1924–5 and 1928–9 on a particular stretch of road. In the first census 55% of the vehicles
were horse-drawn, in the second 27%. The horse population did not drop as sharply as
elsewhere. In 1913 there were 3.8m. horses in Germany, and in 1938 3.4m. In France the
figures were 3.3m. to 2.6m. *International Yearbook of Agricultural Statistics, 1909–21*
(Rome, 1922 and annually thereafter).
[19] R. Hennig, 'Der Stand des deutschen Kraftwagenverkehrs', *Jahrbuch für
Nationalökonomie und Statistik*, 142 (1935), and E. Wagemann, 'Die Motorisierung des
Strassenverkehrs', *Wochenbericht*, 9: 12 suppl. (1937).

TABLE 2.4. *Price movements for cars and commercial vehicles, 1925–1936* (1925 = 100)

		Cars	Commercial vehicles			Cars	Commercial vehicles
1925	Jan.	105.0	97.0	1931	Jan.	59.5	74.5
	June	102.0	101.0		June	57.5	72.5
1926	Jan.	90.0	100.0	1932	Jan.	56.0	71.0
	June	79.0	77.0		June	55.0	70.5
1927	Jan.	70.5	76.0	1933	Jan.	53.0	68.0
	June	68.0	76.0		June	52.0	66.5
1928	Jan.	66.0	75.0	1934	Jan.	51.0	64.5
	June	64.5	75.0		June	50.0	64.5
1929	Jan.	63.0	75.0	1935	Jan.	49.0	63.5
	June	62.0	75.0		June	49.0	63.0
1930	Jan.	62.0	75.0	1936	Jan.	46.5	63.0
	June	60.0	75.5		June	46.5	62.5

Source: Data in WS, 1935–7.

the armed forces, and also continued the process of rural motorization.[20] But professional groups, such as doctors and lawyers, small-scale farmers, and small firms and traders came much more into the market. Agriculture, encouraged by the security of the Reich Food Estate, expanded its demand rapidly. Tractor production had been under 6,000 in 1929, had fallen to 1,500 in 1932, and rose to 28,000 by 1938. Commercial vehicles for use in agriculture increased as fast, since many firms and farms were now working in producer co-operatives.[21] The artisan sector was compelled by law to work in this way wherever possible, and the effects could be seen in the significant proportion of cars purchased by the economic groups 'handicrafts' and 'trade', which amounted to 40 per cent of the whole in 1937.[22] At the same time there developed a steady increase in the sale of cars for private use. Though this came at the expense of motor cycles, the demand for which contracted in the 1930s, private demand for

[20] 'Progress of Motorization in Germany', *Weekly Reports*, 7 (1934), 146–8; 'Die Verbreitungsaussichten des Automobils in Deutschland', *DDV*, Special Issue 5 (1934/5), 16–19; 'Zur Frage der Motorisierungsmöglichkeiten des Verkehrs', *Wochenbericht*, 9: 41 (1937), 1–6. Demand from the armed forces was still only a tiny fraction in the early years of the recovery, rising to an average of 7% of production in 1934–9.
[21] Areas with the lowest number of vehicles per thousand population were the main industrial ones, the Ruhr, the Saar, Silesia, and the Rhineland. See WS 16 (1936), 664.
[22] For artisan industry see E. Grunberg, 'The Mobilization of Capacity and Resources of Small-scale Enterprises in Germany', pt. I, *Journal of Business*, 14 (1941). For details of purchasers in 1937 see WS 17 (1937), 663.

TABLE 2.5. *Capital formation in the car industry, 1933–1936* (RMm.)

Firm	1933		1934		1935		1936	
	A	B	A	B	A	B	A	B
Daimler–Benz	26.9	36.0	30.7	56.0	35.0	60.5	42.6	64.4
Adam Opel	51.2	14.7	68.4	16.8	98.6	24.7	111.5	28.8
Auto-Union	16.4	26.0	18.0	31.3	23.3	30.1	31.9	29.4
Adlerwerke	16.2	9.2	19.2	10.3	20.1	3.6	21.1	6.1
BMW	—	—	20.6	11.0	21.4	3.0	25.0	5.5
Hanomag	—	—	6.1	6.9	13.3	19.5	17.3	21.8

Note: A = own resources; B = outside investors (including government).
Source: 'Die Finanzierung der Kraftwagenindustrie', *Der Vierjahrsplan*, 1 (1937), 417.

cars increased faster than any other category, particularly demand for small cars. By 1937 private demand accounted for 29 per cent of all purchases.[23]

The recovery of the motor-vehicle sector was not all a question of demand. Changes on the supply side were to play an increasingly important role. For one thing the price of vehicles continued to fall as they had done since 1926 without interruption (see Table 2.4), stimulated by cost economies brought about by rationalization, by the lower costs of many key raw materials, and by the easing of the financial situation.[24] The boom in trade so soon after the depression meant that the problem of capital shortage was much reduced. With a general profitability displayed for the first time and a government ceiling on dividend payments, much of the investment in the car industry came from ploughed-back profits (see Table 2.5). The price decline and the expansion of sales also encouraged research and technical improvements (for example in steel alloys, the use of aluminium, bakelite, and other plastics) and this had an effect on

[23] For the spread of private demand see T. Hoehne, *Eine kritische Untersuchung der absatzfördenden Faktoren in der deutschen Automobilindustrie* (Bückeberg, 1936); Fr. von Eltz-Rübenach (Minister of Transport, 1933–8), 'Was kann der Staat für die Motorisierung des Verkehrs tun?', *DDV*, Special Issue 5 (1934/5); and W. Ostwald, 'Die deutsche Automobilindustrie und ihre Käufer', ibid. 35–8. See too the more general discussion in I. Svennilson, *Growth and Stagnation in the European Economy* (Geneva, 1954), 144–52; and Political and Economic Planning, *Motor Vehicles*, PEP Engineering Reports 2 (London, 1950), chs. 8–9.
[24] Rationalization at Opel in 1928/9 had brought a similar response from other large firms. In 1931 the Saxon producers amalgamated to form the Auto-Union, which arranged the pooling of technical resources and the specialization of types.

industrial developments as a whole.[25] Lower prices, too, had a beneficial effect on German vehicle-trading. The favourable trade balance in vehicles, which was established in the depression, continued.[26] Germany became the world's third-largest exporter by 1936, and with this disappeared the threat of overwhelming foreign competition. In 1928 the proportion of foreign cars sold on the German market had been 40 per cent; in 1934 the figure was 9 per cent.[27]

III

Clearly such a striking recovery and expansion were to have a very considerable effect on the scope and scale of the general business revival. The German government deliberately used the motor-car sector and the road-building programme as a lever for this recovery and this it did in two main ways. The first was through the promotion of road-building and construction in the work-creation programmes. The second was the provision of special incentives for car purchasers, which helped to promote car sales immediately.

There was no doubt that some sort of revival was due in 1932. Despite the efforts to maintain the currency, Germany's trading position had been maintained not unfavourably, stocks were almost exhausted, and it was unlikely that prices would fall much further.[28] The main problem for the German government as for those throughout Europe was how to help the recovery along in what was still a pre-Keynesian world.[29] In Germany the efforts of the successive administrations from mid-1932 took the form

[25] See the speech by R. Allmers (Chairman of the Association of German Vehicle Manufacturers) in Das Archiv (1938), 1506–8; J. Werlin, 'Rohstoffplan und Motorisierung', Der Vierjahrsplan, 1 (1937), 12; 'Magnesiumlegierung im Fahrzeugbau', ibid. 3 (1939), 379; K. Uhlemann, 'Anwendung und Verformung von Plexiglas', ibid. 4 (1940), 544–7.

[26] Weekly Reports, 7: 24 suppl. (1934), 3–4; and 10: 7/8 (1937), 16; 'Kraftverkehrsentwicklung und Aussenhandelsbilanz', DDV, Special Issue 5 (1934/5), 20–1; WS 16 (1936), 50–3; 'Die Motorisierung im Rahmen der südosteuropäischen Verkehrsentwicklung', Wochenbericht, 10: 48 (1938).

[27] Weekly Reports, 8: 20/21 (1935), 4.

[28] C. T. Schmidt, German Business Cycles, 1924–1933 (New York, 1934), 56–60; National Industrial Conference Board, The Economic State of Germany (New York, 1933), ch. 1 passim.

[29] There was a certain amount of practical experience already in this field, and of course the problems had been discussed on a theoretical level for some time. For German discussions at the time see H. Drager, Arbeitsbeschaffung durch produktive Kreditschöpfung (Munich, 1932); P. Quante, 'Arbeitsbeschaffung und Rentabilität', Schmollers Jahrbuch, 57 (1933), who concluded that unemployment could and should be solved by public works, provided conservative opposition could be convinced of its efficacy. Men like Luther at the Reichsbank remained unconvinced according to F. von Papen, Memoirs (London, 1952), 209–10. See also D. Keese, 'Die volkswirtschaftlichen Gesamtgrössen für das Deutsche Reich in den Jahren 1925–36' in W. Conze (ed.), Die Staats- und wirtschaftskrise Deutschlands (Stuttgart, 1967).

of work-creation through tax-relief and the provision of government funds for special projects.[30] These work-creation programmes have sometimes been mistaken for rearmament expenditures or 'veiled rearmament'. In fact the schemes of 1932–5 were mainly concerned with infrastructure refurbishment and expansion, the road network in particular. Roads which had suffered badly from the lack of necessary maintenance for three or four years during the depression were now repaired by gangs of unemployed labourers. The work-creation plans from the emergency programmes of 1932 onwards were directed primarily at public works that required a high labour input. Road-repair and road-building constituted a substantial proportion of the work, a course that was recommended by the Brauns Commission of 1931 (set up to report to Chancellor Brüning on the state of the economy), and finalized in the plans proposed by the Finance Ministry in 1932 and 1933. Senior Nazis were talking before the seizure of power about the place that road-building would play in Nazi employment policy.[31] Once in power, the Nazi regime used road-works as a major element in the state-sponsored 'Battle for Work'. Some 60 per cent of the funds released for work-creation public works between 1932 and 1935 went to transport projects, mainly on roads. Public investment constituted 77 per cent of all investment during the same period, so that road-building played a major part in the recovery of German investment in the three years after the trough of the depression.[32]

Proposals for public works were greeted nervously at first by the business and banking community. Limited schemes of this kind had existed since the crisis of 1926, when the provincial governments used unemployment funds to finance local public works.[33] Advances in the construction industry in so-called winter building permitted engineering projects to continue across the winter months, when the unemployment situation was at its worst.[34] Close attention was paid to the experiments in public works in the United States so that any obvious mistakes could be avoided.[35] On this basis, publicly financed re-employment schemes were

[30] L. Grebler, 'Work-Creation Policy in Germany, 1932–1935', pts. I and II, *International Labour Review*, 35 (1937).

[31] Christie Papers, Churchill College, Cambridge, 180/1 4, notes of a talk between Göring and Christie 'summer 1932'; von Papen, Memoirs, 283; H. Schacht, *Account Settled* (London, 1949), 48–9.

[32] Grebler, 'Work-Creation', pt. I, 341, and pt. II, 521.

[33] National Industrial Conference Board, *Unemployment Insurance and Relief in Germany* (New York, 1932), 39, 56–7; K. I. Wiggs, *Unemployment in Germany since the War* (London, 1935), 114.

[34] E. Bernhard, 'Winter Building as a Remedy for Seasonal Unemployment', *International Labour Review*, 24 (1931). This article surveys the extensive experiments carried on in Germany and the United States during the 1920s.

[35] For details see *America's Recovery Programme* (Oxford, 1934) and the debate in *Proceedings of the American Statistical Association*, 28 (1933), esp. the articles by Kahn and Gill; M. Mitnitzky, 'The Effects of a Public Works Policy on Business Activity and Employment', *International Labour Review*, 30 (1934).

perceived to be less risky than had once been thought, and Brüning might well have introduced them earlier in 1932 but for his determination to solve the reparations issue first.[36] Detailed plans for the work-creation schemes were ready by March 1932, designed to give work to more than 600,000 men in the first stage, but only under von Papen, with Dr Warmbold at the Economics Ministry, were they put into effect.[37] This first programme and those that followed in late 1932 and 1933 all concentrated on *Tiefbau*, on construction work on roads, canals, and bridges.[38] In 1934 came the *Autobahnen*, which were intended not only to create work but to encourage the spread of the motor car at the same time. In 1933 all these schemes employed, at the peak, 727,500 directly on the sites. By 1934 the peak number was 992,500.[39] This produced, as expected, a quick revival in some key construction and supply industries. Cement output doubled between 1932 and 1934. The index of the sales of the major supply industries stood at 18.0 (1928 = 100) in January 1933. By September this had climbed to 59 and by the following June to 85.7.[40] Road construction came to play a significant part in the creation of new jobs.

The second way in which the government tried to tie the motor car in with the recovery drive was through the granting of widespread tax concessions. The high level of vehicle and fuel tax in the 1920s hampered expansion.[41] Concessions began in the spring of 1933. On 10 April the motor tax was abolished for all new cars, which meant an immediate reduction in maintenance costs of 10 or 15 per cent.[42] Industry could make deductions for tax purposes for any new vehicle purchased.[43] Acknowledging the importance of the used-car market for the spread of the motor car, a further law of 26 May 1933 allowed owners of second-hand cars to compound all future taxes in a lump-sum payment.[44] The

---

[36] W. J. Helbich, *Die Reparationen in der Ära Brüning* (Berlin, 1962), *passim*.

[37] Ibid. 54–5.

[38] 'Die Bauwirtschaft mitte 1933', *Wochenbericht*, 6: 12 (1933); 'Die Arbeitsbeschaffung im kommenden Winter', ibid. no. 31; 'Arbeitsbeschaffung und Tiefbau', ibid. no. 38; 'Recent Progress in Road and Canal Construction in Germany', *Weekly Reports*, 7: 31 (1934).

[39] Grebler, 'Work-Creation', pt. II, 513.

[40] *Weekly Reports*, 7: 31 (1934), 139.

[41] *DDV* 8: 19 suppl. (1933/4), 18. In 1933 it was calculated that a car costing RM 2,800 would cost a similar sum per year to run and repair.

[42] *Weekly Reports*, 7: 24 suppl. (1934), 1.

[43] Decree of 1 June 1933. As a result a firm could save as much at 70% of the original purchase price of a vehicle. These regulations were part of the general provisions for the Law of the Reduction of Unemployment. In Oct. 1934 the scheme was extended for all vehicles bought by farmers, businessmen, or professional men such as lawyers and doctors. *Weekly Reports*, 9: 7/8 (1937), 15.

[44] *Weekly Reports*, 7: 24 suppl. (1934), 1, and 10: 7 (1937), 15. As a result of this measure the tax on 120,000 cars and commercial vehicles was compounded. For the used-car market see ibid. 7: 24 suppl. (1934), 3.

TABLE 2.6. Vehicle industry: business statistics, 1928–1935

Year	Profit Loss (no. of firms)		Profit (RMm.)	Loss (RMm.)	Dividends (RMm.)	Employment (yearly peak)
1928	11	5	7.7	16.6	3.6	83,751
1929	14	3	8.0	11.7	5.6	76,441
1930	—	9	4.6	38.8	1.9	54,153
1931	3	13	0.2	42.2	0.1	46,134
1932	2	15	0.9	25.8	0.9	34,392
1933	9	—	8.2	23.5	1.2	51,036
1934	13	4	21.8	0.7	2.6	80,858
1935	15	—	27.3	—	8.0	100,937

Source: WS 16 (1936), 49, and 17 (1937), 86.

effect was immediate. Car sales shot up during 1933, and helped to accelerate a trend that had already been noticeable in late 1932.[45] The car firms that had complained during the depression that they needed government subsidy to survive were showing profits for the first time, and the leading producers paid out dividends in 1934 (see Table 2.6). By the end of 1935 the motor industry was working at 93 per cent of capacity, at a time when mechanical engineering as a whole was employing 77 per cent and textiles only 55. The index of production rose very much faster for the motor industry than for industry as a whole, from 100 in 1932 to 250 in 1934 as against 100 and 140 for all industry.[46] Twice as many cars were produced in 1933 as in 1932, and in 1934 twice as many again. This encouraged car firms to employ fully in winter-time as well, thus helping to avoid the difficulties created by seasonal unemployment which had been particularly acute in the winter of 1932–3. Both Opel and Auto-Union began a so-called Winteraktion in 1933–4,[47] which coincided with the first work on the Autobahnen and all-year employment on public works. The government did not follow up the tax concessions with major investment in the vehicle industry to match the investment in roads. Only Daimler–Benz, BMW, and Horch received any substantial sums and this was partly because of the armament work which these firms performed. The necessary investment was rapidly generated through the vigorous revival and by 1934/5 motor-vehicle firms were ploughing back large profits into the expansion of productive capacity.

[45] The upswing in car sales began in October 1932, that for commercial vehicles two months later, in December: Vierteljahrshefte für Konjunkturforschung (1933), pt. B, 20.
[46] Grebler, 'Work-Creation', pt. II, 516; Weekly Reports, 8: 21 suppl. (1935).
[47] W. Kissel. 'Arbeitsbeschaffung durch Automobilerzeugung', DDV, Special Issue 5 (1935), 19–20; 'Motorisierung und Arbeitsschlacht', DDV 8: 20 (1933/4), 850.

The overall effect of the government measures was to restore confidence, both in the role that the Nazi regime was to play in economic affairs and in the expectation of a business recovery. What both the work-creation programme and the tax measures were supposed to do was to provide an initial push. Much of the popular debate in Germany had centred on the idea of the *Initialzündung*, the first spark, a word coined by the economist, Wilhelm Röpke, when working on the Brauns Commission investigating the recession in 1931.[48] This was one of the reasons for choosing *Motorisierung*, though Hitler had a personal preference for it as well. In 1934 at the Berlin Motor Show (in which Hitler took considerable personal interest) he announced to an enthusiastic audience that it was the intention of the

National Socialist leadership not only to crank up the economy through the furthering of the motor-car sector, giving bread and work to thousands of men, but also to offer ever greater masses of our people the opportunity to acquire this most modern means of transport.[49]

The one advantage that this sector had, as the Nazis (among others) pointed out, was that it could affect to some degree every other branch of industry, through the direct manufacture of vehicles and parts, and the provision of service and repair facilities. The roads programme could in addition provide the central core of the recovery in the construction industry, an essential prerequisite if the recovery were to be a sustained one.[50] In 1935 *Der deutsche Volkswirt* looked back on three years of economic recovery and concluded that

the car industry and its suppliers have taken up a very large proportion of the unemployed; the first spark provided here has not left unaffected a large number of corresponding economic sectors, so that motor transportation has played almost the same role in the present business revival as the construction industry played in earlier periods.[51]

[48] W. Röpke, 'Trends in German Business Cycle Policy', *Economic Journal*, 43 (1933).

[49] For the text of the speech see Santoro, *Hitler Germany*, 281.

[50] According to Bernhard, 196, the exceptional importance of road-works 'not only as a part of public works but also in modern national economy can hardly be exaggerated'. Fritz Todt, looking back on five years of road-building, concluded that 'one of the road-building programmes' special tasks was to become the pacemaker for the whole construction sector', *Der Vierjahrsplan*, 3 (1939), 142.

[51] There are numerous references in press and official publications to show that people at the time clearly believed that the motor-car sector was among the most important stimuli for the recovery. Certainly Hitler had intended this to be the case, whatever his views on rearmament. 'Motorisierung', he said, 'was in fact at one and the same time a struggle against unemployment and a struggle *for* employment.' Allmers, head of the industry's organization, believed him. See R. Allmers, 'Die Automobilindustrie im neuen Deutschland', *DDV*, Special Issue 5 (1934/5), 7; and Werlin, 'Vier Jahre Aufbau', 87: 'Following the Führer's initiative, the motor industry has taken first place in the German economic reconstruction and has been an example for the whole economy of drive and pace.'

This contention reappeared the following year when the League of Nations published its survey of European recovery.[52] Whether it was true or not, the motor-car recovery helped considerably in the restoration of business confidence, encouraging the expansion of the heavy industries first— cement, mining, iron and steel, machine tools. On these developments depended the whole success of the upswing in Germany. The motor car and the roads it was to drive along contributed considerably towards its achievement.

These facts about motor transport raise an important question: how important was rearmament? For rearmament has generally been regarded as the 'first spark' in the Nazi economic recovery. Yet in practice rearmament did not get fully under way until 1935, after which it was often a hindrance to economic growth rather than a stimulant.[53] Military expenditure as such was still limited in scope during the early period. In the financial years 1932/3 and 1933/4 budget expenditure remained at the level for 1927/8.[54] In 1933 and 1934 total expenditure on roads and motor transport by the administration was just over RM 2,000m. Total government investment in what can loosely be regarded as rearmament industries came to RM 600m. in the same period.[55] Total military expenditure for the first three years of the Third Reich is estimated at RM 8,000m. to 9,000m., though the exact figures are difficult to calculate.[56] An aggregation of investment in ordinary roads, motor transport, the *Autobahnen*, and road funds in the work-creation schemes gives a figure of RM 5,000m. to 6,000m. (see Table 2.7), with the main weight on the earlier years 1932−4 when the recovery was still not a certainty. Clearly therefore rearmament can only be considered to be one of the reasons why Germany recovered so fast after 1932, rather than the most important one. Some of the orders for vehicles came of course from the armed forces, but this was a tiny percentage before 1936.[57] Although the primary and secondary effects of rearmament and the motor sector were similar, the

[52] League of Nations, *World Production and Prices, 1935−36* (Geneva, 1936), 88.

[53] For the discussion of rearmament see A. Schweitzer, 'Die wirtschaftliche Wiederaufrüstung Deutschlands von 1934−36', *Zeitschrift für die gesamte Staatswissenschaft*, 114 (1958); D. Petzina, 'Hauptprobleme der deutschen Wirtschaftspolitik', *Vierteljahrshefte für Zeitgeschichte*, 15 (1967); R. Erbe, *Die nationalsozialistische Wirtschaftspolitik im Lichte der modernen Theorie* (Zürich, 1958); K. Gossweiler, 'Der Übergang von der Weltwirtschaftskrise zur Rüstungskonjunktur', *Jahrbuch für Wirtschaftsgeschichte*, 7 (1968). For a full discussion of the civilian nature of *Motorisierung*, see Overy, 'Transportation'.

[54] *Statistisches Jahrbuch*, 1928−34.

[55] WS 17 (1937), 330−3, and Klein, *Preparations*, 14, 16, 254−5.

[56] The additional sums came under the secret 'Mefo-Bill' expenditure begun in 1934, which totalled RM 2,140m. in 1934/5 and RM 2,700m. in 1935/6.

[57] USSBS Report 77, *German Vehicle Industry Report* (Washington, DC, 1946), 3, 5. In 1934 the armed forces took 1,700 lorries, in 1935 and 1936 7,000 lorries a year out of a total for the three years of 126,000 produced.

TABLE 2.7. *Military and motor transport expenditure, 1932/3–1934/5* (RMm.)

Fiscal year	Military expenditure	Motor transport
1932/3	766.2	814.0[a]
1933/4	1,360.0	1,139.0
1934/5	1,900.0	1,618.0

[a] Made up from figures for ordinary roads investment, *Autobahnen*, road passenger transport, and work-creation funds for roads and bridges. See Grebler, 'Work-Creation', table 3; Erbe, *Wirtschaftspolitik* 26; and WS, 1936–9.

military expansion before 1935 did not involve large increases in personnel, and was largely carried out in secret. The motor sector, on the other hand, had the advantage that it could rapidly absorb a large number of unemployed with the maximum of publicity. Business confidence was restored, not with threats of foreign war but with the promise of modernization and greater financial security, for which achievement motor transport could lay a considerable claim.

IV

Was this claim in fact justified? The Nazi leadership, for all the talk of first sparks and the 'Battle for Work', knew very little about economics. As far as they were concerned the figures frequently sufficed. Car production increased from 43,000 to 276,000; vast road schemes were planned and put into effect. The propagandists made much of it, but often failed to see what the significance of these changes was, a significance that went well beyond the 'public face' of the revival. The recovery and expansion of the motor industry and the building of new roads had very widespread effects, owing to the peculiar position enjoyed by both, with diverse backward and forward linkages in the economy. These effects continued to play a part long after the crisis was over, in sustaining the recovery through to 1938. The most important effect (and the one which captured the imagination of the government faced with the massive task of overcoming six million unemployed) was on employment levels. Although it is impossible to produce accurate aggregate figures for the employment created by the primary and secondary effects of the sector, some idea can be given. In 1935 Hitler estimated that total employment given by roads and cars

TABLE 2.8. *Estimated employment created by roads and cars, 1938*[a]

Reichsautobahnen	120,000
Ordinary roads (1936)	40,000
Motor industry (excluding parts)	170,000
Components and parts	150,000
Garages (1935)	100,000
Supply industry, roads	250,000
Motor trade	60,000
Chauffeurs, drivers, etc. (1934)	260,000
TOTAL	1,150,000

[a] Estimated jobs, including figures for earlier years where 1938 figure not known.

Sources: WS 18 (1938), 569, and 19: 3 suppl. (1939); *Wochenbericht*, 9 (1936), 553, and 6 (1933), 4–5; *Das Archiv* (1934), 713–14; *DDV*, Special Issue 5 (1934/5), 19–20; *Der Vierjahrsplan*, 5 (1941), 316.

amounted to 1 million jobs.[58] By 1938 the figure had risen to perhaps 1.5 million (see Table 2.8), or one in twelve of the employed work-force.

More important still, this constituted a shift in the pattern of employment, for work on the *Autobahnen* and additional employment in the motor industry and its numerous subsidiaries and subcontractors (estimated at 20,000 firms in 1938) did not just mean the replacement of labour that had suffered during the depression years. It did mean, of course, that employment that might have been created by the railways or horse-transport lapsed, although the number of horses actually increased during the 1930s and the freight traffic of the railways still remained of great significance, since it was high-value goods, low in bulk, that were now shifted by road.[59] Figures for gross sales (though a rather unsatisfactory way of measuring the significance of the industry because it does not indicate the more limited value-added figure) give some indication of the growth in size and vigorous demand for motor products (see Table 2.9). The German industry was not as dominant in the overall industrial economy as its American counterpart, but it was the tip of a sizeable iceberg. Estimates of gross sales of all businesses connected with

[58] *Das Archiv* (1935), 1738.
[59] J. Hellauer, 'Eisenbahn und Kraftwagen', *Zeitschrift für Betriebswirtschaft* (1934); Institut für Konjunkturforschung, *Konjunkturschwankungen im Reichsbahnverkehr*, Special Issue 38 (Berlin, 1936).

TABLE 2.9. Gross sales of some major industries, 1933–1938 (RMm.)

Industry	1933	1934	1935	1936	1937	1938
Coal	1,169	1,309	1,512	1,697	2,047	2,173
Raw iron	282	463	665	833	891	1,093
Raw steel	562	826	1,138	1,405	1,553	1,935
Motor vehicles	483	700	1,148	1,414	1,636	2,017
Synthetic textiles	141	210	248	275	437	557
Cotton goods	303	—	409	446	494	525

Source: Statistisches Jahrbuch, 1935 and 1940.

TABLE 2.10. Export earnings of some major industries, 1934–1938 (RM '000m.)

Industry	1934	1935	1936	1937	1938
Coal	224.5	261.4	277.5	440.4	379.5
Cotton textiles	39.2	41.7	62.1	86.1	92.0
Chemicals	169.0	172.0	177.9	195.3	169.4
Machine tools	87.0	78.2	148.2	209.1	206.9
Electrical goods	218.6	226.0	258.3	312.3	335.4
Precision instruments	62.3	72.4	90.5	116.5	126.0
Pharmaceuticals	104.4	108.6	111.0	139.8	127.7
Vehicles	94.5	120.0	171.2	269.7	259.4

Source: Statistisches Jahrbuch, 1936 and 1940.

the motor vehicle (garages, haulage, etc.) show a figure of RM 4,000m. for 1932, RM 6,000m. for 1936.[60] The motor-vehicle industry also became a major export earner during the period. By 1938 the industry was only exceeded in the value of its exports by the electrical and coal industries. (See Table 2.10).

In discussing these kinds of measurements it must be borne in mind that figures for the motor industry by itself represent only half the story, for the backward and forward linkages increased as rapidly and as significantly as vehicle output itself. The more immediate effects were obvious ones—increases in steel orders, orders for manufactured goods such as lamps, textiles, machinery, and tools. To these may be added the tyre and rubber industry, the fuel industry, retail and repair shops, garages, and roads.

---

[60] The figures are only approximate. DDV, Special Issue 5 (1934/5), 7; Der Vierjahrsplan, 1 (1937), 88.

Some firms grew large and monopolistic through supplying components: Robert Bosch for electrical equipment, Fichtel and Sachs for clutches, Maybach for gears and gearboxes. Others remained small but their numbers increased. In the mid-1930s there were over 55,000 garages. The tyre industry reached the 1929 level of production again by 1934 and output of tyres doubled between 1934 and 1938, while the number of firms increased from 19 in 1934 to 25 in 1936 and employment rose from 7,500 in 1932 to over 17,000 in 1937.[61]

The most conspicuous aspect of *Motorisierungspolitik* were the new motor-roads.[62] Work began in the winter of 1933 laying foundations and clearing earth for the first selected stretches of *Autobahn*, usually in areas with a high unemployment rate.[63] Machinery was used as little as possible at first in order to soak up the maximum amount of labour. By 1934, 40,000 were working directly on the sites, while more than twice that number were working on projects and orders concerned with supplying and planning the construction.[64] By the middle of 1935 Hitler was talking of 400,000 jobs created by road-building, and in June 1936 a peak of 124,000 men working directly on the *Autobahnen* sites was reached.[65] The size of the project was enormous, and although only 3,000 kilometres of road were finished by 1939, well over 3,000 bridges had been constructed, some of them major feats of civil engineering.[66] The cement industry was particularly favoured as a result. At its conference on 4 September 1934 it sent a vote of thanks to Hitler for the road programme that had revived the sector after the disastrous falling off of orders after 1930.[67] By the end of 1935 over one-tenth of cement production since the *Autobahnen* were started was used on the new road network.[68] This sort of impact persisted even after the building of the western fortifications had taken resources from civilian projects. If the actual amount of motorway finished was quite small, the amount of existing road that was completely improved and resurfaced constituted one of the largest engineering projects of the decade. Between 1936 and 1939 over 17,000 kilometres of road were improved,

[61] WS 16 (1936), 93, and 18 (1938), 989.
[62] For details see G. Fischer, 'Die Reichsautobahnen', *Zeitschrift für Betriebswirtschaft* (1935); K. Kaftan, *Die Kampf um die Autobahnen, 1907–1935* (Berlin, 1935); F. Todt, *Drei Jahre Arbeit an die Strassen Adolf Hitlers* (Berlin, 1935).
[63] Todt, *Drei Jahre Arbeit*, 48.
[64] *Das Archiv* (1934), 713.
[65] WS 16 (1936), 553.
[66] By the end of 1937 3,223 bridges had been completed. For details see 'Baustoffe und Bauweisen im Wandel der Zeit', in *Deutscher Beton Verein: 41 Hauptversammlung: Vorträge* (Berlin, 1938), 115–61, and 'Die Donaubrücke der RAB bei Leipheim', ibid. 162–204.
[67] *Das Archiv* (1934), 578–9.
[68] WS 16 (1936), 410; *Statistisches Jahrbuch*, 1936.

maintaining the importance of road construction throughout the recovery period.[69]

Other changes that were linked to the growth of motor transport came to assume a significance of their own. This was certainly the case with the synthetic production of fuel-oil and rubber, which owed something to the motor car as the largest user as it did to the need to prepare for war.[70] The process of producing synthetic fuel followed twenty years of development at IG Farben which ended successfully in the mid-1920s. There is little doubt that Germany's poor trading position in oil, and the advantage of possessing a large coal and chemical industry, provided the initial incentive for research. The industry was an important ingredient of the whole motorization policy, and indeed synthetic fuel was used for civilian consumption to such an extent that stocks for war were often at a dangerously low level.[71] Shortages of fuel also prompted other developments, such as the diesel engine, in which Germany was a leading researcher by the late 1920s. The engines were successfully applied to heavy lorries in the early 1930s and helped to accelerate the growth of road haulage.[72] The diesel engine, like synthetic fuel, was developed and expanded as part of a general process of technological improvement which was transforming the German industrial structure during the inter-war years as it did throughout the industrially developed world. Here, too, the motor industry had an important qualitative role to play, for it was among the pioneers of flow-production methods and advanced factory organization, increasingly demanding from its suppliers the same levels of efficiency and organization that Taylorism had brought to Opel and Ford.

Qualitative changes were often as important as the actual quantities involved. For one thing the inter-war years did see a revolution in transport as a result of the motor car.[73] The distribution of goods speeded up, passengers could be moved faster and more cheaply in towns, and factories were able to incorporate lorry and car into the production and distribution of goods, increasing the general level of industrial efficiency.[74] From 1925–30 only 89,000 commercial vehicles were produced: in the five years after 1933 over 265,000. Agriculture, too, absorbed an ever greater number of tractors—in 1929 there were 25,000 in use, and in

[69] WS 19 (1939), Special supplement, 'Die Kraftverkehrswirtschaft', 34.

[70] T. Hughes, 'Technological Momentum in History: Hydrogenation in Germany, 1898–1933', Past and Present, 15 (1969), 113 ff.; W. Birkenfeld, Der synthetische Treibstoff 1933–1945 (Göttingen, 1963), 3–25; W. Kissel, 'Treibstoffragen in Kraftverkehrswesen', DDV 9: 20 (1934/5).

[71] Nazi Conspiracy and Aggression, 10 vols. (Washington, DC, 1946), iii., Document group 1301-PS, 868–906.

[72] The Modern Diesel (London, 1938), chs. 2, 8, 9.

[73] 'Die Bedeutung der Verkehrsmittel im deutschen Wirtschaftsleben', Verkehrstechnische Woche (1939), no. 12.

[74] Hellauer, 'Eisenbahn', 407–11.

1939 82,000. There was also a marked structural shift in the transport system in favour of motor vehicles for private travel, while the number of passengers on road transport increased sharply as bus services spread into the German countryside.[75] A. P. Sloan of General Motors studied the Germany of 1928 and concluded that in terms of the impact of the motor vehicle Germany was at the level the United States had achieved in 1911. The same could not be said ten years later. Both quantitatively and qualitatively, the motorization of Germany in the 1930s contributed to German recovery and to the long-term technical development of German industry and transport.

V

By 1938, therefore, the German economy had become increasingly dependent on the motor car. The motor industry was firmly in the forefront of German industry, and motor transport had moved from luxury to necessity. Despite the problems of full employment and the competition of rearmament, the prospects for growth seemed as good in 1938 as they had done five years before. The only real limitation now was capacity. By the end of 1938 all lorry production for the following year had been spoken for, and the major car firms were seeking permission to build more factories. The government, anxious that the success that motor cars had had in stimulating and sustaining the economic recovery should not be lessened, elaborated new plans in the Volkswagen project to increase production to ever greater heights, even if this was to mean taking resources away from rearmament, which it inevitably would.[76] The Volkswagen factory was to begin production in 1940, beginning with 150,000 cars a year rising to 1.5 million within two years.[77] This was a production of more than five times as many cars as had been produced in the whole of 1938. Together with the popular car was to come the popular tractor, or *Volkspflug*. This project too was planned in the grand manner, involving the creation of a new town (Waldbröl), the building of four massive factories, and the production first of all of 100,000 tractors a year increasing to 300,000. This would have made it the largest tractor plant in the world.[78] More than that, it would have made Germany among the

[75] Hennig, 'Stand des Verkehrs', 372–9. By 1935 it was estimated that motor traffic took 60% of private journeys, rail 32%, waterways 7%.

[76] For details see Nelson, *Small Wonder* and Hopfinger, *Beyond Expectation*.

[77] P. Kluke, 'Hitler und das Volkswagenprojekt', *Vierteljahrshefte für Zeitgeschichte*, 9 (1960), 361.

[78] R. von Frankenberg, *Porsche: The Man and his Cars* (Henley, Oxon., 1969), 93–8. The information was provided by Porsche's son Ferry, who was in charge of getting the tractor plant into operation.

TABLE 2.11. *Motor transport and motor-vehicle production: statistics, 1907–1913 and 1921–1939*

Year	Vehicle stock	Vehicle production				Vehicle sales (RMm.)	Employment motor industry[a]	No. of firms		Vehicles in agriculture[b]
		Total	Car	Motor cycle	Commercial			All	Cars	
1907	27,026	7,663	3,491	3,776	396	60.9	13,423	69	—	—
1908	36,022	7,721	4,142	3,164	415	56.4	13,136	71	—	—
1909	41,727	11,021	6,682	3,703	636	80.3	19,221	121	—	—
1910	49,941	14,126	8,578	4,758	790	118.4	21,813	114	—	—
1911	56,434	16,672	10,319	4,980	1,373	163.0	28,694	131	—	—
1912	65,450	21,602	14,296	5,524	1,782	221.6	35,877	124	—	—
1913	77,789	19,743	12,400	5,104	1,851	214.0	33,462	109	—	—
1921	118,640	—	—	—	—	—	—	—	—	—
1922	165,315	—	—	—	—	—	—	—	—	—
1923	212,961	—	—	—	—	—	—	—	—	383
1924	293,188	—	—	—	—	—	—	—	86	1,026
1925	425,826	112,506	39,080	55,980	10,304	771.0	86,642	235	—	7,731
1926	571,893	91,832	31,958	48,942	5,211	501.0	55,412	238	41	10,263
1927	723,935	191,010	84,668	84,256	11,972	908.0	83,424	244	—	13,706
1928	933,312	295,929	101,701	162,212	20,960	1,089.0	83,751	140	27	19,007
1929	1,214,059	335,553	96,161	195,686	31,577	994.0	76,441	128	17	25,095
1930	1,419,870	189,509	71,960	104,352	9,985	676.0	54,153	118	16	25,902
1931	1,507,129	129,424	58,774	59,486	8,734	475.0	46,134	102	17	26,686
1932	1,499,724	100,639	43,430	36,262	8,234	309.0	34,392	—	17	27,500
1933	1,682,985	158,894	92,160	40,534	13,261	483.5	51,036	—	17	28,200
1934	1,887,632	274,684	147,350	88,312	27,325	780.0	80,858	—	17	31,000
1935	2,157,811	366,072	205,092	117,651	41,528	1,148.5	100,937	—	17	35,000
1936	2,474,591	449,224	244,289	145,916	57,312	1,414.7	110,148	—	17	45,000
1937	2,848,466	491,224	269,005	159,815	62,404	1,636.5	123,092	—	17	60,833
1938[c]	3,364,503	530,737	276,592	190,018	64,127	2,017.0	140,756	—	17	74,943
1939	3,894,588[d]	289,271[e]	143,602[e]	112,675[e]	32,994	2,096.5	—	—	17	82,077

[a] Yearly employment peak.   [b] Stock of tractors.   [c] Includes Austria.
[d] With Czechoslovakia and Memel approx. 4.1m. vehicles.   [e] production for Jan.–June only for 1939.

Sources: WS 1922, 29; ...

world's leading vehicle producers, approaching for the first time the vast numbers produced each year by the United States. Quite where the resources were coming from was never made clear. The existing car factories were to free some resources by greater rationalization and concentration of production.[79] Clearly, for either project to succeed in its civilian capacity it would also have meant cutting back quite heavily on the level of rearmament achieved by 1938. In any event it was Hitler's intention to make certain that what had been contributed by the motor car to the revival of the economy should not be allowed to lapse.[80]

The recovery of the motor industry and the promotion of motor transport during the 1930s made a significant contribution to speeding up the general revival, in absorbing many of the unemployed, and in sustaining the recovery after the initial upswing. This was the basic premiss behind Nazi policy. The fact that the government could be seen to be providing incentives, protection, and security for a fast-growing industrial sector was also felt to be important for overcoming the psychological barriers to reviving business confidence. Both motor vehicles and road-building were poised to become yet more economically significant when war intervened in 1939. In the 1950s the completion of the *Autobahn* network and the triumphant growth of the German car industry completed the structural shift begun in the 1930s.

[79] See Nelson, *Small Wonder*, 67–8; Kirchberg, 'Typisierung'; Institut für Konjunkturforschung, *Weniger Typen in Deutschland* (Berlin, 1939); 'Das Typenproblem in der Kraftfahrzeugwirtschaft', *Wochenbericht*, 10: 23 suppl. (1937); Adolf von Schell, 'Neue Wege der deutschen Motorisierung', *Der Vierjahrsplan*, 3: 4 (1939).

[80] J. Werlin, 'Die wirtschaftliche und soziale Sinn des Volkswagens', *Der Vierjahrsplan*, 2 (1938), 472–3.

II

INDUSTRY IN THE THIRD REICH

3

Heavy Industry in the Third Reich: The Reichswerke Crisis

ON 24 August 1937 at the Stahlhof in Düsseldorf, meeting-place of the German iron and steel industry, a historic discussion took place. Few of the managers present were enthusiastic Nazis. The wall decoration of the Stahlhof had been clumsily altered to make it impossible to hang a portrait of Hitler.[1] The purpose of the meeting was to discuss a long memorandum drawn up by the heads of the Vereinigte Stahlwerke, Germany's largest steel combine, arguing against the decision to establish a new state-run iron and steel complex, to be known as the Reichswerke 'Hermann Göring'. But there was a broader significance as well. The heavy industry of the Ruhr chose the crisis over the Reichswerke as the occasion to challenge the efforts of the Nazi leadership to alter economic priorities in favour of autarky and large-scale war preparation. This challenge had important political implications, for the rejection of state intervention and autarky was an overtly political act. German heavy industry sought to repudiate the growing *dirigisme* of the Nazi regime, and the explicit subordination of economic interests to political ends, as they had done in the early 1920s and again ten years later when the government flirted with socialization and economic intervention. The conflict must be seen in the context of these earlier political efforts to safeguard the interests of heavy industry.[2] During the Reichswerke crisis this strategy was finally confounded, and the growing divisions between the purposes of Nazism and the purposes of private capitalism made public.

The Reichswerke occupy a central place in the wider discussion of the relationship between state and industry in the Third Reich. Though recent historiography, both east and west, has gone well beyond the crude equation of monopoly capitalism and the Nazi movement, there is a striking reluctance to discuss the detailed interests of German capitalism during this period, or the political dilemmas that confronted businessmen when, after a brief honeymoon, National Socialism turned out to be an

---

[1] IWM, Nuremberg Trials background documents, FO 646 Box 366, Case X, Bülow Defence Document Book 1, 98–106 (cited hereafter as Case X).

[2] See G. D. Feldman, *Iron and Steel in the German Inflation 1916–1923* (Princeton, NJ, 1977) esp. ch. 3; B. Weisbrod, 'Economic Power and Political Stability Reconsidered: Heavy Industry in Weimar Germany', *Social History*, 4 (1979); D. Abraham, *The Collapse of the Weimar Republic* (Princeton, NJ, 1981), 119–74.

increasingly inappropriate structure for their long-term interests. Some businessmen had argued as much before 1933. Others saw Nazism as a means to cement a renewed integration, or *Sammlung*, of conservative forces.[3] But as it turned out integration was imposed not from above, but from below, by forces in popular politics quite beyond the control of German businessmen. By 1939 their interests had more in common with capitalism elsewhere than with domestic politics. There is, of course, no dispute that there were major German businesses which did co-operate closely with the state and derived demonstrable benefits from doing so. Profits could still be made, even if their extent and use were closely controlled. But for the bulk of German heavy industry, particularly in the Ruhr, the extension of Nazi dominance over the economy compromised the businessman's independence of action, and the maximization of profit and economic advantage which that independence permitted. Nazi political hegemony in the end prevented German capitalists from acting as capitalists.

This fact was not immediately apparent after 1933. Once the threat of radical SA activity against individual businesses had been removed in the summer of 1933, big business in informal alliance with the armed forces began to reassert its conventional role in German politics in order to secure a 'national-conservative' solution. Because Hitler wanted a quick economic recovery, he gave businessmen considerable freedom of action. During 1934 the Nazi leaders abandoned the Ministry of Economics, which had been held by Göring's friend Kurt Schmitt since the summer of 1933, and agreed to the appointment of the Reichsbank president, Hjalmar Schacht.[4] Unlike Schmitt, who had been actively hostile to the big concerns and cartels, Schacht was the candidate of the Ruhr and the army. A conservative in domestic politics as well as foreign policy, Schacht favoured rearmament within reasonable limits, the return of German colonies, and sound finances. Though he recognized the temporary necessity for greater state control over trade and the capital market, he was unequivocally committed to the principle of private profit as a sound regulator for business activity. Under his careful guidance the position of

[3] D. Petzina, 'Hitler und die deutsche Industrie', *Geschichte in Wissenschaft und Unterricht*, 17 (1966), 490–1, for a general discussion of the different ways in which historians have classified the relationship between business and Nazism. On the early 1930s see H. A. Turner, 'Big Business and the Rise of Hitler', *American Historical Review*, 75 (1969); id., 'Grossunternehmertum und Nationalsozialismus 1930–33', *Historische Zeitschrift*, 221 (1975); E. Nolte, 'Big Business and German Politics: A Comment', *American Historical Review*, 75 (1969); W. Treue, 'Die Einstellung einiger deutscher Grossindustrieller zu Hitlers Aussenpolitik', *Geschichte in Wissenschaft und Unterricht*, 17 (1966).

[4] A. Schweitzer, 'Organisierte Kapitalismus und Parteidiktatur 1933 bis 1936', *Schmollers Jahrbuch*, 79 (1959), 37–46; F. Facius, *Wirtschaft und Staat: Die Entwicklung der staatlichen Wirtschaftsverwaltung in Deutschland vom 17. Jahrhundert bis 1945* (Boppard am Rhein, 1959), 128.

the large German firms was strengthened. Cartelization was extended further at the expense of small businesses; output and profits rose under the stimulus of government-induced demand.[5] Profits of the leading steel firms rose from RM 32.6m. in 1933/4 to RM 65.3m. two years later, though dividends remained low or were not declared at all.[6] Prospects for the revival of trade and domestic consumption were both good by 1936 though, given the nature of the regime, by no means guaranteed.

It is against this background of reviving economic fortunes and the strengthening of German heavy industry that the sharp change in the direction of economic policy in 1936 must be understood. Hitler had his economic recovery, fragile though it still was. During the course of the year he determined to turn the economy towards his main political goals, military preparation and imperial expansion. To achieve this it was necessary to increase German self-sufficiency, to control trade, currency, and the capital market even more closely, and to invest massively in rearmament and war-essential industry at the expense of consumption and foreign trade. Schacht resisted the change, for it threatened to undermine much of his achievement since 1934. 'Autarky cannot possibly be an ideal,' he wrote early in 1937, 'it is opposed to the general principles of civilisation.'[7] His resistance was weakened by the fact that the armed forces were hoping to take advantage of the reorientation of policy by securing greater control over the economy themselves, and by the growing divisions between different business sectors. The chemical industry was more receptive to autarky because it would produce the synthetic substitutes. The consumer industries wanted greater trade.[8] To resolve all these conflicts and to ensure the primacy of Nazi political goals, Hitler brought the economy progressively under party control.

The main instrument for securing this control was the Second Four Year Plan, deliberately placed under Göring as an indication that the economy was to serve political ends. Unlike Schacht, whom Hitler respected but did

---

[5] S. Merlin, 'Trends in German Economic Control since 1933', *Quarterly Journal of Economics*, 62 (1943), 180–3.

[6] *DDV*, company annual reports. The firms included are Klöckner, Hoesch, Vereinigte Stahlwerke, Gutehoffnungshütte, Mannesmann, Mitteldeutsche Stahl, and Krupp. Only Mitteldeutsche Stahl and Gutehoffnungshütte declared any dividend in 1933 and 1934.

[7] H. Schacht, 'Germany's Colonial Demands', *Foreign Affairs*, 15 (1936/7), 229.

[8] On the army see Nuremberg Trials background documents, Case XI Prosecution Document Book 118A, EC-420, memorandum of the Wehrwirtschaftsstab, Dec. 1936; EC-408, Memorandum of the War Minister, 30 Dec. 1936; International Military Tribunal, *Trial of the Major War Criminals* (hereafter cited as IMT), 42 vols. (London, 1949–51), xxxvi. 243, 244-EC, letter from von Blomberg to Hitler, 22 Feb. 1937. On the chemical industry see J. Borkin, *The Crime and Punishment of I. G. Farben* (London, 1979), 71–5; R. Sohn-Rethel, *Economy and Class-Structure of German Fascism* (London, 1978), 81–8; L. Zumpe, 'Kohle–Eisen–Stahl 1936/7. Unterdrückung oder Interessenprofilierung?', *Jahrbuch für Wirtschaftsgeschichte*, 20 (1980), i. 137–8.

not trust, Göring could be trusted to use his new economic authority to bring the economy into line with German foreign and military policy. Moreover Göring, with his restless pursuit of power and status, saw the contest with Schacht and his allies not as one of economic choices but as a question of political power. Throughout 1936 and 1937, in alliance with more radical elements in the party, Göring wrested responsibility for economic affairs from Schacht and the Ministry of Economics, and from the army, and placed it firmly under Nazi control. By early 1938 the party had achieved a degree of political influence in the economy that it had been unable to secure in 1933 and 1934.[9]

For German business the reorientation of the economy and the sudden change in the political power balance had important implications. Though there was cause for anxiety in the revival of radical economic ideology and talk of 'egoistic capitalism', there was no evidence that this would cause substantial damage to business interests, any more than it had done in 1933. The main threat lay in the overthrow of Schachtian economic strategy. The policy of self-sufficiency threatened the revival of trade. Higher levels of rearmament and heavy state investment threatened financial stability and weakened the private capital market. Export subsidies based on strategic priorities helped the inefficient producer at the expense of the efficient. Industrialists, in the main, disliked having to depend too much on domestic orders and resented the growth of a large economic bureaucracy (and the extra paperwork) which state control brought with it.[10] All of these problems were present in the conflict that produced the Düsseldorf Memorandum. Göring's decision in June 1937 to set up the Reichswerke was chosen by Schacht and heavy industry as a trial of strength between two very different strategies for the German economy.

The Reichswerke conflict had its roots in the 1920s. The iron and steel industry was compensated by the German government for the loss of its Lorraine and Polish holdings under the Versailles settlement. Compensation was paid partly on the understanding that the industry would use the money to investigate ways of utilizing German low-grade iron ores and to reduce dependence on imports, particularly from France. In the event little was done. Germany continued to import large quantities of French and Swedish ores.[11] The project was revived again after 1933 by

[9] A. E. Simpson, 'The Struggle for Control of the German Economy 1936–37', *Journal of Modern History*, 21 (1959), 37, 42–4; D. Schoenbaum, *Hitler's Social Revolution* (New York, 1966), 122–9; A. Schweitzer, 'The Foreign Exchange Crisis of 1936', *Zeitschrift für die gesamte Staatswissenschaft*, 118 (1962).

[10] IMT xxxvi. 569–77, EC-497, letter from Schacht to Göring, 5 Aug. 1937; Bundesarchiv-Militärarchiv (BA-MA) Wi I F 5.203, Vortrag vor Dr Vögler.

[11] Salzgitter Konzernarchiv (SAK), 12/150/3a, Pleiger's notes on the memorandum, 15 Oct. 1937, 1–2; 12/150/2, Pleiger Handakten 'Erzversorgung der deutschen Eisenindustrie,

the Nazi autarkists, chief of whom was Wilhelm Keppler, Hitler's personal economic adviser until 1936. Keppler and his technical assistants argued that Germany should develop additional native sources of iron ore to avoid reliance on world markets. This dependence threatened Germany's military security and compromised her freedom of action. In 1913 Germany supplied 66 per cent of her ore requirements from domestic sources, in 1936 only 26 per cent.[12] Production of ores 'from German soil' was regarded as a geopolitical necessity. By 1936 these arguments had become more pressing. The army complained regularly of the shortages of iron and steel for military contracts, so that the demand for domestic ore production was enlarged into a general demand for substantial increases in the output of finished iron and steel.[13] Though these were rather different questions, they were not unconnected. Because Hitler intended to speed up war preparations and to begin the programme of economic and political expansion into central Europe, it made increasing sense to look to domestic iron ore as a means of guaranteeing a sufficient raw material base for large-scale military production in the future.[14]

For this reason the iron-ore question, now taken out of Keppler's hands by Göring, played a central part in the early months of the Second Four Year Plan launched in October 1936. When Paul Pleiger, Keppler's erstwhile assistant, brought evidence to Göring that similar low-grade ores were being smelted successfully in Britain, at the Stewart and Lloyd's steelworks in Corby, the technical means were found to turn the autarkists' proposals into reality. From December 1936 onwards Göring made it clear that no obstacle was to be put in the way of the domestic iron-ore programme. In a speech to leading industrialists at the Preussenhaus, Göring condemned unhelpful employers 'who still make use of capitalistic methods' and went on to announce with specific reference to the domestic ore-fields that 'if anyone cannot decide himself on the exploitation of the mines, he must sell his property, so that other people

---

22 July 1937'. On the general background see M. Riedel, *Eisen und Kohle für das Dritte Reich: Paul Pleigers Stellung in der nationalsozialistischen Wirtschaft* (Göttingen, 1973), 25–61; Zumpe, 'Kohle', 199–200.

[12] SAK 12/150/2, 'Erzversorgung', 1.

[13] BA-MA Wi I F 5.203, letter from von Blomberg to Göring, 17 Aug. 1936; Wehrwirtschaftsstab, review of the raw materials situation, 2 May 1936; Wi I F 5.114, discussion of iron and steel supply with Göring, 18 June 1937.

[14] W. Treue (ed.), 'Hitlers Denkschrift zum Vierjahrsplan, 1936', *Vierteljahreshefte für Zeitgeschichte*, 3 (1954), 209–10: 'It is further necessary to increase German iron production to an extraordinary degree. The objection that we are not in a position to produce raw iron as cheaply from German ore with a 26% [ferrous] content as from Swedish ore with 45% etc., is unimportant, because for us the question is indeed not what we would prefer to do but only what we can do . . . If the possibility should nevertheless remain for us to import cheap ores, then this is all to the good. But the existence of the national economy, and above all the conduct of war, must not be dependent on it.'

can do so'.[15] During the following months it became evident that the iron and steel industry was far from happy with the prospect of expanding domestic production much beyond the level it had already reached, or of selling its mineral rights to others.[16] In February the industry sent representatives to Göring to argue in favour of more modest proposals.[17] Although Göring had not decided in advance how best to promote domestic production, he was pushed on by the reluctance of private industry, and by pressures from party activists in his own organization, to bring the project under state control.

The arguments in favour of state initiative began to crystallize during the first half of 1937. At the forefront was the question of military preparations. In March Göring told the iron and steel leaders that it was Hitler's unswerving intention 'to mine as much ore from German soil as may be required for war requirements' and that for this reason 'the state must take over when private industry has proved itself no longer able to carry on'.[18] Paul Pleiger later explained to the Finance Minister that the project was 'a military necessity' in view of the 'high iron requirements of a largely motorized and mechanized army'. He thought that the Reichswerke would become 'the inner core of the whole of German rearmament and supplies for the German arms industry in times of peace and war', producing not just iron ore, but large quantities of finished steel as well.[19] The works were also intended to minimize the damage to Germany's rearmament programme if Germany should be cut off from vital foreign supplies, a danger that seemed more real at the time with the success of the Popular Front in France, the problems of civil war in Spain, and the anti-Nazi mood of social-democratic Sweden.[20] Göring used this argument to strengthen his own case for domestic output. 'We are

[15] *Trials of the War Criminals*, 12 vols. (Washington, DC, 1949), xii. 462–3, Doc. NI-051, Göring's speech in the Preussenhaus, 17 Dec. 1936 (cited as *TWC*).

[16] Ibid., Doc. NI-09, minutes of the discussion of the work group on iron and steel production, 17 Mar. 1937; SA 12/150/3a, Pleiger memorandum on 'Widerstand gegen die Verhüttung deutscher Eisenerze, 20 Aug. 1937', 1–8. The heads of the Stahlverein had written in Aug. 1935: 'The completely uneconomic and to a great extent technically questionable smelting of low-grade iron ores in large quantities cannot be contemplated.'

[17] Riedel, *Eisen und Kohle*, 119–20.

[18] *TWC* xii. 469, Doc. NI-09. Hitler had expressed the same sentiment in the Four Year Plan memorandum: 'But if the private economy believes that it is not competent to do this [mine domestic ore] then the National Socialist state will know how to solve it on its own.'

[19] SAK 12/150/9, letter from Pleiger to Schwerin von Krosigk, 2 Dec. 1937, 1, 5.

[20] H.-J. Lutzhöft, *Deutsche Militärpolitik und schwedische Neutralität 1939–1942* (Neumünster, 1981), 26–44. On the ore question see A. S. Milward, 'Could Sweden have stopped the Second World War?', *Scandinavian Economic History Review*, 15 (1967); J. J. Jäger, 'Sweden's Iron-Ore Exports to Germany 1933–1944', ibid. The German finance minister at the time, von Krosigk, has since argued that the Swedish threat was uppermost in his mind during the Reichswerke crisis. See L. Schwerin von Krosigk, *Die grosse Zeit des Feuers: Der Weg der deutschen Industrie*, 3 vols. (Tübingen, 1959) iii. 451–2.

dependent on foreign countries for our iron-ore supply,' he told the industry; 'the Swedish example shows that, if there should occur a general strike for three months, it would have a disastrous effect on our iron industry'.[21] Dependence on iron-ore imports had the added disadvantage that it tied up large amounts of foreign exchange, though it is important not to exaggerate this argument. By 1936 iron-ore imports comprised only 4 per cent of German imports by value, a figure that was more than balanced by the value of exports of iron and steel goods.[22]

The practical arguments were augmented by a renewed effort to compel the economy to conform more with Nazi ideology. The new direction in economic policy was accompanied by a growing chorus of criticism of big business in the Nazi press and among Nazi leaders. Göring accused the iron and steel barons of displaying 'the crassest economic egoism', and returned frequently to arguments about the needs of the community taking precedence over the needs of the individual.[23] Göring could not afford to ignore these ideological pressures since they came at a time when he was still wrestling with Schacht for control over the economy. By playing the card of economic radicalism he was able to strengthen his own political position while at the same time bringing the economy more closely into line with Hitler's wider strategic thinking.[24] Autarky and domestic production became a test of political loyalty, a fact that left German heavy industry in a position of increasing political isolation and insecurity.

Heavy industry was unprepared for the speed with which its political position deteriorated. Göring's speech in December had been greeted, according to the minutes, with 'hilarity'; the industry refused to take Göring's threats very seriously, couched as they were in the conventional language of Nazi propaganda and exhortation. When the foundation of a new state-run integrated iron and steel complex, the Reichswerke AG 'Hermann Göring', was announced to them in July 1937 it came, in Poensgen's words, 'as a bolt from the blue'.[25] From the point of view of private industry the proposal went far beyond what they had expected.

[21] Case XI, Pros. Doc. Book 112, NI-084, minutes of the meeting of 16 June 1937 on 'Iron scarcity and iron rationing', 15.
[22] The total sums were as follows: 1935, RM 123.4m.; 1936, 168.3m.; 1937, 221.9m. (4.1% of all imports). See *Statistisches Jahrbuch für das Deutsche Reich 1937* (Berlin, 1938). See Zumpe, *Kohle*, 138 ff. for a discussion of the importance historians have attached to the foreign exchange question.
[23] T. Emessen (ed.), *Aus Görings Schreibtisch: Ein Dokumentenfund* (Berlin, 1947), 78.
[24] D. Guerin, *Fascism and Big Business* (2nd edn., New York, 1973), 242–4; see too the discussion of the crisis with Göring in 1945 in FO 645 Box 156, interrogation of 10 Oct. 1945.
[25] *TWC* xii. 482, Doc. NI-353, notes of a speech by Göring to leaders of the iron and steel industry, 23 July 1937; H. Schacht, *76 Jahre meines Lebens* (Bad Wörishofen, 1953), 465; SAK 12/150/9, memorandum from Wilhelm Voss to Pleiger, 6 Aug. 1937; for Poensgen's comment see Case X, Bülow Doc. Book 1, 103–4.

Not only was the state planning to exploit the iron-ore deposits, but it also proposed to produce finished iron and steel as well, by-passing the Ruhr in order to secure future supplies for rearmament. The prospect of direct competition from the state forced the industry to think more clearly about its grounds for rejecting the scheme. During August these arguments were brought together by Albert Vögler and Ernst Poensgen of the Vereinigte Stahlwerke in the Düsseldorf memorandum.

The Ruhr industrialists' main line of argument against the project was based on what they regarded as economic rationality. More narrowly interpreted, the proposals as they stood threatened the economic interests of the big iron and steel firms, and promised to slow up or reverse the major improvement of their financial position during 1936 and 1937. Underlying this anxiety was a fear of over-capacity. During the depression the industry had been hit heavily by the low level of output following on a period of large-scale new investment and renovation. Existing plant absorbed the large increase in demand from 1934 onwards, but the industry was unwilling to undertake a large-scale investment programme of the kind implied by the Four Year Plan because it might seriously affect their capital position if the rearmament boom petered out, or if the Nazis fell from power. The simple addition of more capacity whether in iron ore or iron and steel production would not of itself have meant more financial security.

Indeed the Ruhr firms were close to what they regarded as the 'optimal point' in the summer of 1937. The growth of output was slowing down, and productivity per shift was declining through an increasing shortage of skilled metalworkers and miners. With the rising cost of raw materials and increased taxation (particularly the corporation tax), unit cost per ton of coal and steel was increasing, while prices remained controlled under the Four Year Plan. The Ruhr feared a renewed profit squeeze which would make it difficult to maintain dividends or to modernize plant in order to increase operating efficiency.[26] The use of higher-cost German ores would only increase this difficulty. So too would the establishment of a new state-run steel producer, which it was believed would compete for scarce resources of coking coal and skilled labour at an advantage, pushing costs up even further. Vögler argued that it made much more sense to expand within the existing structure, utilizing plant more efficiently, rather than taking funds out of an already overloaded capital market to set up an entirely new complex. This was not mere high-mindedness. The Stahlverein was in the middle of converting further plant to the production

---

[26] G. Stahl, 'Rechnende Schwerindustrie', *DDV* 11 (1936/7), 11–13; ibid. 117 on the Stahlverein. For details on capacity of the industry see L. Zumpe, *Wirtschaft und Staat in Deutschland iii. 1933–1945* (Berlin, 1979), 144. Utilised capacity rose from 23.6% in 1932 to 80.8% in 1937.

of Thomas steel, while the extensive use of German low-grade ores would have meant conversion back to a modified Bessemer process.[27]

The second problem facing the industry was one of markets. Domestic ore was much more expensive to produce and smelt than foreign ore because its iron content was much lower. The effect would be to push up German iron and steel prices and to make German iron and steel products less competitive abroad. This would also squeeze profits. Conditions for the iron and steel industry were particularly favourable on world markets. Because of the relatively high value of the mark, iron-ore imports were much cheaper than they had been in the 1920s. In 1931 7 million tons of imported ore had cost RM 128m. In 1935 14 million tons cost only RM 123m.[28] To revert to using domestic ores meant sacrificing a major market advantage. The iron and steel users also enjoyed benefits in selling abroad, not only because of the lower cost of raw iron and steel, but because of the elaborate system of export subsidies under the New Plan. For the large trusts, most of which produced the raw iron and steel and the semi-finished products, this represented a double boost to profits which they were understandably reluctant to forgo.[29]

With German iron and steel prices some 20 per cent below the world price, exports of semi-finished iron and steel products doubled between 1934 and 1937.[30] It was this highly profitable trade that the Ruhr firms wanted to expand to offset financial difficulties in coal and steel production. Schacht, too, was anxious to maintain the momentum of exports in defiance of the quota system set up by Göring and the army in 1936. During 1937 there was buoyant international demand for iron and steel products. Rather than ease the shortage by using domestic ores, Schacht wanted to expand trade by bringing in more raw iron (particularly scrap iron for which German industry was well suited) and exporting high-value finished or semi-finished goods. Indeed in October, fighting a final rearguard action against Göring, he lowered the tariff on iron and steel imports from RM 10 to RM 1 per ton, in an effort to invigorate international movements of iron and steel goods and preserve the competitiveness of German heavy industry.[31]

[27] SAK 12/150/3a, 'Stellungnahme zur Denkschrift der Vereinigte Stahlwerke von 18 Aug. 1937', 1–2; see too D. Eichholtz *et al.* (eds.), *Anatomie des Krieges* (Berlin, 1969), 154–5, Doc. 52, letter from Hermann Röchling to Göring 27 Mar. 1937; German Economic Dept. Control Office for Germany and Austria, *The Hermann Göring Complex*, GED 43/0/34, June 1946, 4. On the Stahlverein see G.-H. Seebold, *Ein Stahlkonzern im Dritte Reich: Der Bochumer-Verein 1927–1945* (Wuppertal, 1981), 90–2; H. Levy, *Industrial Germany* (Cambridge, 1935), 54–5.

[28] Case XI, Pleiger Defence Doc. Book 3, 120, Puhl affidavit, 3 July 1948.

[29] Ibid. 118–21.

[30] *Statistisches Jahrbuch 1938*, 262–3; DDV 12 (1937/8), 98 on prices.

[31] Ibid. 98: A. Teichova, *An Economic Background to Munich* (Cambridge, 1974), 183–5. Prices for semi-finished goods rose by an average of 57% between June 1935 and Dec. 1937, when the ISC was at its most effective.

Göring, too, was well aware of these arguments. 'Foreign prices are particularly attractive at the present time,' he told a meeting in June 1937. 'Here the egoism of private enterprise is obvious.' Instead of building up iron and steel exports, which he saw as an indirect contribution to the arming of Germany's enemies, he proposed to restrict them sharply: 'Without imperative economic and political reasons I am no longer going to supply foreign countries with semi finished products.'[32] The iron and steel industry, on the other hand, favoured greater trade and greater internationalization of the European steel industry within the context of the International Steel Cartel set up in 1935. Vögler argued for more trade with the Soviet Union. Poensgen looked for further agreements in France. Closer ties were established with representatives of British heavy industry.[33] While the political demands of the party favoured greater efforts for self-sufficiency, the economic interests of German heavy industry lay in the direction of greater European economic integration.

Nevertheless by the time that the Reichswerke project was announced the Ruhr recognized that there was more at stake than economic interest, important though that was. 'The founding of the Hermann Göring Works', Poensgen later wrote, 'was a public challenge against the private iron industry, and was perceived as such by the public.'[34] The industry found itself caught up in a much broader conflict in defence of private initiative against state control, reviving memories of the conflict over post-war socialization. In the Düsseldorf Memorandum the Vereinigte Stahlwerke made it clear that it would be willing to find ways of increasing ore and iron output, but only on its own terms, and under the supervision of private industry. The immediate aim of the industry was to maintain a favourable capital structure and profit levels by strategies of the industry's own choosing.[35] The Economics Ministry supported this view. Schacht insisted that it was up to the private economy to decide what it would do with the ore and when: 'We will get round to it, by and by.'[36] He rejected the idea that the state should directly supplant the functions of the entrepreneur: 'The state should not run business itself and take responsibility away from private enterprise,' a view which he had held

---

[32] Case XI, Pros. Doc. Book 112, NI-084, 7, 11, 14–16.
[33] BA-MA Wi I F 5.203, discussion with Dr Vögler, July/Aug. 1936; Case X, Bülow Doc. Book 1, Poensgen affidavit, 90–8; on contacts with Britain see R. F. Holland, 'The Federation of British Industries and the International Economy 1929–1939', *Economic History Review*, 2nd ser. 34 (1981), 297–8; Teichova, *Economic Background*, 160–1, 187.
[34] Case X, Bülow Doc. Book 1, Poensgen affidavit, 104.
[35] SAK 12/150/3a, draft of the Düsseldorf Memorandum, 24 Aug. 1937; see too Poensgen's remarks to Göring, Case XI, Doc. NI-084, 14–15.
[36] SAK 12/150/3a, letter from Doggerz-Bergbau to Pleiger, 26 July 1937, on a meeting with Schacht on 24 July.

consistently since taking office.[37] The rejection of state control and ownership was widespread in business circles. The corporatism of the 1933 to 1936 period was giving way, according to a prominent business journal, to 'a sort of forced economy . . . in which the independence of private industry would disappear and be replaced by the direction of the state authorities'.[38]

The rejection of state control was not based simply on a preference for self-regulation but on a deeper fear that the Nazi movement would undo many of the gains that the economy had made before 1936, and that this would once again revive the spectre of social unrest. Schacht's strategy since 1934 had been based on the assumption that the threat from radical labour could only be neutralized effectively by maintaining satisfactory living standards, 'a normal, peacetime standard'.[39] Early in August 1937 he warned Göring that the plans for the Reichswerke 'must lead to a further restriction of raw-material supply for those firms working for export and consumption. A shortage of a whole range of consumer goods is already evident today in daily life.'[40] The British ambassador had earlier reported Schacht's fear that food shortages brought about by excessive military demands would make the 'populace restive' and that in the long run 'Communism would be the outcome in Germany'.[41] These views reflected a broadly held conservative fear in 1936 and 1937 that the excesses of the regime might lead once again to political breakdown along the lines of the crisis before 1933. Nazi economic and military policy had now become a threat to the ideal conservative solution operated since 1934 in which the army and industry co-operated with the party in controlling labour and building up the economy. This fear was strengthened by the belief that the Nazis were incapable of running an economy without plunging the country into a second inflation through incompetence and extravagance. The economy, Schacht complained later, 'was now in amateur hands'.[42]

None of these arguments affected the eventual outcome and indeed only confirmed the Four Year Plan officials in their determination to press

[37] Reported in SAK 12/150/9, letter from Voss to Pleiger, 6 Aug. 1937, 3. See too Guerin, *Fascism*, who quotes a speech by Schacht on 30 Nov. 1935: 'The state alone cannot take over a mechanism as vast and ramified into so many branches as that of the economy. Stimulation of individual interests is and will remain the foundation of all economic activity.'

[38] Guerin, *Fascism*, 243, a quotation from *Der Ring*; see too 'Gewerbefreiheit im Dritten Reich', *DDV* 12 (1937/8), 815.

[39] IMT xii. 602, Schacht cross-examination.

[40] Ibid. xxxvi. 577, 497-EC, letter from Schacht to Göring, 5 Aug. 1937; see too SAK 12/150/3a, Doggerz-Bergbau to Pleiger, 26 July 1937, 2.

[41] Phipps Papers, Churchill College, Cambridge, 1/15 letter from Sir Eric Phipps to Sir Samuel Hoare, 7 Nov. 1935, 2; letter from Phipps to Hoare, 5 Dec. 1935, 3.

[42] H. Schacht, *Account Settled* (London, 1949), 92.

ahead with state ownership. Göring called representatives of the industry to see him on 16 June and in 'an agitated voice' told them of his decision 'that German soil will be drained of iron to the utmost'.[43] On 23 July he called them together once again and formally announced the founding of the Reichswerke at Salzgitter in Brunswick. The industry was informed that its mineral rights were to be compulsorily purchased by the state and that compensation would take the form of a minor shareholding in the new works. 'It is not important', he warned them, 'that you fill my ears with your complaints, but that you pull yourselves together.'[44]

What followed was for many industrialists a revealing but uncharacteristic descent into the underground world of Nazi politics. The Ruhr spent the following weeks working with the Economics Ministry to devise tactics to undermine the scheme. Schacht's initial reaction, encouraged by Paul Reusch and Poensgen, was to refuse to release any funds from the Reichsbank for the project.[45] Early in August the leaders of the steel industry agreed in private to a draft memorandum setting out their objections.[46] Poensgen and Vögler drew up a separate memorandum on behalf of the Vereinigte Stahlwerke which was sent to Pleiger on 19 August.[47] A meeting was fixed for 24 August at which all the representatives of the major iron and steel works would be present to sign a formal declaration to be sent to Göring, making clear the opposition of the industry to the scheme in its existing form.

Göring and his officials followed all these moves closely. Telephone-tapping and hidden microphones, controlled from Göring's *Forschungsamt* (Research Bureau), revealed step by step the mounting resistance of the Ruhr. Schacht's attitude was reported back by allies in the Economics Ministry. Another contact smuggled out details of the memoranda and meetings of the Stahlverein.[48] Well before the Düsseldorf meeting Göring had all the information he needed to bring his political weight to bear on the industrialists. His initial reaction was to order their arrest. Pleiger argued against this as a clumsy move and suggested instead that Göring send telegrams to all the firms involved warning them of the serious consequences of further resistance.[49] It was also decided to send Krupp a separate telegram suggesting that co-operation with the Reichswerke

---

[43] Case XI, Pros. Doc. Book 112, NI-084, 3.

[44] TWC xii. 482, NI-353, notes on a speech by Göring to leaders of the iron and steel industry, 25 July 1937.

[45] SAK 12/150/3a, Doggerz-Bergbau to Pleiger, 1–2; 12/150/1, file note on the meeting of 19 Aug. 1937.

[46] Riedel, *Eisen und Kohle*, 193–4.

[47] SAK 12/150/3a, memorandum from Vereinigte Stahlwerke to Pleiger, 19 Aug. 1937, 'Stellungnahme zur Denkschrift, 18 Aug. 1937'.

[48] Ibid., letter from Otto Make to Pleiger, 26 Aug. 1937; 12/150/9, Voss to Pleiger, 6 Aug. 1937.

[49] Riedel, *Eisen und Kohle*, 195–200.

scheme would bring the firm specific financial advantages. On the morning of August 24 telegrams were sent to nine leading industrialists, though not to the heads of the Vereinigte Stahlwerke, warning them not to sign the memorandum, and to avoid intrigues 'that more and more take on the form of sabotage'. To Krupp went a separate telegram from Göring: 'the works will be of special significance for Krupp, because I intend to work out together with you a great plan for German armament. I have already made representations about this to the Führer.' A final telegram was sent to the Finance Minister, Count Schwerin von Krosigk, to prevent Schacht's allies in his ministry from refusing to hand over the necessary funds: 'It comes down to this, whether the interests of the Reich or the crassest economic egoism shall prevail.'[50]

When Poensgen and Vögler arrived at the meeting knowing 'nothing about telegrams', it was clear that the industry's united front had crumbled.[51] The Krupp representative, Arthur Klotzbach, began by urging that the memorandum be sent to Berlin. Poensgen supported the suggestion. One after another the remaining firms counselled caution. Röchling went further and argued that it was better to work with Göring rather than against him for fear of political isolation. In the acrimonious discussion that followed Poensgen offered to resign from his position in the steel cartel, but was dissuaded from doing so by his colleagues. The representatives of Gutehoffnungshütte and Klöckner came round once again to the idea of sending a memorandum, but in the absence of any general agreement the meeting broke up to allow those present to consult with their fellow directors about what to do.[52] In the event the memorandum was not sent. Several days later Poensgen and Vögler were summoned by Göring, who played back to them tape recordings of their meetings.[53]

If the industry had been defeated in its efforts to produce concerted resistance to the Four Year Plan, it avoided a head-on clash that might have provoked a much more serious reaction from the party, given its current mood. None the less, the results of the crisis had substantial repercussions on German industry in general in its relationship to the Nazi system. It was openly evident that Germany's most powerful industrial interest group had been compelled to retreat in the face of party power. The fragile solidarity of the Ruhr collapsed as it had done in 1932. The inner circle of industrialists, the so-called *kleine Kreis*, chaired by Poensgen, broke up over the Reichswerke affair, though some of its members continued to meet informally together until the war. The larger

[50] Emessen, *Aus Görings Schreibtisch*, 82–3, Doc. 33, Telegram from Göring to nine industrialists and Krupp von Bohlen, 24 Aug. 1937; ibid. 81, Doc. 32, telegram from Göring to Schwerin von Krosigk, 24 Aug. 1937.
[51] Case X, Bülow Doc. Book 1, 106.

Ruhrlade circle, led by Paul Reusch of Gutehoffnungshütte, split a few months later with the secession of Krupp.[54] The industry adopted a policy of *sauve qui peut*, an attitude that seems to have been common to many professional groups in the Third Reich.[55] The firms avoided a direct confrontation with Hitler's strategy by retreating into their businesses and conducting policy from behind the protective walls of professional associations and syndicates. Though they could no longer bring industrial interests to bear directly on formal political life, they were determined to prevent the party from invading the industry's own organizations.[56] Firms were left to devise strategies of their own for safeguarding business and shareholder interests at the expense of any longer exercising an important collective influence in national affairs. Gustav Krupp summed up this attitude in a wartime circular to his directors when he argued that in the absence of any general business strategy, 'Krupps interests must be pursued as an opportunity arises'.[57]

Most firms adopted a strategy of timid self-interest. Indeed there was little point in doing otherwise, for their caution kept the substance of the Ruhr intact until 1945, though it left industrial forces fragmented and necessitated industry's co-operation with Nazi racial and slave-labour policy during the war. Though they could still profit from the system, they were forced to do so on the party's terms. Profit and investment levels were determined by the state, on terms much more favourable to state projects. Competition in the market was replaced by competition within the political structure; rational calculation gave way to the 'primacy of politics', completing the disintegration of traditional patterns of social power begun during the depression.

To the Nazi leadership the whole affair demonstrated how untrustworthy an ally big business had proved to be. Göring used the crisis to increase popular pressure against the conservative industrial élite, and to isolate Schacht and the conservative economists around him. Without the open support of big business Schacht was forced to resign in November 1937 from the Economics Ministry and Göring assumed *de facto* control over the whole economy. During the early part of 1938 the ministry was fused with the Four Year Plan and Göring's own appointees

---

[52] SAK 12/150/3a, minutes of the meeting of 24 Aug. 1937 in the Stahlhof, 1–4.

[53] Case X, Bülow Doc. Book 1, 106–7.

[54] L. Lochner, *Tycoons and Tyrants: German History from Hitler to Adenauer*. (Chicago, 1954), 175–7; on the background see H. A. Turner, 'The *Ruhrlade*, Secret Cabinet of Heavy Industry in the Weimar Republic', *Central European History*, 3 (1970), 195–228.

[55] P. Hüttenberger, 'Interessenvertretung und Lobbyismus im Dritten Reich', in G. Hirschfeld and L. Kettenacker (eds.), *The Führer State: Myth and Reality* (Stuttgart, 1981), 429–57.

[56] Case X, Bülow Doc. Book 1, 100–1; Lochner, *Tycoons*, 1974.

[57] On Krupp see Case X, 491, NIK-3990, Krupp circular 24, May 1941.

TABLE 3.1. Profits of leading iron and steel firms, 1933–1938[a] (RMm.)

	Stahlverein	Krupp	GHH[b]	Hoesch	Klö.[c]	Man.[d]
1933/4	8.87	6.65	6.17	1.53	5.21	2.09
1934/5	21.24	9.69	8.38	1.03	3.53	3.39
1935/6	22.85	14.34	9.30	3.67	4.76	5.34
1936/7	27.01	16.22	12.14	5.12	5.52	7.30
1937/8	27.60	21.11	9.62	6.45	6.38	8.35

[a] Figures for year ending Sept. in column 1, for year ending in Mar. for columns 2–3, for year ending June for columns 4–5, and for year ending Dec. for column 6.
[b] GHH = Gutehoffnungshütte.   [c] Klö. = Klockner.   [d] Man. = Mannesmann.
Source: DDV 12–13 (1937–8), company reports.

promoted to key positions. During 1938 state intervention was greatly increased. The Four Year Plan Plenipotentiary for Iron and Steel informed the industry in a conference at Duisberg that the industry's future development would be governed predominantly by 'political considerations of the state'.[58] Huge sums of money were made available for the industrial programmes set in motion under the Plan, amounting in 1938 and 1939 to over half all industrial investment, while investment in the Ruhr was curtailed.[59] It was difficult to find sufficient funds even to renew plant that was rapidly wearing out, a problem compounded with the sharp slowdown in profit growth during 1937–9 experienced by most of German heavy industry (see Table 3.1).[60] The capacity of the Ruhr remained at a level of 16 million tons of steel until the outbreak of war, while its operating efficiency declined. The Reichswerke were the direct beneficiary of the controls over investment, at the expense of the private steel users (particularly the car manufacturers, who complained vigorously of the shortages of sheet steel).[61] Faced by what he regarded as the intransigence of big business, Göring and his officials saw the Reichswerke as an instrument for tackling 'national' tasks beyond the means of private industry. In February 1938 the capital of the Reichswerke was raised to RM 400m. from the RM 5m. allocated in the previous July. The concern embarked on a process of vertical and horizontal concentration, taking

[58] DDV, 12 (1937/8), 50. The Duisberg meeting confirmed the industry's fears that priority in the distribution of iron and steel would go to state projects.
[59] D. Petzina, Autarkiepolitik im Dritten Reich (Stuttgart, 1968), 183.
[60] M. Y. Sweezy, 'German Corporate Profits 1926–1938', Quarterly Journal of Economics, 54 (1940), 390.
[61] On the Ruhr see N. G. Pounds, The Ruhr (London, 1952), 180–97; on car manufacturers see P. Kirchberg, 'Typisierung in der deutschen Kraftfahrzeugindustrie', Jahrbuch für Wirtschaftsgeschichte, 8 (1969), 128–30.

over a large number of smaller firms. In April it absorbed the Rheinmetall–Borsig armaments firm, a move that gave the works a direct interest in manufacturing, despite the army's resistance to the idea that the Four Year Plan should be involved in the actual production of arms, and the Ruhr's hope that the more profitable part of the steel trade would remain in private hands.[62]

The shift in economic control away from conservative circles towards the party was matched by a corresponding shift in foreign policy. In March Austria was brought into the Greater German Reich, and the Four Year Plan extended to cover the Austrian economy. The Reichswerke organization was used indiscriminately to integrate the heavy industry of the area into German preparations for war. For the Ruhr this brought new problems, for it threatened to improve the competitive position of the Reichswerke without any corresponding advantage for private industry. It soon became clear that Göring regarded the spoils of the Austrian economy (and later of the Czech and Polish economies) as gains for the German state and was not prepared to share them with the very same business circles that had proved so politically unreliable in the transition to autarky. Indeed the Reichswerke began almost immediately to trespass on those parts of Austrian industry that were already owned or part-owned by private German firms in the Reich.[63]

Chief of these was the leading Austrian iron and steel company, the Alpine Montangesellschaft, which controlled the production of ore from the Erzberg, the ore mountain. The company was run in the interest of the Vereinigte Stahlwerke which had a 56 per cent shareholding acquired by Hugo Stinnes from Fiat in 1922.[64] Göring had already hinted at his interest in Austrian ore, and the Four Year Plan office had tried unsuccessfully to persuade the Stahlverein to enter into negotiations over the supply of ore for German firms well before the *Anschluss*. When the company came under German jurisdiction in March Göring and Pleiger immediately set out to compel the parent firm to increase the flow of ore very substantially. As an inducement plans were also announced for a vast new iron and steel complex at Linz to be set up by the state as the core of a new mid-European industrial region surrounding the cultural centre of the Reich planned by Hitler. Ore for the new complex was to come from the

[62] SAK 12/150/1, notice of the conference with Göring, 29 Apr. 1938; IWM, Speer Collection, FD 5454c/45, minutes of meeting of 25 Sept. 1937 'Angliederung von weiterverarbeitenden Betrieben an die Reichswerke AG'; on the increase in capital see SAK 12/150/9, letter from Pleiger to von Krosigk, 2 Dec. 1937; NA, Reichswerke files, T83 Roll 76, frames 3447630–42, Pleiger to Schacht 3 Feb. 1938. On the Ruhr's fears see *DDV* 12 (1937/8), 416.

[63] See R. J. Overy, 'Göring's "Multi-National" Empire', in A. Teichova and P. Cottrell (eds.), *International Business and Central Europe 1919–1939* (Leicester, 1983), 270–9.

[64] *Hermann Göring Complex*, 11–12.

Erzberg.[65] The Stahlverein was unenthusiastic. Its leaders reiterated the arguments used against the Reichswerke in 1937, that the plant was privately owned and should be controlled by private interests. They were willing to increase the output of ore at a sensible pace and as the needs of the market dictated. They were prepared to enter into a partnership with the Four Year Plan on an equal footing, but they were not prepared to abandon the Alpine company altogether.[66]

The Plan office devised indirect tactics to achieve the same end. Pleiger bought up a small shareholding of 14 per cent from the Industrie-Kredit Bank in Vienna which gave the Reichswerke a foothold in the company. Then through different Plan departments the Alpine was asked to increase its investment very considerably and at the same time to reduce its prices by between 25 and 40 per cent to bring them in line with German prices. This was an uninviting prospect for the Stahlverein, as the Alpine was a relatively high-cost operation. Its position in Austria became increasingly isolated as one by one the Reichswerke took over all the major Austrian iron, steel, and machinery companies. Unwilling to confront Göring again directly, and anxious about the declining competitive position of the Alpine compared with the vast projected works at Linz, the Stahlverein agreed to sell its controlling participation to the Reichswerke. In return a contract was signed guaranteeing the supply of ore for German companies in the Vereinigte Stahlwerke for thirty years. Even this concession was ignored by Göring, who wanted to provide low-grade Salzgitter ores to German firms instead. The contract was eventually suspended. The 10 per cent holding that the Stahlverein had been given in the new Linz works was bought back by the state to complete the elimination of the Ruhr from the Austrian economy.[67]

Nor did businessmen who were willing to co-operate with the Four Year Plan fare any better. Friedrich Flick's interest in buying up the Petschek lignite holdings, which had been hastily sold to the Czech state, were disregarded when the Germans occupied the Sudetenland in October 1938. Instead they were taken over by the Reichswerke to form the raw-material base of a new synthetic fuel plant set up at Brüx.[68] Krupp was denied the

---

[65] TWC xii. 468–9, Doc. NI-09, minutes of the discussion of the work group on iron and steel production; K. Rothschild, *Austria's Economic Development between the Two Wars* (London, 1947), 79–82.

[66] Riedel, *Eisen und Kohle*, 234–42.

[67] *Hermann Göring Complex*, 11; Case X, Bülow Doc. Book 1, Poensgen affidavit, 107–8.

[68] Flick had taken over some of the German Petschek holdings sold by Julius Petschek in anticipation of their compulsory Aryanization early in 1938; see *Hermann Göring Complex*, 14–15. See also Eichholtz *et al.*, *Anatomie*, 162–5 Doc. 60, Flick notes for meeting with Göring, 19 Jan. 1938; pp. 182–3, Doc. 70, Steinbrinck (Flick) to Neumann (Four Year Plan), 22 June 1938. The holdings of Ignaz Petschek were sold to the Czech state shortly before the takeover of the Sudetenland. These shares were taken over by the Reichswerke and

Skoda Works six months later when the rest of Bohemia fell into German hands. Once again the Reichswerke complex was the beneficiary.[69] As far as the Four Year Plan was concerned the resources of the central European economy became net additions to the domestic resources available for war. It was argued that they were too valuable to be left to private capital to exploit, because its interests were primarily technical and financial, not national.

By 1939 the prospects facing the Ruhr were much bleaker than they had been during the initial Reichswerke crisis. The economy was closely under state supervision and the state itself had begun to move into heavy industry in its own right, and on a much larger scale than had been expected. The decision to expand the capital of the Reichswerke to RM 400m., and to invest an additional RM 180m. in the Alpine company and 390m. in the Sudetenland, meant that a sharp change could be expected in the balance of the economy when the projects were completed. Flick's offer to provide RM 25–30m. to meet the expanded demand for steel, or the RM 60m. proposed by Vögler, paled by comparison.[70] The mood in business circles was one of growing alarm and pessimism at the spread of state control and nationalization. 'Bureaucratic restrictions', complained the *Deutsche Volkswirt*, 'are daily becoming more unendurable. Woe to the industrialist who accidentally fails to fulfil his obligations. The furies are unleashed.' Fritz Thyssen, one of the major industrialists to give initial support to Hitler after the seizure of power, on the assumption that the Nazis would create a paternalistic corporate state, finally broke with Nazism and fled from Germany. His substantial holdings in the Stahlverein were taken over compulsorily by the state. 'Soon Germany will not be any different from Bolshevik Russia,' Thyssen later explained, 'the heads of enterprises who do not fulfil the conditions which the Plan prescribes will be accused of treason against the German people and shot.'[71]

Excluded politically and harassed by the Four Year Plan, the Ruhr still enjoyed one major advantage. Göring lacked direct access to a satisfactory coal basis for the Reichswerke either in Germany or in central Europe. It was evident to the Four Year Plan officials from the outset that this would be a problem. In September 1937 Paul Rheinländer, Pleiger's deputy,

consolidated into the Sudetenländische Bergbau AG, which supplied lignite for the synthetic fuel company Sudetenländische Treibstoff AG. See *Conditions in Occupied Territories*, v. *The Penetration of German Capital into Europe* (HMSO, 1942), 10–11; W. Birkenfeld, *Der synthetische Treibstoff 1933–1945* (Göttingen, 1963), 135–7.

[69] On acquisition of Skoda see Overy, 'Göring's "Multi-National" Empire', 275–6.

[70] On investment see IWM, Speer Collection, FD 264/46, 594–7, 'Konzernverzeichnis HGW, Montanblock', 15 Aug. 1944; on Flick's offer SAK 12/150/3a, notice of a discussion between Pleiger, Flick, and Klöckner 21 Oct. 1937; on the figure of 60m. see 12/150/3a, letter from Make to Pleiger, 28 Aug. 1937.

[71] Guerin, *Fascism*, 245; F. Thyssen, *I Paid Hitler* (London, 1941), 187.

opened negotiations with the Rheinisch-Westfälische Kohlen-Syndikat over supplies of coal and coke for the Reichswerke. Tentative discussions during 1938 produced no settlement.[72] As the first stage of the Salzgitter blast-furnaces neared completion, Pleiger was anxious to ensure that sufficient coal would be available, since the syndicate planned in advance the production quotas of its member companies. The Reichswerke also needed coal at the right price to offset their operating costs which were higher than in the Ruhr. Pleiger demanded coal at less than the market price, at RM 10.7 per ton. Sensing Pleiger's predicament, the syndicate refused. The lowest price at which they would offer coal was RM 13.5.[73] Pleiger and Göring tried to bully the Ruhr into releasing cheap coal. An orchestrated press campaign was started up in the spring of 1939 to discredit the private firms whose 'business egoism' was compromising the achievement of vital national projects. Pleiger refused even to negotiate or reply to syndicate letters for two months and when negotiations were resumed in April and May 1939 he angrily denounced the coal owners' lack of co-operation and hinted once again at the possibility of state action.[74] 'It is clear', Pleiger wrote to the chairman of the syndicate in July, 'that the Field Marshal has not founded the Hermann Göring works in order in the last resort to stake the economic existence and national significance of the works on the coal question.'[75]

'Business egoism' was in practice a two-edged sword, for it invited the state to play one industrialist against another. While talks continued with the syndicate Göring turned to the Harpener Bergbau company owned by Flick, which had large supplies of hard coking coal surplus to the requirements of Flick's steel interests. Where other firms had refused Pleiger's invitation to give mines voluntarily to the Reichswerke, it was hoped that Flick could be induced to do so by an exchange of lignite mines owned by the Reichswerke in which he had previously shown an interest. He was approached informally about the transfer in March 1939.[76] His response was wary but not unenthusiastic. Over the course of the summer fitful negotiations took place. Substantial pressure was put on Flick to agree, although the terms of the exchange were not particularly favourable. The Reichswerke overvalued their Czech holdings in order to acquire more of the Harpener mines, while keeping some of the best lignite

---

[72] SAK 12/150/1, conference with Göring 22 Oct. 1937, 2; NA Reichswerke files, T83 Roll 76, frame 3446846, 'Entwicklung der Verhandlungen zwischen Hermann Göring Werke and RWKS'.

[73] Ibid., frames 3446791–8, Pleiger to RWKS, May 1939; 3446846–7, 'Entwicklung'.

[74] Ibid., frames 3446821–4, Pleiger to Kellermann, 20 July 1939; 3446841–8, Kellermann to Pleiger, 12 July 1939.

[75] Ibid., frame 3446822.

[76] Ibid., frames 3446784–5, 'Verhandlungen über Tausch zwischen Braunkohle aus dem Petschek-Besitz mit Steinkohle', 1 June 1939.

in the hands of the state. Though Flick began the negotiations on the understanding that he would only accept an agreement that benefited Harpener's shareholders, he found himself subject to party pressure and accusations of profiteering.[77] He found that Pleiger changed the terms of the agreement unilaterally meeting by meeting. With some reluctance he agreed to an initial contract shortly after the outbreak of war.[78] But by then the Reichswerke had found alternative sources. The conquest of Poland brought the Silesian coalfield back into the Reich. The Four Year Plan organization immediately laid claim to all the coal deposits there, to be run on a trustee basis for the state. Thyssen's flight brought the additional prospect of more hard coal for the Reichswerke. Flick was made to wait for his agreement, which was not finally ratified until March 1940 on terms far less favourable than he had hoped, and in the knowledge that the Reichswerke had achieved in Poland a major structural shift in German heavy industry in favour of the state-run economy.[79]

Flick's position demonstrated the dilemma facing all the private firms. Industrialists could not afford to ignore the opportunities opening up through rearmament and state building projects because of their fear that other companies would take them instead. Yet co-operation with government contracts forced them into a much closer dependence on the state and weakened still further their ability either to hold up the restructuring of the economy or to prevent the dictation of business strategy by forces beyond their effective control. Nor were they any longer compensated by the political successes of the regime in controlling labour and increasing domestic stability. Under conditions of full employment the labour demands of the Four Year Plan made expansion difficult for other sectors. It was difficult to overcome labour shortages through increased productivity because of the scarcity of capital and the firms' reluctance to commit too much of their own money in the face of growing international instability. War preparation also had the effect of cutting back export growth and domestic demand for consumer goods. To achieve sustainable growth big business argued in 1939 for a freer labour market, a freer capital market, and fewer restrictions on Germany's international

---

[77] Ibid., frames 3446742–7, draft of letter from Reichswerke to Flick, 23 Aug. 1939; frames 3446764–7, Pleiger to Landfried (Economics Ministry), 27 July 1939.

[78] SAK 12/150/12, letter from Flick to Pleiger, 14 Oct. 1939; letter from Flick to Pleiger, 20 Oct. 1939; 'Vereinbarung zwischen Pleiger und Flick, 9 Oct. 1939; 12/150/14, letter from Flick to Pleiger, 27 Sept. 1939.

[79] SAK 12/150/12, letter from Paul Körner to Pleiger over Polish coal deposits, 21 Nov. 1939; 12/150/14, letter from Pleiger to Economics Ministry, 12 Mar. 1940; 12/150/1, conference with Göring, 31 Oct. 1939; letter from Göring to Gauleiter Terboven, 30 Oct. 1939; *Hermann Göring Complex*, 9–10; Thyssen, *I Paid Hitler*, 48–51; Case XI, Pros. Doc. Book 112, NI-932, conversation between Körner and Steinbrinck of Flick AG, 8 Nov. 1939.

TABLE 3.2. *Steel output in Germany and occupied Europe 1938–1944* (m. tonnes)

	1938	1939	1940	1941	1942	1943	1944
Pre-war Germany	23.3	23.7	21.5	23.5	23.3	23.8	21.0
'Ruhr' area	16.0	16.2	13.7	13.6	13.0	13.4	11.7
Austria, Czech.[a]	0.7	0.8	0.8	2.5	2.5	2.8	2.7
Occupied Europe[b]	—	—	—	5.8	6.3	7.9	4.8
TOTAL[c]	24.0	25.0	24.8	31.8	32.1	34.6	28.5

[a] Austria only for 1938–40.
[b] Poland, France, Belgium, Holland 1943/4 figures estimated.
[c] Figures for 1939 and 1940 are estimates only as precise figures for Czech and French output during these years are not available.

Sources: USSBS, *The Effects of Strategic Bombing on the German War Economy*, 246–53; Seebold, *Stahlkonzern*, 86; M. Fritz, *German Steel and Swedish Iron Ore 1939–45* (Göteborg, 1974), 10.

economy.[80] All of these goals were effectively excluded by the nature of Germany's war planning.

These problems were highlighted by the war itself. The Ruhr did much of what was required of it for the war effort. But it was compelled to stand by and watch the growth of the state sector, while its own room for manœuvre was severely circumscribed. Output in the Ruhr was cut back from 16 million tons of steel in 1939 to only 11 million tons in 1944. Increases in steel demand were met by expanding production in the rest of Germany and in occupied Europe (see Table 3.2). By 1942 the Ruhr was producing less steel than in 1936, while the Reichswerke went on to provide one-eighth of all steel output in the last years of war. In all this private heavy industry operated in a structure over which it had very little control, so that support for the state grew increasingly negative. Businessmen were seldom consulted by Nazi leaders, and on the occasions when they were found themselves the victims of Hitler's obsession with defeatism and profiteering.[81] Renewed efforts by the Ruhr leaders to campaign against the Reichswerke in 1939 did little to improve the Ruhr's

[80] Christie Papers, Churchill College, Cambridge, 180/1, 'Memo by members of "Big Business" in Germany', esp. 1–3, 12–13, 22–3. The report concluded that the economy could not be put on to a stable footing without 'the transfer of large parts of the state economy back to the private economy'.

[81] See e.g. A. Speer, *Spandau: The Secret Diaries* (London, 1976), 88–9. According to Speer the industrialists had all too little influence on Hitler: 'they were given the floor only to talk on special technological problems. No military, let alone political, questions were even discussed in their presence... I would not have dreamed of inviting them to armaments conferences at the headquarters. It is an absurd notion that Hitler would have shared power with Flick or one of the others.'

political stock. Though they demonstrated that the project would use up more iron and steel in its construction than its furnaces could produce for three years, Göring insisted that the political significance of the works took precedence over mere economic rationality and ordered their completion.[82]

The war also accelerated the trend to greater state planning and control, not simply to meet the requirements of mobilization but to strengthen the political position of the Nazi state. In Poland the Ruhr firms, which had hoped for the 'repatriation' of the businesses that they had lost to the Polish state, found instead that a great many were taken over by the Reichswerke as trustee for the state in order to avoid what the Four Year Plan representative in Silesia called 'the reintroduction by individual entrepreneurs of colonial methods of seizure'.[83] In Lorraine, where Ruhr claims were harder to dispute, resources were again organized under state control and the most important plants placed under the Reichswerke, including the Thyssen claims and the Arbed concern in Luxemburg. The Ruhr leaders had hoped for compensation in Lorraine for what they had failed to get elsewhere, but Göring and Pleiger refused to 'allow the competition to get together' and once again instituted ambiguous trustee arrangements, leaving the question of ownership until after the war. Poensgen complained that the state only wanted 'the cherries in the cake', leaving the Ruhr with the crumbs. Even Flick and Krupp were disappointed with the outcome in France.[84] By the middle of the war the Reichswerke had swollen to a giant concern with assets of RM 5,000m., almost twice the size of the rest of the German steel industry put together. The balance of the heavy industrial economy in the New Order swung in favour of the state-controlled firms.[85]

Against the background of conflict over the spoils of occupied Europe, the Ruhr found itself subject to further political pressure at home. Independent cartel planning was compromised by the establishment of special Reich associations for coal and iron and steel (the *Reichsvereinigungen*) which brought both industries under closer state supervision, though it avoided the threat of nationalization advocated by

---

[82] BA-MA, Wi I F 5.412, note of a conference with General Thomas, 1 Nov. 1939, 2–3.

[83] NA Göring Stabsamt, T84 Roll 7, frames 6704–5, note on trustee administration, 21 Apr. 1942.

[84] TWC 12, 14885, Pleiger cross-examination: NA Reichswerke files, T83 Roll 76, frame 3447887, minutes of a conference at the Economics Ministry, 27 June 1941. On trusteeship see T83 Roll 55, Rombacher files, frame 3423807, Economics Ministry to Gauleiter Bürckel, 31 Jan. 1941. On the efforts to 'repatriate' the Lorraine firms see Case XI, Pros. Doc. Book 113, NI-049, Wirtschaftsgruppe Eisenschaffende-Industrie to Pleiger, 5 Feb. 1941; NI3513, Flick to Gauleiter Bürckel, 23 June 1940; NI-3548, Flick to Göring, 1 Nov. 1940; Case X, 483–7, NI-048, letters relating to claims on French firms, 10 June 1940.

[85] USSBS, Special Paper 3, 54a; *Hermann Göring Complex*, 112–37.

some Nazi officials in 1941.[86] The threat of further state encroachment brought the final resignation of Poensgen and of General von Hanneken, Plenipotentiary for Iron and Steel. The one-time leader of the *Ruhrlade*, Paul Reusch, was hounded from office in the autumn of 1941 and his son followed him six months later.[87] Ruhr industry now waited for the end of the war to see what reconstruction would bring. With the defeat of Nazism they hoped to rebuild a political structure more appropriate to the needs of German capitalism, allowing the free play of economic forces but avoiding political extremism, a balance that they had failed to achieve under either Weimar or Hitler. The experience of Nazism, it has recently been argued, prepared the ground among German businessmen for acceptance of the *Sozialmarktwirtschaft* ('social market economy') of the 1950s.[88]

At the height of Germany's power in 1942 officials of the Four Year Plan also turned their minds to post-war planning. Paul Rheinländer, now a director of the Reichswerke, produced a detailed report for the Plan on the reconstruction of European heavy industry after the end of the war.[89] The basic principle was to keep control over heavy industry in state hands. State authorities would dictate prices and the flow of raw materials. The Ruhr was to be restricted deliberately to a maximum production based on the figure for 1939 and the large additional demand for iron and steel anticipated under the New Order was to be met by building up a vast integrated industrial region in the centre and east of the German empire, stretching from Linz, through Czechoslovakia and Silesia to the coal and ore deposits of the Donets basin.[90] The production of an additional 20 million tons of steel a year in peacetime was to be accompanied by strict controls over the use of iron ore and coking coal to ensure that the best raw materials were not used up first.[91] National needs, interpreted through the apparatus for state economic intervention, would be satisfied at the expense of private interest. In this sense, state intervention has to be seen not simply as a product of wartime expediency—indeed arguably the German iron and steel industry would have performed better during the

[86] On coal nationalization see Riedel, *Eisen und Kohle*, 277–83.
[87] Case XI, Pros. Doc. Book 116, von Hanneken affidavit, 11 Mar. 1948; E. Maschke, *Es entsteht ein Konzern: Paul Reusch und die GHH* (Tübingen, 1969), 204–5; Case X, Bülow Doc. Book 1, Poensgen affidavit, 90, 100.
[88] See the discussion in L. Herbst, *Der totale Krieg und die Ordnung der Wirtschaft: Die Kriegswirtschaft im Spannungsfeld von Politik, Ideologie und Propaganda 1939–1945* (Stuttgart, 1982), 383–409.
[89] SAK 12/155/4 'Vorschlag zur Ausgestaltung der Eisenindustrie im Grossdeutschen Wirtschaftsraum nach dem Kriege', n.d. [c.1941].
[90] Ibid. 10, 19, 23–31. On the wider plans for the economy see R. Herzstein, *When Nazi Dreams Come True* (London, 1982), 104–12.
[91] SAK 12/155/4 'Vorschlag', 21–2, 34–5.

war free of excessive controls—but as an extension of the political ambitions of the Nazi Party in the context of a wealthy European empire.

These political ambitions lay at the root of the growing division between Nazism and German heavy industry after 1936. Both sides had very different views of what they wanted to do with the economy once it had recovered and the prospect of political unrest had subsided. The Ruhr wanted in the long run to expand the influence of German business through international co-operation and regulation combined with a successful trade offensive into eastern and central Europe; and all to be achieved as far as possible under private initiative and in terms of economic rationality. At the same time the industrialists naïvely supposed that the Nazi movement would provide a stable national-conservative political environment for business to operate in. The Nazi leadership on the other hand looked to industry to serve political ends over which it had no control and which ultimately, through international crisis and domestic uncertainty, threatened its conservative economic strategy. The building of the Nazi empire and the armed forces to secure it could not be reconciled with the narrower financial and political interests of German capitalism. Hence the rapid extension of state power over the economy, and the determination of the Nazis to exclude much of private industry from the profits of territorial expansion, theoretically in the name of the 'community', but in practice as a function of the dynamic power-seeking of the Nazi élite.

The response of the Ruhr leaders, in adopting defensive tactics and giving priority to shareholder interest, increased their dependence on the state while simultaneously reducing their ability to determine the conditions of economic life. To some extent, of course, this reflected the changing pattern of German industry, which in turn was producing new patterns of political commitment. Iron, steel, and coal were declining as a force in German business life, as they were in Britain in the 1930s, where talk of coal and steel nationalization was also widespread. Because of the rise of large new industries with a high growth rate and modern products—the car industry, the aircraft industry, the electrical and chemical industries— the iron and steel industry was forced to abandon the dominant position it had enjoyed before 1914 and to share industrial power. Where heavy industry had provided almost one-third of industrial output in 1913, it provided only one-fifth by 1938.[92] The new industries gave a greater prominence to professional managers, chemists, scientists, and engineers, many of whom were attracted to Nazism not because of its radicalism, but because it offered opportunities through massive state projects to master technical problems without financial constraint—the *Autobahnen* are a

---

[92] Figures are only approximate. They are calculated from *Statistisches Jahrbuch*, 1911– 13, 1937–8.

TABLE 3.3. *Coal, iron, and steel: statistics, 1933–1944*[a]

	1933	1934	1935	1936	1937	1938	1939	1940	1941	1942	1943	1944
Output (m. tonnes)												
Coal	109.7	124.9	143.0	158.3	184.5	187.5	204.8	247.9	248.3	264.5	268.9	249.0
Lignite	126.8	137.3	147.1	161.4	184.7	199.6	211.6	226.8	235.1	248.9	252.5	260.8
Iron ore	2.6	4.3	6.0	7.6	9.8	15.1	14.7[b]	19.5	36.0	33.8	36.0	26.1
Raw iron	5.2	8.7	12.8	15.3	16.0	18.6	18.5	15.5	24.4	25.1	28.0	20.6
Raw steel	7.5	11.7	16.1	18.8	19.4	23.3	23.7	21.5	31.8	32.1	34.6	28.5
Trade (RMm.)												
Iron and Steel												
Imports	3.9	4.9	4.2	5.3	11.2	22.6	23.6	10.0	(No figures have been given for the war period as the basis for calculating trade flows altered after the German occupation.)			
Exports	5.4	7.1	9.2	10.4	7.2	4.3	5.3	8.8				
Rolling-mill products												
Imports	82.8	129.5	56.8	43.1	42.4	43.3	47.0	39.0				
Exports	212.0	200.1	247.3	294.5	406.4	350.9	407.0	325.9				
Iron ore imports	52.8	88.3	123.4	168.3	221.9	281.5	256.7	166.9				

[a] Germany only 1933–1940, Greater Germany 1941–4.   [b] Germany only (excl. Austria).

Sources: WS, 17 (1937), 18 (1938); *Statistisches Jahrbuch für das Deutsche Reich* (Berlin, 1933–41); USSBS, *The Effects of Strategic Bombing on the German War Economy*, 90–105.

striking example.[93] As a result Nazism depended less on the old industrial élite by the 1930s and could afford the risks of confronting and defeating it politically. As elsewhere the traditional entrepreneur and family owner was giving way to the manager and industrial bureaucrat, among whom the Nazis were able to find more amenable assistants.[94] In the long run the movement was moving to a position in which the economic New Order would be controlled by the party through a bureaucratic apparatus staffed by technical experts and dominated by political interests, not unlike the system that had already been built up in the Soviet Union.

[93] On the scale and nature of the new projects see J. Thies, 'Nazi Architecture: A Blueprint for World Domination', in D. Welch (ed.), *Nazi Propaganda* (London, 1983), 45–62; there is a good general account in K.-H. Ludwig, *Technik und Ingenieure im Dritten Reich* (Düsseldorf, 1974).

[94] This point was first made by F. Neumann, *Behemoth: The Structure and Practice of National Socialism 1933–1939* (London, 1942), 314–8. See too Sohn-Rethel, *German Fascism*, 135–6. The gradual take-over of IG Farben by managers sympathetic to the Nazis is a good example. Borkin, *Crime and Punishment*, 55–63, 66–75.

4

'Primacy Always Belongs to Politics': Gustav Krupp and the Third Reich

By chance the active life of Gustav Krupp von Bohlen und Halbach exactly spanned the life of Germany itself. He was born in 1870, three weeks before the German victory at Sedan. He suffered a debilitating stroke early in 1945, three months before the final collapse of the Third Reich. As a result not Gustav, but his son Alfried, was tried by a Nuremberg tribunal for war crimes and sentenced to twelve years in prison. There was no doubt in the minds of the American prosecutors that the head and leading directors of the Krupp concern bore some of the blame for the rise of Hitler, for conspiring to plan and launch aggressive war, and for crimes against humanity in the treatment of slave labour. According to this judgement, the Krupp family shared the responsibility for the historical course which led to the destruction of the Germany Gustav had grown up with.

It is therefore all the more surprising that the Krupps have excited so little attention from historians. The conventional view of a reactionary family tied by self-interest to a rearming Nazi regime, inhabitants of the moral desert of collaboration, has barely been examined since the Trials. In a recent study of industry and politics in the Third Reich the name Krupp does not even appear.[1] Most books on the period see Krupp, like Flick and the directors of IG Farben, as one of the few major businessmen whose close and friendly relationship with the regime is not in doubt. Yet serious historical evaluation of Krupp and the economic history of his firm is largely lacking. Recently about 250 files from the original Krupp central archives have come to light in London, where they have been stored, unused, since 1951. When these are fully available to researchers, it will be possible to write a more comprehensive history of Krupp just before, and during, the Third Reich. This chapter is based on a preliminary survey of the rediscovered archive.[2]

---

[1] J. Gillingham, *Industry and Politics in the Third Reich* (London, 1985). For popular histories of Krupp see W. Manchester, *The Arms of Krupp* (New York, 1968); G. von Klass, *Krupps: The Story of an Industrial Empire* (London, 1954); P. Batty, *The House of Krupp* (London, 1966); E. Schröder, *Krupp: Geschichte einer Unternehmerfamilie* (Göttingen, 1968).

[2] The documents have since been restituted to the Krupp archive at Villa Hügel. I have used the numbering and reference system employed by the Krupp concern to describe each document, though they are now being recatalogued in Germany. References here are to Krupp-Archiv (London) or K-A(L). Xerox copies can be found in the Foreign and Commonwealth Office Library, London.

Any assessment of the role of the Krupp company, and in particular of Gustav Krupp, its head until 1943, must address the questions raised at Nuremberg. It is important to know what the attitude and role of one of Germany's largest companies was during the economic depression and the rise of Hitler. If it is indeed the case that Krupp after 1933 'did an about-face and abased himself before the new ruler', it is important to know why.[3] It is also the historian's task not merely to chronicle the fate of Krupp's forced labourers during the war, but to explain how a business with such high standards of amenity for its own workers, and a reputation for paternalism, could apparently sanction a degree of brutalization almost without parallel among other private German firms. At least some of the answers can be found in the attitudes and values of the Krupp family; but they also lie in the nature and function of the business itself, in its economic history. The problem of reconciling personal history and structural pressure is especially acute in the case of Krupp, since ownership *and* control were vested almost entirely in the family. This synthesis of business strategy and personal interest explains much about the particular character of Krupp's response to the regime after 1933.

I

By the time Hitler became chancellor, Gustav Krupp had been head of the concern for almost thirty years. He achieved this position immediately after marrying Bertha Krupp, the young heiress to the Krupp estate, in 1906. Though not a Prussian, Gustav von Bohlen was in many respects the very model of the Prussian official. His background was in fact from industry—his father was a German-American industrialist who returned to Germany in 1870 to live in the new Reich—but Gustav was directed to a different career. At 18 he served for a year in the Second Baden Dragoons, then read law at Strasbourg, Lausanne, and Heidelberg, graduating into the diplomatic corps. He served in Washington, Peking (during the Boxer Rebellion), and the Vatican, where he met Bertha Krupp. He was a cold, formal, awkward man who relaxed only when hunting or riding. He worked hard and methodically, and always displayed a rigid loyalty to the law and the state. He proved himself an intelligent and assiduous businessman. Indeed, his commitment to the firm was obsessive. At Gustav's wedding Kaiser Wilhelm II performed a unique ceremony at which he presented the bridegroom with a special deed allowing him to add the name Krupp to his own, and permitting the family henceforth to pass on the name Krupp and the family fortune to the eldest

---

[3] H. A. Turner, *German Big Business and the Rise of Hitler* (Oxford, 1985), 399.

son. On handing over the deed the Kaiser told Gustav he must prove himself 'ein wahrer Krupp' (a true Krupp).[4]

This obligation explains much about Gustav Krupp's subsequent career. He was aware that he was an 'outsider' in the family, trying to prove himself worthy of the inheritance he had acquired. Reflecting later in life about his entry into the business, he underlined the importance of his own industrial ancestry: 'I was near enough to this old bloodstream not to be uprooted yet from the "people"; the "economic" tradition was still alive in me.'[5] For Gustav the Krupp dynasty was of primary importance, and the preservation of the firm a lasting responsibility. 'As the trustee of a binding inheritance,' he wrote, 'it was to me an obvious duty to attach myself to the authentic tradition.'[6] When he was imprisoned by the French during the occupation of the Ruhr, he told his brother-in-law, Tilo von Wilmowsky, 'I now really have a perfect right to call myself a *Kruppianer*.'[7] There was never any question in Gustav's mind that the growth and survival of the historic business was an inescapable duty. So too was the survival of the dynasty, an issue with which he became completely absorbed in the last years of his life. In the light of the subsequent crises which Krupp experienced during the thirty years after 1914, the almost regal preoccupation with questions of succession and patrimony assume an added significance.

Not surprisingly Gustav saw it as part of his responsibility to adopt what he saw as the traditional entrepreneurial values of the Krupp business. His model was Alfred Krupp, founder of the enterprise. Like Alfred he saw the heads of big business as defenders of a moral, conservative order. Entrepreneurs had responsibilities to those they employed, which included social provision, education, and decent housing. But in return the work-force had a duty to respect authority unconditionally, to maintain social peace, and to eschew politics. Gustav was an unrelenting paternalist, who looked upon the business as a special community with shared interests. He liked to mix freely, though not as an equal, with the workers: 'I am always careful to establish *personal* contact with as many of my work comrades as possible.'[8] He believed in a social bond, a moral commitment, between the family and the *Kruppianer*. As a result he was fiercely hostile to the left, and operated under the illusion

---

[4] Manchester, *Arms*, 283.

[5] K-A(L), Privatsekretariat, Akten betreffend Reichsregierung 1933–43, first draft of an article for 'das Geschenkbuch für den deutschen Rüstungsarbeiter' entitled 'Betriebsführer und Rüstungsarbeiter', 2. It should be noted that both articles and speeches were written by Krupp himself and can be found in the files in two or even three drafts. They were not, as is sometimes alleged, written for him.

[6] Ibid. 7.

[7] Von Klass, *Krupp*, 345.

[8] K-A(L), 'Betriebsführer und Rüstungsarbeiter', 18.

that Krupp workers, particularly the *Stammarbeiter* (the core work-force), were immune to left-wing politics: 'The infamous agitation of the leftist parties for the most part glances off the solid type of Krupp worker with his deep-rooted sense of loyalty to the firm.'[9] There was nothing unique in these views. Fear of the left, paternalism, the commitment to the concept of 'Herr im Hause' (the master in his house), were common attitudes among the owner-managers of his generation.

So too were Gustav's other views on politics. He favoured a strong and stable state and disliked party politics and the Reichstag, 'the destructive arena of parliamentary conflicts'.[10] His was a traditional, Hegelian conception of the state, to which all other realms of activity were subordinated: 'Economy, law, culture—these are all only emanations, manifestations, segments of the life of the *state*.'[11] He understood that there was a direct correlation between the political fortunes of the German state and the fortunes of the business. But he was also a fierce defender of private economy. Within the economic sphere, the entrepreneurial class alone had responsibility. *Staatskapitalismus* trespassed on the rights and interests of businessmen. He had an instinctive belief that private initiative alone produced sound economics, and that private industry should have the right to determine its own conditions of existence. This was not an altogether *laissez-faire* view, for it left room for private marketing arrangements, and Krupp did expect businessmen to hold some sort of responsibility towards the state: 'Between "free" economy and state capitalism there is a third form: the economy that is free from obligations, but has a sense of inner duty to the state.'[12] The major role of the state was to maintain social peace and an environment for business confidence, but not to act in an entrepreneurial capacity itself.

Not surprisingly, Gustav Krupp was a dedicated nationalist. Though he expressed open views on international affairs only seldom, his sympathies lay almost certainly with the Pan-Germans, and with the idea of an economic *Mitteleuropa*, dominated by Germany. After the *Anschluss* and the occupation of Prague, he publicly welcomed the fact that 'central Europe would be reconstructed', and that 'Greater Germany—the dream of our fathers and grandfathers' was finally created. He was a cultural and economic imperialist, who asserted the superiority of the German way

[9] Ibid. 16.

[10] Quoted in Manchester, *Arms*, 284.

[11] K-A(L), Privatakten: Akten betr. Reden ab 7 July 1933, draft of a speech at Magdeburg, 30 May 1933, 11. He concluded: 'a state lives only through its *politics*—and a state collapses only through its politics too'.

[12] Ibid. 12.

[13] K-A(L), Privatakten: Akten betr. Reden, 1 July 1937–12 Sept. 1941, draft of a speech for 'Feier zur Ehrung der Jubilare', 9 May 1943. Krupp was quoting from the *Jubilarfeier* (Jubilee Festival) of 1916, pp. 1–2, 12.

of life. During the First World War, which he blamed entirely on 'the nets of encirclement', and on enemies who 'hate the German character and German progress', he argued that two different principles were in conflict; the political individualism of the west and 'the German belief in service to the state and the community'. During the Second World War he returned to the nationalist theme, that Germany was defending 'an ancient cultural heritage', and that 'the German people has a *historic mission*'.[13]

Krupp belonged, then, firmly in the political mould of the traditional conservatism and nationalism of the Second Reich, though he would have nothing to do with formal politics. Before the war his energies were devoted to restoring the fortunes of the company, assisted by Alfred Hugenberg, later leader of the German Nationalist Party (DNVP), whom Krupp chose in 1909 to head the *Aufsichtsrat*, and whose views on socialism and politics were very similar to Gustav's own.[14] During the war Krupp played a key role in supplying steel and armaments for the German war effort. By 1917 85 per cent of Krupp output went in war production, and much of the profit from war orders went into building new workshops and in social expenditure to protect the work-force and its families from economic hardship, in the tradition of Krupp paternalism. By the end of the war Krupp had a bleak economic outlook for it had accumulated large assets which were suitable chiefly for war production. In anticipation of this problem Gustav ordered in 1917 high levels of depreciation and low levels of dividend payments.[15]

Nevertheless in the post-war period Krupp suffered more than other firms from the Allied dismantling and destruction of war industry, and was forced to convert to making general equipment and machinery, adapting to the new market conditions as well as it could. The business maintained high levels of employment until 1924, when the post-inflation settlement forced a sharp cut-back in the size of the work-force. During 1923 the Krupp works came under the French occupation force and, following a clash between French troops and Krupp workers, which left thirteen Germans dead, Krupp himself was arrested, tried, and sentenced to seven years' imprisonment. The *Aufsichtsrat* (supervisory board), advised closing the business, but Gustav insisted that the difficulties could be overcome. After his release seven months later, when the French left, the firm was rationalized, the work-force cut, and a programme of new investment undertaken, totalling RM 141m. between 1924 and 1933. Krupp used a $10 m. loan from America to begin the restructuring, and later used 'compensation' funds made available by Stresemann, and a RM 60m. loan

[14] J. A. Leopold, *Alfred Hugenberg* (London, 1977), 2–5.
[15] L. Burchhardt, 'Zwischen Kriegsgewinnen und Kriegskosten: Krupp im Ersten Weltkrieg', *Zeitschrift für Unternehmensgeschichte*, 32 (1987), 76–8, 92, 96.

from a consortium of German banks to put the firm back on a sounder financial footing.[16] It is nevertheless important to recall that throughout the Weimar years economic conditions for Krupp were not generally favourable. As Gustav wrote in 1934: 'The last so-to-say normal balance-sheet for our firm was that of 30 June 1914.'[17] Heavy losses were made during the 1920s, which were survived only because the share capital was concentrated in the family's hands rather than among a wider shareholding public. In 1933 the firm's net assets totalled RM 260m. against RM 333m. in 1914.[18] Though Gustav had preserved his inheritance, he had not enlarged it.

The nature of the firm was forced by circumstances to change during the 1920s too. Coal and steel production became more important, while armaments were abandoned in favour of specialized equipment, bridge-building, and vehicles. Gustav took it as a personal challenge to demonstrate that Krupp could survive without armaments, 'to survive economically without the production of war material'.[19] Though limited research and veiled production of armaments were carried out, they were insignificant in terms of the economic position of the business. Krupp's success in reviving trade abroad was based on agricultural equipment and high quality and specialized steel products. Having made this market readjustment, the recession after 1929 hit Krupp all the harder. Like the rest of German industry Krupp was severely affected by the collapse of world trade and the mounting crisis within Germany. The impact of the recession on Krupp is set out in Table 4.1.[20] It is against the background of a second major period of economic crisis in ten years that the role of Krupp in the 1930s has to be judged.

II

Though Gustav Krupp recognized the relationship between economic and political crisis during the depression, his preference was for a 'natural' economic revival, keeping direct political intervention to a minimum. Running through all his writing between 1931 and 1933 is a strong

---

[16] The details are in K-A(L), Reden ab 7 July 1933, draft of a speech given 10 Jan. 1934, 6.

[17] Ibid. 1.

[18] Ibid. 10–11. Fixed capital was RM 215.8m. in 1914, RM 163.8m. in 1933.

[19] Ibid. 12.

[20] On heavy industry in general see B. Weisbrod, 'Economic Power and Political Stability Reconsidered: Heavy Industry in Weimar Germany', *Social History*, 4 (1979), 247–50. Krupp figures are from K-A(L), Leistungen: Maschinenfabriken, Geschäftsbericht 1927/8; Walzwerke und Schmiedebetriebe: Leistungen 1913/14–1941/2; Fr. Krupp AG, Band I, Jahreserzeugung in Essen, 1913–43; Geschäftsbericht 1929/30, Anlage 12.

TABLE 4.1. *Fr. Krupp AG labour and output: statistics, 1927/8–1931/2*[a]

	Steel, Essen (tonnes)	Coal (tonnes)	Forgings (tonnes)	Labour, Essen[b]
1927/8	514,093	7,907,302	80,187	49,315
1928/9	479,282	8,001,545	74,880	49,166
1929/30	411,282	7,795,047	57,615	40,532
1930/1	380,782	6,139,802	37,791	33,901
1931/2	265,024	4,740,039	22,557	28,332

[a] Business year 1 Oct.–30 Sept.
[b] The final figure is for Oct. 1932, not 1931. The other figures are for the beginning of the business year.

rejection of *dirigiste* policies. In December 1932 he argued: 'It is necessary in future to establish again a clear division between the tasks of the state and those of the private economy.'[21] He was the spokesmen of those businessmen who rejected 'the noxious capital from the "subsidy economy". Every "socialization of losses" is to be refused.'[22] He was incensed in the summer of 1932 when Friedrich Flick sold the major holding in the Gelsenkirchener Bergwerk AG to the state without informing his fellow industrialists. Krupp reprimanded Flick for the damage it did to the public image of private capital, and for failing to offer the shares to other buyers first. Flick's action transgressed Krupp's simple principles about self-responsibility of the entrepreneur, 'a responsibility where the full risk of profit or loss is borne by the person who is responsible himself'.[23] Krupp thought that private industry should set its own house in order, however severe the crisis. The government's responsibility was to maintain the currency at all costs and to run its household on lines of efficiency and financial stringency, something which Krupp doubted was the case under Brüning. For Krupp the main role of the state was still to create a stable environment in which long-term industrial planning could be embarked upon without fear of renewed crisis.

Unlike some industrial circles, Krupp was hostile to the arguments for

[21] K-A(L), Acta Krupp, Privatkorrespondenz 1930–7, letter from Herle to Krupp, 28 Apr. 1933, 'Bemerkungen zur national- und wirtschaftspolitischen Linie des Reichsverbandes seit Beginn der Präsidentschaft Herrn von Bohlen', 7. The quotation comes from the Hauptausschuss-Sitzung, 14 Dec. 1932.
[22] Ibid.
[23] Ibid. Also Albert Vögler to Krupp, 27 June 1932, enclosing a letter for Flick; Krupp to Vögler, 28 June 1932; Flick to Vögler, 30 June 1932; Krupp to Vögler, 5 July 1932. See Turner, *Big Business*, 235, 254–5.

giving agriculture special protection—something which may well explain the cool relations between Krupp and the DNVP—and was generally unsympathetic to the spread of autarkist thinking during the depression. Krupp depended on trade, the Russian trade in particular in 1931–2, and he was anxious that the end of the crisis should see a reopening of world trade links, and a rejection of economic isolationism. In June 1932 he complained to Ludwig Kastl of the Reichsverband der Deutschen Industrie (German Employers Association: RDI) about the dangers for Germany in promoting autarky: 'You know that I too hold the spread of this catchword as extraordinarily objectionable and dangerous and will therefore gladly agree to any steps which lead to a clarification of the situation.'[24] In September 1932 he wrote to Julius Forstmann in Paris that the German economy obviously depended on the revival of the American economy, and the re-establishment of economic interdependence. The strength of Germany's economy lay in its role as a 'Veredelungsland', importing materials and sending finished products back to the primary producers to stimulate their economies in turn.[25] This was a view Krupp returned to in the crisis leading up to the Four Year Plan.

Politics mattered for Krupp only to the extent that it produced a state on a 'sound and stable basis', and avoided external crisis.[26] To restore business confidence and private initiative 'Germany needs above all calm and stability in the realm of internal and external politics.' This could only be produced, Krupp believed, by a rallying of conservative forces. He deplored the growing political divisions of the right and centre, the emphasis on 'egoistical or party-political viewpoints [instead of] the view of the whole'.[27] He was hostile to the German Communist Party (KPD) and German Social Democratic Party (SPD), though less hostile to the trade unions. He blamed labour generally for keeping wage rates to high, but respected the right of both sides to negotiate wage settlements independent of political pressure.[28] In foreign affairs he hoped for an end to reparations, serious steps towards multilateral disarmament, and a restoration of international economic co-operation. In September 1931 he was pushed more firmly into the political limelight than he liked, when he succeeded Carl Duisberg as head of the German Employers

---

[24] K-A(L), Privatkorrespondenz, Krupp to Kastl, 2 June 1932.
[25] Ibid., Krupp to Forstmann, 15 Sept. 1932, 5–6.
[26] Ibid. 2.
[27] Ibid. 2–3.
[28] H. James, *The German Slump: Politics and Economics 1924–1936* (Oxford, 1986), 185, 233; D. Abraham, *The Collapse of the Weimar Republic: Political Economy and Crisis* (Princeton, NJ, 1981), 275. Krupp was instrumental in breaking industry's united front during the steel lockout and accepting the 'Severing award'.

Association (RDI), an appointment designed to reconcile the different big-business lobby groups, while increasing the influence of Ruhr heavy industry.[29]

Krupp used his new position as a platform to promote the views of those who favoured a moderate national-conservative solution to the crisis. He relied heavily on other businessmen for advice, and seldom took the initiative. He supported Duisberg's efforts for the election of Hindenburg as president in 1932 in preference to Hitler.[30] He actively supported the German People's Party (DVP), the party closest to his own ideas on *Staatsreform* and conservative economics. He only withdrew the promise of firm financial support for the party, with the agreement of other DVP industrialists, in January 1932 because the DVP had failed to halt the rise of Nazi support and had encouraged what Paul Reusch called 'the unholy fragmentation of the bourgeois parties'.[31] He approved of Reusch's suggestion to Eduard Dingeldey that 'all the parties standing between the Centre and the National Socialists must unite in a single large party'.[32] Krupp himself wrote to Dingeldey that financial support would be withheld 'so long as the bourgeois parties fail to find a way out of the present unfortunate fragmentation in order to arrive together at common effort'.[33] Krupp's object seems to have been to win the bourgeoisie back from Nazism, and to use the influence of the RDI, such as it was, to encourage a new bourgeois *Sammlung*, or rallying together. But the net effect was to weaken the DVP during the first half of 1932, without effectively halting the Nazi bandwagon. If the object were to reverse the electoral tide of Nazism it was a poor tactic, and there now seems little doubt that Krupp belonged to that section of big business which did not want a Nazi or 'black-brown' [i.e. an alliance of Nazis and Catholic centre] outcome to the political crisis.[34]

For Krupp himself the appointment of von Papen in May 1932 was the ideal solution, the beginning of a new rallying of the centre-right to combat the dangers of extremism. Von Papen represented almost exactly Krupp's own political position. He, too, argued for a political rallying above party, a kind of 'national government', but excluding the socialists

[29] R. Neebe, 'Unternehmerverbände und Gewerkschaften in den Jahren der Grossen Krise 1929–1933', *Geschichte und Gesellschaft*, 9 (1983), 316–19 for the background to this change; Turner, *Big Business*, 163; Abraham, *Collapse*, 214–15.

[30] K-A(L), Privatkorrespondenz, Carl Duisberg to Krupp, 25 Feb. 1932; Krupp to Duisberg, 29 Feb. 1932, giving details of Krupp's contributions to the Hindenburg re-election fund; Dr Dechamps (Concordia Bergbau AG) to Krupp, 1 Mar. 1932, thanking Krupp for his contribution.

[31] Ibid., Paul Reusch to Dingeldey, 30 Jan. 1932; Reusch to Krupp, 2 Feb. 1932.

[32] Ibid., Reusch to Dingeldey, 30 Jan. 1932.

[33] Ibid., Krupp to Dingeldey, 6 Feb. 1932.

[34] See Turner, *Big Business*, esp. ch. 6.

and the Nazis. Von Papen's conception of 'Reformwerk' coincided with Krupp's—rolling back the tide of social welfare politics, maintaining fiscal orthodoxy, and promoting the 'natural' upswing of the business cycle and private initiative. It was the first administration of the recession in which Krupp had real confidence: 'I see in the work of reform undertaken by the regime a serious effort to solve the paralysis in economic life before the onset of winter by reintroducing individual responsibility back into the economy.'[35] When von Papen was replaced by von Schleicher on 2 December, Krupp sent him a personal letter expressing his continued support and offering thanks both from himself and 'from by far the largest part of all those who think of the economy and not just party politics'. He welcomed von Papen's efforts 'to prepare once again a foundation for the revival of Germany through Lausanne and through your economic policy'.[36] Some clue as to why Krupp regarded von Papen so favourably can be found in the ex-chancellor's reply to this letter three weeks later, confirming that he shared Krupp's belief that the way out of the crisis lay 'in a natural way, through the private initiative of the German entrepreneur'.[37]

Krupp placed the blame for the collapse of von Papen's administration and the calling of fresh elections in November firmly on the political parties, whose actions showed, according to Krupp, that they did not have the interests either of the state or the people at heart.[38] From September 1932 onwards Krupp expressed alarm at the growing instability of the political system, coming as it did at a time when the first early signs of an upswing could be detected. But though he regretted the collapse of von Papen's political strategy, and continued to provide funds for his campaigns and, once again, for the DVP, Krupp's active intervention in politics was very limited. In the conditions of political crisis in 1932 the kind of political solution favoured by Krupp was increasingly unrealistic as the bourgeois parties collapsed, the traditional agrarian and military élites reasserted their role in politics, and the economic crisis pushed many Germans towards the populist-nationalist right.

Throughout December 1932 and January 1933 Krupp held to the view that some reasonable conservative solution had to be found in order to permit the fragile but vital economic revival to continue. The real concern for Krupp and for other Ruhr leaders during January was to avoid fresh

---

[35] K-A(L), Privatkorrespondenz, Krupp to Forstmann, 15 Sept. 1932, 1–2.

[36] Ibid., Krupp to von Papen, 3 Dec. 1932. Krupp began his letter by confessing how little he understood what was going on: 'Having wandered too little down the crooked path of party political thinking, I can allow myself no judgement over the development in the last weeks.'

[37] Ibid., von Papen to Krupp, 23 Dec. 1932.

[38] Ibid., Krupp to Forstmann, 15 Sept. 1932, 3.

elections, which would only further undermine business confidence. On 21 January Albert Vögler wrote to Krupp suggesting that the RDI announce formally its opposition to the calling of new elections, though he followed up the suggestion by adding: 'I know that with this we would be treading in the very dangerous sphere of direct politics. What good though would be all our efforts over Russian contracts etc. if the precondition, domestic stability, is not created?'[39] Krupp did not reply until 28 January, when he assured Vögler that he too had been making desperate efforts 'to press for maintenance of stability'. He continued on a pessimistic note: 'But unfortunately, so unfortunately, everything appears once again to come out otherwise than one could have logically expected. I am now very anxious about further development.'[40] The crisis finally provoked Krupp and Kastl to interfere directly in politics when, again on 28 January, they notified the President through Meissner that they placed the greatest emphasis on maintaining a stable regime in which business could have confidence. According to Krupp 'everything should be avoided that disturbs economic life anew'.[41] Krupp was not a Hitler supporter, and it is difficult not to interpret this as evidence that the leadership of the RDI was deeply disturbed at the prospect of a Hitler government.[42] There is no direct evidence that Krupp even knew of the nature of the negotiations going on in January, or that his intervention had the slightest impact on the course of political events.

What is interesting is Vögler's reply to Krupp five days later, on 2 February, with the situation 'overturned'. Vögler regretted that it was impossible to prevent new elections, and notified Krupp that Hugenberg and von Papen would be campaigning on the same list. He added that they would now be confronted with 'a very agitated time'.[43] There was no mention of Hitler, and no sense that the political peace the RDI had been seeking was achieved with the change of government. Indeed the tenor of this, and subsequent letters in the Krupp files, suggests that heavy industry did not see 30 January as a real break at all, but saw it simply as part of the political musical chairs that had been going on since June.[44] Their eyes

[39] Ibid., Vögler to Krupp, 21 Jan, 1933.
[40] Ibid., Krupp to Vögler, 28 Jan. 1933.
[41] Ibid., Kastl and Hamm (RDI) to State Secretary Meissner, 28 Jan. 1933; Kastl to Meissner, 28 Jan. 1933.
[42] H. A. Turner, 'The *Ruhrlade*, Secret Cabinet of Heavy Industry in the Weimar Republic', *Central European History*, 3 (1970), 223–7; id., *Big Business*, 320–1; Neebe, 'Unternehmerverbände', 326.
[43] K-A(L), Privatkorrespondenz, Vögler to Krupp, 2 Feb. 1933.
[44] Neebe, 'Unternehmerverbände', 327–9; U. Wengst, 'Der Reichsverband der Deutschen Industrie in den ersten Monaten des Dritten Reiches', *Vierteljahrshefte für Zeitgeschichte*, 28 (1980), 109–10. As an example in the Krupp file see K-A(L), Privatkorrespondenz, Krupp to Kastl, 28 Feb. 1933: 'In times of such unstable politics as the present...'.

were fixed firmly on the March elections in the hope that this would achieve something of a stabilization. Far from resolving the crisis, the decision of 30 January made it more acute. In the weeks before the election Krupp pursued two separate courses. First he sought to find out what direction Nazi economic policy was going to go in. The opportunity for this came with the meeting on 20 February, at which Krupp, as head of the RDI, addressed a brief vote of thanks to Hitler for a speech outlining the political and social objectives of the regime. Krupp's words, often seen as an early capitulation to the new rulers, amounted to no more than a set of platitudes on the need for a strong state, a national rather than interest-based revival, and an end to the internal political crisis. This was the solution he had hoped for under von Papen.[45]

The second course was to make one last effort to produce the conservative *Sammlung* at the new election along the lines suggested in 1932, based once again around the figure of the new vice-chancellor, von Papen. On 15 February he wrote to Krupp asking him to administer the conservatives' election fund. Von Papen presented himself as the leader of a broad conservative 'black–white–red' front, 'namely the group, embracing several millions, of conservatively inclined men not tied to party, who on principle reject our present party system'.[46] Only by gathering together conservative forces through an energetic campaign, von Papen argued, could a regime be avoided that was too committed to a particular party line. A broad bourgeois front would then permit 'the strengthening of the authoritarian line and the suppression of the excessive claims of party interest in German politics'.[47] Krupp refused to run the fund because of his official position, but he found another administrator for it, and gave money both to von Papen and the DVP. But the strategy had even less chance of success against a background of Nazi terror and intimidation. After the March elections von Papen, much to Krupp's irritation, blamed industry for not giving him enough money.[48] The outcome of the election was the collapse of the national-conservative alliance on which Krupp pinned his hopes, however naïvely, and the triumph of a Nazi-Catholic majority which ushered in the period of totalitarian rule. The chimera of a national-conservative solution, above party, pursuing a firm political line at home, and restoring the prospects of private economy and trade, disappeared.

---

[45] Ibid., Notiz, 22 Feb. 1933.

[46] Ibid., von Papen to Krupp, 15 Feb. 1933, 1–4.

[47] Ibid. 1. Krupp replied that he could not run the fund as head of the RDI, but that he had approached Fritz Springorum, who was willing to undertake the task. See Krupp to von Papen, 16 Feb. 1933; Krupp to Springorum, 18 Feb. 1933.

[48] Ibid., Springorum to Krupp, 25 Mar. 1933.

III

It is generally agreed that Krupp was one of the first and most conspicuous industrial converts to the new regime. While it is certainly true that Krupp, as head of the RDI, accepted the demands of the Nazi radicals in sacking its officials and winding the organization up, Krupp's attitude to the new regime was more complicated than mere compliance. For one thing Krupp found himself uncharacteristically in the political limelight during the *Gleichschaltung* (co-ordination) of the RDI. He had to make choices about accepting or confronting the party which other industrialists did not have to make so directly. Moreover, during April, Fritz Thyssen, who was openly encouraging accommodation with the Nazis, was highly critical of Krupp's leadership of the RDI, and in particular of Krupp's meetings with trade-union leaders with a view to finding a new business/labour compromise, independent of government.[49] Krupp was forced into a difficult position in the spring of 1933. Since he disliked politics and was disillusioned by his own experiences with political life since 1931, he was an unlikely figure to stand out against Nazi pressure. With Thyssen, Wagener, and the party radicals in full cry, Krupp's natural caution was uppermost. The very fact that a man who so disliked the populist, street-based politics of the new party could 'abase' himself before the new rulers suggests how deliberate a tactic it was.[50]

Krupp was also bound by his own values of obedience to the state and independence from politics: 'Primacy always belongs to politics.'[51] After the March elections Hitler was confirmed in power. Krupp had never worked to overthrow the Republic but had adjusted, if reluctantly, to its market conditions and political framework. He did the same after 1933. He was not a courageous or outspoken man. He would never have done what Hugo Junkers did, rejecting Nazi plans for military aviation, and suffering a state takeover as a result. He knew early on what the consequences were for those who did oppose the regime, or who, like Paul Silverberg, were the wrong race. There is a long list of industrialists who did make a break, sooner or later, with the regime: Silverberg and Springorum in 1933, Thyssen in 1939, Reusch, Poensgen during the war.

[49] Neebe, 'Unternehmerverbände', 329; Turner, *Big Business*, 334–6; Wengst, 'Reichsverband', 94–109.

[50] In the Krupp correspondence with members of the family and within the firm, it is striking how little impact the coming of Hitler actually made. Gustav's personal letters, of which there are a great number in the London collection, contain virtually no mention of Hitler or the Nazi movement until the war period. Neither the private letters nor the internal letters and memoranda of the firm carry the 'Heil Hitler' at the foot.

[51] K-A(L), Privatakten, Reden ab 7 July 1933, draft of a speech, 10 Jan. 1934, 13: 'The past year has shown with the greatest forcefulness that primacy always belongs to politics, that a strong, well-ordered state forms the precondition for a prosperous economy.'

Even Krupp's own brother-in-law, von Wilmowsky, and Ewald Löser, Krupp's managing director from 1937 to 1943, ended the war in prison. Maintaining the Krupp tradition meant, under any circumstances, keeping a Krupp in control. Loyalty was not only instinctive, but expedient. But there is another aspect of Krupp's accommodation. After March 1933 there was a sense, however unrealistic it may now seem, that the broad conservative front had in some ways been achieved. Von Papen was still vice-chancellor. Indeed, Krupp was still corresponding with von Papen in 1934, when he helped to organize an industrial fund to subsidize a prominent Catholic journal in trouble with the authorities for criticizing the regime.[52] After 1933 Krupp's contacts with the armed forces and the ministries, still dominated by the old élite, allayed fears that the Nazi revolution would sweep away areas of traditional conservative predominance. The Ministry of Finance was held by a man business respected; and after the fall of Hugenberg as Minister of Economics, his successor, Kurt Schmitt, worked well enough with industry.

The survival of von Papen's conservatism was also underlined for Krupp by the economic strategy of the regime. Krupp found Hitler much less of a threat to economic stability than he had appeared to be before achieving power. Hitler made it clear that economic experiments, inflation, and state control were not part of the government's campaign against the recession. Instead he emphasized areas of economic strategy that almost exactly reflected Krupp's own priorities and attitudes: a national policy, not one based on sectional or party interest; a restoration of parity with other powers and an end to the economic restraints of Versailles; the restoration of social peace; and economic policies based on restoring the self-responsibility of industry. There was nothing particularly National Socialist about these views and they had the effect, as Hitler intended, of calming industrial fears. Krupp, too, wanted the 'avoidance of internal unrest and the maintenance of social peace', and the elimination of the 'communist danger' and 'the antagonism of the German parties'.[53] He welcomed the restoration of what he saw as the 'Herr im Hause' traditions in industry, and Hitler's emphasis on entrepreneurial qualities. In 1939 he looked back on the major achievements of the six years since Hitler came to power. The most important, Krupp claimed, was the improvement in relations 'between leaders and led'.[54] Krupp, like other conservatives, saw in Hitler only what he wanted to see.

[52] Ibid., Krupp to von Papen, 6 Mar. 1934; von Papen to Krupp 7 Mar. 1934. Vögler, who alerted Krupp to the anti-Nazi position of the paper, asked him: 'must we not under these circumstances be somewhat cautious?'

[53] Quoted in Neebe, 'Unternehmerverbände', 328; K-A(L), Privatakten, Reden ab 7 July 1933, draft of a speech 10 Jan. 1934, 14.

[54] K-A(L), Reden 1 July 1937–12 Sept. 1941, draft of a speech 'zur Ehrung Kruppscher Jubilare', 30 Apr. 1939, 8. On entrepreneurship see Reden ab 7 July 1933, draft of a speech, 'Oct. 1933', 2.

For Hitler German heavy industry was an essential component of the drive for recovery in the three years after 1933. His decision to use the expertise of industry and to produce a clear demarcation of responsibility between state and economy helped to break down the distrust between industry and the new government. Krupp would no doubt have felt even more reassured if he had heard Hitler tell Otto Strasser late in January 1933, when asked what he would do with Krupp: 'But of course I should leave it alone. Do you think I should be so mad as to destroy Germany's economy?'[55] As long as Nazi economic and political strategy relied on the co-operation of big business, and corresponded sufficiently with its conservative expectations, notions of 'compliance' and 'resistance' had little meaning.

This was certainly the case as the fortunes of the firms themselves began to improve sharply from the early months of the regime. For Krupp, hit like other producers after 1930 by excess stockholding and wage rates that they regarded as too high, the improved market situation and the weakened position of labour after January 1933 were compelling reasons for suspending judgement on Hitler. By May Krupp's monthly sales were back to the level of 1931, and by August exceeded it. During the first eighteen months of the Third Reich a gradual improvement turned into a sustained upswing, and re-employment itself contributed to social stability. The changes in sales and employment are set out in Table 4.2. For the first time for five years business was expanding. In 1933/4 Krupp declared a profit of RM 6.6m., in 1934/5 of RM 11.4m.[56] Though the relationship between profitability and political acquiescence is a crude one, it is no less valid for that. Krupp was a capitalist before all else.

Yet if Krupp found echoes of his own views in those of Hitler, his attitude to the party was less enthusiastic. After March 1933 the party saw heavy industry as a regular source of income. Demands for party grants, welfare payments, and contribution increased sharply in the first months of 1933. In May the RDI began to discuss a way of approaching the problem, which threatened to get completely out of hand. A decision was made to consolidate all the demands into a single once-and-for-all payment, arranged as a payroll tax for all German industrial and commercial businesses.[57] The fund was called the 'Adolf Hitler-Spende der deutschen Wirtschaft', and Gustav Krupp was its director. The sum was fixed at 5/1000 of the wage bill for 1932 and fell due for the period from June 1933 to May 1934.[58] Though this brought some semblance of order

[55] Quoted in Batty, *House of Krupp*, 156.

[56] K-A(L), Jahresberichte und Bilanzen, 1934/5–1940/1; Jahresbericht für das Geschäftsjahr 1934/5, 13, 17.

[57] K-A(L), Privatsekretariat, Akten betreffend Adolf Hitler-Spende bis 31 July 1934: Krupp to Herle (RDI), 23 May 1933; Krupp to Schacht, 29 May 1933; Poensgen (Vereinigte Stahlwerke) to Krupp, 1 June 1933.

[58] Ibid., RDI to all firms, 'Adolf Hitler-Spende der deutschen Wirtschaft', 1 June 1933.

TABLE 4.2. *Fr. Krupp AG monthly sales and annual employment, 1931/2–1933/4*

	Sales (RMm.)			Labour, Essen Works	
	1931/2	1932/3	1933/4		
Oct.	17.2	11.0	16.6	1 Oct. 1932	26,360
Nov.	15.2	13.4	19.6	30 Sept. 1933	34,789
Dec.	22.5	15.2	20.9	30 Sept. 1934	51,801
Jan.	12.3	12.5	20.6		
Feb.	12.4	14.8	22.2		
Mar.	12.6	17.2	24.5		
Apr.	12.3	13.4	25.3		
May	13.7	17.2	24.5		
June	13.4	16.8	27.8		
July	11.8	16.6	26.7		
Aug.	11.1	22.5	27.1		
Sept.	14.2	19.1	40.6		
	168.7	189.7	297.9		

Sources: K-A(L), Betriebsberichte: Technischer Bericht über das Geschäftsjahr 1933/4, 1934/5; Privatakten Akten betr. Korrespondenz betr. den Aufsichtsrat, Feb. 1903–May 1936.

during 1933, the fund proved not to be a short-term solution at all. It was turned into a regular annual payment, reaching RM 23m. by 1935/6 and RM 77m. by 1940/1.[59] Buying off the party activists in the end simply imposed another kind of tax like the 'impositions' of the Weimar welfare state. Nor was Krupp happy with the efforts to promote the interests of small businessmen in 1933 in the awarding of state contracts, nor with the parity with industry won by handwork, agriculture, and transport on national economic boards.[60] Krupp, like other firms, had to deal with the regular incursions into the independent realm of the entrepreneur from local party enthusiasts. While his admiration for the national renewal inspired by Hitler may well have been real enough, his distaste for the party bosses who came with it was clear. Felix Somary, the Zürich banker, recalled a meeting with Krupp in Berlin late in 1934 at which he complained about the arbitrary nature of party rule: 'Believe me, we are worse off here than the natives in Timbuctoo.' There was, noted Somary, an expression on Krupp's face 'of profound despair'.[61]

[59] Ibid., Band V, Adolf Hitler-Spende May 1940–Dec. 1944.
[60] K-A(L), Akten betr. Reichsregierung 1933–1943, Krupp to von Eltz-Rubenach and Kurt Schmitt, 29 Jan. 1934.
[61] F. Somary, *The Raven of Zürich: The Memoirs of Felix Somary* (London, 1986), 175.

IV

Some of the ambiguity of this relationship with the regime became evident with the development of Nazi economic and military policy after 1934. Krupp was no Thyssen, enthusiastically embracing corporativism, and in the spring of 1934 he tried to resign his office as head of the RDI, in order to devote himself to the affairs of his firm. He remained in the post only because of pressure from Schmitt and Albert Pietzsch, head of the Reichswirtschaftskammer (Reich Economic Chamber), who argued that Krupp's resignation would only lead to economic uncertainty and speculation abroad about his motives for resigning.[62] But in practice Krupp withdrew more and more from his national role, leaving the work to his deputy. After three years at the forefront of national economic life, Krupp, in poor health, retreated into the routine of the business once again.

There were also problems for Krupp with the coming of rearmament on a large scale. Here the firm was faced with a difficult choice. Though Gustav favoured the ultimate aim of *Gleichberechtigung* (parity of treatment), he was unhappy about openly flouting the Versailles settlement. This was not a minor point, since Krupp had bitter memories of the dismantling after 1919 and the French occupation of 1923. For a number of reasons he was also uneasy about the prospect of shifting the balance of the business away from civilian to military work. During the 1920s Krupp had made it his aim to restore the firm's fortunes without relying on armaments output. There was an understandable reluctance to sacrifice areas of the civilian market, where growth prospects in the long term might well be higher, for armaments orders which might well peter out after a number of years leaving the firm over-committed to military capacity. There was, however, very little choice for the firm. Krupp was under strong pressure during 1933 and 1934 from the Defence Ministry to expand arms output and research. The firm was already integrated with the military apparatus during the period of secret rearmament before 1933. For Hitler the firm symbolized German military output.[63] From 1934 onwards Krupp began to expand the military side of the business rapidly, while seeking successfully to retain a share of civilian output and

---

[62] K-A(L), Privatkorrespondenz 1931–1934, Kessler to Krupp, 4 May 1934; Pietzsch to Krupp, 1 May 1934. Springorum was to act as Krupp's deputy.

[63] There is interesting testimony in A. Sohn-Rethel, *Economy and Class-Structure of German Fascism* (London, 1978), 63: 'Krupp could afford to hold out and had no inclination to put hopes for the future at risk by playing with irresponsible policies. Krupp and the Army chiefs were clear-headed enough to know just what would be at stake by embarking on massive rearmament in the face of international opposition.' (Sohn-Rethel worked for a business association, the Mitteleuropäischer Wirtschaftstag, in the early 1930s.)

expanding steel and coal output.[64] As late as 1938 Krupp was still defending his right to go on producing civilian products, prompting Göring's comment: 'Your old Geheimrat would rather make chamber pots than guns!'[65]

Krupp's attitude to armaments also derived from his argument that military production was not necessarily the right way either to solve Germany's economic problems or to get over the international recession. Krupp developed this theme in his letter to Julius Forstmann in September 1932. He wanted Germany to enjoy partiy with other states, but not to embark on a large rearmament drive. Parity in this sense therefore meant disarmament of the other powers, so that Germany was not discriminated against. The path to world recovery was not world-wide rearmament but the restoration of a peaceful international economic system:

I value the development of a generally favourable economic cycle as a result of world peace considerably higher than the economic usefulness of possible arms contracts which are always only isolated and irregular. For that reason I am of the opinion as a businessman that international disarmament must be a general goal.[66]

Of course the other powers did not accept disarmament. As a result Krupp co-operated in achieving military parity, providing the armed forces with a valuable range of advanced weapons and materials. But throughout the 1930s Krupp remained committed to maintaining a mixed range of products. In 1939 the proportion of Krupp capacity devoted to military equipment was no greater than the proportion in the economy as a whole.[67]

Another problem area was trade. Krupp was not an autarkist. He believed that the prosperity of German industry lay in expanding world trade and opening up areas of international co-operation. This made economic sense for a business with such a wide range of business activities. The New Plan was not a solution, argued Krupp in January 1935, but a necessary 'transitional stage' until the point where international recognition of the vital role Germany represented in the world economy would bring 'the return of normal trading conditions'.[68] In May 1935 he publicly attacked the idea that the new Germany should become 'an isolated or autarkist state', cutting economic ties abroad. He called instead for a 'lively, active *trade*, if only in order to be able to acquire the raw

---

[64] Military sales totalled RM 7.07m. in 1932/3, but were RM 20.9m. the following year and climbed to RM 57.4m. in 1936/7. K-A(L), 'Krupp Docs.', second affidavit of Dr Georg Wolff, 15 Oct. 1945.

[65] L. Lochner, *Tycoons and Tyrants: German History from Hitler to Adenauer* (Chicago, 1954), 207.

[66] K-A(L), Privatkorrespondenz, Krupp to Forstmann, 6.

[67] *c.*25%.

[68] K-A(L), Reden ab 7 July 1933, Abschrift, 26 Jan. 1935, 'Krupptag', 2.

materials which Germany does not possess'.[69] Krupp was in the forefront
of firms anxious to extend German trade in weapons, finished products
and large-scale capital goods in the Far East, Middle East (Krupp won the
Turkish order to build the guns to command the Straits), and in Latin
America.[70] In 1939, after the signing of the Nazi–Soviet pact, Krupp
officials made immediate plans to provide a wide range of goods for the
Russian trade which promised 'sales not only measured in millions, but in
billions'.[71] By the late 1930s Krupp's economic strategy was for a mixed
range of production, expanding foreign trade, and international market
co-operation. Like today's weapons makers, Krupp hoped to have the best
of both worlds: a strong, rearmed state providing regular orders and
money for advanced weaponry and weapons research at home (without
actually waging war), and a lively trade abroad among developing and
primary economies keen to build up their own military forces.

The result of this expansion of domestic and foreign demand was a high
rate of growth in the first four years of the recovery, across a whole range
of different products. Employment expanded 250 per cent between 1933
and 1939. The statistics of this growth are set out in Table 4.3. The
government helped with special financial arrangements and interest-free
loans. In 1938/9 Krupp embarked on a large investment programme again,
since the new capacity added in the 1920s was now fully utilized.
But the expansion came at a price. During the six-year period state
intervention in the economy increased continually. Krupp, like the rest of
traditional heavy industry, was not a major beneficiary of the expanded
production programmes of the Four Year Plan. Krupp's managers were
unenthusiastic about the Reichswerke project in 1937. Krupp's armaments
production was almost entirely out of the hands of the firm, controlled
by the military bureaucracy. The vision Krupp had had in 1933 of a
state genuinely committed to the independence of the economic sphere
and the right of the entrepreneur to determine his own conditions of
existence disappeared. What Krupp's attitude was to the growth of
state intervention and the rise of the Göring-apparatus awaits further
research.

By 1937–8 the recovery period was over. Profit and output growth
slowed down. Gustav Krupp, in his late sixties, was aware that the
business needed more forceful management than he could provide. In 1937
he recruited Ewald Löser, Mayor of Leipzig under Carl Goerdeler (who

---

[69] Ibid., Rede für Jubilarfeier, Grusonwerk, Magdeburg, 30 May 1935, 12–13.

[70] The London files have detailed records of Krupp's foreign trade and foreign intelligence
activity in Brazil, Argentina, Bolivia, Ecuador, Colombia, Mexico, Iraq, Egypt, Turkey, Iran,
Portugal, Spain, Greece, Hungary, Romania, the USSR, and Bulgaria.

[71] K-A(L), Task Force 1, 'Subsequent Proceedings', file of original Krupp documents:
Sitzung des engeren Beirats, 29 Sept. 1939, betr. Russland.

TABLE 4.3. *Fr. Krupp AG production, employment, sales, and profits, 1933/4–1940/1*

	1933/4	1934/5	1935/6	1936/7	1937/8	1938/9	1939/40	1940/1
Employment[a]	43,254	60,804	75,954	82,059	90,164	101,113	112,852	121,235
Output ('000 tonnes)								
Coal	6,015	6,852	7,058	7,546	7,635	7,592	8,163	8,278
Coke	1,632	2,020	2,159	2,377	2,559	2,594	2,751	2,697
Iron ore	479	721	920	1,113	1,366	1,455	1,598	1,558
Steel	1,318	1,579	1,833	1,833	2,036	2,104	1,864	1,517
Iron	1,195	1,388	1,616	1,788	1,982	1,965	1,617	1,791
Forgings (tonnes)	48,936	72,908	87,360	98,096	115,247	117,433	105,488	116,832
Castings (tonnes)	60,676	83,519	98,865	98,074	108,320	118,730	104,470	104,832
Sales (RM '000)								
Military output	20,979	39,595	52,809	57,408	52,623	84,598	117,320	152,047
Net declared profits (RM '000)[b]	6,650	11,430	16,680	17,650	21,112	23,830	12,780	12,849

[a] Figure for 1 Oct. The Krupp business year went from 1 Oct. to 30 Sept.
[b] The figures are for Fr. Krupp AG and the major subsidiaries. These are net figures after deduction of taxes, reserves, and social expenditure.

Sources: K-A(L), Jahresberichte und Bilanzen, 1934/5–1940/1; Fr. Krupp AG, Jahreserzeugung 1913–1943, vol. i.

recommended him to Krupp), to revive business expansion.[72] There was little that Löser could do about the political shift away from heavy industry in favour of the industries of the Four Year Plan, or the restrictions on trade expansion and arms exports which the increased rearmament programmes provoked. Though Krupp's weapons output continued to grow during the war, much of the new capacity in iron and steel, shipping, and vehicles was built up elsewhere, much of it under direct state control. Like the other Ruhr firms, Krupp's steel and coal production declined during the war. Nor did Krupp make substantial gains after 1938 outside Germany. Krupp acquired the Berndorfer works in Austria after the *Anschluss*, on the grounds that it was a historic branch of the Krupp concern, but otherwise made relatively modest gains in the New Order. The expansion of participations occurred within Germany rather than abroad. The Skoda Works, in which Krupp expressed an interest, came under Reichswerke ownership. Polish, Russian, French, and Dutch firms were operated on trusteeship during the war, but were not directly owned. The one major new project was the Berthawerke constructed near Breslau by Jewish and forced labour during 1942–3.[73]

Throughout the period after 1936 Krupp appears to have had very little influence on state economic policy. There is much to support von Wilmowsky's later assertion that Krupp was by 1939 nothing more than an executive arm of the state economic apparatus.[74] Nor is there any evidence to suggest that Gustav Krupp, or the firm, had any influence on the course of foreign policy and war planning before 1939, or during the war. Krupp's nationalism and Pan-Germanism embraced revisionism and economic influence in central Europe, both of which had largely been achieved by Hitler without war by 1939. But like so many German conservatives, Krupp was not in favour of jeopardizing this position by provoking a general war. In August 1939 he sent letters to friends in Britain and the United States urging them to work for peace. After the defeat of Poland he echoed the widespread sentiment that a lasting peace could now be achieved in Europe.[75] The failure to achieve this peace, and

[72] Manchester, *Arms*, 440–1. On the slow-down in growth see R. J. Overy, 'Heavy Industry in the Third Reich: The Reichswerke Crisis', *European History Quarterly*, 15 (1985). On the transition from family to managerial concerns see the discussion in V. Berghahn, *The Americanisation of West German Industry* (Leamington Spa, 1986), esp. 13–25.

[73] For a general discussion see R. J. Overy, 'German Multi-Nationals and the Nazi State in Occupied Europe', in A. Teichova and M. Levy-Leboyer (eds.), *Multi-Nationals in Historical Perspective* (Cambridge, 1986); Gillingham, *Industry and Politics*, ch. 7. On the Berthawerke see K-A(L), Fried. Krupp Berthawerke AG, Breslau, monthly reports.

[74] T. von Wilmowsky, *Warum wurde Krupp verurteilt?* (Stuttgart, 1950), 29; also von Klass, *Krupps*, 383–4.

[75] G. Young, *The Rise and Fall of Alfried Krupp* (London, 1960), 49–50; K-A(L), Privatakten, Reden 1 July 1937–12 Sept. 1941, Draft of a speech, 4 Oct. 1939. Krupp hoped the powers would try 'to secure for coming generations a peace based on justice'.

his conviction that neither Hitler nor the German population had wanted a general war in September 1939, inclined him once again to blame the western Allies for launching war against Germany as the Entente had done twenty-five years before.[76] The lack of preparation for general war at Essen was shown by the hasty conferences convened in September to discuss the problem of conversion and mobilization.

For the first two years of war Krupp converted rapidly to war work, within a framework dictated by the military and economic planners. Not until the Speer era, as for other firms, were Krupp directors integrated more fully into the war economic apparatus. Alfried Krupp, Gustav's eldest son, was recruited to Speer's Armaments Council and to the board of Reichsvereinigung Kohle. For Gustav, however, the major question that dominated his final years was the succession of Alfried as head of the firm. The dynastic question became more pressing as Gustav's health declined, and Löser succeeded in changing the character of the firm, from an old-fashioned family business into a modern managerial corporation. The central problem in the succession was the legal form of the business, a joint-stock company, which in the case of a family succession would require the payment of crippling capital gains tax. This would compromise Gustav's intention of passing the entire business on to the next generation.[77]

He first contacted Schwerin von Krosigk at the Finance Ministry about the problem in 1941. For the next two years Krupp waged a personal campaign to get Hitler to allow him to change the nature of the firm into a 'family corporation' and to waive the tax claims on the succession, estimated at RM 70m.[78] The new form was presented to Hitler as a more authentically national-socialist constitution for a major business, but the real motives of the family were transparent throughout. Gustav reaped the reward of Hitler's attachment to the name Krupp. The 'Lex Krupp' was granted, and the firm passed in its entirety into the hands of Alfried. At the same time Alfried ousted Löser as manager and assumed complete control himself. The following year Löser was arrested and imprisoned as Goerdeler's putative finance minister after the July plot.[79] Gustav's last throw was to ensure that his grandson, Arndt Krupp, would also succeed

[76] K-A(L), Privatakten, Reden 1 July 1937–12 Sept. 1941, Entwurf einer Ansprache zur Ehrung der Jubilare am 9 Mai 1943, 2–3.
[77] K-A(L), Privatakten: Akten betr. Umwandlung der Fried. Krupp AG: letter from Krupp to Lammers, 12 Jan. 1943; Krupp to Bormann, 11 Nov. 1942; 'Kurzer Abrisse über die juristische und organisatorische Entwicklung der Firma Fried. Krupp und Fried. Krupp AG, 12 Jan. 1943'.
[78] Ibid., Dr Hedding (Finance Ministry) to Dr J. Joeden, 24 June 1943.
[79] Ibid., Entwurf eines Gesetzes über Familienunternehmen, 23 Dec. 1942; Abschrift, 'Erlass des Führers über das Familienunternehmen der Firma Fried. Krupp von 12 Nov. 1943'; letter from Gustav Krupp to Hitler, 29 Dec. 1943.

if anything should happen to Alfried.[80] It was a significant and predictable conclusion to the relationship between Krupp and Hitler. The survival of the family firm and its dynastic leadership allowed Krupp, almost alone of the leaders of big business, to express his commitment to the regime and the war effort in terms of direct personal interest. This was both a justification and a self-imposed restriction. Dynastic priorities allowed Gustav Krupp to express compliance in terms which made moral and economic sense to him, while it gave very little room for manœuvre—as the fate of Fritz Thyssen showed. Krupp's scrupulous respect for the demands of the regime stemmed from the knowledge that only his person stood between the party and the end of Krupp rule in Essen.

Does this adequately explain the willingness of Krupp to embrace the slave-labour programme, and to pursue it so ruthlessly? There can be little doubt of the ultimate responsibility of the directors of the Krupp businesses for establishing a system which permitted the exploitation of Jewish, foreign, and POW labour in the most inhumane conditions; all the more so since many of them worked under Krupp supervision, and not the control of the SS. The loss of German manpower and the increased arms programmes made emergency labour recruitment necessary on a very large scale. The influx of new workers placed considerable strain on a firm the size of Krupp in disciplining and organizing the work-force. By September 1944 there were over 73,000 foreign and POW labourers working in Krupp plants, and conditions were particularly poor. Even the armed forces, who had to divert resources to sending the Russians to the west to work, complained of the failure to provide living conditions that would allow the labourers to work productively or even survive.[81]

Part of the explanation for such extreme levels of exploitation may lie in the special nature of the Krupp work-force, with its long-established and exclusive social and cultural identity in the face of large numbers of foreign workers, which the regime taught them to regard as inferior. But a more likely explanation must be the progressive brutalization encouraged by the horrors of the war itself. Essen was a major bombing target from 1941 onwards. As the homes and amenities and lives of Krupp workers were destroyed by bombing, as the conditions of daily life deteriorated continually for native German workers, there came a growing indifference to the fate of the slave workers. The urge to survive was common to both Gustav and his German employees. The deterioration of conditions required stricter policing of the foreign work-force (for example, keeping

---

[80] Ibid., Entwurf eines Briefes an Reichsminister Lammers, 16 May 1944.
[81] K-A(L), 'Krupp Docs.', Georg Wolff affidavit, 15 Oct. 1945, 'Ausländer und Kriegsgefangene des Krupp-Konzerns' for figures on foreign labour. For a general account of Krupp's use of foreign labour see U. Herbert, *Fremdarbeiter: Politik und Praxis des 'Ausländer-Einsatzes' in der Kriegswirtschaft des Dritten Reiches* (Bonn, 1985), 190–220.

them out of air-raid shelters which were for German personnel only), and this in turn encouraged the promotion and recruitment of officials and Krupp policemen willing to pursue more ruthless, even vicious, methods. To these changes the Krupp leadership remained strikingly indifferent. The pressures of war maximized the prospects of producing a private police force bent on vengeance and brutalized by their function, while blunting the humanity of an increasingly demoralized German population, itself the victim of bombing, arbitrary death, and declining living standards. Just as German workers insisted on a strict hierarchy of pay and skills, so they accepted a hierarchy of suffering.

V

Even during the Third Reich Gustav maintained what he had set out to achieve in 1906. He succeeded in keeping the Krupp inheritance intact, guaranteeing the family succession, and avoiding excessive interference from the state. He was a traditional businessman, for whom these things mattered greatly. Though he would have preferred a different system, he did nothing to put the enterprise at risk after 1933. His relationship with the regime was played according to its rules. This was not a surprising outcome. Indeed, there is a sense in which we are asking the wrong questions about German capitalists in the Third Reich. If they disliked the party and its lower-class activists, if they disapproved of the drift of trade policy and of *dirigisme* at home, if they feared for the future of Germany by the late 1930s, is it likely that many of them, particularly those as vulnerable as the ageing Krupp, would seriously challenge the aims of the regime and risk personal economic disaster? For many businessmen retreat into the firm and the defensive walls of the cartel was itself of great political significance, for it concerned the survival of private capitalism itself. This involved an expedient co-operation with the regime, in Ernst Poensgen's words, 'um schlimmeres zu verhüten' (to avoid anything worse).[82] It did not make Gustav Krupp into a National Socialist, any more than it made him a Social Democrat in 1919.

Krupp was a traditional conservative and nationalist, whose outlook was shaped in the age of Bismarck, not Hitler. His political inclinations were reinforced during the 1920s by the effects of social unrest and social-welfare policies, and the impact of Versailles and Allied policy towards Germany. His priorities during that period, and during the recession, were the restoration of a sound private economy and freer world trade, and the restoration of traditional social peace at home. But he did

[82] Lochner, *Tycoons*, 174.

not work actively against the Weimar Republic, preferring to adopt strategies that fitted in with the new conditions. The situation was very much the same after 1933. Although he did not want a Nazi government in January 1933, he found Hitler more prepared to work with a conservative economic agenda than many businessmen had expected. Moreover, the vital role that Krupp played in German rearmament tied the business much more closely to the state than other firms. The 'military-industrial' complex, of which Krupp was a part, freed the firm from excessive intervention by the party, but linked it of necessity to the economic strategies of the regime. Given Gustav Krupp's obsessive preoccupation with the survival of the dynasty, and the rapid recovery of the firm's fortunes for the first time since before 1914, a calculated accommodation with the regime, or rather with Hitler, made obvious economic sense. By the time Hitler went beyond conservative aims, with the Four Year Plan in 1936 and the war with Russia in 1941, Krupp was too enmeshed in the system to withdraw, even had he wanted to. His distorted view of the war, based on memories of 1914, the impact of bombing, and his fear of what the 'American and Bolshevik "machine-men"' would do to Germany if they won the war, encouraged first moral abdication, then complicity in the crimes of the regime.[83]

[83] K-A(L), Reden ab 1 July 1937: Ansprache, 9 May 1943, 12.

5

The Reichswerke 'Hermann Göring': A Study in German Economic Imperialism

THE growth of Göring's 'multi-national' business empire was not in the strict sense a business venture. Though it closely resembled the increasing concentration of private heavy industry in Germany during the 1930s, the resemblance disguised certain basic differences. The expansion of Göring's industrial interests was a function of both the internal Nazi power struggle and the development of the wartime economy of occupied Europe.[1] In the first place Göring's growing role in the economy reflected Hitler's conviction that war preparations could only be guaranteed if controlled by leaders whom he could trust to carry out Nazi programmes. In addition Göring's role was a reflection of the growing struggle between more conservative financial and business circles—represented by Schacht and the less Nazified elements of the Ruhr élite—and the Nazi state whose military and international ambitions demanded a greater control over economic policy and industrial development.[2] This conflict took place against the background of the more parochial struggle between rival Nazi potentates for influence in party and state.

In 1936 Göring's position in the Nazi hierarchy was compromised by the loss of his police powers to Himmler's growing security empire, and his subordination in military affairs to the defence minister, von Blomberg, and the economics minister, Schacht. His appointment in October 1936 as head of the Four Year Plan, and his subsequent acquisition of more

[1] The main source for the material used in the preparation of this chapter was the collection of German documents from the Second World War in the Imperial War Museum, London. The most useful collection was that of *Privatfirmen* papers, in particular the partial collection for the Reichswerke 'Hermann Göring', the Rheinmetall-Borsig papers, and the files of Steyr–Daimler–Puch. I have also used the records of the Speer Ministry (available on microfilm), the German Air Ministry (also on microfilm), and the Nuremberg Trials. The Strategic Bombing Surveys also proved invaluable. I am at present working on a more general study of the Reichswerke both in Germany and occupied Europe. The present chapter represents the fruits of that work in one particular area, the setting up of the Reichswerke concern as it affected central and eastern Europe. I have deliberately not included a discussion of Western Europe and Scandinavia, although any more general study would have to include them both.

[2] A. E. Simpson, *Hjalmar Schacht in Perspective* (The Hague, 1969), 111–25; H. Schacht, *Account Settled* (London, 1949), 98–103; A. S. Milward, 'Fascism and the Economy', in W. Laqueur (ed.), *Fascism: a Reader's Guide* (London, 1976), 432–5.

general powers in economic affairs altered the political balance once again in Göring's favour. By early 1938 both Schacht and von Blomberg had resigned. When war broke out Hitler confirmed Göring in his role of mobilizing economic resources for the war effort, giving him the 'special assignment of adapting the economy to the needs of war'.[3] Armed with these instructions, Göring also took over responsibility for the occupied areas, either looting stocks and equipment for use in the Reich, or exploiting resources and industrial capacity where they stood. The chief instrument for industrial exploitation was the state holding company, the Reichswerke 'Hermann Göring', first set up in the summer of 1937 to exploit Germany's low-grade domestic iron ores. The concern grew rapidly beyond its initial brief, for Göring used it as a vehicle for taking over other industrial assets which the state needed for military preparation, or for setting up new state-owned businesses from scratch. The Reichswerke management was closely connected with the personnel of the Four Year Plan organization, and its economic strategy was directed by Göring and a small circle of advisers. The unwieldy and unrationalized character of the enterprise finally led to its demise in 1942, when it was broken up and important sections brought under the Speer Ministry. This transition was made possible by the growing administrative indolence and political isolation of Göring himself.

Because of the important political considerations in the establishment and expansion of the Reichswerke, an interpretation based simply on business grounds is unsatisfactory. Göring insisted from the start that purely economic considerations were less important than political and military ones. The Reichswerke were not built up for Göring's personal profit, nor did he in any sense own the concern. That is not to say that Göring did not personally gain from the enterprise. In a number of well-documented cases payments were made direct to Göring's account from the profits of the concern.[4] But this was merely a by-product. The Reichswerke were run and organized by state-appointed managers and bureaucrats who worked under the umbrella of the Four Year Plan.[5] A

---

[3] *TWC* xii. 575, Doc. NI-125. For a more general discussion of the Four Year Plan see B. Carroll, *Design for Total War: Arms and Economics in the Third Reich* (The Hague, 1968), 142–50; D. Petzina, *Autarkiepolitik im Dritten Reich* (Stuttgart, 1968); Simpson, *Schacht* 132–59.

[4] *TWC* xiii. Doc. NID-15575, letter from Pleiger to Göring 5 Dec. 1941 and Pleiger to Körner 5 Dec. 1941. In this case a sum of RM 3m. was sent to Göring for his personal use out of the profits of Vítkovice and Poldina hut in Czechoslovakia.

[5] Paul Körner was deputy for Göring in the Four Year Plan and chairman of the Reichswerke until 1943. Wilhelm Keppler was Hitler's personal economic adviser and one of the main business supporters of the party. He was made Reich commissioner in Vienna in 1938. Hans Kehrl was an industrial manager who worked in the Economics Ministry. He was brought into the Four Year Plan to help run the raw material department, rising to high office in the war economic structure under Speer as head of the *Planungsamt*. Paul Pleiger,

second point to bear in mind is that the expansion of the concern was not a purely wartime phenomenon, governed only by short-term military necessity. Far from it, for the decision to try to involve Austrian firms, for example, predated the *Anschluss*, and the Reichswerke had already begun to acquire interests in central Europe before the Munich crisis, as part of a growing trade and investment offensive in central and eastern Europe. War accelerated the programme of expansion and acquisition, but the long-term strategy of concern-building predated the war, and was planned to continue after it was over. Göring's industrial empire represented, in this sense, one of the major steps towards restricting private industrial capitalism and substituting a 'völkisch', state-run industrial economy.[6]

It is not the purpose of this chapter to discuss at any length the details surrounding the founding and early growth of the Reichswerke (see Chapter 3 above). By mid-1938 the company had a share capital of RM 400m. and had either acquired or set up a number of related businesses in the Salzgitter–Watenstedt area near Brunswick with long-term plans for the development of low-grade iron ores and iron and steel production.[7]

The progressive realization of Hitler's foreign-policy aims from March 1938 onwards gave Göring considerable opportunities to extend the scope of the Reichswerke. For most of the period up to the invasion of the Soviet Union Göring was given the role of incorporating the economic resources of the captured territories. Though there was strong competition from other Nazi politicians, Göring obtained from Hitler the authority for economic questions in the German 'New Order'. For the invasion of the Soviet Union he obtained further powers directly from Hitler in the face of fierce jurisdictional conflicts over responsibility for policy in the east.[8] In all this Göring had the advantage of being both head of an industrial concern and a senior political and military figure. He could argue from a position of strength, both with his colleagues and with foreign businessmen and officials.

---

son of a miner, became a small Ruhr industrialist and an economic adviser to the Nazis after 1933. He was head of the original Salzgitter works and became chairman of the Reichswerke in 1943. Wilhelm Voss, who helped run the state auditing company Deutsche Revision und Treuhand AG, became a leading figure on the commercial and legal side of the Reichswerke, eventually running the main weapons sector of the concern after 1941.

[6] R. Brady, *Business as a System of Power* (New York, 1943) 3, 49–50, who described the Reichswerke as 'a privatized regrouping of industrial properties previously owned by the Reich'; F. Neumann, *Behemoth: The Structure and Practice of National Socialism, 1933–1939* (London, 1942), 299; Petzina, *Autarkiepolitik*, 105–6. For a contemporary view see E. Schrewe, 'Die Entwicklung der Betriebsgrössen in der gewerblichen Wirtschaft', *Zeitschrift für die gesamte Staatswissenschaft*, 102 (1942).

[7] M. Riedel, *Eisen und Kohle für das Dritte Reich* (Göttingen, 1973), 155–232.

[8] *Nazi Conspiracy and Aggression* (hereafter cited as *NCA*), 8 vols. (Washington, DC, 1946), vii. 543–7, Doc. EC-485 'Conference under the Chairmanship of the Reichsmarshal on October 1 1940 about the economic exploitation of the occupied territories'.

The development of the Reichswerke followed a number of different lines. In conquered areas businesses were either directly confiscated or direct and indirect pressure brought to bear on shareholders to sell to the Reichswerke on favourable terms. The direct seizure of firms was legally justified under the Aryanization legislation, or in cases where firms were owned or part-owned by the defeated state.[9] Industrial spoils in Poland or the Soviet Union were regarded on these grounds as the legitimate fruits of conquest, to be disposed of by the victor as he saw fit. In one curious case—the confiscation of the industrial holdings of Fritz Thyssen following his flight from Germany in 1939—the state used the law of 1934 which gave it the power to expropriate the property of communists.

The practice of 'forced sales' was used typically in the case of private ownership. Sometimes this took the form of direct terror. Count Louis Rothschild was imprisoned after the *Anschluss* and freed only in return for his substantial industrial holdings. Even major German trusts could be compelled to sell. Political pressure was brought to bear on the Vereinigte Stahlwerke for the sale of shares in the Österreichisch-Alpine Montangesellschaft in Austria. Similar pressure was exerted in Czechoslovakia for the sale of shares in the Škodovy závody (Skoda Works) and the Československá zbrojovka akc. spol. (Czech Armaments Works) at Brno, all of which were bought on the open market though at a very favourable price. Thenceforth they were known respectively as Skoda-Werke and Brünner Waffenwerke. A number of devices were used to buy shares at well below their market value, allowing a greater expansion of German financial participation than would have been possible in peacetime.[10] In addition to the exercise of *force majeure* there was expansion generated from within either through the creation of new capital or by the founding of new firms. In such situations it was possible to expand the share capital of foreign firms through Reich loans, and thus turn a minority into a majority holding.

It is important to emphasize here the crucial role played in the course of expansion by the German banks. The Dresdner Bank in particular was largely responsible for actually acquiring or holding shares which were then transferred to the Reichswerke, the government paying a commission to the bank for its agency work. Karl Rasche of the Dresdner Bank, a committed Nazi, was the official responsible for carrying on negotiations

[9] *TWC* xiii. 670, Doc. NID-134636, 'Arisierungsbericht', Böhmische Escompte Bank, 6 Aug. 1941.
[10] A good example was the purchase of Werk Radom in Poland whose book value in 1940 had been zl. 33m. By fixing an arbitrary exchange rate, calculating notional sums for depreciation and by subtracting the assets seized as booty at the time of the invasion, the final agreed purchase price was only RM 7m. instead of the RM 16m. it would have been in 1939. See Speer Collection, FD 787/46, 'Werke in Warschau und Radom', 13 Aug. 1943.

between other banks and businesses with Paul Körner, nominal head of the Reichswerke.[11] In a few cases the banks became shareholders themselves. Göring's political position also gave him access to other banks. The Bank der deutschen Luftfahrt was set up to organize finance for aircraft firms and contractors and through this agency Göring was able to acquire influence in enterprises in which the bank had invested. In fact when the armaments sector of the Reichswerke was taken from his direct control in 1942 the air bank continued to provide some of the finance and a direct line back to Göring.[12] His position as prime minister of Prussia also gave him advantages in using the holdings of the Preussische Staatsbank. In this way he was able to acquire an interest in the Société des Mines de Bor owned by the Banque Mirabeau, which the Prussian bank took over, as well as in other Prussian state holdings.[13]

The chronology of Reichswerke growth more or less followed the course of territorial and military expansion. Göring had expressed a personal interest in gaining control over Austrian iron resources in 1937.[14] A few days after the *Anschluss* both Göring and Pleiger began to plan the exploitation of Austrian ores and the possibility of acquiring an interest in the Österreichisch-Alpine Montangesellschaft. The majority holding was in the hands of the Vereinigte Stahlwerke (VS) and to all intents and purposes apparently safeguarded for the Reich. Nevertheless the Reichswerke took over a 13 per cent stake in Alpine-Montangesellschaft through the purchase of shares held by the Industrie-Kredit Bank in Vienna and continued a campaign for the following six months to compel VS to hand over control to the Reichswerke.[15] One reason for the campaign was the need to guarantee ore supplies for the first of the large subsidiaries founded at Linz, the Reichswerke AG für Erzbergbau- und Eisenhütten 'Hermann Göring', Linz. Its foundation in Linz was not coincidental. For Hitler the area had a special significance. Göring promised to make this company the greatest industrial concern in the world as a compliment to the Führer. There was also the more practical problem that VS control of the Erzberg would not necessarily guarantee a large enough flow of ore for

[11] *TWC* xiii. 666–7, Doc. NID-13927; letter from Kehrl to Rasche, 18 Apr. 1940, 'concerning repayment to the Dresdner Bank of the purchase price of Czech industrial shares'; letter from Reichswerke to Kehrl giving details of a comission of RM 200,000 paid to the Dresdner Bank for agency work. K. Lachmann 'The Hermann Göring Works', *Social Research*, 8 (1941), 33.

[12] IWM Speer Collection, FD 787/46, Steyr–Daimler–Puch records, description of firm, 15 Sept. 1943.

[13] Royal Institute of International Affairs, *Hitler's Europe* (Oxford, 1954), 206.

[14] *TWC* xii. 468–9, Doc. NI-09, Minutes of a discussion of the work group on iron and steel production, 17 Mar. 1937. Göring was reported as saying: 'it is important that the soil of Austria is reckoned as a part of Germany in case of war. Such deposits as can be acquired in Austria must be attended to in order to increase our supply capacity.'

[15] Riedel, *Eisen und Kohle*, 234–42.

war purposes. Instead the ore might be used for private Ruhr firms anxious to expand exports, policies over which conflict had already arisen between the Ruhr leaders and the Nazis.[16] Reichswerke control of the Erzberg and the Linz complex would ensure that political and ideological considerations would be a governing factor. In March 1939 VS gave up the fight and over 70 per cent of the control in the Alpine company passed to the Reichswerke. VS personnel left the board of directors of both their old business and the new foundation at Linz and in June 1939 the name of the company was changed to Alpine Montan AG 'Hermann Göring', Linz.[17] By this time the Reichswerke had penetrated into the rest of the Austrian iron and steel industry and into manufacturing in order to exploit its locational advantages, and to spread the geographical area of war production.

Most of the additional Austrian firms were acquired through the Reich holding company Vereinigte Industrie-Unternehmungen Aktiengesellschaft (VIAG), which had acquired the shares in turn from the Österreichische Creditanstalt–Wiener Bankverein when Austrian financial institutions were absorbed into the Reich. The shareholdings passed on to the Reichswerke were in many cases only minority holdings. Nevertheless through manipulation it proved possible either to acquire more shares or to effect virtual control through political influence. In armaments and engineering the Reichswerke acquired control over the Maschinen- und Waggonbau-Fabriks AG, the Grazer Maschinen- und Waggonbau AG, Paukerwerke AG and the large vehicle and armaments producer Steyr–Daimler–Puch AG.[18] In the case of Steyr–Daimler–Puch there was clear ownership by the middle of the war, but ownership and control were not necessarily interdependent. With this concern it seems likely that its share capital was raised by the Reichswerke to cope with war orders. Since the additional share capital was provided by the Reichswerke, control gradually developed into ownership as well, a device commonly used elsewhere. Through the same VIAG source the Göring concern was able to acquire large holdings in the rest of the Austrian iron, steel, and mining industry. The Steirische Gusstahlwerke AG was taken over completely and large minority holdings acquired in the Feinstahlwerke Traisen AG. A number of small coal workings were also taken over.[19] In addition to this some completely new firms were founded: the Eisenwerke Oberdonau AG for arms production, set up jointly with the high command of the army and the Wohnungsbau AG der Reichswerke 'Hermann Göring', Linz, which,

---

[16] W. Carr, *Arms, Autarky and Aggression* (London, 1972), 62–3.
[17] Riedel, *Eisen und Kohle*, 242–3; *DDV* 13 (1938/9), 1091–2.
[18] Lachmann, 'Göring Works', 30–1.
[19] IWM Speer Collection, FD 264/46, 594–7, 'Konzern Verzeichnis HGW Montanblock' (hereafter cited as 'Konzern Verzeichnis'); Riedel, *Eisen und Kohle*, 241.

together with the takeover of the construction firm Bau AG 'Negrelli', gave the works a stake in the Austrian building trade.[20] The process of vertical integration was completed with the take-over of the shipping company Erste Donau Dampfschiffahrtsgesellschaft from the Alpine-Montan company and the setting up jointly with the Bayerische Lloyd of a new river-shipping company, the Süddeutsche Donaudampfschiffahrts GmbH.[21] Within the space of a few months the Reichswerke had changed from being one of the smaller German iron and steel corporations, to becoming a large concern controlling much of Austrian heavy industry from raw-material production through armaments manufacture to sales and distribution. Moreover, the close interlocking of the industrial and commercial structure of central Europe, and in particular Austrian links with the old Habsburg areas, gave the Reichswerke claims on a large outer circle of smaller firms in which the larger acquisitions had had a stake. By 1944 the Reichswerke coal, iron, and steel bloc alone had a controlling interest in thirty-three firms with a total share capital of RM 226.1m.[22]

The successful penetration of the Austrian economy prepared the way for the expansion into the rest of central Europe and even gave the Reichswerke ownership of companies in Latin America and South Africa.[23] Even before the occupation of Sudetenland and rump Czechoslovakia, the growing German control in Austria led automatically to an increased claim in other economies, in particular the Czechoslovak holdings of the major Jewish families in Vienna which fell to the Reichswerke in the course of 1938 and 1939.

The pre-war acquisitions made certain changes inevitable in terms of the structure of the enterprise. The good iron ores of Austria and the hard coal and lignite deposits from both Austria and Czechoslovakia made the original Salzgitter project to a certain extent redundant. In order to safeguard internal economic resources for long-term Nazi plans, central Europe provided a much more secure base for autarky. The building up of metalworking capacity, particularly the production of armaments, had not been the initial intention. Such a move had the advantage that it gave guaranteed markets for the industrial raw materials produced by the concern, especially for overpriced Salzgitter/Watenstedt iron and steel, and

---

[20] Eisenwerke Oberdonau was set up jointly with OKH to undertake army production. See IWM, Speer Collection, Reel 63, FD 3742/45, File 1, letter from OKH to Eisenwerke Oberdonau GmbH 'betr. Finanzierung des weiteren Ausbaues der Eisenwerke Oberdonau', 1 Apr. 1944. The firm was under the full management of the Reichswerke.

[21] *DDV* 13 (1938/9), 405; Lachmann, 'Göring Works', 31.

[22] 'Konzern Verzeichnis', 594–7.

[23] Acquisition of Steirische Gusstahlwerke gave ownership of three marketing companies in Brazil, Argentina, and Uruguay and of Steel and Machinery Supplies (Pty.) Ltd., Johannesburg, with a capital of £1,000.

gave Hitler and Göring the opportunity to produce a large Nazi-controlled armaments sector, free from interference from the Ruhr and open to manipulation directly in the interests of the developing imperialism. Acquisition by the Göring concern made possible a speedier integration into the war economy and cut through all the delaying negotiations and business arrangements that might have resulted from the more haphazard intervention of private concerns. Certainly the advantages to be won from the Czechoslovak economy were exploited rapidly and systematically, though not always efficiently, by the Reichswerke through control of all the main sectors of Czechoslovak heavy industry.

The Sudetenland provided Göring with the first real opportunity for acquiring large deposits of coal, though in this case it was lignite rather than hard coal. More than half the lignite mines of the area were consolidated into a single company under the combined control of VIAG and the Reichswerke called the Sudetenländische Bergbau AG, Brüx. Some mines were seized as Czech state holdings. Others were the proceeds of the 'Aryanization' of the holdings of the Petschek concern in Prague, of Ignac Petschek of Ústí n.L. and Weinmann of Ústí n.L.[24] As the capital of the lignite concern expanded from an initial RM 50m. to RM 140m. the share of the Reichswerke rose to 78 per cent.[25] On the basis of the lignite, and in support of the Four Year Plan programme for synthetic oil production, the largest planned synthetic oil plant was also set up at Brüx. Originally established under the Four Year Plan and run by the trustee company Mineralölbau GmbH, it was converted by Göring into a massive oil plant under the direct control of the Reichswerke as trustee for the Reich. In October 1939 the Sudetenländische Treibstoffwerke AG was established as a major subsidiary with RM 250m. capital.[26] Again the availability of the raw material and the advantage of distance from Allied bombers probably played a part in the decision. IG Farben was, perhaps rather surprisingly, not given control over the plant, a fact that caused IG Farben directors some concern over whether the Reichswerke was intending to expand into chemical production too.[27] It did mean, however, that Göring's direct control over resources in the captured Czech lands was all-embracing.

Czech heavy industry was concentrated around the big armament firms of Skoda and the Czech Armaments Works, Brno, and the iron and steel

---

[24] USSBS Special Paper 3, *The Effects of Strategic Bombing upon the Operations of the Hermann Göring Works during World War II* (Washington, DC, 1946/7), 42; *Conditions in Occupied Territories*, v. *The Penetration of German Capital into Europe* (HMSO, 1942), 10–11.

[25] Lachmann, 'Göring Works', 32; 'Konzern Verzeichnis', 596.

[26] W. Birkenfeld, *Der synthetische Treibstoff 1933–1945* (Göttingen, 1963), 135–7.

[27] NA Microcopy T83 Roll 74, frames 3445163–4, IG Farben volkswirtschaftliche Abteilung, 'Konzernaufbau und Entwicklung der Reichswerke AG für Erzbergbau and Eisenhütten "Hermann Göring"', 19 Oct. 1939'.

complexes of Poldina huť, Vítkovicke horní a hutní těžířstvo (Vítkovice Mining and Foundry Works), Báňská a hutní společnost (Mining and Metallurgic Company), and Pražská železářská společnost (Prague Iron Company). (Firms were registered under English as well as Czech names, for British shareholders.) In the case of the last of these, control was already exercised before 1939 by the German iron and steel company Mannesmann.[28] In the case of all the remainder the Reichswerke became the predominant influence between 1939 and 1940. Initially the German government maintained the existing Czech industrial and banking structure and concentrated on giving large arms orders, particularly for aircraft and aircraft components, to tie Czech firms more closely to the Reich.[29] This was, to a certain extent, the result of the fact that much foreign capital was still involved in Czech industry—British capital at Vítkovice, French capital in the Mining and Metallurgic Company—and until war was declared the German government could only rely on negotiation to achieve control.[30] It was also the case that many Czech firms willingly transferred to working with their new German masters in order to secure their survival and protect shareholder interests. In some cases a German controlling interest simply replaced, or was superimposed upon, a French or British interest.[31] (The Vítkovice Works were known in German as Witkowitzer Bergban und Eisenhütten Gewerkschaft, the Mining and Metallurgic Company as Berg- und Hüttenwerkgesellschaft.)

Much of the capital of the large concerns lay, however, either with the Czech state or with the major Czech banks. It was the acquisition of these state shares, coupled with the eventual Germanization of the banking system, that supplied the Göring concern with its Czech shareholdings. Through the offices of Hans Kehrl of the Four Year Plan organization and Karl Rasche of the Dresdner Bank, acting on the direct orders of Göring, the Česká eskomptní banka úvěrní ústav (Bohemian Discount Bank and Society of Credit) and the Česká banka Union (Bohemian Union Bank) bought substantial holdings in the following companies:

	% of base capital
První brněnská strojírenská společnost (First Brno Engineering Co.)	37.6

---

[28] A. Teichova, *An Economic Background to Munich* (Cambridge, 1974), 123–7.
[29] NA Microcopy T177 Roll 3, frame 3684568, Wirtschaftsinspektion Prag to RLM, 30 Sept. 1939; BA RL 3/3, Folder 1, report from Udet to Göring, 'Problem der Rüstungsindustrie Dez. 1939'.
[30] Teichova, *Economic Background*, 82–3, 118.
[31] NA Microcopy T83 Roll 77, frames 3449351–5, Jahresabschluss der Brünn-Königsfelder Maschinen- und Waggonbau-Fabriks AG für den 31 Dec. 1939 Prüfungsbericht der Treuarbeit; *TWC* xiii. 710, Rasche Defence Exhibit 3.

	% of base capital
Poldina huť	35.0
Czech Armament Works	49.0
Skoda Works	9.0
Mining and Metallurgic Co.	23.0

The German Finance Ministry reported in October 1939 that 'the Reich Ministry of Economics intends soon to apply for approval ... in order that the Hermann Göring Works (holding) should take over these investments'.[32] By December the Dresdner Bank was in a position to offer the Göring concern 130,528 shares in the Czech Armaments Works and 62,426 Skoda shares where only 12,960 had been available in June; very probably 62,000 shares of those now available had been taken up by the Czech state in 1937.[33] The advantage of acquiring a large share in the capital of the Czech Armament Works was the fact that this enterprise in turn controlled the largest single block of Skoda shares. After acquiring other Czech firms the Reichswerke actively owned 64 per cent of the Armament Works shares and controlled in a syndicate the remaining 36 per cent, thus automatically acquiring an additional 30.5 per cent of the Skoda shares. By acquiring the shares of Omnipol, a Skoda subsidiary, this participation was raised to 54.5 per cent. Through influence in the banking system actual control was exercised over 63.6 per cent of all Skoda shares by October 1940 (see Table 5.1).[34] By the same date the Reichswerke had also acquired a 49.9 per cent holding in the First Brno Engineering Co.[35] Once the position had been clarified German managers were installed under the general direction of Wilhelm Voss and Göring's brother, Albert.[36] Until the reform of the Reichswerke structure in 1942–3 control was exercised over product policy, commercial, and financial affairs, in much the same way as it had been exercised by the French firm Schneider–Creusot before 1938.[37]

Penetration of the Czech iron, steel, and mining sector was as thorough as that in armaments. The Reichswerke acquired only a minority holding

[32] *TWC* xiii. 657, Doc. NID-939, letter from Böhmische Escompte Bank to Kehrl, 12 June 1939; 667, Doc. NID-13927, letter from Reichswerke to Kehrl, 26 Mar. 1940; 668, letter from Reichswerke to Kehrl (n.d.).

[33] *TWC* xiii. 668.

[34] NA Microcopy T83 Roll 77, frame 3449313, 'Verteilung des Aktienbesitzes von Skodawerke und Brünner Waffenwerke, 6 Nov. 1940'; frames 3449318–20, 'Abschrift betr. Beteiligung des Reichs an der Aktiengesellschaft vormals Skodawerke in Pilsen', Oct. 1940.

[35] NA Microcopy T83 Roll 77, frame 3449356, report from Reichsfinanzministerium 'betr. Erste Brünner Maschinen-Fabriks-Ges.', 10 Sept. 1940.

[36] K. Lachmann, 'More on the Hermann Göring Works', *Social Research*, 9 (1942), 397; *Conditions in Occupied Territories*, 11.

[37] Teichova, *Economic Background*, 193–245 for details on Skoda Works before 1939.

TABLE 5.1. *Reichswerke shareholding in Skoda Works and Czech Armaments Works, October 1940*

Skoda Works (687,500 shares)		Czech Armaments Works (300,000 shares)	
A. Reichswerke (direct holding)	59,448	A. Reichswerke (direct holding)	130,528
B. *Controlled by Reichswerke through syndicate*		B. *Controlled by Reichswerke through syndicate*	
Československá zbrojovka	210,000	Skoda Works	61,312
Omnipol	105,000	Česká eskomptní banka a	
Česká eskomptní banka a úvěrní		úvěrní ústav	15,600
ústav	20,850	Anglo-československá banka	15,000
Anglo-československá banka	20,000	Agrární banka	8,229
Živnostenská banka	18,000	Ferdinandova severní dráha	22,223
Agrární banka	4,150	Explosia a.s. pro prumysl	
TOTAL:	437,448	výbušnin	17,375
		Kooperativa	10,973
		Živnostenská banka	15,600
		TOTAL:	296,840

in the Mining and Metallurgic Co. Sufficient shares were bought up in the Poldina huť to give the Reichswerke a 56 per cent stake and to bring it into the Göring fold.[38] The largest complex was the Vítkovice Works, owned mainly by the Rothschilds of Vienna and London. It was to this complex that German leaders paid particular attention when planning the exploitation of the Czech lands.

During the mid-1930s the Rothschilds, in order to improve the competitive situation against Germany, acquired the minority holdings in Vítkovice and then transferred control over the whole business to the Rothschild London-based company, Alliance Assurance. Even though Louis Rothschild was forced to pay for his life with all the remaining Rothschild assets in Austria and Czechoslovakia, the Vítkovice Works was now a British company and could not be expropriated.[39] The works were, nevertheless, occupied at once when rump Czechoslovakia was seized, and handed over for administration to the Reichswerke, which continued to exercise control until the end of the war. Negotiations continued during 1939 with the Rothschilds in Paris for the sale of the company which, through conquest, was already compelled to work for the German war economy. Agreement was finally reached in July 1939 for the purchase of the works for the sum of £2.9m. but the transaction was postponed by the war.[40]

[38] 'Konzern Verzeichnis', 596; TWC xiii. 662–4 Doc. NID-15640 (see n. 32 above).
[39] F. Morton, *The Rothschilds*, (London, 1962), 224–6; Teichova, *Economic Background*, 82–3.
[40] Teichova, *Economic Background*, 91–2. A full managing contract was finally drawn up between Vítkovice and the Reichswerke in Dec. 1942. See TWC, Transcripts Case XI, vol. 231, 14883.

The Czech iron and steel industry complemented the armaments sector. Poldina huť and Vítkovice both provided high-grade steels for army production and continued to supply them for tank production at both Skoda and Linz throughout the war. Vítkovice also had contacts in Slovakia, an area which Göring hoped would be a potential territory for armaments expansion within the structure of the Four Year Plan. Although not much came of the scheme, except for an agreement on aircraft production, what industry there was in Slovakia was attached to the Reichswerke through its controlling interests elsewhere.[41] The take-over of the coal and rail company Ferdinands Nordbahn through the Dresdner Bank, together with some smaller coal-mines, completed the integration of holdings in Czechoslovakia.[42] Figure 5.1 shows the extent of such penetration by 1940–1. In Czechoslovakia the Reichswerke controlled approximately 50–60 per cent of Czech heavy industry by value; in Austria slightly less.[43]

Just as the earlier Austrian invasion opened up the way to penetrate into Czechoslovakia, so the occupation of that country opened the way for expansion into the rest of central Europe, particularly into Poland, Hungary, and Romania. In all these areas actual ownership of assets by the Reichswerke was much smaller, though its influence was considerable. In the case of Poland this was partly due to the seizure policy that followed the invasion. In the case of Romania influence was exercised through enforced 'co-operation' between the Reichswerke and Romanian heavy industry.

After the outbreak of war Göring turned his attention to the need to secure German dominance in central Europe both to safeguard the German war economy and to avoid the problems, particularly with food supplies, experienced during the First World War. A directive issued by Göring in August 1940 made it clear that he wanted personal control over the extension of German firms into the industry of central Europe to the advantage of the Reichswerke.[44] This authority gave him some guarantee

---

[41] BA RL 3/243, report from RLM agent at Firma Letov 17 Aug. 1942 concerning discussions with the Slovakian Luftwaffe; *Conditions in Occupied Territories*, 12. In Slovakia Vítkovice controlled the 'Ruda' Bergbau- und Hüttenbetriebe AG, Bratislava and the Krompacher Kupferwerke AG.

[42] USSBS Special Paper 3, 42; 'Konzern Verzeichnis', 596.

[43] These figures can only be approximations. In Czechoslovakia the Göring Werke clearly had an interest in the mining and metallurgy sector of approximately 60–70% of its total value. In metalworking the proportion was probably closer to 40%. The estimates are based on figures in Teichova, *Economic Background*, 87; 'Konzern Verzeichnis', 594–7; and NA Microcopy T83 Roll 74, frames 3445174–7. Because all the details of minority participations are not available such estimates are probably conservative.

[44] *NCA* vii. 310, Doc. collection EC-137, letter from Göring to Wehrwirtschaft- und Rüstungsamt on 'German influence with foreign enterprises', 9 Aug. 1940, in which he wrote that 'One of the goals of the German economic policy is the increase of the German influence with foreign enterprises'.

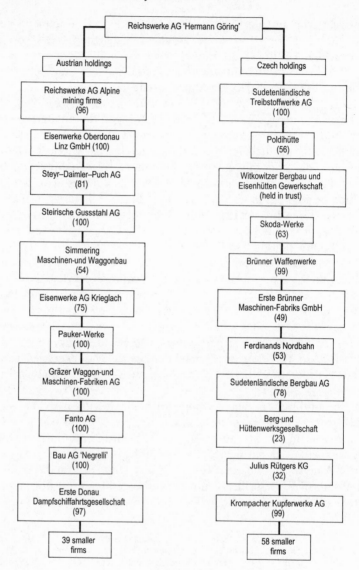

Fig. 1. Reichswerke acquisitions in Austria and Czechoslovakia

of control in a world of competing Nazi empires in which possession was nine-tenths of the law. While a strategy was being prepared for the eventual integration of the Hungarian and Romanian economies into the Nazi European economy, the invasion of Poland returned large areas of pre-1914 German territory back to the Reich. Unlike the case in Austria and Czechoslovakia, Göring was faced with the problem that many of the industrial enterprises seized from Poland had traditional links with private German firms, or had been owned directly by them before 1914. The word commonly used to describe the return of Silesian industry was 'Repatriierung' (repatriation), echoing the view of private heavy industry that its claim to Silesian businesses was legitimate and should be satisfied.[45] Göring's main interest was in hard coal which, despite the acquisitions in other areas, was still in short supply for the Reichswerke concern. Pleiger had already managed an exchange of holdings between the Reichswerke and the Ruhr to secure a larger coal base, but this was clearly not enough for a concern the size of the Göring works, anxious to consolidate its raw material base.[46] In late 1939 Göring demanded that his appointee in Upper Silesia, Max Winkler, arrange the transfer of the coal-mines to the Reichswerke. Many of the mines were owned by the Polish state but were now held in trusteeship by the Haupttreuhandstelle Ost (HTO) for the Reich under the watchful eye of the army. It was agreed that the Reich should, in effect, pay itself for the mines to make the transaction appear 'legal', and a transfer of RM 200m. was effected from the Bergwerkeverwaltung Oberschlesien GmbH der Reichswerke 'Hermann Göring', to whom the money was loaned, to the HTO and thence back to the Reich. As with many other businesses the Reichswerke held the mines on trust for the *Volk*.[47] Through this device it succeeded in gaining control over coal deposits that provided nearly 60 per cent of all the Göring Works' hard coal requirements by 1944 and constituted some 25 per cent of all Silesian production. In addition the Reichswerke had established sizeable participations in a number of allied industries despite the existence of competing claims.[48]

It was only in the iron, steel and armaments sector that there was

[45] D. Eichholtz, *Geschichte der deutschen Kriegswirtschaft, i. 1939–1941* (Berlin, 1969), 185–6 and 294–338 (document collection 'Ruhr–Montankonzerne').

[46] Riedel, *Eisen und Kohle*, 275–6.

[47] TWC xiii. 742–5, Doc. Koerner 177 'Affidavit of Max Winkler, Director of Main Trustee Office East, 7 May 1948'; 749, Doc. NI-598; R. Jeske, 'Zur Annexion der polnischen Wojewodschaft Schlesien durch Hitler-Deutschland im Zweiten Weltkrieg', *Zeitschrift für Geschichtswissenschaft*, 5 (1957), 1073–5, 1087.

[48] USSBS Special Report 3, 42, 73; Riedel, *Eisen und Kohle*, 301–2. The following firms had substantial Reichswerke participation by 1944: Bergbau-Elektrizitäts-AG, Katowitz; Kokerei-Vereinigung GmbH, Katowitz; Oberschlesische Hydrierwerke AG, Blechhammer; Schlesische Elektrizität- und Gas AG, Gleiwitz; Schlesisch-Sandomir' sche Schiffahrts GmbH, Krakow; Sprengstoffwerke Oberschlesien GmbH, Katowitz; Vereinigte Holzindustrie Ost GmbH, Katowitz. (*Source:* 'Konzern Verzeichnis', 595.)

relatively less success. The army entrusted the Reichswerke with operating firms within the General Government that had been owned by Vítkovice and Poldina hut.[49] Most of the large Silesian steelworks were acquired by trustees from Ruhr industry. Other smaller firms were taken over in the Warsaw area, including the Radom and Warsaw factories of the Polish State Armaments Works. Even this take-over had to be ratified by the German Army High Command which was able to exercise much greater control over the Polish economy than it could in areas where Göring dominated the civilian takeover.[50] This position only altered in 1943 with a decision to increase arms production in the General Government, a task with which the Reichswerke was again associated.[51] Interestingly, the experience in Poland prompted Göring to get Hitler to decide beforehand who would have the power in economic affairs in the war with the Soviet Union. Hitler decided in favour of Göring, who was thus able to act as arbiter in distributing economic resources after the invasion, and to attach to the Reichswerke the major portions of the industry of the Ukrainian and Donets Basin industrial region.[52]

Göring's aim in the Soviet Union was to create a monopoly organization of all captured industry, which automatically became the property of the Reich. The Berg- und Hüttenwerkgesellschaft OstmbH (BHO) was set up for this purpose and on 1 September 1941 it took over control, under Pleiger, of the mining installations at Kriwoj-Rog and Nikopol. On 1 March 1942 it took over the coal workings of the Donets basin and the industrial complex at Dniepropetrovsk where, through a programme of heavy investment and the moving of tools, equipment, and engineers from the Reich, a revival of coal, manganese, and steel output was achieved.[53]

---

[49] USSBS Special Report 3, 42–3; Riedel, *Eisen und Kohle*, 300. The firms were Ostrowiecer Hochöfen- und Werke AG, Werk Starachowice (through Vítkovice), and Werk Stalowa Wola (through Poldina Hut).

[50] IWM Speer Collection, FD 787/46, Protokoll über die am 13 Aug. 1943 abgehaltene Sitzung des Aufsichtsrates der Steyr–Daimler–Puch, Beilage 3, 'Werke in Warschau und Radom'.

[51] Speer Collection, Reel 63, FD 3742/45 File 1, Staatssekretär Regierung des Generalgouvernements to Speer, 30 Nov. 1943 'betr. Einsatz polnischer Betriebe in der Rüstungswirtschaft'.

[52] BA/RL3 18, File 1, Kurzbericht 31, 21 Sept. 1941, 1–2; TWC xiii. 847, Doc. EC207 'Decree of the Führer concerning the Economy of the Newly Occupied Eastern Territories of 29 June 1941'.

[53] TWC xiii. 892–5, Doc. NI-5261, letter from Körner enclosing minutes of a meeting on 31 Mar. 1943 of the Verwaltungsrat of BHO; D. Eichholtz *et al.* (eds.), *Anatomie des Krieges* (Berlin, 1969), doc. 176 'Rundschreiben der Wirtschaftsgruppe Eisenschaffende Industrie vom 21 Aug. 1941'. The following firms came under the direct trusteeship of the Reichswerke in 1943: Hütte Kamenskoje group; Hütte Petrowski un Kokschem, Werk Kalinin, in Dnjepropetrowsk; Hütte DSMO in Dnjepropetrowsk; Hütte Komintern I–III in Dnjepropetrowsk-Nishnedneprowsk; Hütte Karl Liebknecht in Dnjepropetrowsk-Nishnedneprowsk; Werke Lenin in Dnjepropetrowsk; Werke Artem in Dnjepropetrowsk-Nishnedneprowsk.

To facilitate the revival of Soviet industry Pleiger and Körner compelled Ruhr firms to take over the running of selected Soviet plants as industrial 'godparents'. It was made clear that this did not imply that the Reich had abandoned its own claims and the Reichswerke distributed the operating franchises under its direct supervision. This was complied with reluctantly by the more radical elements of the party in the east, and only in order to satisfy Hitler's call for expediency in getting experts in the Reich to exploit Soviet and east European industry before it was too late.[54] It is hard to see Göring's ambitions in the Soviet Union as simply expedient. Expansion there was both a natural extension of state industrial penetration elsewhere and also a better guarantee that the party should have a decisive say in the political and economic reconstruction of the area after the war.

By the end of 1941 Göring had achieved his promise to create the largest economic enterprise in Europe. Romania was the only country with significant industrial resources in eastern Europe not drawn into the Reichswerke orbit. The 1939 German–Romanian economic treaty, signed by Göring's representatives, certainly created the framework for co-operation. However, until 1941 the Romanian government was determined to keep as much control over its own industry as it could in order to avoid German penetration, particularly after the outbreak of war, when the Reich regarded Allied oil and industrial holdings in Romania as forfeit enemy property.[55] A way in had been provided, however, through the Reichswerke take-over of Czechoslovak industry. The Czech Armament Works had been a minority shareholder in both the Reşiţa (Uzinele de Fier şi Domeniile din Reşiţa Societate Anonimă) iron and steel complex and the Copşa Mică şi Cugir mines. Although the shares had been deposited with the Westminster Bank in London, which subsequently refused to release them, Göring was able to bring pressure to bear on the Romanian government to produce duplicate shares. These were duly produced in November 1939. The transaction was completed on 24 January 1940 giving the Reichswerke an 8 per cent stake in Reşiţa (soon raised to 13 per cent) and a 19 per cent stake in Copşa Mică. In July 1940 three seats on the board of directors at Reşiţa went to the Reichswerke, while an anti-Semitic campaign forced the resignation of the Jewish general manager, Max Ausschnitt.[56] In January 1940 the Reichswerke

---

[54] A. Dallin, *German Rule in Russia* (London, 1957), 385–8; Eichholtz *et al.*, *Anatomie*, 411–12, Doc. 217 'Grundsätze für die Führung von Patenschaftsbetrieben der BHO vom 3 Nov. 1942'.

[55] E. Campus, 'Die Hitlerfaschistische Infiltration Rumäniens 1939–40', *Zeitschrift für Geschichtswissenschaft*, 5 (1957); N. N. Constantinescu, 'L'Exploitation et le pillage de l'économie roumaine par l'Allemagne hitlérienne dans la période 1939–1944', *Revue roumaine d'histoire*, 3 (1964).

[56] P. Marguerat, *Le IIIe Reich et le pétrole roumain 1938–1940* (Leiden, 1977), 180; Lachmann, 'Göring Works', 34; *Conditions in Occupied Territories*, 29. Two of the directors

turned to the other major industrial complex in Romania, the Malaxa works. A 'Technischer-Hilfsvertrag' (technical assistance agreement) was signed with the company under which arrangement experts were attached to Malaxa to tie it more closely to the German economic strategy in the area.[57] It was not possible to do more until the overthrow of King Carol in 1941 because of Romanian resistance. Göring was able to reach agreement with his successor, Marshal Antonescu, to expand Reichswerke influence in both Reşiţa and Malaxa. In the case of the latter Malaxa himself was put on trial on profiteering charges and the entire complex taken over by the Romanian state, 50 per cent through confiscation, 50 per cent at the price fixed by the government.[58] In March Germany demanded 'the participation of German industries in the management of Romanian heavy industry—considered from the Reich's point of view'.[59] Negotiations continued throughout 1941 and in the autumn a new company was formed called the Rumänisch-Deutsche AG für Eisenindustrie und Handel (Rogifer) in which the capital was divided unequally between the Reichswerke and the Romanian state. The firm operated the Reşiţa and Malaxa works and overall control in technical, financial, and commercial questions passed to the Reichswerke. With this transfer the German company also gained interests in other large firms such as the Astra car and arms works at Braşov.[60] As in Austria, Czechoslovakia, and the USSR the Reichswerke acquired control over almost all the iron and steel output in Romania and maintained this control until it was forced to abandon and destroy the installations by the advance of the Russian armies.

The intervention in Romania also provided Göring with the opportunity to extend his influence over the foreign oil industry. At the end of 1940 Göring appointed an official from the Four Year Plan organization, Dr Neubacher, as 'Plenipotentiary for Natural Oil in the South-East' and set up a holding company, the Kontinentale Öl AG 'to take over companies belonging to enemy and neutral powers in the countries occupied by Germany'. The company was formally constituted on 27 March 1941 with a capital of RM 80m., 30m. provided by the state, which had the sole voting rights in the company.[61] There had already been some penetration

of the company were Albert Göring and Guido Schmidt. The latter had been installed by Göring as general director of the Linz complex in return for his help in the period of the Anschluss.

[57] A. Hillgruber, *Hitler, König Carol and Marschall Antonescu* (Wiesbaden, 1954), 156.

[58] Lachmann, 'More on Göring Works', 396–7; Constantinescu, 'Exploitation', 112.

[59] Constantinescu, 'Exploitation', 110. The demands were made through the Reich envoy, Neubacher.

[60] Ibid. 112; *Conditions in Occupied Territories*, 29. Reichswerke participation was 75th. lei out of a total of 3m. lei.

[61] M. Pearton, *Oil and the Roumanian State* (Oxford, 1971), 231; Hillgruber, *Hitler, König Carol*, 157; British Intelligence Objectives Sub-Committee (BIOS) Final Report 513, *Notes on the Organisation of the German Petroleum Industry during the War*, 7.

of Romanian oil through Czech acquisitions. The first Brno Engineering Company had a large share in Petrol Block AG which came under Reichswerke influence in 1940.[62] Austrian, French, and Dutch holdings were taken under the administration of Kontinentale Öl and there were plans for the company in Russia, where both Hitler and Göring were determined that oil resources would remain permanently Reich properties, operated by firms owned by the Reich.[63] Nevertheless it seems likely that the oil interests lay at the periphery of the industrial empire created around the Göring concern. Indeed within two years any hope of utilizing Russian oil resources had disappeared for good as the Reichswerke organization was forced to retreat westwards with the German armies, contracting, as it had previously expanded, with the path of war. In April 1944 the Economics Ministry wrote to Göring recommending the winding up of his *Ostgesellschaften* (eastern companies) whose personnel had now dwindled to a mere 90.[64] By the end of the war there only remained that part of the German core of the concern that had been left standing in the bombing.

When the period of expansion virtually came to an end in 1941 an unwieldy and untidy industrial colossus had been carved from the spoils of central Europe. Because so much had been acquired so quickly, and under the conditions of war, the need arose for a reorganization of the original structure of the company. Initially the organization had developed through the Reichswerke AG für Erzbergbau und Eisenhütte 'Hermann Göring' set up in 1937. When the capital of the company was raised from RM 5m. to 400m. in 1938, RM 265m. was taken over by the state, the remainder by other private or state agencies which had no voting rights in the company. A new holding company was formed in 1939—the Reichswerke AG 'Hermann Göring'—and most of the non-state participation was taken over at the same time by the government.[65] This organization was kept until January 1941 when, under pressure from the scale and nature of the acquisitions since 1939, the company was broken up into three major blocks, still under the control of the central holding company in Berlin but divided according to the nature of the economic activity. The largest block was the Montanblock made up of the iron, steel, and mining interests. The second block was an armaments sector organized under the Reichswerke AG für Waffen- und Maschinenbau 'Hermann Göring'. The final block

[62] *Conditions in Occupied Territories*, 29.

[63] Eichholtz *et al.*, *Anatomie*, Doc. 190, 'Protokoll der Sitzung des Aufsichtsrats der Kontinentale Öl AG am 13 Jan. 1942'; *TWC* xiii. 863, Doc. NI-440, Körner to economic authorities, 20 Nov. 1941, enclosing a memorandum 'on the essential results of the discussion of economic policy and economic organization in the recently occupied eastern territories'; Pearton, *Oil*, 231.

[64] IWM Speer Collection, Reel 63, FD 3742/45 File 1, Reichswirtschaftsministerium to Göring, 15 May 1944.

[65] Riedel, *Eisen und Kohle*, 231–2; *TWC*, Transcripts of Case XI, vol. 231, 14839.

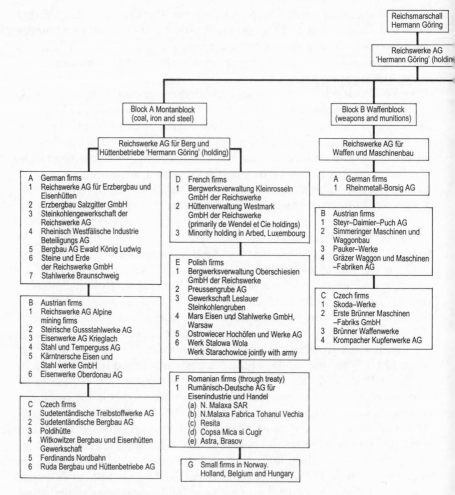

Fig. 2. The structure of the Reichswerke 'Hermann Göring', 1942

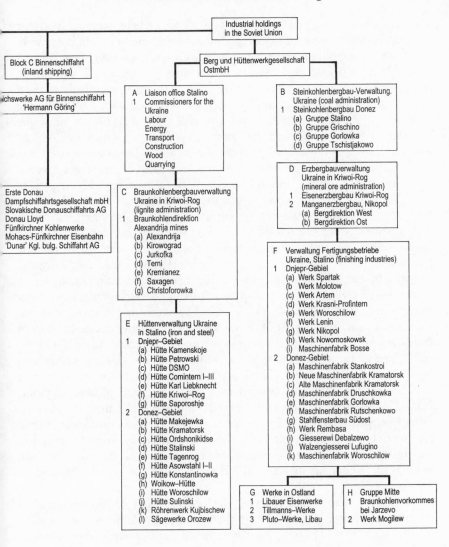

Industrial holdings in the Soviet Union

Block C Binnenschiffahrt (inland shipping)

...ichswerke AG für Binnenschiffahrt 'Hermann Göring'

Erste Donau Dampfschiffahrtsgesellschaft mbH Slowakische Donauschiffahrts AG Donau Lloyd Fünfkirchner Kohlenwerke Mohacs-Fünfkirchner Eisenbahn 'Dunar' Kgl. bulg. Schiffahrt AG

Berg und Hüttenwerkgesellschaft OstmbH

A Liaison office Stalino
1 Commissioners for the Ukraine
  Labour
  Energy
  Transport
  Construction
  Wood
  Quarrying

B Steinkohlenbergbau-Verwaltung. Ukraine (coal administration)
1 Steinkohlenbergbau Donez
  (a) Gruppe Stalino
  (b) Gruppe Grischino
  (c) Gruppe Gorlowka
  (d) Gruppe Tschistjakowo

D Erzbergbauverwaltung Ukraine in Kriwoi-Rog (mineral ore administration)
1 Eisenerzbergbau Kriwoi-Rog
2 Manganerzbergbau, Nikopol
  (a) Bergdirektion West
  (b) Bergdirektion Ost

C Braunkohlenbergbauverwaltung Ukraine in Kriwoi-Rog (lignite administration)
1 Braunkohlendirektion Alexandrija mines
  (a) Alexandrija
  (b) Kirowograd
  (c) Jurkofka
  (d) Terni
  (e) Kremianez
  (f) Saxagen
  (g) Christoforowka

F Verwaltung Fertigungsbetriebe Ukraine, Stalino (finishing industries)
1 Dnjepr-Gebiet
  (a) Werk Spartak
  (b) Werk Molotow
  (c) Werk Artem
  (d) Werk Krasni-Profintern
  (e) Werk Woroschilow
  (f) Werk Lenin
  (g) Werk Nikopol
  (h) Werk Nowomoskowsk
  (i) Maschinenfabrik Bosse
2 Donez-Gebiet
  (a) Maschinenfabrik Stankostroi
  (b) Neue Maschinenfabrik Kramatorsk
  (c) Alte Maschinenfabrik Kramatorsk
  (d) Maschinenfabrik Druschkowka
  (e) Maschinenfabrik Gorlowka
  (f) Maschinenfabrik Rutschenkowo
  (g) Stahlfensterbau Südost
  (h) Werk Rembasa
  (i) Giesserewi Debalzewo
  (j) Walzengiesserei Lufugino
  (k) Maschinenfabrik Woroschilow

E Hüttenverwaltung Ukraine in Stalino (iron and steel)
1 Dnjepr-Gebiet
  (a) Hütte Kamenskoje
  (b) Hütte Petrowski
  (c) Hütte DSMO
  (d) Hütte Comintern I–III
  (e) Hütte Karl Liebknecht
  (f) Hütte Kriwoi–Rog
  (g) Hütte Saporoshje
2 Donez–Gebiet
  (a) Hütte Makejewka
  (b) Hütte Kramatorsk
  (c) Hütte Ordshonikidse
  (d) Hütte Stalinski
  (e) Hütte Tagenrog
  (f) Hütte Asowstahl I–II
  (g) Hütte Konstantinowka
  (h) Woikow–Hütte
  (i) Hütte Woroschilow
  (j) Hütte Sulinski
  (k) Röhrenwerk Kujbischew
  (l) Sägewerke Orozew

G Werke in Ostland
1 Libauer Eisenwerke
2 Tillmanns–Werke
3 Pluto–Werke, Libau

H Gruppe Mitte
1 Braunkohlenvorkommes bei Jarzevo
2 Werk Mogilew

was a small shipping sector under the Reichswerke AG für Binnenschiffahrt 'Hermann Göring'. Subsidiary companies and companies in which a controlling interest was held were grouped roughly according to product into one or other of the blocks.[66] Figure 5.2 shows the structure of the firm in 1942 and its links with other sectors. The most important of these were the linkages with the oil industry, with the holdings of the old Prussian state, through Göring's position as prime minister of Prussia, and with the aircraft economy in which Göring had also established a substantial state-owned sector.[67] The concern itself was made up primarily of businesses either wholly owned by the state or with a majority state holding, though some with a minority holding were included where effective control was exercised through the Reichswerke. Because of Göring's insistence on expansion at all costs there had been little attempt either to concentrate or to rationalize the concern. It soon became clear that unless something was done the concern would become hidebound in its efforts to cope with what Pleiger called its 'inorganic growth'. In 1942 the discussions with Göring on organization finally led to a decision to divide the concern up by removing the armaments block from the control of the Reichswerke and, while state involvement was not abandoned, the manufacturing firms were placed under the leadership of the new armaments production rings set up by Todt and Speer.[68] Göring still insisted on maintaining some links with the armaments sector, appointing his adjutant General Karl Bodenschatz as a liaison officer between them.[69] Effective control over the sector had passed, however, from Göring back to Speer and private industry. The main armaments firms in Czechoslovakia were formed into the Waffenunion Skoda–Brünn and were brought under the control of the production rings organized in the Reich.[70] The Göring concern was left in control of the coal, iron, and steel block which on its own still constituted the largest of its kind in Europe.

One factor that bound together the various parts of the organization was the duplication of personnel in the management of the major branches of the concern. The two most important figures were Paul Körner,

[66] USSBS Special Paper 3, 43–4; *TWC*, Transcripts of Case XI, vol. 231, 14845–55; W. Huppert, 'Konzern-Organisation', *DDV* 16 (1941/2), 844–6.

[67] R. J. Overy, 'German Aircraft Production 1939–1942', Ph.D. thesis, Cambridge, 1978, 117–25, for details on the state sector of the aircraft industry.

[68] *TWC*, Transcripts of Case XI, vol. 231, 14843, 14859–62. The exact timing of the change is unclear. Steyr–Daimler–Puch, for example, officially left the Reichswerke only in 1943 and Voss continued to act as its chairman until replaced by Roehnert in March 1943. See Speer Collection, FD 785/46, Sitzung der Steyr–Daimler–Puch AG; FD 787/46 letter from Roehnert to Göring, 26 Feb. 1943.

[69] IWM, Speer Collection, FD 787/46, Protokoll über die am 13 Aug. 1943 abgehaltene Sitzung des Aufsichtsrates der Steyr–Daimler–Puch AG, 3–4.

[70] *TWC*, Transcripts of Case XI, vol. 231, 14875.

Göring's deputy in charge of the Four Year Plan, and Paul Pleiger, the general manager of the Salzgitter-Watenstedt complex. Until Körner was forced to resign through Hitler's insistence in 1943 that Reichstag deputies should not hold business positions, he was the chairman of the entire concern and of its major subsidiaries. Pleiger, who was also general manager of the iron and steel holding company, became his successor.[71] In addition both men were normally appointed as either honorary chairman or director of the major subsidiaries. There were other appointees who similarly worked on the boards of numerous of the Reichswerke businesses: Dr Wilhelm Voss, prominent in the take-over of banking and industry in Czechoslovakia and mainly concerned with the processing side of the concern; Hellmuth Roehnert, general manager of Rheinmetall–Borsig and later general manager of the Junkers aircraft combine, whose main responsibility was with the armaments works; Karl Rasche, the Dresdner Bank representative of the Reichswerke; Paul Rheinländer, one of the first directors of the concern and deputy for Pleiger. Both Voss and Roehnert had wide responsibilities for the commercial expansion into Austria and Czechoslovakia and the latter took over general direction of the Waffenblock when its constitution was changed in 1942. Pleiger had begun to extend his own responsibility for management into the conquered areas in 1939 but was gradually excluded from Austria by the ambitions of Hans Malzacher, manager of the Donawitz holdings, and from Czechoslovakia by Voss.[72] Göring himself maintained a close link with the various parts of the concern by appointing Bodenschatz as a director of its more important components. While actual production management was decentralized, the central direction of the concern was concentrated in the hands of a relatively small group which, through contact with the Four Year Plan office, the banks, and the armed forces was in a good position to direct the affairs of the concern in the wider framework of the political and economic demands of war.

The structure for policy-making depended on the nature of the decision required. Göring reserved for himself 'all questions of principle as well as matter of special importance'.[73] He took little interest in routine but kept himself informed about the activities of the concern and its links with

[71] *TWC* xiii. 893, Doc. NI-5261.

[72] *TWC*, Transcripts of Case XI, vol. 231, 14859, 14871, 14877, 14893–4. There are numerous references in the documents to individual directors but unfortunately very few complete lists of directors. Certainly in many foreign firms both Germans and native businessmen served side by side on the boards of directors.

[73] *TWC* xiii. 745 Doc. Koerner 177. Although this statement was made in Körner's defence and could thus be interpreted as an attempt to shift responsibility onto Göring, there is enough evidence from contemporary documents of Göring's personal concern to supervise major decision-making to confirm that this was indeed the process. See e.g. IWM, Speer Collection, FD 787/46 Protokoll, 13 Aug. 1943, 9.

other state agencies.[74] Anything to do with administration, information, auditing, budgetary policy, and minor personnel questions was carried out by Körner. Decisions about participation in small enterprises was also left to Körner in co-operation with the appropriate ministries.[75] The main boards and committees met fairly regularly but the huge size of the concern left much of the day-to-day business in the hands of the production management staff at the individual businesses. The independent juridical status enjoyed by the different firms encouraged the decentralization still further. It was in order to restore the balance between local initiative and central control that the reorganization of 1941 took place.[76] The main task of the central controlling body was to achieve greater co-operation and efficiency by 'setting up production programmes in co-ordination, technical experience, joint support between companies, regulating the position of markets, division of market areas among the companies, price regulations'.[77]

The concern was usually financed directly through the Reich Finance Ministry on behalf of the state and only occasionally through other state agencies such as the Bank der deutschen Luftfahrt, which played an important part in financing projects for enterprises producing Luftwaffe material.[78] Some of the finance was found from the occupied territories themselves though few records survive to indicate the relative importance of this method of funding. Many of the assets of the concern were, of course, the product of direct seizure and confiscation and required little or no state investment except to keep them in operation. Moreover, it was policy to encourage firms working for the state war effort to plough profits back into their businesses to relieve the burden on the state. By 1944 the main branches of the concern had advances from the state of more than RM 1,500m., 763m. outside the Reich.[79] More is known about the size and distribution of capital employed in the concern, though only for the Montanblock in the period of the split after 1942. The small shipping sector had assets of RM 89m. and lay largely outside the Reich.[80] The distribution of capital assets by area together with the net worth of the

[74] *TWC*, Transcripts of Case XI, vol. 231, 14842–3.

[75] e.g. IWM, Speer Collection, FD 783/46 letter from Roehnert to Thomas, 3 Jan. 1942 'betr. Verkauf der Beteiligung der Rheinmetall–Borsig AG an die Basch–Jaegar–Lüdenscheider Metallwerke AG, Lüdenscheid'; letter from Roehnert to Wessig, 23 July 1941; letter from Voss to Roehnert, 26 July 1941.

[76] Pleiger confirmed this situation at his trial. Pleiger had in fact produced a memorandum on the inorganic growth of the combine on 21 Apr. 1940 and sent it to Göring. See *TWC*, Transcripts of Case XI, vol. 231, 14843–8.

[77] *TWC*, Transcripts of Case XI, vol. 231, 14847.

[78] *Conditions in Occupied Territories*, 7, 12.

[79] USSBS Special Paper 3, 54*a*, table 8, 'Summary of Assets, Liabilities and Net Worth of Principal Subsidiaries of the Hermann Göring Group'.

[80] Ibid. 55.

TABLE 5.2. *Capital assets, liabilities, and net value of principal Reichswerke plants, 1943/4* (RMm.)

	Fixed capital[a]	Investments in affiliates	Accounts due from affiliates
Pre-war Germany	1,038,910	210,093	148,098
Austria	355,068	42,341	338,033
Czechoslovakia	1,361,493	55,088	123,900
Poland[b]	368,446	45,304	31,357
France	34,800[c]	22,834	24,848
TOTAL:	3,158,717	375,660	666,236

	Other current assets	Total assets	as %
Pre-war Germany	329,103	1,726,204	32.0
Austria	157,851	893,293	16.6
Czechoslovakia	551,275	2,091,756	38.8
Poland	53,591	498,698	9.3
France	96,350	178,832	3.3
TOTAL:	1,188,170	5,388,783	100.0

	Total liabilities	Net worth	as %
Pre-war Germany	1,052,721	672,802	29.9
Austria	583,491	309,802	13.8
Czechoslovakia	1,257,695	835,061	37.1
Poland	99,235	399,463	17.7
France	194,662	34,128	1.5
TOTAL:	3,187,804	2,250,937	100.0

[a] Properties, plants, construction in progress, less depreciation.
[b] Excluding steel mills operated on behalf of Army High Command.
[c] French statements include only capital added after acquisition by Reichswerke.
Source: USSBS Special Paper 3, 54a.

concern are given in Table 5.2. The parent company was heavily dependent on sectors outside the Reich which provided 67 per cent of the fixed assets and 70 per cent of the net assets of the concern. Pleiger estimated that the total capital employed in the concern by the end of 1944 was RM 4,375m. excluding the holdings in Poland and Lorraine, which suggests that a final figure in excess of RM 5,000m. would represent

TABLE 5.3. *Distribution of labour in principal Reichswerke plants, 1941–1944*

(a) *Employment in principal plants 1941–4*

	Germans[a]	%	Foreign	%	POWs	%	Total
Dec. 1941	176,399	57.6	121,822	39.7	8,262	2.7	306,423
June 1942	175,554	55.3	133,210	41.9	8,867	2.8	317,631
Dec. 1942	179,544	51.1	151,289	43.2	20,177	5.7	350,640
June 1943	182,897	49.0	166,045	44.5	23,952	6.5	372,804
Dec. 1943	172,192	42.3	180,394	44.2	54,788	13.5	407,374
June 1944	172,186	41.3	188,979	45.3	55,312	13.4	416,477
Dec. 1944	158,285	42.5	168,845	45.2	46,271	12.3	373,401

(b) *Distribution by area, June 1944*

	Workers	POWs	Total	%
Germany	77,442	15,469	92,911	22.3
Austria	48,096	6,797	54,893	13.2
France	27,617	4,909	32,526	7.8
Czechoslovakia	120,840	12,904	133,744	32.1
Poland	82,403	15,191	97,594	23.4
Others	4,765	42	4,807	1.2
Total in occupied area	283,721	39,843	323,564	77.7
OVERALL TOTAL:	361,163	55,312	416,475	100.0

[a] Includes Germans from Austria and Sudetenland.

Source: USSBS Special Paper 3, 66–8.

the Reichswerke at its fullest extent, more than six times larger than the largest concern in pre-war Germany.[81]

Most of the labour of the concern was drawn from outside the Reich as well. The figures for labour employed in the concern are set out in Table 5.3(a). Figures for 'German' workers in the plants usually included Austrians and Sudeten Germans, so that the proportion of workers from the old Reich area was smaller than the aggregate figures suggest. Table 5.3(b) gives the geographical distribution of labour in the concern, showing that 76.5 per cent of the entire work-force was employed outside the Reich. Some, of course, would have been Germans working as skilled or managerial cadres at foreign enterprises. But employment within Germany was also mixed, as more and more forced labour was brought into the Reich from occupied Europe. There is not much evidence of

[81] Lachmann, 'More on Göring Works', 396; USSBS Special Paper 3, 54–5; Riedel, *Eisen und Kohle*, 359; *Conditions in Occupied Territories*, 5.

labour or capital shortages for the concern. Capital had to be argued for at the Reich Finance Ministry and the Economics Ministry, although this situation was eased by placing officials sympathetic to the Reichswerke in key positions.[82] If anything, there was a tendency to over-manning in the less efficient enterprises, where production was kept going at all costs regardless of the best economic interest of the concern. Productivity declined sharply in the German plants over the war years and it is likely that under the constant pressure of war the same thing occurred at those in occupied Europe. In the competition for capacity and labour resources the Reichswerke concern was well placed to resist intrusions into its own sphere of influence and to hoard its own labour.

Despite the problem of evidence, it is possible to draw some conclusions about the way in which the concern operated, both in terms of product and investment policies, and in terms of its competitive relationship with other concerns. Decisions on investment were largely coloured by the order of priority established for war production. New investment was concentrated in those areas where the greatest gains were to be expected, in particular in Silesia, the Sudetenland, and the Ukraine. Here supplies of coal, which proved to be a substantial bottleneck during the war, were expanded rapidly for the war effort.[83] In other sectors, notably iron and steel, some of the increase in production was the result of the fuller utilization of existing capacity. There is no doubt, however, that substantial investment was undertaken by the Reichswerke concern in its foreign holdings. In the Steyr–Daimler–Puch works some RM 328m. were invested between 1938 and 1943.[84] On taking over control of Skoda investment plans were laid for spending Kčs 200m. in 1940 alone.[85] Such investment was an obvious necessity if the newly acquired industrial booty was going to be fully utilized for the war effort, though at times, as in Romania, much was promised in the way of investment and little given.[86] Although it had been intended that some investment would come from

[82] The Reich Finance Minister himself looked favourably on the Reichswerke. See L. Graf Schwerin von Krosigk, *Staatsbankrott: Finanzpolitik des Dentschen Reiches* (Göttingen, 1974), 233–4. Pleiger's associate Gabel was appointed Chef der Bergbauabteilung in the Economics Ministry at the same time that Funk replaced Schacht. Both these men reduced the resistance of the Economics Ministry to Göring's activities. See Riedel, *Eisen und Kohle*, 231–2.

[83] Reidel, *Eisen und Kohle*, 303. A total investment of RM 120m. was made between Apr. 1940 and Dec. 1944 to raise output from 55,000 to 120,000 tons per day.

[84] IWM Speer Collection, FD 787/46, Protokoll über die Sitzung des Aufsichtsrates der Steyr–Daimler–Punch am 8 Sept. 1944. The investment was made up as follows: improvements RM 52m.; new projects RM 212m.; subsidiary RM 56m.; state loans RM 8m. See also *TWC*, Transcripts of Case XI, vol. 231, 14895–6.

[85] NA Microcopy T83 Roll 77, frame 3449320, Abschrift betr. Beteiligung des Reiches an der Aktiengesellschaft vormals Skodawerke in Pilsen, Oct. 1940.

[86] Constantinecu, 'Exploitation', 111–12.

TABLE 5.4. *Net annual loss of Reichswerke 'Montanblock', 1939–1943* (RM)

1939	1940	1941	1942	1943
5,420,063	11,732,302	6,362,544	8,630,556	4,268,000

Source: USSBS Special Paper 3, 58.

TABLE 5.5. *Combined sales of Reichswerke 'Montanblock', 1941–1944* (RMm.)

	1941	1942	1943	1944
Pre-war Germany	364,294	584,190	683,250	698,604
Alpine group	156,039	205,122	327,067	371,496
Lorraine steel	122,423	131,244	157,638	87,888
Lorraine coal	12,511	29,615	39,386	29,280
Silesian group	242,746	306,923	348,382	344,292
Vítkovice	230,950	235,857	253,917	267,804
Nordbahn, Prague	45,594	59,416	63,907	55,224
Poldina huť	98,360	101,140	117,828	140,364
Sudeten oil	1,999	33,687	139,708	89,736
Sudeten coal	106,485	121,427	148,814	145,056
Polish steel	75,780	89,254	119,043	80,328
Others	33,876	32,132	34,006	31,932
GRAND TOTAL:	1,491,057	1,930,007	2,432,946	2,342,004

Source: USSBS Special Paper 3, 60.

ploughed-back profits, the 'Montanblock' ran at a loss from 1939 to 1943, as is shown in Table 5.4. To this should be added an estimated net loss of RM 75m. in the French companies operated by the Reichswerke from 1941 to 1944.[87] There were profits made in the large Czech firms, particularly Vítkovice and Poldina huť, and these were used to offset the losses in other enterprises. Losses were sustained partly because of the massive investment programme called for in establishing new firms and refurbishing old ones, partly because of high operating costs (including the more expensive Salzgitter iron ore and iron), and partly through poorly utilized capacity together with the impact of bombing, which reduced the efficiency of the plants considerably. Reluctance to work for the German war effort must also have been a factor. In 1941 Rheinmetall–Borsig

[87] USSBS Special Paper 3, 57–9. Alpine was run without loss for the first time in 1944.

calculated that sales in the German plants came to RM 9,900 per head per year, but in Skoda the figure was only RM 6,000 and at Brno only RM 5,500.[88]

Despite losses the gross sales of the concern continued to expand rapidly over the course of the war (see Table 5.5). Again the concern was very heavily dependent for its sales on enterprises outside the Reich. This remained true of production also. The pattern of production followed the lines originally intended. Control over the supplies of iron ore led to control over iron and steel production and back into coal production. Railway industries, armaments, and shipping were added both to utilize the iron and steel and to ship the materials and finished products in central Europe. The geographical breakdown of the distribution of production in Table 5.6 shows the extent to which the concern depended for most of its iron and steel and coal capacity on the occupied areas. There is insufficient evidence to show the pattern of sales between enterprises in the concern or the flow of trade across pre-war frontiers. In Austria, Czechoslovakia, and Romania a considerable amount of the production was used within the country of origin and not sent to the Reich.[89] This was due on the one hand to the existence of an armaments sector in the occupied economies that was used and expanded with the needs of war, and on the other to the gradual dispersal of production into bomb-safe areas.

Unlike a capitalist multi-national concern, the Reichswerke had to worry little about its operating costs and not at all about its shareholders.[90] The only pressures were those of wartime, that the concern should be run as efficiently as possible to guarantee maximum output at a reasonable cost. It was clearly a policy of the directors, particularly Pleiger, to increase efficiency by introducing the best available production methods wherever possible. But any attempt to rationalize the structure of the concern was caught between Göring's insistence that output should be expanded as much as possible, even where the long-term effects of such increases might be damaging, and Pleiger's own desire to keep the Reichswerke concern extended to its fullest capacity for fear of its competitors.[91]

---

[88] Speer Collection, FD 717/46, Rheinmetall–Borsig, 'Bericht über die Entwicklung im Jahr 1941', 20 Apr. 1942, 3.

[89] USSBS Special Paper 3, 60.

[90] *TWC*, Transcripts of Case XI, vol. 231, 14863–4. Pleiger claimed that 'the interests of the Reich in its capacity as shareholder were first of all safeguarded by the Reich Ministry of Economics and . . . later on . . . the Plenipotentiary of the Four Year Plan managed this responsibility'.

[91] Göring wanted to expand output of ore from the Erzberg, against the advice of his deputies, to 20,000 tons per day when the original plan had called for 10,000 tons. Similarly Hitler's demand for an expansion of steel output in 1943 forced Göring to insist upon huge but unmanageable increases in production from the Linz plant whatever the cost elsewhere.

TABLE 5.6. *Distribution of Reichswerke production,*
by product and area, 1941–1944 (%)

	1941	1942	1943	1944
Iron ore				
Pre-war Germany	58.1	59.1	59.9	60.1
Austria	41.9	37.5	36.3	37.4
Slovakia	—	3.4	3.8	—
Pig iron				
Pre-war Germany	24.8	26.8	27.4	31.7
Austria	20.9	21.0	21.9	24.6
Czechoslovakia	24.4	21.2	18.9	20.7
France	29.9	29.5	30.3	22.1
Poland	—	1.5	1.5	0.9
Crude steel				
Pre-war Germany	17.1	22.1	21.4	26.8
Austria	17.0	13.5	13.8	14.9
Czechoslovakia	33.6	27.8	26.0	28.6
France	32.3	32.6	34.5	27.3
Poland	—	4.0	4.3	2.4
Rolling-mill products				
Pre-war Germany	20.3	23.8	19.2	25.2
Austria	12.7	13.0	14.4	16.0
Czechoslovakia	32.1	27.8	28.1	31.6
France	34.9	36.5	33.4	24.5
Poland	—	3.9	4.9	2.7
Bitumous coal				
Pre-war Germany	25.7	22.0	20.3	19.3
Czechoslovakia	17.3	17.4	19.4	19.2
France	1.6	4.9	5.5	4.3
Poland (incl. Silesia)	55.4	55.7	54.8	57.2
Lignite				
Pre-war Germany	20.7	19.8	18.2	18.0
Austria	10.4	9.6	8.8	9.2
Czechoslovakia	68.9	70.6	73.0	72.8

Source: USSBS Special Paper 3, 72–3.

A satisfactory relationship between efficiency and output was never fully developed because of the wider political problems involved. Thus little attempt was made to close down inefficient plants or to transfer resources between plants. The planning of what industry to keep and what to close down was reserved for peacetime.[92] Such a policy was bound to lead to a

[92] RIIA, *Hitler's Europe*, 194 ff.

more wasteful production in the long run. In Austria and Czechoslovakia the Reichswerke operated a near-monopoly in heavy industry (except chemicals) and had the opportunity to run and expand the most efficient units; instead it continued to run them all and indeed set about constructing new units from scratch. However necessary from a political point of view, this tended to spread resources of labour, machinery, and managerial expertise more thinly than was compatible with achieving the highest level of exploitation. The Reichswerke might have achieved more if run along the lines of a private trust rather than a state arsenal. Even attempts to make the Reichswerke accept more rational operating methods often led to dislocation elsewhere. When Hitler insisted that 'experts' from private industry be brought into Soviet iron and steel production, the Ruhr firms complied only with great reluctance, since it meant taking skilled men and materials away from the Reich, which would reduce the ability of the efficient Ruhr firms to produce at their optimum.[93]

Part of the explanation for this failure to take the greatest possible advantages of the Reichswerke capacity lay in the fact that competition provided much less incentive than for the private trusts. What competition there was tended to be a jurisdictional and political struggle between private economic groups and the state and Nazi officials, a struggle that usually favoured the Reichswerke. It proved necessary, however, to conform to some of the pressures of the market. Part of the coal, iron, and steel was sold to private manufacturers and had to be roughly competitive with private production to conform to the structure of costs in government contracts. In the case of iron production at Linz, for example, the state gave a subsidy of RM 20 a ton to cover the difference in production costs between that plant and those of the Reich.[94] On the whole the economic conditions of wartime disguised much of the competition between the private and state concerns. Many of the decisions were made within the broader context of war requirements and increasingly the controls exercised over private firms became indistinguishable from those in state concerns. Where competition did survive, however, it was in terms of who should do the controlling. In some cases the Reichswerke could acquire a special position. When, on the other hand, the Ruhr had a dominant position—as it did in the Reich Iron Union (Reichsvereinigung Eisen), set up in 1942 to oversee iron and steel production—relations between the Reichswerke and private industry were unsatisfactory.[95] Competition was

[93] Dallin, *German Rule*, 384–5; Riedel, *Eisen und Kohle*, 323–4.

[94] USSBS Special Paper 3, 61. Pleiger calculated that the difference in the level of production costs between the Austrian and German part of the concern was 20% in 1938.

[95] Riedel, *Eisen und Kohle*, 279 ff.; Eichholtz and Schumann, *Anatomie*, 451, Doc. 251, 'Bericht von W. Scheiber (Leiter des Rüstungslieferungsamtes) für A. Speer, 23 June 1944'. Pleiger himself claimed that his point of view was 'what is healthful for competition is dangerous to the Hermann Göring Works'. See *TWC*, Transcripts of Case XI, vol. 231, 14842.

more pronounced in the occupied territories where the Reichswerke were able to exclude private firms, or regulate and supervise their activities, but where the Göring organization was itself the victim of jurisdictional and political conflicts with the armed forces, the SS, and local Nazi bosses.[96] The existence of friction on this scale explains why the regime opted to create a giant state industrial concern as the instrument to expel British and French capital from eastern Europe, to safeguard the spoils of war for the German war effort, and to prepare the ground for the new economic order in peacetime Europe.

[96] NCA vii. 310–11, Docs. EC-137, EC-485; E. Georg, *Die wirtschaftlichen Unternehmungen der SS* (Stuttgart, 1963), 52; Lachmann, 'Göring Works', 29.

III

REARMAMENT AND THE COMING OF WAR

6
Hitler's War Plans and the German Economy, 1933–1939

ECONOMIC modernization has created a vital link between military capability and economic strength. Modern technology and modern industry have transformed the nature of warfare and armaments. The larger the economy, and the more sophisticated its scientific and technical base, the greater its military strength. This has been a natural development, made explicit by the slow emergence of an international system dominated by the 'superpowers'. Yet in Europe the nature of this relationship was only fully recognized during the First World War, with the coming of industrialized warfare and the strategy of blockade and attrition. The armies that marched to war in 1914 expected quick victories, with the weapons to hand. By 1918 the concept of total war, the mobilization of all material and moral resources for the war effort, had replaced the traditional strategy, born in an age of agrarian states, of a quick, mobile campaign.

Nowhere was this shift more significant than in Germany, for the Germans blamed their defeat in 1918 on the failure to prepare the economy for war, or to maintain the home front once the war turned into a struggle of material resources. The lesson that the German military took from the First World War was that any future conflict would be a war of economies as well as armies; and that it was the responsibility of the armed forces to ensure that the economy was thoroughly prepared as an instrument for waging that war. The leading spokesman of this view was General Groener, who had signed the army pact with Ebert in 1918, and from 1928 was defence minister in the Weimar coalition governments. During the 1920s he laid down the guidelines for a fundamental shift in German strategy from the age of Moltke and Schlieffen to the age of industry. He argued that the German military had ignored the modern economy at their peril, and that it was now necessary to forge close links between the two. This meant not only industrial preparations, so clearly lacking before 1914, but the organization of the entire labour force, the distribution of adequate resources for the home front, and the maintenance of high morale. 'It is necessary', Groener concluded, 'to organize the entire strength of the people for fighting and working'.[1] Such a strategy presupposed that if war came it would be another titanic struggle like the first, for the German military assumed that powerful modern states would not fight unless it were a matter of life and death. Colonel Georg Thomas, head of the army economic staff set up at Groener's inspiration, argued that 'modern war is no longer a clash of armies, but a struggle for the existence of the peoples involved. All resources of the nation must be made to serve the war.'[2] For Groener too, it was 'the future of the race' that was at stake.

During the 1920s the German army leadership laid the foundation for a strategy of total economic mobilization. They called this conception *Wehrwirtschaft*, the defence-based economy, capable of generating the resources necessary for the conduct of total war. Gradually during the inter-war years the linking of 'defence' and 'economy' became popularly accepted as a crucial component of national security. In Thomas's opinion 'the frontiers between war and peace, state and economy, politics and the conduct of war have disappeared and the defence-based economy has become the definite economic trend of our time'.[3] *Wehrwirtschaft* was as much part of the intellectual apparatus of Germany's military leaders and officials as 'empire' was in Britain. Much recent research has shown that German military and economic preparations for war were not the product of Nazi planning alone, but conformed well with strategic conceptions developed before Hitler ever came to power.[4]

In 1924 the army established an Economics Staff (*Wirtschaftsstab*), whose job was to plan for the time when Germany could embark on rearmament in earnest. A network of ex-officers working in business was set up, to establish close links between industry and the military, a system that was considerably strengthened when the Allied Control Commission left Germany in 1926 and secret rearmament could be undertaken with fewer risks. In December 1925 the Army Armaments Office, together with a number of industrialists, founded a 'statistical society' (*Statistische Gesellschaft*), whose object beneath the innocent exterior was 'to underpin and promote the work of the Defence Ministry' and to establish contact with key firms not yet involved in military production. From 1928

---

[1] Gen. W. Groener, 'Bedeutung der modernen Wirtschaft für die Strategie', repr. in D. Fensch and O. Groehler, 'Imperialistische Ökonomie und militärische Strategie: Eine Denkschrift Wilhelm Groeners', *Zeitschrift für Geschichtswissenschaft*, 19 (1971), 1167–77.

[2] B. A. Carroll, *Design for Total War: Arms and Economics in the Third Reich* (The Hague, 1968), 40.

[3] BA R7 XVI/36, Colonel Thomas, Vortrag vor der Wehrmachtakadamie, 7 Nov. 1935, 4.

[4] W. Deist, *The Wehrmacht and German Rearmament* (London, 1981), esp. chs. 1–2; M. Geyer, *Aufrüstung oder Sicherheit: Die Reichswehr in der Krise der Machtpolitik 1924–1936* (Wiesbaden, 1980); Carroll, *Design*, chs. 2–3; W. M. Stern, 'Wehrwirtschaft: A German Contribution to Economics', *Economic History Review*, 2nd ser. 13 (1960/1), 270–81.

onwards the scope of secret rearmament was enlarged, the economics office increased in size and significance, and with the support of Groener and the efforts of General Kurt von Schleicher, who became chancellor in December 1932, the army began to reassert its traditional political role in Germany, endeavouring through its emphasis on the need for 'total mobilization' to bring military affairs to bear on every area of public life.[5]

There can be no doubt that with Hitler's assumption of power in 1933, the new strategy of Germany's armed forces found an enthusiastic champion. Hitler's world view embraced entirely the link between war and economy. For Hitler no war could be fought, and certainly not a conflict for racial survival, without a strong economy. Like the armed forces he was obsessed with the lessons of 1914 to 1918. To wage a future war successfully it was necessary to prepare the economy for complete conversion in advance. It was essential to provide sufficient food for the home population to prevent another 'stab-in-the-back'. But most of all Hitler's populist conception insisted that only the whole people, morally armed and materially prepared, could prosecute war in the struggle between the races.[6] Hence the Nazi insistence in the war that everyone was a national 'fighter', the soldier at the front, the miner, the factory hand. Hitler also recognized that war was in essence about economic resources. War would be fought to capture fresh resources and *Lebensraum*, living-space for the German people; but it could only be won by mobilizing all existing economic potential. This was almost exactly the argument used by Groener, that any war was about the future of a country's economic life, and that military victory could mean economic power and security.[7]

Hitler's priorities in 1933 thus served to reinforce and enlarge initiatives already undertaken. The Nazi government wanted economic recovery, greater economic self-sufficiency (autarky) to avoid the danger of blockade or boycott, and what Hitler called 'Wiederwehrhaftmachung', or the re-establishment of a broad military capability. This required not only the rebuilding of Germany's armed forces, but also the material and psychological preparation of the whole people for future conflict. There was little here for the army leaders to dispute. The new defence minister, Werner von Blomberg, was on good terms with Hitler before 1933, and the army as a whole at first welcomed the political stability brought about by the establishment of an authoritarian state, and the special role in it

[5] Carroll, *Design*, 54–7, 64–71; E. W. Hansen, *Reichswehr und Industrie: Rüstungswirtschaftliche Zusammenarbeit und wirtschaftliche Mobilmachungsvorbereitungen 1923–1932* (Boppard am Rhein, 1978); P. Hayes, 'Kurt von Schleicher and Weimar Politics', *Journal of Modern History*, 52 (1980), 35–65.

[6] T. Taylor (ed.), *Hitler's Secret Book* (New York, 1961), 26–7, 46: 'in the future the enlargement of people's living space . . . will require staking the whole strength of the people' (p. 96).

[7] Ibid. 13–24; Groener, 'Bedeutung', 1175–7.

promised by Hitler for the armed forces. 'Never', claimed von Reichenau, Blomberg's chief-of-staff, 'were the armed forces more identical with the state than today.'[8] Under Blomberg the High Command was content to leave the wider questions of foreign policy and economic recovery to the government. They concentrated instead on the rearmament programme promised by Hitler in February 1933 and officially launched in December of the same year.

I

In the early years of the Third Reich rearmament was left largely to the armed forces, who continued to build on the narrow foundation established before 1933. Between 1930 and 1932 the army planners prepared a Second Armaments Programme to succeed the first one of 1926, designed to expand the size and effectiveness of the armed forces beyond the level allowed under the Versailles Treaty. In December 1933 the new programme was finally authorized for a 21-division peacetime force, three times the size of the existing army, which was to be established between 1934 and 1938.[9] This was an army much smaller than that of France. The December programme was not expected to offer protection to Germany in the event of a major war. The first priority for the armed forces was to build up again the infrastructure of military power, and the trained men necessary to run the new forces, and to offer at least a limited defence against aggression.

The question of economic preparations was not forgotten either. The army economic office, which was absorbed into the Defence Ministry in 1933 under the title Economics and Armaments Office, continued the work begun in the 1920s, drawing up plans and schedules for mobilization and building the network of economic officers into a national system of armaments inspectorates. At a national level the armed forces, through a new Reich Defence Council, composed of civilian and military leaders, hoped to create a forum in which to influence all major areas of policy in favour of military priorities. During 1934 the army pressed for the appointment of an 'economic dictator' who could centralize economic preparations for war under a single authority. Though the forces would have preferred a military candidate, the choice for the post fell on Hjalmar Schacht, the minister of economics, who had shown himself since 1933 to

[8] K.-J. Müller, *Das Heer und Hitler: Armee und nationalsozialistische Regime 1933–1940* (Stuttgart, 1969), 63.
[9] H. J. Rautenberg, 'Drei Dokumente zur Planung eines 300,000-Mann Friedensheeres aus dem Dezember 1933', *Militärgeschichtliche Mitteilungen*, 22 (1977), 103–39; M. Geyer, 'Das Zweite Rüstungsprogramm (1930–1934)', Ibid. 17 (1975), 25–72.

be sympathetic to the rearmament programmes and an ally of the military and business circles already active in military affairs. In May 1935 he was created Plenipotentiary for War Economy. In November von Blomberg published full 'Guidelines for the unitary preparation of the defence of the Reich', dividing up tasks between the armed forces and Schacht: the former to control all armaments and related production, the latter to supervise the co-ordination of the civilian areas of the economy.[10]

The achievements of the first years of military build-up were modest. (See Table 6.2 in the Appendix to this chapter for military expenditure figures.) Financed by a mixture of ordinary revenue and secret state bills (the Mefo Bills[11]), military expenditure represented 1.9 per cent of GNP in 1933 and 4 per cent in 1934, only reaching economically significant levels in 1935–6. Even Hitler felt the constraint of international opinion, and hesitated to arm too quickly or openly in the first years of Nazi power. Much of the initial expenditure was invested in building up equipment, accommodation, and bases denied Germany under the Versailles Treaty, and which were essential to provide facilities for an extensive training programme. The rapid expansion of the forces had to wait until the infrastructure of military life was fully restored. This explains the slow initial growth of the new German air force. The early production plans were small-scale and improvisatory. The first programme called for 294 aircraft in 1933 and 1934, most of them converted civilian types or trainers. The first full production schedule was drawn up in March 1934, a programme of 17,000 aircraft in five years. Though impressive on paper, 58 per cent of the aircraft were trainers, and only 18 per cent combat aircraft, many of which were obsolescent bi-planes or converted transport aircraft of doubtful usefulness.[12] Air force leaders in Germany called their force the *Risiko-Luftwaffe*, or 'risk air force', as an indication of its obvious weaknesses in the early years of expansion. It was, of course, very difficult to move more rapidly, for Germany possessed no significant aircraft industry in 1933. Large investments and labour retraining schemes were necessary to provide the industrial capacity as quickly as possible. In 1933 aircraft output was valued at RM 37m., and the industry employed 12,000 people; in 1936 output had risen remarkably to RM 527m., with 188,000 employed, and Germany was in the forefront of aviation technology.[13]

---

[10] Carroll, *Design*, 91–2, 108–9, 120.

[11] 'Mefo' = Metallurgische Forschungsgesellschaft, a holding company set up to handle additional secret Reich funds for rearmament.

[12] R. J. Overy, 'German Air Strength 1933–1939: A Note', *Historical Journal*, 27 (1984), 466–9.

[13] E. Homze, *Arming the Luftwaffe: The Reich Air Ministry and the German Aircraft Industry 1919–1939* (Lincoln, Nebr., 1976), 184; NA T177 Roll 32, frames 3720919–36, 'Die Flugzeugindustrie 1933–36', Feb. 1938, 1–5.

The navy, too, expanded slowly, along lines laid down in the Weimar period. Hitler was unenthusiastic at first about expanding German naval power, and not until March 1934, after Admiral Raeder, the commander-in-chief, had persuaded him that there lay some diplomatic advantage in a more powerful navy, was a Replacement Shipbuilding Programme authorized which promised to take German naval strength beyond the levels permitted by Versailles. But shortages of construction capacity and skilled labour, a consequence of the more successful pressure of the army and air force for economic resources, produced a constant lag between the programme and its realization. Naval spending from 1933 to 1936 totalled only RM 2,600m., or 13 per cent of total military expenditure.[14]

There is no doubt that Hitler intended, as did the individual heads of the three services, to build up much larger forces once the economic capacity was available, and once the early problems of organization and expansion were overcome. Indeed the speed with which it was intended to make Germany defence-proof again, within the space of three or four years, was a tribute to the widespread support for rearmament in the civilian and military establishments. With the rapid fall in unemployment and the growth of industrial output, encouraged by government construction and motorization policies, conditions were created that permitted a higher level of rearmament. From 1935/6 economic policy was directed much more at restructuring the economy to conform with the needs of future warfare.[15] Yet neither Hitler nor the War Ministry imposed any overall plan for rearmament, relating service costs and requirements within a set budget on any long-term basis. The three services were allowed to pursue their individual programmes regardless of the cost or of the impact on each other. The subsequent lack of co-ordination brought increasing problems of competition for resources of labour and materials. By 1936 von Blomberg and Schacht began to look for ways of controlling the pace and scope of rearmament to ensure that it posed no danger to the stability of the economy in the early stages of recovery from the depression, while at

[14] Deist, Wehrmacht, 70–4. Figures from J. Dülffer, Weimar, Hitler und die Marine: Reichspolitik und Flottenbau 1920–1939 (Düsseldorf, 1973), 563.

[15] There is still much dispute about how extensive rearmament was in the early years of the regime. Much hinges on how rearmament is defined. Certainly a strong economy would make rearmament easier to achieve. This is the argument of A. Schweitzer, 'Die wirtschaftliche Wiederaufrüstung Deutschlands 1934–1936'; Zeitschrift für die gesamte Staatswissenschaft, 114 (1958); and H.-E. Volkmann, 'Aspekte der ns "Wehrwirtschaft" 1933 bis 1936' Francia, 5 (1977). In the narrower sense of direct military expenditure and investment it is clear that in the first two years of the regime much state and private activity was in non-military areas. See M. Wolffsohn, 'Arbeitsbeschaffung und Rüstung im nationalsozialistischen Deutschland 1933' Militärgeschichtliche Mitteilungen, 22 (1977), 9–19; R. J. Overy, 'Cars, Roads and Economic Recovery in Germany 1932–38', Economic History Review 2nd ser. 28 (1975), 466–83.

the same time fulfilling the wider aim of building a broad, total, preparation for defence.[16]

II

For Hitler the conditions that made for a cautious programme of rearmament—fear of foreign intervention and the weaknesses of the German economy—gave way by 1936 to a quite different set of conditions. In 1935 he declared Germany's rearmament in public, overturning the Versailles Settlement. In March 1936 German troops reoccupied the demilitarized zone in the Rhineland, permitting industry there to be brought into the rearmament programme. Neither action provoked any significant reaction from the Treaty powers. The Ethiopian crisis, the Spanish Civil War, and Russian rearmament suggested the need for greater speed in the military build-up. The obvious failure of the League to provide a system of collective security provided the opportunity for action. The economy in 1936 was nearing full employment and had recovered to a degree that made the next stage of Hitler's foreign and military programme possible. For Hitler the object was not merely to make Germany capable of defending herself again, and to harness the economy to that end, or even to reverse the territorial clauses of Versailles, but to use Germany's new economic and military strength to embark on a period of active expansion in Europe, and eventually the achievement of German world-power status.

This was a conception that went well beyond what the army or the conservative politicians expected. Indeed Schacht was by 1936 anxious lest the uncoordinated expansion of German armament would threaten the economy by denying opportunities to expand consumer goods and exports. The armed forces also expressed concern about the economy, though for different reasons. The army now believed that the initial plan for a 300,000-man force could not guarantee the defence of Germany. During the first half of 1936 the army staff worked on a new plan, eventually published in August, for the build-up of an 800,000-man army, whose equipment would make even greater demands on the German economy. Calculations showed that the new forces would cost RM 8,000m. in each year 1937–9, instead of the RM 3,600m. originally scheduled.[17] To cope with these new requirements, von Blomberg and the army leaders tried during 1936 to exert a greater degree of military control

---

[16] IWM, Wehrwirtschaftsstab papers, Mi 14/317, German War Ministry 'Grundsätze für die wirtschaftliche Mobilmachung' 1 Feb. 1936.

[17] Deist, *Wehrmacht*, 44–7.

over the economy, particularly raw materials and trade, and to achieve the rational defence economy first mooted in the 1920s. Absence of such control would, they feared, endanger the whole military programme. According to the armed forces, uncontrolled civilian demands increased pressure on imports and diverted resources from exports, which were essential to earn foreign exchange to buy raw materials for military industries. Civilian demand created undesirable pressures on investment and finance as well. In August 1936 von Blomberg wrote to Göring:

Measures of the armed forces themselves will not suffice to overcome the difficulties . . . Everything must be postponed that does not serve export and expanded armaments. That includes the work of the Labour Front, the *Autobahnen* and also house construction . . . It also appears to be necessary to direct domestic policy in such a way that damage to export prospects will be avoided.

What the armed forces wanted was the 'right to instruct all the highest offices of state for the unitary conduct of all preparations for war'.[18]

Yet just at the point where the military leaders believed they could create the new 'military-economic' state, and would have support from Hitler for doing so, the terms of the political situation changed fundamentally; and they changed primarily because of rearmament. During 1936 there was growing evidence of pressure in the economy in certain sectors, brought about by rapid military expansion since 1934. Schacht and his supporters now argued that rearmament should accordingly be slowed down: expanding rearmament further threatened to create serious economic crisis, which in turn compromised the prospects for fulfilling existing rearmament plans. The armed forces were caught in a dilemma. They did not want either to provoke an economic crisis, or to reverse the tempo of rearmament. At first efforts were made to reconcile economic and military priorities. In April 1936 Hitler appointed Göring, with the qualified approval of von Blomberg and Schacht, as commissioner for raw materials and foreign exchange, responsible for extending state control over how these resources should be used.

Despite Göring's appointment, the situation continued to worsen over the summer. While the army pushed ahead with its vast new plans for equipment, the air force launched a major phase of modernization and expansion. It was impossible for the armed forces to agree to less rearmament, for this contradicted the whole trend of military policy since 1932. The loose alliance between von Blomberg and Schacht, between the military and German conservatives, was severed. To Hitler it was evident

---

[18] BA-MA Wi I F 5.203, von Blomberg to Göring, 31 Aug. 1936; Wi I F 5.3615, Jodl to von Blomberg, 'Vortragsnotiz über Vierjahresplan und Vorbereitung der Kriegswirtschaft 30 Dec. 1936'.

from the squabbling and confusion between the two sides that to have both a stable economy and more rearmament it was necessary to bring both under more direct government and party control. Moreover, now that the economy had recovered and unemployment was no longer a political issue, it was possible to exploit the economy more generally and deliberately for war. This meant in the main a policy of greater economic self-sufficiency, and more comprehensive controls over labour, raw materials, and investment; and, of course, more arms. Hitler was no longer prepared to put such an economic and military strategy at risk by leaving it to military or financial experts critical of Nazi policy.

There remained none the less a close identity of interest between Hitler and the military. Both wanted to gear economic development to military requirements, not just in the production of armaments but in all areas of economic life. Who should bear responsibility for this was a political, not an economic, question. Hitler had to make sure that war preparations were in the hands of those who shared entirely his foreign-policy ambitions, and who would be politically capable of overcoming domestic resistance to their achievement. Hitler revived the idea of an 'economic dictator', but instead of choosing an army officer, he decided to expand the powers already exercised by the air force leader, Göring. It was not in the end a surprising choice. Göring combined high military and civilian office, and was a major figure in the Nazi movement. He was a keen autarkist and rearmer: 'Carrying out of the armaments programme according to schedule and planned scale', he claimed in July 1936, 'is *the* task of German politics.'[19] Göring was, according to Hitler, 'the best man that I possess, a man of the greatest will-power, a man of decision who knows what is wanted and will get it done.'[20] No one else was so uncompromisingly committed to large-scale preparations for war. In August 1936 Hitler retired to his summer retreat where he worked on a memorandum which formed the basis of the Second Four Year Plan. In September Göring was formally given the twin tasks of preparing the economy and the armed forces for war. When he described his new office to his cabinet colleagues he told them that 'all measures have to be taken just as if we were actually in the stage of imminent danger of war'.[21]

The creation of the Four Year Plan was a decisive step towards preparing Germany for total mobilization. Göring later argued that the Plan 'was a basic prerequisite for the entire building-up and expansion of the armament industry'. The Plan was the instrument which was to enable the Nazis 'to determine the whole of Germany's economic and social

[19] Ibid., Göring to von Blomberg, 19 June 1936.
[20] E. Gritzbach, *Hermann Göring* (Berlin, 1938), 104.
[21] IMT xxxvi. 491, Council of Ministers, 4 Sept. 1936.

policy'.[22] Although the Plan was never in practice quite as far-reaching as this, Göring was never constrained by its terms of reference, but willingly trespassed in any area of economic policy if it furthered Hitler's aims. There is no doubt that it symbolized a major change of pace and direction in German war preparations. Indeed, it marked the point at which the armed forces' conception of a recovery of defensive strength gave way to Hitler's conception of large-scale preparations for aggressive imperialism, over which the armed forces were to have less and less say.

The core of the Four Year Plan was the increase in the domestic production of vital raw materials: synthetic rubber, fuel-oil, and iron ore, all of them resources essential for waging war. The synthetics programme dated from well before 1936, for the Nazis had favoured autarkist solutions from the start. But Hitler was dissatisfied with the slow rate at which the schemes were developing and, in the case of domestic iron ore, the unenthusiastic response of German heavy industry. During 1937 large plans were laid for synthetic rubber, or 'Buna', and synthetic fuel produced from coal. Both schemes were to be completed by the mid-1940s. The expense and complexity of the programmes made it difficult to accelerate them, and much of the initial planning and development was finished only in 1938 and 1939. In the area of domestic iron ores, the Four Year Plan, in the face of considerable hostility from the iron and steel industry and from Schacht, insisted on exploiting the low-yield ores of central and southern Germany to reduce dependence on Swedish and French supplies, neither of which could be guaranteed in wartime. As shown in Chapter 5, Göring founded a large state-owned concern to carry this policy into effect. The Reichswerke 'Hermann Göring' was within eighteen months the third largest concern in Germany, and branched out from iron ore into the production of finished steel and armaments. The object was to turn the Reichswerke into 'the core of the whole of German rearmament, of supplies for the arms industry in peace and war'. By 1940 it was the largest concern in Europe, engrossing almost all the industrial and raw-material supplies of the territories acquired in 1938 and 1939. The Reichswerke symbolized in a very literal sense the close connection in Hitler's strategy between economy and war.[23]

During the years between its inception and the outbreak of war the Four Year Plan encroached on all the major areas of economic policy-making, so much so that Schacht resigned in November 1937 in protest, and his

---

[22] IMT ix. 450. See too D. Petzina, *Autarkiepolitik im Dritten Reich* (Stuttgart, 1968).
[23] G. Meinck, *Hitler und die deutsche Aufrüstung 1933–1937* (Wiesbaden, 1959), 159–69; R. J. Overy, 'Heavy Industry and the State in the Third Reich: The Reichswerke Crisis', *European History Quarterly*, 15 (1985), 316–23; M. Riedel, *Eisen und Kohle für das Dritte Reich* (Göttingen, 1973), esp. 25–61; on synthetic fuel see W. Birkenfeld, *Der synthetische Treibstoff 1933–1945* (Göttingen, 1963), 77 ff.

place was taken by Walther Funk, a political nonentity, entirely subordinate to Göring. By 1938 Göring was 'economic dictator' in all but name, with the ultimate say over areas of the economy vital for war: agriculture, necessary to provide the food for the home population; labour, which was to be trained and distributed as the needs of rearmament dictated; trade and foreign exchange, necessary in order to give priority to strategic imports; and over prices to ensure that rapid increases in armaments and strategic heavy industries should not bring about a serious risk of inflation. Though Schacht and other conservative economists predicted swift economic disaster as a result of these policies, Göring was able to use a large circle of officials, businessmen, and officers, sympathetic to the general drift of Hitler's strategy, to implement the detailed industrial and financial policies. The army economic office continued its own work in loose association with the Four Year Plan, sometimes duplicating, sometimes complementing, what was being done by Göring.

During this period control over the economy gradually passed to the state, while control over and influence upon the economic aspects of war preparation were gradually removed from the armed forces. The army in particular regarded this as a far from satisfactory outcome. Even though Göring's policies were precisely those anticipated by the 'total-war' strategists of the 1920s, army leaders only very reluctantly accepted their reduced responsibility for *Wehrwirtschaft* within the changed political balance, and resented encroachment on what they saw as soldiers' work. Even the explosives programme was removed from army control and placed under a commissioner from the Four Year Plan. So, too, was the building of the *Westwall* fortifications in 1938, which became the responsibility of Fritz Todt, head of the *Autobahn* project; and the oil, motor vehicle, and machinery industry, came under Four Year Plan supervision in order to integrate them into the overall plan for economic mobilization.

These programmes were not pursued without difficulty. Shortages of skilled labour and raw materials were apparent as early as 1936, and the financing of the new schemes (the Four Year Plan took over 50 per cent of all industrial investment in 1938 and 1939) placed new demands on the brittle German financial system. Nevertheless strict regulation and state intervention prevented serious crisis. 'Measures', Göring said, 'which in a state with a parliamentary government would probably bring about inflation, do not have the same results in a totalitarian system.'[24] Under state control interest rates were forced down, while prices and wages were maintained at the levels of the early 1930s, with only minor adjustments.

---

[24] *NCA* iii. 883, Meeting of Council of Ministers, 12 May 1936.

Even by 1939 the state debt in Germany was lower than in Britain and the United States.

In a great many respects the extension of state power over the economy was a logical outcome of the rapid and uncoordinated growth of armaments between 1933 and 1936. Though the armed forces carped at the loss of responsibility for areas that they regarded as properly military in nature, rearmament and economic stability were both safeguarded after 1936, while the economy was directed in a much more specific way to the needs of defence than had been possible before. Preparations for war dominated economic and political decisions in Germany after 1936. A momentum was built into German rearmament thereafter, fuelled by the protection it received from Hitler in state policy, the enthusiasm of the movement's leaders, and the unwillingness of the armed forces to turn down the offer of more arms.

III

What increasingly worried financial and military circles in Germany was the exact nature of Hitler's plans. The armed forces expected rearmament to peak in 1937–9 and then for the level of expenditure to be gradually reduced by two-thirds, leaving enough to maintain a large conscript armed force with modern weapons. Some civilian ministers and officials assumed that rearmament would be completed even earlier, in 1937–8, and would then be progressively scaled down. Yet the whole tenor of Hitler's strategy from autumn 1936 onwards, when he talked privately about the need to solve living-space through conflict in the east, was to prepare Germany for large-scale war at some date in the future. There were plenty of indications about what Hitler's aims were. The construction of *Mitteleuropa* (union with Austria, the return of the Sudetenland and Silesia, domination of the Balkans) was common knowledge by 1937 and was widely supported.[25] But in November 1937, talking to the service chiefs, Hitler gave formal notice that his ambitions were much greater than this. The first stage was to create a large, resource-rich area in central Europe, to be achieved without general war. This was to be followed 'by 1943–5' by major war with the great powers in order 'to solve Germany's problem of space'. Hitler's strategic plan foresaw a conflict for continental hegemony, and war with Russia for a Eurasian empire. Beyond that lay his imperial fantasies: world dominion, war with the United States and the British Empire.[26]

[25] R. J. Overy, *Goering: The 'Iron Man'* (London, 1984), 76–8.
[26] M. Hauner, 'Did Hitler Want a World Dominion?', *Journal of Contemporary History*, 13 (1978); M. Michaelis, 'World Power Status or World Dominion?', *Historical Journal*, 15

As Germany grew militarily and economically stronger, Hitler moved from consolidation to active expansion. He did so against the background of economic restructuring already described. Yet many historians have argued that before 1939 German rearmament was deliberately restricted, that Germany's leaders set out to pursue short, limited wars which would make the minimum of demands on the civilian economy. This was partly, it is argued, from fear of the political repercussions of cutting living standards, partly because of the difficulties in mobilizing resources inherent in the confused administrative jungle of the Nazi state. In 1961 A. J. P. Taylor, in an influential and controversial book, challenged the very idea that Hitler even planned to do more than build up limited armed strength in order to reverse the territorial clauses of Versailles, and that he had achieved all he wanted by 1939. The evidence that Hitler wished to go further than this is now overwhelming. But whether he sought to achieve this by total or limited war is still very much in dispute.[27]

As more evidence comes to light on detailed service programmes and economic preparations under the Four Year Plan, it seems clear that the Nazi leaders intended to establish the army vision of total mobilization. How successfully they did so is another question. Much of the argument, of course, hinges on how rearmament or military preparations are defined. Though formal expenditure on armaments and military investment was higher than that of any power save the Soviet Union before 1939, it is the investment in the military infrastructure and the heavy industrial and engineering base of the economy for strategic purposes that demonstrates the wider economic commitment to war. In 1939 Colonel Thomas noted: 'the Führer stands by the view that any mobilization must be a total one, and that the three pillars, military, economy, and party, have their own great tasks in wartime'.[28] According to Göring: 'The Four Year Plan has the task of preparing the German economy for total war.'[29] The surviving documents from 1938 onwards are littered with references of this kind.

The point that is always overlooked is that Hitler wanted total economic

(1972); G. Weinberg, *World in the Balance* (Hanover, Mass., 1981), esp. ch. 3 on Hitler's attitude to the United States; id., *Hitler's Foreign Policy 1937–1939* (London, 1980); K. Hildebrand, 'La Programme de Hitler et sa réalisation', *Revue d'histoire de la Deuxième Guerre Mondiale*, 21 (1971); W. Michalka, *Ribbentrop und die deutsche Weltpolitik 1933–1940* (Munich, 1980), esp. 172–6, 220 ff.; J. Thies, *Architekt der Weltherrschaft: Die Endziele Hitlers* (Düsseldorf, 1976). There is interesting, if unreliable, testimony in H. Rauschning, *Hitler Speaks* (London, 1939).

[27] A. J. P. Taylor, *The Origins of the Second World War* (London, 1961); id., '1939 Revisited', German Historical Institute Annual Lecture, 1980; A. S. Milward, *The German Economy at War* (London, 1965), ch. 1; W. Carr, *Arms, Autarky and Aggression* (London, 1972).

[28] IWM Mi 14/377 (file 2), Thomas memorandum, 28 Mar. 1939, 'Gesichtspunkte für die Änderung der Mob. Vorbereitungen der Wirtschaft', 2.

[29] BA-MA Wi I F 5.412, conference with Göring, 16 July 1938, 1.

mobilization in any war with other great powers whether the conflict was a short one or a long-drawn-out struggle. The outcome of military campaigns could not be planned in advance, as the failure of the Schlieffen Plan in 1914 had shown. Hence the need for thorough economic preparation and conversion in case the worst happened. In May 1939 Hitler told his generals:

Everybody's Armed Forces and Government must strive for a short war. But the government must, however, also prepare for a war of from ten to fifteen years' duration. History shows that wars were always expected to be short. In 1914 it was still believed that long wars could not be financed. Even today this idea buzzes in a lot of heads. However, every state will hold out as long as it can.

Either way, to gamble with the economy was to court the disaster of the Great War again. 'The idea of getting out cheaply is dangerous,' Hitler continued; 'there is no such possibility'.[30] This view was a central part of Groener's argument in 1928, that the economy should be adjusted in such a way that it could be quickly and completely converted to war in order to utilize, in one great campaign, all the resources of the nation. The object of German war preparations was to win the war next time, whatever its nature.

Limited war could be fought with stocks of weapons and raw materials (imported and home-produced) while making very little additional claim on the civilian economy and labour force. The Four Year Plan involved quite a different strategy. Its programme of import substitution was expensive and long-term. Investment in the Reichswerke at Salzgitter, Linz, and Brüx (in the Sudetenland) totalled RM 800m., more than all the investment in the aircraft industry from 1933 to 1937. The rubber, fuel, and explosives plans called for sums of the same magnitude. The state invested RM 280m. directly in Buna production, out of a total investment of RM 940m. The explosives plan finalized in 1938, the so-called Schnellplan (Accelerated Programme) required a 40 per cent increase in the output of heavy machinery in Germany, and 480,000 additional tons of steel a year.[31] The programme for expanding food output was to enable Germany to withstand a long war of attrition. Controls over investment directed capital away from consumer industries to armaments and war-related tasks, which took well over 60 per cent of all capital invested between 1936 and 1939. The controls over labour, which took the form of

[30] *Documents on German Foreign Policy*, ser. D, vol. 6 (HMSO, 1956), 577.

[31] For details see G. Plumpe, 'Industrie, technischer Fortschritt und Staat: Die Kautschuksynthese in Deutschland 1906–1944/5', *Geschichte und Gesellschaft*, 9 (1983), 594; on the Reichswerke IWM FD 264/46, 'Konzernverzeichnis HGW Montanblock'; on the Schnellplan A. Bagel-Bohlan, *Hitlers industrielle Kriegsvorbereitung im Dritten Reich 1936 bis 1939* (Koblenz, 1975), 117–21.

compulsory retraining and labour conscription, though used sparingly before 1939, anticipated the mobilization of the entire working population for war tasks. Propaganda efforts were focused on preparing the population 'spiritually for total war'.[32] The fact that many Germans found such a prospect unthinkable in the late 1930s only demonstrated what a gulf existed between popular perceptions of foreign policy and the extravagant war plans of their leaders.

The Four Year Plan provided the economic substructure which permitted the expansion of the superstructure of actual armaments production, the guns, aircraft, and submarines. It was the very scale of these armament programmes that led to the growing economic commitment after 1936. During the course of 1938, with the original aircraft production plans coming to an end, and the army still struggling to complete the August 1936 programme on schedule, Hitler ordered the expansion of the armed forces to a scale well beyond anything that the services had asked for, or could reasonably cope with. Between the 'Hossbach conference' in November 1937 and the conference called with the commanders-in-chief on 28 May 1938, Hitler discussed at length prospects for a new level of arms output. Exact records of the May conference are missing, but the surviving evidence suggests that Hitler's purpose was to match military output with his now much enlarged foreign policy aims. Not only did this mean more weapons, it also meant more money. Hitler authorized a radical change in Reich financial policy, ending the system of Mefo Bills which had helped to finance rearmament since 1934, and resorting instead to Reich loans, increasing the public debt by 30 per cent in the fiscal year 1938/9.[33]

The navy was a major beneficiary of this increased commitment to armaments. Because Britain and France were now potential enemies, it won a higher priority from Hitler. He called for more battleships, and a speeding up of construction on those already laid down, as well as an expanded programme of submarine building. During 1938 the navy worked out plans for a large battle fleet for war with Britain which formed the basis of the so-called Z-Plan, published in January 1939, for 6 battleships, 4 aircraft carriers, 8 heavy cruisers, 233 submarines, and

[32] Overy, *Goering*, 84. The place of propaganda in German war preparations is an important one. Both the army and Hitler put great value on morale—attitudes to authority, the willingness to accept sacrifices, psychological orientation to military goals. See J. Syottek, *Mobilmachung für den totalen Krieg: Die propagandistische Vorbereitung der deutschen Bevölkerung auf dem Zweiten Weltkrieg* (Opladen, 1976), 94–103, 194–201; D. Aigner, *Das Ringen um England: Die öffentliche Meinung 1933–1939* (Munich 1969), 349–53.

[33] M. Geyer, 'Rüstungsbeschleunigung und Inflation: Zur Inflationsdenkschrift des OKW von November 1938', *Militärgeschichtliche Mitteilungen*, 23 (1981); L. Graf Schwerin von Krosigk, *Staatsbankrott: Finanzpolitik des Deutschen Reiches 1920–1945* (Göttingen, 1974), 281–5.

numerous destroyers and smaller craft.[34] The air force won its share of the new spending too. During the summer of 1938 a new production programme, Plan 8, was drawn up which would take the Luftwaffe from the initial stage of training and establishment to the creation of a large fleet of combat aircraft, 16,000 aircraft in all in two years. The new aircraft were among the most advanced air weapons in the world. On 14 October Hitler confirmed these plans with a commitment to increase the size of the air force fivefold, including a large core of 4,300 medium and heavy bombers.[35] The army was told to speed up the activation of its forces, and to expand motorization. Explosives production, which lagged significantly behind the output of finished weapons, was now planned to reach the levels of the last months of the First World War; and it was placed under the Four Year Plan with the publication in July of the 'Wehrwirtschaftliche neue Erzeugungsplan' (New defence economy production plan).[36] In October Göring announced to his staff Hitler's general decision to raise 'the level of armament from 100 to 300 . . . a gigantic programme compared with which previous achievements are insignificant'.[37]

It is difficult to see how such programmes taken together can be regarded as limited rearmament. No area of the economy remained untouched by the demands of war. The effect on consumption was clear. Consumer industries were held back during the recovery period. Investment in the consumer industries failed to reach the level of 1929 where investment in heavy industry exceeded it by 170 per cent. Real earnings, after allowance for increased taxation and party levies, as well as declining quality of goods, failed to regain the levels of the late 1920s, even though real GNP per head was 31 per cent higher. Consumption as a share of National Income declined from 71 per cent in 1928 to 59 per cent in 1938, while consumer industries came bottom of the list in the allocation of raw materials and capital. The deliberate containment of consumption encouraged higher levels of saving, which was then channelled via the banks and savings institutions into government loans for the war economy. Nazi leaders were well aware that this was part of the price for the economic strategy pursued after 1936. For Hitler it was a necessary, if regrettable, outcome. When he was told bluntly about economic problems

---

[34] Deist, *Wehrmacht*, 82–4; Dülffer, *Marine*, 488–504. At the time the German navy possessed only 3 small battleships, no heavy cruisers or aircraft carriers, and only 36 submarines.

[35] NA 177, Roll 14, frames 3698585–8, letter from Luftwaffe General Staff to Generalluftzeugmeister, 9 Aug. 1939; R. J. Overy, 'From "Uralbomber" to "Amerikabomber": The Luftwaffe and Strategic Bombing', *Journal of Strategic Studies*, 1 (1978), 155–7.

[36] Bagel-Bohlan, *Kriegsvorbereitung*, 118–20.

[37] *NCA* iii. 901; IMT xxxii. 413, note on the meeting of the Reich Defence Council, 18 Nov. 1938.

in June 1939 by Emil Puhl, deputy head of the Reichsbank, he responded by saying 'yes, he feared it might be so and he knew that the German housewife must be having a hard time to make both ends meet. But he wondered whether she does not sometimes consider that this is a relatively small price to pay for the great advantages which had been gained for Germany.'[38] As early as 1934 Thomas recorded that it was 'Hitler's own insistence that the people take deprivations and curtailments upon itself'; while on the eve of the war in 1939 Hitler told Birger Dahlerus, the envoy between Göring and the British government, 'War does not frighten me. If privation lies ahead of the German people, I shall be the first to starve and set my people a good example.'[39] The German people was expected to bear its part of the sacrifices during the period of German expansion. The scale of preparations made this unavoidable.

So extensive were the new plans from 1938 that the armed forces themselves began to question their feasibility. The rearmament programme was increasingly out of their control. Admiral Raeder tried to resign in January 1939 rather than attempt to meet Hitler's extravagant naval programme. Hitler, though sometimes painted as a leader remote from the day-to-day workings of the economy and military affairs, played a central role in dictating not just the broad outlines of policy, but details of individual programmes. It is not clear that he himself ever seriously questioned how realistic his programmes were, although he did claim during the war that he exaggerated requirements in order to achieve more than his timid commanders would have asked for. He admired men like Erhard Milch, Göring's deputy, for whom 'there was no such word as impossible'.[40] This made it harder for those who wanted rearmament to take a more modest course, or who could not understand what Hitler wanted the forces for. Yet during the summer of 1938 the army found it impossible to meet its scheduled expansion on time, and find all the raw materials and labour to provide the weapons. By the second half of the year the armed forces were taking almost one-third of all iron and steel production, while future programmes promised to claim more copper, tin, zinc, and aluminium than Germany could produce or import. In November the army, though still enthusiastic for a carefully prepared armament in depth, sent a long report to Hitler, explaining that inflation appeared unavoidable, and that this would threaten internal stability and

[38] Bank of England, Central Bank Papers (Germany), OV 34, ix, notes of a conversation with Dr Puhl in Basle, 12 June 1939.

[39] Carroll, *Design*, 89; see too BA-MA Wi I F 5.114, 'Aufrüstung und Export', lecture by Thomas to Reichsgruppe Industrie, 10 June 1937, 21: 'Everything that only serves to increase amenities or concerns the improvement of the living conditions of the people must take second place.'

[40] D. Irving, *The Rise and Fall of the Luftwaffe: The Life of Erhard Milch* (London, 1973), 150.

the continuation of rearmament.[41] The finance minister made the same point: expenditure would have to be cut or German finances would face serious difficulties. At the Reichsbank Schacht made one more concerted effort to deny Hitler access to the financial resources he needed to carry the new programmes out.

Another political crisis, like that of 1936, appeared likely. But Hitler was determined to maintain the tempo of military preparation at all costs. He saw it as the responsibility of the state to take the necessary measures to ensure that economic crisis could be avoided, a view briskly summed up by Göring the previous June: 'There is no place for the collapse of parts of the economy. Ways will be found. The Reich will step into the breach to help.'[42] Rather than cut back, Hitler sacked Schacht and other critics. Schwerin von Krosigk and Funk were authorized to work out new financial arrangements, and in April 1939 a New Finance Plan was made law, designed to accommodate the state's new expenditure without inflation. Despite a major increase in the state debt, the official price index rose by less than 1 per cent in 1939. Serious planning was initiated for wartime finance and rationing, and for current savings in non-military expenditure. Göring embarked on a programme of industrial and administrative rationalization designed to free labour and resources for war preparation at the expenses of the 'inessential industries'.[43] Ignoring all the warnings, Hitler permitted military expenditure to rise sharply in 1939, consuming more in the first nine months than the whole of 1938, while avoiding serious economic crisis.

What Hitler wanted such forces for was far from clear to the critics of rearmament, and has remained an area of controversy ever since. They were certainly not designed, as Taylor argued, to defeat Czechoslovakia and Poland and establish German domination of central Europe. The forces available to Germany by 1938 and 1939 were more than equal to such a task, as they showed in the rapid defeat of Poland. The new rearmament programmes only made sense in terms of a major war with other great powers, in the east to establish *Lebensraum*, and in the west, against Britain and the United States, to defend Germany's claim to world-power status. The naval programme and the strategic bomber plans, including the 'Amerikabomber' which Messerschmitt began work on in 1939, and the range of advanced technological projects on which German

---

[41] Geyer, 'Rüstungsbeschleunigung', 125–7.
[42] Ibid. 136.
[43] *NCA* iii. 902–3, 1301-PS, conference with Field Marshal Göring, 14 Oct. 1938; BA-MA, Wi I F 5.560, Sitzung des Reichsverteidigungsrats 18 Nov. 1938: 'not food but the increase in armaments is the most important thing . . . review of the economy must concern itself with which production units are really necessary. Those that are not essential will be converted.'

research was working, all indicate clearly the drift of Hitler's strategy. The important point was the question of timing. As Hitler indicated in November 1937, the major programmes would be completed by 1943–5. The air force plans would not be completed until 1942 at the earliest. The Z-Plan covered the whole period from 1939 to 1949. The army motorization and its training schedules for officers and technicians would run on to 1943. More important, the raw material programmes, in oil, rubber, and iron and steel, including the incorporation of the captured resources of central Europe, would not be finished until the same date. The plans to modernize and strengthen the railway system, begun seriously only in 1939, would carry on until 1944.[44] Had Germany enjoyed a further four or five years of peace, the military forces and economic resources available would have made her, like Russia and America, one of the military superpowers of the 1940s.

Hitler's problem was to avoid major conflict until these programmes were complete, and it is here that his strategic competence and political judgement were seriously questioned. He expected that Britain and France would not fight in 1939 for Poland. There were good grounds for this belief: Britain and France had been only too willing to sell out Czechoslovakia and were still talking of settlement and compromise in the summer of 1939; military intelligence in Germany suggested that western rearmament was still far behind German; and Hitler's political instincts told him that western leaders would not risk plunging their countries into war for fear of political collapse at home. The strength of this conviction was recalled by a German official later in the war:

When the German leadership decided on a final solution through force of the conflict with Poland in September 1939, they were firmly convinced that it would only come to a war with Poland ... On the basis of certain information from England and France, and despite numerous warnings, they had a fixed belief that these two countries would not stand by the obligations of their guarantee to Poland and at the very least would not enter into any serious war against Germany.[45]

The German non-aggression pact with Russia in August 1939 was a diplomatic coup of the greatest importance, for it came at just the right psychological moment from Hitler's point of view, and seemed to remove once and for all the threat of a serious crisis in the west.

It is clear now that Hitler misjudged the political situation in both France and Britain. His intelligence on their war preparations was badly

[44] R. J. Overy, 'Hitler's War and the German Economy: A Reinterpretation', *Economic History Review*, 2nd ser. 35 (1982), 276–7.
[45] IWM AL 2719, 'Deutschlands gegenwärtige Wehrwirtschaftliche Lage, Juni 1944', Dr Tomberg, 7 Aug. 1944, introduction, 1.

flawed, and his personal judgement of his adversaries, though in a great many respects correct, failed to take account of the pressures for war with which both Daladier and Chamberlain were faced. The whole nature of German economic preparations runs against the thesis that Hitler deliberately sought a general war in 1939. On 21 August the German High Command (OKW) was specifically instructed by Hitler only to prepare for a limited economic mobilization against Poland, not general mobilization. Not until after Britain and France had finally declared war on 3 September did Hitler order the total mobilization of the economy.[46]

By September 1939, as Hitler and the Nazi leaders knew, German preparations were far from complete. Germany entered the war with no operational heavy bomber, only 5 battleships and 50 submarines, and only 300 of the most up-to-date Mark IV tank. The factories of the Four Year Plan were in some cases still on the drawing-board. The large programme of armaments set in motion in 1938 was only in its early stages. The aircraft production plans were revised downwards during 1939 to achieve what the Air Ministry thought was a more realistic match between plan and industrial capacity. Of the new generation of advanced aircraft only 1,800 had been produced by April 1939 (11 per cent of the programme), while 15,500 remained to be produced.[47] The army faced the same problems. Motorization was slow, so much so that a special commissioner, General von Schell, was appointed under the Four Year Plan to speed up the rationalization of the motor industry and to adjust it more to military needs. In 1939 the armed forces took only 8 per cent of the output of the vehicle industry. When the war broke out stockpiles of weapons and munitions were low, and there was a serious shortage of bombs and shells; and the horse remained the main form of traction for the German forces at the front throughout the war.

The most obvious difficulties for rearmament lay in the supply of labour and raw materials, and it was here that government efforts were directed in 1938 and 1939. After regular promptings from the army, Göring set up a comprehensive register of all workers so that less essential labour could be transferred to where it was most needed, and the 'Wehrarbeiter', workers vital for the defence industries, could be given protected status. Efforts were made to increase female labour, already at a high level by western standards. More foreign labour was recruited, reaching a level of 435,000 by the spring of 1939. The unemployed in Austria, the Sudetenland, and Bohemia were rapidly absorbed into the German industrial effort. The Four Year Plan and the Labour Front also embarked

---

[46] IWM Mi 14/328 (d), OKW, minutes of meeting of Wehrwirtschaft inspectors, 21 Aug. 1939; OKW, Wehrmachtteile Besprechung, 3 Sept. 1939, 1; *Dokumente der deutschen Politik*, vii (Berlin, 1941), 403–4, Kriegswirtschaftsverordnung, 4 Sept. 1939.

[47] Overy, 'German Air Strength', 470.

on programmes of retraining and apprenticeships to produce more of the skilled workers needed by the armaments industry. By 1939 the supply of trained, skilled metalworkers, a bottleneck in the First World War, actually exceeded demand. In 1938–9 513,000 workers were retrained under the new schemes; industry retrained an estimated 500,000 itself; and another 223,000 were retrained under other programmes. Labour was attracted away from consumer sectors by the prospect of fuller and more regular hours, and higher earnings, in heavy industry and engineering.[48]

Military claims on raw materials, and on machinery and equipment, were also a constant source of friction. Expansion of investment in armaments and strategic sectors starved other areas of the economy—the Ruhr coal and steel industry, the railways—of sufficient resources to cope with the high level of military demand. And the difficulties of finding sufficient foreign exchange to buy important materials abroad remained an endemic one, rendered more difficult by growing demands in world markets for materials from the other rearming powers. In the light of these problems, it is easy to see how important to German rearmament were the areas acquired in central Europe: iron ore and engineering in Austria, lignite in the Sudetenland for synthetic fuel production, coal, iron, steel, and armaments in Bohemia. Austria became the site in 1939 for a huge new integrated steel and armaments complex at Linz; and the industries of Bohemia were integrated at once into the programmes of the Four Year Plan. The occupation of western Czechoslovakia in March 1939 had been carried out, Göring told his staff in July 1939, 'in order to increase German war potential by the exploitation of the industry there'.[49]

Such problems were made more difficult than they might have been through the failure to establish a satisfactory organization for war production and mobilization planning under the Four Year Plan. Although Göring was the ultimate authority on these questions, as head of the Plan and chairman of the Reich Defence Council, formal central control was not exercised on any regular or systematic basis. As a result decisions at local level were often made by the armed forces' armaments inspectorate, which was relatively experienced and had a large organization already in being. The armed forces abandoned their special powers in the economy only with great reluctance after the summer of 1938, when Göring and Hitler tried to confine their responsibility to 'armed combat' alone. The armed forces and the War Ministry (which became OKW in February 1938) continued their work in preparing the necessary legislation and decrees for mobilization, and did much of the groundwork for 'Mob. Plan

---

[48] J. Gillingham, 'The "Deproletarianization" of German Society: Vocational Training in the Third Reich', *Journal of Social History*, 19 (1985/6), 427–8; see too IWM Mi 14/478, Heereswaffenamt, 'Die personelle Leistungsfähigkeit Deutschlands im Mob. Fall', Mar. 1939.
[49] NCA viii. 202, R-133, note of a conference on 25 July 1939 with Field Marshal Göring.

Wirtschaft', the technical schedules for economic mobilization should war break out. The military thus retained much more influence than Hitler intended, and were able almost by default to reassert this when war came in September 1939.[50]

It would nevertheless be wrong to exaggerate the extent to which the rearmament effort was affected by organizational problems, any more than by shortages of raw materials. It should not be forgotten that a very great deal was achieved by 1939 in the space of only five or six years. Yet it is certainly true that Germany was not fully prepared for a general war in 1939. In many cases work had only just begun in 1939 for a war still assumed to be some years distant, if it ever came. The register of labour and of firms, the mobilization plans for each major industrial sector, the preparations for war finance and rationing, only started during the course of the year. When war broke out the registers were barely two-thirds completed and nothing had been settled about how to finance a war. Many sectors vital to any war effort lacked any mobilization plan at all. On 8 August, just three weeks before the war, OKW drew up a list of industrial sectors for which mobilization plans already existed, those in preparation, and those still to be produced (see Table 6.1). It is significant that the mobilization plans that were complete were exclusively in the heavy-industrial sectors, the foundations of the war economy, and were almost entirely lacking in the manufacturing sectors, reflecting closely the priorities established under the Four Year Plan in 1936.

Even in the heavy-industrial sectors there was still much that needed to be done. On 3 September, at a meeting called by OKW for all three services, Colonel Thomas explained how much basic preparation was incomplete:

The position is clear. The total mobilization of the economy has been ordered . . . a whole number of programmes are still at this time in progress, which should actually have been ready by the outbreak of war: the giant explosives plan; the programme for munitions production; the substitution of scarce materials; the Ju-88 programme; the building up of the oil industry; the expansion of Buna, aluminium and magnesium production; the construction of fortified airfields; further necessary building on the *Westwall* and the construction of public air-raid shelters.[51]

These were all projects due for completion during the following four or five years.

---

[50] IWM Mi 14/294 (file 5), OKW, 'Die Munitionslage 1939', Nov. 1939; Mi 14/328 (d), OKW, Wehrmachtteile Besprechung 3 Sept. 1939, 1: 'direction of the production plans obviously comes from the armed forces themselves as only they can judge what they need'; Carroll, *Design*, 163–5.

[51] IWM Mi 14/328 (d), OKW, Wehrmachtteile Besprechung, 3 Sept. 1939, 1–2.

TABLE 6.1. *Mobilization planning, by industry, August 1939*

Completed	In preparation	No mob. plan
Iron and steel	Mining (coal)	Motor vehicles
Chemicals (in part)	Semi-finished metal goods	Aircraft industry
Mineral oil	Machine tools	Precision instruments
		Optical goods
		Iron and steel manufactures
		Metal goods
		Refining processes
		Electrical industry
		Construction industry

Source: IWM M; 14/294 (file 5), Major Neef, 'Grundlagen und Werfahren zur Schaffung von Mob. Erzeugungsplänen', 9 Aug. 1939, 9.

Given the nature and timing of the rearmament drive and the loose strategic guidelines from Hitler, this situation should not surprise us. Yet much of the problem was self-inflicted. The whole strategy of 'armament in depth' was a counsel of perfection, reflecting the ambitions of highly trained and professional armed forces, but in many respects unrealizable at the optimum. The military planners insisted from the outset on the highest-quality equipment, and on the right of the soldiers to interfere at every stage in the production process or in the development of weapons, with little regard for productivity, industrial priorities, or costs. According to a war academy lecture in 1936: 'Armament is for us a question of quality in every sense, but particularly in the technical sense...an armament that overemphasizes quantity and speed of production is only to be achieved at the expense of material and individual quality.'[52] Hence the reluctance of the army to mobilize the mass-production car industry in Germany either before or after 1939, in stark contrast to the practice in Britain and the United States. From 1938 onwards the Four Year Plan initiated policies to achieve greater rationalization and a simplification of weapons and production methods, but with little effect. Even in the most advanced sector, the aircraft industry, traditional work methods, excessive use of skilled labour, and wasteful material policies undermined the drive to greater output started by Hitler in 1938.

In the end much of this problem stemmed from the excessive competition for resources and duplication of effort between the three services, who refused to co-ordinate their production, leading to a multiplicity of weapons types and components and far too little standardization. Prospects for economies of scale and long production

[52] BA R7 XVI/36, Wehrwirtschaftsstab memorandum, 25 Feb. 1936, 5.

runs, of which German industry was perfectly capable, were poor from the outset. The military preferred close links with small, specialized firms which were more responsive to individual requirements rather than with new mass-production industries. Not surprisingly, therefore, the armed forces found it difficult to win the confidence and co-operation of industry. This was partly because many businessmen hoped that the economic recovery would bring more exports and consumer demand, where long-term prospects for growth and profits seemed better. Many assumed that rearmament would soon slow down and hesitated to risk putting too many resources into military work in case the market collapsed and they were left with unusable capacity. Businessmen, particularly in the private sector, resented the spread of state controls made necessary by rearmament, and the subordinate role they were expected to play to the armed forces and the Four Year Plan. Manufacturers complained all the time about planlessness and incompetent procurement policies, but since, in the end, the marriage of military and industry, the dream of the total-war strategists, was a military affair, the businessmen and engineers were ignored.[53] The 'military-industrial' complex was a very one-sided arrangement, creating through military priorities and technical ignorance a high-cost, wasteful, and poorly organized armaments economy. If Hitler's demands in 1938 were beyond what Germany could currently produce, they were not beyond what a better-organized and more rational productive system could have achieved with more years of preparation.

IV

Some historians have argued that it was precisely the contradictions represented by this failure to match Hitler's exaggerated demands with economic reality that created the pressure to go to war in 1939. The threat of inflation and popular unrest which lurked behind it is said to have produced a situation of economic chaos, a contradiction that could only be resolved by embarking on short wars of plunder to keep the German people quiet.[54] The evidence for such a view is slender. Hitler was much

---

[53] A. Schröter and J. Bach, 'Zur Planung der wehrwirtschaftlichen Mobilmachung durch den deutschen faschistischen Imperialismus vor dem Beginn des Zweiten Weltkrieges', *Jahrbuch für Wirtschaftsgeschichte*, 17 (1978), 42–5; W. Treue, 'Die Einstellung einiger deutschen Grossindustriellen zu Hitlers Aussenpolitik', *Geschichte in Wissenschaft und Unterricht*, 17 (1966), 103–4. On the attitude of industry to mobilization planning see IWM Mi 14/294 (file 5), Wi Rü Amt, 'Die mangelnde Vorbereitung der Industrie durch den GBW', 24 Nov. 1939. On industry and the business cycle see Geyer, 'Rüstungsbeschleunigung', 134–6.

[54] T. W. Mason, 'Innere Krise und Angriffskrieg', in F. Forstmeier and H.-E. Volkmann (eds.), *Wirtschaft und Rüstung am Vorabend des Zweiten Weltkrieges* (Düsseldorf, 1975),

more concerned with the pressures of foreign rather than domestic policy. Economic pressures suggested that general war should be avoided until the programmes begun in 1937–8 could be completed, a view Hitler reiterated in May 1939, after the plan to defeat Poland had been drawn up. Nor is there any conclusive evidence that the working class was politically restive in 1939, and much evidence to the contrary. The state apparatus was more widespread and more effective by 1939 than at any previous stage in the Third Reich.[55] 'Revolution from within is impossible', Hitler told his commanders-in-chief in November 1939.[56] The propaganda of the regime was highly effective in creating nationalist support among the population in 1939 against the new 'Encirclement' plans of Britain and France. Local party and security reports in the summer of 1939 show little sign of serious discontent and much support for Hitler's policies. 'Trust in the Führer', ran one report, 'and pride in German policy among the population is boundless. Everyone is sympathetic.'[57]

Nor is there compelling evidence that Hitler was worried about living standards to the extent that such fears forced him to choose war. A reasonable minimum was achieved by 1939 and would be guaranteed in wartime thanks to a thorough system of rationing and welfare payments designed to avoid the poverty and hardships of the First World War. Until rearmament was completed and German power secured in Europe and Asia, consumption was to remain suppressed. Reports from Berlin suggested that there was 'plenty of minor grumbling, but no serious discontent'[58] as a result of rationing and mobilization measures. Consumption had been deliberately suppressed and wages kept low well before 1939. Even after the war Hitler's plans for the reconstruction of German cities on a vast scale promised to take up whatever resources might have been available for boosting living standards.[59] There was no effective way this political situation could be reversed, as long as the state was willing, forcefully, to impose economic regulations, including effective

---

158–88. See too C. Bloch, 'Die Wechselwirkung der Nationalsozialistischen Innen- und Aussenpolitik 1933–1939' in M. Funke (ed.) *Hitler, Deutschland, und die Mächte* (Düsseldorf, 1976), 205–21.

[55] Something along these lines has already been argued by Mason himself. See T. W. Mason, 'Die Bändigung der Arbeiterklasse im ns Deutschland', in C. Sachse *et al.* (eds.), *Angst, Belohnung, Zucht und Ordnung: Herrschaftsmechanismus im Nationalsozialismus* (Düsseldorf, 1982), 48–53.

[56] NCA iii. 578, 789-PS, Führer conference with heads of armed forces, 23 Nov. 1939.

[57] IWM, *Aus deutschen Urkunden 1935–1945*, 211, Kreisleitung report, Kreis Darmstadt, Aug. 1939.

[58] Bank of England, Central Bank Papers (Germany), OV 34, ix, memorandum on the German situation, 23 Oct. 1939.

[59] J. Thies, 'Hitler's European Building Programme', *Journal of Contemporary History*, 13 (1978).

price and wage controls, and to repress fiercely any dissidence. Moreover, as we have seen, great efforts were made in 1938 and 1939 to cope with the economic problems thrown up by rearmament—the New Finance Plan, greater savings, labour retraining. In many respects the German economy was stronger in 1939 than its enemies or critics supposed, and very much more so than during the severe slump of 1929–33. It was the second-largest industrial economy in the world, with increasing domination of the smaller economies around it, capable by 1939 not only of devoting 23 per cent of GNP to military spending, but of building huge public projects and the *Autobahnen*, as well as maintaining living standards at a level unlikely to provoke serious political dissent. It was an economy which, far from collapsing from 'overheating' as British leaders hoped, or later cracking under blockade and bombing, took the combined might of the other three largest industrial economies to defeat during four years of bitter conflict.

Of course rearmament did have political effects. It dominated the political scene after 1933. Under Hitler pursuit of rearmament was a means to political advancement, and any policy that promised to enlarge or protect the defence capability of the state, however tenuous, found all doors open. The major political changes in 1936–8 were concerned essentially with the economic consequences of rearmament. State policy was more and more concerned with promoting war preparations at the expense of every other priority. Göring's rapid rise to become 'economic dictator' can be attributed very largely to his defence of rearmament and his promise to provide an alternative, Nazi-led economy to the more conservative schemes of Schacht. The seizure of the political initiative in directing resources to war stemmed from the Nazis' own view of the role of the economy in the state: 'It is the duty of the leadership of the state politically to develop and direct the economy, so that it may best serve the preservation of the nation... the economy must conform itself with defence, and defence with the economy, and politics must take care that defence and economy correspond to one another and increase each other's power.'[60] Rearmament was both a technical problem and a political one. Hitler expected the forces and the Four Year Plan to solve the technical side, but only the Nazi movement itself, through a revival of national consciousness and political will, could be trusted to solve the ultimate questions about Germany's future. This view led logically and inexorably to the point later in the war when Nazi appointees and the SS finally assumed control over the means of waging war.[61]

[60] BA R7 XVI/36, Wehrwirtschaftsstab memorandum, 25 Feb. 1936, 1.
[61] A. Speer, *The Slave State: Heinrich Himmler's Masterplan for SS Supremacy* (London, 1981); E. Georg, *Die wirtschaftliche Unternehmungen der SS* (Stuttgart, 1963).

From the point of view of German military and economic preparations, the war that broke out in the the autumn of 1939 was the wrong war. There was not even any serious planning for conflict with the western powers, no Schlieffen Plan. When on 1 September Dahlerus warned Hitler of British firmness, his response was spontaneous: 'if necessary I will fight for ten years'.[62] When general war came on 3 September a state of full economic mobilization was declared at once, putting all the nation's resources at the service of the war. Widespread rationing was introduced, immediately cutting civilian consumption to low levels. Within two years 60 per cent of the German industrial work-force was working on military orders, a higher proportion than in Britain. Hitler himself, still closely involved in drawing up the production plans for the war economy, put his signature in the winter of 1939 to arms programmes 'with the highest possible figures', that exceeded even the unrealistic schedules of 1938. 'We Germans', Hitler confided in what proved to be one of the last of his private audiences, in October 1939, 'have learnt much from our experiences in the First World War and are fully prepared, both militarily and economically for a long war.'[63] The wheel had come full circle. Groener's 'total mobilization' was finally realized in Hitler's 'struggle for national existence'.

Appendix

TABLE 6.2. *Military expenditure, 1933/4–1938/9* (RMm.)

Fiscal year	I Budget expenditure				II Mefo-bills	Total I + II
	Total	Army	Air Force	Navy		
1933/4	750	—	—	—	—	750
1934/5	1,953	815	642	496	2,140	4,093
1935/6	2,772	1,041	1,036	695	2,720	5,492
1936/7	5,821	2,435	2,225	1,161	4,450	10,271
1937/8	8,273	3,537	3,258	1,478	2,690	10,963
1938/9	17,247	9,465	6,026	1,756	—	17,247

Note: Fiscal year 1 April–31 March.

Sources: Dülffer, *Marine*, 563; BA R2/21776–81, Reichsfinanzmin., 'Entwicklung der Ausgaben in der Rechnungsjahren 1934–1939', 17 July 1939; Schwerin von Krosigk, *Staatsbankrott*, 230–1.

[62] B. Dahlerus, *Last Attempt* (London, 1948), 119.
[63] Sven Hedin, *German Diary* (Dublin, 1951), 46–7.

TABLE 6.3. *Aircraft production, 1933–1939*

	1933	1934	1935	1936	1937	1938	1939
Total	368	1,968	3,183	5,112	5,606	5,235	8,295
Combat	—	840	1,823	1,530	2,651	3,350	4,733

Source: R. Wagenführ, *Die deutsche Industrie im Kriege* (Berlin, 1963), 74.

TABLE 6.4. *Production programmes of the Four Year Plan* ('000 tonnes)

	1936	1942[a]
Mineral oil	1,714.0	4,920
Aviation fuel	76.0	1,200
Aluminium	98.0	255
Buna rubber	0.0	114
Artificial fibres	26.7	142
Leather substitutes	14.5	70
Explosives	38.0	450
Basic chemicals	2,765.0	5,334
Synthetic textiles	88.0	395
Iron ore	7,570.0	20,932[b]
Coal	158,300.0	264,500
Lignite[c]	161,400.0	248,900
Machinery and machine tools (RMm.)	2,570	5,550

[a] The figures for 1942 are for Greater Germany, and are based on the monthly production figures for May.

[b] Figure for 1941 (excluding occupied areas).

[c] Known in Germany as 'brown coal', lignite was a vital material in the production of synthetic fuel.

Source: BA R26 I/18, 'Ergebnisse der Vierjahresplan-Arbeit', 20–40.

7

Germany, 'Domestic Crisis', and War in 1939

THE outbreak of war in 1939 is one of the most prominent issues to divide 'intentionalist' and 'functionalist' historians of the Third Reich. The former stress the individual responsibility of Hitler and his ministerial and party entourage in framing and carrying out a programme of foreign expansion, whose final goal was the achievement of world power.[1] The latter, while not ignoring the Nazis' foreign-policy objectives, emphasize the primacy of structural or functional pressures in explaining the German push for war in 1939. Such pressures are presented as the product of an increasingly bankrupt political system, which sought to stave off the inevitable social tensions between masses and leaders brought about by rapid rearmament and subsequent economic crisis. In this sense the situation is similar to that which provoked the old ruling class into risking European war in 1914, and at least one German historian has argued that the primacy of *Innenpolitik* is a key and continuous explanation for the nature of German foreign policy in the era of the world wars.[2]

These are not by any means exclusive historical categories, and there can be few historians of modern Germany who do not find themselves striking some kind of analytical balance between stated intention and the circumstances and pressures which limited or diverted it. In a recent article, Tim Mason has argued that there is a half-way house, that Hitler's declared intentions and their flawed realization are evidence of a dialectical

---

[1] K. Hildebrand, *The Foreign Policy of the Third Reich* (London, 1973), esp. 91–104; id., 'La Programme de Hitler et sa réalisation', *Revue d'histoire de la deuxieme Guerre Mondiale*, 21 (1971), 7–36; A. Kuhn, *Hitlers aussenpolitisches Programm* (Stuttgart, 1970); J. Thies, *Architekt der Weltherrschaft: Die Endziele Hitlers* (Düsseldorf, 1976); M. Hauner, 'Did Hitler want a World Dominion?', *Journal of Contemporary History*, 13 (1978); F. Zipfel, 'Hitlers Konzept einer Neuordnung Europas', in D. Kurse (ed.), *Aus Theorie und Praxis der Geschichtswissenschaft* (Berlin, 1972), 154–74; M. Michaelis, 'World Power Status or World Dominion', *Historical Journal*, 15 (1972), 331–60; B. Stegemann, 'Hitlers Ziele im ersten Kriegsjahr 1939/40', *Militärgeschichtliche Mitteilungen*, 27 (1980), 93–105. There are many more.

[2] F. Fischer, *Bündnis der Eliten: Zur Kontinuität der Machtstruktur in Deutschland 1871–1945* (Düsseldorf, 1979). There is a general survey on the literature in E. Hennig, 'Industrie, Aufrüstung und Kriegsvorbereitung im deutschen Faschismus', in *Gesellschaft: Beiträge zur Marxschen Theorie 5* (Frankfurt am Main, 1975), 68–148; and also in I. Kershaw, *The Nazi Dictatorship* (London, 1985), 106–29. For a general functionalist view see H. Mommsen, 'National Socialism: Continuity and Change', in W. Laqueur (ed.), *Fascism: A Reader's Guide* (London, 1976), esp. 177 ff.

relationship between actors and historical context which gives primacy to neither. In Hitler's case he chooses to call this relationship 'struggle', the interplay between Hitler's crude and literal idealism and the reality of economic and administrative circumstances in the Germany of the 1930s.[3] But in the case of the outbreak of war Mason argues that Hitler could not, for once, resolve this tension, so that circumstances got the better of him. He had to choose war in 1939 'because of domestic pressures and constraints which were economic in origin and also expressed themselves in acute social and political tension'.[4] Hitler, Mason argues, did not want to fight the war he was faced with in September 1939, but he had little choice: 'These were the actions of a man who had lost control of his policies.'[5]

This is still a widely held explanation for the origins of the Second World War, and indeed has been so since these ideas were first formulated some twenty years ago. In the complex politics of the Third Reich two key elements have been observed: first, the effort to push through a programme of rearmament in a short period of time to satisfy the demands of the military élites, the party hawks, and Hitler's own expansionist dreams; secondly, the desire that rearmament should not be compromised by provoking the masses into political opposition by reducing living standards and courting economic crisis. It is argued that the administrative confusion and political contradictions of the Nazi system made it increasingly difficult to deliver both arms and consumer goods/food and produced instead regular crises (foreign exchange and food in 1936, labour and the balance of payments in 1938). By 1938–9 the crisis is assumed to have reached a climax, with trade, finance, labour, and agriculture all producing irreconcilable pressures for an economy conditioned by full employment and an overvalued mark. Knowing that economic stability, and thus domestic political peace, could not be maintained under these conditions, and yet unwilling to cut back sharply on government expenditure and rearmament, Hitler launched war in 1939 in order to gain plunder with which to stave off a crisis in living standards, permit further rearmament, and divert domestic political conflicts to a patriotic struggle against a new encirclement.[6]

---

[3] T. W. Mason, 'Intention and Explanation: A Current Controversy about the Interpretation of National Socialism', in G. Hirschfeld and L. Kettenacker (eds.), *The Führer State: Myths and Realities* (Stuttgart, 1981), 23–40.

[4] Ibid. 39.

[5] T. W. Mason, conference abstract, 'Zur Funktion des Angriffskrieges 1939', 3 (conference on 'Rüstung und Wirtschaft am Vorabend des 2. Weltkrieges', Freiburg, 1974).

[6] Mason, 'Intention and Explanation', 38–9; id., 'Some Origins of the Second World War', *Past and Present*, 10 (1964), 67–87; id., Innere Krise und Angriffskrieg', in F. Forstmeier and H.-E. Volkmann (eds.), *Wirtschaft und Rüstung am Vorabend des Zweiten Weltkrieges* (Düsseldorf, 1975), 158–88; id., *Sozialpolitik im Dritten Reich* (Opladen, 1977),

The product of this tension between economic reality and military planning was the strategy of Blitzkrieg. Short wars would mean fewer arms and the maintenance of living standards; and would also accommodate the constraints on the military economy produced by the competing party and administrative hierarchies which, it is claimed, made it inherently difficult to prepare effectively for any larger military effort, while at the same time making war more likely. The emphasis here is on the primacy of domestic politics and economic circumstances as explanatory approaches to the outbreak of war.[7] These arguments have not been without their critics. Blitzkrieg, for example, as a coherent military and economic concept, has proved to be a difficult strategy to defend in the light of the evidence.[8] This conclusion alone must throw increasing doubt on current analyses of the relationship between domestic affairs and foreign policy in the Third Reich. The purpose of this chapter is to explore alternative ways of looking at German economic performance in the late 1930s, and to reassess the threat of serious political disorder in 1938–9. These approaches present a quite different conclusion about the outbreak of war in 1939 and Hitler's motives in attacking Poland.

I

The question of evidence is clearly crucial here, since it is on the basis of a large quantity of apparently unambiguous documentary material that the conceptual apparatus of 'domestic crisis' has been founded. And yet the evidence in question is in some important respects highly ambiguous. In the first place the absence of a body of documents expressing Hitler's recognition that foreign policy in 1938–9 was governed by domestic political priorities is taken to imply that the evidence has been lost or destroyed, rather than that it simply did not exist.[9] Though far from

esp. ch. 6. For a variation on this theme see C. Bloch, 'Die Wechselwirkung der nationalsozialistischen Innen- und Aussenpolitik 1933–1939', in M. Funke (ed.), Hitler, Deutschland, und die Mächte (Düsseldorf, 1976), 205–21, who argues that Hitler, like Bismarck, used foreign policy manipulatively to maintain political popularity at home.

[7] See esp. A. S. Milward, 'Hitlers Konzept des Blitzkrieges', in A. Hillgruber (ed.), Probleme des Zweiten Weltkrieges (Cologne, 1967), 19–40; id., 'Could Sweden have stopped the Second World War?', Scandinavian Economic History Review, 15 (1967), 135 ff. See too W. Murray, The Change in the European Balance of Power 1938–39 (Princeton, NJ, 1984), 18–27.

[8] R. J. Overy, 'Hitler's War and the German Economy: A Reinterpretation', Economic History Review, 2nd ser. 35 (1982), 272–91; id., Goering: The 'Iron Man' (London, 1984), 82–9; J. Dülffer, 'Der Beginn des Krieges 1939: Hitler, die innere Krise und das Mächtesystem', Geschichte und Gesellschaft, 2 (1976), 443–70; M. Cooper, The German Army 1933–1945 (London, 1978), 116–66.

[9] Mason, 'Some Origins', 86.

complete, there is a very great deal of evidence on what Nazi leaders were doing and thinking in 1939, very little of which suggests the primacy of domestic pressures. Though it does demonstrate some confusion of purpose and error of judgement (far from an exclusively German failing before 1939), there are clear strands of strategy which provide an alternative and perfectly plausible explanation for German policy. The bulk of the positive evidence for economic and domestic political crisis came either from unsympathetic conservative circles within Germany, or exiled opponents of Nazism, or, significantly, from British pre-war assessments of the nature of the Nazi regime.

The roots of the argument about domestic pressures can be traced back to the critical discussions in British political and economic circles of the nature and prospects of Hitler's Germany. The rise of economic nationalism in Germany, following on the serious credit crisis of 1930–3, inclined British politicians to view the German economy even before 1933 as a fragile structure, highly susceptible to financial and trading problems, faced all the time with serious economic difficulties, which might bring social discontent.[10] It was this situation that prompted the onset of economic appeasement. Western statesmen assumed that if Hitler were granted economic concessions, he could be brought to the conference table to work out a general European settlement. 'Might not', asked Chamberlain, 'a great improvement in Germany's economic situation result in her becoming quieter and less interested in political adventures?'[11] Cordell Hull, Roosevelt's Secretary of State, argued that in a freer world economy, prepared to extend concessions to Germany, 'discontent will fade and dictators will not have to brandish the sword and appeal to patriotism to stay in power'.[12] In western eyes a demonstrable relationship existed between economic prosperity and peace.

This perception of German weakness affected British strategy in a number of ways. Chamberlain's hope was that a policy of concessions to Hitler on economic questions might bring about a Grand Settlement on British

[10] On British reactions during the depression see H. James, *The Reichsbank and Public Finance in Germany 1924–1933* (Frankfurt am Main, 1985), esp. ch. 6.

[11] Quoted in L. R. Pratt, *East of Malta, West of Suez: Britain's Mediterranean Crisis 1936–1939* (Cambridge, 1975), 158. These views underlined Chamberlain's personal belief that economic questions dominated the policy of any leader: 'The ultimate aim of this government, and I believe that it must be the ultimate aim of every government,' he told the House of Commons, 'whatever its complexion may be, is the improvement of the standard of living of the people'; in N. Chamberlain, *The Struggle for Peace* (London, 1939), 347 (debate of 1 Nov. 1938). There is evidence that the French government thought in the same way. In 1937 Paul Elbel told the French Chamber, following a Franco-German trade agreement, that 'Germany will cease to appear "a nation of dispossessed" and, with prosperity, shall return a love of calm and a will to collaborate'; quoted in J. Gillingham, *Industry and Politics in the Third Reich* (London, 1985), 104.

[12] A. W. Schatz, 'The Anglo-American Trade Agreement and Cordell Hull's Search for Peace 1936–1938', *Journal of American History*, 57 (1970/1), 89.

terms.[13] By holding out the prospect of economic improvement, the British government hoped to win over the moderates around Hitler, including the Reichsbank President Schacht and Hermann Göring, who would then put pressure on him to adopt a more conciliatory foreign policy. The British were alive to all kinds of rumours about political conflicts among Germany's leaders as evidence that they would finally see political good sense.[14] But at the same time the government began large-scale rearmament and a policy of increasing firmness towards Germany, in the belief that Hitler could be deterred from waging war by demonstrating the superiority of Franco-British economic resources.[15] By calling his bluff the Allies supposed that Hitler would face political hostility at home and might even be overthrown. Carl Goerdeler, a leading member of the German conservative opposition, told the British in April 1939 that a policy of firmness might see the 'Hitler adventure... liquidated before the end of June'.[16]

There was, of course, much wishful thinking in all this; and such a strategy carried a considerable risk that Hitler might commit what the British Foreign Office called a 'mad-dog act' if he were pushed into an economic corner in 1939. Intelligence sources sent a stream of information to London suggesting that 'Hitler would have to explode in 1939'.[17] After Munich there was increasing evidence of what the British saw as economic crisis and social unrest in Germany. The 'X-documents', memoranda by a British businessman, A. P. Young, of conversations with Goerdeler, included the view that 'the working classes are nervous, distrustful of the leader. Their allegiance is doubtful'.[18] The second document, in September 1938, gave an even franker assessment:

---

[13] K. Feiling, The Life of Neville Chamberlain (London, 1946), 332–4.

[14] C. A. Macdonald, 'Economic Appeasement and the German "Moderates", 1937–1939', Past and Present, 18 (1972). A good example of these rumours was the message from the British ambassador in Paris, Sir Eric Phipps, to Halifax in Jan. 1939 to the effect that Göring was about to be appointed German chancellor: see Documents on British Foreign Policy (HMSO, 1953), ser. 3 (hereafter DBFP), vi. 9–10, Phipps to Halifax, 25 Jan. 1939.

[15] D. Dilks, 'The Unnecessary War? Military Advice on Foreign Policy in Great Britain 1931–1939', in A. Preston (ed.), General Staffs and Diplomacy before the Second World War (London, 1978), 120–7; G. C. Peden, 'A Matter of Timing: The Economic Background to British Foreign Policy 1937–1939', History, 66 (1984), 19–22; R. Shay, British Rearmament in the Thirties (Princeton, NJ, 1977), 228 ff.

[16] Lord Gladwyn, The Memoirs of Lord Gladwyn (London, 1972), 87.

[17] Ibid. 86–7. The Foreign Office view was that Hitler's object 'was to divert attention away from the German economy, to suppress his own moderates, and to secure supplies of raw materials'. See too F. H. Hinsley, British Intelligence in the Second World War, i (HMSO, 1979), 67–9, who records Halifax's view that the sacking of Schacht was evidence that economic problems were pushing 'the mad dictator to insane adventures'.

[18] DBFP vi. 708, app. I (v), enclosure in letter from Orme-Sargent to N. Henderson, 23 June 1939, 'conversation with 'X' June 13 1939'. Interestingly, Henderson's response to the letter (app. I (vii), 709–10) was that the army would march behind Hitler 'as one man', and that the view that workers were unreceptive to Nazism 'rubbish', when even the most intelligent Germans believe it'. A Foreign Office note adds, however, that: 'evidence from other sources shows that the working classes are not so impressed as the intelligentsia'.

the feeling among the people against war is welling up at an alarming rate. His [Goerdeler's] recent talks with leading industrialists had satisfied X that the workers' feelings have been bitterly roused to the point where, if they were in possession of arms, they would physically revolt against the present regime.

Sending the report to British officials Young added the comment: 'We know exactly the economic and financial conditions in Germany. Nobody can deceive us. This knowledge in itself would be a big inducement to go to war, if we did not believe passionately in the divine cause of peace.'[19] Four months later Goerdeler's views hinted at imminent disaster: 'Economic and financial situation gravely critical. Inner situation desperate. Economic conditions getting worse.'[20]

Though there was some evidence to the contrary, the general drift of British strategic thinking hardened during 1939 into a conviction that Hitler was walking a tightrope. He might launch a sudden war which the Allies would win because of their greater economic resources and the alleged inability of the German economy to sustain more than a short war once subjected to blockade and bombing; or he might back down and Germany be brought back to the conference table to complete the task of economic and political restructuring begun seriously in 1938. Either way Germany was the victim of a deep socio-economic crisis which would bring an end to Hitlerism as it then stood. Right up to the declaration of war the Allies gambled on German weakness. Indeed the French decision to declare war was allegedly influenced by a letter received by the French prime minister, Daladier, at the end of August from Berlin asking the French only to stand firm to bring Hitler to his knees.[21]

It is difficult not to conclude that British politicians, who found Nazism so hard to understand, deluded themselves into believing that Germany was much weaker and Hitler's position more precarious than was actually the case. The German economy did not collapse in 1939, nor was Hitler overthrown. Yet the British attitude is more understandable if it is remembered that much of the intelligence fed to London before 1939 came from circles within Germany, or exiles, hostile to Hitler, who had their own motives for painting a bleak picture of Germany's room for

[19] A. P. Young, *The 'X' Documents* (London, 1974), 78–82, X doc. 2, 'conversation with Carl Goerdeler, Zürich, Sept. 11th 1938'.

[20] Ibid. 156–7, 'Memorandum based on most trustworthy information received before Jan. 15th 1939, conversation between Carl Goerdeler and Reinhold Schairer'. Goerdeler's reports were received unkindly by the Foreign Office, not because they were disbelieved, but because the British regarded him as an old-fashioned German nationalist.

[21] P. Reynaud, *In the Thick of the Fight, 1930–1945* (London, 1955), 235–6. See too R. J. Minney (ed.), *The Private Papers of Hore-Belisha* (London, 1960), 216, where Hore-Belisha records his meeting with Daladier on 21 Aug. 1939: 'He thought that in the event of war we should derive great help from those hostile to the regime in Germany and attached importance to assistance by German émigrés, who were extremely anxious to disrupt the regime.'

manœuvre. There were many books and pamphlets published in Britain, France, and the United States in the 1930s by German men and women with 'inside' knowledge of German conditions, most of whom were deeply hostile to Nazism.[22] This literature contributed to popular western perceptions of German difficulties, and suggested strategies for exploiting them. Contacts with prominent Germans through official channels or through intelligence added weight to the popular view. Hjalmar Schacht, the German economics minister until November 1937, tried to persuade foreign opinion that conditions in Germany would deteriorate unless the western powers made concessions.[23] There were numerous contacts with the German conservatives, who were disgruntled at being displaced by party appointees whom they thought incapable of running an economy or conducting foreign affairs sensibly, and who hoped to win friends abroad to help them reassert their influence. There were German businessmen, too, who disliked the economic controls and red tape and were seriously worried about the economic effects of rearmament and Nazi extremism. They again had their foreign contacts to whom they submitted their complaints about the new Nazi masters.[24] All of these groups contributed one way or another to building up a picture of impending economic crisis and political unrest in Germany, and it constitutes a large part of the evidence used by historians that this was so.[25]

Of course German conservatives thought their anxieties justified by what they saw around them. Even those close to Hitler in the armed forces or the government believed that by 1938–9 Hitler had gone too far. The army produced a long memorandum on the danger of inflation in December 1938, which contributed to a wider discussion of the acceptable levels of armaments expenditure and prompted some limited proposals for cutting government spending.[26] The finance minister also called for

[22] e.g. A Member of the German Freedom Party, *Hitler Calls this Living* (London, 1939); H. Hauser, *Hitler versus Germany: A Survey of Present-Day Germany from the Inside* (London, 1940); H. Rauschning, *Germany's Revolution of Destruction* (London, 1939); A. Kolnai, *The War against the West* (London, 1938); E. Hambloch, *Germany Rampant: A Study in Economic Militarism* (London, 1939). There are numerous others.
[23] F. Leith-Ross, *Money Talks: Fifty Years of International Finance* (London, 1968), 232–6, 254–5; Macdonald, 'Economic Appeasement', 106–10.
[24] Christie Papers, Churchill College, Cambridge, 186/1 4, Rough Notes from a recent conversation with a German industrialist, 1 June 1939; 180/1 25 'Memo by members of "Big Business" in Germany, 1937'; letter from a senior industrialist to Christie, 7 July 1939; Young, 'X' *Documents*, 78, 137.
[25] See Mason, 'Intention and Explanation', 39, who argues that 'The view that this was a major urgent problem was common to many top military and political leaders in Germany, to top officials in Britain, to some German industrialists and civil servants, to German exiles and members of the conservative resistance, and to non-German bankers and academics', without seriously assessing the motives or interests of those involved, or evaluating their evidence.
[26] M. Geyer, 'Rüstungsbeschleunigung und Inflation: Zur Inflationsdenkschrift des OKW von November 1938', *Militärgeschichtliche Mitteilungen*, 23 (1981), 121–69. For Göring's

extensive cuts in government investment projects and greater rationalization in the public sector. Late in 1938 wide publicity was given abroad to a speech by the Reichsbank director Rudolf Brinkmann highly critical of Nazi economic policy. 'The situation in the private economy is critical,' he told the Reich Chamber of Industry at Dresden. 'For one thing, there are far more orders than can be filled in a lifetime. For another, production has deteriorated to a much greater extent than we can answer for. There are unmistakably genuine inflationary symptoms, and it is high time to call a halt and to promote exports.'[27] A few weeks later Schacht himself was removed as president of the bank, which was used as further evidence abroad that all was far from well with the German economy. 'Very bad! Lots of repercussions in the foreign market' was the reaction of the American Treasury Secretary, Morgenthau, to the news.[28]

Underlying German worries about the financial situation was the deeper fear, evident well before 1938, that Nazi economic profligacy would endanger the currency and produce a political backlash against military spending, or might threaten to topple the regime altogether and plunge Germany back once again into political turmoil. Conservatives found Nazi economics unorthodox. They disliked excessive government control and distrusted deficit financing, as did their counterparts in the west, where fears circulated about the end of capitalism in Germany. Economic orthodoxy and political good sense seemed to indicate the need for moderation. Conservative fears for German political stability were exported to a foreign audience only too willing to believe that Nazism was a shallow, crisis-ridden movement, trying to stave off the consequences of overheating the economy.

II

To use this conservative fear as evidence that a crisis of these proportions existed in Germany is to distort the economic reality. It also ignores other contemporary evidence which suggested the opposite: that the German economy was actually considerably stronger than its critics believed in

response to these fears see IMT xxxii. 412–17, note on the meeting of the Reich Defence Council, 18 Nov. 1938.

[27] NA, Reichsfinanzministerium, T178, Roll 15, frames 3672058–9, Schwerin von Krosigk tó Göring, May 1939; IMT xxxvi. 493–7, id. to Hitler, 1 Sept. 1938. The Brinkmann speech is reprinted in Hauser, *Hitler versus Germany*, 114–16.

[28] J. Blum (ed.), *From the Morgenthau Diaries: Years of Urgency, 1938–1941* (Boston, 1965), 80, Morgenthau to Roosevelt, 20 Jan. 1939. On fears for the future of capitalism in Germany see G. Hutton, 'German Economic Tensions: Causes and Results', *Foreign Affairs*, 17 (1939), 524–33; 'V', 'The Destruction of Capitalism in Germany', ibid. 15 (1937), 596–603.

1939. Schacht had his own reasons for informing Hitler that the economy was facing 'desperate' problems.[29] But he told Sir Frederick Leith-Ross on a visit to London in December 1938 'in a very depressed mood' that 'the German control of wages and prices was working well and could be maintained indefinitely'.[30] Frederick Ashton-Gwatkin's report for the Foreign Office on economic conditions in Germany in February 1939 did not confirm earlier reports from the British embassy of impending economic collapse. He concluded that: 'Economic conditions inside Germany are not brilliant, but they are certainly not disastrous... Most Germans with whom I spoke believe that these difficulties will be surmounted; they do not think that their country is heading for the "economic collapse" which has been long prophesied. An "economic collapse" is almost impossible in a country so well regimented as Germany.'[31] British economic intelligence confirmed this picture. The research of the Industrial Intelligence Committee for the Sub-Committee on Economic Pressure on Germany suggested that Germany faced no serious financial difficulties in 1939, and would face raw-material shortages of damaging scale only after the second year of the war, if a British blockade could be made to work.[32]

Chamberlain preferred to listen to those who predicted economic disaster, since this encouraged his hope of deterring Hitler, but there were others in the administration who knew that the real picture was less hopeful. In July the Chancellor, Sir John Simon, produced a report on 'the German Financial Effort for Rearmament' which suggested that Germany was in a better economic position than Britain, with greater financial flexibility, higher taxation, and growing economic power over her eastern neighbours: 'The question of the means of payment for overseas imports in war—an ever present anxiety in our case—scarcely arises in Germany.'[33] It was the Treasury view that Germany was better prepared for a long war than Britain, who would require extensive American loans to survive, a prediction that proved to be remarkably accurate.[34]

[29] Hinsley, *Intelligence*, 68.

[30] Leith-Ross, *Money Talks*, 254. On another occasion during his visit Schacht reportedly 'pooh-poohed the suggestion that they [the German people] would not bear a good deal more than they were suffering already, and said that the standards of living could still be reduced a long way'; in Bank of England, unclassified German file, S. 89(2), 'Germany: Notes of a Discussion which took place on the 12th Dec. 1983', 2.

[31] *DBFP* iv. 598–601, app. II, 'Report by Mr Ashton-Gwatkin on his visit to Germany and interviews with German Statesmen, Feb. 19th to Feb. 20th 1939'.

[32] Hinsley, *Intelligence*, 60–4; R. J. Young, 'Spokesmen for Economic Warfare: The Industrial Intelligence Centre in the 1930s', *European Studies Review*, 6 (1976), 480–2.

[33] Hinsley, *Intelligence*, 69–70. See too Peden, 'Matter of Timing', 23–4, who discusses in detail the Treasury assessment of Germany's financial position in 1938–9.

[34] On the British position see W. F. Kimball, 'Beggar My Neighbour: America and the British Interim Finance Crisis 1940–41', *Journal of Economic History*, 29 (1969), 758–72.

Much of this assessment hinges on what historians mean when they talk about economic crisis. The German economy was certainly not facing a conventional economic crisis in 1938–9, with rising unemployment, sharp falls in prices and profits, widespread credit restriction, a slump in foreign trade; nothing, in other words, to match the crisis of 1929–32.[35] The words used to describe the German 'economic crisis' are general and economically imprecise—an overheated economy, forced rearmament, economic contradictions—but they all imply that if Germany continued to pump money into military spending she would be faced with rapid inflation, serious balance-of-payments problems, financial collapse. It is important in this context, however, to distinguish between structural weaknesses and frictional problems. There is no doubt that Germany did face a difficult situation with foreign exchange and payments, and that full employment produced increasing friction in a job market with wage controls. Yet all industrial economies continually face the problems of distributing and balancing their resources. This is a characteristic feature of modern industrial states, and recent evidence suggests that the British and French economies experienced difficulties every bit as great in this respect in 1936–9 as did Germany, if not greater since they were subject to much less regulation. To see such problems, though, as evidence of economic collapse or economic chaos, as some historians have done, is to misinterpret the nature of economic life. Of the more fundamental components of economic stability none assumed what economists would regard as a critical position in 1939, and indeed it is difficult to find a contemporary economist who thought otherwise.[36]

Germany had surmounted major difficulties well before 1939. In 1933 the country had 8 or 9 million unemployed (with 6 million on the registers), trade had collapsed, credit was sharply restricted, international payments questions still unresolved. Recovery was steady, based on high government demand and close controls over trade, investment, wages, and prices. But it was by no means certain, and at points in 1934–6 there were fears of renewed crisis. By 1938–9 the worst of these fears were past. Germany's external debt was stabilized, falling in nominal terms from RM 20,000m. in 1932 to RM 9,000m. in 1938. Interest rates fell continually over the 1930s, from 6 per cent in 1932 to 3 per cent six years later. The

[35] R. J. Overy, *The Nazi Economic Recovery 1932–1938* (London, 1982), 16–21.

[36] See e.g. C. W. Guillebaud, *The Economic Recovery of Germany 1933–1938* (London, 1939), 267: 'so far as the reasonably near future is concerned... it would seem more probable that the German economy will grow stronger than that it will collapse or decline'. See too M. Palyi, 'Economic Foundations of the German Totalitarian State', *American Journal of Sociology*, 46 (1940/1), 472–85; T. Balogh, 'The National Economy of Germany', *Economic Journal*, 48 (1938), 490–7; S. Merlin, 'Trends in German Economic Control since 1933', *Quarterly Journal of Economics*, 57 (1943), 169–72, 185–95; G. Parker, 'Economic Outlook of Germany', *Lloyds Bank Review*, July 1937, 347–67.

German capital market was closely controlled by the state. Increases in state funding were covered by taxation, Reich loans, and treasury bills, which were taken up by businesses, insurance companies, and savings banks at government insistence. Up until 1938 the bulk of government expenditure was covered by taxation, and only in 1939 was there a substantial increase in the cumulative government deficit. Though this alarmed Schacht, it was not an unacceptably high debt by modern standards, and certainly not for an economy under close state regulation. Firms in receipt of government contracts were also forced through dividend and profit controls to reinvest substantial industrial funds and thus carry some of the cost of rearmament themselves. By 1938 private investment once again exceeded public.[37]

At the centre of the economic strategy was control of prices and wages to prevent inflation and excessive consumer demand in competition with rearmament, and to encourage investment and savings. Although there were some limited price rises, particularly in foodstuffs, and earnings were higher in the engineering trade than in textiles, the policies were sufficiently successful to prevent any serious pressure on prices or wages, as Table 7.1 demonstrates. The pressure of consumer demand was relieved by withholding goods from the shops, by high taxation, and through propaganda campaigns to encourage savings and investment. So extensive were government controls—making money into what one economist called a 'passive instrument'—that it is difficult to see how inflation could have became a factor of crisis proportions in 1939; nor did it do so until the very last stages of the war.[38]

Of course this is not to deny that the German economy faced some financial strain. Rearmament consumed very large sums of money; so too did the motorways and the Nazi Party buildings. Military expenditure in 1938 was also much higher than anticipated because of the mobilization

[37] On financial controls see S. Lurie, *Private Investment in a Controlled Economy: Germany 1933–1939* (London, 1947), 33–5; K. E. Poole, *German Financial Policies 1932–1939* (London, 1939), 157–66. Government revenue exceeded stated expenditure from 1933/4 to 1937/8, but fell short of it by RM 6,000m. in 1938/9, or 4% of GNP at current prices. The overall burden of government debt, RM 25,000m., cannot be regarded as excessive in an economy where GNP had grown by 75% in five years and tax revenue had almost doubled. Total government debt was considerably less than in Britain, where servicing of the debt alone consumed a substantial portion of government expenditure, equivalent to 4–5% of GNP. On Germany's external debt see H. Ellis, *Exchange Control in Central Europe* (London, 1941), 231. In real terms the fall in the debt was from RM 14,000m. to RM 7,700m.

[38] M. Wolfe, 'The Development of Nazi Monetary Policy', *Journal of Economic History*, 15 (1955), 398; R. Lindholm, 'German Finance in World War II', *American Economic Review*, 37 (1947), 124–8; J. J. Klein, 'German Money and Prices 1932–1944', in M. Friedman (ed.), *Studies in the Quantity Theory of Money* (Chicago, 1956), 135–6. By 1939 money supply had increased by 60% over the depression level of 1932, but GNP had increased by 81% over the same period (current prices).

TABLE 7.1. *Wages, earnings, and cost of living, 1929–1940*

	Money wages (1913/14 = 100)	Real wage rates (1913/14 = 100)	Real earnings (1925/9 = 100)	Cost-of-living index (1913/14 = 100)	Wholesale prices (1925 = 100)
1929	177	115	107	154.0	96.8
1932	144	120	91	120.6	68.1
1933	140	119	87	118.0	65.8
1934	140	116	88	121.1	69.3
1935	140	114	91	123.0	71.8
1936	140	112	93	124.5	73.4
1937	140	112	96	125.1	74.7
1938	141	112	101	125.6	74.6
1939	141	112	n.a.	126.2	75.4
1940	141	109	n.a.	130.1	n.a.

Sources: G. Bry, *Wages in Germany 1871–1945* (Princeton, NJ, 1960), 331, 362; BA RD51/21–3, Deutsche Reichsbank, Statistische Tabellen, Jan. 1944, 20.

costs in the Austrian and Sudeten crises, and the expense of building the *Westwall* at high speed. Plans to expand expenditure further in 1939 were revised and restrictions introduced on less essential civilian projects, though with less success than the government hoped. But all these pressures can be seen not so much as contradictions which could no longer be checked, but as problems to be coped with by adjustments in Reich financial and economic policy. The New Finance Plan, for example, introduced by Walther Funk in April 1939, was designed to see the Reich over the following three years of high state demands on the capital market.[39]

Similar controls governed the development of German trade and payments. Both were closely monitored by the state in response to the serious difficulties in this area that had developed during the 1929–33 recession. German trade revived faster after 1933 than that of Britain or the United States or France. The volume of German trade fell 50 per cent from 1929 to 1934, but recovered by 1938 to almost three-quarters of the 1929 levels. The Germans' determination to control foreign trade and

[39] On the 'New Finance Plan' see Lurie, *Private Investment*, 33. The core of the plan was the issue of a new type of tax certificate. All firms working on government contracts were to be paid 40% in tax certificates, one type redeemable after 7 months, the others after 37 months. There were tax advantages if firms held on to the certificates beyond redemption date, and they could be exchanged between firms. In this way the government could get industry involuntarily to finance a share of current arms expenditure. By Sept. 1939 certificates to the value of RM 3,000m. had been issued. See too R. Stucken, *Deutsche Geld- und Kreditpolitik 1914 bis 1963* (Tübingen, 1964), 150, 155–7.

payments forced them towards a policy of exchange agreements and barter trade. Though this arguably inhibited the expansion of German trade in the 1930s, it removed serious balance-of-payments difficulties, and gave Germany privileged access to markets where agreements could be reached, particularly in eastern Europe, Latin America, and the Middle East. Helped by export subsidies and a managed currency, Germany enjoyed an active trade balance for most of the 1930s, with a very modest deficit in 1934 and 1938.[40] Most important of all, controlled trade removed the need to link the Reichsmark more closely to the world market and the dollar, which would have involved devaluation, increased import prices, and produced fears at home of renewed inflation. Such fears were partly responsible for pushing Germany towards import-substitution after 1933. Though self-sufficiency was far from complete in 1939 in those areas where it was deemed feasible and strategically necessary, Germany was less dependent on the world economy and much less affected by world market fluctuations than were Britain and France, whose financial and trading position faced a range of difficulties once rearmament got seriously under way.[41] Sir Alexander Cadogan, permanent under-secretary at the Foreign Office, complained after Munich that 'Germany was far more self-sufficient than were we, who, in order to keep alive, had to import the bulk of our food and maintain the value of the pound.'[42] British gold reserves fell from £800m. in the spring of 1938 to £460m. in September 1939, while the pound fell sharply against the dollar, making supplies for rearmament purchased abroad even more expensive.[43]

At the core of the argument about crisis lie the questions of employment and living standards. By 1938 the German economy faced selective labour shortages which led to pressure on wages in the heavy-industrial and engineering industries. These problems led to widespread complaints about poaching of labour and some evidence of labour exploiting its improved bargaining position. The problem was alleviated to some extent by foreign labour, which had reached 435,000 by March 1939, drawn mainly from

[40] H. James, *The German Slump: Politics and Economics 1924–1936* (Oxford, 1986), 332 for comparative trade performance. On controlled trade see D. Kaiser, *Economic Diplomacy and the Origins of the Second World War* (Princeton, NJ, 1980), esp. chs. 9 and 10; H.-E. Volkmann, 'Die NS-Wirtschaft unter dem "Neuen Plan"', in W. Deist *et al.*, *Das Deutsche Reich und der Zweite Weltkrieg*, i. *Ursachen und Voraussetzungen der deutschen Kriegspolitik* (Stuttgart, 1979), 254–9; F. Child, *The Theory and Practice of Exchange Control in Germany* (London, 1958), 208–30; Palyi, 'Economic Foundations', who argued that the great strength of the German economy lay in its ability to reduce dependence on the world economy.

[41] On Germany see D. Petzina, *Autarkiepolitik im Dritten Reich* (Stuttgart, 1968), 91–109, 183; on France R. Frankenstein, *Le Prix du réarmement français, 1935–1939* (Paris, 1982), 289–99; and on Britain, R. A. C. Parker, 'The Pound Sterling, the American Treasury and British Preparations for War 1938–39', *English Historical Review*, 98 (1983), 261–79.

[42] Gladwyn, *Memoirs*, 86.

[43] Parker, 'Pound Sterling', 262–3.

central and southern Europe. Very large-scale retraining and apprenticeship programmes were set up, reversing the shortage of skilled metalworkers by 1939, and putting 1.2 million workers through appropriate training programmes.[44] The government also responded by introducing a measure of labour conscription which proved unpopular and was used only sparingly; and by initiating efforts at rationalization, partly by reducing the competing claims of government agencies on labour resources, partly by insisting that firms modernize factory methods and reduce labour requirements that way.

All these policies were in the early stages of application when war broke out, but they do demonstrate the extent to which the government was aware of the problem and had devised strategies to cope with it. Labour problems created frictional pressures which, because they were regularly reported by the labour supervisory offices and the internal security service (SD), whose task it was to highlight such complaints, have assumed a prominence in the surviving documentation quite out of proportion to their intrinsic economic significance. Labour problems were hardly so intractable as to compel Hitler to abandon his chosen course, and opt for a war of expansion 'at any price'. If anything they suggested the opposite, that a reallocation of labour resources within the economy, and the training of additional skilled labour, was a necessary prelude to launching any major war. This is certainly what the armed forces and Göring's Four Year Plan thought was the case with the labour strategy set up in 1938–9.[45] It might be said that any government which had successfully weathered the political and economic storms of 1933–5, and large-scale unemployment, was unlikely to be thrown sharply off course by a temporary shortage of farm-hands.

The labour problem was related politically to the question of living standards. It is claimed that Hitler was particularly sensitive to the need to maintain living standards or even make concessions to the working class in order to maintain support for the regime. This was increasingly incompatible with large-scale rearmament and the impending clash of these two elements, a distributional crisis between the military and civilian

[44] H. Vollweiler, 'The Mobilisation of Labour Reserves in Germany, Part I', *International Labour Review*, 38 (1938), 448–9; the figure for foreign labour is from *Statistisches Jahrbuch für das Deutsche Reich 1939/40* (Berlin, 1940), 382. For figures on the training programmes see J. Gillingham, 'The "Deproletarianization" of German Society: Vocational Training in the Third Reich', *Journal of Social History*, 19 (1985/6), 427–8. On the labour problem in general see T. W. Mason, 'Labour in the Third Reich', *Past and Present*, 12 (1966); D. Petzina, 'Die Mobilisierung deutscher Arbeitskräfte vor und während des Zweiten Weltkrieges', *Vierteljahreshefte für Zeitgeschichte*, 18 (1970).

[45] IMT xxxii. 150–3, Second Meeting of the Reich Defence Council, 23 June 1939, 413, Note on the meeting of the Reich Defence Council, 18 Nov. 1938; BA-MA Wi I F 5.412, results of a conference with General Göring, 16 July 1938; IWM EDS Mi 14/478, Heeres Waffenamt, 'Die personelle Leistungsfähigkeit Deutschlands im Mob.-Fall', Mar. 1939.

economies, forced Hitler to go to war.[46] Aside from the problem of evidence, this argument fails to do justice to the nature of German strategy from 1936 onwards. The Nazi leaders knew that high government spending and rearmament would cut back on living standards but insisted that military spending took priority. Moreover, far from making concessions to the working class by maintaining civilian consumption and limiting armaments—the argument at the heart of the *Blitzkrieg* conception—Nazi plans were for full mobilization and armament in depth, leading already by 1938 to reductions in consumption, rationing, and shortages. Consumption as a share of National Income declined from 71 per cent in 1928 to 59 per cent in 1938. Consumer goods output increased 38 per cent between 1932 and 1938, while output of capital goods increased 197 per cent. Colonel Thomas noted that 'the Führer stands by the view that any mobilisation must be a total one'.[47] The nature of Hitler's extravagant arms plans made this inevitable.

Nazi propaganda was designed to persuade the population that shortages now were necessary sacrifices for prosperity in the future. The British Embassy in Berlin reported in July 1939 that the Nazi leaders seemed well aware of the effects on living standards ('the poor quality of food and the lack of amenities which a greater supply of consumable goods would provide'), but despite this knowledge Hitler showed himself 'intolerant lately both of argument and of misgiving'. Government financial strategy, the report continued, aimed to divert 'surplus earnings' away 'from a demand for consumable goods'.[48] Any extra purchasing power available by the late 1930s was soaked up by high levels of taxation, or by saving, which was channelled back to the government by the banks and savings institutions to fund high government expenditure. There was, of course, no intention of allowing serious shortages to develop, but there was no question that the workers should be given butter before guns, or that the failure to provide sufficient of both pushed Nazi economic policies 'out of control'. By 1939 consumption and investment were both closely controlled precisely in order to avoid this sort of crisis.

It is possible to see the German economy in a more positive light in

---

[46] Mason, *Sozialpolitik*, 299–312.

[47] IWM EDS Mi 14/377 (file 2), Thomas memorandum, 28 Mar. 1939, 'Gesichtspunkte für die Änderung der Mob. Vorbereitungen der Wirtschaft', 2. For a more general discussion of the effect on consumption see Overy, *Goering*, 83–7. The statistical evidence makes it clear that the growth of consumption after 1933 was restricted to the benefit of capital goods and government expenditure. See also K. Mandelbaum, 'An Experiment in Full Employment: Controls in the German Economy 1933–1938', in Oxford University Institute of Statistics, *The Economics of Full Employment* (Oxford, 1944), 189–96; Stucken, *Geld- und Kreditpolitik*, 160–1, who discusses 'indirect' rationing, controls over the quantity, and price of goods in the shops.

[48] Bank of England, Central Bank Papers (Germany), OV 34, ix, memorandum from British Embassy Berlin, 'Germany: Financial Position', 21 July 1939, 5, 10–11.

1939, on as sound a footing in terms of finance, employment, output, and balance of trade as the two western powers, increasingly shielded from the effects of the world market, building up a powerful trading and Reichsmark bloc, whose resources were to be used to wage a major war in the mid-1940s. The primary goal of increasing the investment ratio and government demand substantially, while restricting consumption and avoiding inflation, had in large measure been achieved by 1939. The economy was in a transitional stage as it adjusted to the demands of large-scale war preparations. This pattern of economic development brought its fair share of frictional difficulties, political arguments, and evidence of mismanagement. But to claim that this is prima-facie evidence of impending economic collapse understates the extent to which the Nazis were able to impose their political will on economic circumstances. The degree of planlessness and polycratic confusion in the economic policy of the Third Reich has been much exaggerated by measuring it against some kind of 'ideal' of rational, totalitarian economics. To claim that political conflicts and administrative discordance of themselves were a determinant of economic and social instability is to greatly distort the reality of economic policy-making, and to underplay the powerful coercive effects of economic intervention in a one-party state.

This was not, of course, a 'normal' economy, like those of the industrial west, any more than was Stalin's Soviet Union, with which the Nazi control system had something in common (and whose prospects of survival the west also regularly misjudged in the inter-war years). It was none the less a relatively stable system in the short term, which because of its economic strength and size had by 1939 formed the major core of the economic region of central and eastern Europe. It would be fair to assume, had major war not broken out in 1939, that Germany would have established further important complementarities with neighbouring and dependent economies, and would have extended economic and political dominance over a wide area of Europe, including Poland, drawing the sinews of the continental economy inexorably towards Berlin, and preparing for the great war to the east.[49] What emerges from such a perspective is not a crisis-ridden economy dragged out of control by grumbling managers and labourers, but an economy remarkably resurgent after experiencing a real economic crisis of such severity that it brought

[49] This was a process begun well before 1939. See Kaiser, *Economic Diplomacy*, 130–69; Gillingham, *Industry and Politics*, 90–108, 139–59; M. Broszat, 'Deutschland–Ungarn–Rumänien: Entwicklung und Grundfaktoren nationalsozialistiscer Hegemonial- und Bündnispolitik 1938–1941', *Historische Zeitschrift*, 206 (1968), 45–96; P. Einzig, 'Hitler's New Order in Theory and Practice', *Economics Journal*, 51 (1941), 1–16; S. Newman, *March 1939: The British Guarantee to Poland* (Oxford, 1976), ch. 3 and pp. 107–20 on German economic penetration of the Balkans.

Germany to the brink of bankruptcy and threw German politics into the melting-pot.

III

It could well be maintained that it makes little difference to the argument whether an objective crisis existed in Germany in 1938–9 or not, but only whether the Nazi leadership, and Hitler in particular, *perceived* this as a crisis, and reacted accordingly. It is clear that German leaders knew much of what was going on in the economy, and that Hitler was closely involved in major decision-making, and in more trivial issues as well. But it is difficult to see them as passive onlookers, drifting with economic events and social pressures. Being aware of the problems, Nazi policy-makers and state officials adjusted policy to take account of circumstances, developing new instruments of economic management and social control. Hitler expected the state to intervene and solve problems as they arose, a view summed up concisely by Göring in June 1938: 'There is no place for the collapse of parts of the economy. Ways will be found. The Reich will step into the breach to help.'[50]

The development of these policy instruments dated from the early years of the regime. Indeed it could well be argued that the real period of political and economic instability was 1935–7, while the economy was still in the throes of recovery, and while the Nazis were forced to take account of popular political pressures and the interests of the old élites.[51] It was during the crisis over foreign exchange, imports, and rearmament in 1936 that Hitler insisted on taking a firmer grip on the economy to meet his military requirements for an active foreign-policy programme, aimed primarily at the Soviet Union. The political difficulties that Göring met in establishing the new economic framework provoked the party leaders into eliminating the conservatives as a major force in domestic politics and extending the political dominance of the movement's leaders. At the same time Himmler increased the movement's grip at a local level, extending the terror and surveillance tactics and stamping out remaining centres of resistance. From this period onwards the political influence of the non-Nazis was reduced and the population subjected to more widespread propaganda and coercion. Both sets of control, over economic and political life, were elaborated and institutionalized between 1936 and

---

[50] Geyer, 'Rüstungsbeschleunigung', 136.

[51] Overy, *Goering*, 68–73; W. Deist, *The Wehrmacht and German Rearmament* (London, 1981), ch. 3; I. Kershaw, *Popular Opinion and Political Dissent in the Third Reich* (Oxford, 1983), 120–32; A. E. Simpson, 'The Struggle for Control of the German Economy 1936/37', *Journal of Modern History*, 21 (1959).

1939, reducing the prospects of the economic strategy going wrong, and the prospects for effective political opposition. There was certainly something in Göring's claim that, 'Measures which in a state with a parliamentary government would probably bring about inflation, do not have the same results in a totalitarian state.'[52]

Although Hitler was alive to the dangers of provoking the 'home front', he was determined to forge ahead after 1936 with the plans to create a powerful economic springboard for his military adventures. This springboard was to include the industrial areas of central Europe, which were necessary to provide the Germans with continental resources for war. When diplomatic circumstances permitted expansion into Austria and Czechoslovakia, their economies were immediately integrated with the Reich, under the auspices of the Four Year Plan.[53] This was clearly the case with Poland too, and with economic penetration of the Balkans, as Hitler made clear to his military and civilian leaders in March 1939:

German dominion over Poland is necessary, in order to guarantee the supply of agricultural products and coal for Germany.

As concerns Hungary and Roumania, they belong without question to the area essential for Germany's survival. The Polish case, as well as appropriate pressure, will doubtless bring them round, bring them down a peg or two. Then we will have unlimited control over their immeasurable agricultural resources and their oil reserves. The same can be said of Jugoslavia.

This is the plan, which shall be completed up to 1940[54]

There were certainly economic *motives* at work here, but these are not the same as economic *pressures* produced by impending crisis at home. This economic conception did not simply emerge as rearmament found growing difficulties, but was central to the *Lebensraum* strategy from the start. Economic expansion was as much the cause as the consequence of rearmament.

Hitler's commitment to living-space in eastern Europe dates from well before 1938–9, and was consistent with the general intention to prepare the economy for large-scale military mobilization. Neither could be achieved without cuts in living standards, and made necessary greater disciplining of the work-force. It also made it necessary to prepare the country, in Göring's words, 'psychologically for total war'. The development of a moral commitment to military expansion was the work of the armed forces and of the apparatus of propaganda, whose object was to persuade

[52] Overy, *Goering*, 55.
[53] Overy, *Goering*, 110–16; R. J. Overy, 'Göring's "Multi-National" Empire', in A. Teichova and P. Cottrell (eds.), *International Business and Central Europe 1919–1939* (Leicester, 1983), 270–8.
[54] D. Eichholtz *et al.* (eds.), *Anatomie des Krieges* (Berlin, 1969), 204, Doc. 88, Bericht von Wilhelm Keppler über die Rede Adolf Hitlers am 8 März 1939.

the people that guns now would mean butter later.[55] Although both efforts were less productive than the authorities might have liked, they demonstrate that Nazi leaders had a grasp of the possible consequences of their economic and military strategy from the outset, and were not caught out in 1938–9 by an unpredictable and uncontrollable social and economic crisis. Indeed they were better prepared to meet it should it occur in 1939 than perhaps at any stage since 1933.

But the truth is that there was no such crisis in 1939 for the Nazis to perceive. There is no evidence at government and ministerial level of a 'crisis' in the summer of 1939. There were no suggestions that the economy was in severe difficulties, 'out of control', in either the Finance Ministry, the Foreign Office, the Economics Ministry, the Four Year Plan Office, the armed forces' economic office, or the Labour Front. Not even Schacht, least likely to disguise the amateur economics of his Nazi successors, suggested that a serious crisis existed in 1939, however much he disapproved of the way in which German finances were being run.[56] 'Crisis' is an inappropriate characterization of the German economy in the months before war.

Much the same can be said of the German working class in 1939. After six years of repression and party rule and propaganda, the working class was demoralized, powerless, and fearful. The revolutionary potential of the class was negligible. The so-called Sopade reports, produced by SPD exiles, show the development of a mood of resignation and apathy among the working class, even of hostility towards those who preached to them of the virtues of struggle.[57] When the socialist Hilda Monte visited Germany early in 1939 she was struck by the negative attitude of workers to the political situation:

---

[55] M. Balfour, *Propaganda in War 1939–1945* (London, 1979), 148, who quotes Otto Dietrich's remark in 1939: 'The German people must be roused to a readiness for sacrifice and for maximum participation.' The remark by Göring is in BA-MA Wi I F 5.412, conference with General Göring, 16 July 1938. See also W. Wette, 'Ideologien, Propaganda, und Innenpolitik als Voraussetzungen der Kriegspolitik des Dritten Reiches', in Deist et al., *Ursachen und Voraussetzungen*, 121–36, and the general discussion of efforts to mobilize the population for total war in L. Herbst, *Der Totale Krieg und die Ordnung der Wirtschaft: Die Kriegswirtschaft im Spannungsfeld von Politik, Ideologie und Propaganda 1939–1945* (Stuttgart, 1982), chs. 2–3; and J. Sywottek, *Mobilmachung für den totalen Krieg: Die propagandistische Vorbereitung der deutschen Bevölkerung auf dem Zweiten Weltkrieg* (Opladen, 1976), 94–103, 194–201.

[56] H. Schacht, *76 Jahre meines Lebens* (Bad Wörishofen, 1953), 495–514; Lutz Graf Schwerin von Krosigk, *Memoiren* (Stuttgart, 1974), 191 ff.; H. Kehrl, *Krisenmanager im Dritten Reich* (Düsseldorf, 1973), 145–55; N. Henderson, *Failure of a Mission* (London, 1940), 227–36. Interestingly there is no hint of a crisis in the detailed reports prepared on Germany in the Bank of England, though the Bank had access to a wide range of information on the state of the German economy. Yet the reports up to 1937 are full of comments on critical difficulties facing Germany.

[57] Kershaw, *Popular Opinion*, 94–5, 108–10; J. Stephenson, 'War and Society: Germany in World War II', *German History*, 4: 3 (1986), 16–23.

I wish I could say that the terror alone stemmed a powerful wave of rebellion, which was ready to break out at any moment. But that would not be true . . . The terror, in common with the misery, despair, and fatigue, have worked on people's minds. It has made them acquiesce in and find excuses for the system. The result is resignation and indifference rather than rebellion . . . Since the future held out no hope or promise to them I was convinced beforehand that the masses in Germany would not, as some expected, turn round their rifles on to their leaders the moment Hitler wanted to drive them into war. The German people are not revolutionary in character, and worse things will have to happen before a rebellion breaks out.[58]

This is not to condemn the German working class for not confronting Nazism, but to understand the reality of working-class life in pre-war Germany. The working class itself was far from homogeneous, and opportunities for organization and agitation almost entirely lacking. Nazi propaganda played up working-class patriotism and racialism, creating in important ways some kind of identity of interest between rulers and ruled.[59] Labour service, the Hitler Youth, and military training achieved something of the same effect. Mason himself has recently adopted Wilhelm Leuschner's argument that the condition of the working class was like life in a 'convict prison' (*Zuchthaus*), where the workers were deliberately cut off from other social groups, and from communication with the outside world, and were subjected to propaganda and coercion diluted with limited welfare concessions.[60] Though this view possibly overstates the extent to which the working class was excluded from party office and understates the degree of social mobility in a highly militarized society, there can be no doubt that the Nazi regime was particularly effective as an instrument of social control, rewarding normative actions but fiercely and deliberately repressive of dissent. 'Revolution from within', Hitler told his commanders in November 1939, 'is impossible.'[61]

Hitler's motive for controlling the working class in this way was to ensure that it should have no opportunity to repeat November 1918—

---

[58] H. von Rauschenplat and H. Monte, *How to Conquer Hitler: A Plan of Economic and Moral Warfare on the Nazi Home Front* (London, 1940), 190, 201. See too the letters reproduced in *Hitler Calls this Living!* (n. 22 above), 2–3, 'letter from a workman, Mar. 1938', and 4–5, 'letter from a young employee, Jan. 1939', both of which convey vividly the isolation and demoralization of the work-force.

[59] D. Aigner, *Das Ringen um England: Die öffentliche Meinung 1933–1939* (Munich, 1969), 349–53.

[60] T. W. Mason, 'Die Bändigung der Arbeiterklasse im nationalsozialistischen Deutschland', in C. Sachse *et al.* (eds.), *Angst, Belohnung, Zucht und Ordnung: Herrschaftsmechanismen im Nationalsozialismus* (Düsseldorf, 1982), 48–53. See too H. Mommsen, *Arbeiterbewegung und nationale Frage* (Göttingen, 1979), 366 who reproduces Leuschner's views in a letter to a friend on 20 Aug. 1939: 'We are imprisoned in a great convict prison. To rebel would amount to suicide, just as if prisoners were to rise up against their heavily armed overseer.'

[61] *NCA* iii. 578, Doc. 789-PS, Führer conference with heads of armed forces, 23 Nov. 1939.

hence the efforts to maintain a reasonable minimum level of food consumption, to offer improved factory conditions, and to provide comprehensive welfare care in the event of a major war. These were not temporary concessions, extorted in the face of growing social unrest, but were a consistent component of the regime's political strategy, and also, it should be noted, of the 'social strategy' of the armed forces, equally fearful of another stab in the back. But the priority of both the party and the army was to provide only a minimum standard guaranteed for all, in contrast to the inequities of the Great War. Such a minimum had to be compatible with a high level of military expenditure and output. For those workers who objected to the restrictions involved in Nazi labour strategy by slack working, absenteeism, or veiled strikes, there were fines, work-education weekends with the Gestapo, the threat of conscription, or dismissal.[62]

Nazi propaganda was designed with the strategy of social control in mind. The media isolated and pilloried slackers and saboteurs.[63] Public opinion was manipulated so that it should appear as if Germany were threatened by hostile encircling powers once again, led by capitalist enemies of the German worker. Patriotism was appealed to, particularly in the summer of 1939 when it was suggested that foreign powers were trying to break the Germans' nerve. Reluctant to appear as the unpatriotic Germans, and fearful of reprisals, it is hardly surprising that most workers chose, with resignation, to accept full employment and restricted consumption rather than confront the regime head-on. Moreover there is evidence that Hitler's personal popularity increased during 1938 and 1939, as he achieved a reversal of Versailles without war. If there was little of the overt enthusiasm of 1914 when war finally came, there was little popular hostility.[64]

The irony is that Hitler perceived crisis not in Germany in 1939, but in the democracies, precisely because they lacked the repressive political apparatus and propaganda machinery at his disposal. Henderson reported to London in January 1939 that leading Nazis thought the weakness of Britain's position lay in 'the opposition within', and one of Hitler's own

---

[62] S. Salter, 'Class Harmony or Class Conflict? The Industrial Working Class and the National Socialist Regime 1933–1945', in J. Noakes (ed.), *Government, Party and People in Nazi Germany* (Exeter, 1980), 84–9.

[63] In very much the same way as 'social security scroungers' and 'moonlighters' have been isolated as general enemies of the community in recent efforts to mould public opinion in Britain.

[64] I. Kershaw, *Der Hitler-Mythos: Volksmeinung und Propaganda im Dritten Reich* (Stuttgart, 1980), 112–13, 122–6; Balfour, *Propaganda*, 49–50, 148. According to a report sent to the Bank of England from Berlin in Oct. 1939, 'there is plenty of minor grumbling but no serious discontent', Bank of England, Central Bank Papers (Germany), OV 34, ix, memorandum on German situation, 23 Oct. 1939, 2.

arguments for pressing ahead with action against Poland was that a firm German response would lead to the overthrow of the Chamberlain and Daladier governments and plunge the Allies into political crisis.[65] There was plenty of evidence of widespread labour unrest, political violence, and party conflict to suggest that this was a very real possibility. He was later to apply the same arguments to the Soviet Union.[66] But there is little evidence that he ever entertained the same fears about Germans, or that such fears governed his foreign-policy decisions; nor in fact did a serious threat of popular political resistance emerge at any stage between 1939 and the end of the war.

IV

Any analysis of the relationship between domestic problems and the outbreak of war in 1939 must in the end take account of international circumstances and the conduct of foreign policy. There are strong arguments for suggesting first of all that German expansion in 1938 and 1939 was governed primarily by Hitler's exploitation of diplomatic opportunities within a strategic and ideological framework already accepted well beforehand. And secondly that, far from seeking a major war in September 1939 to avert domestic disaster, Hitler was convinced that the Polish crisis could be localized, and Poland brought within the German orbit with possibly no war at all, as had Austria and Czechoslovakia. In other words, that the main explanation for the outbreak of a war in September 1939 rather than at a future date lies with British and French decision-making rather than German.[67] If Hitler did not expect a major war in 1939, it can hardly be argued that he deliberately provoked one to avoid domestic crisis.

Hitler's strategic conception is not difficult to uncover. He wanted Germany to achieve continental hegemony, to seek living-space in an

---

[65] *DBFP* iv. 593, app. I (v), N. Henderson to Halifax, 22 Feb. 1939; E. Kordt, *Wahn und Wirklichkeit* (Stuttgart, 1948), 168, 192. Hitler was no doubt influenced by von Dirksen's reports from London which stressed the political fears of Chamberlain and the appeasers. Chamberlain realised, according to Dirksen, 'that the social structure of Britain, even the conception of the British Empire, would not survive the chaos of even a victorious war': see G. Craig and F. Gilbert (eds.), *The Diplomats 1919–1939* (Princeton, NJ, 1953), 482–3, 492–3, 500–1. There is an interesting instance of Hitler's attitude in Ernst von Weizsäcker, *Memoirs* (London, 1951), 203, who records that after an interview with Henderson on 23 Aug., during which Hitler had appeared in an agitated mood, he 'slapped himself on the thigh, laughed and said: "Chamberlain won't survive that conversation: his cabinet will fall this evening"'.

[66] F. Taylor (ed.), *The Goebbels Diaries 1939–1941* (London, 1982), 413–15.

[67] This is certainly the direction taken by much recent research. See A. Hillgruber, 'Zum Kriegsbeginn im September 1939', in G. Niedhardt (ed.), *Kriegsbeginn 1939* (Darmstadt, 1976), 163–77.

eastern empire, and to become a world power in place of the declining western 'plutocracies'. It was for that reason that he embarked on large-scale rearmament, initiated the Four Year Plan to make Germany as nearly self-sufficient as possible in oil, chemicals, rubber, and iron ore, and began a trade and financial offensive into central and eastern Europe as a prelude to the extension there of military and political influence. *Mitteleuropa* was essential to this conception, because only very great economic resources would permit Germany to achieve world-power status, an obvious lesson Hitler drew from Germany's experience in the First World War. These resources would permit Germany to build up huge military capability. There is little hint in German planning of limited rearmament—army motorization, a fivefold increase in air strength from 1938, a large battle fleet, strategic bombers, synthetic fuel and rubber production, and explosives output greater than the levels of the First World War—these were hardly the armoury for *Blitzkrieg*, and of course they proved more than enough to bring Germany's immediate neighbours under German influence.[68]

Much of this conception was shared by others in German society and was not exclusively Hitler's. The armed forces also argued that major war was likely to be a long-drawn-out affair, a battle of economies as well as armies. Pan-German and imperialist circles in Germany had been arguing for some such strategy since before 1914. In this sense Hitler was not an isolated actor, but was representative and spokesman of ideas about international and military questions which had a wide currency in Germany. Nor was this conception simply conjured up to cope with Germany's domestic situation in 1938–9, desperate wars of booty to stave off collapse. Nazi leaders made it plain that they wanted a free hand in eastern Europe from at least 1936 onwards: Austria first, then Czechoslovakia, then Poland.[69] There were, as we have already noted, strong economic motives in this. Lignite from the Sudetenland for synthetic fuel, the Austrian Erzberg, the coal and machinery industry of Czechoslovakia and Silesia were slotted immediately into the German economic structure under the Four Year Plan once they were occupied by German troops.[70]

[68] Overy, *Goering*, 84–6; Dülffer, 'Beginn des Krieges', 451–7, 467–8.

[69] Christie Papers, 180/1 5, report of a meeting which Göring, 28 July 1937; notes of a coversation with Göring, 19 Sept. 1937; notes of a conversation with Göring, 3 Feb. 1937. Gladwyn, *Memoirs*, 66, records Göring's remark to Lady Stanley at Christmas 1937: 'You know of course what we are going to do. First we shall overrun Czechoslovakia, and then Danzig, and then we shall fight the Russians. What I can't understand is why you British should object to this.' Leith-Ross, *Money Talks*, 236–7, reports a conversation with a Romanian oil industrialist in early 1937 who told him that Hitler 'wanted to get back Danzig, reabsorb Austria, perhaps to slice off part of Czechoslovakia . . . The sort of country that he wanted for his colonies was to be found in Russia.'

[70] Overy, 'Göring's "Multi-National" Empire', 272–8; N. Schausberger, 'Der Anschluss und seine ökonomische Relevanz', in R. Neck (ed.), *Anschluss 1938* (Vienna, 1981).

The timing of this expansion depended on circumstances: on the achievement of domestic political stability and the growth of German economic power, as well as on international conditions. Above all it was to be achieved without general war, for which Germany would not be fully prepared, as Hitler himself argued, until 1943–5.[71] That Germany should achieve a more powerful economic and political position in central Europe was conceded by Britain and France during 1938, not without misgivings. The Czech crisis and the Munich Pact proved a vital turning-point in Hitler's calculations. He interpreted it, with some justification, as a green light for further German advances in eastern Europe. Rump Czechoslovakia was treated almost as a German satellite after October 1938; Hungary, Yugoslavia, and Romania were brought into the German economic sphere of influence. These were not the acts of a leader whose policies were out of control, but a co-ordinated diplomatic and economic offensive into eastern and south-eastern Europe promoted by the German government and its officials, whose short-term object was to strengthen Germany's war potential, and whose long-term aim was to cement permanent German control.[72]

Munich brought two important diplomatic lessons as well. Hitler formed a conviction, underlined by the Anglophobe von Ribbentrop, that the 'men with umbrellas' had abandoned eastern Europe and were too timid and too unprepared to prevent Hitler achieving the final consolidation of eastern Europe under German domination.[73] Young reported to the Foreign Office Goerdeler's claim that

it is vitally important to realise that Hitler is deeply and definitely convinced that after his unexpected victory at Munich, anything is possible to him . . . He says that he [Hitler] is now convinced that England is degenerate, weak, timid, and never will have the guts to resist any of his plans. No war will ever be needed against either France or England.[74]

This conviction was to stay with Hitler throughout the period leading up to war. The second lesson was that something had to be done about the

---

[71] Documents on German Foreign Policy, ser. D, i. 3, 'Minutes of the meeting in the Reich Chancellery, Nov. 5th 1937' (Hossbach Memorandum); ser. D, vi. 580, 'Minutes of a conference on May 28th 1939': 'the armaments programme will be completed by 1943 or 1944'.

[72] A. Teichova, An Economic Background to Munich (Cambridge, 1974), passim.

[73] I. Kirkpatrick, The Inner Circle (London, 1959), 135. Hitler was reported as saying after Chamberlain's departure from Munich: 'If ever that silly old man comes interfering here again with his umbrella, I'll kick him downstairs and jump on his stomach in front of photographers.' 'Thank God,' he told an audience later in the year, 'we have no umbrella politicians in this country.'

[74] Young, 'X' Documents, 159. See too F. von Papen, Memoirs (London, 1952), 445: 'Hitler apparently still hoped to solve the Polish corridor question without a general war, it still being Ribbentrop's conviction that Britain was only bluffing.' Schwerin von Krosigk, Memoiren, 191, recalls a similar conversation with Ribbentrop in July 1939.

Soviet Union, whose actions had been unpredictable during the Czech crisis, and who might be persuaded to join Britain's policy of encirclement. The answer was to move closer to the Soviet Union, even in the end promising her the economically less significant eastern areas of Poland, in return for the promise of non-aggression by both parties. Once it became clear that Britain and France were taking the Polish crisis seriously, Hitler speeded up the moves to achieve such a rapprochement in the belief that this would lead to the collapse of British strategy and bring Poland into the German camp after a brief military campaign.

There is abundant evidence that Hitler's decision to solve the Polish question in 1939 stemmed not from domestic considerations but from diplomatic and military. He and Ribbentrop were convinced that the Polish war could be limited. The state secretary at the German Foreign Office, Ernst von Weizsäcker, recorded in his diary from February 1939 until after the outbreak of war regular assertions from Hitler that war would be localized; and he later recalled that 'on Sept. 3, when the British and French declared war, Hitler was surprised, after all, and was, to begin with, at a loss'.[75] Formal military preparations during 1939 were predicated on this assumption of a local war. As late as 21 August Hitler instructed the High Command to prepare only for limited economic mobilization against Poland.[76] The western powers were expected to make substantial gestures but not actually to fight Germany. This assessment was based on political and military intelligence which suggested first of all that the democracies were in too fragile a state politically to risk war, and secondly that they were still far too unprepared militarily.

Secret interception of British diplomatic correspondence with Warsaw and Berlin lent weight to this view, for it seemed that the British wanted the Poles to give up something, perhaps Danzig, to the Germans rather than risk major war (and there were certainly those in London and Paris who favoured just such a course).[77] The answer to the question 'why did Hitler take the risk?' lies much more in considerations of this kind than in domestic pressures. Of course the final attack on Poland did carry a greater risk than Hitler had expected, but he ran it because he thought he had the measure of Chamberlain—'Our enemies are little worms. I saw

[75] L. E. Hill (ed.), *Die Weizsäcker-Papiere 1933–1950* (Frankfurt am Main, 1974), 149 (entry for 1 Feb. 1939), 153 (entry for 16 Apr. 1939), 155–6, 159 (entry for 23 Aug. 1939), 160, 164 (entry for 7 Sept. 1939); von Weizsäcker, *Memoirs*, 205. See too M. Muggeridge (ed.), *Ciano's Diplomatic Papers* (London, 1948), 284, conversation with Ribbentrop, 6/7 May 1939: 'It is certain', said Ribbentrop, 'that within a few months not one Frenchman nor a single Englishman will go to war for Poland'; and pp. 297–8, conversation between Ciano and Ribbentrop, 11 Aug. 1939: 'France and England cannot intervene because they are insufficiently prepared militarily, and because they have no means of injuring Germany.'
[76] IWM EDS Mi 14/328 (d), OKW, minutes of meeting of *Wehrwirtschaft* inspectors, 21 Aug. 1939.
[77] A. Cienciala, *Poland and the Western Powers 1938–39* (London, 1968), 241–19.

them at Munich'[78]—when in fact he had not. The answer to why war broke out in September must very largely be found by explaining British and French firmness at a time when political and military reality suggested to Hitler that they would back down; and in the British and French cases there is a good argument for saying that economic and political pressures at home played a very considerable part in that decision.

It is important to recall that with the coming of major war to Germany sooner than Hitler wanted it, the German economy had to be converted to total mobilization several years before it was ready to do so. Nevertheless Hitler proceeded as if it were now possible to have the 'big war'. To the large plans drawn up in 1938 were added economic demands even greater. Hitler authorized production programmes in the winter of 1939 that eclipsed anything achieved even by the end of the First World War.[79] By the beginning of 1941 almost two-thirds of the industrial work-force was engaged on direct military orders, a higher proportion than in Britain; living standards, already low before 1939, were cut back still further and the country smothered with controls.[80] None of this produced economic crisis, though it produced widespread inefficiency and muddled planning; neither did it prompt social or political unrest of a critical kind, because this time, unlike 1914, the government was prepared with effective rationing, welfare payments, and mechanisms of control to ensure that the home front did not crack as it had allegedly done in 1918.

V

Interpreting the outbreak of war in this way does not impose intention over structures, though the relationship between them is different. It could

---

[78] NCA iii. 584–5. See too A. Speer, *Inside the Third Reich* (London, 1970), 164–5.

[79] Hitler called for a 'programme with the highest possible figures': BA-MA Wi I F 5.412, minutes of a meeting with General Thomas, 13 Nov. 1939. The army programme (Fertigungsplan 1940/2) planned for artillery production four times greater than the peak level of the First World War, and machine-gun and rifle production ten times greater. See IWM EDS Mi 14/521 (part I), Munitionslieferung im Weltkrieg, Anlage 2, Munition.

[80] On the German figure, see IWM Speer Collection, FD 5450/45, Gen. Thomas to Field Marshal Keitel, 6 July 1941; Nuremberg Trials, background documents, Case XI, Prosecution Document Book 112, 301, lecture by State Secretary Neumann at the Verwaltungsakademie, 29 Apr. 1941. See too R. Wagenführ, *Die deutsche Industrie im Kriege* (Berlin, 1963), 159, who gives the figures produced by Reichsgruppe Industrie during the war. The proportion working on military orders for all German industry in 1941 was 54.5% if consumer industries are included, 66% if they are excluded, and 58% if construction is excluded, but consumer production included. The British figure is calculated from P. Inman, *Labour in the Munitions Industries* (London, 1957), 5, and H. M. Parker, *Manpower* (London, 1957), 112, 483. The figure for industry (excluding services and construction) is 50.9% working on supplies and orders for the armed forces in June 1941. This is directly comparable with the figure of 58% for German industry given above.

well be argued that in a very general sense the rise of Nazism and the seizure of power were directly related to the failures of the world economy to cope with structural crises brought about by the First World War and the 1929 crash. These were problems that many Germans were aware of in the 1930s, as were economic nationalists in Italy or Japan. But once Hitler was securely in power he actively sought, with support among military and administrative circles in Germany, to pursue a strategy that would free Germany from the western economy and western political interests, and establish German international power. Because this could not be achieved without further economic resources, the expansion of German influence into central Europe became imperative. But before that could be begun it was necessary to establish a firm political base, to initiate rearmament, and to achieve economic recovery. It is possible to stand the structural argument on its head and to argue that domestic political peace and a more stable economy, neither of which was guaranteed before 1936, were essential *preconditions* for the period of active European expansion, rather than its consequence. Pressure of circumstances was more significant in the mid-1930s than in 1938–9.

The arguments over strategy were finally resolved in favour of the party in 1937–8, representing the triumph of the Pan-German tradition over the Prussian, and opening the way to active imperialism and racial politics. This meant the undermining of conservative influence and the strict regimentation of the working classes, and it drew its strength from the support of those party hacks and German nationalists who hoped to profit from the establishment of a wealthy German empire. In establishing the complex system of political and economic control, the subjective ambitions of the leader became a crucial reference point, holding the whole structure together, so that in the end Hitler's obsessive historical vision became willy-nilly that of Germany as a whole. In this sense the structures of the Nazi political system interlocked with the literal intentions of its leader, producing an ideological determinism that led to the Holocaust and the pursuit of world power. The more Hitler sensed this power, the more positivistic his foreign policy became, the more he risked. It seems inherently unlikely, therefore, that general war was a scrambled reaction in 1939 to domestic crisis. The acquisition of Poland was on the agenda long before this; Germany was not prepared for war with the great powers for four or five more years. It was the obvious weakness and diplomatic ineffectualness of the Allies that tempted Hitler to solve the Polish crisis and complete the first stage of German expansion. The 'structural' pressure that really mattered at this juncture was the disintegration of the established international power constellation during the 1930s.

If domestic factors have any bearing on the outbreak of war in September 1939, they are to be found in the response of the British and

French empires to the decline in their relative international strength and the cost and political difficulties of reversing this trend. For Britain in particular it soon became obvious that a sustained rearmament and increased government spending would produce crisis in the balance of payments, a decline in exports, more imports, a threat to the currency, labour difficulties, and so on.[81] By 1939 a Treasury official warned that Britain was sailing economically 'upon uncharted waters to an unknown destination'.[82] If Hitler were to be confronted militarily, while Britain and France maintained economic stability and domestic political peace, then 1939 was in some respects the best time to do so. Allied rearmament was planned to peak in 1939/40, while the advantage of using up unemployed resources and avoiding inflation was not expected to last beyond the winter of 1939. Oliver Stanley, President of the Board of Trade, concluded that 'there would come a time which, on a balance of our financial strength and our strength in armaments, was the best time for war to break out'.[83]

Neither Britain nor France was prepared to accept an end to her imperial power and world influence, though neither could really afford the military effort of defending it. Caught between these two pressures, but reasonably confident of the brittle nature of the Nazi system, they opted for war.[84] By June 1940 France was defeated and in political turmoil. By December 1940 Britain was almost bankrupt, entirely dependent on United States finance and war production to keep going. The economy and political system of the Third Reich was only brought to collapse by the combined efforts of the United States, the Soviet Union, and Britain after four years of total war.

[81] R. A. C. Parker, 'British Rearmament, 1936–1939: Treasury, Trade Unions and Skilled Labour', *English Historical Review*, 96 (1981), 306–43; F. Coghlan, 'Armaments, Economic Policy and Appeasement', *History*, 57 (1972), 205–16.

[82] Shay, *Rearmament*, 276.

[83] Ibid. 280.

[84] Peden, 'Matter of Timing' 15–28; P. Kennedy, *The Realities behind Diplomacy* (London, 1981), 301–16.

8
Hitler's War and the German Economy: A Reinterpretation

WHEN the Allied intelligence services at the end of the Second World War examined the performance of the German war economy a paradox was uncovered. Instead of operating at full throttle, the German economy appeared to have been only partially mobilized for war until 1942, despite the fact that Germany had embarked on a programme of European conquest in 1939 for which it was assumed by the Allies that large military and economic resources were necessary. The traditional explanation that this prompted was that the German economy, encumbered with the apparatus of Nazism, performed its tasks inefficiently.[1] This view laid the foundation for an interpretation based on the concept of the *Blitzkrieg*.[2] According to this explanation the German economy was mobilized at a low level because Hitler had intended it to be that way, partly to complement the military concept of the 'lightning war'; partly to take account of the peculiar administrative and political circumstances of the Nazi state; but primarily because he wanted to reduce the burden of war on the German people and thus remove the prospect of an internal upheaval. It was to be 'a system of waging war without reducing civilian consumer standards'.[3] According to these arguments the fear of an internal crisis reached a peak in 1939 and made necessary the launching of the first of those short wars for which the German economy had been specially

I would like to thank Prof. B. Bond, Dr W. Deist, Dr Z. Steiner, and Prof. A. Teichova for advice in the preparation of this chapter.

[1] B. H. Klein, 'Germany's Preparation for War; A Re-examination', *American Economic Review*, 38 (1948), 56–77; id., *Germany's Economic Preparations for War* (Cambridge, Mass., 1959).

[2] A. S. Milward, 'Der Einfluss ökonomischer und nicht-ökonomischer Faktoren auf die Strategie des Blitzkrieges', in F. Forstmeier and H. E. Volkmann (eds.), *Wirtschaft und Rüstung am Vorabend des Zweiten Weltkrieges* (Düsseldorf, 1975), 189–201; A. S. Milward, 'The End of the Blitzkrieg', *Economic History Review*, 2nd ser. 16 (1963/4), 499–518; id., Milward, *The German Economy at War* (London, 1965); id., 'Hitlers Konzept des Blitzkrieges', in A. Hillgruber (ed.), *Probleme des Zweiten Weltkrieges* (Cologne, 1967), 19–40.

[3] A. S. Milward, 'Could Sweden have stopped the Second World War?', *Scandinavian Economic History Review*, 15 (1967), 135.

prepared.[4] This was rearmament in 'width' rather than 'depth'; war in short bursts rather than 'total war'.

Although the military concept of the *Blitzkrieg* has been critically re-examined, the idea of a *Blitzkrieg* economy, and the reasons for it, still remain an orthodoxy. The purpose of this chapter is twofold. First of all to carry out the same critical examination of the concept of *Blitzkrieg* economics to show that in most respects the concept does not fit with the actual facts of German economic life between 1936 and 1942. Secondly to suggest an alternative interpretation based on a reassessment of Hitler's intentions and the response of the German economy to the demands of war in 1939. It will be argued below that Hitler's plans were large in scale, not limited, and were intended for a major war of conquest to be fought considerably later than 1939. The fact that the large armament failed to materialize was not due to any *Blitzkrieg* conception, but to the fact that economic preparations were out of step with the course of foreign policy; a dislocation that was exacerbated after 1939 by a combination of poor planning, structural constraints within German industry, and weaknesses in the process of constructing and communicating policy. The intention was large-scale mobilization. Hitler's object, in the long run, was European conquest and world hegemony.[5]

I

If the idea of the *Blitzkrieg* economy is to work, it must be shown that Hitler, strongly influenced by short-term economic and political considerations, conceived of, planned, and launched a war based on this economic policy in the late summer of 1939.[6] Yet all the evidence—or rather lack of it—suggests that short-term economic and social considerations played only the smallest part in Hitler's foreign-policy

---

[4] On the question of the internal crisis: T. W. Mason, 'Innere Krise und Angriffskrieg', in Forstmeier and Volkmann, *Wirtschaft und Rüstung*, 158–88; T. W. Mason, 'Labour in the Third Reich', *Past and Present*, 12 (1966), 112–41; id., 'Some Origins of the Second World War', *Past and Present*, 10 (1964), 67–87; E. Hennig, 'Industrie, Aufrüstung und Kriegsvorbereitung im deutschen Faschismus', in *Gesellschaft: Beiträge zur Marxschen Theorie 5*, (Frankfurt am Main, 1975), 68–148.

[5] For criticism of the military *Blitzkrieg* conception see: W. Deist *et al.*, *Das Deutsche Reich und der Zweite Weltkrieg*, i. *Ursachen und Voraussetzungen der deutschen Kriegspolitik* (Stuttgart, 1979); L. Herbst, 'Die Krise des nationalsozialistischen Regimes am Vorabend des Zweiten Weltkrieges und die forcierte Aufrüstung', *Vierteljahreshefte für Zeitgrschichte*, 26 (1978), 347–92; J. Dülffer, *Weimar, Hitler und die Marine: Reichspolitik und Flottenbau 1920–1939* (Düsseldorf, 1973). J. Thies, *Architekt der Weltherrschaft: Die Endziele Hitlers* (Düsseldorf, 1976).

[6] T. W. Mason, *Sozialpolitik im Dritten Reich* (Opladen, 1977), 305–10; Milward, *German Economy*, 8–14.

calculations. If anything it was the part that he deliberately chose to ignore, since those who understood the intelligence available tried without success, throughout the year leading to war, to demonstrate that the Allies were economically stronger than the Axis and that German economic preparations were inadequate.[7] The reason for this situation is clear enough. Hitler did not think in narrow 'economic' or 'social' terms. He was happy for the economy to perform the political tasks which he set it to do—the creation of employment before 1937, preparation for war thereafter; but he left Schacht and big business to achieve the first and, unwisely, expected Göring to achieve the second. His concerns were not primarily to do with the day-to-day problems of economics, living standards, and social peace, as were those of his contemporaries, but to do with questions of race and foreign policy. What economic views he had were placed in the context of his broader military or social ambitions in a general and uncritical way. Of plans for a *Blitzkrieg* economy before 1939 there is little sign. Hitler provided no detailed analysis of how such an economy might work, no systematic intervention in economic affairs, no plan to switch abruptly from consumer goods to arms and back again whether in response to raw material shortages or the monthly reports of his internal security police. Economic questions, when considered at all, were all subsumed into his great plans for the future; the plans for *Lebensraum* and the plan to wage a 'life-and-death struggle' for the survival of the race.[8]

Indeed the tenor of all Hitler's statements before the outbreak of war pointed towards, not *Blitzkrieg*, but its exact opposite, the prospect of a massive and long-term war of the continents from which Germany would emerge either victorious or destroyed;[9] and towards which he believed himself to be progressively restructuring the German economy. For this struggle he announced in May 1939 that 'the government must be prepared for a war of ten to fifteen years' duration' during which the

---

[7] IMT xxxvi. 493–7, Doc. 419-EC, Finance Minister to Hitler, 1 Sept. 1938; W. Warlimont, *Inside Hitler's Headquarters* (London, 1964), 24; on Gen. Thomas's efforts to convince Hitler of Germany's poor economic position see H. B. Gisevius, *To the Bitter End* (London, 1948), 355–7; B. A. Carroll, *Design for Total War: Arms and Economics in the Third Reich* (The Hague, 1968), 178.

[8] NCA vii. 847, 850–1, Doc. L-79, report of a conference with Hitler, 23 May 1939. For a general discussion see E. Jäckel, *Hitler's Weltanschauung* (Middletown, Conn., 1972), 27–46; K. Hildebrand, *The Foreign Policy of the Third Reich* (London, 1973), 91–104; A. Kuhn, *Hitlers aussenpolitisches Programm* (Stuttgart, 1970), 96–140.

[9] A. Speer, *Inside the Third Reich* (London, 1970), 166, who recorded Hitler's statement to his generals that 'if the war were not won, that would mean that Germany had not stood the test of strength; in that case she would deserve to be and would be doomed'; H. Rauschning, *Hitler Speaks* (London, 1939), 125, 'even if we could not conquer then, we should drag half the world into destruction with us, and leave no one to triumph over Germany'; also ibid. 126–8.

requirements of the army in particular would become a 'bottomless pit'.[10] Most important of all, the lesson he drew from the First World War was not that the hardships of total mobilization should be avoided but on the contrary the belief that 'the unrestricted use of all resources is essential'.[11] To the leaders of the armed forces to whom Hitler delivered this lecture, the sentiments were unrealistic to say the least. But for the historian it is almost the only evidence available on what Hitler's long-term intentions with the economy were; and it is hardly the language of *Blitzkrieg*. Any review of the projects that Hitler had authorized under the Four Year Plan and German rearmament confirms this wider intention. The naval programme, the enormous fortifications designed to be completed only in the 1950s, the synthetic oil and rubber programmes, the steel programme of the Reichswerke 'Hermann Göring' were large and expensive projects, launched with Hitler's blessing, but designed for completion only in the long term. Such projects had already begun, well before 1939, diverting resources of labour, raw materials, and machinery from the consumer sector to the sectors necessary for large-scale war.[12] If it is argued that Hitler's intention had been a limited war fought in 1939 together with the safeguarding of domestic living standards, such preparations did not make sense. But that is not what Hitler intended. Hitler wanted a healthy and expanding economy so that he could convert it to the giant task of European and Asian conquest.

Some of the confusion over Hitler's intentions has been fuelled by his own uncertainty about how an economy worked. He expected much more to be delivered than was actually possible, and had only a very hazy idea of economic time-scale. He wanted a high level of preparation for war and at the same time wanted *Autobahnen* and the *Volkswagen* for the purposes of completing the material structure of the *Volksgemeinschaft* (the racial community).[13] He wanted massive building programmes on an unprecedented scale. Speer calculated the cost at RM 25,000m.[14] Significantly the buildings were scheduled for completion by 1950 to coincide with the achievement of total victory, suggesting that Hitler had

[10] NCA vii. 851–3, Doc. L-79. This conviction is echoed in M. Muggeridge (ed.), *Ciano's Diplomatic Papers* (London, 1948), 284, 'Conversation with the Reich Foreign Minister, 6–7 May 1939', when Ribbentrop assured Ciano that 'preparations are being made to carry on a war of several years' duration'.

[11] NCA vii. 851.

[12] W. Birkenfeld, *Der synthetische Treibstoff 1933–1943* (Göttingen, 1963), 112–40; M. Riedel, *Eisen und Kohle für das Dritte Reich* (Göttingen, 1973), 155–232; D. Petzina, *Autarkiepolitik im Dritten Reich* (Stuttgart, 1968); Dülffer, *Marine*, 498; Thies, *Architekt*, 151–2, 186–7.

[13] R. J. Overy, 'Transportation and Rearmament in the Third Reich', *Historical Journal*, 16 (1973), 389–409.

[14] Speer, *Inside the Reich*, 176; J. Dülffer, J. Henke, and J. Thies (eds.), *Hitlers Städte: Baupolitik im Britten Reich* (Cologne, 1978).

already seen his coming war as a long-term struggle of heroic proportions.[15] These many ambitions betrayed Hitler's inability to see the economy as a whole, to grasp that cars and tanks could not be produced at the same time, that fortifications vied for resources with the rebuilding of Berlin. It is this inability that has been mistaken for a positive desire to restrict military production in favour of the civilian sector. This was not so. It was a result of Hitler's curiously compartmentalized view of German affairs which persuaded him that each was possible simultaneously. His petulant reaction to all advice during the war to restrict his 'peacetime' projects demonstrated the confusion in his economic thinking.[16]

But, it will be objected, how can the outbreak of war in 1939 be accounted for if not in terms of a short war designed to suit the special economic and social crisis of 1939? Put another way, can it be explained in terms of the large-scale total war effort which Hitler's plans clearly did express? The answer to both questions lies in the particular circumstances of the Polish crisis. It is necessary to digress a little to examine the explanation because it is on Hitler's intention that so much of the argument rests. The first point to make is that Hitler did not expect a European war to break out in 1939. Of course there was an element of risk as there is in any act of aggression. But all the evidence shows that from 1938 onwards, and increasingly after March 1939, Hitler had persuaded himself that the western Allies would not take action over Poland and, by implication, further German action in the east.[17] As late as August 1939 Hitler expressed his conviction to Ciano 'that the conflict will be localized' and that it was 'out of the question that this struggle can begin war'.[18] The head of Hitler's military planning staff was allowed to take leave during August and even to have it extended until 18 August, so confident were the armed forces that a general crisis would not develop over the Danzig question.[19] When news of the pact with Stalin arrived

---

[15] J. Thies, 'Hitler's European Building Programme', *Journal of Contemporary History*, 13 (1978), 423–4; Speer, *Inside the Reich*, 174.

[16] On the *Autobahnen* in wartime; K. Lärmer, 'Autobahnenbau und Staatsmonopolistischer Kapitalismus', in L. Zumpe (ed.), *Wirtschaft und Staat im Imperialismus* (Berlin, 1976), 253–81; Speer, *Inside the Reich*, 171, 245. For more details of the economic cost of all these projects see J. Dülffer, 'Der Beginn des Krieges 1939; Hitler, die innere Krise und das Mächtesystem', *Geschichte und Gesellschaft*, 2 (1976), 457–9.

[17] L. E. Hill (ed.), *Die Weizsäcker-Papiere 1933–1950* (Frankfurt am Main, 1974), 149, 153, 155–6; A. Bullock, 'Hitler and the Origins of the Second World War', *Proceedings of the British Academy*, 53 (1967), 280–1; E. M. Robertson, *Hitler's Pre-war Policy and Military Plans* (London, 1963), 160–2; Hildebrand, *Foreign Policy*, 84–90. According to Rauschning, *Hitler Speaks*, 123–4, Hitler had already reached this conclusion in 1934.

[18] *Ciano's Papers*, 301–2, 'First Conversation with the Fuehrer, 12 Aug. 1939'; ibid. 303, 'Second Conversation with the Fuehrer, 13 Aug. 1939'.

[19] Nuremberg Trials (see Ch. 3 n. 1 above), Case XI documents, Foreign Office Library (hereafter Case XI), Körner Defence Doc. Book IB, 154–5.

Hitler was finally and, it could be argued, sensibly convinced that the west would not attack.[20] Any hesitation before the invasion of Poland was caused by Italy's panic and the prospect of a second Munich but on no account did the outbreak of a general war seem any more likely to Hitler in August 1939 than in September 1938—if anything less so. Indeed all the intelligence available to the Germans of Allied rearmament and strength confirmed that neither Britain nor France was in a position to risk war with the Axis powers.[21] The general war for which Hitler was preparing was not supposed to break out in 1939 and even when it did would, according to Hitler, peter out as the western powers grew tired of their gesture.[22] He did not shirk the war when it came, not because he had any *Blitzkrieg* economic plan prepared, but for a quite different reason: he believed that in the long run the economic and moral resources of the Reich, when stretched to their utmost, would prove greater than those available to the Allies.[23] In other words even when general war broke out against his expectations in 1939 Hitler immediately thought in terms of the large-scale contest which had coloured so much of his thinking beforehand.

The second point to emphasize is the long-term nature of Hitler's imperial ambitions. The fact that the Polish question led to general war prematurely in 1939 obscured the character of the imperialism, which was designed in two complementary stages.[24] The first was to create a military-economic core for the new German empire comprising Germany, Austria, Czechoslovakia, and parts of Poland, to be achieved without a general war. This core was to be protected by fortifications to east and west and was to provide the resources of the autarkic economy.[25] The achievement of this first stage was to be guaranteed by neutralizing the threat of intervention by concessions to one or other potential enemy, Britain in

[20] Speer, *Inside the Reich*, 161–2; W. Carr, *Arms, Autarky and Aggression* (London, 1972), 123; *Weizsäcker-Papiere*, 159–60; J. Toland, *Adolf Hitler* (New York, 1976), 548.
[21] E. Homze, *Arming the Luftwaffe* (Lincoln, Nebr., 1976), 244–5; W. Baumbach, *Broken Swastika* (London, 1960), 30–1; *Ciano's Papers*, 298, 'Conversation with the Reich Foreign Minister 11 Aug. 1939'.
[22] *Weizsäcker-Papiere*, 164.
[23] NCA vii. 854, Doc. L-79; according to B. Dahlerus, *The Last Attempt* (1948), 163, Hitler told him: 'If the enemy can hold out for several years, I, with my power over the German people, can hold out one year longer.'
[24] There is considerable debate on how many such 'stages' there were. Since there is general agreement that Hitler's policy involved some kind of primary imperialism to make possible the final war for wider dominion, I have concentrated on this broader strategic intention. It did not seem necessary to enter the discussion about how many minor 'steps' each stage required. See M. Hauner, 'Did Hitler Want a World Dominion?', *Journal of Contemporary History*, 13 (1978), 15–31; A. Hillgruber, *Hitlers Strategie: Politik und Kriegsführung 1940–41* (Frankfurt am Main, 1965); B. Stegemann, 'Hitlers Ziele im ersten Kriegsjahr 1939/40', *Militargeschichtliche Mitteilungen*, 22 (1980), 93–105.
[25] Carr, *Arms*, 72–80.

1938, the Soviet Union in 1939. The second stage involved using this larger economic region as the base for launching war against the major powers. It was for this racial struggle that the German economy was to be prepared. Much of the evidence from the pre-war period shows the extent to which Hitler's view of foreign policy was coloured by such irrational biological and geo-political perspectives. France, the Soviet Union, Britain, and even the United States were the main enemies, a conviction that wavered only with the tactics of diplomacy.[26] This interpretation of Hitler's economic and military ambitions, which required a large rearmament and a continuing militarization of German society, accords much more satisfactorily with the evidence of war preparations, most of which pointed to a war to be fought in the mid-1940s or later. The first stage of the build-up of the Luftwaffe was not to be completed until 1942, and it was to be prepared for a long war only by 1947 or 1950.[27] The naval programme was due for completion only by the mid-1940s.[28] The plans for refurbishing the German rail network laid down in 1939 were to reach fruition in 1944.[29] Hitler himself authorized Keitel to inform the armed forces that they should concentrate on training and internal development until at least 1944 or 1945.[30] And the impression that was given to the Italian leadership throughout 1938 and 1939 was that the war with the major powers, the larger, and inevitable, conflict, would be postponed until 1942 at the earliest.[31]

Finally it must be remembered that German strategy was very much dictated by Hitler's personal and fantastic perspectives on world affairs, so different from those of his contemporaries abroad. The *Blitzkrieg* strategy suggests a degree of economic and political realism, and of careful calculation, which the evidence of Hitler's activities does not confirm. He

[26] Ibid. 5–20; K. Hildebrand, 'La Programme de Hitler et sa réalisation', *Revue d'histoire de la deuxième Guerre Mondiale*, 21 (1971), 7–36; F. Zipfel, 'Hitlers Konzept einer Neuordnung Europas', in D. Kurse (ed.), *Aus Theorie und Praxis der Geschichtswissenschaft* (Berlin, 1972), 154–74; Rauschning, *Hitler Speaks*, 126–37; A. Speer, *Spandau: The Secret Diaries* (London, 1976), 70, who recalls Hitler's remark: 'But I'll still have to lead the great clash with the USA. If only I have time enough, there would be nothing finer for me than to stand at the head of my people in that decisive struggle as well'; Thies, *Architekt*, 165–6, 187.

[27] BA-MA RL3 234 'Industrielle Vorplanung bis 1 Apr. 1945', 15 Oct. 1940; IMT 37, Doc. 043-L, 'Organisationstudie 1950', 2 May 1938. IMT 9, 60, Milch cross-examination; R. J. Overy, 'The German Pre-War Aircraft Production Plans: Nov. 1936–April 1939', *English Historical Review*, 90 (1975), 779–83; Homze, *Arming*, 242–50.

[28] Hauner, 'World Dominion', 27; Dülffer, 'Beginn des Krieges', 467–8.

[29] NCA vi. 729, Doc. 3787-PS, Second Meeting of the Reich Defense Council, 10 July 1939.

[30] Case XI, Körner Defence Doc. Book 1B, 140.

[31] *Ciano's Papers*, 242, 'Conversation between the Duce and the Foreign Minister of the Reich, 28 Oct. 1938'; *Documents on German Foreign Policy*, (HMSO, 1956), ser. D, vol. 6, Doc. 211, 'Unsigned Memorandum, Discussion with Göring, 16 Apr. 1939'.

became throughout 1938 and 1939 more and more preoccupied with the fulfilment of a German destiny to which he alone claimed the insight, and for which he was quite prepared for the German people to bear the severest consequences. 'War does not frighten me,' Hitler told the Swedish businessman, Birger Dahlerus. 'If privation lies ahead of the German people, I shall be the first to starve and set my people a good example. It will spur them to superhuman efforts.'[32] When he told his generals in 1939 that he was the first man since Charlemagne to hold ultimate power in his own hand 'and would know how to use it in a struggle for Germany',[33] he was stating his firmly held belief that the destiny of Germany lay in his hands alone. Hence the reasons which Hitler himself gave for the attack on Poland; that he was growing old and could afford to wait no longer to create the new German empire; and that what counted in foreign policy was will. Lacking the will to restrain Hitler before 1939, the western nations had forfeited their claim to the status of great powers and would not fight.[34]

The fact that Hitler's wider intentions failed to produce the large-scale armament that he wanted was not because he lowered his sights and chose *Blitzkrieg* but because of the premature outbreak of a general war in 1939 and the difficulties experienced thereafter in mobilizing an economy starved of strategic guidelines and a satisfactory wartime administration.

II

The *Blitzkrieg* economy is just as elusive in the wider context of German war preparations. The restructuring of the economy implied by the Four Year Plan and the acceleration of Hitler's diplomacy after 1937 showed what the ultimate purposes of the regime were. If Hitler's precise intentions were not always clear, or were not always taken seriously by the business or military élites, there could be no doubt that the restructuring was taking place.[35] It was a necessary step in preparing for large-scale war and German hegemony. In fact it was precisely because this was a long-term goal that exact details were lacking. The reorientation of the economy was bound to be a lengthy and clumsy process. The absence of precise economic planning confirmed that the intention was not to wage a

[32] Dahlerus, *Last Attempt*, 63; Hauner, 'World Dominion', 28–9.

[33] Speer, *Inside the Reich*, 165.

[34] Gisevius, *Bitter End*, 361–2; Rauschning, *Hitler Speaks*, 276–87, for a record of Hitler's increasing morbidity and isolation in 1939.

[35] Case XI, Körner Defence Doc. Book 1B, 140, Fritsche Affidavit, 29 June 1948; 155–6, Warlimont cross-examination; Gisevius, *Bitter End*, 277–360; according to D. Orlow, *The History of the Nazi Party*, 2 vols. (Newton Abbot, 1973), ii. 263, the party itself had no indication that a general war might break out in 1939 and was taken by surprise.

short, carefully calculated war in the near future but a big war at a later date.

It was Hitler's intention that Göring should co-ordinate the efforts to prepare the economy as a whole, using state agencies and party supporters to carry the programme out. Göring's view of the economy was, like Hitler's, concerned with its role in the future conquest of Europe and world war. Like Hitler he assumed that the scale of preparation must involve the whole economy. His task as head of the Four Year Plan organization, set up in October 1936, was to reorientate the whole economy to war purposes. That he was unsuccessful in doing so by 1939 was an indication not only that he was an inappropriate choice as plenipotentiary but also of the fact that Göring expected to have much more time to complete his task.[36] Working on a wide range of uncompleted projects, Göring was among the foremost of those who argued against risking war in 1939 and who accepted Hitler's assurances that the crisis in August would be localized.[37] Göring worked on the assumption that any war would be a general and large-scale conflict; hence his anxiety to prevent war until Germany was fully prepared. To the *Gauleiter* (provincial party leaders) in 1938 he spoke of the 'new war' of 'great proportions' to come.[38] To industry in October 1938 he stressed that 'the economy must be completely converted'.[39] A year later he warned industry that 'Today's war is a total war, whose end no one can even approximately foretell'.[40] In December 1939 he wrote to all Reich authorities telling them to 'direct all energies to a lengthy war'.[41] The picture he presented to the German economy at large was of a future and large-scale conflict for which the complete transformation of the economic structure was required.[42]

The same contingency was prepared for by the armed forces, compelled to perform their functions in partial ignorance of the exact nature of

---

[36] W. Treue, 'Hitlers Denkschrift zum Vierjahresplan', *Vierteljahrshefte für Zeitgeschichte* 3 (1955), 184–210; D. Petzina, 'Vierjahresplan und Rüstungspolitik', in Forstmeier and Volkmann, *Wirtschaft und Rüstung*, 65–80.

[37] R. Manvell and H. Fraenkel, *Göring* (London, 1962), 154–65.

[38] Case XI, Körner Defence Doc. Book 1B, 8, statement of Gauleiter Uiberreither, 27 Feb. 1946; see also IMT xxxviii. 380, Doc. 140-R, Göring address to aircraft manufacturers, 8 July 1938, in which he called for the achievement of a long-term production of 'a colossal quantity' of aircraft.

[39] IMT xxvii. 161–2, Doc. 1301-PS, 'Besprechung bei Göring, 14 Okt. 1938'.

[40] IWM, Milch Documents (MD), vol. 65, 7302–3, letter from Gen. Brauchitsch, 6 May 1939.

[41] MD, vol. 65, 7299, letter from Göring to Reich authorities, 7 Dec. 1939.

[42] Case XI, Prosecution Doc. Book 112, Doc. NI-090, minutes of meeting of iron industry and Four Year Plan Office, 17 Mar. 1937; Doc. NI-084, minutes of meeting held by Göring, 16 June 1937; Doc. NI-8590, Report from Loeb to Göring, 30 Oct. 1937, 'Results of work done during the first year of the Four Year Plan'; *Documents on German Foreign Policy*, Ser. D, vol. 6, 260, Doc. 211.

Hitler's long-term intentions. The lack of precise information reflected Hitler's own secretiveness and administrative methods. To Halder, the army chief-of-staff, he remarked 'my true intentions you will never know. Even those in my closest circle who feel quite sure they know my intentions will not know about them.'[43] In this light the armed forces geared preparations to a wide number of major contingencies which they regarded as reasonable. It was generally agreed that all such contingencies required preparations for a total war economy, and the army developed during the 1930s the theory of the *Wehrwirtschaft*—the defence-based economy—to cope with the requirement.[44] General Thomas, head of the army economic office, planned economic mobilization as though any war might mean total war, hoping to avoid the mistakes of 1914. Preparations for this 'armament in depth' existed throughout the 1930s and continued after the outbreak of war in 1939, coinciding with Hitler's view of warfare.[45]

Thomas himself complained after the war that such preparations had been much less successful than he had expected. Part of the reason for this lay with the administrative confusion surrounding rearmament, what Thomas called 'the war of all against all'.[46] But a major explanation lay in the general unwillingness of much of German industry to co-operate in preparing for total war, the more so as many industrialists regarded a general war as unthinkable in 1939. Industry was faced in 1939 with the prospect of rising. trade and a consumer boom based on the continued modernization of the German economy. Instructions from Göring and Thomas were circumvented or ignored.[47] The whole structure of controls and *Wehrwirtschaft* preparations was sabotaged by the unwillingness of many industrialists, happy enough to take rearmament orders, to follow the logic through to actual war. The problems with which private industry and banking were concerned were those of markets—including the newly won areas of central Europe—investment, and money supply.[48] This was

---

[43] Case XI, Körner Defence Doc. Book 1B, 81, Halder cross-examination. See also Gisevius, *Bitter End*, 353; R. J. Overy, 'Hitler and Air Strategy', *Journal of Contemporary History*, 15 (1980), 407–8; W. Carr, *Hitler: A Study in Personality and Politics* (London, 1978), 41–5.

[44] W. Warlimont, *Inside Hitler's Headquarters* (London, 1964), 17–23.

[45] Carroll, *Design*, 192–212.

[46] Milward, *German Economy*, 23.

[47] On the resistance of the car industry see Overy, 'Transportation', 404–5; on industry as a whole see A. Schröter aríd J. Bach, 'Zur Planung der wehrwirtschaftlichen Mobilmachung durch den deutschen faschistischen Imperialismus vor dem Beginn des Zweiten Weltkrieges', *Jahrbuch für Wirtschaftsgeschichte* (1978), i. 42–5. By May 1939 only 60% of the mobilization plan could be accounted for by the existing industrial agreements.

[48] Christie Papers, Churchill College, Cambridge; 180/1 25, letter from 'a senior German industrialist' to Christie, 7 July 1939; 'Memo by members of Big Business in Germany 1937', 2–23; 'Rough Notes of a recent conversation with a German industrialist, 1 June 1939'.

not, of course, true of all industrialists. The large state sector developed after 1936 was designed to provide the Nazis with the goods needed for war which private industry might have been reluctant to provide. There were also sympathizers in those private firms whose boardrooms were penetrated by the Nazis willing to co-operate in the economic restructuring. But the increasing tension between these elements and the rest of the economy, symbolized by the clash over the Reichswerke and the *Volkswagen*, placed limits on the pace and extent of the Nazi war-economic programme.[49] The emergence of just such a division showed clearly that the *Blitzkrieg* solution of a small arms sector and protected consumer output was not the option that the Nazis had chosen. The purposes of Nazism and the purposes of German capitalism no longer coincided as they had appeared to do in 1933. The resistance of business was caused by the crude attempt to force the whole economy after 1936 along the path towards the successful prosecution of major 'racial struggle'.

III

In the light of this interpretation of Nazi intentions it is not surprising to find that in most important respects the *Blitzkrieg* economy does not fit with the actual circumstances of German economic life during the period in question. The first problem is the sheer scale of Nazi rearmament. If it is looked at from a pre-war perspective, military expenditure in Germany up to 1940 was very large, much greater than that of any other power, with perhaps the exception of the Soviet Union, and much greater as a proportion of GNP than that of any power.[50] In May 1939 General Thomas boasted that in the following twelve months German rearmament would have almost reached the levels of the First World War.[51] Far from avoiding the total commitment of the previous conflict, the German economy was on the brink of exceeding it. It will be argued later that Hitler did not get value for money, but to contrast German 'limited' mobilization with the 'total' mobilization of the Allies is, before 1941, historically misleading.[52]

---

[49] Riedel, *Kohle und Eisen*, 167–78, on the Reichswerke; P. Kluke, 'Hitler und das Volkswagenprojekt', *Vierteljahreshefte für Zeitgeschichte*, 8 (1960), 376–9.

[50] Carroll, *Design*, 184–8.

[51] IMT xxxvi. 116, Doc. 028-EC, 'Vortrag gehalten von General-major Thomas am 24 Mai 1939 im Auswärtigen Amt'.

[52] To some extent this is a statistical illusion. The percentage increase in British military expenditure was much greater than that of Germany in 1939–40 and 1940–1 because it was growing from a much smaller base. It is difficult, too, to compare like with like since the structure of state finances and the definition of military expenditure differed between the two countries.

More important, however, is the fact that economic mobilization was intended to continue at a high and rising rate. Where the *Blitzkrieg* economy represented the peak of a short-term armaments effort to be used up in a short campaign, the German economy in 1939 was already operating at a high level of military production and was designed to reach even higher levels in the future. Nearly all the plans indicate this. The navy's 'Z-Plan' launched in January 1939 required a huge industrial effort which had only just begun when the Polish crisis arose.[53] Such a programme was essential to the waging of the larger, long-term conflict that Hitler had in mind. Moreover Hitler gave priority to the 'Z-Plan' over every other service programme, even over exports, something which made no sense at all in terms of a *Blitzkrieg* economy.[54] Demands for the air force followed the same course. Germany already possessed a large force of modern aircraft by 1939, if smaller than those of the Allies together.[55] In addition to this Hitler demanded a fivefold increase in air strength in late 1938, something that would have required an annual production of 20,000 aircraft in peacetime, 30,000–40,000 in wartime.[56] Although German aircraft production planners scaled these plans down substantially during 1939, they were almost exactly the sort of plans that Britain was laying down at the same time for 'total' mobilization.[57] Even the Luftwaffe itself, less ambitious than Hitler, planned a much larger output of aircraft than it in fact got from 1939 onwards. The last peacetime programme for the Luftwaffe planned for an output of 14,000 aircraft a year by 1941, nearly three times the output for 1938.[58] The *Wehrmacht* mobilization plans for the air force expected production to rise to over 20,000 aircraft in the first full year of war: actual production was 10,247.[59] All this suggests that Hitler wanted a great increase in the proportion of the economy devoted to military purposes, even if war had not broken out in 1939.

[53] M. Salewski, *Die deutsche Seekriegsleitung 1939–1945*, 2 vols. (Frankfurt am Main, 1970), i. 58–65.

[54] Ibid. i. 59. The order was given on 29 Jan. 1939 and was confirmed in May. See *NCA* vii. 854.

[55] French, British, and Polish front-line air strength was marginally greater than German in quantity, though not in quality, in Sept. 1939. See R. J. Overy, *The Air War 1939–1945* (London, 1980), 23.

[56] K.-H. Völker, *Dokumente und Dokumentarfotos zur Geschichte der deutschen Luftwaffe* (Stuttgart, 1968), 211, 'Festlegung der Planungen zur Vergrösserung der Luftwaffe, 7 Nov. 1938'; *NCA* iii. 901, Doc. 1301-PS, 'Conference at General Field Marshal Goering's, 14 Oct. 1938'; R. Suchenwirth, *Historical Turning Points in the German Air Force War Effort* (New York, 1959), 23–4.

[57] M. M. Postan, *British War Production* (HMSO, 1952), 21, 66–8.

[58] BA-MA RL3 159, 'Lieferprogramm Nr. 15, 1 Sept. 1939'.

[59] NA T177, Roll 31, frame 3719681, 'Nachschubzahlen für Luftfahrtgerät, 1 Apr. 1938'; MD, vol. 65, 7410–11, 'Vortragsunterlagen für den Vortrag vor dem Herrn Generalfeldmarschall, 13 Dec. 1938'.

To carry such an expansion out the Nazi leadership began, from 1937–8 onwards, to build up a large state-owned and state-operated industrial structure designed to speed up the reorientation of the economy for war. In aircraft production most new investment came from the state and much of it was concentrated in building large-scale production units.[60] In 1938 Göring demanded the construction of three giant aero-engine works capable of producing 1,000 engines a month each, to be followed by plans for a 10,000-a-year bomber factory.[61] In iron and steel Göring used the Reichswerke, set up in 1937, for the extraction of low-grade iron ore, but was also able to employ the business as a convenient cover for large-scale expansion of state involvement in industry, taking over control of the armaments firm Rheinmetall–Borsig, almost the whole of the Austrian and Czech iron and machinery industry, and slices of the Thyssen industrial empire.[62] The purpose of it all, as Göring privately admitted, was to construct an industrial empire sensitive to the demands of Hitler's imperialism and on the largest scale.[63] The investments involved were very substantial. The hydrogenation plant at Brüx alone cost RM 250m., more than all government investment in the aircraft industry in 1939/40.[64] Moreover the investments were largely long-term, making very little sense if the object were to design a *Blitzkrieg* economy. In fact the very scale of all these projects proved to be a drain on productive potential in the early years of war, thus explaining part of the paradox between Hitler's large-scale planning and expenditure and the poor return in the shape of finished armaments. Hitler's intention had been to create this necessary industrial substructure first before developing the superstructure of actual armaments production. War in 1939 interrupted the programme and threw industrial planning into confusion.

The industrial evidence is unhelpful to the *Blitzkrieg* as well. The

---

[60] For example the Heinkel works at Oranienberg, the Messerschmitt works at Wiener-Neustadt and the large new investments in the Junkers aero-engine and aircraft factories. Details on state investment can be found in BA-MA RL3 46, Chart 1 'Investitionen; Zellenbau'; Chart 2, 'Investitionen; Motorenbau'.

[61] MD, vol. 65, 7429, 'Besprechung in Berlin, 29 Nov. 1938'; vol. 51, 451, letter from Milch to Göring on the Volkswagen factories, 21 Sept. 1938.

[62] K. Lachmann, 'The Hermann Göring Works', *Social Research*, 8 (1941), 35–8; on Austria see NA T83, Roll 74, frames 3445159–77, I. G. Farben volkswirtschaftliche Abteilung, 'Konzernaufbau und Entwicklung der Reichswerke AG Hermann Göring', 19 Oct. 1939; on Rheinmetall-Borsig see NA T83, Roll 74, frames 3445356–60.

[63] NAT 83, Roll 75, frame 3445754, Pleiger to heads of firms in Reichswerke organization, 29 Apr. 1942; frames 3445997–8, Göring to Gritzbach, 23 Mar. 1942; T83, Roll 74, frames 3445207–10, 'Gründung und Wachsen der Hermann Göring Werke 1937–1942'.

[64] IWM, Speer Collection, Reichswerke documents, FD 264/46 'HGW Konzern-Verzeichnis, 15.8. 1944'. The Reichswerke alone cost RM 400,000m., 93% from state sources. Although many of the factories were set up outside the old Reich, much of the money had to be found from Reich sources.

conversion of industry was planned comprehensively by the armed forces under Thomas, who worked on the 'total-war' contingency.[65] The new *Volkswagen* complex for example, which Hitler, with his fragmented view of the economy had detailed as a peacetime project, was assigned to the Luftwaffe in the event of war. Whilst its conversion was hopelessly planned, as with so much of the effort to convert, the intention to do so was certainly there.[66] The plan was to draw on the civilian industries to make up for the inadequate provision of factory capacity and to close down inessential consumer production. In February 1940 Göring made it clear that such capacity had to be found 'to a much greater extent in the idle factories, even if in one way or another this does not correspond to all wishes'.[67] The head of the air industry economic group instructed air firms in October 1939 to take over any spare capacity in those sectors that were being closed down or on short time.[68] So rapid and wide-ranging was this conversion that the Four Year Plan Office estimated that the proportion of the work-force employed for military purposes had risen from 20 per cent in 1939 to 60 per cent by early 1941.[69]

Not surprisingly this led to reductions in civilian goods production. That this did not happen is a crucial part of the thesis of *Blitzkrieg* economy. 'There can be little doubt', wrote Professor Milward, 'that the impact of war on the German people over these years was very small.'[70] Consumer spending and civilian output, it is argued, were maintained in the face of the demands of war, while the military budget only rose sharply after the end of the *Blitzkrieg* in 1942. The facts show otherwise. Looking at the German economy as a whole, military spending rose in virtually a straight line between 1938/9 and 1943/4. There was no abrupt change in 1942, nor any halt in expenditure in 1940 and 1941, as Table 8.1 demonstrates. In fact the greatest percentage increases in military expenditure were in the

---

[65] Carroll, *Design*, 162–4; NA T177, Roll 3, frame 3684363, Thomas to heads of services 'betr. wehrwirtschaftliche Räumung, 29 Sept. 1939'; frame 3684308, Göring to all Reich authorities, 24 Sept. 1939; B. Mueller-Hillebrand, *Die Blitzfeldzüge 1939–41* (Frankfurt am Main, 1956), 23–39 on the work of the army.

[66] BA-MA RL3 20, letter from Göring to Ley, 15 Sept. 1939; MD, vol. 51, 451, letter from Milch to Göring, 21 Sept. 1938. On the difficulties of establishing production there see BA-MA RL3 247, report of a meeting at Junkers, Dessau, 17 Oct. 1939; Speer Collection, FD 4969/45, Bayerische Motorenwerke 'Ablauf der Lieferungen seit Kriegsbeginn', 5. On Göring's determination to convert all or any firm see *NCA* iii. 901–4, Doc. 1301-PS.

[67] MD vol. 65, 7285, report of a conference with Göring, 9 Feb. 1940; T. Mason, *Arbeiterklasse und Volksgemeinschaft* (Opladen, 1975), 1044, Doc. 174, 'Rede Görings in den Rheinmetall-Borsig-Werke, Berlin am 9 Sept. 1939', in which he said: 'In so far as we don't have the production facilities they will be created through conversion, expansion, and new construction.'

[68] NA T83, Roll 5, frame 3745418, letter from Admiral Lahs to all aircraft firms, 10 Oct. 1939.

[69] Case XI, Prosecution Doc. Book 112, 301, Doc. NID-13844, lecture given by State Secretary Neumann at the Verwaltungsakademie, 29 Apr. 1941.

TABLE 8.1. *Military expenditure, state expenditure, and National Income, 1938/9–1943/4* (RM '000m., current prices)

Year	Military expend.	State expend.	National Income
1938/9	17.2	39.4	98
1939/40	38.0	58.0	109
1940/1	55.9	80.0	120
1941/2	72.3	100.5	125
1942/3	86.2	124.0	134
1943/4	99.4	130.0	130

Note: Based on revenue from occupied Europe and the Reich; '000m. = US billion.

Sources: W. Boelcke, 'Kriegsfinanzierung im internationalen Vergleich', in Forstmeier and Volkmann, *Kriegswirtschaft und Rüstung*, 55–6; Klein, *Economic Preparations*, 256–8.

years 1939 to 1941. This pattern confirms the fact that German rearmament and war expenditure followed a relatively smooth course of expansion over the period with none of the implied discontinuities of the *Blitzkrieg* economy. As a proportion of National Income and GNP the figures also compare favourably with the performance of the Allied economies.[71] Since military expenditure grew at a faster rate than the German economy as a whole, this could only have been at the expense of civilian consumption.

And so in fact it was. Car production, for example, hungry for raw materials and labour, was dramatically cut back from a peak of 276,592 in 1938 to a mere 67,561 in 1940 and 35,195 in 1941. Of the total in 1940 the military took 42 per cent, in 1941 77 per cent.[72] It is the same story for the construction industry. The number of housing units completed fell from 303,000 in 1938 to 117,000 in 1940, and 80,000 in 1941; again with many of the latter for military use. The volume of construction as a whole fell from RM 12,800m. in 1939 to RM 8,000m. in 1940 and RM 6,900m. in 1941.[73] These were the important areas from which resources could be released into the military economy. Those goods whose survival is supposed to demonstrate the maintenance of consumer spending were either those which would be expected to increase under war conditions (such as basic foodstuffs, the output of which increased

[70] Milward, *German Economy*, 29.
[71] Carroll, *Design*, 264–5.
[72] USSBS Report 77, *German Motor Vehicles Industry Report*, 8.
[73] Number of housing units from R. Wagenführ, *Die deutsche Industrie im Kriege* (Berlin, 1963), 37, 56; volume of construction from Klein, *Preparations*, 105. By 1942 80% of all construction was for military or industrial purposes.

enormously in Britain as well during the war[74]) or those whose production was divided between military and civilian use, a division disguised by the gross figures. In fact it was the high quality of the equipment that the *Wehrmacht* demanded for its members that swallowed up much of the consumer-goods production as well as the increased output of food.[75] For the ordinary civilian consumer much less was available than before the war. By 1943 the armed forces took 44 per cent of all textile production, 43 per cent of all leather goods, 40 per cent of all paper produced.[76] Of course Hitler kept a propaganda eye on domestic living standards, and the conquest of Europe allowed greater flexibility than might otherwise have been possible, but many of the concessions made were, literally, cosmetic.[77]

The result of such a diversion to military purposes was widespread and increasingly comprehensive rationing, some of it before 1939.[78] The Four Year Plan Office itself openly admitted the need to cut back on consumption. In a speech early in 1941 State Secretary Neumann acknowledged that

not only almost all articles of daily use but also practically all other goods have become increasingly scarce in recent years—even prior to the outbreak of war . . . a higher standard of living is the ultimate goal, not the immediate object of the Four Year Plan. Whatever was available by way of labour, materials, and machines had to be invested in the production of military-economic importance according to an explicit Führer order . . . The fact that consumer interests had to be put second is regrettable but cannot be helped.[79]

---

[74] K. A. Murray, *Agriculture* (HMSO, 1955), 375. British grain production increased from 4.6m. tons in 1939 to 8.2m. in 1944; potatoes from 5.2m. tons in 1939 to 9.8m. in 1943; vegetables from 2.3m. tons in 1939 to 3.4m. in 1943. There seems little remarkable about the German economy, better endowed with agricultural potential than Britain, increasing its domestic food production, much of it destined for the well-fed armed forces. It should be noticed that in those areas where the German agricultural economy was weakest—dairy products, fats, oils—production dropped sharply. Milk output fell by a third between 1938/9 and 1939/40; vegetable oils by the same amount.

[75] Case XI, Prosecution Doc. Book 112, 296–7, Neumann lecture; see the discussion in W. Williams, *Riddle of the Reich* (London, 1941), 10–14.

[76] Wagenführ, *Deutsche Industrie*, 174.

[77] One feature of the 'survival' of consumer goods industries was Hitler's insistence that cosmetics, stockings, etc. should still be produced to keep up home morale. Cigarettes, for which there was a large domestic demand, were heavily restricted and of poor quality. In 1941 a heavy tax was placed on tobacco and women were restricted to a ration half that of men (1.5 cigarettes a day). See L. Lochner, *What about Germany?* (London, 1943), 144–5.

[78] M. Steinert, *Hitler's War and the Germans* (Athens, Ohio, 1977), 53, 64–5, 92–3; Lochner, *What about Germany?* 142–5, who wrote that both before and after 1939 'the simplest articles of daily life were lacking . . . Things made of leather, rubber, metal, wool or cotton were almost non-existent'; NCA vi. 723, Doc. 3787-PS, 'Second Meeting of the Reich Defense Council, 10 July 1939', on the intention to take resources away from 'the vital industries which are of importance to the life of the people'.

[79] Case XI, Prosecution Doc. Book 112, 293–4, Doc. NID-13844, Neumann lecture.

TABLE 8.2. *Expenditure on selected armaments, 1939–1941* (RMm., 1941/2 prices)

	1939[a]	1940	1941
Aircraft	1,040.0	4,141.2	4,452.0
Ships	41.2	474.0	1,293.6
Armour	8.4	171.6	384.0
Weapons	180.0	676.8	903.6
Explosives	17.6	223.2	338.4
Traction vehicles	30.8	154.8	228.0

[a] Sept.–Dec.

Source: Calculated from Wagenführ, *Deutsche Industrie*, 29.

Civilian production as a whole was severely cut back from the outbreak of war, while the bulk of surviving consumer-goods production was diverted to the armed forces. The problem facing the German economy was not the release of resources but the ineffective use to which they were put once released.

The final question concerns the degree of 'flexibility' in the German economy; the extent to which, under the terms of the *Blitzkrieg* economy, production could be switched within weeks from one weapons group to another or back to civilian production, as strategy dictated.[80] Now while it is true that priority changed, as would be expected, under the circumstances of war, there occurred little substantial shift between weapons groups in practice over the period. The air force, for example, found it impossible to increase production significantly after the fall of France while enjoying a production priority, but was able (for different reasons) to expand output to new levels when the priority was removed and given again to the army.[81] In practice the production of all the services expanded over the whole period 1939–41 more or less continuously, for it was difficult to disrupt production programmes at short notice, and the services jealously guarded their own economic spheres of influence.[82] The same is true of the switch back from arms to the civilian economy. Hitler certainly explored the idea of running down arms production in 1940 and again in 1941, not in response to any *Blitzkrieg* conception or preparation, but in reaction to the extraordinary degree of success that his relatively

---

[80] Milward, *German Economy*, 32; Milward, 'Der Einfluss', 195.

[81] R. J. Overy, 'German Aircraft Production 1939–42' Ph.D. thesis, Cambridge, 1978, 23–32.

[82] Klein, *Preparations*, 161; Carroll, *Design*, 154–5; Warlimont, *Hitler's Headquarters*, 8–9.

underarmed but well-run forces were able to achieve. But it must be stressed that Hitler did no more than explore the possibility. Success did not blind the Nazi leadership to the fact that enemies remained undefeated, and expenditure on weapons, like overall military expenditure, rose steadily and continuously over the whole period, helped by the expansion of output in the dependent territories in central Europe (see Table 8.2). The problem which Hitler faced was not the degree of commitment from what was, after all, a large and heavily industrialized economy, but the fact that despite such a commitment the output of finished weapons failed to match the extent of revenue and resources devoted to arms production. This made necessary a significant change in the level of productivity in 1941–2, rather than in the level of aggregate resources.

IV

It is to this question that we must now turn: why was there such a gap between what Hitler wanted and what was actually produced? The immediate explanation is that the war broke out before the economy could be satisfactorily converted. Both the military and economic leadership were caught in the middle of restructuring the economy, and were compelled to divert energies to the needs of war before the economy was prepared for it. But that is not the whole answer. There were structural problems in the German economy that were not satisfactorily solved by 1939. There were also difficulties that arose from the very nature of German rearmament. This had started late in terms of a war to be fought in 1939, only reaching significant levels by 1937–8. There was little time to build up the plant and resources Hitler's plans warranted.[83] Not only was the question of time crucial, there was also the fact that so much of the money was spent on refurnishing Germany with a military infrastructure (airfields, barracks, etc.) which had been destroyed or prohibited under the terms of the Versailles Treaty. This was an expensive business made more so by the fact that German weapons were also expensive. The insistence on very high standards of workmanship, and the preference for small-scale over large-scale mass-production, contributed to this. So too did the cost-plus system of contracts which gave no incentive to reduce prices and actually encouraged firms to produce inefficient methods and a high-priced end product.[84] The RM 50,000m. spent on

[83] On rearmament totals see BA R2 21776–81, Reichsfinanzministerium, Abteilung 1, 'Entwicklung der Ausgaben in den Rechnungsjahren 1934–9', 17 July 1939. Rearmament from 1933/4 to 1935/6 averaged RM 3,445,000 per year, including the *Mefo Bills*.

[84] On the cost of the fortifications see Dülffer, 'Beginn des Krieges', 457. On German arms finance see A. Schweitzer, 'Profits under Nazi Planning', *Quarterly Journal of Economics*, 61 (1946), 9–18.

rearmament by 1939 could have been expected, as Hitler no doubt did, to yield more in terms of military goods than was in fact the case.[85] This situation continued into the war. In 1940 Germany spent an estimated $6,000m. on weapons, Britain $3,500m. Yet Britain produced over 50 per cent more aircraft, 100 per cent more vehicles, and almost as many tanks as Germany in 1940.[86] If German armaments had been less well made and more efficiently produced and paid for, the number of weapons available in 1940 would have been considerably greater.

Another answer lay in Hitler's limited access to accurate information on the performance of the economy. This was partly a product of his style of government. But during the war it was as much a product of self-delusion and misinformation. Having spent large sums on rearmament with the most modern weapons Hitler failed to ensure that they were produced in quantity. He accepted new developments uncritically. He found it difficult to accept the long time-scale involved in developing a weapon or in distinguishing between weapons that were mere prototypes and those that were battle-ready.[87] The element of self-delusion was complemented with a good deal of poor or misleading intelligence. This was very much a product of the regime. Subordinates in the hierarchy hesitated to take initiatives in the economy and preferred to provide only that information which would present as optimistic an impression of their achievements as possible.[88] The information that finally reached Hitler was often partial and unrealistic, reflecting the intelligence that it was believed Hitler wanted to hear. Hence Hitler's reproaches to Göring over the failure of aircraft production later in the war; and hence Hitler's bitterness that the range of advanced weapons shown to him in 1939 as virtually ready for combat had failed in every case to materialize by 1942.[89] Hence, too, the persistent underestimation of enemy economic strength provided by German intelligence from 1939 to the invasion of the Soviet Union.[90]

One of the main culprits in this process of misrepresentation was Göring. His eagerness to enlarge his political empire through the economy, and his anxiety to present to Hitler the most optimistic picture of his

[85] Military expenditure had to cover investment in industry, military installations, and airfields, as well as military mobilization preparations over the Rhineland crisis, the *Anschluss* and the Munich crisis.

[86] Wagenführ, *Deutsche Industrie*, 34; R. J. Overy, 'Die Mobilisierung der britischen Wirtschaft während des Zweiten Weltkrieges', in Forstmeier and Volkmann, *Kriegswirtschaft und Rüstung*, 289.

[87] Overy, 'Air Strategy', 406, 415–16; F. H. Hinsley, *Hitler's Strategy* (Cambridge, 1951), 1–4.

[88] D. Kahn, *Hitler's Spies* (1979), 386–7; on the misrepresentation of the strength of the Luftwaffe see D. Irving, *The Rise and Fall of the Luftwaffe* (London, 1973), 65–8; R. Suchenwirth, *Command and Leadership in the German Air Force* (New York, 1969), 75–81.

[89] Irving, *Rise and Fall*, 73–4, 155–6.

[90] Homze, *Arming*, 244; W. Schwabedissen, *The Russian Air Force in the Eyes of German Commanders* (New York, 1960), 48–51.

achievement with war production, obscured much of the true state of preparations. Göring was then able to shelter behind the German victories, until the poor performance of the economy became more obvious in the course of 1941 and Göring was gradually excluded from its direction.[91] Before then he had taken up all his tasks in the economy with much political enthusiasm, little economic or technical understanding, and exceedingly poor relations with sections of heavy industry, the Reichsbank, and the Finance Ministry.[92] He insisted on treating his office as if he were responsible personally for preparing the future war economy, demanding that other agencies should be fused with his to increase the centralization of the economy under his direction.[93] Yet the civilian and military economic leadership did not want to work under Göring, and sought to circumvent his jurisdiction whenever possible, while Göring himself was unequal to the tasks of organization that Hitler had set him. The result was that during the crucial years of build-up towards war and in the early years of conflict the military economy was either not directed in a co-ordinated way or was under the influence of a man incapable of doing so.[94] Up to 1938 under Schacht, after 1942 under Speer, the German economy did what was expected of it. Between those dates came what Speer later saw as an era of 'incompetence, arrogance and egotism'.[95]

The main characteristic of the 'era of incompetence' was the ineffective way in which the resources released for war were taken up and the general inefficiency and confusion of the military economy. Not that German industry, particularly large-scale industry, was uncompetitive commercially. The problem lay in adopting the same practices in the armament factories. Not only was this slow to happen, but those commercial firms brought into war work became infected by the incompetence and inflexibility of the system as well. One obvious explanation for ineffective mobilization was the fact that industry was caught by surprise by the actual outbreak of war in 1939, and had to divert resources from long-term military projects and from civilian life without a competent central authority for the economy. When war broke out industry was unprepared for the scale of demands and anxious, like much of the military leadership, that war should be over as soon as possible. Moreover the firms expressed in many cases a marked hostility to too high a level of government intervention or military interference and

[91] Speer, Inside the Reich, 252–66.
[92] A. E. Simpson, 'The Struggle for Control of the German Economy 1936–1937', Journal of Modern History, 21 (1959), 37–45; H. Schacht, 76 Jahre meines Lebens (Bad Wörishofen, 1953), 461–74.
[93] Case XI, Prosecution Doc. Book 112, 283–8, Neumann lecture; MD vol. 65, 7299, letter from Göring to all Reich authorities, 7 Dec. 1939.
[94] Carroll, Design, chs. 7–8.
[95] Speer, Diaries, 63.

failed to co-operate in achieving high levels of arms output in the way in which American or British businessmen did.[96] It is perhaps not surprising that in a situation where not even Hitler's closest subordinates could guess his intentions, business in Germany was unable to comprehend the scope of what was happening in 1940 and 1941 and to prepare accordingly. Moreover German business was anxious not to lose the prospect of rising profits and expanding trade which had been held out at the end of the 1930s, and the first years of war saw a continuation of the silent struggle over the nature and destination of the German economy.[97] Too much energy was used up in combating excessive state interference on the one hand and in competing for contracts and influence abroad on the other. This, combined with the incomplete nature of preparations for a war in 1939, and the lack of a competent war economic administration, substantially reduced the quantity of war goods.

There were also industrial constraints. This was not simply a result of a lack of central planning, jurisdictional confusion, and poor co-ordination, or of a shortage of raw materials, the lack of which has been much exaggerated. There were problems within the armaments industry itself. There was too high a reliance on skilled labour in areas of manufacture where increasing automation might have been expected. The reluctance of the work-force to accept dilution during the 1930s and the early years of war brought many difficulties in introducing mass-production methods and made labour more of a problem than was necessary.[98] So, too, did the conservatism of management faced with the requirements of making the transition from small-scale to large-scale manufacture. This was less of a problem with established firms, such as Krupps. But many of the firms that grew large on government orders in the 1930s were small firms faced with all the strains of making the transition to a different style of management at a vital stage in German war preparations.[99] Only when industrialists from the large commercial firms were brought in to run the war economy in 1942 were some of these difficulties overcome.[100]

[96] Overy, 'German Aircraft Production', 170–88.

[97] In particular the struggle over the whole question of state ownership. See Christie Papers, 180/1 25, 'Die deutsche Staatswirtschaft'. On the Reichswerke and state ownership see NA T83, Roll 74, frames 3445207–10, 'Gründung und Wachsen der Hermann Göring Werke 1937–42'; Case XI, Prosecution Doc. Book 112, 149, Doc. NID-13797, Körner to Schwerin von Krosigk, 7 Oct. 1940.

[98] Overy, 'German Aircraft Production', 159–61.

[99] NA T177, Roll 14, frames 3698887–916, Gen. Bauer 'Rationalisierung der Luftwaffengerät-Fertigung, 1 Jun. 1941'; Roll 12, frames 3695910–12, Gen. Bauer, 'Fertigungsvorbereitung, 1935'; Roll 3, frames 3684551–4, 'Klein- und Mittelbetrieb oder Grossbetrieb', GL Report, 24 Apr. 1939.

[100] For aircraft production this process began early in 1941 with the establishment of an *Industrierat*. See MD vol. 54, 1555; D. Eichholtz *et al.* (eds.), *Anatomie des Krieges* (Berlin, 1969), 331, Doc. 161.

One final problem industry could do very little about: the exceptional degree of control exercised over armaments firms by the armed forces. In the absence of a strong civilian economic administration this was perhaps inevitable. But it meant that the military kept a tight control over contracts, product selection, and production methods which stifled industrial initiatives.[101] The most damaging problem was the extent to which minor technical demands from the armed forces at the front held up the introduction of mass-production methods and encouraged only short and expensive production runs.[102] When the more successful commercial firms were drafted into war production, their productive performance was similarly blighted by contact with the poor planning of the military production authorities.[103] When Todt, Speer, and Milch revolutionized production in 1941 and 1942 they did so not by a massive redirecting of resources but simply by using existing resources better. The aircraft industry in 1942 produced 40 per cent more aircraft than in 1941 with only 5 per cent more labour and substantially less aluminium.[104] What produced the low level of war output was not a lack of resources but the problem of coping with a premature war in an economy lacking effective central control, dominated by military requirements and guided by an impulsive strategist whose understanding of the economy was deliberately obscured. Under these circumstances it was possible to produce just enough for the early German campaigns, but not enough for Hitler's 'big war'; not enough to defeat Britain in 1940 or the Soviet Union in 1941.

V

The first conclusion to draw from this interpretation of the German war economy is the inappropriateness of applying a *Blitzkrieg* conception. In terms of economic planning, industrial conversion, consumer-goods production, civilian consumption, and strategic 'flexibility', the model breaks down. The idea that Germany deliberately sought to restrict the economic costs of war and that German civilian consumption levels were maintained intact over the early war period while the military economy

---

[101] Schröter and Bach, 'Zur Planung der Mobilmachung', 45–7; A. Bagel-Bohlan, *Hitlers industrielle Kriegsvorbereitung im Dritten Reich 1936 bis 1939* (Koblenz, 1975), 137–8.

[102] Overy, *Air War*, 179–80.

[103] Opel claimed e.g. that when the firm began military production output per man-hour dropped 40% compared with peacetime output. See British Intelligence Objectives Sub-Committee, Final Report 537, 7. On the poor utilization of the car industry as a whole see USSBS Report 77, 5–11.

[104] By contrast in 1941 some 50% more labour was diverted to aircraft production but only a 5% increase in aircraft output achieved. See USSBS European Report 4, Chart VI-11; USSBS Report 20, *Light Metal Industry of Germany* (Part I), 17a; Irving, *Rise and Fall*, 167; IWM, Speer Collection, FDC 9, Zentrale Planung, 789.

had its resources skilfully switched from one weapon group to another fits with neither the general strategic picture nor with the details of economic life in Germany between 1939 and 1941.

Hitler's intention was, by contrast, to prepare for a long and total war, using all Germany's resources to achieve a final victory. This perspective explains the nature of the autarkic and rearmament programmes initiated from 1936 onwards, many of them quite redundant for the purposes of a limited and conventional 'short war'. The evidence shows that Hitler expected such a confrontation in the mid-1940s, after an initial period of consolidation in central Europe achieved without a general war, and protected by a series of diplomatic *coups* of which the Nazi–Soviet Pact was the most important. It was this initial stage of preparing a large economic and military bloc in central Europe that backfired in 1939 into a more general war, against Hitler's expectations. That is why the German economy appeared to be prepared for a limited war. It was caught half-way towards the transformation planned by Hitler, with a military base capable of achieving the limited first stage but not the second, more general, one.

It is clear that Hitler, faced with the fact of war in 1939, changed his mind about the time-scale involved in his imperialism, accelerating the move towards the 'big' war which found him in conflict with Britain, the Soviet Union, and the United States by the end of 1941. That he did so was in part because he believed that the economic time-scale could be speeded up and conversion to the needs of the larger war be achieved in the early 1940s instead of later. This expectation was in turn derived from misinformation or lack of information on how the economy was developing. This failure of communication was crucial. It was compounded of Göring's anxiety that the achievements of the Four Year Plan should be presented in as favourable a light as possible and Hitler's own predilection for secretiveness and fragmented administration. The failure was helped, too, by Hitler's own limited contact with issues of production and finance, which led him to expect that military goods could be produced much more quickly and cheaply than was in fact possible. Göring's remark that Hitler was only interested in how many bombers there were, and not in how many engines each had, was symptomatic of this approach.[105]

Most important of all, however, in persuading Hitler that the 'big' war was possible was the remarkable military success enjoyed between September 1939 and June 1940 against enemies whose combined material strength was more than equal to that of Germany. This success was not due to any *Blitzkrieg* economy. The victories were due, first and foremost, to the staff work, leadership, and fighting qualities of the German forces,

[105] Overy, 'Air Strategy', 407.

together with the weaknesses, poor leadership, and wrong intelligence on the part of the Allies. Hitler's belief that the 'big' war could now be won still required a huge economic effort based on the large-scale plans laid down, but not yet completed, between 1936 and 1939. It is true that the extent of the military victories, which surprised Hitler as well as the generals, tempted him at times to question the need for a greater economic effort and to rely more on military prowess. But these second thoughts were very much *post hoc*, reflecting the changing circumstances of war, and were not preplanned; nor, it must be emphasized, did Hitler ever hold back the continued expansion of the aggregate arms economy over the whole of the period 1939 to 1942. Moreover such second thoughts were soon dispelled by the failure against Britain in 1940 and the failure to defeat the Soviet Union in 1941, both of which showed the limit of German military potential and the extent to which the German armed forces were under-armed. As it turned out the German forces were able to perform remarkably in the face of massive material superiority throughout the war. That they were comparatively under-armed was due to the fact that the German economy could not be converted satisfactorily in 1939–41 to the needs of a large-scale war.

This failure to convert satisfactorily, to adjust to the 'big' war when asked to do so, had many causes. At one level the failure was simply a result of the fact that the war broke out prematurely while many of the preparations were of a long-term character. Hitler's own uncertainty and impulsive strategy left the economy itself uncertain about the strategy it should be adopting. The economy was caught in two minds, one hoping for the survival and extension of the economic recovery, the other only part-way towards completing the programme of preparations laid down since 1936. This lack of appropriate planning was made more acute by the lack of a satisfactory central economic administration in wartime. In the absence of such central direction the military had a much greater say in economic affairs, concentrating on factors (such as tactical suitability) that concerned the front line, and not on factors to do with large-scale industrial production and distribution. When this was added to a reluctance on the part of much of industry to convert for war, and the rapid and unpredictable shifts in strategy, the economy failed to rise to the challenge of a large-scale war as it did in Britain, the United States, and the Soviet Union. The failure to solve the problem of arms production (disguised by the very good use to which the *Wehrmacht* put what weapons it had) was caused not by a preference for consumer-goods production over armaments, nor by *Blitzkrieg* campaigns deliberately based on a small military economy, but by the fact that Hitler's larger war arrived before preparations for it were complete. A low level of weapons production was not deliberate, but was a product of this contradiction between economic and diplomatic reality.

IV

THE GERMAN WAR
ECONOMY, 1939–1945

9

Guns or Butter? Living Standards, Finance, and Labour in Germany, 1939–1942

AT the end of the Second World War the United States Strategic Bombing Survey uncovered what appeared to be a remarkable contradiction. Germany, the country of totalitarian politics and massive rearmament, had apparently mobilized her economy to a very limited extent in the early stages of the conflict, and to a much smaller extent than her enemies, particularly Britain. 'The Germans did not plan, nor were they prepared for, a long war,' ran the *Overall Report*, '. . . measured by the standards of other belligerents, there was no "total mobilization" . . . The production of civilian goods was only restricted to a moderate extent, there was no further mobilization of women, and no great transfer of labour from the non-essential to the essential industries.'[1]

The basis for this assessment was to be found in the work of Rolf Wagenführ of the Statistische Reichsamt, whose manuscript on the German war economy provided much material not only for the Bombing Survey, but for much subsequent historical writing. Wagenführ claimed that the characteristic feature of the German economy in 1939 and 1940 was 'business as usual' in the 'peace-like war economy'.[2] Evidence of the low level of actual armaments output in Germany before 1942, coupled with the knowledge of how much Germany was capable of producing at

[1] USSBS, *Overall Report* (European War), Sept. 1945, 31. See too USSBS, *The Effects of Strategic Bombing on the German War Economy*, Oct. 1945, 9: 'Germany entered the war with a "guns *and* butter" philosophy which was continued well after the initial defeats in Russia.'

[2] IWM FD 3057/49, FIAT Report 1312, 'Economic History of the Second World War' by Dr R. Wagenführ, 6–8. This manuscript was later rewritten and published as *Die deutsche Industrie im Kriege* (Berlin, 1963). Almost all subsequent discussions of the nature and performance of the German war economy have been based on a combination of the work of Wagenführ and the Bombing Survey—indeed Wagenführ uses the conclusions of the Survey in the later edition of his own work. It is necessary, however, to bear in mind the conditions under which the Bombing Survey officials operated. A large amount of material was processed very rapidly at the end of the war and reports produced within weeks by intelligence officers who were not historians, and whose main brief was to assess the effectiveness of the bombing campaign. The evidence used to support their conclusions about the German economy was limited. Great reliance was placed on oral testimony, and there was neither the time nor the necessity to produce a more searching evaluation. It is remarkable that conclusions produced under these difficult circumstances have been able to support such a weight of later historical writing, and have attracted so little critical attention.

the end of the war, confirmed this view. Although Albert Speer in his interrogations always insisted that his success was due to greater rationalization and better organization rather than a substantial redirection of resources from civilian to military production, the conclusion was drawn that the coming of the Speer era signalled the onset of fuller economic mobilization, in sharp contrast with the limited commitment of the *Blitzkrieg* phase.[3]

The conclusions of the Bombing Survey have been accepted almost without question by economists and historians since the war. The economist Nicholas Kaldor, writing in 1946, argued that Germany 'made no serious attempt to exploit her own war potential fully... there is no evidence of ruthless sacrifices having been imposed upon her own people for the sake of victory'.[4] The same view was put forward by Burton Klein in his history of the German war economy. According to Klein the *Blitzkrieg* strategy 'did not involve a large use of resources' and allowed the Nazi government to maintain a 'prosperous civilian economy'.[5] But the most systematic analysis of the whole question was offered by Alan Milward, who argued that the reasons for the low level of mobilization were to be found in the political system within Germany. Hitler favoured short, economically limited wars, in order to avoid the political costs of alienating the population by reducing living standards and to compensate for polycratic confusion in the Nazi state. The *Blitzkrieg* strategy was a 'system of waging war without reducing civilian consumer standards'. 'There can be little doubt', he wrote, 'that the impact of war on the German people over the years 1939–1941 was very small.'[6] Others studies stressed the failure to mobilize labour effectively before 1942, and in particular the failure to mobilize female labour, again a marked contrast to the labour policies of the other belligerent states.[7] The conception of

---

[3] IWM Box S368, Interrogation Report 56, Speer Interrogation, 31 Oct. 1945; Report 54, Speer Interrogation, 13 July 1945, esp. 5–6.

[4] N. Kaldor, 'The German War Economy', *Review of Economic Statistics*, 13 (1946), 20.

[5] B. H. Klein, *Germany's Economic Preparations for War* (Cambridge, Mass., 1959), 27.

[6] A. S. Milward, 'Could Sweden have Stopped the Second World War?' *Scandinavian Economic History Review*, 15 (1967), 195; id., *The German Economy at War* (London, 1965), 29. See too id., 'Hitlers Konzept des Blitzkrieges', in A. Hillgruber (ed.), *Probleme des Zweiten Weltkrieges* (Cologne, 1967), 19–40.

[7] There are numerous books and articles discussing the 'Blitzkrieg' phase of the economy. See esp. D. Petzina, 'Die Mobilisierung deutscher Arbeitskräfte vor und während des Zweiten Weltkrieges', *Vierteljahrshefte für Zeitgeschichte*, 18 (1970), 449–52; E. R. Zilbert, *Albert Speer and the Nazi Ministry of Arms* (London, 1981), esp. 33–9; L. Herbst, *Der Totale Krieg und die Ordnung der Wirtschaft* (Stuttgart, 1982), 95–174; S. Salter, 'Class Harmony or Class Conflict? The Industrial Working Class and the National Socialist Regime 1933–1945', in J. Noakes (ed.), *Government, Party and People in Nazi Germany* (Exeter, 1980), 89–91; L. Burchardt, 'The Impact of the War Economy on the Civilian Population of Germany during the First and Second World Wars', in W. Deist (ed.), *The German Military*

limited war has become incorporated into wider political analyses of the nature of the Nazi state and its *Herrschaftssystem* (system of domination). Short wars of booty, designed to stave off domestic political unrest, can be seen as a characteristic feature of populist authoritarian regimes, caught in the dilemma of offering economic benefits and a nationalist foreign policy together.[8]

Yet however plausible such an analysis seems in terms of the Nazi system, it is in almost every respect misleading. The impact on the German consumer between 1939 and 1941 was not 'very small'. Civilian consumer standards were cut by a considerably wider margin than in Britain. Labour was diverted to war tasks well before the Speer era, so that by the summer of 1941 almost two-thirds of the industrial work-force were working on military supplies and war work. The proportion of women in the German work-force remained higher than that in Britain throughout the war. Direct comparisons are, of course, difficult to make, for the structure of the working population was very different in each country. But there can be no doubt about the central conclusion that between 1939 and 1942 Germany did not enjoy a 'peace-like' war economy when compared with her enemies. It is the object of this chapter to explore these three major components of the *Blitzkrieg* argument—the financing of the war and the level of consumer spending, the diversion of labour to war, and the role of women in the German war economy—in order to dispel the myth of Germany's easy war.

---

in the Age of Total War (Leamington Spa, 1985), 40–70; B. Kroener, 'Squaring the Circle: Blitzkrieg Strategy and Manpower Shortage 1939–1942', in Deist, *Total War*, 282–303, who writes of 'a Blitzkrieg plan with a precisely calculated use of resources' (p. 295). Some recent historical writing has found difficulty in reconciling the growing evidence of shortages and cut-backs before 1942 with the established 'Blitzkrieg economy' argument. See F. Grube and G. Richter, *Alltag im Dritten Reich: So lebten die Deutschen 1933–1945* (Hamburg, 1982), 169–73, who argue both that consumption was kept at peacetime levels in 1940, and that food consumption (except bread) was 50% lower than the last year of peace!; W. F. Werner, *Bleib übrig! Deutsche Arbeiter in der nationalsozialistischen Kriegswirtschaft* (Düsseldorf, 1983), 138–41, who demonstrates a sharp decline in the provision of consumer goods in the Ruhrgebiet in 1940, while accepting the figures which show that consumption in Germany was the same in 1940 as in 1938. He leaves the contradiction unresolved: 'Looked at purely statistically, consumer output in 1941 lay only a little below that of 1938. However, the morale reports on the provisioning situation significantly contradict the statistics.' See also S. Bajohr, *Die Hälfte der Fabrik: Geschichte der Frauenarbeit in Deutschland 1914 bis 1945* (Marburg, 1979), 251–60; and J. Stephenson, 'War and Society in Württemberg 1939–1945: Beating the System', *German Studies Review*, 8 (1985), 89–105. The only recent study to challenge the conventional view is W. Boelcke, *Die deutsche Wirtschaft 1930–1945: Interna des Reichswirtschaftsministerium* (Düsseldorf, 1983), 153–9, although even here the author fails to relate his findings to the wider issues of German strategy.

[8] See esp. T. W. Mason, 'Intention and Explanation: A Current Controversy about the Interpretation of National Socialism', in G. Hirschfeld and L. Kettenacker (eds.), *The Führer State: Myths and Realities* (Stuttgart, 1981), 23–40.

I

A large-scale financial commitment to war and restrictions on consumption were already in evidence before 1939, and stemmed from the nature of German war preparations and strategy. Hitler and the armed forces were committed to extensive re-militarization. These demands reached new and extravagant levels in 1938 with the expanded naval programme, the requirement for a fivefold increase in air strength, and the new munitions and explosives programmes started in the summer.[9] But well before this Hitler had recognized what the army leaders had been arguing since the 1920s, that any future war must involve the fullest mobilization of the fighting and labour power of the nation. This meant that the economy had to be geared as far as possible to long-term military needs, particularly in building up the basic foundation in iron and steel production, chemicals, machinery, non-ferrous metals, and fuel-oil, without which any future war between great powers could not be fought. Hitler, like the generals, was obsessed with the lessons of 1914–18. Germany had to become immune to blockade; and had to avoid the danger of an economy unready for war as in 1914. This explains the introduction of a Plenipotentiary for War Economy in 1935, and the establishment of the Four Year Plan in 1936. The economic strategy behind the Plan was based on the assumption that Germany must become self-sufficient enough to be able to fight major war on her own, and that large financial and industrial resources should be devoted in the short term to producing an economy capable of total war.[10]

By 1939 Germany already devoted a very large proportion of her output to military purposes—some 23 per cent—while investing heavily in the synthetic production of fuel and rubber, and in the domestic production of iron ore, and in Austrian (and later Czech) iron, steel, and armaments

[9] On rearmament in general in 1938 see M. Geyer, 'Rüstungsbeschleunigung und Inflation: Zur Inflationsdenkschrift des OKW von November 1938', Militärgeschichtliche Mitteilungen, 23 (1981); W. Deist, The Wehrmacht and German Rearmament (London, 1981), chs. 3–5; A. Bagel-Bohlan, Hitlers industrielle Kriegsvorbereitung im Dritten Reich 1936 bis 1939 (Koblenz, 1975), 118–20. On the navy see J. Dülffer, Weimar, Hitler und die Marine: Reichspolitik und Flottenbau 1920–1939 (Düsseldorf, 1973), 488–504; on the air force R. J. Overy, 'The German Pre-war Aircraft Production Plans', English Historical Review, 90 (1975), 782–3. For the wider framework of economic preparations for war in 1938 (raw material, machinery, chemicals, etc.) see BA R25/84–5, Reichsamt für Wirtschaftsausbau, 'Wehrwirtschaftliche Neue Erzeugungsplan, 12 Juli 1938', 1–4; R26 I/18, Four Year Plan, Central Office, 'Ergebnisse der VJP-Arbeit', 20–49.
[10] IWM EDS AL 2652/1, Dr Tomberg, 'Deutschlands gegenwärtige wehrwirtschaftliche Lage', 7 Aug. 1944, 1–4; B. A. Carroll, Design for Total War: Arms and Economics in the Third Reich (The Hague, 1968), 54–71; G. Förster, Totaler Krieg und Blitzkrieg (Berlin, 1967), 67–82; A. Schröter and J. Bach, 'Zur Planung der wehrwirtschaftlichen Mobilmachung durch den deutschen faschistischen Imperialismus vor dem Beginn des Zweiten Weltkrieges', Jahrbuch für Wirtschaftgeschichte, (1978), I. 42–7.

production. Between 1937 and 1939 over 60 per cent of all capital investment in Germany went into these sectors, while another 10 per cent went into the aircraft and shipbuilding industries.[11] This strategy made very little sense in terms of a limited commitment to short wars, and Hitler himself made it clear on numerous occasions that his conception went well beyond that, for a major war to be fought when the armaments were finally ready in 1943–5; and when the economic resources of central and south-eastern Europe had been integrated with those of the Reich, to provide a large economic platform for the launching of war.[12] Göring argued that the Four Year Plan had 'the task of preparing the German economy for total war',[13] while Hitler told Colonel Thomas in 1939 'that any mobilization must be a total one, and that the three pillars, military, economy, and party have their own great tasks in wartime'.[14] When general war came in September 1939 the strategy of total economic mobilization was activated on Hitler's instructions.[15]

An obvious consequence of this economic strategy, in which rearmament had priority over every other consideration, was the deliberate suppression of consumer demand. Controls over trade and wages, and the starving of the consumer sector of raw materials and labour, produced an economy quite different in character from that of Weimar. Investment in the consumer industries failed to recover the levels of 1929, while investment in producer goods exceeded 1929 by 172 per cent. Real earnings, after making allowance for increased taxation and party levies,

[11] D. Petzina, *Autarkiepolitik im Dritten Reich* (Stuttgart, 1968); R. J. Overy, *Goering: The 'Iron Man'* (London, 1984), 60; on synthetic fuel, W. Birkenfeld, *Der synthetische Treibstoff, 1933–1945* (Göttingen, 1963); M. Riedel, *Eisen und Kohle für das Dritte Reich* (Göttingen, 1973), 25–61; G. Plumpe, 'Industrie, technischer Fortschritt und Staat: Die Kautschuksynthese in Deutschland 1906–1944/5', *Geschichte und Gesellschaft*, 9 (1983).

[12] See the general discussion of strategy in R. J. Overy, 'Hitler's War and the German Economy: A Reinterpretation', *Economic History Review*, 2nd ser. 35 (1982), 276–7. The date 1943/5 was used at the 'Hossbach' conference on 5 Nov. 1937 (see *Documents on German Foreign Policy* (HMSO, 1949), ser. D, vol. 1, 34–6). At some time in 1937 Hitler decided on a rough timetable to resolve the international order in Germany's favour. He gave the same dates to Goebbels in conversations earlier in the year (E. Frölich (ed.), *Die Tagebücher von Joseph Goebbels: sämtliche Fragmente* (Munich, 1987), part 1, iii. 55). There is further corroboration in the evidence from Erich Walter, adjutant's clerk to Admiral Raeder before the war: 'I realised from the discussions and conferences which the Supreme Commander had with Hitler—and from the later talks with the Naval Operational Staff— that they were counting on a war in the year 1943/4.' See Foreign Office Library, London, 'Miscellaneous Communications from the Public', part i, doc. D722, Erich Walter, 'The Story of My Life', 19 Feb. 1946, 2.

[13] BA-MA Wi I F 5.412, Ergebnis der Besprechung bei Generalfeldmarschall Göring am 16 Juli 1938, 1.

[14] IWM EDS Mi 14/377 (file 2), Thomas memorandum, 28 Mar. 1939, 'Gesichtspunkte für die Änderung der Mob.-Vorbereitungen der Wirtschaft', 2.

[15] IWM EDS Mi 14/328 (d), OKW Wehrmachtteile Besprechung, 3 Sept. 1939, 1–2: 'The position is clear,' wrote Thomas, 'the total mobilisation of the economy has been ordered'; OKW, Wehrwirtschaftsstab an Wehrwirtschaftsinspektionen, 7 Sept. 1939.

failed to regain the levels of the late 1920s, even though real GNP per head was 31 per cent higher by 1939. Private consumption as a share of National Income declined from 71 per cent in 1928 to 59 per cent in 1938, a fall of remarkable magnitude in such a short space of time. By the same date 68 per cent of the industrial work-force were employed in the producer-goods sectors and earned 75 per cent of all industrial incomes.[16] In this respect Germany was already in a different economic condition from Britain and the United States even before the outbreak of war. In Britain in the 1930s consumer spending expanded considerably, helped by cheapter imports. In Germany consumer spending was restrained, and the additional resources generated in the economy were diverted to rearmament and major capital projects.[17] When war came there was already less consumer production and spending to cut back on than there was in Britain.

This factor is of critical importance. Germany was not a 'rich' country in the 1930s in the sense of Britain, France, or the United States. The impact of war, inflation, and recession left large areas of poverty and deprivation. Recovery policies encouraged re-employment or substitute-employment at low wages. Wage controls kept wage rates at depression levels. Real wage growth between the wars was substantial in most other industrial countries, but was much less in Germany. By 1938 real wages had grown 9 per cent since 1913 in Germany, but 53 per cent in the United States, 33 per cent in Britain, and 28 per cent in France. In 1939 average *per capita* incomes in Germany were two-thirds of average British incomes and only 46 per cent of American, while in Germany prices for many products were higher, or the quality considerably lower than in the west.[18] Consumer durables sold less well in Germany, while food consumption patterns showed a tendency for coarse foods (rye-bread, potatoes) to increase and higher-quality foods to decline. *Per capita* consumption of meat was 75 per cent of levels in Britain.[19] A British

[16] BA R7 xvi/7 (IWM Microfilm Reel 145), Professoren-Ausschuss an Reichswitschaftsminister Funk, 16 Dec. 1939, 3; R. Erbe, *Die nationalsozialistische Wirtschaftspolitik 1933–1939 im Lichte der modernen Theorie* (Zürich, 1958), 100, 111, 177–8.

[17] By 1938 producer goods output in Germany was 35% higher than in 1928, but output of consumer goods was only 7% higher, an increase entirely absorbed by the growth in population between 1928 and 1938, from 64.3m. to 68.4m. In Britain there was a 14% increase in real consumer expenditure per head between 1925/9 and 1935/9.

[18] C. D. Long, *The Labor Force under Changing Income and Employment* (Princeton, NJ, 1958), 369; on real wages (weekly earnings) I. Svennilson, *Growth and Stagnation in the European Economy* (London, 1954), 235.

[19] O. Nathan and M. Fried, *The Nazi Economic System* (London, 1944), 358. Consumption of rye bread in working-class families increased 20% between 1927 and 1937, potatoes by 4%, while consumption of meat was 18% lower, of fats 37% lower, wheat bread 44% lower. Comparative figures on meat consumption in USSBS Special Paper 4, *Food and Agriculture*, 105. A great number of products declined in quality as well, a factor that deserves much more research.

businessman visiting Germany in 1937 noted: 'In the country itself, the standard of living seems low compared with ourselves ... The difficulty of the poorer classes obtaining what may be called "lesser luxuries" i.e. the things just above the limit of necessities is very marked.' One American journalist reported that standards in Germany were so low that American labour would not have tolerated them: 'We thus encounter two standards of living and attitudes towards daily life which differ from each other so profoundly that they cannot easily be compared.'[20] Of course, Germany was not poor by the standards of less developed countries in Europe and beyond but, because of her recent economic crises, simply lacked the depth of wealth available in Britain and the United States. Comparing the German war effort with that of richer economies, geared more to consumer demands, distorts the perspective. Changes in Germany during the war, real though they were, intensified a situation already in being.

The extravagant levels of military demand brought forward in 1938 and 1939, and confirmed again personally by Hitler after the outbreak of war, required ever greater cuts in the non-war sectors of the economy.[21] This was not a situation that arose merely from the inflated and uncoordinated demands of the individual armed forces, but was the explicit policy of Hitler's government, expressed in the War Economy Decree published at the beginning of the war, and planned for in detail through the numerous instructions on economic mobilization issued to local economic chambers during 1939.[22] On 9 September Göring, as head of the Reich Defence Council, called for the 'complete employment of the living and fighting power of the nation economically for the duration of the war'. Thomas informed Reichsgruppe Industrie that the political and military leadership wanted 'an exertion of strength by the German economy which, in its scope and rapid effort, must leave the Hindenburg Programme far behind it'.[23]

[20] Bank of England, file S.89 (2) Germany, letter from R. L. Barclay to Montagu Norman, 8 July 1937. I am grateful to the Bank for permission to quote from this unclassified file. See too L. Stoddard, *Into the Darkness: Nazi Germany Today* (London, 1941), 81, who concluded that 'the German population put up with privation because it had become the normal condition of life. No German under 40 has more than childhood recollections of the "good old times".'

[21] IWM Speer Collection, FD 1434/46 169, 'X-Fall für die Wirtschaft'; *Dokumente der deutschen Politik* (Berlin, 1940), vii. 403–9, Kriegswirtschaftsverordnung, 4 Sept. 1939; IWM EDS Mi 14/328 (d), OKW Wehrwirtschaftsstab an Wehrwirtschaftsinspektionen, 7 Sept. 1939: 'The Führer has also ordered on 3 Sept. 1939 together with the total mobilization of the economy, the planned introduction of Production Plan "Wehrmacht".'

[22] e.g. NA, Microcopy T71, Roll 45, frames 439440–54, Wirtschaftskammer Sachsen, 'Ein Ausschnitt aus der Kriegswirtschaftlichen Tätigkeit der Wirtschaftskammer Sachsen und ihrer Gliederung'; frames 439455–7, Wehrwirtschaftsbericht, Dec. 1939.

[23] IWM, Case XI background documents, Book 118-A, Doc. 3524-PS, speech by Economics Minister Funk, 14 Oct. 1939; IWM, Speer Collection, FD 5454 d/45, speech by Thomas to Reichsgruppe Industrie, 29 Nov. 1939, 1. Thomas reminded his audience of the mistakes of the First World War: 'It follows precisely on the basis of experience in the World War in this sphere, that the most extreme concentration of resources on the production of direct and indirect war needs is the compelling requirement.'

Discussions between Hitler, Göring, and the armed forces' chiefs in November led to a further policy statement for 'co-ordinating all efforts for increasing production for the armed forces... The war requires the greatest efforts in building up armaments. The High Command... recommends guidelines which have as their goal the strongest mobilization of all economic resources in the service of national defence.'[24] In December the High Command (OKW) reported Hitler's order that 'the conversion of the economy should be pursued with all energy' in order to produce what Hitler called 'a programme with the highest possible figures'.[25] None of this suggests a strategy based on limited mobilization. The armed forces' own preparations were conducted on the assumption that economic mobilization would be general and thorough, and Hitler, who as Supreme Commander was in the best position to supervise this policy, not only endorsed it but produced his own plans for production which made conversion on a large scale unavoidable.

The plans for military output confirmed at the end of 1939 demonstrate clearly the drift of Hitler's thinking. For Hitler the object was to produce weapons and munitions in such quantities that Germany would never have to run the risk of losing war again. Behind the British and French threat, which he hoped to eliminate with a great surge of armaments output, lay the growing menace from a less neutral United States and fears of Soviet action in the east.[26] The armaments programmes announced in December

[24] IWM, Speer Collection, FD 5454 d/45, OKW Kriegswirtschaftlicher Lagebericht 3, 1 Dec. 1939; FD 5445/45, OKW 'Richtlinien zur Zusammenfassung aller Kräfte zur Steigerung der Fertigung für die Wehrmacht', 29 Nov. 1939.

[25] IWM, Speer Collection, FD 5445/45, OKW Kriegswirtschaftlicher Lagebericht 3, 1 Dec. 1939; BA-MA Wi I F 5.412, Aktenvermerk über Besprechung am 11 Dez. 1939 über das neue Pulver- und Sprengstoffprogramm, die Mineralöl-Erzeugung and Aluminium Herstellung, 1: 'in the Reich Chancellery interest in the munitions question stands at the moment in the forefront. The Führer presses for clarity and demands a programme with the highest possible figures.'

[26] It is evident that Hitler believed from late 1939 onwards that even with the rapid defeat of France and Britain on the Continent, Germany would still be faced with the problem of the USSR and the USA, for which very large military and economic resources would be necessary. The war for world power could, Hitler believed, be postponed but not avoided. For his views on the USSR and USA see H. Groscurth, *Tagebücher eines Abwehroffiziers* (Stuttgart, 1970), 414, minutes of a talk between Hitler and the heads of the armed forces, 23 Nov. 1939; IWM EDS AL 1571, Aktennotiz, 4 Dec. 1939, Chef WiRüAmt; OKW Inspekteur-Besprechung, 24 Mar. 1940; Aktennotiz über die Entwicklung der Rüstungslage im Sommer 1940, 3: 'This new directive from the supreme leadership appears to base itself on the recognition that (1) the collapse of England in the year 1940 is under the circumstances no longer to be counted upon; (2) in the year 1941 the intervention of America can come into the question; (3) the relationship to Russia in the year 1941 can experience a change.' This last document should be read together with Chef WiRüAmt, notice of a meeting, 13 Sept. 1940, in which Hitler discussed the various options with the USSR and the USA again. It is clear that OKW already included the USA when discussing enemy war potential, and had done so since Sept. 1939. See IWM EDS AL 1492, WiRüAmt, Aktenvermerk, 26 Sept. 1939 and Mi 14/441, WiRüAmt Lagebericht West, 'Die Leistungsfähigkeit der USA-Flugzeugindustrie', 25 Nov. 1939.

1939, and repeated and extended again in the summer of 1940 after the defeat of France, were for the great war for world power. Hitler argued that it was necessary to prepare for war as if it might last five, seven, or even thirty years.[27] To cope with all or any of the contingencies in the future required the total mobilization of the economy for the present.[28] For Hitler the very nature of modern warfare dictated that supreme economic efforts had to be made, whether the war turned out to be a long one or a short one. He made this clear to his military leaders in May 1939:

Everybody's Armed Forces and Government must strive for a short war. But the government must, however, also prepare for a war of from ten to fifteen years' duration. History shows that wars were always expected to be short. In 1914 it was still believed that long wars could not be financed. Even today this idea buzzes in a lot of heads. However, every state will hold out as long as it can . . . The idea of getting out cheaply is dangerous, there is no such possibility.[29]

This is the only satisfactory explanation for the scale of Hitler's economic plans, which by 1939 already anticipated the production levels of the last year of the Great War, and which his anxious ministers and officials argued could not be fulfilled even with an economy converted to total war. The problem can be illustrated by looking at the figures drawn up by the Heereswaffenamt (Army Weapons Bureau) comparing the production of 1918 with the new armaments 'Production Plan 1940/2', based on Hitler's own figures set down in December 1939 (see Table 9.1). The army also calculated what was available on the basis of existing armaments capacity.[30] Other munitions were planned to increase by 200–300 per cent during 1940 and 1941.[31] Aircraft production was supposed to increase by 100 per cent in the first year of war, and Hitler's own

[27] BA-MA, Wi I F 5.412, Aktenvermerk, Besprechung am 17 Nov. 1939, betr. 'Erhöhung der Eisen- und Stahlkontingente zur Durchführung des Krauch-Plans, 12: 'on the other hand all preparations should be carried out in order to carry through a five-year war'; *Documents on German Foreign Policy (DGFP)*, ser. D, vol. 8 (HMSO, 1954), 193; memorandum of a conversation between the Führer and Count Ciano, 1 Oct. 1939; p. 141, memorandum of a conversation between the Führer and M. Dahlerus, 26 Sept. 1939.

[28] This is a point that is often overlooked. Hitler wanted as large an economic and military commitment as possible in order to give himself greater political flexibility. See e.g. IWM EDS AL 1571, Aktennotiz über die Entwicklung der Rüstungslage im Sommer 1940, 2–3. After the defeat of France Hitler ordered the creation of much larger and more heavily armed services because 'one must prepare for the year 1941 for every possible political situation'.

[29] *NCA* vii. 851–3, report of a conference with Hitler, 23 May 1939.

[30] IWM EDS Mi 14/487, OKW WiRüAmt, 'Vom Führer am 17 Dez. 1940 genehmigten Programm'; Chef OKW an von Brauchitsch, 19 Jan. 1940, betr. 'Denkschrift über die Steigerung der Munitionsfertigung auf Grund der Führerforderung von 12 Dez. 1939'; Mi 14/521 (prt. 1), Heereswaffenamt (Waffenstab 1c), 'Die personelle Leistungsfähigkeit Deutschlands im Mob.-Fall' n.d. [spring 1939]. HWA calculated that the Fertigungsplan 1938/9 would require 7.4m. new workers, and that Hitler's final goal would need 21m. workers altogether. The report concluded: 'One way or another there remains an enormous mismatch between what is and what is supposed to be.'

[31] IWM, Speer Collection, FD 1434/46, 169, Vergleichende Übersicht über die Munitionsprogramme 1938–1942.

TABLE 9.1. *Production plans for armaments, December 1939*

	1918	1940/2	Hitler's 'Endziel'*	From current capacity
(per year)				
Light artillery (incl. Flak)	15,550	110,893	151,780	36,290
Heavy artillery	1,903	3,334	3,334	887
Machine-guns	196,578	2,179,449	2,179,449	603,350
(per month, tonnes)				
Gunpowder	12,100	18,100	18,100	14,000
Explosives	14,000	17,700	19,700	16,000

Source: IWM Mi 14/521 (part 1), 'Munitionslieferung im Weltkrieg'.

* 'Final aim'.

preference was for an output of powder and explosives of over 60,000 tons a month, the figure laid down in the 'Schnellplan' drawn up by Carl Krauch in 1938.[32] If these sums were unrealistic in the conditions of 1939, as the figures on available capacity make clear, they do show that Hitler, characteristically, thought in terms of colossal schemes and utmost efforts. It should also be remembered that if general war had broken out later, as German leaders hoped, many of the armaments and materials programmes would have been completed, and Hitler's figures would have appeared less exaggerated than they now do.

II

The nature of German military and economic strategy in the early stages of the war made very great demands on German financial resources. It was widely understood in government circles that financial strategy was a decisive element in the war economy, one of the major ways in which the government could directly influence the macro-economic structure in favour of the war effort. There was general agreement that the mistakes of the 1914–18 war should be avoided. The dependence on voluntary war loans, the failure to prevent high levels of inflation, and the rise of the black market and war profiteering undermined Germany's ability to continue the war and provoked widespread social unrest.[33]

[32] IWM Case XI documents, Book 118a, Doc. NI-7835, 'Development of the production plans for gunpowder and explosives, 15 July 1940'; EDS Mi 14/521 (pt. 1), OKW 'Pulver-, Sprengstoff- und Kampfstoffherstellung, 12 Dec. 1939'. On aircraft output see NA T177 Roll 31, frame 3719681, 'Nachschubzahlen für Luftfahrtgerät', 1 Apr. 1938.

[33] C.-L. Holtfrerich, *The German Inflation 1914–1923* (Berlin, 1986), 102–8; W. A. Boelcke, *Die Kosten von Hitlers Krieg* (Paderborn, 1985), 83–99; L. Graf Schwerin von

TABLE 9.2. *Government military and civilian expenditure, 1938/9–1943/4* (RM '000m., current prices)

	Military expend.	Civilian expend.	Total state expend.	GNP[a]
1938/9	17.2	22.2	39.4	115
1939/40	38.0	20.0	58.0	129
1940/41	55.9	24.1	80.0[a]	132
1941/42	72.3	28.2	100.5[a]	137
1942/43	86.2	37.8	124.0[a]	143
1943/44	99.4	30.6	130.0[a]	160

[a] Includes contributions from occupied territories.

Sources: W. Boelcke, 'Kriegsfinanzierung im internationalen Vergleich', in F. Forstmeier and H.-E. Volkmann (eds.), *Kriegswirtschaft und Rüstung am Vorabend des Zweiten Weltkrieges: 1939–1945* (Düsseldorf, 1977), 55–6; Klein, *Preparations*, 256.

From the outbreak of war in 1939 there was a very great increase in both military and civilian expenditure by the central government. Military spending in 1939/40 was double the level of the last peacetime year, and had doubled again by 1941/2. The largest absolute increase in expenditure and the fastest rate of growth of expenditure both occurred in the years before 1942, not after (see Table 9.2). The decision to convert the economy to full mobilization in 1939 made extraordinary demands on the German financial system. In the first four months of war military costs were RM 12,000m., and the armed forces expected the first full year of war to cost RM 40,000m.–45,000m.[34] In order to permit the high levels of military expenditure and war production, and to avoid inflation and financial crisis, it was necessary to solve the question of financing the war above all others.

There were a number of options open to the government. There was general agreement among ministers and officials that consumption would have to be cut back sharply: 'It is necessary,' ran a report from the Finance Ministry in February 1940, 'to limit the consumption of goods for private use to the very lowest level.'[35] The second step was to take up the personal income released by these restrictions and

Krosigk, *Staatsbankrott: Finanzpolitik des Deutschen Reiches 1920–1945* (Göttingen, 1974), 295–6.

[34] BA R7 xvi/7 (IWM Reel 145), OKW to GBW betr. Geldbedarf der Wehrmacht im Kriege, 7 Oct. 1939; RWM Aktenvermerk, Staatssekretärbesprechung im RFM, 3 Jan. 1940, 1.

[35] NA T178 Roll 15, frames 3671791–3, RFM 'Denkschrift über Kaufkraft und Kriegsfinanzierung 1940', 13 Feb. 1940. See too frames 3671852–6, Preiskommissar Wagner to von Krosigk, 21 Dec. 1939 and frame 3671873, Funk to Schwerin von Krosigk, 19 Jan. 1940.

channel it towards the war effort: 'to soak up as quickly and widely as possible the purchasing power released by restricting the possibility of buying'.[36] The object was to restrict personal consumption, through rationing, to an *Existenzminimum*; 'only enough ... to meet essential consumer requirements and unavoidable financial obligations'[37] (rent, insurance etc.). Rationing was the most effective way of achieving these aims in the short term, and it promised to avoid the wide inequalities in consumption that developed during the First World War. Rationing involved not only control over the demand for goods, by establishing a standard ceiling for buying food and clothing, but also over the supply of goods. It was assumed that people would try to turn their surplus income into luxury or non-rationed goods. Once stocks were cleared out in the autumn and winter of 1939 by hoarders, the so-called *Hamsterkäufer*, rigid restrictions were placed on the sale and production of any non-rationed goods, confining personal expenditure to a limited range of permitted products.[38]

The second way of controlling consumption levels was to increase taxation. Again there was little disagreement that some increase in taxes was desirable, and an emergency surtax (*Kriegszuschlag*) was imposed on all German taxpayers from the beginning of the war.[39] Indirect taxes were also increased, and in January 1940 Hitler personally authorized increases in taxation on cinemas, travel, and theatre-going.[40] Taxes on beer and tobacco were increased, and the range of products covered by the sales tax expanded. Despite some vigorous opposition to increasing the tax burden of industry, on the grounds that it discouraged productive investment, corporation tax receipts increased from RM 2,400m. in 1938/9 to RM 5,100m. in 1941/2.[41] The net result of all these measures was a doubling

[36] NA T178, Roll 15, frame 3671816, Schwerin von Krosigk to Funk, 21 Nov. 1939.

[37] BA R7 xvi/7, Finance Ministry (Reinhardt) 'Die Möglichkeit der Kriegsfinanzierung', 22 July 1939, 3. This view was widely supported. See for example letter from Posse (Four Year Plan) to Landfried (Economics Ministry), 7 Aug. 1939; Labour Front to Landfried, 19 Dec. 1939, 1–2; NA 178, Roll 15, frames 3671805–7, Ley to Funk, 13 Dec. 1939.

[38] On rationing see BA R7 xvi/7, Labour Front to Economics Ministry, 19 Dec. 1939, Anlage, 'Aufstellung der Lebenskarten pro Woche'; Popitz to Funk, 26 Oct. 1939, 1–2; Reichswirtschaftskammer to Lange, 21 Oct. 1939, enclosing 'Ansprache Präsident Pietzsch bei der Besprechung mit Minister Funk am 20 Oktober 1939', 5–7, 14; Reichsbank, volkswirtschaftliche Abteilung, 'Zur inneren Währungslage', 14 Sept. 1939, 2: 'the possibilities of consumption have already experienced a reduction through the rationing measures. This situation will considerably worsen because—leaving aside the hoarders—the transfer of the economy to war and export needs must substantially narrow the availability of consumer goods.'

[39] NA T178, Roll 15, frames 3672285–92, Finance Ministry, 'Die steuerlichen Massnahmen während des gegenwärtigen Krieges', n.d.; L. Schwerin von Krosigk, *Staatsbankrott: Finanzpolitik des Deutschen Reiches 1920–1945*, (Göttingen, 1974), 298.

[40] BA R7 xvi/7, Staatssekretärbesprechung in RFM betr. Kriegsfinanzierung, 3 Jan. 1940, 4.

[41] NA T178, Roll 15, frames 3671878–80, Funk to Schwerin von Krosigk, 19 Jan. 1940;

TABLE 9.3. *Central government tax receipts, tax years 1938–1943* (RMm., current prices)

	1938	1939	1940	1941	1942	1943
Income and business tax	8,186	12,227	14,790	19,185	21,808	21,954
Sales tax	3,356	3,734	3.929	4,148	4,160	4,177
Purchase tax[a]	2,833	4,425	5,582	6,193	6,202	5,943
Customs	1,818	1,696	1,413	1,121	833	639
Misc. revenue	1,517	1,491	1,506	1,658	1,707	1,664
TOTAL:	17,710	23,573	27,220	32,305	34,710	34,377
(1938 = 100)	100	133	154	182	196	194
Total in 1938 prices:	17,710	23,370	26,181	30,317	31,758	30,887

[a] Includes war tax on beer, tobacco, travel, entertainment.

Sources: NA T178, Roll 15, frames 3671912–7, Reichsfinanzmin., 'Statistische Übersichten zu den Reichshaushaltsrechnungen 1938 bis 1943' Nov. 1944; price adjustments according to BA RD-51 (IWM Reel 168), Reichsbank, 'Deutsche Wirtschaftszahlen', Mar. 1944, 2.

of domestic tax revenues between 1939 and 1941 (see Table 9.3). With only a small increase in the price level, the real burden of taxation increased significantly. For those earning RM 1,500–3,000 a year tax payments increased by an average of 20 per cent; for those earning between RM 3,000 and 5,000, by 55 per cent.[42] In 1940 and 1941 military expenditure was covered half by taxation, half by government loans and contributions from occupied territories.[43]

But neither rationing, nor increases in taxation, provided a complete solution, for there remained substantial amounts of surplus personal income available with no goods to spend it on. The Finance Minister, Graf Schwerin von Krosigk, with the support of the so-called Committee of Professors set up in autumn 1939 to advise on war finance policy, hoped to absorb the surplus purchasing power during 1940 with larger increases

BA R7 xvi/7, Ergebnis der Chefbesprechung am 1 Feb. 1940, 7; minutes of a meeting in the Finance Ministry, 16 Jan. 1940, 4–5, 8; Staatssekretärbesprechung, 3 Jan. 1940, 6–7.

[42] BA R7 xvi/8, Statistisches Reichsamt to Economics Ministry (Josten) 3 Feb. 1943, Anlage 'Zur Frage der Erhöhung des Einkommens- und Vermögenssteuer'. For those earning over RM 100,000 a year the proportion going in taxation rose from 38% in 1938 to 54% in 1940.

[43] NA T178, Roll 15, frames 3671762–3, Finance Ministry, General Bureau, 'Finanzieller Überblick über die vergangenen vier Kriegsjahre, 1 Sept. 39–31 Aug. 43'; R. Lindholm, 'German Finance in World War II', *American Economic Review*, 37 (1947), 123–7.

in income tax.[44] There was strong resistance to these proposals on the grounds that increases in direct taxation would demoralize the population and provoke opposition, and Hitler finally vetoed the policy in the spring of 1940.[45] Instead the government pursued a policy of indirect war finance by encouraging high levels of saving. The argument behind this approach was partly political: the authorities started from the assumption that ordinary Germans would only identify with the war effort if they felt they would get something out of it.[46] With surplus income put into savings banks, the problem of purchasing power was solved, while the government got access to very large liquid assets. This system avoided the problem that worried Hitler, of having to depend on public war loans as in the First World War, which had encouraged inflation and undermined saver confidence.[47] From 1939 onwards German earners were bombarded with propaganda on saving and, in the absence of anything in the shops to spend their money on, they diverted very great sums from consumption to saving of all kinds (see Table 9.4).[48] This development was particularly marked among small investors. The number of post office savings books increased from 1.5 million in 1939 to 5.5 million in 1941 and 8.3 million in 1942.[49] But what savers did not know was that all the savings institutions were compelled to transfer their deposits to the government by buying Treasury bills or taking up long-term loans, thus providing the funds needed for the war effort without arousing public anxieties. Schwerin von Krosigk described the system after the war in his history of German finances: 'The saver became indirectly, without realizing it, a creditor of the Reich.'[50]

[44] BA R7 xvi/7, letter from Schwerin von Krosigk to Göring, Frick, Funk, and Wagner, 12 Jan. 1940; Report from the 'Professoren-Ausschuss' to Funk, 16 Dec. 1939, 14–16. There was also support from the Reichsbank to increase income tax; Reichsbank-Direktorum to Lange (Economics Ministry), 8 Nov. 1939.

[45] Schwerin von Krosigk, Staatsbankrott, 298–9. Popitz thought that higher tax levels were akin to bolshevization, because they gave too much power and discretion to the state. See BA R7 xvi/7, Ergebnis der Chefbesprechung, 1 Feb. 1940, 3. On Funk's objections see minutes of the meeting in the Finance Ministry, 16 Jan. 1940, 4–6.

[46] This was the prevailing view at the Economics Ministry, not the Finance Ministry. See BA R7 xvi/7, Economics Ministry Memorandum 'Zur Kriegsfinanzierung', n.d. [Dec. 1939?], 2–3: 'The best means for it is saving'; Staatssekretär Neumann to Posse, 1 Jan. 1939; Lange to Funk and Landfried, 7 Jan. 1940, 5–11.

[47] BA R7 xvi/7, Staatssekretärbesprechung, 3 Jan. 1940, 3; von Krosigk, Staatsbankrott, p. 297; Holtfrerich, Inflation, 116–19.

[48] BA R28/98, Deutsche Reichsbank, Entwurf einer Ansprache von Vizepräsident Kurt Lange in Budapest am 8 Juni 1943: 'Die deutsche Finanz- und Wirtschaftspolitik im Kriege', 11–12.

[49] BA R7 xvi/7, Economics Ministry report, 'Die Bayerische Wirtschaft an der Jahreswende 1942/3, 75–6 (these figures are for the Reich as a whole); R2/31681, Reinhardt Akten, Unterlage für die Besprechung mit den Gauwirtschaftsberater am 19 Feb 1942, Anlage 'Mehr an Sparanlagen'; Boelcke, Kosten, 103–4.

[50] Schwerin von Krosigk, Staatsbankrott, 297. See too Boelcke, Kosten, 104; J. J. Klein, 'German Money and Prices 1932–1944' in M. Friedman (ed.), Studies in the Quantity Theory of Money (Chicago, 1956), 135–6.

TABLE 9.4. *Sources of private credit creation, 1937–1941* (RM '000m.)[a]

	1937	1938	1939	1940	1941
Credit bank deposits	1.2	2.2	4.2	8.7	8.1
Savings banks deposits	1.9	2.7	2.6	8.9	14.5
Private insurance	1.4	1.7	1.7	3.3	4.2
Private shareholding, treasury bills, and tax certificates	1.1	2.5	6.9	8.1	12.4
TOTAL:	6.2	10.9	19.2	31.3	44.6

[a] Net annual increase; '000m. = US billion.

Source: BA R7 XVI/22 (IWM Reel 147), O. Donner, 'Die Grenzen der Staatsverschuldung', 1942, 4.

By these various means the high level of liquidity in the economy in 1939–41 was prevented from creating inflationary pressures. The government acquired direct access to the financial resources that it needed, and levels of consumption were rapidly reduced. But the confidence of savers, on which the whole system depended, required visibly effective controls over prices and wages. This was a central feature of German policy during the war, necessitating a comprehensive system of controls and the exemplary punishment of those who ignored them.[51] Although the official price and wage indexes take no account of the sharp deterioration in the quality of goods during the war, and understate price rises for non-rationed goods, they do indicate a quite different situation from that of the First World War (see Table 9.5).[52] Moreover the wide publicity given to price controls served to maintain confidence in the government's determination to defend the currency, and to postpone recognition of the economic difficulties that might be expected to arise after the end of the war.[53]

While the indirect system of financing the war and the price-control mechanism produced a more complicated and riskier strategy than one that relied on exceptionally high levels of direct taxation, there is no doubt

[51] BA R7 xvi/7, Wagner to Schwerin von Krosigk, 3 Feb. 1940; Economics Ministry (Josten) to Posse, 24 Aug. 1939, 1: 'In order to avoid the destructive result which the high industrial wages in 1917/18 produced, the armed forces, the Price Commissioner, and the Trustees of Labour must work together as closely as possible to secure the stability of wages and prices'; BA R2/31681, Reinhardt-Akten, von Krosigk to Fischboeck (Price Commissioner) May 1942; BA R28/98, Deutsche Reichsbank, 'Die deutsche Finanz- und Wirtschaftspolitik', 10, 15–17.

[52] On the official indices see Boelcke, *Kosten*, 134–6.

[53] The government would have faced the greatest difficulty in controlling consumption when the war was over and people tried to spend what they believed they had saved, but which had been used up to fund the war. In this sense the problems of war finance were only postponed, not avoided altogether.

TABLE 9.5. *Official indices of prices and wages, 1939–1943*

Year	Cost-of-living index (1913 = 100)	Nominal weekly earnings (1936 = 100)	Real weekly earnings (1936 = 100)
1939	116.2	112.6	111.1
1940	119.6	116.0	111.0
1941	122.3	123.6	116.0
1942	125.0	124.3	114.2
1943[a]	126.9	126.5	114.5

[a] Figures for earnings in 1943 are for Jan./Feb.

Source: BA RD-51/21–3 (IWM Reel 168), Deutsche Reichsbank, Volkswirtschaftliche Abteilung, 'Deutsche Wirtschaftszahlen', Berlin, Mar. 1944, 2.

that it worked effectively enough from the regime's point of view. The great sums needed to pay for the war were found from domestic sources, supplemented by compulsory contributions from the occupied territories (12 per cent of the total), while inflation was kept at bay for most of the war. The consumer lost out. People paid higher taxes and saved more, rather than buying goods and services. Taxation and public expenditure doubled between 1939 and 1941; private savings increased more than 130 per cent, and the share of the state in Gross National Product increased from 32 to 53 per cent. Over the same period the economy as a whole expanded by only 6 per cent.[54] In other words, increases in tax revenue and savings did not come as a result of the expansion of the economy but as a substitute for private consumption. The financial strategy of the regime gave expression to its desire to mobilize economy and society as fully as possible for war; at the same time the transfer of financial resources provided the means by which the transfer of physical resources from civilian to military purposes could be carried out.

III

Within its own terms, the policy for reducing consumption and diverting excess purchasing power was successful enough. In February 1940 *Die Bank* reported that: 'Restrictions on consumer goods, through ration cards

[54] NA T178, Roll 15, frames 3671912–17, Finance Ministry, 'Statistische Übersichten zu den Reichshaushaltsrechnungen 1938 bis 1943', Nov. 1944; frames 3671758–63, Finance Ministry General Bureau, 'Finanzialler Überblick über die vergangenen vier Kriegsjahre', 15 Oct. 1943.

and the points and certificate system are almost entirely completed.'[55] It was estimated that approximately RM 13,000m. of consumption was removed in 1940, including RM 5,000m. of clothing consumption and RM 4,000m.–5,000m. of food consumption, while more funds were released for the government by sharply curtailing restocking in the wholesale and retail trades and refusing permits for regular repairs and maintenance.[56] As a result large sums were diverted to saving and investment out of the surplus between net income and net consumer expenditure, a gap which totalled RM 14,000m. in 1939, RM 23,000m. in 1940 and RM 31,000m. in 1941.[57]

There are a number of ways of measuring more precisely the reduction in consumer spending during the period 1939 to 1941, either through *per capita* real consumer expenditures or through *per capita* retail sales. It is necessary to use figures per head during this period since there were major changes in population size. Figures for consumption based on aggregate consumer expenditures can be misleading unless these changes are kept in mind. Before the *Anschluss* the German population was 69 million. By the end of 1938 it was 79 million, and by the end of 1940, through the incorporation of new territories in the west and east, it had risen to 92 million.[58] Without adjusting for an increase of almost a third in three years, the aggregate statistics show a slower decline in consumption. It is also important to look at consumer expenditure rather than consumer output (the measurement favoured by Wagenführ and Milward), since, as will be shown below, a very large proportion of the surviving consumer production was devoted to military orders for consumer goods. Another obstacle in obtaining accurate figures on consumer spending arises from the fact that full national economic accounts were not published during the period, and were calculated after the war by the Bombing Survey on the basis of reports and statistics produced in the Economics Ministry, the Reich Statistical Office, the Reich Economic Chamber, and the Wagemann Institute both before and after 1945. While these figures, like all national economic data, are necessarily crude, they all indicate a decisive trend in

[55] BA R7 xvi/7, Auszug aus *Die Bank*, 10 Jan. 1940, 1.

[56] BA R7 xvi/28 (IWM Reel 147), Vortrag vor Dr E. W. Schmidt, Direktor der Deutschen Bank vor der Auslandspresse, 7 Feb. 1941, 2–3. According to Schmidt, 'The supply of consumer goods decreased, since in war productive capacity must be concentrated on producing the goods necessary for the war effort.'

[57] BA R7 xvi/28, statistics on national income, n.d.

[58] BA NSD/51 (IWM Reel 168), German Labour Front, 'Die Rohstoffbasis des grossdeutschen Wirtschaftsraumes', June 1941, gives the following figures for the German pre-war and wartime population: pre-1935 German area, 68,474,000; Saarland, 843,000; Austria, 6,650,000; Sudeten areas, 3,408,000; Memel, 155,000; Danzig, 391,000; Polish territories, 10,043,000; Eupen/Malmedy, 69,000; Alsace-Lorraine, 1,915,000; Luxembourg, 301,000. The total population in Germany immediately before the war was 79,530,000. By 1941 'Greater Germany' had 92,249,000 inhabitants.

the decline of consumer spending.[59] Table 9.6 sets out the data for the war years, based on *per capita* consumer spending as a whole (that is, including housing and services) and on retail sales. The British figures are included for comparison. They show that for the whole war, including the years 1939 to 1941, real levels of consumption per head were maintained at a higher level in Britain than in Germany.

There are a number of points to be made about Table 9.6. The first calculation is based on figures given by Klein, which are drawn from the documents used by the Bombing Survey at the end of the war. These statistics are for the pre-war German area including Austria, the Sudetenland, and Memel.[60] Far from supporting Klein's thesis about limited war, his figures show that consumption per head was already falling in 1939 and by 1942 had declined by 25 per cent, approximately the amount recommended in autumn 1939 by the Finance Ministry. Indeed, Klein's figures actually show that the bulk of the fall in consumer spending came *before* 1942, not after. If all the increases in population and territory are taken into account, as they were in the wartime calculations of Dr Grünig, who worked for the Reichswirtschaftskammer (Reich Economic Chamber), the figures show an even sharper fall in expenditure per head, set out in line three of the table. The difference can largely be accounted for by the fact that the areas brought into the Reich in 1940 in

[59] These reports were used as the basis for the figures in the USSBS Special Paper 1, *The Gross National Product of Germany 1936–1944*, 4–6. The figures selected by the survey suggest a slow decline of consumer expenditures during the early part of the war, but they are unadjusted for population changes and include private civilian investment as well, rather than simply consumer spending on goods and services. No source is given in the paper for the figures, but they correspond almost exactly for the early years with the figures produced during the war by Dr Grünig of the Reich Economic Chamber, whose work was known to the Bombing Survey officials (see Table 9.5). These figures are in fact for the old, smaller Reich area for 1938, but thereafter reflect the expansion of Germany eastwards and westwards. On this basis the real *per capita* figures for consumption and private investment in the period 1938 to 1944 calculated from the USSBS data are as follows (1938 = 100): 1939, 93.2; 1940, 86.2; 1941, 83.9; 1942, 75.9; 1943, 74.8; 1944, 67.9. This gives a picture of a much sharper decline in consumption levels than the gross unadjusted figures on their own suggest.

[60] Klein, *Preparations*, 256–7. The figures provided by Wagenführ, *Deutsche Industrie*, 36–7, on which so many authors rely, were in fact taken from Kaldor, 'War Economy', 25, and Kaldor used the figure from the Bombing Survey already discussed in n. 59. The whole weight of the argument about consumer expenditure rests on a single, and less than adequate, source, which has been recycled in various forms ever since. Neither Wagenführ nor Milward provide statistics from the original sources for calculating Germany's national accounts, and neither gives a *per capita* calculation of consumer expenditure. Both authors rely also on another USSBS source on the volume of consumer goods output. Wagenführ (p. 37) argues that consumer goods output declined only marginally in 1940, and actually went up again in 1941. Yet this takes no account of the diversion of consumer sectors to war work, which Wagenführ admits elsewhere (p. 49) reached at least 30% of aggregate consumer output. Many firms designated as 'consumer goods' producers were by 1940 making components out of ceramic, leather, paper, etc., which bore little resemblance to their peacetime production. Gross figures of volume or value of consumer industry output are meaningless on their own.

the east were much poorer than the rest of Germany.[61] These figures conform well with the other evidence of an increase in savings and the level of decline of retail sales over the same period. Retail sales (lines five and six of Table 9.6) are in some respects a better indication of consumption trends because they reflect actual sales in the shops and exclude from the calculation fixed expenditures such as rent (which could not be reduced in wartime), fuel, and essential services. Once again the figures show that retail sales fell faster between 1939 and 1941 than at any other stage of the war, achieving only 74 per cent of the 1938 level by 1942. Retail sales fell more slowly than overall *per capita* expenditure because consumers cut back on non-essential services and goods faster than on food and household articles, and the supply of rationed goods meant a guaranteed minimum in the shops.

The gross figures of cuts in real levels of consumption match the changes in levels of taxation and government spending between 1939 and 1942. Far from these being the easiest years of the war, they were the years when the reduction in the civilian economy was at its most rapid. This situation is confirmed by the surviving documentary evidence, and by statistics of industrial output and sales per head of population. The government's economic strategy from the autumn of 1939 onwards was designed to restrict civilian production sharply in favour of military and war-related production and to cut back on civilian imports. This was done through the closing down or restriction (*Stillegung* or *Verdrosselung*) of civilian producers. The purpose of these restrictions was 'to concentrate important war production in certain particularly suitable businesses, and to close down large parts of the productive economy, or to prepare this capacity for other war purposes in a planned way'.[62] The Economics Ministry and the Labour Ministry were instructed by Göring to carry out this programme over the winter months and by May 1940, despite the evident reluctance of many businessmen to comply with closure or conversion, was close to completion.[63] The Reich Economic Chamber produced regular reports on the economy during this period, based on the detailed

---

[61] IWM FD 3958/49, Referat Dr Grünig vor dem Beirat der Reichswirtschaftskammer am 14 Dez. 1944, 'Volkswirtschaftliche Bilanz für Deutschland, Grossbritannien und die Vereinigten Staaten von Amerika'. See too BA R11/11 (IWM Reel 152), Dr Grünig to Albert Pietzsch, 17 Nov. 1044, Anlage 2, 'Die Entwicklung von Erzeugung und Nettoeinkommen seit 1936', 2–3; Dr Grünig to Pietzsch, 16 June 1941, 'Kriegswirtschaftlicher Bilanz'. The figures in this enclosure show a *per capita* fall in 1940 to 87.4% of the level of 1938 for all food, clothing, consumer durables, fuel, and services (pre-war area).

[62] BA-MA Wi I F 5,412, minutes of a conference in the Economics Ministry, 3 Oct. 1939, 1; see too BA R41/64, Handakten Hultig: 'Stilllegung von Betrieben'.

[63] IWM Speer Collection, FD 4809/45, Four Year Plan Report, 3 May 1940; on the problems of getting firms to comply see IWM EDS Mi 14/294 (file 5), OKW WiRüAmt, Dr Tomberg, 'Die Probleme der deutschen Rüstungswirtschaft im Kriege', Sept. 1940, 56–8; BA-MA Wi I F 5.412, conference with Gen. Thomas, 13 Nov. 1939.

TABLE 9.6. Consumption and retail sales, 1938–1944

	1938	1939	1940	1941	1942	1943	1944
Consumer expenditure (RM '000m., 1939 prices)	70.0	71.0	66.0	62.0	57.0	57.0	53.0
Index of real per capita consumption (1939 area)	100.0	95.0	88.4	81.9	75.3	75.3	70.0
Index of real per capita consumption (Greater Germany)	100.0	98.0	80.2	74.4	68.0	67.2	—
Index of real per capita consumption in Britain	100.0	97.2	89.7	87.1	86.6	85.5	88.2
Retail sales (Greater Germany, RM '000m.)	33.1	37.8	35.7	35.4	33.7	33.0	31.5
Index of retail sales per capita (current prices)	100.0	97.3	79.5	77.8	74.2	72.7	69.5
Official cost-of-living index (1913 = 100)	125	126	130	133	136	138	139

Sources: Calculated from IWM FD 3058/49 'Volkswirtschaftliche Bilanz für Deutschland, Grossbritannien und die Vereinigten Staaten von Amerika', compiled by Dr Grünig, 14 Dec. 1944. The figures for Germany are confirmed in BA R11/11 (IWM Reel 152), Reichswirtschaftskammer file, letter from Grünig to Albert Pietzsch, 17 Nov. 1944, Anlage 2, 'Die Entwicklung von Erzeugung und Nettoeinkommen seit 1936'; letter from Grünig to Pietzsch, 16 June 1943 'Kriegswirtschaftliche Bilanz'. This letter shows a 30% fall in per capita consumption between 1936 and 1943 (1939 area). BA RD 51/21–3, 'Deutsche Wirtschaftszahlen', Deutsche Reichsbank, Mar. 1944; BA R7 xvi/28, Josten files, statistics on national income and retail sales; Klein, Preparations, 256–7. For the British figures see R. Stone and D. Rowe, The Measurement of Consumers' Expenditure and Behaviour in the United Kingdom (Cambridge, 1966), ii. 125–6, 147.

information provided by local economic chambers, which show that at a local level the regulations on closure and conversion were being enforced. The report for January 1940 noted: 'The conversion of the economy to war production is, according to the view of all reporting offices, in all substantial respects fulfilled', while production of non-war goods was 'further reduced'. Non-war sectors were starved of raw materials, transport licences, and labour. By July 1940 the economic chambers reported: 'Conversion to war production has been allowed to be carried through to such an extent that production for anything other than war and

vital civilian supply is as good as completely halted.' By November direct
and indirect war production was eating into the capacity and resources
allocated for producing rationed goods as well.[64]

These reports make it clear that not only was conversion to war pursued
energetically from September 1939, but it was not allowed to slacken even
after the defeat of France in the summer of 1940. Of course, many officials
and businessmen, and no doubt much of the population, assumed that
civilian production would be restarted and that a punitive peace treaty
would be imposed on Britain and France. But this was not to be. For the
war economy there was no 'pause' in the summer of 1940. Within a
month of the defeat of France, Hitler decided to expand the army to 180
divisions with a core of 20 armoured and motorized divisions (double the
number in May 1940), in order to prepare for the next stage of the 'big
war' to the east.[65] He ordered a further wave of cuts from the civilian
economy to accommodate the new programmes: 'a complete shutting
down of all tasks not of the utmost urgency by both the armed forces and
the civilian sector'.[66] Göring's response to the early efforts of the
Economics Ministry to ease the strain on the civilian side was sharp and to
the point: 'You tell those people: armaments come first.'[67] To later
accusations from the OKW that the Economics Ministry had not pursued
the conversion to war enthusiastically enough, Landfried replied with a
long memorandum setting out in full the policies of 1939 and 1940 in
cutting back civilian output, converting labour and factory capacity to war
work, drawing up lists of proscribed consumer goods and diverting raw
materials to military needs.[68]

---

[64] BA R11/77, Reichswirtschaftskammer, Wirtschaftslagebericht, 24 Jan. 1940; 18 June
1940; 13 July 1940; 22 Nov. 1940.

[65] IWM Speer Collection, FD 5447/45, Notiz über die Besprechung bei Chef
Heeresrüstungsamt, 19 July 1940: Hitler wanted an army 'as large as all enemy armies put
together'. Thomas calculated that such a programme would require seven years to complete
at current levels of tank production, or 3.5 years if tank production were doubled. IWM EDS
AL 1571, Chef WiRüAmt, notes for a meeting, 13 Sept. 1940, 1–2; Mi 14/463 (file 1), Chef
OKW to heads of armed forces, 27 Sept. 1940. 'Steigerung der Rüstung', 1–3. These
programmes marked a significant shift in the military and economic effort, for not only did
Hitler want a large new motorized army, but additional naval and aircraft output, and
increase in Flak shells from 400,000 a month to 1m., and large increases in the output of
strategic materials, esp. aluminium. Both Todt and Thomas thought that the economy was
already converted so extensively for military purposes that the new programmes could not
possibly be fulfilled.

[66] IWM EDS Mi 14/433 (1), WiRüAmt, 'Steigerung der Rüstung', 25 Sept. 1940.

[67] IWM EDS AL 1571, WiRüAmt, Amtschef-Besprechung am 15 Aug. 1940 betr.
Dringlichkeit, 1; see too BA-MA Wi I F 5.118, pt. 2, Göring to Economics Ministry, 22 July
1940.

[68] IWM EDS Mi/463 (file 2), Landfried to Field Marshal Keitel (OKW), 14 Nov. 1940.
See too Mi 14/463 (file 3), OKW WiRüAmt, 19 Mar. 1941, Vortragsnotiz,
'Zusammenstellung der Massnahmen zur Durchführung der materiellen Rüstung von 1 July
1940–10 Mar. 1941'; Boelcke, *Deutsche Wirtschaft*, 255–6, for details on the lists of
proscribed goods.

By the spring and summer of 1941, as the armed forces prepared for the invasion of the Soviet Union, efforts to squeeze more out of the civilian economy were bearing much less fruit. The process of conversion was in large part completed, though demands from the armed forces continued to rise. In July Hitler intervened again to authorize further increases in aircraft, naval and army armaments, and cuts in essential civilian output.[69] For Hitler relaxation of the economic effort was still out of the question, for the war would continue after the defeat of the Soviet Union. The reduction in the output of a number of munitions during the late summer and autumn, which some historians have seen as evidence of a second 'pause' in anticipation of rapid defeat of Soviet forces, have to be set against the major expansion planned for other major programmes. The reductions had been planned the previous winter, after adequate stocks had been built up, so that the resources released could be used for other urgent production. As it turned out the labour involved, some of which was to have been released for naval and air production, was all kept by the army to help with Hitler's new army programmes. There was never any question that it would be returned to the civilian sector.[70]

If historians have misjudged the 'pause' in the summer of 1940, they have almost entirely ignored the vast new programmes set in motion by Hitler in the summer of 1941 for the period after the expected defeat of the Soviet Union. In July 1941 Hitler announced plans to keep a very large, and more extensively equipped, army in being after the Russian campaign. This army was to be even more fully motorized than the 180-division army planned in summer 1940, making, as Fritz Todt observed, exceptional demands on the industrial economy. Instead of 20 armoured and motorized divisions, Hitler ordered preparations for 36 Panzer and 18 additional motorized divisions, figures which required an 80 per cent increase in tank and vehicle productive capacity, and an increase in tank strength from the current 4,000 to 15,400.[71] The very real prospect of war with both the Anglo-Saxon powers called for increases in aerial and naval strength as well, both of which made very much greater

[69] IWM EDS Mi 14/433 (2), WiRüAmt, 'Umstellung der Rüstung' 17 July 1941. Hitler also ordered the further expansion of basic industries (aluminium, oil, chemicals, etc.). This kind of expansion could only serve warfare after 1941, not the attack on the USSR.

[70] IWM EDS Mi 14/463 (file 3), OKW Vortragsnotiz, 'Neue Fertigungszahlen Heer für Waffen und Munition'. The reduction in munitions output from Apr. 1941 was supposed to free 192,671 workers, 67,260 of whom were to be kept for other army contracts, leaving 125,411 for other war-essential tasks. In the end the army kept them all.

[71] IWM EDS Mi 14/451 (1), Aktennotiz über die Besprechung am 17 July 1941, 'Richtlinien des Führers von 14 July 1941'; RüII, Aktenvermerk über die Sitzung des Panzerausschusses an 17 July 1941. The figures for the proposed new tank force were: Panzer II, 4,608; Panzer III, 7,992; Panzer IV, 2,160. Total strength: 15,444. Initial plans were laid to raise monthly production from 600 to 900, and eventually to 2,000. Without the bombing this final figure would have been achieved by 1944.

demands on industrial capacity and resources than army equipment. The Luftwaffe produced new plans in July to raise output by 50 per cent in 1942. The navy too, having won back some of the priority lost in 1940, submitted the most extensive plans for shipbuilding of the whole war.[72] And while the current production of some munitions was reduced, that of a great many others was increased, particularly Flak, where the new plans required a doubling of the labour available for anti-aircraft shells in the summer of 1941.[73] Taken together, the plans of the three services in 1940 and 1941 for large quantities of technically complex and expensive weapons made demands on the economy far in excess of those of the First World War.

The strategy pursued throughout the period from 1939 to 1941 was not a limited economic effort at all, but a constant escalation of the demands for weapons and resources to wage global war. Even during the summer of 1940, or in the autumn of 1941 when the Soviet Union seemed close to defeat, Hitler continued to ask for ever-greater sacrifices from the civilian sectors to meet ever greater levels of military output. The cut-backs on civilian consumption were even more severe in practice than they might have been because of government and military plans to establish stocks of foodstuffs and essential materials either from current German production or from the stocks in the captured areas, so that the aim of a fair minimum for all could be maintained in the long term, and so that the armed forces could continue to be supplied to a very high standard. German policy was not to maintain a high level of living standards or peacetime standards, but to establish the *Existenzminimum* below which living standards should not be permitted to fall. This was to avoid at all costs another 'Turnip Winter'. Hitler's real priority was equal distribution, not unlimited consumption. The issue was to ensure that no one sector of the native population suffered more than another, that sacrifices were equally shared.

Real output *per capita* of all consumer goods (including those for the armed forces) fell by 22 per cent between 1938 and 1941. The civilian economy was starved of raw materials and equipment. The armed forces were allocated a quota of iron and steel in 1940 greater than that of 1918, and even this met only 70 per cent of their requirements. The allocation of

---

[72] On aircraft production: IWM Speer Collection, FD 5450/45, Vortragsnotiz für Chef OKW, 'Erweitertes Luftrüstungsprogramm', 6 July 1941; BA-MA RL3/146, Liefer-Plan 20/2, 'Göring-Flugzeug-Lieferplan', 15 Sept. 1941. On the navy: Mi 14/451 (1), Marinewaffenamt to WiRüAmt, 30 July 1941; G. Weinberg, *World in the Balance* (Hanover, Mass., 1981), 89. The new naval programme comprised 25 battleships, 8 aircraft carriers, 50 cruisers, 150 destroyers, and 400 submarines.

[73] IWM EDS Mi 14/451 (2), Besprechung Chef OKW mit den Wehrmachtteilen, 16 Aug. 1941, 9. Todt reported that if Hitler's request for Flak munition at a level of 2m. a month was confirmed, 66,000 more workers would be needed in addition to the extra 19,000 already allocated.

iron and steel for manufacturing industry other than armaments was cut by 75 per cent, even though many of these firms were working on other orders for the armed forces. Metal allocation for all essential civilian goods was cut by 50 per cent in September 1939 and cut again in June 1940. The situation in the supply of iron and steel was typical. The consumer sector had to accept reductions of 75 per cent of its peacetime quota. For the construction industry the figure was 85 per cent, for the Four Year Plan projects it was 83.5 per cent. Even sectors essential for war, the railways and the basic industries (coal, steel, chemicals), had to accept cuts of half their normal iron and steel allocations.[74] By the second quarter of 1940 the armed forces took a high proportion of all metals—62 per cent of copper, 61 per cent of chrome, 73 per cent of nickel, 78 per cent of aluminium, and so on.[75] These restrictions severely limited output from the first weeks of the war. Consumption of food, clothing, and household articles fell steadily thereafter, in line with planned reductions. Once stocks of unrationed goods had been bought up in the scramble to buy anything left in the shops, available supplies fell sharply. This meant higher than average sales in the first months of war and then a sudden decline. Sales of textile articles of all kinds were 10 per cent higher in January 1940 than the previous year. By June sales were more than 20 per cent lower. Furniture sales were 11 per cent higher in January, 40 per cent lower in June. The figure for metal and household goods was 5 per cent up in January, 20 per cent down by June: and so on.[76] Consumer durables such as motor vehicles ceased production almost entirely except for the armed forces, while domestic housing was cut back to a bare minimum.[77] By 1940 there were numerous complaints at a local level of shortages of food and clothing to meet the rationing allowances, and of boots and overalls for manual workers. By 1941 it was difficult to provide replacement goods for bombed-out families, while the provision of food and clothing rations was irregular and the standards poor.[78] In 1943 the production of certain

[74] IWM EDS AL 1905, General von Hanneken, 'Überblick über die Lage auf dem gewerblichen Sektor der Wirtschaft', 2 Sitzung des Generalrats der Wirtschaft, 3 Jan. 1940, pp. 4–6.

[75] For full details on raw material allocation for the armed forces from 1939 to 1942 see EDS Mi 14/261, OKW 'Rohstoff Bilanzen, Stand vom 1 März 1942', 6 Mar. 1942.

[76] BA R11/11, Grünig to Pietzsch, 16 June 1941, Anlage 7, 'Entwicklung der Umsätze des Facheinzelhandels Januar bis Juni 1940'; see too BA R7 xvi/7, Wagner to Schwerin von Krosigk, 3 Feb. 1940, giving details of the 'wave of consumption' in the autumn of 1939. Demand for furs went up 420%, for leather goods 76%, radios 80%, carpets 260%, etc, The result, according to Wagner, was that 'purchasing power must very soon come up against a blank'. See Boelcke, Deutsche Wirtschaft, 254–5.

[77] Car production fell from a peak of 276,592 in 1938 to 67,561 in 1940 (42% military) and 35,195 in 1941 (77% military). See USSBS Report 77, German Motor Vehicles Industry Report, 8. The number of housing units fell from 303,000 in 1938 to 80,000 in 1941, with most of the latter built for war-related purposes.

[78] IWM EDS Mi 14/521 (part I), OKW WiRüAmt, 'Bemerkenswerte Punkte aus den zum

classes of consumer goods actually went up from the levels of 1941–2 in order to supply bare household essentials for bomb victims. But throughout the early years of war consumption was restricted to a limited amount of foodstuffs, essential clothing when available, and a small range of permitted household goods.

Rationing was introduced for a wide range of goods in September 1939, although some goods, notably butter, had been rationed earlier than this. Only bread and potatoes remained unrationed, and bread was later rationed as well. The bread rations were set at a high level so that calorie intake would remain relatively stable early in the war, despite the disappearance of many foodstuffs and shortages of others; but the result was a monotonous, grain-based diet.[79] Meat was restricted to 500 grammes a week per head, butter to 125 grammes, margarine to 100 grammes, sugar to 250 grammes, cheese to 62.5 grammes, and eggs to one a week. There were special rations for those with physically strenuous jobs and for night-shift workers. The standard ration for meat and fats was much the same as in Britain, but food rationing in Germany covered a wider range of products than in Britain and was introduced much earlier in the war.[80] Milk was kept for children and infants, while adults made do with extracts or substitutes. In addition to reductions in foodstuffs other than bread, the quality of many foods deteriorated rapidly, again continuing a process begun before the war. Most foods were produced as standard and adulterated *Einheit* products, including coffee, flour, marmalade, margarine, pudding powder, and powdered milk.[81] Tea and

15 Juli erstatteten 28 Lagebericht der Rüstungsinspektionen über die wehrwirtschaftliche Lage', 2 Aug. 1941, 6–7: e.g. report from Armaments Inspectorate XVIII, 'supply for the clothing ration card becomes more and more difficult'; Inspectorate XXI, 'supply of shoes is completely inadequate'; Inspectorate XIII, 'sharp fall in morale and confidence of the city population. Cause is the niggling daily struggle to find food'. See too H. Boberach (ed.), *Meldungen aus dem Reich: Auswahl aus den geheimen Lageberichten der Sicherheitsdienst der SS, 1939–1945* (Berlin, 1965), 43–4, report for 6 Nov. 1939; 53–4, report for 12 Dec. 1939; 73–4, report for 18 Mar. 1940; 79, report for 3 May 1940; 121–4, report for 21 Nov. 1940; Werner, *Bleib übrig*, 138–40, 216; M. Steinert, *Hitler's War and the Germans*, (Athens, Ohio, 1977), 59, 94.

[79] USSBS Special Paper 4, *Food and Agriculture*, Exhibits D, E; Steinert, *Hitler's War*, 51–3; W. Russell, *Berlin Embassy* (London, 1942), 136–9.

[80] BA R26 IV/vol. 51, Four Year Plan, Geschäftsgruppe Ernährung report, 11 Mar. 1942, 2–7 and Anlage, 'Rationen in den europäischen Ländern'. Rations in early 1942 were (Britain/Germany, gr. per week): bread, unrationed/2,000; meat, 440/300; fats, 226/206. On British rationing see A. Calder, *The People's War: Britain 1939–1945* (London, 1969), 81–2, 275–6, 318–20. On Germany see too Stoddard, *Into the Darkness*, 72–4; W. Frischauer, *The Nazis at War* (London, 1940), 20–2; H. Focke and U. Reimer, *Alltag unterm Hakenkreuz: Wie die Nazis das Leben der Deutschen veränderten* (Hamburg, 1980), 179–81.

[81] W. D. Bayles, *Postmarked Berlin* (London, 1942), 18–20, 24. Berliners nicknamed *ersatz* coffee 'nigger-sweat', milk powder 'cadavar juice', and the ubiquitous boiled potatoes 'Four Year Plan nuggets'. See too Stoddard, *Into the Darkness*, 90; Stephenson, 'War and Society', 90–3.

coffee were in the main ersatz, the former made out of a wide range of plants and berries, the latter out of roasted barley. Real coffee was reserved for the soldiers at the front before combat and the wounded, or for those made homeless through bombing.[82] Supplies of fresh fruit and vegetables, or fish, which though unrationed were virtually unobtainable, were irregular and of poor quality. A joke circulating in Berlin in 1940 asked what was the difference between India and Germany. The answer was: 'Well in India one man [Gandhi] starves for everybody. In Germany, everybody starves for one man!'[83]

Einheit products also included washing supplies, which were rationed to one small bar of ersatz soap per month, and a shaving stick every five months. Hot water was also rationed to two days a week where it was realistic to do so, that is in apartment blocks, lodging houses, and institutional buildings.[84] Clothing was not only rationed but very difficult to obtain once stocks had been bought up. Sales of the textile industry fell 40–50 per cent in the first months of war, those of the clothing industry by 70 per cent. On 1 November 1939 clothes rationing was officially introduced to replace temporary controls on sales introduced in September.[85] Each man and woman had a limited clothing allowance of 100 points a year. For women a dress cost 40 points, a suit 45 points, a blouse 15 points. For men a suit or coat cost 60 points, and could only be obtained, as could shoes, after giving up the old ones.[86] This reduced average clothing consumption by half in 1940, and after stricter rationing in October 1941, to a quarter of peacetime levels (against a fall of only 16 per cent in Britain during 1940). Quality also deteriorated with the compulsory use of synthetic materials.[87] Other minor regulations were introduced to make sure clothes lasted as long as possible. Shoes or boots issued at work could not be worn outside the office or factory. Many families made do with clogs or metal and wood shoes, while government propaganda highlighted the importance of mending and making do.[88] Waste disposal was also closely controlled. All households had to sort

[82] Stoddard, *Into the Darkness*, 102–3; Bayles, *Postmarked*, 20.

[83] Russell, *Berlin Embassy*, 140–3.

[84] Frischauer, *Nazis at War*, 43; Bayles, *Postmarked*, 20.

[85] F. Wunderlich, *Farm Labor in Germany 1810–1945* (Princeton, NJ, 1961), 267–8. By Aug. 1943 all clothing sales were suspended except for bomb victims and children.

[86] Bayles, *Postmarked*, 40–1; Russell, *Berlin Embassy*, 144–5; Stoddard, *Into the Darkness*, 77–8; Wunderlich, *Farm Labor*, 268.

[87] The fall in the quantity of clothing sold is disguised by substantial price increases introduced by the government from autumn 1939. By Aug. 1942 clothes had increased in price by an average of 30%. See BA R7/2496, 'Die Bayerische Wirtschaft an der Jahreswende 1942/3', 81; Wunderlich, *Farm Labor*, 267–8.

[88] J. Stephenson, 'Propaganda, Autarky and the German Housewife', in D. Welch (ed.), *Nazi Propaganda* (London, 1983), 117–38.

their waste into one of five categories for regular collection for recycling or for animal fodder.[89]

It is difficult to reconcile this picture of life in Germany with claims of 'business as usual'. One American commentator writing of life in Berlin in the winter of 1939 described it as 'Spartan throughout'.[90] The world of shortages, queuing, ersatz supplies, declining health standards, and deprivation was shared by many Germans from the beginning of the war. The government was well aware of the sacrifices this imposed. In a number of ways efforts were made to show that sacrifices were shared equally. Soldiers' families were provided with welfare payments paid partly by the armed forces, partly by the local community, equal to 60 per cent of the man's previous income, but paid mainly in kind with coupons for coal, potatoes, milk, bread, rent, and school fees. This policy avoided the very real problems experienced by soldiers' families in the First World War, while leaving them no better off than other rationed households.[91] Prosecutions for violation of the strict rules on consumer production and rationing were highlighted in the press, and black marketeers, both seller and buyer, were liable for heavy fines, imprisonment, or, in the worst cases, death.

Despite the shortages, there was no repeat of the spontaneous efforts in the First World War of townspeople scouring the countryside for black-market goods. While there was plenty of evidence of widespread grumbling, there was little open dissatisfaction. The government also introduced small concessions, which, against a background of monotonous food and scarce goods, assumed an added prominence. For Christmas week 1939 the government made available for children 250 grammes of sweets or 150 grammes of cake, and for adults an additional 100 grammes of meat (including fowl where it could be found), and the chance to buy a necktie or a pair of stockings free of coupons, under the slogan 'Germany will enjoy Christmas!'[92] In December Goebbels engineered a propaganda stunt when he announced that butter rations would be increased; but the margarine ration was reduced by the same amount, and the butter then adulterated with the margarine. The government also insisted that shops

[89] Stoddard, *Into the Darkness*, 90–1. Waste categories were: (1) paper, (2) rags, (3) bottles, (4) old metal, (5) broken furniture.

[90] Ibid. 80; also 181, where Stoddard claims that over the winter of 1939/40 'war's impoverishing grip drew ever tighter, producing cumulative shortages and scarcity'.

[91] Details in Bayles, *Postmarked*, 109. German welfare payments during the war were as follows (RM 1000m.): 1939, 1.6; 1940, 3.9; 1941, 4.7; 1942, 5.2; 1943, 5.9. Details are to be found in NA T178, Roll 15, frame 3671912, 'Statistische Übersichten zu den Reichshaushaltsrechnungen 1938 bis 1943'. It should be recalled that similar welfare payments were made in Britain for the families of serving soldiers. There was nothing unique about this in the German war effort.

[92] Bayles, *Postmarked*, 103–4; Stoddard, *Into the Darkness*, 182–3.

and department stores keep their window displays in place even though the goods shown were frozen for the duration; and a certain number of magazines were permitted to continue publication and prominently displayed. None of this appears to have fooled the German public, though it may certainly have fooled historians.[93]

Of course not all Germans shared this degree of restriction. Peasants could produce more of their own food, and indeed the risks of black marketeering were so high that many chose to consume much more of their surplus themselves. But for the small farmers there were problems in buying feedstuffs for animals, fuel for tractors or vans, replacement tools, or the full range of foodstuffs permitted on the ration cards. Fixed food prices turned the terms of trade sharply against farmers, making shortages of goods even more intolerable.[94] Wealthier Germans could get access to non-rationed goods, at least for a short time, while Nazi leaders and party officials could use the free-market area in Hamburg where foreign diplomats could buy supplies from overseas, until the war with the United States. But there is no doubt that the qualititative evidence reinforces the general quantitative picture for the period. German living standards were suppressed before the war and were already falling in 1939. Declining quality, shortages, and restriction of supply were continued and intensified after September 1939 when, abruptly and comprehensively, people found themselves forced to live within the limits imposed by a rapidly expanding and very expensive military machine.

IV

It might well be asked why the surveys at the end of the war and the histories that were based on them failed to discover the true impact on civilian lives, and the direction that Reich financial and industrial policy was taking. One answer lies in the low level of arms output during the early years of war. But it is important to remember that this was a supply, not a demand, problem. Indeed the scale of Hitler's requirements were such that officials doubted that the German economy even fully mobilized could supply them. There were many reasons for this gap between programmes and output. The war broke out earlier than expected, so that major programmes of industrial expansion, raw-material substitution, and additional armaments capacity were still being completed in the early

---

[93] Bayles, *Postmarked*, 26; Frischauer, *Nazis at War*, 22. On butter and margarine rations see USSBS Special Paper 4, Exhibit E. Some of the increase in the butter ration was also achieved by cutting back on liquid milk supplies in order to save transport capacity.

[94] See e.g. BA R26 IV/vol. 51, 'Bericht über die Lage der Landwirtschaft im Wehrkreis XIII (Nürnberg)', 10–11.

stages of the war. These non-armament projects absorbed very great resources, and cannot be ignored in discussing the degree of commitment to war after 1939. Armaments represented only one part of the economic war effort, with the result that the economy was pulled in two different and competing directions, trying to complete the major capital projects and produce weapons at the same time.[95] Another fundamental problem was the surprisingly poor efficiency of the militarized economy. Inefficient use of resources arose partly from the lack of any formal, centralized control of the war economy and industrial output, partly from the stifling effects of military controls and interference, which very greatly reduced the capacity of the economy to produce weapons in the quantities Hitler wanted, and which Speer, with a more flexible civilian establishment, was able to achieve by the end of the war. Speer himself informed his interrogators in 1945 that 'OKW had seen the necessity of total mobilization at the beginning of the war. Preparations to this end were made' but there was 'a faulty manner of execution'.[96]

Another explanation is a statistical one. At least some of the information relied upon at the end of the war, and notably the statistics produced by the Wagemann Institute, took war year 1939/40 as the starting-point, missing altogether the sharp fall in consumption introduced at the onset of hostilities, and suggesting a relatively small decline in consumption throughout the war. Figures supplied to the Reich Economic Chamber in 1941 showed that there had in fact been a fall in *per capita* consumption in 1940 to 87.3 per cent of the level of 1939.[97]

---

[95] IWM EDS Mi 14/463 (file 3), OKW WiRüAmt, 'Bericht über die Leistungen auf dem Gebiet der materiellen Wehrmachtrüstung in der Zeit von 1 Sept. 1940 bis 1 März 1941', 10 July 1941, 1–7. On the substructure of the economy see BA R26/ I 18, 'Ergebnisse der Vieriahresplan-Arbeit', 20–49. Not until June 1941 did Hitler realize what this dual effort meant in terms of economic mobilization, when he decided to depend more on foreign conquests than on domestic investment programmes in heavy industry. According to Keitel, Hitler said: 'The course of the war shows that we went too far in our efforts for autarky . . . the whole effort for autarky claims an enormous quantity of manpower, which simply cannot be covered. One must follow another path and conquer what you need but do not possess.' Gen. Thomas had realized this a year before: 'We are overburdened. *Programmes are too many and too large!*' See IWM EDS AL 1571, Chef WiRüAmt Aktennotiz, 20 June 1941; 'Aussprache mit Industriellen über Verkehrsprobleme', 16 Feb. 1940, 2.

[96] IWM Box S368, Report 56, Speer interrogation 31 Oct. 1945, 8. For a general discussion of the problems facing the economy at this stage of the war see R. J. Overy, *Goering: The 'Iron Man'* (London, 1984), 150–63, 180–91.

[97] IWM Speer Collection, FD 3058/49, Wagemann Institute, National Income estimates, 5 July 1945. The figures given in this report were for the war years 1939/40 to 1942/3, giving a *per capita* annual consumer expenditure as follows (at current prices): 1939/40, RM 863; 1940/41, RM 756; 1941/42, RM 773; 1942/43, RM 784. But *per capita* consumer expenditure in 1938 was RM 1,014. Using this as a base the figures produced by the Institute show a much sharper fall in wartime consumption. Adjusted to constant prices, the Wagemann Institute figures are close to the figures given above in Table 9.5.

But perhaps the most important statistical problem arises through excessive reliance on aggregate levels of consumer-goods output. These figures were at the centre of Wagenführ's argument, for they seemed to show that living standards went up slightly in 1940 and declined only very slowly thereafter. These conclusions are very misleading, for in *per capita* terms consumer-goods production declined 22 per cent between 1938 and 1941 in line with the falls in *per capita* spending already discussed.[98] Even these figures disguise the fact, which is clear from all the surviving evidence, that a very large part of consumer-goods output in 1940 and 1941 ẏent to the armed forces, not to civilian consumers. The armed forces had very high standards of dress and equipment, almost certainly the highest in Europe, and the forces had already begun to make significant claims on consumer-goods capacity even before the war. After September 1939 these claims multiplied as consumer sectors found themselves inundated with demands for consumer goods designated as military necessities, or with subcontracts for military equipment made out of wood, ceramic, leather, or textiles.

Priority for military demands was a central principle of German war-making approved even by Hitler himself. Soldiers made a special sacrifice, acknowledged in the propaganda of war and in its economic strategy: 'The higher claim on clothing, on food, above all on luxuries, belongs to the soldier at the front.'[99] The standard of diet was much higher in the armed forces than among the civilian population. *Per capita* meat consumption in the forces in 1940–1 was three times that of civilians, and in 1941–2 over four times as great. During the same period raw sugar consumption was 70 per cent higher for soldiers and bread grain consumption 250 per cent

---

[98] For the figure of 22% see IWM Speer Collection FD 5454b/45, Deutsche Institut für Wirtschaftsforschung, 'Die deutsche Industrieproduktion im Kriege und ihre Messung', June 1942. The figures for *per capita* output of consumer goods are as follows (1928 = 100): 1936, 93; 1937, 104; 1938, 110; 1939, 103; 1940, 91; 1941, 86. This gives a fall of 22% between 1938, the last peacetime year, and 1941. These figures also include production for the armed forces, so that the fall in consumer goods output for *civilian* use was considerably greater. The gross figures given by Wagenführ, *Deutsche Industrie*, 36–7, are taken from the USSBS reports once again, and make no allowance either for *per capita* changes or the diversion of goods to the military. The Statistisches Reichsamt continued to classify firms according to their pre-war status as 'consumer' or 'capital' goods producers, and not on the basis of war or non-war production. This meant in practice that the output of the consumer industries was technically classified as consumer output throughout the war, even when firms were converted to military orders. This helps to explain the extraordinary claim by the Bombing Survey that civilian consumption levels were maintained at peacetime levels until 1944! (*Effects of Strategic Bombing on the German War Economy*, 8). During the war consumer production did not mean the same as civilian consumption, and the failure of the Bombing Survey to realize this was the source of all subsequent claims that the German economy was not fully converted to war.

[99] BA R7 xvi/7 (IWM Reel 145), Economics Ministry, 'Zur Kriegsfinanzierung', n.d. [Oct. 1939].

higher.[100] Soldiers enjoyed relatively secure supplies of cigarettes, tobacco, chocolate, and alcohol, even real coffee. In occupied areas it was the military who took most advantage from captured supplies. Details of soldiers' rations were published in the press, partly perhaps to confirm for families with serving soldiers that the propaganda calling for sacrifices at home and everything for the fighters at the front was actually a reality; though whether workers in the Reich were really buoyed up by news of the ham, fresh fish, butter, jams, pressed meats, and tinned vegetables enjoyed by the troops is surely questionable.[101]

The extent of the military claims on non-food civilian production was even higher, estimated at between 40 and 50 per cent by 1941.[102] In some cases the proportion was higher still. In January 1941 a meeting of all the main economic groups in the consumer sector was called at which details were supplied of the contribution each was making to the war effort. The main conclusion of the conference was that: 'The economy outside the narrower armaments sector is already working overwhelmingly for the armed forces or other offices vital for the war effort.'[103] The figures supplied by the economic group leaders supported this conclusion. The proportion of male workers engaged on direct and indirect orders for the armed forces was 55 per cent in clothing, 47.5 per cent in leather goods, 43.6 per cent in textiles, 34.5 per cent in glass, 27.3 per cent in ceramics. This was the situation after the first full year of war, up to September 1940, and was a proportion of a work-force that was steadily contracting in absolute size as labour left for arms factories and the armed forces. Such a situation made it difficult to supply even the 'economic requirements essential for the war', or exports, or goods needed by organizations such as the Organization Todt or the Arbeitsdienst (Labour Service), while it left very much less for the ordinary consumer.[104]

---

[100] USSBS Special Paper 4, *Food and Agriculture*, Exhibits G, J, M; BA R26 IV/vor1. 51, Four Year Plan, Geschäftsgruppe Ernährung, 11 Mar. 1942, 6: the Wehrmacht bread ration was 'double the normal entitlement, with meat as much as three and a half times'. See too IWM Case XI, Prosecution Doc. Book 112, lecture by State Secretary Neumann to the Verwaltungsakademie, 20 Apr. 1941, 296–7; W. Williams, *Riddle of the Reich* (London, 1941), 10–14.

[101] Bayles, *Postmarked*, 25–6.

[102] IWM FD 5444/45, Protokoll über die Inspekteurbesprechung am 22 Feb. 1942 bei OKW, 'Die Ersatzlage der Wehrmacht', 42. These proportions were approximately the same in 1943. See Wagenführ *Deutsche Industrie*, 174. The armed force in Feb. 1941 already took 40% of textiles output, 44% of clothing, 44% of leather goods, etc.

[103] IWM EDS AL 1571, WiRüAmt, Niederschrift einer Besprechung 9 Jan. 1941, 'Arbeitseinsatz und Einziehungen in der nicht zum engeren Rüstungsbereich gehörenden Wirtschaft', 1.

[104] Ibid. 2–8. According to a spokesman of Reichsgruppe Industrie: 'The demand for production for the armed forces is in every branch of consumer industry greater than one in general imagines.'

A look in detail at a number of major consumer industries illustrates the point. In the woodworking industry over 50 per cent of goods produced by September 1940 were direct orders from the armed forces and the remainder allotted 'to civilian requirements essential for war, in particular the requirements of public authorities'. By January 1941 the figure was 60 per cent, but for furniture output it was 80–90 per cent. Some 60 per cent of plywood production went to the armed forces, the rest to war-essential industry; 60 per cent of paint-brushes was for the armed forces; 60 per cent of all wooden boxes; 60 per cent of all barrels; 70 per cent of all wooden tools; and 50 per cent of all desks, the rest for the civilian administration. In the textile industry 34 per cent of all sales went direct to the forces in May 1940; and with uniforms for the railways, Organization Todt, Arbeitsdienst, SS, and the police, the figure was 50 per cent. The remaining 50 per cent was divided between materials for other industries working on war-related contracts or to fulfil ration-card quotas. Only 0.75 per cent of textile output was used for goods not under one of these categories. In the printing industry it was reported that: 'Almost all contracts have become *war-essential* in some connection.' The Propaganda Ministry was unable to get its material bound properly, and OKW faced problems in getting its essential circulars printed. The paper industry was converted almost exclusively to the output of specialized paper products used in a wide variety of essential products for war, from gas masks to submarines. In the consumer chemicals sector (excluding heavy chemicals) 80 per cent of production was destined for the forces, including toothpaste and shoe-polish. And so difficult did the armed forces find it to get sufficient quantities of confectionery produced that sweet production for the military was placed under priority ranking I (*Dringlichkeitsstufe* I) in the allocation of labour.[105] All consumer industries complained about falling labour supply and excessive military demands. Yet as General Thomas told the representatives of the consumer sectors, Hitler was determined to push through the new military programmes at all costs: 'The difficult situation elsewhere does not therefore interest him.'[106]

This situation got worse as the war went on. By the time Speer was appointed, the major consumer industries had lost yet more labour, while the remorseless increases in military demands ate into even that productive capacity left to satisfy the most essential needs of the population. The

---

[105] Ibid. 5–32. The detailed evidence was supplied by a spokesman representing each of the major Economic Groups. The evidence and conclusions of their reports make it clear beyond reasonable doubt that consumer goods production cannot be regarded as production for the civilian market.

[106] Ibid. 48. Thomas admitted to his audience at the meeting that he was surprised at the extent of military production in the consumer sectors, but insisted that Hitler's programmes for the war economy were 'unalterable', requiring even higher levels of conversion from the civilian economy than hitherto.

looting of occupied countries was of benefit mainly to the military and the party faithful, or was used to maintain existing ration-card quotas where shortages were developing. Without foreign agricultural supplies the food rations would have been considerably lower. As it was the rationing system became increasingly unstatisfactory, with less chance of finding even the clothes or houshold goods to which the population at large, or mothers with small children, or bombed-out families were entitled.[107] What is striking is how rapidly and comprehensively controls were established over consumption, and how extensive were the claims of the armed forces on consumer production. By the spring of 1941 Germany was nearing a situation of full-scale mobilization for war.

V

The same picture appears in labour policy and in the distribution of the work-force. Indeed extensive controls over consumption, high levels of military spending and military industrial demand, and increased taxation and saving could have had no other effect than to divert labour away from the civilian sectors to war work. This was, of course, very much the line of government policy. Claims by historians that labour was not mobilized extensively for Germany's war effort until 1942–4, or that the bulk of industrial labour was put to war work only after 1942 fly so much in the face of the available evidence that it is difficult to see why they were ever sustained in the first place.[108] Ironically enough, the evidence of extensive labour mobilization for war before 1942 was actually presented in the statistical appendices of both Wagenführ's book and the Bombing Survey *Overall Report*, although its implications were ignored in the text.[109]

German labour policy before September 1939 was based on the need to retrain large numbers of Germans to perform tasks in the economy where there were identifiable shortages if war should break out, and also on the necessity of closing down inessential production in wartime and diverting labour to war tasks wherever possible.[110] The Economics Ministry was

[107] Werner, *Bleib übrig*, 216–17. For a recent discussion of conditions on the home front later in the war see E. Beck, *Under the Bombs: The German Home Front 1942–1945* (Lexington, Ky., 1986).

[108] See esp. Petzina, 'Mobilisierung', 452–4; Klein, *Preparations*, 142–6; Herbst, *Totale Krieg*, 118–21.

[109] Wagenführ, *Deutsche Industrie*, 159; USSBS, *Effects of Strategic Bombing*, 213, which showed that by May 1942 70% in the engineering and metalworking industries were engaged on direct military orders, and 54.5% in industry as a whole, against 21.9% in May 1939.

[110] See e.g. IMT xxxiii. 151, 'Zweite Sitzung des Reichsverteidigungsrats', 23 June 1939; IWM EDS Mi 14/478, Heereswaffenamt, 'Die personelle Leistungsfähigkeit Deutschlands im Mob.-Fall', Mar. 1939. See also J. Gillingham, 'The "Deproletarianization" of German Society: Vocational Training in the Third Reich', *Journal of Social History*, 18 (1984/5),

entrusted with the task by Göring, in loose co-operation with the Labour Front and the Labour Ministry. Registers of labour were drawn up, although uncompleted by September 1939, which recorded what labour was available, where skills were in short supply, and what capacity was available for conversion when war broke out.[111] This policy was set in motion in September 1939. By the spring of 1940 there were widespread complaints from all sides that labour was insufficient to meet the contracts of the armed forces.[112] Göring activated special *Auskämmaktionen* (combing-out operations), designed to examine the labour force in the civilian sectors, in handicrafts, and in the administration, in order to find labour to divert to war work. These actions continued through 1940. Once again, the reports from the local economic chambers make it clear how rapidly labour was diverted to essential tasks related to the war effort. In May 1940 it was noted that: 'Through the closing down and combing through of businesses which do not produce goods essential for the war or vital consumer goods, it is attempted to cover the urgent requirement of the armaments plants for labour.' By July the chambers reported the 'requisitioning of almost all suitable labour for production directly or indirectly vital for the war'. But even this labour did not suffice 'to cope with the production programmes'. Labour working on civilian consumer production was cut back month by month during 1940, even at the expense of essential rationed goods.[113]

427–8; E. Homze, *Foreign Labor in Nazi Germany* (Princeton, NJ, 1967), 11–13. By 1938–9 513,000 workers had been retrained under the Four Year Plan and German Labour Front training schemes; industry had trained an estimated 500,000 on its own behalf, and 213,000 were retrained or trained from scratch in other official programmes.

[111] Overy, *Goering*, 84; H. Vollweiler, 'The Mobilization of Labor Reserves in Germany', pts. I and II, *International Labour Review*, 38 (1938); T. W. Mason, *Sozialpolitik im Dritten Reich* (Opladen, 1977), 214–28.

[112] BA-MA Wi I F 5.3352, Göring-Erlass betr. Facharbeitermangel, 28 Sept. 1939; IWM EDS Mi 14/478, Göring-Erlass, 29 May 1940; Labour Ministry, Mangelberufliste. 24 Apr. 1940; IWM, Speer Collection FD 5078/45, Beitrag für die Rü-In Besprechung, 5 Jan. 1940, betr. Auskämmaktionen; FD 5446/45, Aktenvermerk über Arbeitseinsatzlage, 15 Dec. 1940. There are many more examples.

[113] BA R11/77, Reichswirtschaftskammer, Wirtschaftslageberichte: report 18 June 1940, 1; report for 13 July 1940, 2, 7. In Nov. the chambers reported the following: 'The "combing through" of firms for the purpose of freeing labour for contracts in special and priority cases is pressed further... Different reports however point out that the withdrawal of further workers from firms working for the supply of the civil population has already considerably exceeded what is bearable' (report of 22 Nov. 1940, 1); 'Almost all available economic resources are claimed to the fullest extent by the demands of the war economy. Firms are either directly incorporated in arms production, or must make a very considerable proportion of their labour available for the arms industry' (Report of 21 Mar. 1941, 1). See too IWM EDS Mi 14/294 (file 5), OKW, Dr Tomberg, 'Die Probleme der deutschen Rüstungswirtschaft', Sept. 1940, 18–19: 'In August 1940 the closures were finally stopped since it had been demonstrated more and more that most of the metal works, whose workers were the main concern, already worked for the armed forces in one form or another'; EDS AL 1775, Labour Ministry to OKW (Warlimont), 24 Oct. 1941.

To meet the military demands strict control was established over the allocation of all labour for what Göring called 'totale Kriegsführung' (total war effort).[114] Large numbers of workers were conscripted and then allowed back, if they were skilled, on short-term release.[115] But by the beginning of 1941 these expedients were bearing less fruit. The armed forces simply took replacement labour for the workers they released, leaving many firms in the same position as before, even those with so-called special status, protected from the claims for conscription. As it was, this protection extended only to 4.8 million workers throughout the country.[116] By the spring of 1941 there were demands for at least another million workers, in addition to the 1.5 million Hitler wanted for the expanded armed forces. The new combing-out operations released only another 100,000 men. Thomas concluded that the civilian economy simply could not provide any more without seriously endangering essential consumer production: 'On cutting back civilian production, on dispersal and closure there is nothing more to say.'[117]

By the summer of 1941 both OKW and the Four Year Plan Labour Office concluded that approximately 60 per cent of the industrial work-force was engaged on orders directly for the armed forces and their agencies.[118] Reichsgruppe Industrie supplied figures in August 1940 to show that 57 per cent was working on war-related contracts.[119] Both these figures were considerably higher than the level of labour mobilization achieved in Britain by the same date.[120] Fuller figures supplied by Reichsgruppe Industrie later in the war also showed that the mobilization

[114] IWM EDS Mi 14/478, Entwurf eines Göring-Erlasses, 29 May 1940.

[115] IWM EDS Mi 14/433 (1), OKW Führerbefehl, 28 Sept. 1940; IWM, Speer Collection, FD 5078/45, Aktenvermerk über die Staatssekretärbesprechung, 24 Jun. 1940; FD 5444/45, Thomas conference with Minister Todt, 10 Jan. 1941.

[116] IWM Box S368, Fritz Schmelter (Amtsgruppe Arbeitseinsatz) interrogation, 20 Dec. 1945, Appendix 1, 'The Call-Up of Workers from Industry for the Armed Forces', 7–8.

[117] IWM, Speer Collection, FD 5444/45, Protokoll über die Inspekteurbesprechung am 22 Feb. 1941 bei OKW, 34–67. See too Landfried's comment to Keitel in Nov. 1940: 'I am convinced that the freeing of labour in greater quantities is no longer possible' (IWM EDS Mi 14/463 (file 2), Landfried to Keitel, 26 Nov. 1940).

[118] IWM, Speer Collection, FD 5450/45, Thomas to Keitel, 6 July 1941, giving a figure of 68%; Case XI, Pros. Doc. Book 112, Neumann lecture, 29 Apr. 1941, gives a figure of 55% of all industrial workers engaged directly on military orders in Feb. 1941.

[119] IWM EDS Mi 14/463 (file 2), Landfried to Keitel, 26 Nov. 1940: 'Of the male labour force in industry as a whole the proportion put to work on military production in the course of the first year has risen from 25.5% to 57.6%; in the branches of industry particularly important for the war (mining, iron and metal industry, and chemical industry) from 28.5% to 64.0%.' With the inclusion of the female work-force the figure was still 55.2% of the gross industrial work-force working on military orders.

[120] By June 1941 this figure had reached approximately 50% in Britain. See H. M. Parker, Manpower (London, 1957), 112, 483; P. Inman, Labour in the Munitions Industry (London, 1957), 5. These figures do not include building workers. If building is deducted from the figures in Table 9.6, the proportion of those working in German industry on war orders rises from 54.5% to 58% in May 1941.

TABLE 9.7. *Industrial labour force working on orders for the armed forces, 1939–1943*[a] (%)

	1939	1940	1941	1942	1943
All industry	21.9	50.2	54.5	56.7	61.0
Raw materials	21.0	58.2	63.2	59.3	67.9
Manufacturing	28.6	62.3	68.8	70.4	72.1
Construction	31.5	57.6	53.8	45.2	46.2
Consumer goods	12.2	26.2	27.8	31.7	38.3
Index (1939 = 100)	100	229	249	256	278

[a] Figure for 31 May each year.

Source: IWM FD 3056/49 'Statistical Material on the German Manpower Position during the War Period 1939–1944', FIAT EF/LM/1, 31 July 1945, table 7.

of the work-force for direct war work occurred largely before 1942, not afterwards. These statistics are set out in Table 9.7. Taking these figures as a minimum and Thomas's figures as a maximum, it is evident that between 55 and 60 per cent of the industrial work-force was engaged on direct military orders, against a roughly comparable figure of 50 per cent for Britain in June 1941. Nor can we assume that the rest of the work-force was engaged on 'civilian' production, for the figures exclude those working in areas such as railway equipment and equipment for the fuel and energy industries, all of which could properly be regarded as *kriegswichtig* (vital for war). Nor do the figures support the idea that there was a major redistribution of the work-force after 1942 when Germany is supposed to have switched to total war. In the manufacturing sectors where armaments output was concentrated the figure for 1943 is barely above that for 1941. The largest part of Germany's industrial work-force and industrial capacity was mobilized for war work in the first two years of war, an increase of 149 per cent between 1939 and 1941, but an increase of only 11 per cent between 1941 and 1943.

The same pattern emerges in the distribution of the work-force. The percentage figures above disguise the fact that the number of workers in the construction and consumer sectors declined in absolute quantities, while the number working in heavy and engineering industry, and particularly in the armaments-related sectors, rose substantially. In consumer-goods production the absolute number working fell from 3.58 million to 2.54 million between 1939 and May 1942. These changes are set out in Table 9.8. The table uses the pre-war classification according to the main industrial branches, but it must be remembered that under the industries designated as 'consumer' a very large proportion was actually

TABLE 9.8. *Labour force: selected statistics, May 1939–May 1943* (m. workers)

	May 1939	May 1940	May 1941	May 1942	May 1943
All industry	10.9	10.1	10.3	9.9	10.6
All heavy/manufacturing ind.	3.75	3.87	4.21	4.36	4.81
Iron and steel	0.35	0.33	0.36	0.36	0.41
Mining	0.59	0.58	0.61	0.62	0.69
Metalwork, machinery	1.97	2.08	2.31	2.44	2.67
Electrical ind.	0.51	0.50	0.55	0.58	0.61
Chemicals	0.59	0.58	0.62	0.63	0.69
Metal goods	0.46	0.51	0.52	0.53	0.62
Building ind.	0.91	0.71	0.72	0.51	0.44
All consumer ind.	3.58	2.94	2.84	2.54	2.59
Textiles	1.24	0.98	0.94	0.83	0.84
Clothing	0.34	0.28	0.28	0.26	0.27
Wood products	0.30	0.25	0.24	0.23	0.28
Leather goods	0.25	0.18	0.18	0.17	0.19
Food	0.57	0.48	0.45	0.42	0.42

Source: Calculated from R. Wagenführ, *Die deutsche Industrie im Kriege* (Berlin, 1963), 140–1.

producing military orders, not civilian. In addition, the restructuring of the work-force before 1939, by which date almost 70 per cent of industrial labour was employed in the producer-goods sectors, meant that much of the redistribution had already occurred in peacetime, reducing the numbers who could realistically be transferred from civilian sectors. The gross figures also disguise the redistribution within sectors between different firms. Krupp's total employment increased three times faster between 1939 and 1940 than total employment in heavy industry.[121] It is also interesting to note that in 1943, against the trend, labour in the consumer sectors actually increased. This is to be explained partly by the continuing demands made by the armed forces for goods from the light-industrial sectors, partly to the need to provide essential clothing and equipment for bombed families.

The local evidence again supports the broader conclusions about labour mobilization before 1942. The aircraft industry, for example, already the single largest manufacturing industry before 1939, expanded its

[121] Foreign and Commonwealth Office Library, Krupp Collection, file Fr. Krupp AG 1, Gefolgschaft der Fried. Krupp AG einschl. Tochterunternehmungen 1932–1942.

TABLE 9.9. Occupational origins of conscripts, June 1941

Economic sector	Conscripts
Agriculture	1,114,986
Metal workers	827,363
Building workers	584,588
Transport workers	485,897
Labourers and gen. workers	604,928
White-collar workers	907,974
All others (e.g. school leavers)	2,121,944
TOTAL:	6,647,680

Source: IWM EDS Mi 14/433(2), 'Die Lage auf dem Arbeits-einsatzgebiet' für Chef OKW, 30 June 1941.

employment from 900,000 to 1.8 million between 1939 and 1941.[122] The work-force at the main Junkers aircraft plants increased from 30,000 to 45,000 during this period, but expanded only by a further 7,000 up to 1944. The figures for the aero-engine factories at Dessau were 22,000 in 1939 and 40,000 in 1941.[123] Some of the increases came from diverting industrial labour from other products (the car industry, for example), some from subcontracting in what had previously been consumer sectors, some from mobilizing Handwerker more effectively for the war. Local SD reports on the Auskämmaktionen showed a similar picture. In Leipzig by May 1940 the numbers working in less vital or non-vital occupations had fallen from 124,000 to 90,000 with a further 10,000 about to be transferred to war production. Leipzig's quota for skilled labour in the combing-out operation was set by the armaments inspectors at 11,600, but by May 1940 only 3,500 had been found because so many had been conscripted or were already engaged in war work.[124]

There is no doubt that the difficulties in mobilizing labour were due to a considerable extent to high levels of conscription, which by June 1941 had

[122] BA-MA RL3/33, Beschaffungslage der Luftfahrtgerät, 5 June 1941; IWM Milch Documents, vol. 58, 1018. These are figures for all those working directly or indirectly on aircraft orders, and not just the final assembly of airframes and aero-engines.

[123] IWM, Speer Collection, FD 5665/45, History of Junkers: v. General statistical Data, chart 3; FD 5504/45, Junkers Motorenbau, Dessau: statistical survey, chart C. There were also increases in hours worked. At the BMW plants for aero-engines overtime as a percentage of all hours worked increased as follows: early 1939, 1.4; end of 1939, 7.1; end of 1940 9.1; end of 1941, 23.0; end of 1942, 23.1. BMW's work-force also increased in size, from 28,800 in Sept. 1939 to 53,600 by 1942. See Speer Collection, Deutsche Privatfirmen, FD 927/46, BMW Kriegsleistungsbericht, 10 Mar. 1943.

[124] BA NS 29/775, Sicherheitsdienst reports for Leipzig, 16 May 1940, 12–16.

taken 6.6 million men out of the labour market (see Table 9.9). When OKW protested to the Labour Ministry about shortages of workers for the arms industry, the ministry showed that while it had allocated a further 737,000 workers for the arms industry from February to August 1941, the services had removed another 1.3 million between February and June from other vital economic areas. The ministry was compelled to find labour not only for armaments, but for agriculture, repair industries, coalmining, and the railways, all of which were by 1941 seriously short of the numbers of personnel needed to provide what the war effort demanded.[125] The conscription of this quantity of labour into the armed forces in 1940 and 1941 in itself makes it difficult to accept that the impact of war on civilian sectors was limited, for only some of these losses were compensated for by foreign labour before 1942, mainly in construction and agriculture.

This tension between military conscription, military orders for industry, and the supply of labour, which took the form of endless administrative squabbles and arguments, accusations of sabotage, ruthless poaching of labour, and so on, simply cannot be reconciled with the conventional picture of limited war. Indeed the frantic efforts to return skilled workers from the forces, 600,000 of whom were released by Hitler on short leave in autumn 1940, would have been unnecessary if there had still existed large untapped reserves of skilled labour in the civilian sectors.[126] The evidence from the consumer industries themselves shows that this was not the case. From the onset of war they were subjected to strenuous efforts on the part of the armed forces, the armaments inspectors, and the Labour Ministry to release labour for essential war work or to convert their own production to military contracts. By the end of June 1940 the decline in male consumer-industry employment had developed as set out in Table 9.10. The decline in male employment in the food industry was much smaller because the bulk of men were in supervisory, managerial, or technical positions with a largely female work-force, and could not be released so easily for war work. Numbers employed in the alcohol industry went up because spirits were used as a fuel during the war.[127] If the workers employed in these sectors who were working on armed forces orders are also deducted, the true decline in the male work-force available for civilian consumer production can be shown. These figures, which are set out in Table 9.11, show a level of decline very similar to the decline in the actual quantity of consumer goods available for civilians, well over 50 per cent for the clothing, leather, textiles, and woodworking industries.

[125] IWM EDS AL 1775, Labour Ministry to OKW, 24 Oct. 1941, 1–2.
[126] IWM EDS Mi 14/433 (1), Führerbefehl von 28 Sept. 1940; Mi 14/463 (file 2), Der Führer: 'Personelle Massnahmen für Rüstungsindustrie und Bergbau', 20 Dec. 1940.
[127] IWM EDS AL 1571, Niederschrift der Besprechung am 9 Jan. 1940, betr. 'Arbeitseinsatz und Einziehungen...', 11–19.

TABLE 9.10. *Decline in the male work-force in consumer industry in the first year of war*

Economic Sector	Pre-war	1 June 1940	% decline
Leather industry	126,515	87,437	30.9
Textile industry	424,795	294,819	30.6
Clothing	54,302	40,598	25.2
Woodworking	217,833	167,351	23.2
Ceramic industry	57,013	44,202	22.5
Brewing	71,742	56,720	20.9
Paper	43,987	35,047	20.3
Metal goods	116,371	94,991	18.4
Glass industry	70,909	58,492	17.5
Printing	149,300	125,019	16.3
Foodstuffs	169,478	151,015	10.9
Sugar industry	24,926	24,432	2.0
Spirits industry	17,571	21,891	+24.6

Source: IWM EDS AL 1571, 'Arbeitseinsatz und Einziehungen in der nicht zum engeren Rüstungsbereichgehörenden Wirtschaft', OKW Bericht, 9 Jan. 1941, 2.

TABLE 9.11. *Male work-force in consumer industries working on civilian orders, June 1940*

Economic Sector	Pre-war	June 1940	Decline	
			(nos.)	(%)
Leather industry	98,515	45,437	53,078	53.9
Textile industry	360,795	165,819	194,976	54.0
Clothing	44,302	18,598	25,704	58.0
Woodworking	178,833	71,351	105,482	59.7
Ceramic industry	47,013	32,202	14,811	31.5
Brewing	70,742	48,720	22,022	31.1
Paper	39,987	26,047	13,490	34.9
Metal goods	94,371	49,991	44,380	47.0
Glass industry	59,909	38,492	21,417	35.7
Printing	143,300	103,019	40.281	28.1
Foodstuffs	166,478	124,015	42,463	25.5
Sugar industry	24,427	20,432	3,995	16.4
Spirits industry	14,571	15,891	+1,320	+9.1
TOTAL:	1,343,243	760,014	583,229	43.4

Source: As Table 9.10, p. 3.

This process of reduction continued after June 1940, as the experience of individual branches of industry shows. In the glass industry, which by October 1940 had lost 30 per cent of its male work-force, three-quarters of those lost were skilled workers, the only ones remaining being too old for military service, or apprentices who were too young. Levels of output, much of it for the military, could only be met 'through extensive overtime by the remaining work-force'.[128] Woodworking also lost over 30 per cent of the male work-force by October 1940, again including many specialists and master-craftsmen, who were recruited into metalworking whether their skills were compatible or not. The food industry was hit particularly badly because so many of the men in the work-force were the skilled machine operators and technicians who were difficult to replace. The growth of more mechanized or technically sophisticated food processing in the 1930s, such as milk production, also meant that many of the skilled workers were relatively young, among groups most likely to be conscripted. Economic group 'foodstuffs' complained that labour was especially vulnerable in regions where the arms industry was concentrated, and that skilled workers were often taken and sent to arms factories to perform jobs that could be learned by unskilled or semi-skilled personnel. In the textile industry labour had fallen 200,000 before the war broke out, and fell by another 810,000 by October 1940 (30 per cent of the male work-force, 17 per cent of the female). Even industries like chemicals, whose work-force remained more or less constant during 1939 and 1940 (585,000 in July 1939, 583,000 in November 1940), lost 79,000 workers to conscription, increased the number of women to 33 per cent of the work-force, substituted two 12-hour for three 8-hour shifts, and had to fill losses with unskilled female and older male workers. Finally, agriculture lost 30 per cent of its wage-labour force in the first year of war, and 45 per cent of its male workers. 'In particular farms', ran a report, 'only the disabled, the old, and the ill are available.'[129]

A central feature of the labour force between 1939 and 1941 was its rapid redistribution, both within and between different sectors, in favour of war production and military service. The total native German civilian work-force fell through conscription by 8 million between 1939 and 1942,

---

[128] Ibid. 5–7.

[129] Ibid. 7–10, 25–9, 44–7. The textile industry also suffered from the rapid withdrawal of its most skilled workers (usually men), who were required to mend machinery etc. This made it even harder to maintain the efficiency of the remaining work-force. This situation is corroborated in EDS Mi 14/463 (file 2), Landfried to Keitel, 26 Nov. 1940, 3–4. The male work-force in textiles fell from 424,000 to 294,000, while the proportion working on war orders in the industry rose from 15% to 43.6%. Economic Group Textile Industry reported that military orders could no longer be guaranteed, while the clothing ration simply could not be met. 'Similar reports are available for all consumer sectors,' wrote Landfried. 'Recently reports from different parts of the Reich are being submitted which say that the supply of clothing for the population guaranteed on the ration card has come to standstill.'

but by only another 2.2 million by 1944. The key areas from which labour was drawn for the armed forces and war-related industry were commerce, agriculture, and craft trades. The last of these was particularly important as a source of labour, for older craftsmen were drafted into armaments factories and the women in handicraft occupations either redirected to war work in local factories or given subcontracts for war orders. By January 1940 the number of male craftsmen had fallen by almost a million, and *Handwerk* employment as a whole was 20 per cent down on the level in September 1939, a significant reduction in a sector traditionally associated with consumer production. The figures for the fall in craft employment by sector are set out in Table 9.17 below. They show a rapid decline in the first six months of the war. Wagenführ's argument that the fall in craft employment after 1942 illustrates a sharp change in state labour policy ignores the very substantial reductions already achieved by 1941. Indeed by May 1942 over four-fifths of the wartime reduction in craft employment had already been achieved.[130] At that point craft employment stood at 60 per cent of the level in May 1939. For the remainder of the war the fall was much more modest, reaching 52 per cent of the 1939 level by 1944. The overwhelming majority of artisans who were removed from handicraft industries during the war left before the Speer reforms of 1942, not after.

There was also a modest fall in levels of administrative employment, although this was more than compensated by the increase in the huge military bureaucracy which absorbed large numbers of female workers. The overall distribution of the labour force is given in Table 9.12. As young men went into the armed forces, firms either experienced an absolute drop in the size of their work-force if they were in a less essential sector, or had to find substitute employment (female workers or older or very young men). The reallocation of workers towards the central parts of the war effort was a laborious administrative task, a constant effort to keep pace with the growing appetite of the armed forces, and to keep intact those sections of the work-force needed for armaments production.

Though Germany might well have mobilized its work-force more efficiently, it can hardly be maintained that the German administration did

---

[130] Wagenführ, *Deutsche Industrie*, 47–8, gives misleading figures on the redirection of the work-force by using the year 1941 as the baseline, rather than 1939. The decline in artisan employment of 20% between 1941 and 1944 is used by Wagenführ to suggest a significant shift in labour policy after 1941. But the major change in artisan employment occurred between May 1939 and May 1941, a decline of 30%. Almost two-thirds of the total decline in employment in this sector came before the Russian campaign. By leaving out figures for the first two years a very distorted view of the restructuring of the work-force is produced. Table 9.18 below gives the decline in artisan employment for the whole war period, and shows that, irrespective of baseline, by May 1942 82% of the reduction in artisan employment was already achieved.

TABLE 9.12. *Distribution of the native German work-force, by occupation, 1939–1944* ('000)

	1939	1940	1941	1942	1943	1944
1. Agriculture	11,104	10,007	9,262	9,252	9,008	8,708
2. Industry and transport	18,482	15,857	15,206	13,836	13,324	12,489
(a) Industry	10,836	9,551	9,200	8,370	8,170	7,640
(b) Handwork	5,307	4,122	3,730	3,207	2,957	2,745
(c) Transport	2,109	1,982	2,072	2,064	2,010	1,927
(d) Power	230	202	204	195	187	177
3. Commerce	4,595	3,719	3,358	3,124	2,933	2.679
4. Administration and services	2,670	2,605	2,626	2,373	2,340	2,228
5. Armed forces' administration	689	710	804	1,184	1,292	1.294
6. Domestic workers	1,575	1,505	1,460	1,388	1,370	1,307
7. Homeworkers	—	—	—	—	—	279
TOTAL:	39,115	34,403	32,716	31,157	30,267	28,984

Note: Figures for 31 May.

Source: IWM FD 3056/49, 'Statistical Material on the German Manpower Position during the War Period 1939–1944', FIAT EF/LM/1, 31 July 1945. These figures are based on the annual *Kräftebilanz* figures published by the Statistische Reichsamt.

not try from 1939 onwards to mobilize labour as extensively as possible for the war effort. As in Britain, this was not a smooth process, nor did it happen all at once, but gradually over a two-year period. But unlike in Britain, mobilization was made more difficult by the peculiar structure of the work-force. Very large numbers were employed in agriculture: 11.1 million in 1939, 9.2 million still in 1942. This was a direct consequence of the labour-intensive and small-scale nature of German farming. It has often been argued that this represented a wasteful diversion of labour resources; but such arguments ignore the fact that food production was a top priority in Germany because of the blockade. To have transformed German agriculture during the war by making it significantly less labour-intensive would have required a social and economic revolution of such scale that it might well have jeopardized food supplies altogether. Germany suffered too from accidents of geography. Population was more evenly scattered among small towns and villages and was less concentrated in urban areas than in Britain, requiring in Germany a wider spread of employment in services and the distributive trades, with larger numbers of retail outlets. Though both farming and retailing employed increasing numbers of women as single owner-workers, and the young men quickly disappeared from both industries, it was difficult, even politically undesirable, to undermine the fabric of local services too severely.[131]

But there were serious problems with labour mobilization which were man-made. Although the military paid lip-service to the idea that reserved occupations should be immune from conscription, the demands of the forces continued to take priority, particularly in sectors where the special protective category of 'S' or 'SS' could not be obtained, but where the labour was none the less vital for the industrial war effort. These problems might well have been avoided if a single, central authority for labour distribution had existed, but in practice labour policy was divided among a number of agencies, not one of which could impose its overall policy on the rest, and certainly not on the military. When in the early spring of 1941 Göring ordered the reallocation of labour freed from army munitions output to the armaments production of the other services, the army simply refused to release it, arguing that the demands of additional tank and weapons programmes would absorb any spare labour they had.[132] Firms working exclusively for one of the services were encouraged to keep their labour even if it was not fully employed on war orders for fear that they would not get the workers back again when new contracts came in. But most important of all, the armed forces' insistence on high levels of skilled work and regular modifications and changes in design placed a much greater strain on the supply of skilled labour than was really necessary.[133]

The productivity of German labour in the war sectors after 1939 was poor in relation to pre-war standards and to what was achieved later in the war with more mechanization and serial production and a more rational distribution of labour. The aircraft industry produced almost four times as many aircraft in 1944 as in 1941 without substantial increases in total labour supply, and with a large component by the end of the war of less productive forced labour.[134] The muddled administration, competition between the services for skilled men, and the poor productivity of much industrial labour, in a context where demands for military output grew continually, made labour an increasingly scarce commodity. These shortages finally compelled the government in 1941 to adopt new

---

[131] See e.g. IWM EDS AL 1571, Besprechung am 9 Jan. 1940, 35–41.

[132] IWM EDS Mi 14/463 (file 3), Chef Heeresrüstung to OKW, 11 Apr. 1941: 'giving up labour resources from the army sector is not to be reckoned with'.

[133] Overy, *Goering*, 159–62, 190–1. See IWM EDS Mi 14/433(3), Vortrag des Oberst Neef (OKW), 21 Jan. 1942: 'Our economy was orientated much more towards handwork methods of special quality than to the machine methods of mass production, and is still substantially orientated that way today.'

[134] At the height of the war effort in the summer of 1944 aircraft production had 2.3 million workers, against 1.85 in autumn 1941, yet 39,000 aircraft were produced in 1944 against only 11,700 in 1941, with a structure weight 120% greater.

strategies for labour use. The most important change was the emphasis on rationalization, on mass production and modern methods in the factories, and on the simplification and standardization of weapons design. During the 'Battle for Work' after 1933 and later during the frantic efforts to increase armaments production in the late 1930s, too little attention was paid to questions about the most efficient use of labour. Demands were expressed in terms of the mere numbers of workers needed, rarely in terms of how they might be utilized in the productive process most effectively. This situation was highlighted by General von Hanneken, Göring's Plenipotentiary for Iron and Steel, in a circular on rationalization sent to the heads of Economic Groups in December 1941:

Since 1933 the main tasks of the German economy have been the overcoming of unemployment and the rapid build-up of armaments. The fulfilment of these pressing tasks necessarily had the consequence that the rationalization of production was comparatively less important. The conquest of unemployment was directly opposed to rationalization; and the strongly growing armaments led to an extensive exclusion of German industry working on armaments from competition in the world market and therefore to the exclusion of a substantial incentive for rationalization. This deficiency, which had already arisen before the war, could not be counteracted in the first war years. The necessity at first of creating for the Reich the necessary room for manoeuvre led to a *rapid* conversion of the German economy to the thoroughly unfamiliar production of war equipment. In engaging these firms in this production, the aspect of the rational exploitation of available productive capacity and labour often played a subordinate role to the necessity of a quick increase in initial output.[135]

Hitler's acceptance of the need to concentrate all efforts on a broad-based productivity drive in the early summer of 1941 marked a significant turning-point in the German war effort. Nevertheless there was no way of avoiding labour shortages until rationalization became effective. As a result in May 1941 Hitler authorized greater use of prisoner-of-war and foreign labour, while the forces argued for the further expansion of female labour and compulsory conscription of the work-force.[136]

VI

It is usually argued that at this stage of the war the German war effort failed to take advantage of a large reservoir of unused female labour, in

---

[135] BA R7/2229, von Hanneken (Economics Ministry) to Economic Groups and Offices, 24 Dec. 1941, on 'Richtlinien für die Gestaltung der Fertigung in der Eisen- und Metallverarbeitenden-Industrie', 1–2.
[136] IWM EDS Mi 14/463 (file 3), OKW Aktennotiz über die Besprechung bei Chef OKW, 19 May 1941. This was a report of a meeting with Hitler and Todt on 18 May at Berchtesgaden. The meeting marks the start of Hitler's drive for greater efficiency and rationalization which continued throughout 1941.

contrast to the mobilization of women workers on a large scale in Britain, the United States, and the Soviet Union. Had Germany done so, the argument implies, much greater productive efforts might have been achieved. The barrier to doing so was Nazi ideology, which preached the virtue of women as housewives, and fear of popular discontent if excessive demands were made on the German population. The evidence that this was the case rests on the ground that the absolute total number of women in the work-force increased hardly at all during the war, and in the early stages actually fell slightly.

Yet this argument, like that on labour in general, is a considerable distortion of reality. It fails to take sufficiently into account the fact that Germany had an exceptionally high level of female employment in the late 1930s, and that on the outbreak of war the female work-force too underwent a redistribution to war tasks away from the civilian sector. The first of these points is of great importance. Female employment expanded rapidly from 1935 onwards, partly a result of the re-employment policies of the government, partly encouraged by tight wage controls which encouraged households to expand the number of wage earners to increase gross earnings.[137] In some industrial sectors the increase in the proportion of female workers was striking: from 13 per cent to 19 per cent in iron and steel and engineering; from 12 to 29 per cent in the electro-technical industry; from 18 to 25 per cent in precision and optical instruments.[138] By 1939 the total number of women in the work-force was 14.8 million, or 37.4 per cent. In Britain the corresponding proportion was only 26.4 per cent. During the war the proportion in Germany rose to 51 per cent, but in Britain it reached a peak of only 37.9 per cent.[139] More women were brought into the British work-force because a great many more

---

[137] C. W. Guillebaud, *The Economic Recovery of Germany 1933–1938* (London, 1939), 190; D. Winkler, *Frauenarbeit im Dritten Reich* (Hamburg, 1977), 196. See too BA R7/2496, Economics Ministry, 'Die Bayerische Wirtschaft...', 7, which shows an increase in female employment in Bavaria of 40% between 1933 and 1940, from 533,000 to 749,000.

[138] A. Tröger, 'Die Planung des Rationalisationsproletariats: Zur Entwicklung der geschlechtsspezifischen Arbeitsteilung und das weibliche Arbeitsmarkt im Nationalsozialismus', in A. Kuhn and J. Rüsen (eds.), *Frauen in der Geschichte*, ii (Düsseldorf, 1982), 260–1.

[139] Bajohr, *Frauenarbeit*, 252; Parker, *Manpower*, 482. Both figures are net of military service. Almost all the discussions on female employment have concentrated on the absolute increase or decrease in the size of the female work-force, not on the proportion of women employed in the total work-force, nor the participation ratio (the proportion of all women of employable age in employment). See Herbst, *Totale Krieg*, 118–19, who claims that 'a great potential reserve of women remained relatively unutilised'; Salter, 'Class Harmony', 89, who gives the proportion of women working in the American economy, but not the German; Bajohr, *Frauenarbeit*, 259–60, talks misleadingly of 'a rapid decline' in female employment in 1939–40, when the fall was only 2%. J. Stephenson, *Women in Nazi Society* (London, 1975), 101, is almost alone in identifying clearly the already high proportion of women in the German work-force on the outbreak of war.

TABLE 9.13. *Proportion of women in the native civilian work-force, Germany, UK, and USA 1939–1944 (%)*

Germany		United Kingdom		United States	
May 1939	37.3	June 1939	26.4	—	—
May 1940	41.4	June 1940	29.8	1940	25.8
May 1941	42.6	June 1941	33.2	1941	26.6
May 1942	46.0	June 1942	36.1[a]	1942	28.8
May 1943	48.8	June 1943	37.7[a]	1943	34.2
May 1944	51.0	June 1944	37.9[a]	1944	35.7

[a] Includes women in part-time work.

Sources: Germany: Bajohr, *Frauenarbeit*, 252; Britain: calculated from Parker, *Manpower*, 482; United States: Rupp, *Mobilizing Women for War*, 188.

unemployed or non-employed women were available in Britain than in Germany. Even so a very considerably higher percentage of Germany's work-force was made up of women than was the case in Britain throughout the war. It should also be noted that the German figure in 1939 included some 6.4 million married women (36 per cent of all married women), and that 88.7 per cent of all single women aged 15–60 were already employed by the same date, a remarkably high figure which fits uneasily with claims about Nazi resistance to female employment. The 'participation ratio' of women aged 15–60 was already 52 per cent in Germany *in 1939*. In the United States it reached a peak of only 36 per cent in 1944 and in Britain a peak of 45 per cent.[140]

Not only was the proportion of women employed very high by international standards, but there was also a significant redistribution of female employment during the early years of war, in favour of war production. Such redistribution is, of course, disguised by the raw figures on female labour, which show absolute totals but not shifts within the work-force. Redistribution took two very distinct forms. The first was redistribution within industry, away from consumer-goods sectors towards more war-related sectors. This shift was most marked between May 1939 and May 1942 as Table 9.14 shows. But it must be remembered that a large proportion of those working in consumer sectors were actually working on military orders, so that the number of women working for the civilian market was much smaller still. Again the evidence from individual firms confirms these movements within the female work-force, while it

[140] Winkler, *Frauenarbeit*, 198; L. Rupp, *Mobilizing Women for War* (Princeton, NJ, 1978), 186; *Statistical Digest of the War* (London, 1951), 8 (7,253,000 in 1943 out of a female population of 15–60 years old totalling 16,084,000).

TABLE 9.14. Distribution of female industrial work-force in Germany, 1939–1943 ('000)

	May 1939	May 1940	May 1941	May 1942	May 1943
Producer goods					
Chemicals	184.5	197.4	204.7	215.8	255.9
Iron and Steel	14.7	18.4	29.6	36.3	64.9
Engineering	216.0	291.3	363.5	442.0	603.0
Electrical	173.5	185.4	208.1	226.3	264.7
Precision tools, optical	32.2	37.2	47.6	55.6	67.2
Metal goods	139.1	171.3	172.0	192.2	259.5
TOTAL:	760.2	901.3	1,025.7	1,168.4	1,515.4
Consumer goods					
Printing	97.2	88.8	92.6	73.9	60.1
Paper goods	89.5	84.3	79.2	71.9	73.1
Leather	103.6	78.7	85.0	81.8	95.6
Textiles	710.1	595.4	581.3	520.9	546.3
Clothing	254.7	226.5	225.3	212.8	228.9
Ceramic goods	45.3	41.4	39.5	37.1	42.8
Food	324.6	273.5	260.9	236.8	238.0
TOTAL:	1,625.3	1,388.7	1,364.0	1,235.4	1,284.5

Source: Wagenführ, *Deutsche Industrie*, 145–7.

shows a high level of female employment before the war as well.[141] Local evidence from Labour Offices around the country submitted to the Labour Ministry during 1939 and 1940 also bears out the statistical picture. Armaments firms sent regular requests for female labour, while Labour Offices did their best to allocate women from less essential work to war work when and where available.[142]

The second kind of redistribution was more indirect, but none the less significant. A great many women worked in agriculture; indeed, female

[141] Winkler, *Frauenarbeit*, 197, who shows that at Siemens electrical works in Berlin female employment expanded rapidly in the two years *prior* to the outbreak of war, from 10,265 in Sept. 1937 to 15,112 by Dec. 1938, and 17,443 by Dec. 1939. By Dec. 1941 the figure had increased only to 19,335, or almost double the figure four years before.

[142] BA R41/158, Labour Ministry report, 'Fraueneinsatz in der Rüstungsindustrie 1939–1940'. It is important to bear in mind that in the autumn and winter of 1939/40 many women in the consumer sectors were put on short time or laid off as the consumer-goods sectors contracted, and that it took time to place these women back in full-time employment. When they did get back it was increasingly into war and war-related production, or in consumer goods production for the armed forces. These movements in the female work-force are concealed by the aggregate figures.

employment increased by 230,000 between 1933 and 1939 on the land, while male employment declined by 640,000. During the war women workers in agriculture made up 54.5 per cent of the native work-force in 1939, 61.6 per cent in May 1942, 65.5 per cent by 1944.[143] As the farmers and labourers were called up for military service—over 1 million by June 1941—more and more women were compelled to take on the task of running the small family farm on their own, using foreign or POW labour where available, but having to bear a very much greater burden of the actual farm-work than hitherto, especially in the early years of the war.[144] Kaldor's assertion that women in agriculture should not be considered when talking about labour mobilization is thus misplaced, for Germany's war effort depended just as much on harvesting potatoes as it did on filling shells. Agriculture was a vital area of production, and a great deal of the physical effort involved was undertaken by women during the war, not by men. The extra help for agriculture at times of peak activity was found mainly among evacuated mothers, schoolchildren, and students, or women temporarily unemployed by the closure of civilian production. In the summer of 1942, for example, out of 1 million German workers recruited for work on the land (both permanent and temporary) from 58,660 communes, 948,000 of them were women. Much of this part-time work—helping with the harvest, relieving peasants' wives of routine housework so that they could work on the farm—did not appear in the full-time employment figures, but was none the less essential for agriculture.[145]

The peculiar nature of German agriculture also helps to explain the high level of so-called domestic servants in the German work-force. This again is usually adduced as evidence that Germany failed to adapt its work-force to war; but it ignores the fact that a very large number of servants were in practice helpers on farms or in small businesses, and were not servants in the conventional sense at all. In 1933 the International Labour Office calculated that only 44,000 of those registered as 'servants' in Germany, out of a total of 1.2 million were actually domestic household servants.[146] One concession the government did introduce was to set up a 'home help' service, where women were paid to give short-term assistance to families in special need, work which in Britain, for example, was done instead by voluntary service. But none of this should obscure the central fact that for

[143] Wunderlich, *Farm Labor*, 297–9; Kaldor, 'War Economy', 28–30.

[144] BA R26 IV/vorl. 51, Bericht über die Lage der Landwirtschaft im Wehrkreis XIII (Nürnberg), 10–11: 'A peasant wife whose husband is at the front must work until the very last hour before her release from labour, and must look after her children; she has not a single quiet minute from 4 in the morning until 9 at night.'

[145] Wunderlich, *Farm Labor*, 339–40.

[146] M. Thibert, 'The Economic Depression and the Employment of Women; part II', *International Labour Review*, 27 (1933), 622.

many women war simply meant carrying on working, and working often harder than ever.

The same thing applies to other sectors of the work-force. In retailing, from which over 600,000 men had been recruited by June 1941, women were forced to keep the business going as best they could, with the additional burden of rationing, which brought a great deal of paperwork, and fines or imprisonment for any major discrepancies. At least part of the slight fall in female employment in early 1940 can be explained by the fact that female workers left wage-employment to return to the family farm or business to replace conscripted men.[147] In sectors of the wage-labour force the same diversion occurred, away from civilian, non-essential jobs to more essential services. This meant women taking on jobs as postmen, transport and railway workers, bus drivers, and so on. In white-collar employment it meant a different kind of work, related more to the industrial war effort, or the rationing system, or the stream of new offices and departments that followed in the wake of large-scale conscription (and led to a doubling of the military bureaucracy between 1939 and 1942).[148] With such a large proportion of married and unmarried women already working by 1939 this kind of redefinition of role within employment categories could go on without any real increase in the absolute total of women employed. But any argument that seeks to prove that 14 million women in employment in 1941, or 42 per cent of the native work-force, constitutes a failure to mobilize German women has a strange sense of reality. Perhaps part of the problem is the failure to appreciate fully that what women farmers, women domestic helpers, or women retailers and their family assistants were doing was really 'work', just as housework is not regarded as 'work' in this sense. But this is simply not so. With the loss of ever-increasing numbers of men to the armed forces between 1939 and 1942 women found themselves having to perform new tasks, and take on more responsibility, while struggling to keep up a household and, in the cities, searching for rationed goods.

It is this situation which helps to explain why it was so difficult to increase the absolute number of women in work during the war. Although estimates made by the Four Year Plan and by OKW showed that between 3.5 and 5 million more women could be recruited into the work-force (almost all of whom would have been married women), and plans were made before the war to increase the number of females in work substantially, these figures were ideal, optimal figures, ignoring the reality of a situation where women were already employed in great numbers,

[147] IWM EDS AL 1571, Besprechung 9 Jan. 1941, report of Economic Group Commerce; Williams, *Riddle of the Reich*, 56–7.

[148] Stephenson, *Women*, 106–7. For figures on administrative employment see Table 9.11 above.

often for long hours and for considerably less pay than men.[149] Already by 1939 there was widespread evidence of declining health standards among working women, exhaustion, increased absenteeism, and hostility to differential pay.[150] During 1940 and 1941 many firms were compelled to move to 10- or 12-hour shifts instead of 8 hours, and to insist on much more overtime and weekend working. This had the effect of further reducing both the productivity and work-willingness of female workers. During the early months of war there was high labour turnover as women reached exhaustion point, left employment, and then returned to it at a later stage. Agricultural work was particularly resented, for hours were long and poorly paid, and conditions for women from the cities were so primitive that many tried to escape from the land as soon as they could. 'Conditions of nervous depression are piling up', wrote one doctor to the local *Landrat* in his report on the health of female labour in his area. He predicted a 'rapid decline in productivity'.[151]

It was considerations of this kind rather than ideology which prevented more draconian recruitment of women. Indeed, female employment was a central plank of the government's labour strategy both before September 1939 and thereafter. Propaganda was directed at women to work for the war effort. Women were seen as the 'home army', a vital part of Germany's total war effort, whether their work was voluntary (the army of women who collected scarce materials, visited hospitals, repaired clothes) or paid wage-labour.[152] Between 1939 and 1941 all the official correspondence and discussions show evidence that women were accepted as an integral part of the economic war effort.[153] What Hitler could not bring himself to accept was the call from the armed forces for a *Generalmusterung* (general conscription) of all German women, since this would mean for the most part compelling older women and women with young children to take up full-time work. Hitler seriously believed that such a move would damage the health of those women necessary to raise further sons for the fatherland, and it would certainly have led to a much

[149] Bajohr, *Frauenarbeit*, 251; Winkler, *Frauenarbeit*, 86.

[150] IWM EDS Mi 14/294 (file 5), OKW, 'Die Probleme der deutschen Rüstungswirtschaft...', 19–25; BA R41/158, President of Provincial Labour Office, Lower Saxony, to Labour Ministry, 25 Nov. 1939, who reported that some women were working 9 to 10-hour shifts with a one or two hour journey to and from work; Bajohr, *Frauenarbeit*, 259–60; Stephenson, *Women*, 106–8.

[151] BA R41/158, Staatliches Gesundheitsamt to Landrat, Genthin, 23 Nov. 1939, 1–2: 'It is particularly noteworthy that already before the war, indeed considerably before, the employment of women in this region was extraordinarily intensive, as a result of the very great rapidity in the development of the arms industry.'

[152] Rupp, *Mobilizing Women*, 116–17.

[153] BA R41/158, Labour Ministry, 'Fraueneinsatz in der Rüstungsindustrie'. See too IWM EDS Mi 14/307, OKW Besprechung am 4 Feb. 1941 mit den Wehrersatzinspekteuren, 21–2; Mi 14/463 (file 1), Chef OKW to heads of armed forces, 22 Sept. 1940, 1–2.

more extensive mobilization of women than in Britain or America.[154] As it was by 1944 over 3.5 million women were working part-time (four times the number in Britain), and those not in work were coping with evacuation and child-rearing under a growing hail of bombs, or were engaged in some kind of voluntary activity.[155] Though Germany had its share of idle upper- and middle-class women, and the spoilt party wives, there were real limits to the extent to which higher numbers of women could be recruited to full-time work on any long-term basis. When later in the war renewed efforts were made to employ more women, only 1.4 million were found to be capable of work (*einsetzbar*), and many of them were difficult to engage permanently.[156] The experience of German women during the war was thus not very different from that of the other belligerent countries, and worse in a great number of respects than in the west, particularly once the bombing had begun in earnest. The very great demands made of German women in the crisis years of 1945–7, with so much of the male work-force unavailable, stretched back to the beginning of the war. For working-class and peasant women in particular the idea of an 'easy war' has a hollow ring about it.

Nor in the end could the ruthless mobilization of female labour have solved Germany's labour problems, which were the result of low productivity in the armaments sectors and the high levels of military demands. It was for these reasons that the decision was taken in 1941 to employ more foreign labour, to use POWs more productively, and to disperse contracts for less vital production to the occupied territories. By 1944 almost 7 million foreign workers were working in Germany.[157] Their conditions of work, pay, and diet were, as is well known, strikingly lower than those of German workers. But this situation should not obscure

[154] IWM EDS Mi 14/433 (2), Beitrag zum Vermerk über Steigerung der Luftwaffenfertigung, 27 June 1941: 'A general mustering of all male and female persons of a certain age recommended'; BA-MA Wi I F 5.2602, Fritz Sauckel memorandum, 'Das Programm des Arbeitseinsatzes', 20 Apr. 1942, 10–12. Sauckel argued that Hitler's objection was to the general conscription of all women, and to placing additional burdens on women with young children or peasant women, but was not an objection to female employment as such.

[155] IWM Box S368, Report 69, interrogation of Fritz Schmelter, 20 Dec. 1945, 5. This is an important point, for in the British figures on female employment part-time workers were included in the ratio of 2:1. Deducting part-time work from the British figures on female employment gives a smaller total, 375,000 fewer in June 1943 and 450,000 fewer in June 1944. This reduces the proportion of women in full-time employment in the British work-force to 36.4% in 1943 instead of 37.7%.

[156] Bajohr, *Frauenarbeit*, 290.

[157] U. Herbert, *Fremdarbeiter: Politik und Praxis des 'Ausländer-Einsatzes' in der Kriegswirtschaft des Dritten Reiches* (Berlin, 1985), 270–1; and Homze, *Foreign Labor*, ch. 2. The German Labour Ministry was already convinced by the end of 1941 that the prospects for recruiting more women for work was not good and that female employment was close to a ceiling. See IWM EDS AL 1775, Labour Ministry to OKW (Warlimont), 24 Oct 1941.

the heavy demands made by the Nazi state on its own women workers from the beginning of the war.

VII

There can be no doubt that the conventional picture of Germany's war effort must be redrawn. The *Blitzkrieg* phase of the economy turns out to be an illusion. Whatever the outcome of the military campaigns, the high levels of military demand and of government spending made it necessary to convert the economy to war, on Hitler's instructions, as fully as possible from the start. There was no major turning-point in the German war effort in the winter of 1941/2, or later in 1943. The biggest increases in taxation came between 1939 and 1941. The fastest growth of military spending came in the same two years. Personal consumption and civilian output also fell faster during 1939–41 than at any other time in the war, and the mobilization and redistribution of the work-force was carried out largely before the spring of 1942, not thereafter. Of course worse was to come. By 1944 many rationed goods were unobtainable, the black market was beginning to take shape, and bombing, perhaps more than any other factor, made civilian life harsher and deprivation more widespread than would otherwise have been the case. Nevertheless, this represented only a continuation and intensification of changes initiated from the very first weeks of war, or even before war broke out.

If there is a difference between 1939–41 and the last years of war it is a psychological one. In the early stages of the war the quick victories bred a sense of relief and a willingness to share sacrifices. Much of the population believed the war would be over quickly. By the end of the war there was no escaping the fact that Germany faced the real prospect of defeat by enemies apparently bent on vengeance. This engendered a psychological commitment to the very greatest efforts. In this sense, at least, total war, the complete mobilization of the moral and material strength of the nation, which Hitler and his generals had looked for in 1939, was finally realized. But in its material sense, in terms of the use of industrial capacity, the cut-backs in civilian consumption, the mobilization of the work-force, both male and female, total war was pursued from the start.

This becomes clear once Germany's war effort is compared with that of Britain. It has always been assumed that Britain converted her economy to total war long before Germany, that by 1941 the British work-force was more thoroughly recruited for war, and civilian consumption much lower. While it is certainly true that in a great many categories Britain produced more armaments than Germany, and more cheaply, this was largely a result of the very poor management of Germany's resources early in the

TABLE 9.15. *German and British war effort: selected statistics, 1939–1944*

	1939	1940	1941	1942	1943	1944
Index of consumer expenditure (*per capita*; 1938 = 100)						
Germany	95.0	88.4	81.9	75.3	75.3	70.0
Britain	97.2	89.7	87.1	86.6	85.5	88.2
Industrial work-force working on war orders (% of work-force)						
Germany	21.9	50.2	54.5	56.1	61.0	—
Britain	18.6	—	50.9	—	—	—
Proportion of women in the native civilian work-force (%)						
Germany	37.3	41.4	42.6	46.0	48.8	51.0
Britain[a]	26.4	29.8	33.2	34.8	36.4	36.2
War expenditure as a percentage of National Income (current prices)						
Germany	32.2	48.8	56.0	65.6	71.3	n.a.
Britain	15.0	43.0	52.0	52.0	55.0	54.0

[a] Excluding part-time workers.

Sources: Consumer expenditure as Table 9.6; industrial work-force as Table 9.7 for Germany, and Parker, *Manpower*, 112, 483; women in work-force as Table 9.13. National Income for Germany from Klein, *Preparations*, 257, and NA T178, Roll 15, frame 3671912, RFM Statistische Übersichten zu den Reichshaushaltsrechnungen 1938 bis 1943, Nov. 1944; for Britain from W. K. Hancock and M. M. Gowing, *British War Economy* (HMSO, 1949), 75, 199, 347.

war.[158] Measured in terms of the diversion and conversion of resources the picture is quite different. By 1941 Germany was more fully mobilized than Britain, and remained so for the rest of the war (see Table 9.15). The great success that Speer had in multiplying war output by 1944 was not a result of converting more civilian resources to the war effort, but of using the resources already converted more rationally. There is no doubt that Germany's leaders did not get what they wanted out of the military economy in the early stages of the war. It was Hitler himself who, later in the war, acknowledged that although the commitment to large-scale war was there from the start, things had been 'mismanaged'.[159] The question that historians have now got to answer is why the one country, whose

[158] The details can be found in C. Webster and N. Frankland, *The Strategic Air Offensive against Germany*, 4 vols. (London, 1961), iv. 469–70.
[159] A. Speer, *Inside the Third Reich* (London, 1970), 202.

political and military leadership had thoroughly grasped the importance of *Wehrwirtschaft*, and prepared for economic mobilization on a large scale, failed to produce weapons in the quantities expected and called for. The answers to this question are to be found in the nature of the Nazi state, in the role and attitudes of the military leaders and officials, and in the structure and performance of German industry.

The idea of a limited, *Blitzkrieg* economy must now be replaced by a different conception: that of 'total mobilization' which in the early stages of the war went badly wrong. Total economic commitment was not mere propaganda, but corresponded to Hitler's own view of how an economy should be managed in any war between major states, based on the experience of 1914–18, and reflected in the economic transformation of Germany between 1936 and 1941.[160] For Hitler, as for the military leadership, the economy had to be capable of providing the largest quantity of weapons and resources that it could to meet every political and military eventuality, for short campaigns and for long-drawn-out wars of attrition. Hitler did not simply want to defeat Poland, then France, but wanted to achieve, and hold on to, global power. It was with this ambition in mind that he ordered the rapid conversion of the economy to war in autumn 1939, and increased his demands again in the summer of 1940 and the summer of 1941. According to Speer, Hitler told him in 1942 that 'he anticipated an intensification of the war ... he had repeatedly drawn attention to the dangers of the second front or of additional theatres of war'.[161] Massive war production was to give him the sort of freedom of manœuvre that the generals of the First World War had lacked.

[160] The propaganda of the period 1939 to 1941, and before the outbreak of war as well, was not, as might be expected for a Blitzkrieg war, designed to show how successful the government was at keeping up living standards, but was the opposite: preparation of the population to accept sacrifices, when the time came, in the name of total war. Indeed all the 'psychological' preparation before 1939 was predicated on the need to prepare 'the spiritual attitude of the people towards a total war' (BA-MA Wi I F 5.412, Göring conference 16 July 1938, 2). There is interesting testimony on this in Stoddard, *Into the Darkness*, 54: 'Nazi spokesmen tell you frankly that they cracked down hard from the start and made things just about as tough as the civilian population could bear. Indeed, they say that severe rationing of food and clothing from the very beginning was done not merely to avert present waste and ensure future supplies, it was done also to make people realise that they were in a life-and-death struggle for which no sacrifice was too great.' On propaganda see J. Sywottek, *Mobilmachung für den totalen Krieg: Die propagandistische Vorbereitung der deutschen Bevölkerung auf dem Zweiten Weltkrieg* (Opladen, 1976), 94–103, 194–201; W. Wette, 'Ideologien, Propaganda und Innenpolitik als Voraussetzungen der Kriegspolitik des Dritten Reiches', in W. Deist *et al.*, *Das Dentsche Reich und der Zweite Weltkrieg*, i. *Ursachen und Voraussetzungen der deutschen Kriegspolitik* (Stuttgart, 1979), 121–36.

[161] IWM Box S368, Report 54, Speer interrogation, 13 July 1945, 2: 'He knew', Speer continued, 'the supply figures of the last war in detail and could reproach us with the fact that the output in 1917/18 was higher than we could show for 1942 ... I only knew that these were the requirements which had been fixed in his mind for a long time. They were in nearly every case three to six times the armament production of 1941.'

Appendix

TABLE 9.16. *Reductions in steel allocation to non-war sectors, 1940 (%)*

Sector	Reduction from 1939
Consumer industry	75.0
Railways	45.0
Party projects, road-building	94.0
Construction industry	85.0
Four Year Plan	83.5
Basic industries	55.0

Source: IWM EDS AL 1905, General von Hanneken, 'Überblick über die Lage auf dem gewerblichen Sektor der Wirtschaft', 2 Sitzung des Generalrates der Wirtschaft, 2 Jan. 1940, 4–6.

TABLE 9.17. *Decline in male artisan employment with the outbreak of war ('000)*

Handicraft sector	1 July 1939	1 Jan. 1940
Iron and steel	877	737
Building and woodwork	1,972	1,370
Paper	31	27
Clothing and dry-cleaning	702	596
Foodstuffs	594	499
TOTAL:	4,176	3,229

Source: BA R11/11, Reichswirtschaftskammer, Kriegswirtschaftliche Bilanz, 16 June 1941, Anlage 6, 'Die Beschäftigung im Handwerk'.

TABLE 9.18. *Decline in artisan employment, 1939–1944*

	(1941 = 100)	(1939 = 100)
May 1939	142.3	100.0
May 1940	110.5	77.6
May 1941	100.0	70.3
May 1942	85.9	60.4
May 1943	79.2	55.7
May 1944	73.6	51.7

Source: Wagneführ, *Deutsche Industrie*, 47–8.

10
German Multi-Nationals and the Nazi State in Occupied Europe

DURING the Second World War the relationship between German industry and industry elsewhere in Europe was transformed. By 1941 Germany was master of large parts of the industrialized continent. German leaders sought to co-ordinate the industrial resources of the conquered and dependent areas with the long-term economic interests of the Reich. An important part of this strategy was direct investment by German firms in the industry of the occupied areas. The opportunities opened up by conquest to extend German multi-nationalism were substantial, though much of the new multi-national activity was promoted through state ownership and was governed in the main by political considerations and the needs of war. The relationship between government and multi-national development is therefore of central importance.

This fact raises some problems of definition. Much of the new multi-national activity did not spring in the main from commercial motive. Indeed the state sought to suppress purely economic motives and to substitute some rough notion of 'racial political' priority when supervising industrial acquisitions or controlling existing German subsidiaries. The government, dominated by radical nationalist politicians, became the self-appointed guardians of the national interest. Firms that co-operated with the state were given greater freedom of action than others, but all German firms were subject to a set of regulations and controls over investment policy, product policy, and labour dictated by the state economic apparatus. The New Order raised other problems of definition as well. German businesses which owned shares in Austrian or Czech firms found their holdings converted into German businesses as Germany's frontiers expanded. The same was true of western Poland and eastern France, areas absorbed back into Greater Germany. Elsewhere in occupied Europe constitutional questions were left in abeyance, so that the exact national status of captured businesses remained unclear. In many cases German private firms acquired temporary trusteeship over foreign firms, leaving the question of ownership open until the end of the war, particularly in the case of those taken over by the Commissioner for Enemy Property which were still legally owned by Germany's enemies. For the purpose of this chapter multi-national activity is taken to mean all direct investment in industry, whether state or private capital, outside the frontiers of the pre-1938 Reich.

There is no doubt that the political context within which this German penetration of European industry took place is unique in the history of multi-nationalism. None the less, this example does raise questions about the relationship between government and industry at an important stage in the development of large-scale German businesses, and provides an extreme example of political power used to further industrial expansion along multi-national lines.

I

Before the Second World War German multi-nationalism was less developed than that of other industrialized countries. There were a number of reasons for this. German firms lost a large proportion of their foreign assets after the war and had to start rebuilding again from scratch. They concentrated on reconstruction and reorganization inside Germany. German firms also faced both political barriers and economic constraints in extending activities outside Germany in the 1920s and 1930s. In the case of Poland, for example, German industry was gradually excluded by the Polish government and German business taken over by the state. In Czechoslovakia and France there was strong resistance to the penetration of German capital. German investment in Czech industry comprised only 7 per cent of all foreign investment there in 1937.[1] Political uncertainty, fear of nationalization, and the poor state of German finances combined to limit German multi-national expansion. German firms preferred to export direct from Germany, particularly to hard-currency areas which could provide foreign exchange to buy raw materials abroad. Only in cases where foreign governments made it difficult to export did German firms set up subsidiaries producing direct for foreign markets; or in cases where it was necessary to safeguard sources of raw material supply.[2] On balance German firms lacked the financial strength and opportunity of French, British, or American industry, and where they could, arrived at marketing or sales agreements with foreign competitors rather than undertake direct capital penetration. By 1939 the share of German industrial activity conducted by subsidiaries abroad was relatively small.

[1] J. Tomaszewski, 'German Capital in Silesian Industry in Poland between the two World Wars', in A. Teichova and P. Cottrell (eds.), *International Business in Central Europe 1919–1939* (Leicester, 1983), 227–44; A. Teichova and R. Waller, 'Der tschechoslowakische Unternehmer am Vorabend und zu Beginn des Zweiten Weltkrieges', in W. Dlugoborski (ed.), *Zweiter Weltkrieg und soziale Wandel* (Göttingen, 1981), 292.

[2] This was the exception. On preference for exports over investment see V. Schröter, 'The IG Farbenindustrie AG in Central and South-Eastern Europe 1926–38', in Teichova and Cottrell, *International Business*, 139–62; H. Schröter, 'Siemens and Central and South-East Europe between the two World Wars', ibid. 173–89.

This situation was encouraged after 1933 by the German government with its controls over trade and preference for domestic production. But after the announcement of the Second Four Year Plan in 1936 the domestic political context began to change. Firms were encouraged with state backing to push more forcefully into central and south-eastern Europe. At the same time the state extended more and more controls over the industrial economy and the domestic capital market in order to divert the necessary resources to war preparation. Greater state control over the economy was an important prerequisite for the period of expansion which began with the *Anschluss* in March 1938. Nazi leaders hoped to build up a German-dominated economic bloc in central and eastern Europe which could be used to contribute some of the vast military and strategic resources needed to wage major war. Through its foreign policy the Nazi state sought to ease the conditions of access to the economies of the region through direct occupation and incorporation or through diplomatic and military pressure. After 1938 multi-nationalism became a device to further the political aims of the German government in using the resources of other countries to make up for what was lacking inside the Reich; direct investment in the region was closely monitored by the state.

The industrial spoils acquired in the first wave of expansion before the war were largely taken over by the state holding company, the Reichswerke 'Hermann Göring', with the help of the Dresdner and Deutsche banks which co-operated in shielding the Reichswerke from publicity in the company's share dealings, while buying up the major Austrian and Czech businesses on its behalf. The vacuum created in central Europe by the flight of western and Jewish capital was filled not in the main by private German firms but by state holding companies. The Reichswerke had begun life as a state company set up by Göring in the summer of 1937 to exploit low-grade German iron ores in the framework of the Four Year Plan. Instead, as Göring came to acquire extensive controls over the economy, it was used as the foundation for building up a vast industrial conglomerate to secure the gains of occupied Europe for Germany's strategic needs. It was not in this sense a true multi-national, seeking to set up profitable subsidiaries abroad to the benefit of the parent company, but was a political instrument of the Nazi state designed to defend the interests of 'national economy' and to secure for the party extensive control over its imperial gains. 'Profits' came in the form of arms and resources for the Reich. The development of the Reichswerke undertaking was closely bound up with the political ambitions of those who ran it, a mixture of nationalist bureaucrats and small businessmen generally hostile to German big business. It was not simply an instrument for incorporating the spoils of Europe quickly into the German war machine but became a key institution in planning a post-war state-controlled economy dominated by bureaucratic managers, very different from the Reichswerke set up to cope with armaments contracts in the First World War.[3] (For details see Chapter 5 above.)

The role of the state was made explicit from the outset of German expansion. The Austrian economy, said Göring, must be kept 'firmly in the hand of the state'.[4] The German Economics Ministry issued a decree a week after the *Anschluss* preventing any unauthorized capital transfers in Austria, to be enforced retroactively. Authorization of share transactions was granted to Göring as head of the Four Year Plan. When the Sudetenland was occupied in October 1938 the Plan was immediately extended to cover the area, and the chief industries taken under the supervision of the Economics Ministry pending their distribution.[5] Major private firms got very little from the take-over of Austria and Czechoslovakia, with the important exception of the chemical giant, IG Farben, and there were limits even in this case. The chemical industry had the advantage that it was already closely integrated with the industrial programmes of the Four Year Plan, but IG Farben was particularly well placed because of the prograssive Nazification of its leading managerial circles.

IG Farben was involved in the takeover of foreign assets from the start, after a decade of growing influence in the chemical industry of central Europe. In Austria it acquired ownership from the Rothschilds of the Skoda-Werke Wetzler, after its general manager, Isador Pollack, had unsuccessfully tried to merge with other European firms to avoid German control. IG Farben was also able to use its Czech subsidiary, Dynamit AG Bratislava, to gain entry to the Austrian and Czech chemical industry. In July 1938 Dynamit took over two Austrian chemical works, Carbidwerke Deutsch-Matrei and Österreichische Dynamit Nobel AG. In early 1939, before the occupation of Czechoslovakia, IG Farben was finally successful in penetrating the largest Czech chemical producer by taking over the Aussig and Falkenau plants in the Sudetenland jointly with Chemische Fabrik von Hayden, both of which held 50 per cent of the shares. With the break-up of Czechoslovakia, IG Farben acquired full control over its Slovakian subsidiary, which the Czech government had previously obstructed, and enjoyed a dominant position from which to launch further expansion into south-eastern Europe.[6]

---

[3] For details on the Reichswerke see R. J. Overy, 'Göring's "Multi-National" Empire', ibid. 269–93.

[4] *Der Vierjahresplan*, 2 (1938), 602–3.

[5] *TWC*, Case X, 475–6, Economics Ministry decree, 19 Mar. 1938.

[6] H. Radandt, 'Die IG Farbenindustrie AG und Südosteuropa 1938 bis zum Ende des Zweiten Weltkrieges', *Jahrbuch für Wirtschaftsgeschichte*, 1967 pt. I, 78–84, 97–9: J. Borkin, *The Crime and Punishment of IG Farben* (London, 1979), 95–8.

By comparison other private transactions in Austria were much less important. Krupp was allowed to increase participation in the Berndorfer Metallwarenfabrik though on the condition laid down by Göring that Krupp 'will do everything possible to raise the Austrian economy to the level which is desirable not only in the interests of Austria but also in that of Germany'.[7] The Stahlverein increased its participation in Böhler AG from 39.5 to 67 per cent.[8] But the bulk of non-German businesses were brought under the control of the state. When Flick expressed interest in the Petschek holdings which had fallen into German hands in the Sudetenland, Körner, Göring's state secretary, replied that the German Petschek mines, some of which Flick had already acquired, would be 'the last coalfields to be transferred to private ownership... any lignite coalfield which would become available in the course of further Aryanization would have to be taken over or come under direct control of the state'.[9] This was a disappointment for the private firms which had been given to understand by officials in the Finance Ministry who were either unsympathetic towards or ignorant of Göring's economic plans, that the Sudeten lignite mines would be sold off to IG Farben or Flick. Instead the state took them all over, reorganized them into a single business, and transferred them as a whole to the Reichswerke.[10]

The same pattern was followed in Czechoslovakia. When the Skoda works fell into German hands both Flick and Krupp expressed interest. But the works were instead taken over by the Reichswerke, which gradually built up a majority shareholding. The state went even further than this and put pressure on German firms that already had a multi-national stake in Austria to transfer the interest to the state in order to produce a unified exploitation of the area. The Vereinigte Stahlwerke were compelled to sell their controlling interest in the Alpine Montangesellschaft to the Reichswerke, eventually losing even the 10 per cent stake they had been given as compensation in a new steel complex set up by the Reichswerke at Linz. Mannesmann sold out its 50 per cent interest in Kromag to the state-controlled Steyr–Daimler–Puch, though it was able to keep its interest in the Prague Iron Company after the German

[7] *TWG*, Case X, 477, Doc. NI-766, Keppler to von Wilmowsky, 2 Apr. 1938. Krupp acquired a holding of 86.9%.

[8] N. Schausberger, 'Die Auswirkungen der Rüstungs- und Kriegswirtschaft 1938–1945 auf die soziale und ökonomische Struktur Österreichs', in F. Forstmeier and H.-E. Volkmann (eds.), *Kriegswirtschaft und Rüstung 1939–1945* (Düsseldorf, 1977), 259.

[9] IWM Case V, background documents (hereafter Case V), Steinbrinck Doc. Book iv, 172, Final report on the liquidation of the Petschek transaction, 26 Nov. 1938.

[10] Case XI, background documents, Pleiger Doc. Book viiB, 'The Economic Development of the Sudetenländische Bergbau AG during the years 1939–1945', 30–2: Pros. Doc. Book 168, NID-15635, file note of Reichs Finance Ministry, 17 Feb. 1939; NID-15636, RFM Memorandum, 25 Feb. 1939, 'Transfer of Czech coal interests in the Sudetenland'.

occupation.[11] Foreign multi-nationals in the occupied areas were also brought under considerable pressure to sell their shares to the German state, though a great number of non-German firms had abandoned the area before the German occupation. Only with American firms were German negotiators more cautious, for there were strong indications that German holdings in the United States were vulnerable to expropriation if undue pressure were put on American shareholders in European firms.[12]

There were certainly elements in the German administration and in German industry who were hostile to these developments. The Finance Ministry remained strongly critical of the Reichswerke concern, with its demands for state subsidy and tendency to monopoly. When the Czech lignite mines fell into German hands the ministry felt that the claims of the Reichswerke were 'quite out of the question' and 'cannot be complied with'.[13] IG Farben was distrustful of Reichswerke ambitions too, particularly after the Sudeten mines were acquired by Göring to provide the raw material for a large synthetic oil plant at Brüx under state control, paying a licence to IG Farben in respect of the process; and even more so when the Reichswerke began to trespass on IG Farben interests in the production and distribution of domestic gas.[14] But as Göring's economic and political strategy began to crystallize during 1938 and early 1939 the claims of the state became more insistent and wide-ranging. In Austria the Reichswerke gradually acquired ownership of the major iron, steel, and machinery sectors, including Steyr–Daimler–Puch, and the Alpine Montangesellschaft. In Czechoslovakia it took over all the lignite mines of the Sudeten area, major iron and steel businesses, including Ferdinands Nordbahn and Poldihütte and Vítkovice, and the arms and machinery works of Skoda, Erste Brünner Maschinenfabrik, and Brünner Waffenwerke, extending the share of German capital in total foreign investment in Czechoslovakia to 47 per cent by 1940. Shares in these companies were collected over a period of time from Austrian and Czech banks and from private shareholders. Full Reichswerke control of Poldi and Skoda took longest to acquire; in both cases the German state issued new shares against capital invested by the Reichswerke, which finally gave

[11] IWM G.ED. 43/0/34, German Industrial Complexes: The Hermann Göring Complex, June 1946, 11–13.
[12] Case V, Steinbrinck Doc. Book iv, 152–3, Steinbrinck memorandum, 1 Feb. 1938; 157–8, 'Status of Negotiations with the Petschek Group', n.d. The US negotiators representing the Petscheks threatened that the US government would expropriate German holdings in America if the Germans did not agree to buy the Petschek shares on reasonable terms.
[13] Case XI, Pros. Doc. Book 168, NID-15636.
[14] NA, Reichswerke Collection, Microcopy T83 Roll 74, frames 3445163–4, IG Farben report 'Konzernaufbau und Entwicklung der Reichswerke AG', 19 Oct. 1939; Hermann Göring Complex, 15.

it a controlling interest.[15] Only in the case of Vítkovice was there any difficulty since the ownership had been hastily transferred to the London-based Alliance Insurance before the German occupation. The works were occupied and operated by the Reichswerke, which attempted to annul the London shares and gain full ownership on the grounds that the business was Jewish as defined in Reich law. The Reich Protector of Bohemia, Konstantin von Neurath, refused to allow the London shares to be annulled and instead the Reichswerke had to be content with a special operating treaty signed in 1941 which gave it trustee status but left the question of ownership until the end of hostilities.[16]

The Reichswerke concern was not the only state-funded institution to share in these acquisitions, though it was by far the most important, assuming a controlling participation in almost two-thirds of the heavy industry of the two countries. The ease with which the transfers were made can be explained in part by the absence of any large private German shareholding in the region which might have forestalled the growth of state ownership. Private firms were given access to industry that was either too small or too specialized technically for the Reichswerke to cope with. The German state also enjoyed the advantage that significant shareholdings had been sold by private owners to the Austrian and Czech states in anticipation of German expansion. These share packets were simply bought up on very favourable terms by the German state when Austria and Czechoslovakia ceased to exist as sovereign units. These circumstances made it possible to pursue a policy of direct state investment straight away, in order to bring the new businesses quickly into the production programmes of the Four Year Plan and the armed forces.

II

The expansion into Austria and Czechoslovakia set the pattern for the war years. The guidelines for the economies of the captured areas were laid down by the state. At the centre of German economic strategy was a policy of direct investment, as the best guarantee of securing a dominant position for Germany in the post-war European economy and to exclude as far as possible the other major investing countries from participation in European industry. The process of direct capital penetration was authorized by Göring in September and October 1939, when the Finance

---

[15] Overy, 'Görings "Multi-National" Empire' 272–7; Teichova and Waller, 'Unternehmer', 293.

[16] Case XI, Pleiger Doc. Book viiA, Dr Nowak, 'The Legal Position of the Witkowitz Gewerkschaft, 23 Oct. 1939'; Minutes of the 14th meeting of the Aufsichtsrat, 17 Feb. 1941; Resolution of the Aufsichtsrat, Witkowitz Gewerkschaft, 14 Dec. 1942.

Ministry was instructed that foreign acquisitions were to be kept in state hands on the grounds that it was essential that the economic extension of 'Germandom' should be properly co-ordinated.[17] Göring expanded these arguments in his directives on the Polish economy: 'Any wild confiscations, and any profiteering of individuals will be prosecuted... The essential point is that Polish property liable to confiscation shall be utilized in the interests of the Reich, i.e. of the community but not for the benefit of individuals.' The area under German occupation 'formed a *homogeneous economic area* with manifold, mutual obligations which makes necessary a co-ordinated supervision from Berlin'.[18] Even in cases where the state would not acquire ownership, particularly of property already owned by German nationals, all industry held abroad was to be 'staatlich gelenkt' (guided by the state).

The same policy was authorized after victory over France in 1940. Occupation authorities throughout Europe were instructed before any final peace settlement to take every opportunity in questions of future shareholding 'to make it possible for the German economy to obtain access even during the war to material of interest in the occupied countries'.[19] 'One of the goals of German economic policy', Göring announced in August, 'is the increase of German influence in foreign enterprises... I reserve for myself the granting of permission for the purchasing of enterprises, participations etc.... situated in the occupied territories'.[20] The decrees on shareholding outlawed any attempt to sell shares in the conquered areas to a third party, whether they had been sold before the decree was published or not. Nor were the military or the occupation authorities allowed to make 'independent commitments of any kind to individual German interested parties'.[21] All enemy property was seized immediately and placed under the Commissioner for Enemy Property; all other acquisitions came directly under the supervision of the Four Year Plan.

The state's role in all this was explained by Göring's state secretary in the Four Year Plan journal at the end of 1940. 'In a national economy highly developed technically and politically, which should serve not the

[17] TWC xii: 665, NID-15640.

[18] Case V, Flick Doc. Book xiA, EC-410, Letter from Göring to all Reich authorities, 19 Oct. 1939, 1–3 (italics in the original); para. 4 read: 'In order to exploit the territories, and especially those to be incorporated in the Reich, in the best way for the achievement of the Führer's goal, the property in real estate, plants, mobile objects, and all rights taken out of Polish hands must be safeguarded and administered in a co-ordinated way.'

[19] 'Letter from Goering to Reich commissioners, 2 Aug. 1940', in Royal Institute of International Affairs, *Hitler's Europe*, (Oxford, 1954), 194.

[20] NCA vii. 310, Göring to Thomas, 9 Aug. 1940.

[21] Ibid. EC485, Göring conference, 1 Oct. 1940, 'about the economic exploitation of the occupied territories'.

profit motive of the individual but the common good, there will always exist huge tasks which have outgrown the private sphere and will be soluble only through the forces of the community.'[22] Behind these functional arguments can be detected important political motives. The extension of German control over Europe's economy meant more permanent power for the party in economic affairs. The Nazi government did not want the balance of power in the economy to tilt back decisively in favour of the big German concerns by handing them European economic resources on a plate. Paul Pleiger, managing director of the Reichswerke, believed that the private firms were only interested in buying foreign assets to set them off against high tax liabilities in the Reich.[23] Nor could the party afford to ignore radical nationalist opinion, whether in the party or the administration, by openly rewarding German big business with the spoils of a war fought ostensibly on behalf of the German community as a whole. Economic populism and Prussian statist traditions met on common ground in resisting purely commercial pressures. There was also the question of sheer power. Nazi leaders by 1941 had a degree of personal authority in conquered Europe inconceivable a decade before. It is not difficult to understand their hesitancy in sharing this power unconditionally with industrial circles outside the favoured party few.

The response of German industry to these circumstances was far from uniform. Victory in 1939 and 1940 presented German industry with the opportunity to reverse the situation it had faced between the wars, to roll back foreign capital, particularly British and French, and to gain revenge for the losses brought about through the Versailles settlement. There is no doubt that sectors of German heavy industry did feel strongly that they deserved some form of compensation for the economic losses forced through political changes after 1919: 'I could write novels about that,' minuted Friedrich Flick in 1938.[24] There was strong support for this view in the Economics Ministry which in response to Göring's decree ordering the acquisition of shares by German firms discussed whether or not 'the stocks should be bought for private economy or for the Reich'. The outcome of the discussion was a general agreement that the transfers should be made to private hands via the German banks and that Göring must bow to 'superior opinions' in 'undertaking to hand them over to private industry. Under all circumstances, a further extension of control by trust is to be avoided.'[25] Both Walther Funk, the Economics Minister, and Schwerin von Krosigk, the Finance Minister, preferred this policy, the one

---

[22] *TWC* xii. 536–8, NI-002.
[23] *TWC*, Case XI transcripts, 14891.
[24] Case V, Flick Doc. Book xA, NI-3249, Flick file note, 19 Jan. 1938.
[25] *NCA* vii. 258–9, EC-43, RWM discussion, 16 Aug. 1940.

because of his fears of backdoor 'bolshevization', the latter because of his dislike of state subsidy and bureaucratized industry.[26]

But this view was by no means shared by German industry as a whole. The growth of state power in the economy backed by influential figures in the party made businessmen wary of undertaking initiatives abroad in competition with the Four Year Plan. They were also constrained from setting up multi-national organizations by lack of capital or skilled managerial personnel, which the state was not, or at least not until the conquest of the western Soviet Union. Krupp's reasons for not taking up fresh commitments in Poland were based partly on considerations of this kind.[27] For even the largest private businesses the economic cost of taking up ownership of foreign assets during wartime, with the political and military situation unclear and no guarantee of long-term financial security (Ruhr leaders warned Göring in 1940 of the dangers of challenging both the Soviet Union and the United States), made the strategy of foreign expansion less inviting than the private industrial lobby realized.[28]

There was another political consideration too. The occupied areas were taken over by Nazi appointees whose view of their new territories was a very proprietary one. In Lithuania, for example, the newly installed *Gauleiter* Hinrich Lohse prohibited German firms from entering captured businesses and rejected private claims in favour of some kind of state monopoly. AEG was expelled from an electricity works which it had occupied without permission; Flick's advice to his representatives in the area was to 'proceed with caution'.[29] In Poland the SS and Governor Frank between them tried to pursue an independent economic policy, restraining both IG Farben and the Reichswerke from buying up captured Polish plants. Even established affiliates were not immune. The Osram plant in Poland was taken over by a Reich commissioner for alleged inefficiency in 1942.[30]

This world of 'Intrigenspielen' (games of intrigue), as one exasperated accountant put it, was nowhere more evident than in the conflicts over the industry of Polish Silesia and eastern France.[31] The conquest of Poland brought back the Upper Silesian heavy-industrial region into German hands. Here there were old German claims going back before

---

[26] Case XI, Pleiger Doc. Book vA, 80–1, letter from Schwegin von Krosigk to Funk, 11 Dec. 1940.
[27] NA Reichswerke files, T83, Roll 76, frames 3446876–7, letter from Pleiger to Körner, 10 Apr. 1940; 3446884–6, Pleiger to Krupp, 8 Apr. 1940.
[28] Case X, background documents, Bülow Doc. Book 1, 102.
[29] Case V, Flick Doc. Book xiiiD, NI-3100, notes of a meeting on Phoenix AG, 17 Oct. 1941: 'It was Gauleiter Lohse's aim for the present to consolidate the larger and medium enterprises into monopolistic companies,' under the *Gauleiter*'s own supervision.
[30] NA Göring Stabsamt, T84 Roll 8, frames 7309–10, Göring decree, 31 Oct. 1942.
[31] Ibid., Reichswerke files, T83 Roll 75, frame 3445814, Dr Müller HGW Wirtschaftsabteilung, 'Bericht der Arbeitsgruppe für Verkaufsfragen'.

1914. The Four Year Plan hoped to pre-empt these claims by keeping the industry of the region under state control, and if possible directly in state hands, by transferring it wholesale to the Reichswerke. A special trustee office was set up under Hans Winkler, the Haupttreuhandstelle Ost, which took over all captured property on behalf of the Reich. As in Czechoslovakia this transfer was made easier by the fact that many of the coal-mines and steelworks were directly owned by the Polish state and could be expropriated as enemy property. Göring met some resistance from Winkler himself, who thought it wrong to place all industry under one owner and was backed up by the Economics Ministry.[32] Göring insisted on obtaining at the very least the coal-mines of the region to serve Reichswerke needs at Salzgitter and Linz. Winkler agreed to this, though the coal gave Göring strong influence on the steelworks as well, which were dependent on the Silesian coalfield. The mines were consolidated into a single company, the Bergwerksverwaltung Oberschlesien GmbH. Krupp and Röchling, who were both interested in buying up Silesian plants, urged Göring to restore the mines serving Katowice and the Bismarckhütte to private ownership, but Göring refused.[33] The outcome was that the iron- and steelworks on their own were a much less inviting prospect. Flick, who had owned the Bismarckhütte before 1914, lacked the financial resources to compete with the Reichswerke after acquiring new lignite assets from the state in 1939, and was, after June 1940, more interested in acquiring something in Lorraine. Krupp abandoned the contest for the Dubenskogrube on grounds of cost, but presumably from political caution as well, since Göring had personally intervened to acquire it for the Reichswerke.[34] The Vereinigte Stahlwerke succeeded in getting operating contracts at the Katowice steel plants but was denied ownership on the grounds that this would strengthen the position of the Ruhr in an area where 'in the future, as now during the time of war economy, the people's economic necessities would have to stand ahead of private contracts'.[35]

Indeed it was by no means clear at first that private industry would gain

[32] Ibid., T83 Roll 76, frames 3446860–1, Pleiger to Körner, 13 Mar. 1940; *TWC* xiii. 744–5, Winkler affidavit, 7 May 1948.

[33] Ibid. 749, NI-598, Agreement between HTO and Reichswerke Hermann Göring: NA Göring Stabsamt, T84 Roll 7, frames 6704–6, Winkler memorandum, 21 Apr. 1942; *Hermann Göring Complex*, 21–2: Case XI, Pros. Doc. Book 115, NG-044, RWM note 'incorporation of Upper Silesian coal in the mining administration of the Reichswerke Hermann Göring, 9 Nov. 1941'.

[34] On Flick see Case XI, Pros. Doc. Book 113, NI-3548, Flick to Göring, 1 Nov. 1940; Case V, Flick Doc. Book xiB, NI-3529, notes of a conversation with von Hanneken, 27 Aug. 1940; on Krupp, Case XI, Pleiger Doc. Book viii, Winkler affidavit, 6 Mar. 1948, 4; NA Reichswerke files, T83 Roll 76, frames 3446860–1, Pleiger to Körner, 13 Mar. 1940; frames 3446876–86, letter from Pleiger to Körner, 10 Apr. 1940 eclosing a letter from Krupp to Pleiger, 27 Mar. 1940; 3446891–2; Aktenvermerk Pleiger 'Dubenskogrube'.

[35] Case XI, Pros. Doc. Book 115, NG-044, 4.

very much of the iron and steel capacity either. The Reichswerke took over control of Berg- und Hüttenwerke AG at Trzynietz, the largest steelworks in the region, and then, with the fall of Paris, succeeded in getting the shares bought outright by the Dresdner and Deutsche banks from the Union Européene Industrielle et Financière which held them on behalf of Schneider et Cie. Berg- und Hüttenwerke then took over the other steelworks, Bismarckhütte and Königshütte, with a view to integrating them into the Reichswerke. In the end the shares were sold to a group of private buyers and not to the Reichswerke, though they were sold in such a way as to avoid a dominant position for any of the big concerns. Most of the shares were sold to smaller German Silesian companies that had lost out in 1922 and 1937 with Polish nationalization of German participations. These same circles were successful in winning back the Hohenlohe zinc works too, which Göring had taken over along with the coal-mines, but which he was forced to relinquish to the other zinc producers after vigorous lobbying.[36] Nevertheless Reichswerke nominees still dominated the boards of directors of the privatized iron- and steelworks and through Otto Fitzner, the local head of administration, and Hans Winkler, the Four Year Plan representative, the state was able to monitor the activity of the private firms.[37]

The same conflict developed over the heavy industry of Lorraine, Luxemburg, and north-eastern France. Here again there were well-established German claims and here again Göring's initial response was to claim all the industry of the region for the state. Paul Pleiger argued that this strategy was based on a fear of the Ruhr firms 'getting together' in the area to challenge the position of the Reichswerke in the rest of Europe.[38] It was his view that the Reichswerke should try to get as much as it could in Lorraine 'for the reason that the rest of the German iron industry, particularly the west German industry, still considers the Hermann Göring Works to be superfluous'.[39] These arguments were put to Göring in June 1940. He ordered that 'the endeavour of German industry to take over enterprises in the recently occupied territory must be rejected in the sharpest manner. Travel of industrialists into the occupied territory must not be permitted for the present'.[40] Trustees and special commissioners

---

[36] Hermann Göring Complex, 21–2.

[37] R. Jeske, 'Zur Annexion der polnischen Wojewodschaft schlesien durch Hitlerdeutschland im zweiten Weltkrieg', Zeitschrift für Geschichtswissenschaft, 5 (1957), 1073–5.

[38] NA Reichswerke files, T83 Roll 74, frame 3445217, 'Gründung und Wachsen der HGW 1937–1942'; Case XI, Pleiger Doc. Book x, 1–2, Gritzbach affidavit; TWC, Case XI transcripts, vol. 231, 14890.

[39] Ibid., Book vB, minutes of the meeting of the Aufsichstrat of the Reichswerke, Nov. 1944.

[40] Case V, Flick Doc. Book xiA, 1155–PS, Notice of Göring conference, 19 June 1940, 1.

were sent in to take temporary control over the iron-ore mines and the steelworks of the area. Funk wrote to the iron and steel industry that it should 'repress any desire for annexation'.[41] Four Year Plan officials made it clear that the decision on ownership of the captured plants was Göring's responsibility and that there could be no guarantees that private ownership on the basis of past claims would be re-established in the region.

Pleiger's fears were well founded. Industrialists met with General von Hanneken, the Four Year Plan Plenipotentiary for Iron and Steel, on 10 June. At this meeting they pressed their claims for 'repatriation'. Firms with historic claims were to get their plant back; other private firms should also be considered; the iron-ore mines should be consolidated and the flow of ore controlled jointly by all the steel companies of the area and those of the Ruhr and Saarland. The industrialists also put pressure on von Hanneken to ask Pleiger to abandon building the Reichswerke at Salzgitter altogether, as the acquisition of Lorraine solved the problem of output and threatened to produce a large surplus of sheet steel capacity if Pleiger persisted with the original scheme. His reply was 'write to Göring yourself'. Even von Hanneken, whom they regarded as an ally, was surprised by the stampede to acquire the best plants: 'Everybody is scrambling after Rombach, Hayingen, and Differdingen, and in a little while the other plants will be offered like sour beer!'[42] By 26 June the industry had produced a set of principles on which the distribution of captured plants should be based, giving preference to old claims, but also to those firms in the Reich which had a poor ratio of coal to steel output and needed more steel capacity. These included Flick, Hoesch, and Mannesmann, but adversely affected the claims of Vereinigte Stahlwerke and Klöckner, where the ratio went the other way. There was general agreement that in the future French participation in the region was to be excluded completely. By mid-August the claims had largely been filed. Lists of these were sent to the Economics Ministry, to Göring, and to the local administrators in Lorraine.[43]

By this time, however, it was known that Göring had plans of his own.

[41] *TWC*, Case X, 484, NI-048, letter from Poensgen to Reichert, 10 June 1940, reporting meeting of the Kleiner Kreis, 7 June. Funk told the industrialists present that any attempt to push the interests of big business would arouse political hostility.

[42] Case V, Flick Doc. Book xiB, NI-3516, note of discussion with von Hanneken, 10 June 1940, 1–2; NI-3529, consultation with von Hanneken, 27 Aug. 1940, 2.

[43] Case V, Flick Doc. Book xiB, NI-048, Poensgen to Funk, 10 June 1940, NI-8518, proposals made by the Reich Office Iron and Steel for the Distribution of the Iron Industry in Luxemburg and French Lorraine, 26 July 1940; on French claims see NI-3533, Weiss memorandum for Burkart, 6 Aug. 1940. It is clear from these documents that W. Dlugoborski's claim (Teichova and Cottrell, *International Business*, 301) that the Germans wanted to co-operate with the French industrialists 'to win friends rather than to seize by force' was not the case. When Flick took over the Rombach plant all the French managers were sacked and sent back to France.

It is not clear exactly when or why Göring was made to reduce his claim to take over everything. Even by August it was rumoured that the Reichswerke sought 5 million tons of steel capacity in the region.[44] Göring was clearly influenced by Pleiger's advice. Since it was impossible to expect a take-over of all plants and mines, Pleiger's strategy was to divide the minette ore mines from the foundries, as the coal had been divided from steel production in Silesia, in order to reduce the economic influence of any of the successful German claimants. The ore mines were reorganized and placed under a Reich trustee, Karl Raabe of the Reichswerke, where they remained until recaptured by the Allies.[45]

The Reichswerke then laid claim to the largest slice of the available steel capacity, the huge Arbed trust in Luxemburg, the de Wendel concern, itself a multi-national with business interests in Holland, Germany, and Luxemburg, and to the former Thyssen holdings which were now forfeit to the state after his flight from Germany in 1939; in all a total of 1.4 million tons of steel capacity. Mannesmann, Krupp, Gutehoffnungshütte, Hoesch, and the Stahlverein were all denied what they had asked for. The remaining French plants were allocated to German firms on a trustee basis. Flick, after pressing his claim forcefully on Göring as compensation for 'losses' in Silesia, was successful in acquiring trusteeship of the Rombacher Hüttenwerke. The remainder was distributed among a number of smaller Ruhr and Saar companies, Röchling, Klöckner, and the Neunkircher Eisenwerke. There was to be no question of French participation.[46]

The question of ownership was sidestepped by introducing a system of trusteeship, though there was little alternative since the former French owners refused to sell their participations voluntarily.[47] Trusteeship was, however, unpopular with the Ruhr firms, which according to Ernst Poensgen, head of the Stahlverein, 'wanted a free hand in the companies. Any attempt to gain control over the statutes or the appointment of the board of directors would not be suitable.' Nor was the Ruhr satisfied with the scale of Reichswerke gains, 'the cherries in the cake', complained Poensgen.[48] No doubt the Ruhr was influenced by the widespread feeling

[44] Case V, Flick Doc. Book xiB, NI-3539, Flick conference, 16 Aug. 1940.

[45] Case XI, Pleiger Doc. Book x, 3–9, Beckenbauer affidavit, 8 June 1948, who claims that Pleiger too had wanted to keep the mines and steelworks together before he found out the extent of Ruhr claims; NA Reichswerke files, T83 Roll 81, frames 3452359–60, 'Liefergemeinschaft der Eisengruben in Lothringen, 1944'.

[46] Case XI, Pros. Doc. Book 113, 1–3, NI-049, Göring decree on the distribution of smelting works in Lorraine and Luxemburg, 5 Feb. 1941; NI-3548, Flick to Göring, 1 Nov. 1940; Case V, Flick Doc. Book xiB, NI-3539, Flick conference, 16 Aug. 1940, 3; NI-2508, Chief of Civil Administration of Enemy Property to Flick, 20 Feb. 1941.

[47] Case V, Flick Doc. Book xiA, NI-5385, interview between Herr Frohwein and M. Couve de Murville, 4 Oct. 1941.

[48] Ibid., Book xiB, NI-3542, Flick memorandum, 2 Oct. 1940; NA Reichswerke files, T83 Roll 76, frame 3447887, RWM discussion, 27 June 1941.

that the war was effectively over with the defeat of France, and could not see why the state would not permit the immediate sale of the plants where this was feasible rather than institute a trustee system. Though they were able to make qualified gains in both Poland and France, the state kept overall control of both regions, dictating prices, product policy, and conditions of access to the captured plants, while local Nazi officials, Frank and Winkler in Poland, Bürckel in Lorraine, pursued ambitions of their own.

III

From the world of industrial 'games of intrigue' it is possible to disentangle four distinct types of multi-national activity within the New Order economy of occupied Europe; direct state ownership, monopoly organizations with mixed participation; trusteeship; and direct private ownership.

1. Direct State Ownership or Participation

The German state, via the state holding companies Vereinigte Industrieunternehmungen AG (VIAG) and Vereinigte Elektrizitäts- und Bergwerke AG (VEBA), or state-owned German industrial undertakings, was the largest single beneficiary of the German strategy of direct investment outside the Reich. The foremost example was the Reichswerke, which took over ownership of a large part of Austrian, Czech, and Polish industry and mining, setting up an enormous conglomerate with assets in excess of RM 5,000m. Reichswerke participation was also built up through the activity of the major subsidiaries that it took over. Rheinmetall–Borsig for example, had substantial holdings in the Dutch armaments firms NV Nederlandsche Maschinenfabriek Artillerie Inrictungen and the ship-engine company Werkspoor NV, Amsterdam. In France Rheinmetall was given the management of the major armaments works, including Schneider et Cie, on a trustee basis.[49] In Slovakia the Reichswerke eventually acquired ownership of the subsidiary of the Brünner Waffenwerke, Pod brezova Berg- und Hütten AG, from the Slovakian government in 1941; and via Vítkovice it acquired the Ruda Bergbau und Hüttenbetriebe.[50] Reichswerke activities were also expanded through setting up new plants in occupied territories: the Linz iron and steel complex, the massive Eisenwerke Oberdonau (which was by the end of the war the major supplier of tank hulls and turrets), and the

---

[49] *Hermann Göring Complex*, 24.   [50] Ibid. 20–1.

hydrogenation plant at Brüx. All of these new plants were supplied with resources of coal, iron ore, or steel from other businesses taken over by the Reichswerke. In some cases the Reichswerke co-operated with private firms in buying up foreign assets, as in the case of Krupp in Yugoslavia, where the Reichswerke prevented exclusive control over raw materials from falling into private hands.[51]

The regime was also able to use the state-owned multi-nationals as a 'battering ram' for entering economies that were not occupied territory. Capital participation in Romanian heavy industry, including oil, was made possible by acquiring assets in Austria and Czechoslovakia which held shares in Romanian firms. Political pressure was put on the Romanian government to accept German capital penetration through German state-owned firms. The Reichswerke by 1941 enjoyed a 50 per cent stake in a joint German–Romanian holding company, 'Rogifer', which managed the affairs of the bulk of Romanian heavy industry.[52]

2. Monopoly Organizations

Early in the war the Four Year Plan office arrived at the decision to set up in the New Order economy a number of continental monopoly organizations made up of a mixture of state-owned and private firms regulated by the state, which would accept responsibility for investment policy, pricing, and trade. The first of these organizations were for textiles and oil. The state also set up territorial monopoly organizations; the best example was the Berg- und Hüttengesellschaft Ost in the Soviet Union, which took over control of all the industry in a given region on behalf of the state. The object of the monopoly organization was to vest control of important industries in state hands, so that the final structure of the New Order economy could be determined in German interests and not simply through market forces.[53]

The oil monopoly, Kontinentale Öl, was set up for strategic purposes as well. Göring argued that a commodity so vital in wartime would have to be kept permanently in state hands after the war. Set up in March 1941, the oil monopoly was run by Funk on Göring's behalf. Capital was fixed initially at RM 50m, RM 30m. to be held by the Reichswerke subsidiary Borussia GmbH, the remaining RM 20m. to come from a mixture of state

[51] Ibid. 12; on Yugoslavia see R. Schönfeld. 'Deutsche Rohstoffsicherungspolitik in Jugoslawien 1934–1944', *Vierteljahreshefte für Zeitgeschichte*, 24 (1976), 220–33.

[52] Overy 'Göring "Multi-National" Empire', 279–82.

[53] M. Riedel, *Eisen und Kohle für das Dritte Reich* (Göttingen, 1973), 305–9. The monopoly was set up according to Göring's officials 'to prevent violent competition by German industrial firms for the Russian plants'; see Case XI, Pros. Doc. Book 124, NI-5581, circular of Wirtschaftsgruppe Eisen- und Stahlindustrie, 21 Aug. 1941; Case V, Flick Doc. Book xiiiC, NI-5262, note of a conversation with Col. John, for Flick, 13 Aug. 1941.

and private chemical and oil companies. The Borussia shares carried multiple voting rights so that control would always be vested in the state. The monopoly was not only responsible for all oil exploration and production within Germany, but took over the oil holdings of enemy powers as well. This included the Belgian Concordia company, in which 45 per cent of the capital was in German hands, the French Colombia firm, and Südost-Chemie, which was linked with the Romanian Petrol-Block, in which the Reichswerke had direct participation. By 1941 Germany effectively controlled 47 per cent of Romanian oil output. Negotiations began in 1941 with Standard Oil for the transfer of their Hungarian oilfields, valued at $30m., but were interrupted by the outbreak of war in December. It was also planned to take the whole of the Russian oil industry, once it was captured, under the monopoly's control.[54]

The general drift of state thinking on the post-war economy can be illustrated by the recommendations drawn up by Paul Rheinländer a Reichswerke director, for the control of the European iron, steel, and coal industries after the war. The long-term goal was to reorganize the industry on co-ordinated lines on a continental basis. The Ruhr would be restricted to its pre-war level of output and the large planned increases in iron and steel output would come in Austria, Czechoslovakia, Silesia, and from the captured resources in the Soviet Union. The whole industry was to be subject to regulations on resource use and price determined by the state, which would also provide the investment to build up the eastern economy. In this way major economic resources—the coal and ore—would be utilized on the basis of national needs and not for quick economic returns.[55] The monopolies were designed to enable the state to plan economic policy on major industries in a large multi-national empire in which the sheer scale of the operation precluded reliance on private initiative, though it did not exclude the survival of private ownership.

3. Trusteeship

In addition to direct ownership and monopoly organizations, the state also set up a trustee system in which private and state firms alike took over and operated captured businesses on behalf of the state. This did not imply ownership, as party and state officials were at pains to point out, but was

---

[54] NA Reichswerke files, T83 Roll 81, frame 3452276, Göring decree on the eastern economy, 27 July 1941; Case XI, Pros. Doc. Book 124, NI-10797, memorandum on the founding of Kontinentale Öl AG, 21 Jan. 1941; NI-10162, minutes of the second meeting of the managing board of Kontinentale Öl, 13 Jan. 1942; M. Pearton, *Oil and the Roumanian State* (Oxford, 1971), 228–31.

[55] Salzgitter Konzernarchiv (SAK), 12/155/4, Paul Rheinländer, 'Vorschlag zur Ausgestaltung der Eisenindustrie im Grossdeutschen Wirtschaftsraum nach dem Kriege', 1941.

dictated by the wartime necessity of getting captured industries working again as quickly as possible on war orders. Trusteeship involved the granting of a special operating contract to the firm involved on the understanding that most of the money and equipment necessary would be provided by the state, and that the trustee was responsible for operating the works as economically as possible. There were various grounds for justifying trusteeship. It was used in cases where sheer confiscation or purchase was not possible, for example enemy property whose future had to be decided after the war, or the property of foreign nationals whose identity or whereabouts could not be discovered. It was used most commonly by the armed forces when allocating foreign armaments capacity to German firms, an area where there was in general less direct German investment; or in those cases where the question of ownership had formal political implications and could not be dealt with adequately until after the war, for example in Lorraine or the Soviet Union.[56]

For private German firms trusteeship was a rather mixed blessing. It left considerable control in the hands of the state and gave a difficult responsibility to the trustee, under wartime conditions, to fulfil the state's requirements. The state could also decide who the trustees should be, discriminating against firms on political grounds. This was certainly the explanation on a number of occasions for the exclusion of the Stahlverein from trustee arrangements.[57] Trusteeship also meant the loss of personnel and equipment from the German parent company which, in the case of the trustee system in the USSR, many could ill afford to supply by the middle of the war, and much of which might have been more effectively utilized in Germany. Nor did they operate on equal terms with the state firms. The Reichswerke in Russia had better access to equipment and labour than the private firms, and when the area was evacuated in 1943, helped itself to large amounts of machinery from all the Russian plants while allocating almost nothing to the other trustees.[58] It was hardly surprising given that the BHO was run by Reichswerke managers, who had only agreed to allow private firms access to Soviet production on the grounds that the state simply could not manage to provide the resources quickly enough to get the area working again.

When the private firms did assume trusteeship, the agreement bound

[56] NA Göring Stabsamt, T84 Roll 7, frames 6704–6, memorandum on trusteeship by Hans Winkler, 21 Apr. 1942.

[57] Case V, Flick Doc. Book xiiiB, NI-3665, memorandum of a discussion between Pleiger and Flick, 11 Nov. 1942. Pleiger said he would prefer to exclude the Vereinigte Stahlwerke, and divide up the trustee plants between Flick and the Reichswerke. On VS claims in the region see ibid., NI-5722, Flick memorandum 26 June 1941.

[58] Ibid., Flick Doc. Book xiiiB, NI-4500, minutes of a conference 21 Feb. 1944 and NI-5737, Burkart to Flick, 29 Apr. 1944; Case XI, Pros. Doc. Book 124, NI-2695, BHO Notiz, 17 June 1943 and NI-4437, BHO circular to all trustee firms, 1 Nov. 1943.

them closely to the state. Flick's agreement with the BHO was so one-sided that his advisers recommended that he demand a leasehold instead: 'whoever signed this contract would be delivering himself body and soul to the BHO'.[59] But under pressure Flick accepted trusteeship. The contract spelt out that 'The sponsored plant is neither legally nor economically part of the home plant of the sponsor.' All objects produced became automatically the property of the Reich, prices were determined by the BHO, and sales as well. The trustee was not allowed under any circumstances to negotiate for credit for operating the plant, and could use his own funds only with the approval of the BHO.[60] In Lorraine Flick found that his trusteeship of the Rombach plant did not even entitle him to tax concessions available in the Reich, which he argued would result (given the difficulties of starting up capacity in the region again) in an operating loss to the trustee. Nor did the contract contain any reference to trustees having preferential claims for direct ownership of the plants after the war.[61] Although some officials in the Economics Ministry and the Finance Ministry were in favour of selling the plants held in trust to private industry after the war, and said as much, it was by no means clear that this would have been the outcome. Nazi administrators were reluctant to make any firm commitments and kept their options open on the future of state control. While this did not exclude privatization, trusteeship did not provide a full guarantee of future ownership by any particular trustee.

4. Direct Private Ownership and Participation

Direct investment by private German firms was limited during the war by the claims of the state firms and the reluctance of the state to offer more than operating contracts in captured plants to meet war requirements. There were German firms with foreign affiliates, Mannesmann, AEG, IG Farben, and the Stahlverein among the most prominent, but apart from the example of IG Farben these do not seem to have been used as stepping-stones to the substantial expansion of multi-national activity during the war. Some businesses acquired by the state in the first instance were returned to private ownership during the war, particularly in Silesia. Where this did happen the state and party authorities appear to have given preference not to the big concerns but to smaller firms which could not become 'multi-national' without state help. This may well have fitted with ideological preferences but it also had the effect of creating a number of

---

[59] Case V, Flick Doc. Book xiiiC, NI-3622, letter from Bernhard Weiss to Siemag, 12 Dec. 1942.

[60] Ibid., NI-3659, 'Principles of the management of trustee plants of the BHO, Nov. 1942'.

[61] Ibid., Flick Doc. Book xiB, NI-1651, Flick file note, 7 May 1941.

smaller, less organized, and more dependent multi-nationals which would relatively strengthen the influence of the state. It had the further result of strengthening the competitive position of the big state-backed multi-nationals against domestically based heavy industry by restricting its access to foreign assets necessary for post-war competition (which was almost certainly Pleiger's object).[62]

The most successful private firm to operate on multi-national lines was IG Farben. There are a number of explanations for this. In the first place the firm was closely identified with the aims of the Nazi state from at least 1936 onwards, even to the extent of sharing personnel with the Four Year Plan. It was able to use state power quite unscrupulously in its pursuit of corporate strategy. Secondly, IG Farben was the largest pre-war German concern, in a very capital-intensive and technically advanced sector. It possessed as a result the personnel and organizational skills necessary to make the transition to multi-nationalism rapidly which other firms lacked. After the defeat of Poland IG Farben defended its claims in the Polish chemical industry on the grounds that 'Only the IG is in a position to make experts available.'[63]

IG Farben policy in Europe was conditioned not only by its commitment to the state's plans for building up a resource base for major war in central Europe, but by its desire to develop a continental-wide organization to serve its commercial interests as well. IG Farben planned to set up chemical raw-material plants in south-eastern Europe to meet the needs of local agriculture, but to keep more sophisticated processing in the hands of the parent company in Germany and its affiliates in Austria and Czechoslovakia, which it acquired in 1938–9. During the war IG Farben used its Dynamit AG plant in Slovakia as a stepping-stone to expansion into central Europe and the Balkans. It acquired shares in six other chemical companies as well as setting up seven new plants, mainly to meet expanded demand for basic chemicals from the German armed forces. However, the main Czech chemical producer, the Prager Verein, remained independent of IG Farben during the war, and became its major competitor in south-eastern Europe. Nor was IG Farben successful in its efforts to take over any of the Belgian Solvay company holdings, since ownership was vested in two Swiss holding companies.[64] In Poland chemical works were either bought outright by IG Farben or operated as trustee through arrangement with Frank and the SS. In France IG Farben again used the power of the state in its negotiations with the French dyestuffs industry, which was forced to accept reorganization into a single

[62] Case XI, Pleiger Doc. Book vB, 51–2, minutes of the meeting of the Aufsichtsrat of the Reichswerke AG, 15 Nov. 1944.
[63] Borkin, *IG Farben*, 98.
[64] Radandt, 'IG Farbenindustrie', 79–84, 99–103.

holding company, Francolor, in which IG Farben would have a 51 per cent interest, in return for transferring to French industrialists 1 per cent of IG stock. The agreement was drawn up and signed in November 1941, drafted in such a way that IG Farben hoped to be able to retain its position in the French industry, even if Germany were to lose the war. This agreement gave IG Farben effective control over the European chemical industry of occupied Europe, and placed it in a strong position in negotiating marketing agreements with Italian and Swiss competitors.[65] The ability of IG Farben to exercise considerable influence on Nazi officials in its efforts to acquire interests in foreign businesses and in discussing the shape of the post-war European economy gave it a uniquely privileged position during the war years.

IV

The scope and character of multi-nationalism in occupied Europe was dependent in almost all cases on the role of the German state, either directly or indirectly. The same was true of the operation of multi-national firms, which were conditioned by policies over which they had only limited control. Of course the war distorted this development, by placing priority on industrial strategies to help the German war effort; so much so that on occasion firms resisted or obstructed efforts by the state to promote what they regarded as costly or poorly planned projects, aluminium production in Norway, for example.[66] Though war production involved a notion of efficiency—the justification given by the state for the reorganization of the Sudeten lignite mines, or the rationalization of ore supply from Lorraine— purely financial considerations were never a decisive factor. Pleiger claimed, not altogether truthfully, that 'money plays no part'.[67] It was certainly the case that the war encouraged rising costs and large sectors of the Reichswerke organization never made an operating profit during the war, despite the efforts of the Finance Ministry to restrict subsidies to those cases where a fixed contract for regular repayments of Reich loans could be established. Where operating profits were made in the occupied areas, they were usually swallowed up through reinvestment, helped by generous tax allowances for depreciation which released more funds to be ploughed back. The effect of this financial policy was to reduce the flow of

---

[65] Borkin, *IG Farben*, 100–9.
[66] A. S. Milward, *The Fascist Economy in Norway* (Oxford, 1972), 180, 207–8.
[67] NA Reichswerke files, Roll 76, frames 3446885–6, letter from Pleiger to Krupp, 8 Apr. 1940; on France see Roll 80, frame 3452713, 'Rationalisierung innerhalb der lothringisch-luxemburgischen Eisenhüttenindustrie, 20 Mar. 1942; on the Sudetenland, Roll 77, frames 3448199–200, Aktennotiz 'Befahrung der Sudetenländische Bergbau AG', 16 July 1943.

payments to the Reichswerke concern from its major subsidiaries, which in turn inhibited profit growth and the repayment of state loans.[68] Firms acting as trustees rather than owners had a better chance of securing a regular return because they depended for most of their operating capital on the state.

But the government also had long-term plans for the development of European industry that went well beyond military priorities. The large iron, steel, and armaments complex at Linz, for example, not only met war needs but was to be the core of a new central European industrial region deliberately centred in Hitler's homeland. The same was true of the large new investments at Vítkovice, which were designed to turn it into 'the eastern industrial pillar of the Reich supplying steel to the industries of the Protectorate, Poland and the Ukraine'.[69] It is clear that at least some of the state's capital penetration strategy was based on the need to secure adequate supplies of industrial raw materials to feed the finishing plants of the captured region, and to rationalize the transfer of resources between them, or from the occupied areas to the Reich. How extensive these transfers were and how rationally multinational operations were conducted is, however, difficult to tell from the available evidence.

It would be wrong to conclude from all this that the German government had a co-ordinated programme for its industrial policy abroad. Differences in the political and socio-economic conditions of the occupied areas produced different treatment from the German rulers, particularly in places like Belgium and northern France, where the army kept control. Political conflicts and the pressures of war made it difficult to be consistent in dealing with cases in different parts of Europe, or to be able to see the situation clearly as a whole. By the end of the war industrial planning was simply improvised. The largest multi-national, the Reichswerke, was a model of inorganic growth. Its policy of grabbing everything that came its way guaranteed foreign resources for the war effort, but created considerable confusion, giving it what one manager called a 'Warenhauscharakter' (the character of a department store).[70] The

---

[68] Overy, 'Göring's "Multi-National" Empire', 289; Case XI, Pleiger Doc. Book vB, meeting of the Aufsichtsrat of the Reichswerke AG, 15 Nov. 1944; on reinvestment and depreciation at Vítkovice see ibid., Doc. Book viiA, Extraordinary meeting of the shareholders of the Witkowitzer Gewerkschaft, 28 Aug. 1940 in which it was decided to suspend any distribution of profits in 1939–40 in favour of new investment.

[69] Case XI, Pleiger Doc. Book viiA, 57, fiscal report of the Gewerkschaftsvorstand of Witkowitzer Gewerkschaft, 1941.

[70] NA Reichswerke files, T83 Roll 75, frame 3446010, Vorschlag Pleiger zum Aufbau der HGW, 9 Nov. 1941.

reorganization of 1941 and 1942, brought about through the complaints of its leading managers, highlighted the unsystematic growth of the concern. During 1941 the organization was rationalized into product groups, smaller, less essential firms were weeded out and closed down, and a clearer demarcation of managerial roles worked out. In 1942 the Reichswerke abandoned armaments production altogether, which was then brought into Speer's system of industrial committees, though it remained predominantly in state hands. Steyr and Rheinmetall were held by the Bank der deutschen Luftfahrt, and Skoda and the Brünner Waffenwerke were converted into a state-backed holding company, the Waffenunion. Efforts by Krupp and the Stahlverein to assume ownership were vetoed by Göring.[71]

On the whole Reichswerke managers in the remaining sectors displayed a good grasp of the problems facing a large multi-national organization and were eventually able to implement operational strategies to cope with them. The role of the central organization was, according to Pleiger, 'setting up production programmes in co-ordination, sharing technical experience, joint support between companies, regulating the questions of markets, division of market areas among the companies, price freight questions, etc.'[72] Issues concerning the nature of corporate strategy and management were not ignored during the war and may well have provided important lessons for the post-war period. Pleiger, for one, was well aware that peace would bring a very different economic environment. So too was IG Farben, the other major multi-national, whose main priority was to strengthen its market position through direct investment and trading agreements, while getting the government to share in the cost of capital growth and to alter the political conditions for its negotiations. In return IG Farben co-ordinated its product and labour policy with military requirements.

The government did, however, play a central part in providing the investment funds needed to expand abroad, through either buying up shares, setting up new plants, or expanding existing ones. This was true not only for state firms, but for private firms and trustees as well. The government did so to help the war effort, but also because the current state of the private capital market in Germany might have made it difficult for the state to rely to any great extent on private funds for expansion. Shares

---

[71] For details on the background to reorganization see R. J. Overy *Goering: The 'Iron Man'* (London, 1984), 144–6, 212–14; *Hermann Göring Complex*, 27–9.

[72] NA Reichswerke files, T83 Roll 75, frames 3446008–17, Vorschlag Pleiger zum Aufbau der HGW, 9 Nov. 1941; 3445813, Bericht der Arbeitsgruppe für Verkaufsfragen des Ausschusses für Konzernorganisation, n.d. [June 1941?]; *TWC* trial transcripts, Case XI, 14847–8.

abroad were acquired in the main through the major German banks, which were then paid a commission by the state in addition to the purchase price of the shares where the state itself acquired ownership. New investment abroad was met either directly from state funds, usually via the major state financial institutions, or from occupation levies or forced loans from blocked clearing accounts with other European countries.[73]

There were a number of motives for investment, though they were all closely related to the war, or to Göring's strategy on direct investment. The state also found it necessary to promote technology transfer in order to raise foreign plants to the same operating level as German ones, which involved considerable investment in new machinery and equipment. Rheinmetall calculated that its sales per head in 1941 were 50–100 per cent higher than the machinery and arms plants taken over in Austria and Czechoslovakia.[74] The Finance Ministry report on the Czech Brünner Maschinenfabrik in 1940 pointed out that its capacity had been poorly organized and underutilized, and that it required some Kčs 32m. of new investment over three years to modernize it. During that period it was recommended that all profits should be ploughed back into the firm.[75] In other cases large investments were needed to repair war damage, as in the case of the BHO, which was set up with an initial capital of RM 100m. In all areas where the state directly acquired ownership or exercised trusteeship very large funds were spent on investment or authorized to be spent on future expansion. The details are set out in Table 10.1. These were very large sums indeed, and gave the Reichswerke organization, which was granted Reich loans totalling RM 1,500m. during the the war, considerable economic influence through sheer scale in the areas where it was active. By comparison, IG Farben only invested an additional Kčs 124m. in its Slovakian subsidiary between 1938 and 1943, less than one-tenth of Reichswerke investments in Czechoslovakia.[76] The state's long-term plans were greater still. Investment at Vítkovice was to increase by a total of Kčs 995m. in a programme planned to go on into peacetime; at Sudetenländische Treibstoff the increase was RM 607m., and in Silesia RM 803m.[77]

---

[73] RIIA, *Hitler's Europe*, 205–7; on the activities of the Dresdner Bank see FO 646 460, Office of Military Government of Germany (US), *Report on Dresdner Bank Investigation*, esp. 71–3.

[74] NA Reichswerke files, T83 Roll 77, frames 3449374–5, Rheinmetall-Borsig, report on monthly sales, 26 Feb. 1943.

[75] Ibid., frames 3449351–8, RFM report 10 Sept. 1940.

[76] Radandt, 'IG Farbenindustrie', 92.

[77] NA Reichswerke files, T83 Roll 76, 3447016, 2nd report of Sudetenländische Treibstoff, Sept. 1942; Case XI, Pleiger Doc. Book viiA, 51, 5th meeting of Aufsichtsrat, 30 June 1942; Doc. Book viii, 58–60, BO to Reichswerke, 24 June 1941.

TABLE 10.1. *German state investment in European industry: selected statistics 1938–1945*

Austria (RMm.)		
Steyr-Daimler-Puch	328	1938–44
Alpine Montangesellschaft	140	1939–45
Steirische Gussstahl	7	1939–45
Czechoslovakia (Kčsm.)		
Sudetenländische Treibstoff (RMm.)	420	1939–42
Skoda	455	1939–41
Erste Brünner Maschinenfabrik	32	1939–42
Brünner Waffenwerke	300	1939–41
Vítkovice	504	1940–2
Poldi	235	1940–4
Poland (RMm.)		
Bergwerksverwaltung Oberschlesien	120	1940–4
France (RMm.)		
Hüttenwerksverwaltung Westmark	55	1941–4
Soviet Union (RMm.)		
Berg-und Hüttenwerksverwaltung Ost	100	1942

Sources: TWC, Case XI transcripts, 14895; IWM Speer Collection, FD 787/46, Sitzung des Aufsichtsrats der Steyr–Daimler–Puch, 8 Sept. 1944; NA Reichswerke files, T83 Roll 76, frames 3447016–43, second report of Sudetenländische Treibstoff, 1941/2, Sept. 1942; *Hermann Göring Complex*, 19; Case XI, Pleiger Doc. Bk. viiA, p. 51, Bk. viiB, pp. 30–4, 51–3, Bk. x, p. 65; Riedel, *Eisen und Kohle*, 303; Case V, Flick Doc. Bk xiiiA, NI-4332, first report of the BHO, Jan. 1943, 3

The state also influenced other aspects of multi-national decision-making. The Four Year Plan fixed prices for major commodities, and did so to fit as far as possible with the interests of the war economy. Russian iron ore and coal, for example, was sold at 50 per cent of the price in the Reich to speed up the recovery of the iron and steel industry of the Donets basin. In Austria the Four Year Plan forced the Alpine Montangesellschaft to reduce its prices in line with Reich prices so that the new works at Linz could be guaranteed a cheap supply of ore.[78] It was also possible for the government to fix the exchange rate between Germany and the occupied

[78] *Hermann Göring Complex*, 11.

areas in German favour so that the transfer of resources between plants from abroad could be effected to the advantage of the German company. The Reichswerke plant at Salzgitter was supplied with coking coal from coal resources in Poland at a price below that offered by the Ruhr coal syndicate. In the early stages of the war foreign acquisitions, particularly in Czechoslovakia, were used to provide exportable goods which could no longer be produced in Germany but which were essential to provide the foreign exchange to buy strategic imports. Much more research needs to be done on the transfer of resources from occupied Europe to industry in the Reich, or between subsidiaries of the same multi-national, before anything more definite can be said about sales or costs.[79]

The government's role was also important in labour policy. The management boards of the major state-owned multi-nationals were filled with state appointees, party members, civil servants, bankers and local collaborators. The state was also represented on the boards of the major private firms, and appointed the trustees responsible for administering captured businesses. There was a considerable degree of integration and overlap in managerial appointments, which made it easier to co-ordinate the activities of the major subsidiaries.[80] With manual labour there were great difficulties. The mobilization of foreign labour reserves for work in the Reich made it difficult to exploit foreign acquisitions to the full, and forced many to operate below capacity throughout the war. It also increased demand for labour in the occupied territories and pushed up costs. The wage bill at Vítkovice increased from Kčs 588m. in 1939 to Kčs 844m. in 1940 with only a 9 per cent increase in the work-force.[81] The transfer of foreign labour to the Reich forced foreign subsidiaries to use more semi-skilled and unskilled labour which was cheaper, or to use more machinery which improved labour productivity. Real wages and conditions of work deteriorated throughout occupied Europe as the war went on and the German authorities adopted more draconian and exploitative labour policies.

The effect of the foreign labour programme was to make it difficult for foreign subsidiaries to supply what was required of them; and to make them more dependent on prisoners and slave labour, which was much less productive because of the appalling conditions under which forced labourers worked. In Russia the workers were paid only one-eighth of German wages, and produced less than half the amount of coal per head

[79] Overy, 'Göring's "Multi-National" Empire', 290.
[80] For a full list of Reichswerke directors and managers see NA Reichswerke files, T83 Roll 74, frames 3445227–362.
[81] Case XI, Pleiger Doc. Book viiA 40, business report for financial year 1940, Witkowitzer Gewerkschaft.

of German miners.[82] The poor co-ordination between the investment priorities of the state and its foreign labour policy, which saw a stream of capital flowing out of Germany and a stream of labour flowing in, considerably reduced the usefulness of captured industry, and compromised German war-production plans. The exploitative and ill-thought out labour strategy showed that there could also be real limits to the usefulness of state help in running multi-national organizations. Some of the large sums allocated for foreign investment might from the German point of view more usefully have been kept in the Reich to encourage rationalization and productivity growth at home, which would in turn have reduced the frantic demand for foreign labour and have allowed the state real benefits in keeping an adequate supply of domestic labour in the occupied territories.

V

The Nazi occupation or conquest of most of Europe opened up for German industry the possibility of developing multi-national organization in areas where political and financial constraints had prevented expansion during the inter-war years. In practice the vacuum created by the expulsion of foreign capital was filled largely by the state in order to safeguard the region for war purposes and also to permit the Nazi government to decide what the shape of the post-war economy would be. German private capital, with the exception of IG Farben, had to be content with modest gains and a system of trusteeship. The Nazis' purpose was to prevent a scramble for the spoils of Europe by replacing the free market with a state-dominated and co-ordinated economic order embracing the whole continent. Pleiger deplored 'earlier organizations in the economy formed as pure interest groups to safeguard the interests of their members against competitors and even against the state'. The new economic order, he told Speer, was to replace the old liberal economy with the supervision of the Nazi state.[83] These political ambitions gave the policy of direct investment a highly political character. This fact, coupled with the growing risks as the war situation deteriorated, seems to have restrained most of private German industry from pressing its claims in Europe too forcefully, except in France and Silesia, where the risks seemed less and the gains much greater. The high point of private industrial ambitions was the summer of

---

[82] Ibid., Pros. Doc. Book 124, NI-5261, minutes of meeting of BHO Verwaltungsrat, 31 Mar. 1943; Case V, Flick Doc. Book xiiiA, NI-4332, first report of the BHO, Jan. 1943, 7–8.
[83] SAK 14/150/12, Pleiger to Speer, 11 Aug. 1944.

1940, when many businessmen, and other Germans, assumed that the war was over and that Germany could return to the position she enjoyed in 1914.

For the duration of the war corporate strategy was determined primarily by the needs of war. Investment and labour programmes were both geared to German war demands, though often so poorly co-ordinated that less was extracted from the host countries than German leaders wanted. The relationship between Germany and the host countries was one of exploitation, in the sense that the state used its political power to ensure the most favourable terms for German foreign participation even in areas not actually occupied by German forces. There was, however, a transfer of resources from the Reich of considerable size, involving a certain amount of technology transfer (though in the case of the Soviet Union and France it was all transferred back again to the Reich as German forces retreated). Host countries gained benefits only in the sense that some domestic production and employment was maintained, and even expanded in selected sectors, though on unfavourable terms, particularly for labour. In all other respects the relationship was very one-sided, and there is every reason to suppose that, had Germany won the war, this relationship would have been a permanent feature of the New Order.

11

Rationalization and the 'Production Miracle' in Germany during the Second World War

THE rationalization of industrial production played a significant part in transforming the productive performance of all the major warring states between 1939 and 1945. Wartime economic pressure, brought about as a result of the high demand for industrial products and the limited resources available, compelled efforts to use industrial capacity more efficiently. The state had a primary interest in getting the most out of industry: 'the greatest output is to be achieved with the smallest expenditure of resources,' ordered Hitler in March 1942.[1] Rationalization in the context of war production meant, according to the Luftwaffe's time-and-motion expert, 'the systematic saving of materials and manpower in order to achieve the highest possible quantities of output'.[2] This involved the application of modern mass-production techniques and the scientific management of labour and material resources, not with the profit motive in mind, but in order to approach as far as possible the optimum use of national resources for the country's war effort.

Rational production made most progress in the United States before the war. Automated production and scientific management had become characteristic of a range of industries, but was associated chiefly with the motor and electrical industries. Rational methods had begun to appear in Europe in the 1920s, but the impact of the slump and the depressed state of the European economy in the 1930s inhibited its development. It featured mainly in the European car industry, and was not general even there. During the war rationalized production spread rapidly in American war industry. When British officials and industrialists visited the United States in 1942 on a mission to investigate the American aviation industry, they found an unbridgeable gap between British practice and the scale and modernity of American plants. Efforts were made in Britain in the last

---

[1] NA, Microcopy T83, Roll 76 frame 3447503, OKW, Führerbefehl, 21 Mar. 1942.
[2] NA T177, Roll 14, frame 3698898, 'Rationalisierung der Luftwaffengerät-Fertigung', 1 June 1941.

years of war to plan production and the flow of resources and components more rationally, and to modernize British factory practice.[3]

Progress was also slow in Germany. When British technical experts visited German plants at the end of the war they found factory practice there was not as different from their own as they had expected. In both states industry exploited rational methods where it was feasible to do so. The degree of automation and rational labour and resource utilization was considerably higher in both economies by the war's end. The United States Strategic Bombing Survey concluded in 1945 that 'the expansion of German industrial output from 1939 to 1944 was made possible largely by improvements in the productivity of labour'. The survey found that most of the 30 per cent increase occurred in the later period of the war and was brought about by 'simplification, standardization, and a certain modernization of industry long accustomed to highly skilled workers and multi-purpose machines'.[4] It has long been accepted that rationalization played a part in the so-called 'production miracle' in Germany between 1942 and 1944, though its nature and effects have not been assessed or measured in much detail. The survey that follows here is a preliminary assessment of how and why rationalization was introduced into the German war economy and of the extent to which it was responsible for the trebling of weapons output in Germany between 1941 and 1944.

I

The impact of rationalization after 1941 can only be understood in the wider framework of the development of Germany's military economy from the late 1930s. During the period of accelerated rearmament in Germany after 1936 the demands of the state for military production and the development of strategic heavy industry together placed enormous demands on German resources. It was recognized that greater rationalization would reduce these strains and some efforts were made before the outbreak of war to encourage better factory practice and more

[3] Public Record Office, Kew, London (PRO), AVIA 10/104, 'Report of British mission to USA to study production methods, Sept.–Oct. 1942'. Aircraft assembly plants in the USA were four to five times the size of a typical British plant. On changing practice in British firms see W. Hornby, *Factories and Plant* (HMSO, 1958), 299–334. On planning in Britain and America see A. Cairncross, *Planning in Wartime* (London, 1991), esp. 7–41, 158–71.

[4] USSBS, Report 134A, *Industrial Sales, Output and Productivity, Pre-War Area of Germany 1939–1944* (Washington, DC, Mar. 1946), 17, 23. For more recent accounts see L. Zumpe, *Wirtschaft und Staat in Deutschland, i. 1933 bis 1945* (Berlin, 1980), 340–3; D. Eichholtz, *Geschichte der deutschen Kriegswirtschaft 1939–1945, ii. 1941–1943* (Berlin, 1985), 265–316; H.-J. Braun, *The German Economy in the Twentieth Century* (London, 1990), 129–32.

rational labour use, and to simplify and standardize major products and components. Much of this activity took the form of recommendations from semi-official commissions set up to advise firms about new production systems and forms of labour use. In December 1938 Hermann Göring as head of the Four Year Plan gave the Economics Minister, Walther Funk, the task of raising the overall level of industrial efficiency through 'improvements in the layout of factories, in production means and production methods'.[5] On the whole such efforts met with only limited success. Funk's powers were ill-defined and industry was generally hostile to bureaucratic intervention in the actual processes of production or in commercial strategy. In the aircraft industry, which boasted a great deal of up-to-date equipment, officials appointed to encourage standardization and scientific management found resistance from both managers and workers, who could either not understand the new processes or were reluctant to change from more conventional skilled-work methods. Industrial sectors such as motor vehicles, where modern rational production was more widespread, were poorly integrated into the military economy, and remained so in the early years of the war.[6]

With the outbreak of war in September 1939 the demands made of the industrial economy for military production expanded rapidly and substantially. The proportion of the industrial labour force engaged on orders for the armed services leapt from 21 to 55 per cent by early 1941, and was not much higher than this by 1944. In the metalworking and engineering industries, where armaments production was concentrated, almost 70 per cent of the work-force was committed to military orders by the summer of 1941, and remained at or around this level until 1944. Both these figures exceeded levels of mobilization in Britain. At the same time the output of goods for the civilian market declined sharply; by late 1940 most of the consumer industries were devoting between 40 and 50 per cent of their output to the military, leaving very little for the civilian population.[7] Labour and raw-material shortages for both military and civilian production became widespread during 1940 and 1941. When Albert Speer was appointed Armaments Minister by Hitler in February 1942 on instructions to expand war production even further, he and his

---

[5] Cited in R. Hachtmann, *Industriearbeit im 'Dritten Reich': Untersuchungen zu den Lohn- und Arbeitsbedingungen in Deutschland 1933–1945* (Göttingen, 1989), 71–2. See too M. H. Geyer, 'Soziale Sicherheit und wirtschaftliche Fortschritt: Überlegungen zum Verhältnis von Arbeitsideologie und Sozialpolitik im Dritten Reich', *Geschichte und Gesellschaft*, 15 (1989), 388–9.

[6] NA T177, Roll 14, frames 3698898–903, General-Engineer Bauer, 'Rationalisierung der Luftwaffengerät-Fertigung'; on the motor industry see BIOS, Overall Report 21, *The Motor Car Industry in Germany during the Period 1939–1945* (HMSO, 1949), 7–11.

[7] Details in R. J. Overy, 'Mobilization for Total War in Germany 1939–1941', *English Historical Review*, 103 (1988), 626–9.

colleagues regarded the task as 'scarcely soluble' on account of the 'extraordinary degree' to which the economy was already committed to war.[8]

During the first years of war the problem for the German leadership was not the extent to which resources were converted to the war effort, but the poor productive performance of the military industries for which the resources had been released. The large increase in the proportion of the industrial work-force involved in military production did not produce a proportionate increase in military output. The supply of weapons grew much more slowly than the supply of resources to produce them. Output per worker in the arms industry fell by 24 per cent between 1939 and 1941. In certain branches the performance was much worse than the average. The output of aircraft stagnated between 1939 and 1941. Though the industry got 50 per cent more labour, the output of finished aircraft increased by only 15 per cent. The output of tanks and armoured vehicles was only one-third of British levels in 1941; the output of heavy vehicles actually declined between 1940 and 1941. Britain outproduced Germany in most major classes of weapon in the first three years of war, even though a smaller proportion of the British industrial labour force was converted to war production, and despite the fact that Germany had more than twice the steel output and a total labour force half as large again as the British.[9] This was not what Hitler wanted. In December 1939, and again in the summer of 1940 and the summer of 1941, he ordered very great increases in military output of all kinds. Hitler wanted German production to exceed the levels of the First World War. Speer told his interrogators in 1945 that Hitler 'knew the supply figures of the last war in detail and could reproach us with the fact that the output in 1917/18 was higher than we could show in 1942'. According to Speer 'these were requirements which had been fixed in his mind for a long time. They were in nearly every case three to six times the armament production in 1941.'[10] In the end the output of finished weapons matched neither the quantity of resources transferred to war production nor the plans insisted upon by Hitler.

There are plenty of explanations for the low level of productive performance, many of which were recognized by officials at the time. The

[8] IWM, Speer Collection, FD 4369/45, Albert Speer, 'Rede auf der Grosskundgebung im Sportpalast, Berlin, 5 Juni 1943', 6–7.

[9] On aircraft production see BA-MA RL3/46 'Gefolgschaft für Flugzeugzellen-Herstellung, 1 Apr. 1940'; USSBS, European Report 4, Aircraft Industry Division Report, (Washington, DC, Jan. 1947), charts 6–7; on lorries, USSBS Report 77, German Motor Vehicles Report (Washington, DC, 1946), 8.

[10] IWM, Speer Collection, Box 368, Report 54, Speer Interrogation 13 July 1945. The technical interrogation reports were based mainly on written submissions from the German officials rather than on oral testimony. Some officials had access to reports and statistics in compiling their responses.

economy had to cope with completing expensive capital projects in industrial sectors essential for war as well as producing larger quantities of finished weapons. The synthetic oil and rubber programmes, the chemical plans essential for expanding the output of explosives, the expansion of domestic iron-ore and steel output, the expansion of facilities and plant for armaments, all of these soaked up substantial quantities of labour, materials, and managerial effort. The problems produced by the competition for resources might well have mattered less if there had existed an effective and co-ordinated administration for the war economy to sort out the different claims and organize priorities. In practice priority was claimed for every new programme, so that a real ordering of needs was difficult to produce. The armed forces demanded more resources and capacity on a pro rata basis to meet every new programme. The wartime economic administration developed in a fragmented and piecemeal way with a great deal of jurisdictional conflict and little centralization and co-ordination.

The situation was made worse by the tension that existed between the military and the civilian authorities. Once war had broken out the armed forces argued that weapons procurement was largely their responsibility. The technical branches of the services took the lead in developing new weapons and updating existing types, planning the quantities needed and monitoring what industry did with the orders. This was done with almost no co-operation between the three armed services, which led to endless duplication of productive effort and the jealous guardianship of resources and factory space. It was also done with virtually no attention to the wider problems of the industrial economy or with rational production methods in mind.[11]

Instead the armed forces insisted on very high technical standards at the expense of greater quantities of production, and generally remained hostile to suggestions that they should simplify the design of weapons, or reduce the number of different types, or embrace a production strategy favourable to mass production. The forces regarded mass production as something inherently incompatible with the high standards of workmanship and careful attention to technical detail and finish required by modern weaponry. They gave priority to the technical requirements of the front-line soldiers, which were assessed and communicated to industry by the engineering officers who jealously guarded their specialized and professional function.[12] Looked down on by the more glamorous combat

---

[11] For a general discussion of the role of the military see B. A. Carroll, *Design for Total War: Arms and Economics in the Third Reich* (The Hague, 1968), 213–31; R. J. Overy, *Goering: The 'Iron Man'* (London, 1984), 158–62.

[12] IWM Box 368, Report 59, interrogation of Alfried Jodl, 31 Oct. 1945; Report 95, interrogation of Friedrich Geist, 1–7, 16–17; Report 81, interrogation of Kurt Weissenborn, 5 Dec. 1945, 'German Methods of Design and Production in the Manufacture of Weapons', 1–7; Report 83, interview with Geist, Oct. 1945, 12–16.

officers, the engineers were keen to establish their authority over mere civilians. They insisted that industry would have to accept military interference at every stage of the production process, including the regular refinement and modification of weapons already in production even at the expense of the flow of finished weapons. Under these circumstances it proved very difficult to sustain long production runs and to achieve the economies in labour and resource use that large-scale production permitted. The officers responsible for procurement rarely consulted the manufacturers and saw no reason why they should. Civilian ministers were tolerated only to the extent that they continued to supply the men, materials, and machines to fuel the armaments sector. Even the Speer Ministry was regarded, according to officials of the Army Ordnance Office, as 'an inexperienced intruder'.[13] The product of poor co-ordination, inter-service rivalry, and the relative exclusion of industry from decision-making was a war economy characterized, as one official of the Labour Front put it in the autumn of 1940, by 'a steady decline in efficiency'.[14]

Manufacturers complained regularly about the disorganization and apparent planlessness of the war economy. They resented the subordinate role assigned to them by the military authorities, and argued that they could do the job better themselves.[15] But in the face of encroaching state power, industry sat back and did what it was told. Under the circumstances there was little incentive to rationalize production further. Since the mid-1930s a great many German businesses had relied on state orders. The rearmament boom brought guaranteed contracts and a steady rate of profit. Contracts were negotiated on a cost-plus basis. The state reimbursed costs in full and gave a profit rate of between 3 and 6 per cent of the costs.[16] The more expensive and inefficient the production, the higher the profit. Rather than operate existing capacity more productively, many firms built additional factory capacity and enlarged their capital assets at the expense of the state. By 1941 only a small proportion of war industry worked more than one shift, while large resources were tied up building new plant. In the absence of commercial pressure to adopt

---

[13] IWM Box 368, Report 83, 'Relationship between the Army Ordnance Board and the Speer Ministry', Oct. 1945, 2. It was Speer's view that 'the General Staff lacked any understanding of technical and economic matters', Speer interrogation, Report 56, 31 Oct. 1945, 1.

[14] IWM, EDS papers, Mi 14/294, Dr Tomberg (OKW), 'Die Probleme der deutschen Rüstungswirtschaft im Kriege, Sept. 1940', 24.

[15] e.g. BA-MA Wi I F 5.412, discussion between Col. Thomas and leading industrialists, 18 Dec. 1939. 'Industry could manage much more if clear tasks are given to it', Wilhelm Kissel of Daimler–Benz told Thomas. See too IWM EDS Mi 14/521, Bochumer Verein to Army High Command, 4 Mar. 1940.

[16] IWM Box 368, Report 90 I, interrogation of Karl Otto Saur, 3.

rational methods, industry adopted a conservative position. The collusion between armed forces which placed a premium on old-fashioned production and high quality, and industries which profited from high-cost production and asset-building, pushed up the cost of Germany's war effort and greatly exaggerated the resource problem. It also encouraged a low level of exchange of information and resources between businesses, which preferred to maintain an exclusive relationship with particular sectors of the military establishment. By the summer of 1941 German industry had arrived at a state which Karl Otto Saur, Speer's deputy in the Armaments Ministry, later described as 'completely unrationalized'.[17]

Nor did efforts to improve the productive performance of labour have much greater success. Since under the cost-plus system wage costs were passed on to the consumer—in this case the state or the armed forces—firms were under little pressure to rationalize labour use. Wage controls and limited bonuses reduced the incentive for labour to increase earnings, unlike British or American workers who benefited substantially more from war employment. Even workers on piece-rates found it difficult to increase earnings by working harder or suggesting improvements in labour use from the shop floor. When their hourly output increased the rate per unit produced was renegotiated to a lower level, so that they ended up earning the same amount of money for harder work. Foremen and workers colluded together to deceive the time-fixers and work at the pace of the slowest workers.[18] In this way labour, too, had a vested interest in maintaining high-cost, unrationalized output and workers resisted where they could attempts to reorganize factory practice or methods of payment.[19]

II

The German war economy reached an impasse in 1941. It lacked any centralized control of its key physical resources. The armed forces had adopted practices in procuring weapons which strongly militated against the introduction of mass or automated production and encouraged old-fashioned skills. Neither industry nor labour had incentives for greater efficiency and both had vested interests in preserving unrationalized, high-

---

[17] Ibid. 4.

[18] IWM Box 368, Report 85, Dr T. Hupfauer, 'Incentives used to increase the output of labour in Germany during the Second World War', 10 Sept. 1945, 5; T. Siegel, 'Wage Policy in Nazi Germany', *Politics and Society*, 14 (1985), 20.

[19] In aircraft production see BIOS Final Report 537, *Investigation of Production Control and Organisation in German Factories*, 7–8; Combined Objectives Sub-Committee (CIOS), Report XXV-42, *Survey of Production Techniques used in the German Aircraft Industry*, 6; Hachtmann, *Industriearbeit*, 198–206.

cost production. The military planners continued to pile up demands one on top of the other for technically complex weapons, with little eye to the effect these demands had on the economy as a whole; and no civilian office, whether the Four Year Plan, the Economics Ministry, or the Ministry of Munitions set up under Fritz Todt in February 1940, had sufficient political strength to compel the forces to use the economic resources more efficiently.

From the late autumn of 1940 there was a growing awareness in official circles that the demands made of the economy were producing a crisis. In November General Georg Thomas, head of the War Economy Office at Supreme Headquarters, complained that it was 'a generally acknowledged fact with all those offices concerned with formulating and carrying out the demands of the supreme leadership that they bear no relationship to the capacity of the German economy'.[20] That same month the State Secretary in the Economics Ministry, Friedrich Landfried, wrote to Hitler's headquarters to insist that the armed forces confine their programmes to the productive capacity of industry. According to Landfried, production for the military threatened to endanger not only the production of basic ration-card goods for the German consumer, but even the production of heavy-industrial goods for the war effort, and the maintenance of the transport network. By this stage of the war the armed forces took almost three-quarters of all German steel production, leaving only 5 per cent for exports and 20 per cent for all remaining industrial, service, and civilian needs.[21] In the case of most other metals the armed forces took between two-thirds and four-fifths of German supplies. Almost two-thirds of the industrial work-force were engaged in war or war-related work. By the spring of 1941 Thomas reported to a meeting of armaments inspectors that little more could be squeezed out of the remaining non-war sectors: 'On the question of cutting back civilian production, on conversion and closures there is nothing more to say.'[22]

The pressures in 1941 were especially acute in labour supply. By the spring of 1941 there were outstanding demands for a further 2.5 million men for the armed services and the arms industry. When Hitler ordered a new programme for aircraft production in July 1941 for quadrupling the size of the air force, it was calculated that another 2.9 million workers would be needed, in addition to current demands for 1.9 million from the

[20] IWM EDS Mi 14/463 file 2, OKW (WiRüAmt), memorandum 20 Nov. 1940, 'Überhöhung der Programme', 1.

[21] IWM EDS Mi 14/463 (file 2), Landfried to Keitel, 14 Nov. 1940, 1–3; Landfried to Keitel, 26 Nov. 1940, 2–4. Landfried concluded: 'I am convinced that the release of labour in larger quantities is no longer possible.'

[22] IWM, Speer collection, FD 5444/45, 'Protokoll über die Inspekteurbesprechung, "Die Ersatzlage der Wehrmacht"', 22 Feb. 1941, 64.

rest of war industry. This problem was compounded with the declining quality of labour. By 1941 a great number of skilled men had been taken by the armed forces—Thomas calculated that over 800,000 metalworkers had been conscripted by July 1941—leaving less skilled, older, or very young workers in industry. During 1941 high levels of conscription reduced the stock of young male workers by a total of 6 million, while industry was compensated for their loss with labour that was less skilled or completely untrained. The result was increasing pressure on firms to apply labour more rationally or face further falls in productivity.[23]

There was no simple solution to the labour problem. It was recognized that not much more was to be gained by increasing hours. Average hours worked per week peaked in 1941. There were limits to increasing labour input. The addition of more female workers, foreigners, and prisoners of war in 1941 failed to compensate for the loss of workers to the armed forces. The only remaining option was to utilize existing labour resources more productively in order to raise output. In February 1941 General Thomas called for *'the use of more rational methods'*.[24] It was soon discovered that much was to be gained from rationalization. That same month Thomas's office undertook a widespread survey of industrial production methods. The survey demonstrated how great was the gap between the best and worst firms producing army weapons. In the production of fuses for bombs the worst firm, AEG in Berlin, used 9.2 workers for every 1,000 fuses produced; the best firm used only 4.1. In the production of cartridge cases the best firm used 3, the worst firm 60 workers per 1,000 cases. According to the report 'the first firm worked completely mechanically, the second with handworker methods'.[25]

The same situation was evident in aircraft production. Although the air industry was the largest and most recently developed industry in Germany, with a great deal of modern plant and equipment, habits of handwork and unit rather than mass production persisted. Its productive performance since the beginning of the war was a key element in the overall production failure. Large additional resources for aircraft production produced a negligible increase in output. Lack of rationalization was by no means the only cause of the problem. Poor technical planning and leadership in the Air Ministry and major misjudgements in the development of new types of aircraft made it very difficult for aircraft producers to plan rational

[23] IWM EDS Mi 14/433 (file 2), Vortragsnotiz für Chef OKW, 'Die Lage auf dem Arbeitseinsatz', 30 June 1941; 'Vermerk über Steigerung der Luftwaffenfertigung', 27 June 1941.
[24] IWM, Speer Collection, FD 5444/45, 'Inspekteurbesprechung', 65 (italics in the original).
[25] IWM EDS Mi 14/463 (file 3), OKW (WiRüAmt),' Einwirkung des Beschäftigungsgrad auf dem Arbeitsbedarf', 7 Mar. 1941, 2–3.

production or develop long production runs. In the spring of 1941, at the prompting of the State Secretary in the Air Ministry, Erhard Milch, efforts were finally made to improve planning and productive performance.[26] In May Göring appointed an Industrial Council for the air industry, staffed by engineers and industrialists, to investigate the production crisis and recommend ways of rationalizing the industry and reducing the planning muddle.[27]

At this stage Hitler became aware of the growing economic crisis. In February he let it be known that 'he would not allow these economic difficulties to influence his plans'.[28] The planned invasion of the Soviet Union had a strong economic impulse behind it. Soviet labour, food, and raw material resources were to be seized for the German war effort. But this would not bring immediate benefits, neither would the Soviet economy supply skilled labour and factory capacity for the output of German weapons. At some point in the spring of 1941 Hitler, like Thomas, arrived at the view that rationalization was the way to increase output. On 18 May he invited Thomas and Todt to meet him at Berchtesgaden, where he outlined to them his plans for increasing the efficiency of the war economy.

Hitler took as his starting-point the view that the armed forces made too many technical demands on industry which worked against mass production, simplified construction, and ease of maintenance at the front line. He argued that military insistence on very high quality equipment 'overburdened industry excessively and endangered the whole military output in relation to the utilization of labour'. He called for a return to 'more primitive, robust construction', which would permit 'the promotion of crude mass production'.[29] His chief-of-staff, Field Marshal Keitel, drew up a decree based on Hitler's instructions, calling on the three commanders-in-chief to reduce the number and complexity of weapons ordered from industry and to promote designs which saved on raw materials and manpower.[30]

Over the next four months the original order was supplemented by further directives from Hitler's headquarters. In July Hitler authorized

[26] R. J. Overy, 'German Aircraft Production 1939–1942: A Study in the German War Economy', Ph.D. thesis, Cambridge, 1978, 23–39.

[27] IWM, Milch Documents (hereafter MD), vol. 54, 1555, Göring order establishing the Industrierat, 14 May 1941; D. Eichholtz et al. (eds.), Anatomie des Krieges (Berlin, 1969), Doc. 161, 'Rundschreiben von Generaloberst Ernst Udet von 22 Mai 1941 über die Berufung eines Industrierats für die Luftwaffenindustrie'.

[28] IWM EDS AL 1571, OKW/WiRüAmt, Aktennotiz 8 Feb. 1941.

[29] IWM EDS Mi 14/463 (file 3), OKW, Aktenvermerk über die Besprechung bei Chef OKW, Reichskanzler, Berchtesgaden, 19 May 1941, 2–3; Draft OKW directive, May 1941.

[30] IWM EDS Mi 14/463 (file 3), Chef OKW, 'Technische Ausstattung der Wehrmacht', May 1941.

substantial new programmes for the war economy, including a large battle-fleet, a quadrupling of air force strength, and an army with thirty-six motorized divisions. The new plans could only be met by more efficient production. Hitler ordered the military and civilian authorities to squeeze out any remaining inessential production 'even more than hitherto'. In August he ordered contracts to be concentrated in 'the firms that worked most efficiently'.[31] The armed forces were again directed in October to co-ordinate and rationalize their planning and procurement policy, and to adjust designs to make them suitable for modernized production methods.[32]

There was already some basis on which to build the new production policy. German industry may have been poorly rationalized but it was certainly modern. A large amount of new factory capacity and machinery was acquired during the rearmament period. Between 1936 and 1941 some RM 26,000m. was spent on capital equipment.[33] There were pockets of rationalized production in German industry, particularly in sectors which had pioneered modern processing before 1939. Even in the aircraft industry highly rationalized sectors coexisted with suppliers and producers where rational methods had made very little progress.[34] For many firms the problem was not lack of equipment or experience but the failure to plan programmes in ways which permitted the use of rational methods, or provided sufficient incentive to rationalize. Despite Hitler's directives, progress towards reversing this situation was slow during 1941. This was partly because Hitler did not at the same time resolve the problem of military intervention in the economy, or the lack of central, co-ordinated direction. Bureaucratic self-interest and political conflict continued to militate against more rational and co-operative planning; the armed forces vigorously resisted efforts by civilians to interfere with procurement policy.[35]

Indeed, the slow development of rationalization during the second half of 1941 prompted Hitler to take firmer steps. On 3 December he published a widely circulated Führer Order on 'Simplification and Increased

[31] IWM EDS Mi 14/433 (file 2), Keitel (OKW) to General Becker on 'Umstellung der Rüstung', 10 Aug. 1941.
[32] IWM EDS Mi 14/433 (file 2), Keitel (OKW) to the commanders-in-chief, 10 Oct. 1941; NA T84 Roll 8, Göring-Stabsamt, frames 8005–6, 'Notiz betr. die Rede des Herrn Reichsmarschalls am 20 Mai 1942'.
[33] K.-H. Ludwig, *Technik und Ingenieure im Dritten Reich* (Düsseldorf, 1974), 421.
[34] NA T177, Roll 14, frames 3698898–903, Bauer report, 1 June 1941; IWM MD vol. 57, 5288, Besprechungsnotiz beim Reichsmarschall, 29 June 1942.
[35] IWM EDS Mi 14/433 (file 3), OKW, Vortrag des Oberst Neef, 21 Jan. 1942, 21–31; OKW/WiRüAmt, 'Rationalisierung des Menscheneinsatzes in zivilen Sektor', 27 Jan. 1942, 2–12; IWM, Speer Collection, Box 368, Report 54, interrogation of Albert Speer, 13 July 1945, 5–6: 'you cannot imagine the bureaucracy and red tape with which we had to contend in the Army Ordnance Board and other offices'.

Efficiency in Armaments Production', which provided the foundation for the more thorough rationalization of the military economy in 1942. Hitler in this decree returned to the argument that the increases in military output he had ordered in 1940 and 1941 could only be met by industry if there were corresponding improvements in productivity. This could be achieved through 'a correction in the construction of our weapons and equipment, in the sense of making possible mass production on modern principles, and by this means achieving the rationalization of our manufacturing methods'.[36] Increased efficiency, he added, could also be achieved by giving orders only to the most rationally organized and best-operated firms, and finally through the strict limitation of military products to those most suitable for mass production. All this would produce 'considerably simplified manufacturing methods' and would 'save raw materials, skilled labour and time'. Industry was instructed to make recommendations for increased productivity, simplification, and standardization; the armed forces were ordered to comb through their programmes in order to reduce the number of types in production, to adapt designs for mass production, and to avoid excessive modification or technical complexity.[37]

This time Hitler was determined that his objectives would be met. He threw his political weight behind the strategy to increase efficiency, which had been patchily pursued during 1941. Rationalization was finally recognized to be a political issue as well as a practical problem. 'It is significant', Saur later reflected, 'that rationalisation in Germany was only really put into operation for all practical purposes after Hitler's order of December 3rd 1941 and that his intervention was needed to carry it from theory to practice'.[38] The power structure of the Reich was such by 1941 that only Hitler could resolve the problems of who organized and directed the industrial economy, and on what terms. During December Fritz Todt won Hitler's backing for a complete overhaul of army production. On 20 December Todt established a system of Main Committees (*Hauptausschüsse*), each one responsible for directing the production of a particular class of weapon or equipment. The first committees were set up for armoured vehicles, munitions, weapons, machine tools, and general military equipment. In aircraft production a similar system of production 'Rings' was introduced by Erhard Milch, in which all the firms involved in the production of each aircraft type were grouped under the direction of the main producers. These reforms increased the degree of centralization

[36] IWM EDS Mi 14/433 (file 2), Der Führer, 'Vereinfachung und Leistungssteigerung unserer Rüstungsproduktion', 3 Dec. 1941, 1.
[37] Ibid. 2–4.
[38] IWM Box 368, Report 90 I, 'The Rationalisation of the German Armaments Industry', 8.

and co-ordination, and gave much greater responsibility to industrialists in organizing production.[39]

After the December decree rationalization came to be regarded as the panacea that would resolve all the dilemmas facing the war effort. All the major departments scrambled to meet Hitler's objectives, now that rationalization was politically fashionable. Special commissioners for rationalization were appointed by the Four Year Plan organization, and, in February 1942, by the Economics Ministry. Todt appointed Dr Theodor Hupfauer to produce a survey of German industry in order to register levels of efficiency. He told his interrogators in 1945 that his research proved that 'the degree of efficiency in German industry and even in the most modern firms was bad'. The results of the efficiency comparison showed that 'the production times of individual processes varied often between fifteen- and twentyfold, though for total operations it was only four- or fivefold... As this was not a rare occurrence the slogan for the rest of the war became: INCREASED EFFICIENCY on as broad a basis as possible, using all possible means.'[40]

One of the factors governing Hitler's decision to enforce rationalization was his intention, in the light of reverses on the Soviet front, to increase arms production again in January 1942, even before solutions had been found to the problems raised by the increased production ordered the previous July. Another factor was his desire to involve industrialists and engineers much more fully in running the productive side of the economy, and to reduce the responsibility of the armed force and the Four Year Plan organization. Hitler favoured strengthening the position of Todt's Munitions Ministry and the industrial committees set up by Todt in 1941. On 6 February 1942 Todt called together the heads of the new Main Committees to discuss the establishment of a central organization for production and the distribution of resources. Two days later Todt was killed in an air crash. Hitler took the opportunity of his death to complete the restructuring of the organization of the war economy in ways that gave him a much more direct say in economic affairs than he had enjoyed hitherto.

He appointed Albert Speer, Todt's deputy and the party's pet architect, as Minister of Armaments with wide executive powers, and deliberately reduced the role of the armed forces and the Göring apparatus. His object was to try to eliminate the political infighting and jurisdictional arguments that had characterized the first two years of war, and to reduce the stifling effect of excessive bureaucratization, which produced, he told Himmler,

---

[39] Zumpe, *Wirtschaft und Staat*, 339–41; W. Boelcke, *Die deutsche Wirtschaft 1930–1945: Interna des Reichswirtschaftsministeriums* (Düsseldorf, 1983), 281–3.
[40] IWM Box 368, Report 85 II, 4 (emphasis in the original).

the 'satrap's mentality'.[41] Speer enjoyed Hitler's direct political support, which no other war economic leader had been able to count on until then. 'The backing of the Fuehrer', Speer wrote in his memoirs, 'counted for everything.'[42] Speer was able to resolve the disputes over technical and economic issues by reference to Hitler. When Speer arrived at his post the new rationalization drive was in full swing. He quickly saw that the only way to increase output in an economy already committed to war 'to an extraordinary degree' was the widespread adoption of 'new production methods'.[43]

III

The so-called 'production miracle' of 1942–4 was based largely on the revolution in levels of industrial efficiency initiated during 1941. The watchwords of the economy were announced by Walther Funk in April 1942: 'Rationalization and Concentration'.[44] Rationalization took two forms. The first involved a more general rationalization and centralization of the administration and tighter central control over important physical resources—raw materials, factory equipment, and labour. The second comprised the rationalization of factory practices and labour processes and the imposition of common production standards across German industry.

An effective rationalized administration was the essential precondition for the success of reforms in distributing resources and production practices. The framework for the administration of war production was provided by the Speer Ministry. In discussions with Hitler in the weeks following his appointment Speer was given full executive power 'to achieve a greater centralization and simplification of the leadership of the whole economy'.[45] This was achieved in a number of ways. In April Speer established a Central Planning agency (Zentrale Planung), which became an inner economic cabinet concerned with the allocation of material resources for all German industry. Labour supply was placed under a single Plenipotentiary, the Gauleiter Fritz Sauckel. The work of Fritz Todt in establishing a system of industrial committees was continued and

---

[41] H. Trevor-Roper (ed.), Hitler's Table Talk 1941–1944, 2nd edn. (London, 1979), 129, entry for 16 Nov. 1941.

[42] A. Speer, Inside the Third Reich (London, 1970), 210.

[43] IWM, Speer Collection, FD 4369/45, 'Rede auf der Grosskundgebung im Sportpalast Berlin, 5 Juni 1943', 7–8.

[44] Boelcke, Deutsche Wirtschaft, 281; see too Eichholtz et al., Anatomie des Krieges, 383–7, Doc. 199, 'Besprechung von Wilhelm Zangen mit den Geschäftsführer der Wirtschaftsgruppen, 5 März 1942'.

[45] IWM EDS AL 1371, OKW/WiRüAmt, Aktennotiz über Besprechung mit Minister Speer', 3 Mar. 1942, 1.

strengthened. In addition to the Main Committees set up in December, Speer added committees for shipbuilding, vehicles, airframes, aero-engines, air armament, and radio apparatus. Each Main Committee was served by subordinate Special Committees (*Sonderausschüsse*) which were responsible for a particular model of weapon or a particular piece of equipment. All the firms involved in the production of weapons were controlled by the committees, and work practices, the flow of resources, and the allocation of labour were placed under central review. Finally a number of Armaments Commissions were established to oversee the technical development of weapons in co-operation with the armed forces, in order to avoid as far as possible duplication of effort, or excessive complexity of design. The development commissions worked closely with the Main Committees on production questions.[46]

At Hitler's prompting Speer was encouraged to continue the work begun by Todt in staffing the new offices and committees with men from an engineering and business background. In February Hitler told Speer that 'in industry there stands ready an enormous amount of untapped expertise among designers and engineers'.[47] Speer brought younger men with business experience into his ministry. His deputy, Karl Saur, had been responsible for rationalization at Vereinigte Stahlwerke in the 1930s before working for the Organisation Todt. The Main and Special Committees were staffed almost entirely by industrialists. Their appointment helped to bridge the gulf that had developed between the state apparatus and industry, and gave industrial leaders the kind of responsibility they had argued for since the beginning of the war. The 'self-responsibility principle' gave industry the chance to put its own house in order under the guiding hand of the Ministry and the Committees.[48]

At the same time the state altered the way in which industry was paid for war production in order to provide real financial incentives for the reform of factory methods and labour use. The cost-plus contract gave way to the fixed-price contract, which forced firms to adjust production to meet what the contractor was prepared to pay, or risk making a loss. The decree on fixed-price contracts was signed by Göring in October 1941, despite strong hostility from other ministries and from the army, but not until January was Todt able to introduce it.[49] Under Speer it became one of the main instruments in encouraging greater efficiency. The new

[46] IWM Box 368, Report 81, 'German Methods of Design and Production in the Manufacture of Weapons', Dec. 1945, 6–8; Report 95, 'Design and Development of Armaments in Germany during the War', 10–26.

[47] IWM, Speer Collection, FD 1434/46, no. 167, Speer speech to Gau economic advisers, 17 Apr. 1942; see also NA T83, Roll 76, frames 3447503–4, Führerbefehl, 21 Mar. 1942.

[48] A. Speer, 'Selbstverantwortung in der Rüstungsindustrie', *Der Vierjahresplan*, 7 (1943), 242–3.

[49] IWM Box 368, Report 90 I, 3.

contract prices were worked out on the basis of official investigation of the production costs of a particular weapon. Firms could either opt to work to a fixed price which reflected average performance, and be freed from corporation taxes if they could produce at 10 per cent below the norm, or they could accept an even lower fixed price and try to rationalize production further to undercut the agreed price and make higher profits. Either way profitability was linked to productive performance: the more successful a business was in promoting rationalized production, the greater the margin of profit.[50]

With the new administrative structure in place it proved possible to organize the production and distribution of materials on a national, co-ordinated basis, and to utilize existing industrial capacity more fully. Speer's priority was to use existing plant and facilities more thoroughly, rather than rely on building expensive new plant. When Speer visited twenty major firms in Berlin one night in the spring of 1942 he found not a single one operating a double shift. At the time 1.8 million men were engaged in constructing new plant, and RM 11,000m. had been spent on expanding floor-space, much of which could not be fully utilized because of shortages of energy supply and machine tools. Speer authorized the termination of RM 3,000m. worth of industrial building and other construction projects, and would have closed down more but for Hitler's resistance. The Ministry encouraged higher levels of shift work and the more rational use of floor-space as a substitute for constructing new plant.[51]

The most important policy adopted to cope with the better exploitation of factory space was the concentration of production, reducing the number of different firms engaged in the manufacture of weapons, components, and equipment of all kinds and concentrating output in the largest or most efficient. The effect was actually to reduce the amount of floor-space needed and to increase output at the same time. At Messerschmitt production of the Me 109 fighter increased from 180 per month in seven factories to 1,000 per month in three. The production of machine tools was distributed among 900 firms; by October 1943 the figure was reduced to 369. The strategy was also applied to consumer goods. It was discovered that out of 117 carpet firms still in operation, 5 produced 90 per cent of the output, while 112 accounted for only 10 per cent. The 112 were closed down and their capacity and labour made available for war work.[52]

[50] Zumpe, *Wirtschaft und Staat*, 341–2.

[51] IWM, Speer Collection, FD 1434/46, no. 167, Speer speech to Gau economic advisers, 17 Apr. 1942, 10–12.

[52] IWM EDS AL 1746, interrogation of Saur, 10 Aug. 1945, 14; FD 4921/45, folder 1, Papers of Sonderausschuss F2 (Messerschmitt) general report, 6; on the machine-tool industry, Eichholtz, *Kriegswirtschaft*, ii. 314–15.

Concentration of production was particularly significant for the supply of small parts and components. It was recognized that without rationalizing the small subcontractors the gains in the assembly plants would be vitiated. The small firms tended to be less efficient than the larger ones, yet the supply of components and equipment had to match the increased pace of production in the larger firms. The component industries were subjected to strict control for the first time. Production was concentrated in the most efficient, and the range of products greatly reduced in number. In 1942 there were 300 different types of prismatic glass produced; by 1943 the number was reduced to 14, and the 23 firms engaged in production were reduced to 7. Fire-fighting equipment for the air force was produced at 334 factories in 1942; by the beginning of 1944 the figure was 64, with a saving of 360,000 man-hours per month: and so on.[53] By this means great savings could be made in manpower, equipment, and floor-space, and output raised with fewer resources. As well as concentrating production, the Ministry, in co-operation with the Main Committees, set up a centralized control over and statistical review of the flow of parts and components, to avoid excessive stockholding and to ensure that products went to where they were needed at the right time. A delicate supply web was established to make sure that a continuous stream of industrial resources, components, and sub-assemblies fed the final assembly plants. The large firms introduced more effective stock control systems using the new Hollerith calculating machines. Bottlenecks could be quickly identified and efforts concentrated on products temporarily in short supply.[54]

The same controls were established over the distribution of raw-material stocks. When the rationalization drive began it was found that the armed forces had greatly inflated the demand for raw materials by exaggerating the quantity needed for each unit of production. The large firms held substantial stocks of scarce materials, particularly aluminium, which had been allocated on the basis of 16,000 lb. for each aircraft, regardless of the fact that a fighter required only a quarter of this quantity. Aircraft firms had so much ingot aluminium in store that they used it to produce non-essential goods—ladders, greenhouses, even mosquito-nets—with the unused material.[55] Once the problem was identified firms were forced to give up their stocks, and allocations were based on the actual quantity of

[53] IWM Box 368, Report 90 V, 'Rationalisation in the Components Industry', 34.

[54] T. Spandau, 'Abgrenzung der Rüstungsaufgaben zwischen Handwerk und Industrie', *Der Vierjahresplan*, 8 (1944); H. Block, 'Industrial Concentration and Small Business: The Trend of Nazi Policy', *Social Research*, 10 (1943); on Hollerith machines BIOS Final Report 537, app. 1, 'Production Control in the Heinkel Aircraft Organisation', 1–3. See too CIOS Report XXX-94, 'Administration, Plastics, Production Tooling, Spare Parts and Servicing in the German Aircraft Industry', 17–23.

[55] IWM, Speer Collection, Zentrale Planung, 14th Meeting, 4 Sept. 1942, 417; IWM MD vol. 53, 1162.

raw material required by the most efficient factory for a given unit of production. This encouraged widespread rationalization, for firms risked losing their quotas of material if they failed to meet the new performance criteria. An extraordinary degree of wastage and scrapping was discovered in existing work processes, much of which was due to the survival of handwork and the use of general-purpose tools. In the production of a single aero-engine it was found that 1,500 lb. of aluminium was wasted. With better control over stocks, the centralized distribution of material, and the introduction of more rational raw material use, substantial savings were recorded. The quantity of aluminium allocated to the aviation industry fell in 1942, but the structure weight of finished aircraft increased by 43 per cent.[56] The supply of all major raw materials for the armed forces either declined or remained stagnant from 1942 and 1944, while the quantity and weight of weapons produced increased steadily.

Some of the savings in raw materials can be explained by the internal redistribution of resources within the military economy. Up to 1942 large capital projects deemed to be essential for the war effort soaked up large quantities of raw materials. By 1942 much of this building was either completed or suspended. The end of the phase of heavy industrial and engineering industry expansion released raw materials and manpower for the production of finished weapons. Internal redistribution of resources also came from imposing priority rankings on military contracts, weeding out non-essential or less essential military output, and transferring those resources to more urgent projects.[57] The same effect was derived from the better co-ordination of the different service programmes to avoid duplication where there were products in common. Rationalization was in this sense a case of using resources already earmarked for the military economy more effectively, rather than transferring additional resources from civilian sectors.

The next step was to improve efficiency at the level of the individual firm. Rationalization was brought about in a number of different ways. First of all it proved necessary to find out what constituted optimum production performance. Engineers trained in scientific management techniques were recruited to examine the production processes for all major products and components. It was found that even the best factory undertook some parts of the production process less efficiently than firms with a lower overall efficiency level. The production norm was arrived at by breaking down the production of a weapon or machine into the

[56] In 1941 200,000 tons of aluminium produced 11,700 aircraft with a structure weight of 64m. lb. In 1942 185,000 tons of aluminium produced 15,400 aircraft with a structure weight of 92m. lb.
[57] See e.g. IWM Box 368, unnumbered file, Reichswirtschaftsministerium, 'Development of German metal supplies from the beginning of the War, and projected to 1946', July 1943.

different processes involved in order to discover the most efficient form of each process. Once this was done aggregate norms could be established and contract prices fixed which reflected the optimum use of resources through the production line. A team of consulting engineers then toured the plants, teaching managers how to put optimum time schedules into effect. Production was reviewed every six months to see if further savings had been made or new approaches introduced.[58] Information on new processes or savings were then sent to all the firms involved in the production of a particular item. The exchange of information between businesses was made compulsory, and this, together with the widespread introduction of suggestion schemes designed to involve the work-force more in the rationalization programme, contributed to the rapid dissemination of rational practices throughout industry.[59] Where the ratio between the best and worst practice had averaged 1:5, rationalization reduced it to 1:1.5. In the production of some weapons the performance of all firms after rationalization was better than the practice of the best firm beforehand.[60]

The major gains in productivity were made by utilizing existing space, labour, and equipment more rationally. The gains reflected how poorly resources had been exploited in the early years of war. In some cases greater efficiency involved a transition to mass-production techniques, though great gains were made simply by better stockholding, more rational use of machinery, and a better distribution of workers using existing techniques. The application of flow production using conveyor belts or overhead cables to supply the production line, together with a higher level of automation, spread more slowly than changes in layout and the pattern of operations. Where it was feasible to do so the work-force was spread out along an assembly line where the product was brought to the workers, in contrast to unit or batch production where a team of workers moved from product to product. Flow production was generally more suitable for large components, such as engines, or major sub-assemblies, but towards the end of the war it was used in the final assembly of tanks and fighter aircraft.[61] Great savings were also made in reducing the degree of finishing demanded by the armed forces. The

---

[58] IWM Box 368, Report 90 I, 4, 6–7.

[59] Ibid. 12.

[60] Ibid. 4; Report 90 IV, 'Rationalization of the Munitions Industry', 44: 'This idea of compelling firms under the leadership of the most competent one was the first big step towards the realisation of successful rationalization' (testimony of Otto Merker, head of Main Committee, Shipbuilding).

[61] On the progress of automation in the aircraft industry see Overy, 'German Aircraft Production', 266–8. Messerschmitt converted where possible to flow production in 1942; Heinkel, Junkers, BMW, and Henschel by 1943. See too IWM Box 368, Report 90 V, 32–5 on the components industry, where flow production was widely introduced from 1942.

polishing, lacquering, and grinding of external surfaces was reduced or scrapped and cruder machining or higher tolerances permitted where this did not seriously affect the quality of a product. Finally considerable savings were achieved through simplifying the packaging and delivery of goods.[62]

The switch to rational, automated production depended to a considerable extent on the degree to which the new economic administration could persuade the armed forces to reduce the number of modifications to products in the pipeline, and to accept both a reduction in the number of types of weapon and a standardization of parts and components. Though the forces resisted as long as they could the right to order design changes at any stage in the production process, the only way to ensure large-scale production was to insist on longer production runs and fewer interruptions. The number of minor design changes could run to enormous figures. By the end of 1942 some 18,000 design alterations had been recommended for the Junkers Ju 88 bomber. For the Heinkel He 177 heavy bomber there were fifty-six files of modifications stored in Heinkel's design offices. The reduction in the number and frequency of modifications was a major aim of the Speer Ministry, but although longer production runs did become possible it proved very difficult to eliminate the pressure to modify designs altogether. In tank production the army only accepted the reduction of technical modification in 1944, when it was agreed to establish a committee to reduce and screen product refinement.[63]

What could be achieved was a greater simplification and standardization of equipment. Here the gains were chiefly in the production of components and machinery, for the armed forces resisted as long as they could efforts to simplify the number of models currently in production because of their fear that the quality of weapons would suffer. In 1943 Speer established an Armaments Commission to bring greater co-ordination between weapon design and production needs. The Commission recommended that for the production drive in 1944 the war economy should concentrate on a narrower range of weapons best suited for mass production. In January 1944 the army finally announced plans to reduce the number of types of weapon in production as follows:[64]

---

[62] IWM Box 368, Report 90 I, 8: 'Much could be saved in the finishing processes, such as polishing, varnishing and grinding of parts not subject to wear'; also 90 VI, 'Rationalization of the Optics and Precision Instrument Industry', 39.

[63] On Junkers see BA-MA RL3/247, Aktenvermerk Sonderausschuss F1, 16 Nov. 1942; on Heinkel see E. Heinkel, He 1000 (London, 1956), 203. See Göring's views on modification in IWM MD vol. 62, 5314–15, 'Bericht über Besprechung des Reichmarschall Görings mit Vertretern der Luftfahrtindustrie', 13 Sept. 1942.

[64] IWM EDS Mi 14/133, Army High Command (OKH), 'Studie über Rüstung 1944', 25 Jan. 1944. The army general staff ordered 'simplification of construction' in order 'to assist the mass production of the main equipment'.

light-infantry weapons	from	14	to	5
heavy-infantry weapons		6		3
anti-tank weapons		12		1
light and heavy Flak		10		2
artillery		26		8
flame-throwers		10		6
vehicles		55		14
tanks, armoured vehicles		18		7

When Speer took over air production fully in the spring of 1944 the number of aircraft models was progressively reduced from 42 to 20, then to 9, and finally to 5.[65]

The concentration of production on a narrow range of standard products made much greater ground in the components industry and in non-armaments engineering. The number of lorries was reduced from 151 to 23 in 1942, and the number of motor-cycle models from 150 to 26. The coal industry reduced the number of types of one machine from 120 to 12, of another from 80 to 8. The number of mechanical and hydraulic presses was reduced from 440 models to 36; and so on. In one year alone the number of types of cylinder produced was cut from 3,232 to 1,138. Standardization simplified production. The Ju 88 bomber used over 4,000 different types of bolt and screw. Its successor, the Ju 288, used only 200 and was put together with automatic riveting machines rather than by hand.[66] The process of standardization continued down to the end of the war, freeing labour and resources for other production essential for war.

The whole programme of simplification, standardization, and reorganisation of production processes was designed to permit more rational use of labour resources. The introduction of higher levels of automation and special-purpose machine tools reduced the need for skilled workers. The new machinery allowed a more rational division of labour to take account of the dilution of the work-force with female, foreign, or untrained labour. The long apprentice training was replaced with short courses lasting a few weeks to familiarize the new labour with simple and repetitive mechanical operations. Skilled German workers took on the responsibility of inspection and work discipline. In general, areas of production that had previously required a high level of skilled handwork were reduced in favour of processes requiring only semi-skilled labour operating more specialized equipment. The introduction of time-and-

---

[65] IWM EDS AL 1746, Saur interrogation, 6.

[66] Details from Zumpe, *Wirtschaft und Staat*, 342; Ludwig, *Technik*, 421; Speer, 'Selbstverantwortung', 242; CIOS Report XXX-94, 21; Eichholtz, *Kriegswirtschaft*, 314.

motion studies on a widespread basis was intended to find norms for average work efficiency that could be applied across the work-force.[67]

The result of de-skilling, increased automation, and the greater division of labour was a sharp rise in the productivity of labour in the armaments industries of over 100 per cent between 1941 and 1944. But in practice there remained a great number of obstacles to the more efficient use of labour, and the productivity gains reflected how prodigally labour had been used before 1942 rather than great gains in labour output per hour. The authorities recognized that labour needed greater incentives to compensate for fixed wages, longer hours, the deteriorating supply of consumer goods and food, and the demoralizing effects of strategic bombing. Many firms offered welfare payments, social amenities, and bonuses in kind for German workers.[68] Improvements were made in overtime pay, holiday, and Sunday working payments. A range of state-sponsored improvements in conditions were also introduced, similar to those promoted in Britain or the United States during the war. Working women were provided with crèche facilities. Hostels were built for German and foreign workers. Canteen facilities were provided to ensure that all German workers got a hot meal once a day. Leave rosters were introduced, and health and safety provision in German firms improved.[69]

The German Labour Front had also argued for some time the need to overhaul the whole wage structure in German industry to remove what was regarded as an anachronistic division into skilled, semi-skilled, and unskilled categories. The rationalization drive provided the opportunity to introduce a wage structure based on a graded measure of achievement (*Leistung*) rather than on acquired skill. The wartime dilution of the work-force led to a situation where the gap between unskilled and skilled pay levels narrowed while the division in function actually became more diverse.[70] To reverse this trend, and find a wage structure which fitted better with the actual achievement of individual workers under rationalized production, a new pay structure was introduced in the iron and metalworking industries. The new system involved eight graded wage groups, from Group I for unskilled labourers to Group VIII for highly skilled operatives. Under the new system the gap in pay between the

[67] Hachtmann, *Industriearbeit*, 81–9; E. Homze, *Foreign Labor in Nazi Germany* (Princeton, NJ, 1967), 240–63. On the position of women see A. Tröger, 'Die Planung des Rationalisierungsproletariats: Zur Entwicklung der geschlechtsspezifischen Arbeitsteilung und das weibliche Arbeitsmarkt im Nationalsozialismus', in A. Kuhn and J. Rüsen, (eds.), *Frauen in der Geschichte* (Düsseldorf, 1982), 245–313.

[68] Hachtmann, *Industriearbeit*, 254–301; on Daimler–Benz, H. Pohl, S. Habeth and B. Brüninghaus, *Die Daimler–Benz AG in den Jahren 1933 bis 1945* (Stuttgart, 1986), 172–80.

[69] IWM Box 368, Report 85, 'Incentives used to increase the output of labour', 1–3.

[70] Ibid., Report 85 I, 5; Siegel, 'Wage Policy . . .', 20–1.

highest and lowest wage group was 66 per cent, considerably greater than the gap between skilled and unskilled workers of 25 per cent. It was hoped that the graded structure of pay would encourage workers to acquire new skills and improve their achievement level so that they could move up to a higher wage category and improve the productive efficiency of the work-force.[71]

For the wartime authorities there were other motives involved. The wage-group system gave factories a clear check on the rational use of their labour resources, and permitted state officials to see more easily where firms were holding on to excess skilled labour. The wage catalogue was introduced in the iron and metalworking industries in 1942, but it spread only slowly and was used very little in other industrial sectors. Some firms were worried that the system would leave many workers worse off and were concerned about the effect that this would have on labour relations and efficiency. In January 1943 the Labour Front insisted that other industries should develop their own wage catalogue but by 1944 little was achieved and the idea was shelved (though it was revived again after the war).[72] Where possible the authorities tried to produce a more rational piece-rate system, which like the wage catalogue would operate across whole industries for work of a comparable kind, and which would give incentive to better workers to increase earnings above the norm. But this programme of *Akkordbereinigung* (piece-rate rationalization) was held up on the resistance of workers and the Trustees of Labour, and the shortage of time-and-motion engineers to fix the piece-rate norms.[73]

By the last years of war the pressures to maximize production militated against further steps to provide incentives to German labour through restructuring pay. In 1943–4 a great number of foreign workers were introduced into the factory work-force, for whom the division of labour and new factory practices were necessary not as incentives but as a means of control and coercion. By this stage of the war absenteeism and low morale among the German work-force led to high labour turnover (particularly of the female workers) and declining discipline. At the Ford factories in the Ruhr it was estimated that the absenteeism rate for German labour increased from 4 per cent in 1940 to 25 per cent in 1944. Foreign workers could be disciplined much more easily. The rate of absenteeism for foreign workers at Ford was a steady 3 per cent between

[71] Hachtmann, *Industriearbeit*, 207–12; the system was first pioneered at Daimler–Benz from 1938. See B. P. Bellon, *Mercedes in Peace and War: German automobile workers, 1903–1945* (New York, 1990), 224–6.

[72] M.-L. Recker, *Nationalsozialistische Sozialpolitik im Zweiten Weltkrieg* (Munich, 1985), 242–50; Siegel, 'Wage Policy', 23.

[73] IWM Box 368, Report 85 I, 6–7. Efforts were also made to raise hours worked by paying overtime and bonuses above 48 hours.

1942 and 1944.[74] To keep up the morale of German workers later in the war the regime resorted to short-term incentives such as increases in rations, or special bonuses known as 'Speer recognition' paid to workers for exceptional efforts. These payments were made in kind, since cash was no guarantee that goods could actually be acquired in the shops.[75] Foreign workers, on the other hand, were subjected to a much harsher regime in the large automated assembly halls, under the watchful eye of German foremen and company policemen. Despite deteriorating conditions and widespread brutality, and despite the fact that foreign workers performed at an estimated 50–80 per cent of the level of German workers, the high gains in productivity brought about by new production methods were sustained through 1944.[76]

IV

There are a number of ways in which the achievements of the rationalization programme can be measured. Expressed in its simplest terms an increase in labour input of 8 per cent over the course of the war produced a 30 per cent increase in aggregate industrial output. This says very little about the performance of different sectors of the economy or about the timing of changes in productivity performance. According to Professor Eichholtz's calculations, based on a crude assessment of increased output per head, the productive performance of the different sectors of the economy was as shown in Table 11.1.[77] The table demonstrates a remarkable increase in the productive performance of the armaments sector from 1942 onwards, with an increase in output per head of 110 per cent between 1941 and 1944. By 1943 the bulk of the industrial work-force was concentrated in arms production, and it was here that the greatest efforts were made to achieve rationalization. The

[74] IWM, Speer Collection, FD 4369/45, British Bombing Survey Unit, 'Manuscript Notes on Ford, Cologne'. On rising illness and absenteeism rates see Eichholtz, *Kriegswirtschaft*, 264–5.

[75] IWM Box 368, Report 85 II. It was apparently proposed to militarize factory labour in 1944 but this was judged to be too risky and was abandoned in favour of increased incentives.

[76] U. Herbert, *Fremdarbeiter: Politik und Praxis des 'Ausländer-Einsatzes' in der Kriegswirtschaft des Dritten Reiches* (Bonn, 1985), chs. 8–9. A. S. Milward, 'Arbeitspolitik und Produktivität in der deutschen Kriegswirtschaft unter vergleichendem Aspekt', in F. Forstmeier and H.-E. Volkmann (eds.), *Kriegswirtschaft und Rüstung 1939–1945* (Düsseldorf, 1977), 82–4.

[77] Eichholtz, *Kriegswirtschaft*, ii. 265. The USSBS arrived at rather different figures in 1945. According to Special Report 134A, overall productivity in German industry grew by 23% between 1939 and 1944, but by 30% in manufacturing industry, and 50% in the metalworking and engineering sectors. The final figure is only slightly lower than the Eichholtz calculation.

TABLE 11.1. *Output per head in German industry, 1939–1944 (1939 = 100)*

	1939	1940	1941	1942	1943	1944
Primary industry	100	104.1	114.6	113.5	108.7	87.6
Arms industry	100	87.6	75.9[a]	99.6	131.6	160.0[b]
Consumer industry	100	115.9	133.3	121.1	124.7	132.3

[a] Provisional figure. [b] Minimum figure.

consumer industry improved productive performance in the early years of war as a result of the rapid decline in its work-force as workers were drafted into the armed forces or into war work. Later in the war productive performance was sustained by the effects of rationalization. There were limits to what could be achieved in the primary sector, partly because the coal and iron and steel industries were already rationalized before 1939, partly because of shortages of skilled miners and steelworkers, which got worse as the war went on.[78]

Eichholtz's figures make it evident that something quite remarkable occurred during the war in the productive performance of war industries. But this is not the whole story, and much more needs to be discovered about the performance of individual industries and firms before the whole pattern becomes clear. Nor do the crude figures take full account of the changing nature and quality of the work-force. The high productivity achievements of the final years of war were established with a work-force that was much less skilled and in which a substantial proportion were subject to harsh treatment and bomb attack. The proportion of German skilled workers in arms factories declined steadily during the war. By 1944 the proportion of skilled German males in the Messerschmitt work-force had fallen from 59 per cent in 1941 to only 21 per cent. Over 40 per cent of workers in the Daimler–Benz concern were foreigners or prisoners of war by 1945.[79] Given the declining quality of the work-force and its progressive demoralization through poor conditions and bombardment, the actual productivity achievement between 1941 and 1945 is all the more remarkable. It can partly be explained by the willingness of the regime to exploit its foreign labour force more intensively than German workers; but it was partly the result of the fact that rationalization was

[78] See above pp. 296–9 for a discussion of employment in the consumer sector. On the very real limits to extending the productivity performance of the iron and steel industry see IWM Box 368, Report 90 II, 'Rationalisation of the iron and steel industry', prepared by Walter Rohland.

[79] IWM, Speer Collection, Messerschmitt papers, FD 4904/45, Konzernbericht zum 31 Okt. 1943; Pohl *et al.*, *Daimler–Benz*, 145–7.

easier to introduce and enforce where there were smaller numbers of German workers to defend old skills or methods of payment. The disorganized and powerless foreign labour force could more easily be moulded to fit the new requirements.

The gains in productive performance can also be measured by comparing the rate of growth of output with the rate of growth of productive resources (raw materials, labour, etc.). There were increases in the resources available to war output between 1941 and 1944, due partly to a redistribution within the military economy, partly to the fuller exploitation of European resources, partly to the gradual concentration by 1944 on a narrow range of priority weapons. But these additional resources grew at a rate very much below the rate of increase in output. In some cases output increased with almost the same resource base. Aircraft output quadrupled between 1941 and 1944, but the quantity of aluminium available for aircraft production increased by only 5 per cent, while the labour force only grew from 360,000 to 390,000 between 1942 and 1944. At Junkers aircraft production in 1942 increased by 42 per cent over 1941, and aero-engine production by 75 per cent, while the total labour force grew only 7 per cent.[80] The same picture emerges from examining the labour force as a whole. The proportion of the industrial work-force engaged on orders for the armed forces grew by 159 per cent between 1939 and 1941, but by only 11 per cent between 1941 and 1943. Yet between 1941 and 1943 the production of all weapons expanded by 130 per cent, the production of aircraft by almost 200 per cent and the production of tanks by over 250 per cent.[81] During the same period the quantity of steel available for military production actually declined from a peak in the first half of 1942, yet by 1944 the output of army weapons had increased by 200 per cent.[82] However they are measured, gains in output were the direct result of using Germany's physical resources more productively.

The aggregate figures nevertheless disguise differences between industrial sectors or types of weapon. Nor do the gross figures reveal where the savings were made, whether in the use of raw materials, in labour effort, in time, or price. Not all factors were of equal importance. Improvements in

---

[80] IWM, Speer Collection, Junkers papers, FD 5504/45, charts C, D, and E; at Henschel output of aero-engines increased sixfold between 1939 and 1943, but the labour force only trebled. It was planned to increase output by 100% in 1944 with only a 9% increase in labour.

[81] Figures on labour input, IWM FD 3056/49, 'Statistical material on the German manpower position during the war period, 1939 to 1944', 31 July 1945, tables 2, 7. According to USSBS Special Report 134A labour input in German industry increased by only 8% over the war period, taking account of longer hours worker and the use of foreign labour.

[82] B. H. Klein, *Germany's Preparations for War* (Cambridge, Mass., 1959), 131–3.

efficiency depended to some extent on the complexity of the product, or the ease with which production could be reorganized. Great savings could be made with large and complicated weapons. In submarine production, for example, where rationalization made little headway until Speer appointed a car manufacturer in 1943 to reorganize the industry, the gains were very substantial. The production time for each submarine was reduced from forty-two weeks to sixteen. The saving was achieved by breaking down the production of a submarine into eight sections, each one produced by a different firm with standard parts and to standard times. The final product was assembled at a central yard.[83] The production of tanks was also notoriously inefficient before 1942, leaving room for quick gains in productivity. When tank production was converted to flow production in 1943 the number of man-hours expended on the Panzer III was reduced from 4,000 to 2,000.[84] In the production of aircraft very striking gains were made. By 1944 rationalization of the production of the Messerschmitt Me 109 brought a 53 per cent saving in production time, 50 per cent fewer man-hours, and a saving of 25 per cent in raw materials used.[85]

Gains like this were the result of a whole range of smaller rationalizations achieved in the production of components and sub-assemblies, as well as improvements in the layout and flow of production in the final assembly of major products. The reform of raw material distribution and the increased automation of the production process yielded remarkable savings in raw-material use. Raw-material wastage was reduced through better machining methods, and through the automatic pressing and stamping of parts which had previously been machined by hand.[86] These savings were encouraged particularly in the use of scarce materials such as copper or tin, which were substituted by more plentiful materials where possible. So-called Savings Engineers (*Sparingenieure*) were employed by the Speer Ministry to advise firms on raw-material use.[87] By May 1943 Speer was able to report that for every ton of munitions produced industry used less than half the iron and steel, one-sixth of the aluminium, and one-twelfth of the copper that was used in 1941 (see Table 11.2). In the production of every artillery piece the quantity of steel was reduced by 50 per cent, of copper by 80 per cent, of aluminium by 93 per cent. The weight of materials used in the production

[84] IWM Box 368, Report 65, interrogation of Ernst Blaicher, head of Main Committee Tanks, 12; Report 52, interrogation of G. Stieler von Heydekampf, 6 Oct. 1946, 11.

[85] IWM, Messerschmitt papers, FD 4921/45 (folder 1), papers of Sonderausschuss F2, 6.

[86] IWM Box 368, Report 90 I, 8, 10, 90 V, 'Rationalization of the components industry', 34–5.

[87] IWM, Speer Collection, FD 4369/45, Speer speech, 5 June 1943, 14. On savings made see e.g. Table 11.3 below.

TABLE 11.2. *Metals used on the BMW 801 aero-engine, 1940–1942* (kg.)

	mid-1940[a]	end 1942
Aluminium	750.0	425.0
Lead	10.0	1.1
Copper	136.0	22.8
Zinc	13.0	2.0
Tin	6.9	0.0
Iron and steel	4,000.0	3,200.0

[a] At start of production.

Source: IWM, Speer Collection, FD 927/46, BMW Kriegsleistungsbericht, 10 Mar. 1943, 73.

of each 88 mm. Flak shell fell from 29 kg. to 15. By the end of the war industry was producing four times as many munitions from the same quantity of steel.[88] Despite military fears, the cuts in the use of scarce materials did not affect the quality of weapons too adversely. As one official later pointed out, the armed forces insisted on quality that was unnecessarily high: 'generally speaking weapons were designed to last 25 years ... that was unfeasible in wartime'.[89] With these margins reduced, much larger quantities of finished weapons were provided from the same quantity of raw material.

The second source of increased efficiency was better use of labour on the shop floor. Reduced man-hours meant faster and larger output and reduced prices (though some of the savings in costs came through employing cheaper labour, women, foreign workers, and youths). Some of the savings came simply from economies of scale once long production runs were established and the armed force were persuaded to reduce modifications that interrupted the production line. Other savings came from adjusting patterns of work and the redistribution of workers in the plant in response to increased automation and the use of special-purpose machine tools. At BMW man-hours per aero-engine fell from 3,260 in the summer of 1940 to 1,860 by the summer of 1943 and 1,250 in 1944. The

[88] IWM FD 4363/45, Speer speech, 5 June 1943, 16–20; Box 368, Report 90 I, 6; 90 VIII, 'Rationalization in the munitions industry', 44.

[89] IWM Box 368, Report 90 I, 8. On reductions in tank quality see Report 65, 11: 'considerable reductions in the quality of parts could be achieved without diminishing their technical value' (testimony of Ernst Blaicher, head of Main Committee Tanks, 1943–5).

[90] IWM FD 927/46, BMW Kriegsleistungsbericht, 10 Mar. 1943, 40; FD 4969/45, BMW report, 'Ablauf der Lieferungen seit Kriegsbeginn', n.d., 25.

number of workers per engine produced fell from 1,470 in 1940 to 380 in 1943.[90] At Henschel the savings on hours per engine was higher still, 64 per cent per engine in 1943 compared with 1939. At the Junkers aircraft assembly plant savings of 30 per cent in man-hours for each Ju 88 bomber were recorded for 1942 alone. At Messerschmitt the labour time on the Me 109 fell by 53 per cent; and so on.[91]

Finally productivity gains owed much to the reorganization of production layout, the better distribution of materials and parts, the more rational use of existing equipment and machinery, and the addition of special-purpose machinery for flow production and the automatic machining of parts. The effect of these changes is difficult to quantify. It can be expressed in the reduction of floor-space per unit produced. At Henschel floor area per engine was 60 per cent lower in 1943 than 1939, and further savings were anticipated for 1944 to reduce the figure by 70 per cent.[92] It can also be expressed through the reduction in the time taken for a product to move along the production line, the *Durchlaufzeit*. For the Me 109 this time was reduced by 30 per cent by the end of 1943. At least one firm, BMW, produced a detailed survey in 1943 and 1944 of the effects of the general rationalization of work-processes and plant layout, and the results of these surveys show a wide range of different kinds of savings brought about 'through improvements in manufacturing processes ... simplification of construction and the introduction of special machines and flow production'.[93] The performance at BMW is set out in Table 11.3.

Improvements in throughput time and man-hours per unit produced owed a great deal to the adoption of special-purpose machinery which was designed to carry out processes automatically which had previously been done by hand. Karl Saur singled out special tools as the most important single factor in explaining efficiency gains. He found that in some cases the time taken to produce an article by machine was 1/100 of the time previously taken by hand.[94] The output of special machine tools rose steadily over the war, though more slowly than demand because of the failure to anticipate what could be achieved with better use of machinery. By the middle of the war there were waiting lists of two or three years for special-purpose tools, and the machine-tool industry itself was thoroughly rationalized in order to speed up delivery of vital equipment.[95] These

[91] IWM FD 3224/45 I, Henschel report, 'Leistungssteigerung seit Kriegsbeginn, 22 Dez. 1943'; FD 783/46, 'Kurzbericht der Junkers Flugzeug- und Motorenwerke AG für den Kalenderjahr 1942', 2; FD 4921/45 (folder 1), Sonderausschuss F2 report, 6.
[92] IWM FD 3224/45 I, Henschel, 'Leistungssteigerung' (n. 91 above).
[93] IWM FD 4969/45, BMW, 'Ablauf der Lieferungen', 25.
[94] IWM Box 368, Report 52, p. 11; Report 90 I, 10.
[95] Overy, 'German Aircraft Production', 215–19; A. S. Milward, *The German Economy at War* (London, 1965), 92–3.

TABLE 11.3. *Production of the BMW 801 aero-engine: statistics, 1940–1944*

	1940	1941	1942	1943	1944
Total labour force	8,396	9,787	10,787	11,050	9,339
Output of engines	2,044	1,842	3,942	5,540	7,395
Man-hours per engine	2,400	2,500	2,050	1,700	1,250
Price of engine (RM)	80,700	68,800	59,400	45,000	n.a.
Raw materials (kg.)	5,145	—	3,651	—	2,790
Wage-costs per engine	3,387	3,474	2,640	2,169	n.a.

delays certainly inhibited the rationalization drive until the bombing in 1944 forced a widespread decentralization of production and a higher reliance again on general-purpose tools and hand operation.

The difficulty in supplying special-purpose tools was one of a number of factors inhibiting the development of rationalized production. The spread of new procedures was uneven, and despite the gains made, areas of less rationalized production remained. Tank production remained closely under military supervision and was not subjected to full-scale rationalization until 1944. Naval production was only taken under Speer's control in 1943, and aircraft production, though it showed significant improvements in productive performance over the poor levels of 1939– 1941, was only fully rationalized in 1944, when aircraft output was almost double the level of 1943.[96] Even when rationalization was introduced, there was a shortage of engineers who understood the new methods, or men skilled in time-and-motion practices who could fix new timings on the factory floor. The conservatism with which rational methods had been received in some firms before 1942 did not evaporate overnight, and labour hostility held up the pace of reform, particularly in sectors with a high proportion of skilled German workers.[97]

Nor was rationalization free of other political pressures. The armed forces accepted their exclusion from the war economy with a poor grace and arguments continued throughout the war between civilian officials and soldiers over the simplification of weapons, standardization, and product quality. A great deal of departmental self-interest and jurisdictional rivalry survived into the Speer era.[98] Nor did local authorities, notably the

[96] BA R13/V/vorl. 100, Göring Erlass über Jägerstab, 4 Mar. 1944; letter from Speer to all Economic Groups, 1 Mar. 1944, 'Die Entwicklung des Jägerstabs'.
[97] Hachtmann, *Industriearbeit*, 216–23; Recker, *Sozialpolitik*, 243–50; IWM Box 368, Report 85 I, 5–7.
[98] IWM Box 368, Report 81, 'German Methods of Design and Production', 7–8; Report 83, 'Relationship between the Army Ordnance Board and the Speer Ministry and the Control of Armaments Development', Apr. 1946, 2–6, 12–14.

Gauleiter (provincial party leaders), always welcome the closure and concentration of production if it meant making economic sacrifices in their region.

What effect all these frictional issues had on the rationalization programme is impossible to assess quantitatively, though in their absence it is fair to assume that rationalization would have achieved even higher levels of output in 1942–4. Even by 1944 the German economy was not operating at the optimum. What can be measured is the impact of strategic bombing, which did have clear physical effects on efforts to promote rationalization. By 1944 rationalization was in full swing throughout the military economy, and the large gains in increased scale and speed of production promised large additional gains in output. Bombing placed a ceiling on this achievement by undermining some of the more important features of the rationalized system. Bombing had obvious effects in reducing worker morale and destroying facilities. But it also had the effect of interrupting in arbitrary and unpredictable ways the web of supplies of materials and parts on which the whole industrial structure depended. The gradual collapse of the supply system forced firms to carry larger stocks again, and left regular gaps in the supply of components or scarce materials.[99] Bombing also forced the authorities to disperse production at just the time that concentration was providing rich dividends. Dispersal meant longer transport hauls between factories, a greater reliance on skilled labour in small firms, and eventually a large programme of underground construction which once again took resources away from arms production. The effects of bombing could only be mediated by insisting on even more rigorous rationalization—concentrating production on a handful of weapons, reducing all unnecessary and sophisticated equipment, and cutting back on all military production not directly concerned with priority weapons.[100] It also meant higher levels of exploitation for the work-force, with fewer goods available and the regular threat of bombardment. The foreign labour force was subjected to harsher discipline and poorer diet, and the SS and Gestapo increased the level of terror and intimidation to keep the work-force in place.

In January 1945 German officials from the Ministry of Armaments assessed what might have been produced in 1944 without the bombing. They estimated that German industry turned out 35 per cent fewer tanks,

[99] IWM Box 368, Report 67, 'Causes of the Decline in German Industrial Production', Dec. 1945, 2: 'The decline in production was caused by the fact that raw material, semi-finished products and components could not be delivered in sufficient quantities' (evidence of Otto Messer); 'The ever increasing air attacks on the transport system led to the fatal paralysis of the regular supply of materials and semi-finished products and finally made allocation impossible' (evidence of Dietrich Stahl), 4.

[100] IWM EDS AL 2786/3, 'Reichsminister Speer auf der Sitzung des Rüstungsstabs am 21 Aug. 1944', 1–9; Mi 14/133, OKH-Studie, 'Sturm-Programm 9 Jan. 1945'.

31 per cent fewer aircraft, and 42 per cent fewer lorries than would otherwise have been possible. This would have given Germany over 55,000 aircraft in 1944 and 30,000 tanks.[101] Without the diversion of men and weapons to combat the bombing offensive, output of weapons for the front would have been higher still. After the war the major department heads of the Ministry were interviewed by Allied intelligence teams to help them assess the effect of bombing. All the officials interviewed stated that bombing was the factor responsible for the declining gains from rationalization and for the eventual collapse of the economic structure after January 1945.[102]

V

If rationalization might have achieved more under different political and military conditions, there can be little doubt that it was the chief factor responsible for transforming Germany's war economic performance from 1942 onwards. In August 1944 Dr Tomberg from OKW, in a general review of the war economy, pointed out that the great gains in military output were 'less a result of expansion of capacity than of rationalization'.[103] In a speech made the same month, Speer told an audience of officials from the Main Committee for Munitions that 'the recruitment of industrialists and engineers to the task of modernizing the economy had achieved efficiency levels 'which had previously appeared to be impossible'. He attributed the quadrupling of munitions output with virtually the same quantity of steel to better production methods, savings in raw materials, and the better distribution and allocation of resources. He called on the industrialists present to return to their firms with the urgent question: 'what can still be simplified, and what can be made better?'[104]

---

[101] IWM Box 368, Report 67, Saur evidence, 14. See too Report 65, 18. Ernst Blaicher claimed that 28,000–30,000 tanks could have been produced without bombing. Output of 36,000 was planned for 1945. These figures show considerably higher losses than those calculated by the bombing survey teams in 1945. The survey estimated a loss of 14% in arms production in 1944, 19% for aircraft production, and 16.5% for tanks. See PRO AIR 10/3871, BBSU 'Potential and Actual Output of German Armaments in Relation to the Combined Bombing Offensive', 7, 11, 23.

[102] IWM Box 368, Report 67, 'Causes of the Decline in German Industrial Production Autumn 1944', Dec. 1945, 1–14.

[103] IWM EDS AL 2719, OKW (Dr Tomberg), 'Deutschlands gegenwärtige wehrwirtschaftliche Lage: Stand Anfang Juni 1944', 19. See too BA-MA RL2/9, General Unruh, 'Probleme der deutschen Rüstungsindustrie', report dated 25 Mar. 1945, 42–3, on the success of the rationalization drive.

[104] IWM EDS AL 2786/2, 'Rede Reichsminister Speer auf der Arbeitstagung des Hauptausschusses Munition, 11 Aug. 1944', 12–13.

Since the war this perspective on the German economy has given way to the view that the increases in output were largely the result of switching resources from the civilian to the military economy after 1942. This view does not exclude rationalization as a contributory factor, but it places most emphasis on the conversion of unused resources. The evidence presented here shows a different story. The change in economic strategy was conditioned before 1942 by the discovery in the spring and summer of 1941 that there were few significant resources left to switch to arms production, and that the only way to fulfil Hitler's ever-escalating demands for weapons was to conquer more resources or to use existing ones more productively. Both were tried simultaneously. The failure to defeat the Soviet Union in 1941 undermined the first option. Rationalization became the primary instrument for raising levels of military output, and would have achieved even more but for the effects of surviving structural and institutional constraints and the effects of bombing.

Rationalization needed the backing of the state and the co-operation of industry to be successful. Until these were secured in the winter of 1941–2 the German war economy remained dominated by military rather than productionist priorities, and German industry, though capable of producing weapons and machinery of the highest quality, had neither the economic incentive nor political opportunity to challenge military control. Under military direction German industry fell back on its traditions of skilled craftsmanship and high-quality, high-cost production; under civilian control quality was not abandoned, but the emphasis shifted to the modernization of work practices and the scientific management of resources. In this lay the key to the 'Production Miracle'.

FURTHER READING

The following list includes essential reading in German, but is otherwise confined to books available in English. It is by no means a complete bibliography, but is designed to introduce students of the subject to the main historical arguments discussed in the foregoing essays. For a more general historiographical guide to the Third Reich see J. Hiden and J. Farquharson, *Explaining Hitler's Germany: Historians and the Third Reich* (2nd edn.; London, 1989).

I General Books

BERGHAHN, V., *Modern Germany: Society, Economy and Politics in the Twentieth Century* (London, 1982).

BOELCKE, W. A., *Die deutsche Wirtschaft 1930–1945: Interna des Reichswirtschaftsministeriums* (Düsseldorf, 1983).

BRAUN, H. J., *The German Economy in the Twentieth Century* (London, 1990).

DEIST, W., *The German Military in the Age of Total War* (London, 1984).

EUCKEN, W., 'On the Theory of the Centrally Administered Economy: An Analysis of the German Experiment', *Economica*, 15 (1948).

FISCHER, W., *Deutsche Wirtschaftspolitik 1918–1945* (Opladen, 1968).

HARDACH, K., *The Political Economy of Germany in the Twentieth Century* (London, 1980).

HERF, J., *Reactionary Modernism: Technology, Culture and Politics in Weimar Germany and the Third Reich* (Cambridge, 1984).

HIRSCHFELD, G., and KETTENACKER, L. (eds.), *The Führer State: Myths and Realities* (Stuttgart, 1981).

KERSHAW, I., *The Nazi Dictatorship* (London, 1985).

KINDLEBERGER, C., *The World in Depression 1929–1939* (London, 1973).

KRAMER, A., *The West German Economy 1945–1955* (Oxford, 1991).

MAIER, C., HOFFMANN, S., and GOULD, A. (eds.), *The Rise of the Nazi Regime: Historical Reassessments* (London, 1986).

MASON, T. W., 'The Primacy of Politics. Politics and Economics in National Socialist Germany', in Woolf, S. (ed.), *The Nature of Fascism* (London, 1968).

MILWARD, A. S., 'Fascism and the Economy', in Laqueur, W. (ed.), *Fascism: A Reader's Guide* (London, 1976).

NEUMANN, F., *Behemoth: The Structure and Practice of National Socialism 1933–1939* (London, 1942).

NOAKES, J. (ed.), *Government, Party and People in Nazi Germany* (Exeter, 1980).

REICH, S., *The Fruits of Fascism: Postwar Prosperity in Historical Perspective* (London, 1990).

SOHN-RETHEL, A., *Economy and Class-Structure of German Fascism* (London, 1978).

STOLPER, G., *The German Economy: 1870 to the Present* (London, 1967).
SVENNILSON, I., *Growth and Stagnation in the European Economy* (Geneva, 1954).
THIES, J., *Architekt der Weltherrschaft: Die Endziele Hitlers* (Düsseldorf, 1976).
TURNER, I. (ed.), *Reconstruction in Post-War Germany* (Oxford, 1989).
WOOLF, S., 'Did a Fascist Economic System Exist', in Woolf, S. (ed.), *The Nature of Fascism* (London, 1968).
ZUMPE, L., *Wirtschaft und Staat in Deutschland*, iii. *1933–1945* (Berlin, 1980).

II *Economic Recovery and Economic Policy*

ABRAHAM, D., *The Collapse of the Weimar Republic: Political Economy and Crisis* (Princeton, NJ, 1981).
BALDERSTON, T., 'The Beginning of the Depression in Germany 1927–30: Investment and the Capital Market', *Economic History Review*, 2nd ser. 36 (1983).
BALOGH, T., 'The National Economy of Germany', *Economic Journal*, 48 (1938).
BARKAI, A., *Nazi Economics: Ideology, Theory and Policy* (Oxford, 1990).
BORCHARDT, K., *Perspectives on Modern German Economic History and Policy* (Cambridge, 1991).
CHILD, F., *The Theory and Practice of Exchange Control in Germany* (London, 1958).
CORMI, G., *Hitler and the Peasants* (Oxford, 1990).
EICHENGREEN, B., 'The Origins and Nature of the Great Slump Revisited', *Economic History Review*, 2nd ser. 45 (1992).
ERBE, R., *Die nationalsozialistische Wirtschaftspolitik im Lichte der modernen Theorie* (Zürich, 1958).
FALKUS, M., 'The German Business Cycle in the 1920s', *Economic History Review*, 2nd ser. 28 (1975).
FARQUHARSON, J., *The Plough and the Swastika: The NSDAP and Agriculture in Germany 1928–1945* (London, 1976).
GARVY, G., 'Keynes and the Economic Activists of Pre-Hitler Germany', *Journal of Political Economy*, 83 (1975).
GUILLEBAUD, C. W., *The Economic Recovery of Germany 1933–1938* (London, 1939).
HOPFINGER, K., *Beyond Expectation: The Volkswagen Story* (London, 1954).
JAMES, H., *The Reichsbank and Public Finance in Germany 1924–1933* (Frankfurt am Main, 1985).
—— *The German Slump: Politics and Economics 1924–1936* (Oxford, 1986).
KERSHAW, I. (ed.), *Why Did Weimar Democracy Fail?* (London, 1990).
KLEIN, J. J., 'German money and prices 1932–1944', in Friedman, M. (ed.), *Studies in the Quantity Theory of Money* (Chicago, 1956).
LEE, J. J., 'Policy and Performance in the German Economy 1925–35: A Comment on the Borchardt Thesis', in Laffan, M. (ed.), *The Burden of German History 1919–45* (London, 1988).
LEOPOLD, J. A., *Alfred Hugenberg* (London, 1977).

LURIE, S., *Private Investment in a Controlled Economy: Germany 1933–1939* (London, 1947).

NEAL, L., 'The Economics and Finance of Bilateral Clearing Agreements: Germany 1934–8', *Economic History Review*, 2nd ser. 32 (1979).

NELSON, W., *Small Wonder: The Amazing Story of the Volkswagen* (London, 1967).

OVERY, R. J., *The Nazi Economic Recovery 1932–1938* (London, 1982).

PENTZLIN, H., *Hjalmar Schacht* (Berlin, 1980).

PETERSON, E. N., *Hjalmar Schacht: For and Against Hitler* (London, 1954).

PETZINA, D., 'Germany and the Great Depression', *Journal of Contemporary History*, 4 (1969).

—— and ABELSHAUSER, W. (eds.), *Industrielles System und politische Entwicklung in der Weimarer Republik* (Düsseldorf, 1974).

SCHACHT, H., *Account Settled* (London, 1949).

SCHNEIDER, C., *Stadtgründung im Dritten Reich: Wolfsburg und Salzgitter* (Munich, 1979).

SCHWERIN VON KROSIGK, L. GRAF, *Staatsbankrott: Finanzpolitik des Deutschen Reiches 1920–1945* (Göttingen, 1974).

SIMPSON, A. E., *Hjalmar Schacht in Perspective* (The Hague, 1969).

TEICHERT, E., *Autarkie und Grossraumwirtschaft in Deutschland 1930–1939* (Munich, 1984).

TEMIN, P., 'The Beginning of the Depression in Germany', *Economic History Review*, 2nd ser. 24 (1971).

—— 'Soviet and Nazi Planning in the 1930s', *Economic History Review*, 2nd ser. 44 (1991).

WOLFE, M., 'The Development of Nazi Monetary Policy', *Journal of Economic History*, 15 (1955).

WULFF, B., 'The Third Reich and the Unemployed: National Socialist Work-Creation Schemes in Hamburg 1933–4', in Evans, R. J., and Geary, R. (eds.), *The German Unemployed* (London, 1987).

III *Rearmament and War Economy*

BAGEL-BOHLAN, A., *Hitlers industrielle Kriegsvorbereitung im Dritten Reich 1936–1939* (Koblenz, 1975).

BENNETT, E. W., *German Rearmament and the West 1932–33* (Princeton, NJ, 1979).

BERGHAHN, V. (ed.), *Germany in the Age of Total War* (London, 1981).

BEYERCHEN, A. D., *Scientists under Hitler: Politics and the Physics Community in the Third Reich* (London, 1977).

BLAICH, F., *Wirtschaft und Rüstung im 'Dritten Reich'* (Düsseldorf, 1987).

BOELCKE, W. A. (ed.), *Deutschlands Rüstung im Zweiten Weltkrieg: Hitlers Konferenzen mit Albert Speer 1942–45* (Frankfurt am Main, 1969).

—— *Die Kosten von Hitlers Krieg* (Paderborn, 1985).

CARR, W., *Arms, Autarky and Aggression* (London, 1972).

CARROLL, B. A., *Design for Total War: Arms and Economics in the Third Reich* (The Hague, 1968).

DEIST, W., *The Wehrmacht and German Rearmament* (London, 1981).

—— et al., *Germany in the Second World War*, i (Oxford, 1990). (Published in Germany as *Das Deutsche Reich und der Zweite Weltkrieg*, 10 vols. (Stuttgart, 1979–).

DINARDO, R. L., and BAY, A., 'Horse-Drawn Transport in the German Army', *Journal of Contemporary History*, 23 (1988).

DÜLFFER, J., *Weimar, Hitler und die Marine: Reichspolitik und Flottenbau 1920– 1939* (Düsseldorf, 1973).

EICHHOLTZ, D., *Geschichte der deutschen Kriegswirtschaft*, i. *1939–1941* (Berlin, 1969); ii. *1941–1943* (Berlin, 1985).

GEYER, M., *Aufrüstung oder Sicherheit: Die Reichswehr und der Krise der Machtpolitik 1924–1936* (Wiesbaden, 1980).

—— 'Traditional Elites and National Socialist Leadership', in C. Maier (ed.), *The Rise of the Nazi Regime: Historical Reassessments* (London, 1986).

HANSEN, E. W., *Reichswehr und Industrie: Rüstungswirtschaftliche Zusammenarbeit und wirtschaftliche Mobilmachungsvorbereitungen 1923– 1932* (Boppard am Rhein, 1978).

HAUNER, M., 'Did Hitler Want World Dominion?', *Journal of Contemporary History*, 13 (1978).

HERBST, L., 'Die Krise des nationalsozialistischen Regimes am Vorabend des Zweiten Weltkrieges und die forcierte Rüstung', *Vierteljahrshefte für Zeitgeschichte*, 26 (1978).

—— *Der Totale Krieg und die Ordnung der Wirtschaft: Die Kriegswirtschaft im Spannungsfeld von Politik, Ideologie und Propaganda 1939–1945* (Stuttgart, 1982).

HOMZE, E., *Arming the Luftwaffe: The Reich Air Ministry and the German Aircraft Industry* (Lincoln, Nebr., 1976).

IRVING, D., *The Rise and Fall of the Luftwaffe; The Life of Erhard Milch* (London, 1973).

KAISER, D., MASON, T. W., and OVERY, R. J., 'Debate: Germany, Domestic Crisis and War', *Past and Present*, 35 (1989).

KALDOR, N., 'The German War Economy', *Review of Economic Statistics*, 13 (1946).

KEHRL, H., *Krisenmanager im Dritten Reich* (Düsseldorf, 1973).

KLEIN, B. H., 'Germany's Preparation for War: A Reexamination', *American Economic Review*, 38 (1948).

—— *Germany's Economic Preparations for War* (Cambridge, Mass., 1959).

LINDHOLM, R., 'German Finance in World War II', *American Economic Review*, 37 (1947).

McISAAC, D. (ed.), *The United States Strategic Bombing Survey*, reprinted; 8 vols. (New York, 1980).

MARTENS, S., *Hermann Göring* (Paderborn, 1985).

MEINCK, G., *Hitler and die deutsche Aufrüstung 1933–1937* (Wiesbaden, 1959).

MESSERSCHMIDT, M., 'The Wehrmacht and the Volksgemeinschaft', *Journal of Contemporary History*, 18 (1983).

MIERZEJEWSKI, A. C., *The Collapse of the German War Economy 1944–1945* (Chapel Hill, NC, 1988).

MILWARD, A. S., *The German Economy at War* (London, 1965).

MÜLLER, K.-J., *The Army, Politics and Society in Germany 1933–1945* (Manchester, 1987).

MURRAY, W., *The Change in the European Balance of Power 1938–39* (Princeton, NJ, 1984).

—— *Luftwaffe* (London, 1985).

O'NEILL, R. J., *The German Army and the Nazi Party* (London, 1966).

OVERY, R. J., 'The German Pre-War Aircraft Production Plans, 1936–April 1939', *English Historical Review*, 90 (1975).

—— 'From "Uralbomber" to "Amerikabomber": The Luftwaffe and Strategic Bombing', *Journal of Strategic Studies*, 1 (1978).

—— *Goering: The 'Iron Man'* (London, 1984).

—— 'Mobilization for Total War in Germany 1939–1941', *English Historical Review*, 103 (1988).

—— 'Did Hitler want Total War?' *History Sixth* 1 (1989).

PETZINA, D., *Autarkiepolitik im Dritten Reich* (Stuttgart, 1968).

RECKER, M.-L., *Nationalsozialistische Sozialpolitik im Zweiten Weltkrieg* (Munich, 1985).

ROBERTSON, E. M., *Hitler's Pre-War Policy and Military Plans* (London, 1963).

SCHMIDT, M., *Albert Speer: End of a Myth* (New York, 1982).

SPEER, A., *Inside the Third Reich* (London, 1970).

—— *The Slave State: Heinrich Himmler's Masterplan for SS Supremacy* (London, 1981).

STEINERT, M., *Hitler's War and the Germans* (Athens, Ohio, 1977).

STEPHENSON, J., 'Emancipation and its Problems: War and Society in Württemberg, 1939–1945', *European History Quarterly*, 17 (1987).

STERN, W., 'Wehrwirtschaft: A German Contribution to Economics', *Economic History Review*, 2nd ser. 13 (1960/1).

STUEBEL, H., 'Die Finanzierung der Aufrüstung im Dritten Reich', *Europa-Archiv*, 6 (1951).

THOMAS, C. S., *The German Navy in the Nazi Era* (London, 1990).

THOMAS, G., *Geschichte der deutschen Wehr- und Rüstungswirtschaft 1918–1943/5*, ed. W. Birkenfeld (Boppard am Rhein, 1966).

UEBERSCHÄR, G., 'General Halder and Resistance to Hitler in the German High Command 1938–40', *European History Quarterly*, 18 (1988).

WALKER, M., *National Socialism and the Quest for Nuclear Power* (Cambridge, 1990).

ZILBERT, E. A., *Albert Speer and the Nazi Ministry of Arms* (London, 1981).

IV *Economic Foreign Policy: Expansion and Exploitation*

DALLIN, A., *German Rule in Russia*, 2nd edn. (London, 1981).

FORBES, N., 'London Banks, the German Standstill Agreements and Economic Appeasement in the 1930s', *Economic History Review*, 2nd ser. 40 (1987).

GEORG, E., *Die wirtschaftliche Unternehmungen der SS* (Stuttgart, 1963).

HERBERT, U. (ed.), *Europa und der 'Reichseinsatz': Ausländische Zivilarbeiter, Kriegsgefangene und KZ-Häftlinge in Deutschland 1938–1945* (Essen, 1991).

HERZSTEIN, R., *When Nazi Dreams Come True* (London, 1982).

HOMZE, E., *Foreign Labor in Nazi Germany* (Princeton, NJ, 1967).

JÄGER, J.-J., 'Sweden's Iron-Ore Exports to Germany 1933–1944', *Scandinavian Economic History Review*, 15 (1967).

JENSEN, W., 'The Importance of Energy in the First and Second World Wars', *Historical Journal*, 11 (1968).

KAISER, D., *Economic Diplomacy and the Origins of the Second World War: Germany, Britain, France and Eastern Europe 1930–1939* (Princeton, NJ, 1980).

MACDONALD, C. A., 'Economic Appeasement and the German "Moderates", 1937–1939', *Past and Present*, 18 (1972).

MILWARD, A. S., *The New Order and the French Economy* (Oxford, 1970).

—— *The Fascist Economy in Norway* (Oxford, 1972).

ORLOW, D., *The Nazis in the Balkans* (Pittsburgh, 1968).

OVERY, R. J., 'The Luftwaffe and the European Economy', *Militärgeschichtliche Mitteilungen*, 21 (1979).

RICH, N., *Hitler's War Aims*, 2 vols. (London, 1973–4).

ROYAL INSTITUTE OF INTERNATIONAL AFFAIRS, *Hitler's Europe* (Oxford, 1954).

TEICHOVA, A., *An Economic Background to Munich* (Cambridge, 1974).

—— and COTTRELL, P. (eds.), *International Business and Central Europe, 1919–1939* (Leicester, 1983).

THIES, J., 'Hitler's European Building Programme', *Journal of Contemporary History*, 13 (1978).

WENDT, B.-J., *Grossdeutschland: Autarkiepolitik und Kriegsvorbereitung des Hitler-Regimes* (Munich, 1987).

WITTMANN, K., *Schwedens Wirtschaftsbeziehungen zum Dritten Reich 1933–1945* (Munich, 1978).

V Industry and Labour in the Third Reich

BAJOHR, S., *Die Hälfte der Fabrik: Geschichte der Frauenarbeit in Deutschland 1914 bis 1945* (Marburg, 1979).

BECK, E., *Under the Bombs: The German Home Front 1942–1945.* (Lexington, Ky., 1986).

BELLON, B. P., *Mercedes in Peace and War: German Automobile Workers 1903–1945* (New York, 1990).

BERGHAHN, V., 'Big Business in the Third Reich', *European History Quarterly*, 21 (1991).

BESSEL, R. (ed.), *Life in the Third Reich* (London, 1988).

BLAICH, F., 'Why Did the Pioneer Fall Behind? Motorisation in Germany between the Wars', in Barker, T. (ed.), *The Economic and Social Effects of the Spread of Motor Vehicles* (London, 1987).

BORKIN, J., *The Crime and Punishment of I.G. Farben* (London, 1979).

BRY, G., *Wages in Germany 1871–1945* (Princeton, NJ, 1960).

DE WITT, T., 'The Economics and Politics of Welfare in the Third Reich', *Central European History*, 11 (1978).

ENGELMANN, B., *In Hitler's Germany: Everyday Life in the Third Reich* (London, 1988).

EVANS, R. J. (ed.), *The German Working-Class 1888–1933: The Politics of Everyday Life* (London, 1992).

—— and GEARY, R., (eds.), *The German Unemployed* (London, 1987).

GILLINGHAM, J., *Industry and Politics in the Third Reich* (London, 1985).

—— 'The "Deproletarianization" of German Society: Vocational Training in the Third Reich', *Journal of Social History*, 19 (1985/6).

GRUNBERGER, R., *A Social History of the Third Reich* (London, 1971).

GUERIN, D., *Fascism and Big Business*, 2nd edn. (New York, 1973).

HACHTMANN, R., *Industriearbiet im 'Dritten Reich': Untersuchungen zu den Lohn- und Arbeitsbedingungen in Deutschland 1933–1945* (Göttingen, 1989).

HAYES, P., 'Carl Bosch and Carl Krauch: Chemistry and Political Economy of Germany 1925–1945', *Journal of Economic History*, 47 (1987).

—— *Industry and Ideology: IG Farben in the Nazi Era* (Cambridge, 1987).

HERBERT, U., *Fremdarbeiter: Politik und Praxis des 'Ausländer-Einsatzes' in der Kriegswirtschaft des Dritten Reiches* (Bonn, 1985).

HOMZE, E., *Foreign Labour in Nazi Germany* (Princeton, NJ, 1967).

HUGHES, T., 'Technological Momentum in History: Hydrogenation in Germany 1898–1933', *Past and Present*, 15 (1969).

LOCHNER, L., *Tycoons and Tyrants: German Industry from Hitler to Adenauer* (Chicago, 1954).

LUDWIG, K.-H., *Technik und Ingenieure im Dritten Reich* (Düsseldorf, 1974).

MASON, T. W., 'Labour in the Third Reich', *Past and Present*, 12 (1966).

—— 'Women in Germany 1925–1940: Family, Welfare and Work' *History Workshop*, 1 and 2 (1976).

—— *Sozialpolitik im Dritten Reich* (Opladen, 1977).

MOLLIN, G., *Montankonzerne und 'Dritten Reich': Der Gegensatz zwischen Monopolindustrie und Befehlswirtschaft in der deutschen Rüstung und Expansion 1939–1944* (Göttingen, 1988).

OVERY, R. J., 'Business and the Third Reich', *History Review*, 13 (1992).

PEUKERT, D., *Inside Nazi Germany: Conformity, Opposition and Racism in Everyday Life* (London, 1987).

POHL, H., HABETH, S., and BRÜNINGHAUS, B., *Die Daimler–Benz AG in den Jahren 1933 bis 1945* (Stuttgart, 1986).

RICHTER, G., *Alltag im Dritten Reich: So lebten die Deutschen 1933–1945* (Hamburg, 1982).

RIEDEL, M., *Eisen und Kohle für das Dritte Reich: Paul Pleigers Stellung in der nationalsozialistischen Wirtschaft* (Göttingen, 1973).

SACHSE, C., *et al.*, *Angst, Belohnung, Zucht und Ordnung: Herrschaftsmechanismus im Nationalsozialismus* (Düsseldorf, 1982).

SALTER, S., 'Structures of Consensus and Coercion: Workers' Morale and the Maintenance of Work Discipline', in Welch, D. (ed.), *Nazi Propaganda* (London, 1983).

SCHOENBAUM, D., *Hitler's Social Revolution* (London, 1967).

SCHWEITZER, A., 'Profits under Nazi Planning', *Quarterly Journal of Economics*, 60 (1946).

—— *Big Business in the Third Reich* (Bloomington, Ind., 1964).

SIEGEL, T., 'Wage Policy in Nazi Germany', *Politics and Society*, 14 (1985).

SIMPSON, A. E., 'The Struggle for Control of the German Economy 1936/37', *Journal of Modern History*, 21 (1959).

SMELSER, R., *Robert Ley: Hitler's Labor Front Leader* (London, 1988).

STEPHENSON, J., *Women in Nazi Society* (London, 1975).

VOGELSANG, R., *Der Freundeskreis Himmlers* (Göttingen, 1972).

WEISBROD, B., 'Economic Power and Political Stability Reconsidered: Heavy Industry in Weimar Germany', *Social History*, 4 (1979).

WERNER, W. F., *Bleib übrig! Deutsche Arbeiter in der nationalsozialistischen Kriegswirtschaft* (Düsseldorf, 1983).

WINKLER, D., *Frauenarbiet im Dritten Reich* (Hamburg, 1977).

WUNDERLICH, F., *Farm Labor in Germany 1810–1945* (Princeton, NJ, 1961).

INDEX